Contents

INTRODUCTION	4
FUNCTIONAL REQUIREMENTS	7
DETAILING PRINCIPLES	29
MATERIALS	43
FOUNDATIONS & FLOORS	65
FOUNDATION DETAILS	74
FLOORS	92
FLOOR DETAILS	102
BASEMENTS	147
BASEMENT DETAILS	158
FRAMES	177
PORTAL FRAME DETAILS	190
WALLS AND CLADDING SYSTEMS	213
WALL DETAILS	226
ROOFS	299
ROOF DETAILS	310
BIBLIOGRAPHY & FURTHER READING	337
FIGURE INDEX	340
2D DETAIL INDEX	342
3D DETAIL INDEX	345

All information contained in this ebook and associated digital files are for educational purposes only.

All rights reserved. No part of this publication may be reproduced, distributed, or transmitted in any form or by any means, including photocopying, recording, or other electronic or mechanical methods, without the prior written permission from the author.

Users of this guide are advised to use their own due diligence when it comes to working up construction details, and should be verified by qualified professionals.

Under no circumstances should any of the contents of this book be used as construction drawings. Drawings must always be checked and verified by a fully qualified architect or associated professional.

Materials and textures used in the 3D details have been selected for clarity of information - the materials or textures are not always an accurate representation of the colour of the element or product used in reality.

Copyright © 2018 by Emma Walshaw
First In Architecture
978-1-9163343-6-6

INTRODUCTION

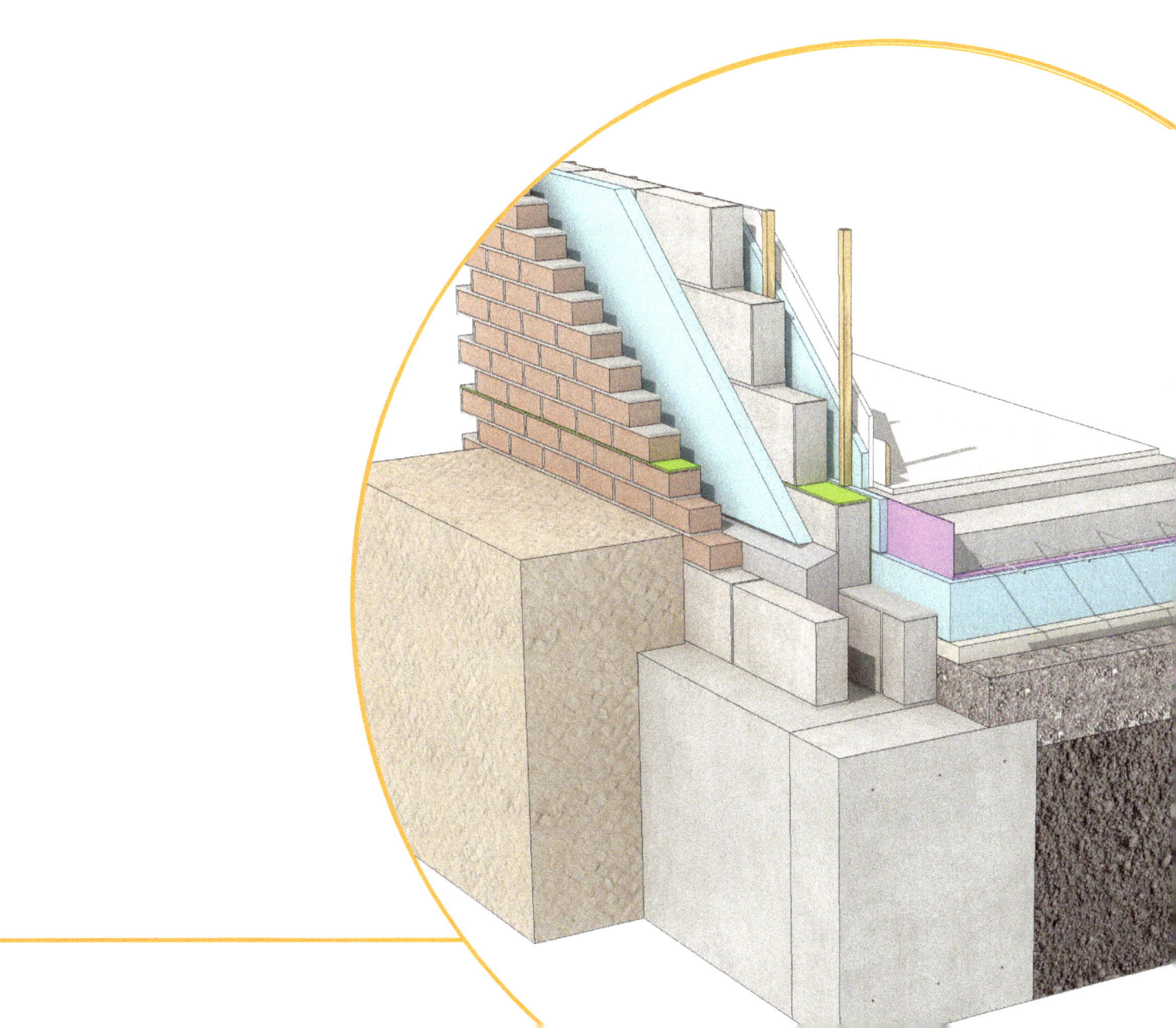

INTRODUCTION

This is the third book in the series from First In Architecture - Understanding Architectural Details. The success of the first two books, Residential Construction and Basements, made me want to dig deeper, to see what other information I could put together that would prove a vital resource for any student or professional.

This second edition now includes more details, more 3d images and plenty more information to help you expand your knowledge of construction detailing.

Commercial construction, specifically, steel and concrete framed construction, is an area I struggled with during my student days and beyond. I found it hard to locate detailed information and guidance, and spent many an hour searching the internet and library for useful resources. Hopefully this book will fill that gap, and help save you some time searching for information, and give a solid basis for understanding.

As with the previous books, I have included both 2D and 3D details to help the reader really grasp the elements of construction and understand how the building is put together. Being able to compare the 2D details with the 3D detail gives a far better explanation than a black and white detail alone.

I am not an expert, and I do not know everything there is to know about architectural detailing, does anyone? You are forever learning and evolving, as is the construction industry. The drawings in this book have been produced for educational and instructional purposes only. Some information has been removed or omitted for clarity in description/information. These details are not to provide ready made solutions, but to inform and be used as an instructional tool, a base level.

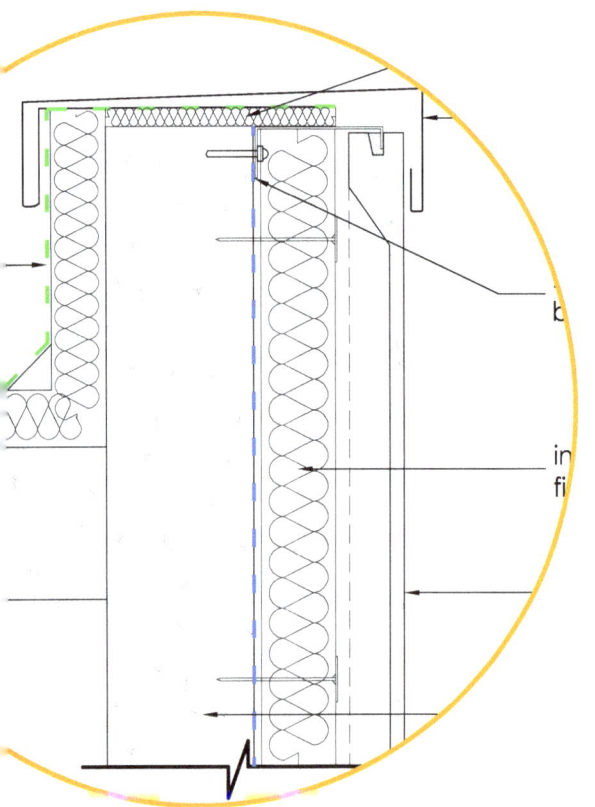

I invite you to study the details, and decide for yourself whether you can find a better solution to the problems we face in construction - air leakage, water leakage (and so on). Question every aspect of the detail presented to you, in order to gain a full understanding. How do these details relate to your project? Be aware that there are often many solutions to one problem, and here we are only able to demonstrate a fraction of the solutions available to us.

I hope you find this book useful, and that it helps you improve your knowledge and understanding of basic architectural detailing.

Best of luck.

Emma
First In Architecture

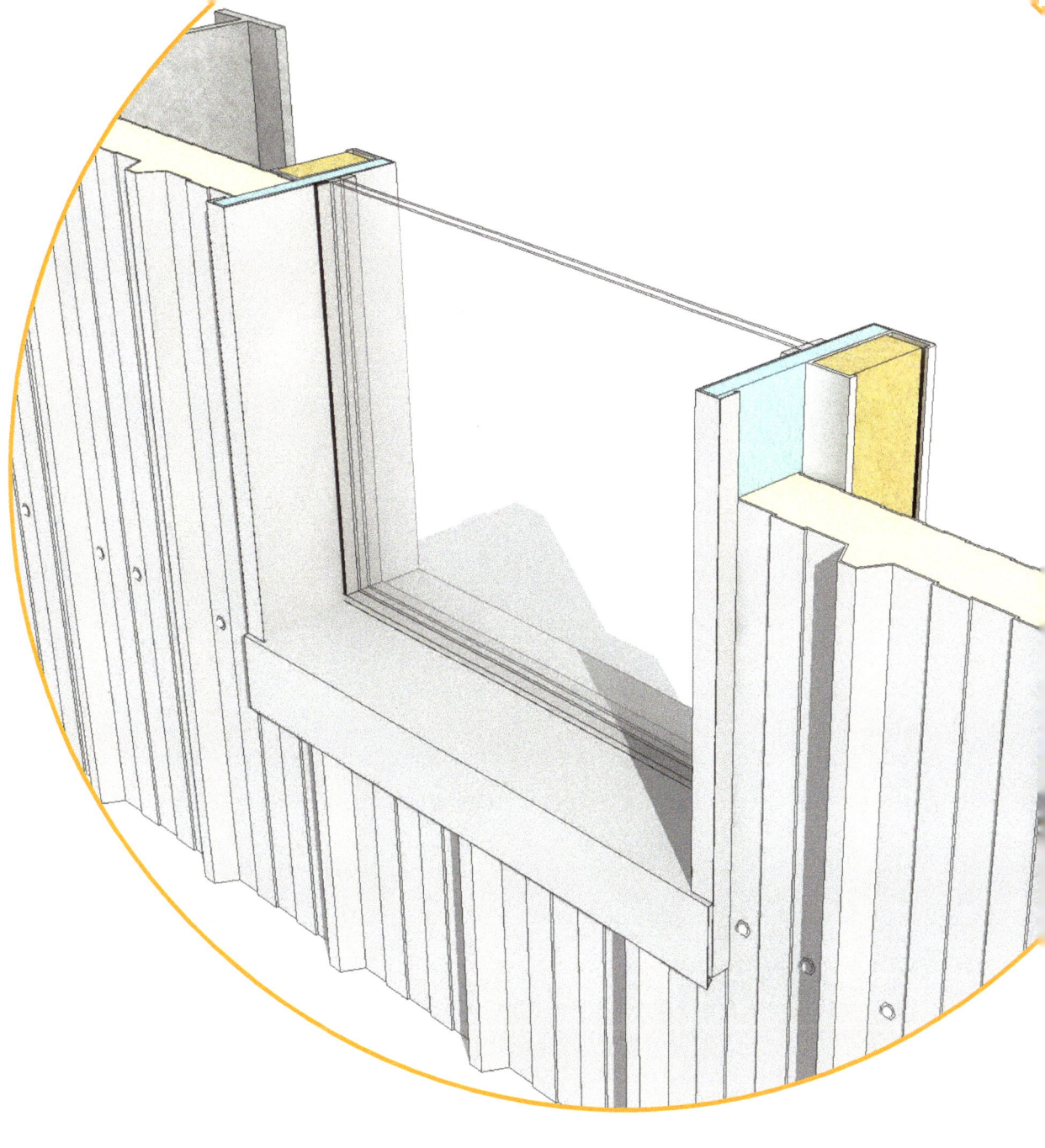

Blank Page

FUNCTIONAL REQUIREMENTS

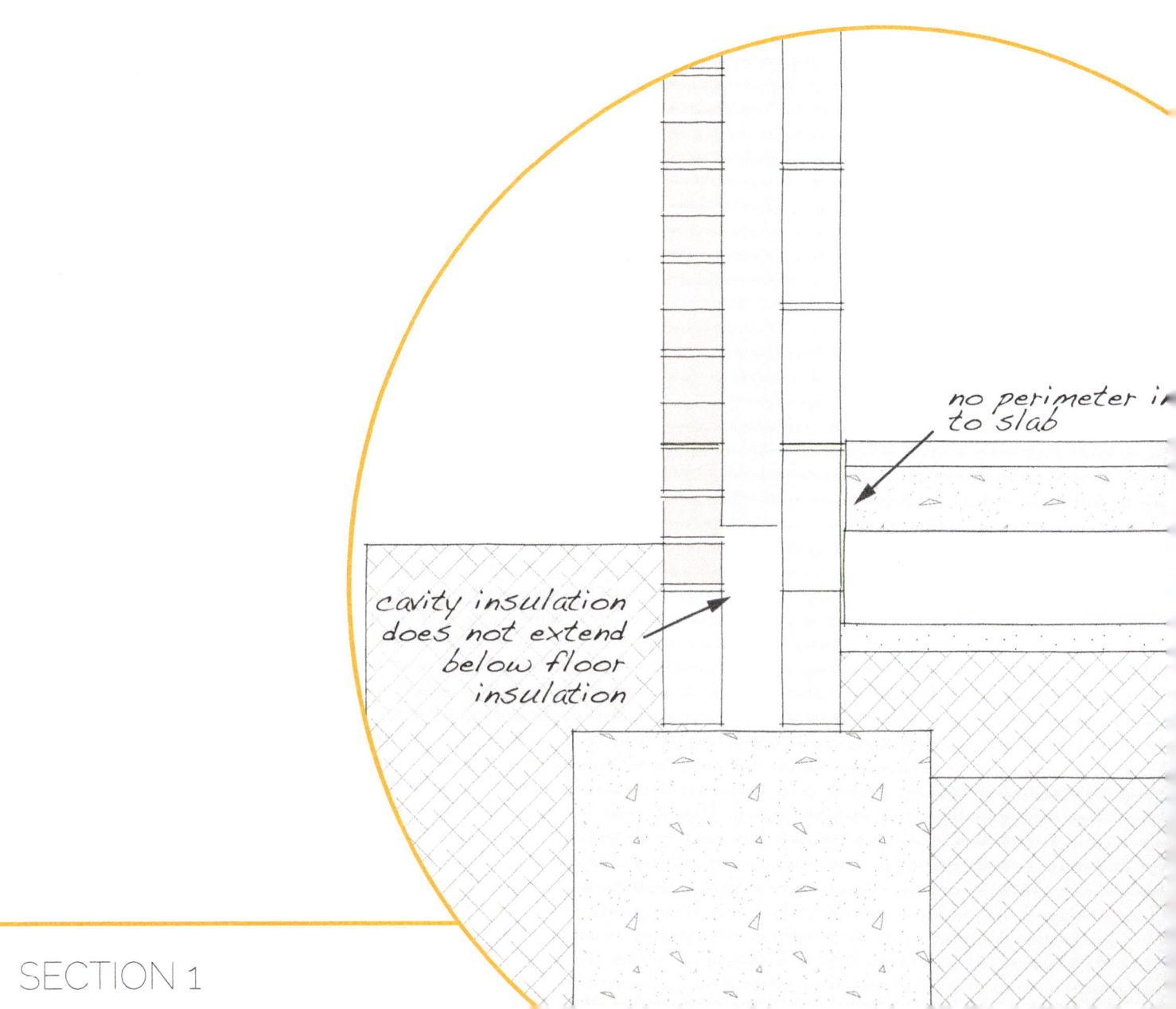

SECTION 1

FUNCTIONAL REQUIREMENTS

In this section we look at the key requirements of a building. Much of the best work in the area of the principles underlying architectural detailing has been done in a north American context, by authors such as Edward Allen, and John Sraube and Joseph Lstiburek at the Building Science corporation. Construction methods and climate in the UK differ from north America and this section draws on the work of these authors but applies it to the UK context.

In Book 1 we looked at the functional requirements of residential buildings, reflecting the Building Regulations. In this book, we will revisit those functional requirements, but study them from a perspective of the commercial building, or buildings other than dwellings.

It is estimated that we now spend on average 90% of our time in buildings - much more than in the past. Buildings are structures that enclose human activities, and their primary function could be thought of as enabling people to carry out their activities of daily life in comfort.

The building fabric and building services should be designed so as to separate the external environment from the internal environment in order to produce a comfortable internal environment, by ensuring that the transfer of water, air, heat, light and sound is appropriately regulated. Of course, buildings cannot carry out that purpose unless they are sound and safe structures, in other words that they are strong and stable structures that do not pose a hazard to people in and around them.

The requirements we are placing on buildings are changing. The scope of the regulatory framework has come to embrace a wider range of requirements; for example as well as keeping weather out, we now require buildings to be more air tight than in the past. This can have an effect on occupants' health and comfort and we need to take this into account in considering the impact of changing building requirements.

The Building Regulations define the functional requirements of buildings, through the individual Parts and the associated Approved Documents provide guidance on how these requirements can be met. There are 14 Parts to the Building Regulations, and this section examines the requirements relating to the following:

- Strength and stability
- Environmental protection
- Conservation of heat and power
- Airflow and ventilation
- Light
- Acoustics
- Fire

1 - STRENGTH AND STABILITY

Approved Document A - Structure, covers this requirement.

"Strength is the ability of a structure to resist a force (e.g. wind, load or gravity) and is a function of tensile and compressive strength of most of the commonly used materials."

"Stability is the ability of a structure to remain in or return to a stable, balanced position when forces act on it."

Approved Document Part A stipulates that a building should be constructed so that the combined dead, imposed and wind loads are sustained and transmitted by it to the ground safely and without causing such deflection or deformation of any part of the building, or such movement of the ground, as will impair the stability of any part of another building. The building must be constructed so that in the event of accident the building will not suffer collapse to an extent disproportionate to the cause.

So that buildings do not deflect, deform or collapse they must be strong and stable. A structure's ability to withstand a load depends on its overall strength. Failure of building structures is caused either by material failure (governed by material strength) or by structural instability (governed by geometry and size).

The Approved Document Part A sets out the codes, standards and references for all building types that should be referred to, many of which are British Standard or Eurocode publications.

2 - ENVIRONMENTAL PROTECTION

The building envelope or enclosure effectively separates the external environment from the internal environment. Approved Document Part C requires that the building enclosure should:

- Resist the passage of moisture from the ground to the inside of the building
- Not be damaged by moisture from the ground and not carry moisture from the ground to any part which would be damaged by it
- Resist the penetration of precipitation to components of the structure that might be damaged by moisture
- Resist the penetration of precipitation to the inside of the building
- Be designed and constructed so that their structural and thermal performance are not adversely affected by interstitial condensation
- Not promote surface condensation or mould growth

2.1 - EXTERNAL ENVIRONMENT

The building envelope must be designed to cope with temperature variation, wind, rain and snow. These forces can act in combination to produce severe effects, for example, wind-driven rain. The effect of the external environment on a building depends on its altitude, latitude and longitude.

Figure 1.1 shows the considerations that will influence the impact of the external environment:

- number of storeys
- building's exposure
- way in which architectural features provide shelter
- complexity of the building envelope

Risk	Number of storeys	Exposure to driving rain	Shelter provided by architectural features	Envelope/cladding complexity
↓ Increasing Risk	Low level	Sheltered	Good shelter provided by features	Simple envelope
	Mid level multi storey	Moderate	Adequate shelter provided by features	Simple envelope with some cladding complexity
	High rise multi storey	Severe	No shelter provided by features	Complex envelope with varied cladding and features

Fig 1.1 - Factors influencing the impact of the external environment

2.2 - WATER

It has been estimated that 75% of building failures are due to water. These occur mainly through rain water penetration, but also interstitial condensation that occurs within the building fabric and surface condensation affects building finishes.

Water also affects the performance of the building in other ways, particularly in terms of thermal performance and the effect on human health. For example, damp external walls exhibit considerably lower thermal resistance, while surface condensation on the inside of houses causes moulds, which are not good for human health.

Water is attracted to hygroscopic materials (which have capillary pores) in both the liquid and vapour state. Liquid water is sucked into very small tubes or capillaries which are present in porous materials. The sucking, or wicking, of interconnected capillaries is what causes water to be drawn up into a brick for example, or into the end grain of timber. Hydrophobic materials, such as glass, steel and plastics, repel water, which causes water to bead, for example, rain on oil soaked concrete.

Liquid water tends to exist in large clusters, because of molecular attraction. When liquid water evaporates as its temperature increases, the clusters break up into their individual vapour molecules. The size difference between liquid water molecule clumps and lone water vapour molecules explains how materials such as Gore-Tex and breather membranes such as Nilvent, Spirtech and Tyvek can simultaneously be watertight and vapour permeable.

All buildings are made of relatively small components. Each joint between materials is a potential leak, and moisture has many ways to move through any gap in the structure:

- Gravity: water will naturally move downwards
- Surface tension: causes water to cling to underside of a surface where it can run through into an opening
- Capillary action: water can also move upwards - cracks or holes with smooth sides may act as capillaries and by mechanisms of surface tension, draw in water
- Momentum: wind-driven rain possesses momentum that can move it through an opening
- Pressure differential: water will move from areas of higher pressure to areas of lower pressure

Deflection is the first line of defence against moisture ingress. Driving rain can be minimised by good siting, plantings, landscaping and choice of building height.

Figure 1.2 shows the forces leading to moisture ingress and Figure 1.3 how they can be neutralised (adapted from Lstiburek).

Forces	Neutralised by
Gravity	Wash and overlap
Surface tension	Overhang and drip
Capillary action	Capillary break
Absorption	Drain and weep
Momentum	Labrynth
Air pressure differentials	Rainscreen assembly

Fig 1.2 Forces leading to moisture ingress

Wash	A slope on a horizontal surface to drain water away from vulnerable areas of a building eg. window or door sill, sloping roof, slopes to drain, pitch to drain, ground slope away from building
Overlap	A higher surface extended over a lower surface so water moved by the force of gravity cannot run behind or beneath them. Cannot be used on a level surface e.g. roof slates, timber cladding.
Overhang and drip	Water running down wall can be kept away from openings by creating a projecting profile above the opening (overhang) and by creating a continuous groove in the underside of the projection (drip) so that gravity will pull the adhering water free of the overhang e.g. door and window sills
Capillary break	Water can be pulled by capillary action through a narrow crack; a capillary break is a crack/gap large enough so that a drop of water cannot bridge it e.g. cavity wall.
Drain and weep	Collect and conduct away water that may leak through the outer leaf e.g. cavity tray and weep hole
Labrynth	A joint in which a straight line cannot be constructed through it without passing through solid material
Rainscreen	A detail that blocks air currents passing through a joint to prevent water being pushed through by differential pressures e.g. ventilated cavity

Fig 1.3 Neutralising moisture ingress

Once water is on the wall it will form a film and begin flowing downward under the force of gravity. Wind flowing over the surface will tend to deflect the flow from this path and may even force the water upward. Surface features such as trim (slopes and drip edges), surface texture and openings influence the flow paths, either concentrating or dispersing surface flows.

Siting, building shape and surface rainwater control rarely provide complete rain control therefore some strategy to deal with rainwater that penetrates the surface has to be used. There are three fundamental strategies, as outlined by Straube and Lstiburek:

- Mass walls: this requires the use of, for example solid masonry with enough storage mass and moisture tolerance to absorb all rainwater that is not drained or otherwise removed from the outer surface. This moisture is eventually removed by evaporative drying before it reaches the inner surface of the wall. A large mass of material is required to provide sufficient moisture storage. Examples include adobe, solid masonry.
- Perfect barriers: stop all water penetration at a single plane e.g. some window frames, some metal and glass curtain walling systems. Some systems use factory built wall elements that are perfect barriers. The joints between them may also be designed as perfect barriers e.g. a single line of caulking/sealant. These are not very effective.
- Screen-drained walls: this strategy assumes some rainwater will penetrate the outer surface and remove this water by designing an element that provides drainage within the wall e.g. cavity wall.

3.0 - CONSERVATION OF HEAT AND POWER

The requirement for buildings to be energy efficient is one of the key requirements imposed on designers and builders. The burning of fossil fuels to provide the energy to heat, cool and power buildings contributes nearly half the UK's CO_2 emissions. The Government is committed to reduce the UK's greenhouse gas emissions by 80% by 2050 and reducing emissions from buildings is a key way of achieving this. Approved Document Part L of the Building Regulations is the vehicle by which the Government seeks to improve energy efficiency by reducing heat loss from buildings.

3.1 - HEAT LOSS

Heat is lost from buildings in two ways. It is lost through the fabric of the building (the building envelope) by radiation, convection and conduction exchanges. This is known as **fabric heat loss**. Buildings are not completely airtight and heat is also lost by heated air leaving the building through gaps in the building fabric and being replaced by colder air that needs to be heated. This is known as **ventilation heat loss**.

Total Heat Loss (Q) = Fabric Heat Loss (Qf) + Ventilation Heat Loss (Qv)

3.1.1 - FABRIC HEAT LOSS

The amount of heat that is lost through this route (Qf) depends on three things:

- The difference between the inside design temperature and the outside temperature (ΔT)
- The area of the different building elements exposed to the temperature differential (A)
- The rate at which heat flows through the different building elements exposed to the temperature differential, known as the U-value (U)

This can be represented as the equation:

$Qf = \Sigma (U.A.\Delta T)$ measured in Watts (Σ simply means 'the sum of')

The temperature differential and area of the building elements are straightforward, but the U-value is an important concept that needs further explanation.

3.1.2 - U-VALUES

A measure called a U-value, (also called the thermal transmittance coefficient) is the conventional way of expressing the rate at which heat flows through a building element such as an external wall, window, ground floor or roof. Its formal definition is:

"The rate at which heat flows, in Watts, through one square metre of a building element when the air temperature either side differs by one degree (K or °C)"

The units in which the measure is expressed are therefore:

W/m^2K

Watts per square metre per degree Kelvin (the formal SI unit of temperature: a change in temperature of 1K is the same as a change in temperature of 1°C).

The U-value is a measure of the rate at which a building element transmits heat. The higher the U-value, the more heat is transmitted, or lost, through the building element. From an energy conservation point of view therefore, **the lower the U-value of a building element the better**.

The Building Regulations specify maximum U-values that should not be exceeded for different building elements. Approved Document Part L2A sets out the limiting fabric parameters shown in Figure 1.5, however designers are encouraged to design to higher performance than set out in Figure 1.5.

Element	Limiting U value (fabric elements of building) (W/m^2K)	Notional building specification U value (W/m^2K)
Wall	0.35	0.26
Floor	0.25	0.22
Roof	0.25	0.18
Windows/Doors	2.2	1.6

Fig 1.4 - Table of U Value requirements for buildings other than dwellings

3.1.3 - CALCULATING U-VALUES

A U-value is a measure of thermal transmittance. Heat flow through a material is usually expressed in terms of thermal resistance (R). Transmittance is the inverse of resistance and can therefore be expressed as the reciprocal of resistance:

Thermal Transmittance (U-value) = $\dfrac{1}{\text{Thermal Resistance (R)}}$

A building element is composed of a number of materials, each of which has a resistance to the flow of heat. The U-value of a building element can therefore be calculated by adding together the thermal resistances of the components of the building element (ΣR) and dividing the result into one (taking its reciprocal). The shorthand expression of that, and the formula for calculating a U-value (U) is:

$$U = \dfrac{1}{\Sigma R} \quad \text{(Units } W/m^2K\text{)}$$

1.3.4 - THERMAL RESISTANCE

The amount of resistance that a material offers to the heat flow through it depends on the thermal properties of the material and its thickness. It can be calculated from the following formula:

$$R = \frac{d}{\lambda}$$

R is the thermal resistance of a material (m²K/W)
d is the thickness of the material (in metres)
λ is the thermal conductivity of the material (W/mK)

3.1.5 - SURFACE AND AIRSPACE RESISTANCE

In a building element it is not only materials that provide a resistance to the transfer of heat; surfaces and airspaces or empty cavities also offer resistances that need to be taken into account in calculating U-values. These are usually standard values that can be found from tables such as those published by CIBSE.

3.1.6 - THERMAL CONDUCTIVITY

The thermal conductivity (λ) of a material is the heat flow in watts across a thickness of 1 square meter when the air temperature either side differs by one degree.

Materials which have a high thermal conductivity, such as copper, are good conductors of heat and therefore poor thermal insulators. Conversely, materials that have a low thermal conductivity, such as expanded polystyrene, area poor conductors of heat and therefore good thermal insulators. A table of the thermal conductivity of common construction materials is shown below.

Material	Thermal Conductivity (W/mK)
Aluminium	190.00
Steel (mild)	60.00
Concrete (medium density)	1.13
Tiles (clay)	1.00
Brickwork	0.77
Lightweight concrete block	0.57
Plaster (dense)	0.57
Plasterboard	0.21
Aircrete block	0.18
Timber	0.13
Glass fibre insulation	0.04

Fig 1.5 - Table of thermal conductivity of common construction materials

The thermal conductivity figures are based on measurements in controlled environments and make standard assumptions about, for example, moisture content. If practice, the moisture content of materials may be higher than assumed. If a material, such as mineral wool insulation, becomes wet then its thermal conductivity will be higher (because thermal conductivity of water is greater than that of air).

3.17 - CALCULATING A U-VALUE: WORKED EXAMPLE

Calculation of a U-value for an external cavity wall.

The structure of the wall is shown in the diagram below along with information on the thermal conductivities of the materials and standard values for surface and air gap resistances. From this information, the thermal resistances of the components of the wall are calculated. These are then added to the resistances of the surfaces and air gap. The total resistance is then divided into one to determine the U-value.

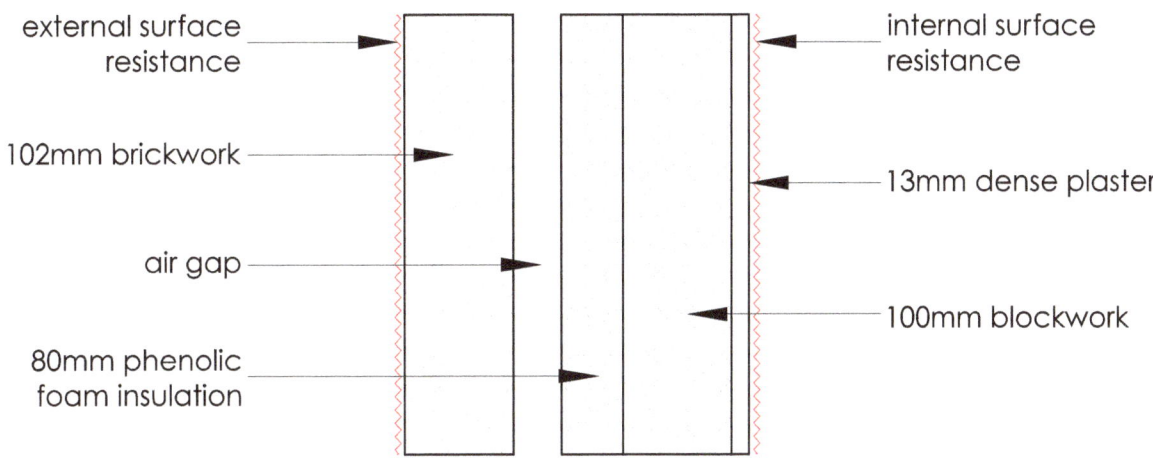

Thermal conductivities (W/mK)
Dense plaster   0.50
Lightweight blockwork   0.11
Brickwork   0.84
Phenolic foam insulation   0.02

Surface and air gap resistances (m^2K/W)
Internal surface   0.12
External surface   0.06
Air gap   0.18

	Thickness (d)	Thermal Conductivity (λ)	Thermal Resistance $R=d/\lambda$
Internal Surface	-	-	0.120
Plaster	0.013	0.50	0.026
Blockwork	0.100	0.11	0.909
Insulation	0.080	0.02	4.000
Air gap	-	-	0.180
Brickwork	0.102	0.84	0.121
External Surface	-	-	0.060

Total Resistance (ΣR) = 5.416

U-value = 1/ ΣR = 1/ 5.416 = 0.18 W/m^2K

U-value = 0.18 W/m^2K

3.1.8 - THERMAL BRIDGING

Standard U-value calculations assume that the materials in the building element are homogeneous, in other words that the thermal resistance is constant in the plane of the material. In practice that is not always the case. There may be gaps in the layer of material, or the material may be 'bridged' in some way.

For example in a timber frame external wall construction, the timber studs interrupt, or bridge, the insulation layer in the framed wall. In a cold roof the ceiling joists interrupt the layer of insulation placed between the joists. In a cavity wall, a combined lintel bridges the cavity. These are all examples of thermal bridging.

A thermal bridge is created when materials that are poorer insulators than surrounding materials come in contact, allowing heat to flow through the path created. Thermal bridging has become a significant source of heat loss as insulation standards have improved and this has to be allowed for in estimating the heat loss from buildings.

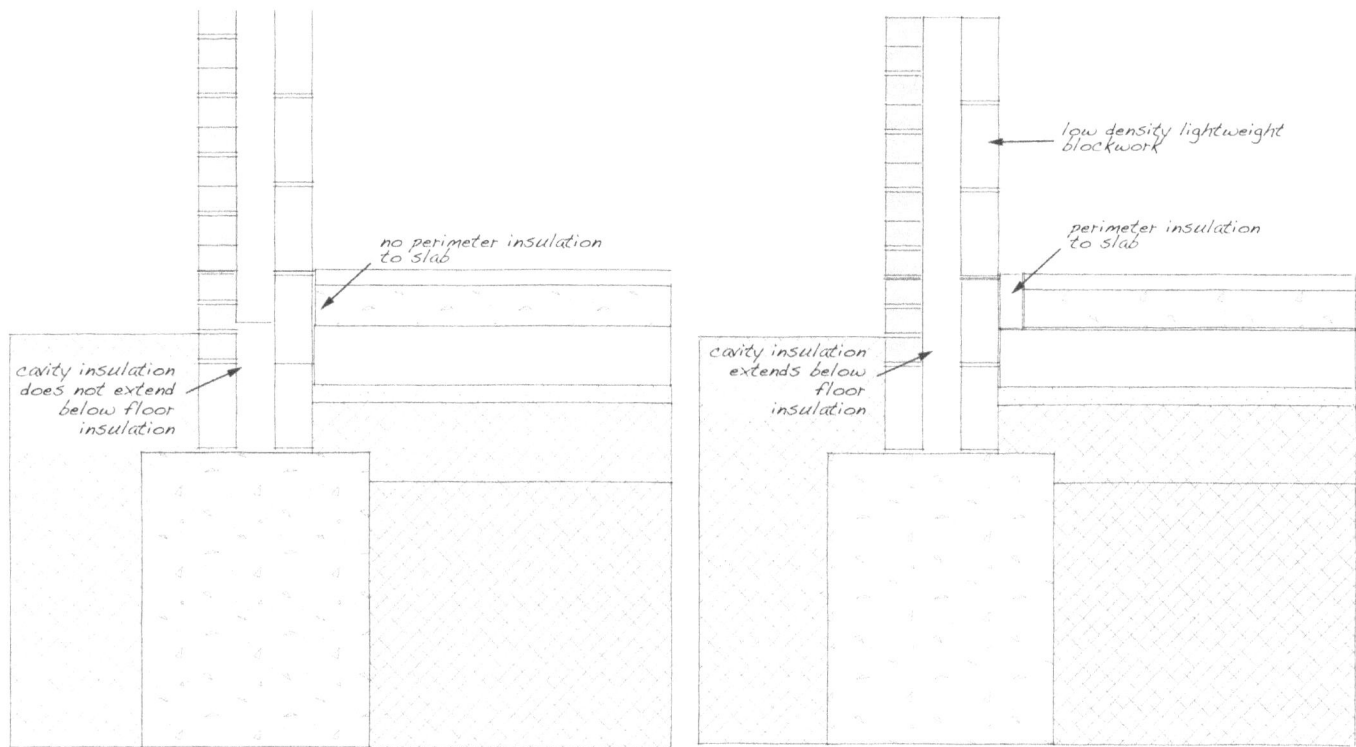

Fig 1.6 - Image showing thermal bridge at junction, and solution to improve performance

3.2 - VENTILATION HEAT LOSS

Building fabric has improved over time to meet more stringent Building Regulation requirements, U-values have therefore declined and building fabric heat loss has decreased. There has been less regulatory concern with airtightness with the result that ventilation heat loss can now account for up to a third of total heat loss in a new dwelling.

The ventilation heat losses in a building are determined by:

- the volume of air passing through the building that requires heating to achieve the desired internal temperature (calculated by the number of air changes per hour multiplied by the volume of the building)
- the amount of heat energy required to raise the air temperature by one degree (the specific heat capacity of air)
- the difference between the temperature to which the inside of the building is designed to be heated and the temperature outside of the building

Ventilation heat loss can therefore be estimated using the following equation:

$$Q_v = \frac{C_v \cdot N \cdot V \cdot \Delta T}{3600}$$

Qv is the ventilation heat loss (Watts)
Cv is the specific heat capacity of air - usually given as 1210 J/m³K
N is the number of air changes per hour (ach): divided by 3600 gives air changes per second, which is the correct unit as Qv is measured in Watts, or Joules per second
V is the volume of the building that is conditioned, or heated
ΔT is the difference in temperature between the inside and outside of the building

3.3 - HEAT LOSS: THEORY AND PRACTICE

The above equations are only an approximation of what is called 'steady state' heat transfer, in which variables such as temperature differential do not change. Such formulations cannot provide a dynamic picture of heat transfer over time, which would be necessary to assess for example, whether summer overheating is likely to occur. To do this, much more complicated dynamic models are required.

Furthermore, thermal models tend to seriously underestimate actual heat loss from a building. Research carried out by Leeds Beckett University has shown that a significant discrepancy exists between the energy performance of a dwelling as designed and that realised in practice, typically around 20% higher than predicted by modelling. The difference between measured and predicted performance can be accounted for by factors such as:

- Thermal bypasses. A thermal bypass is set up whenever air movement is able to take place in such a way as to reduce the effectiveness of an insulation layer, for example via the party wall cavity or if insulation boards in a cavity wall are not butted firmly up to the blockwork.
- Higher than predicted thermal bridging, for example as a result of the timber fraction in a timber frame wall being significantly higher than the nominal value.
- Real fabric U-values higher than nominal, for example installing windows who 'centre page' U-values equate to the design U-value buy whose 'whole window' U-value is significantly higher. Another example would be where components such as insulation become damp, resulting in higher heat loss than predicted using manufacturer's data on thermal conductivity in laboratory conditions.
- As-built differing from design intent. This can happen in relation to the fabric in many ways, for example the omission of a perimeter insulation detail. It can also happen in relation to airtightness, for example service penetrations not being properly sealed.

4 - AIRFLOW AND VENTILATION

Ventilation is dealt with in Approved Document Part F of the Building Regulations. The requirement is that there should be adequate means of ventilation provided. The ventilation system should:

- extract water vapour from areas with high rates of generation (e.g. kitchens, utility rooms and bathrooms) before it can spread widely;
- extract hazardous pollutants from areas where they are produced in significant quantities, before they can spread widely;
- rapidly dilute pollutants and water vapour in habitable rooms, occupiable rooms and sanitary accommodation;
- provide a minimum supply of outdoor air for occupants and disperse residual pollutants and water vapour;
- perform in a way in which is not detrimental to the health of people in the building;

The control of airflow is important for several reasons: to control moisture damage, reduce energy losses, and ensure occupier comfort and health.

- Moisture control: water vapour in the air can be deposited within the building envelope by condensation and cause health, durability and performance problems.
- Energy savings: warmed air leading out of a building is replaced by (usually) colder air which requires energy to heat it - about a third of space heating energy consumption is due to air leakage through the building enclosure.
- Comfort and health: cold draughts and excessively dry wintertime air that result from excessive air leakage directly affect human comfort, airborne sound transmission control requires good airflow control and external odours and gases can cause health and comfort problems.

Airflow across buildings is driven by wind pressures, stack effects, and mechanical air handling equipment such as fans. A continuous, stiff, durable, air permeable barrier system is required between the external and internal space to control airflow driven by these forces. Uncontrolled air leakage through the building envelope is a major cause of building performance problems.

Increased airtightness must be matched by an appropriate ventilation system to dilute pollutants, provide fresh air and control humidity levels.

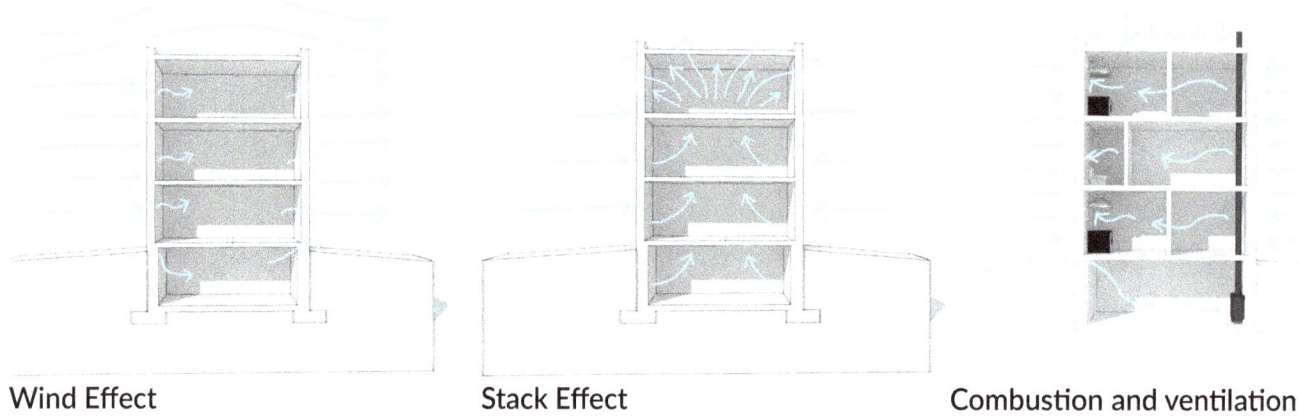

Wind Effect **Stack Effect** **Combustion and ventilation**

Fig 1.7 - Forces driving airflow through the building enclosure

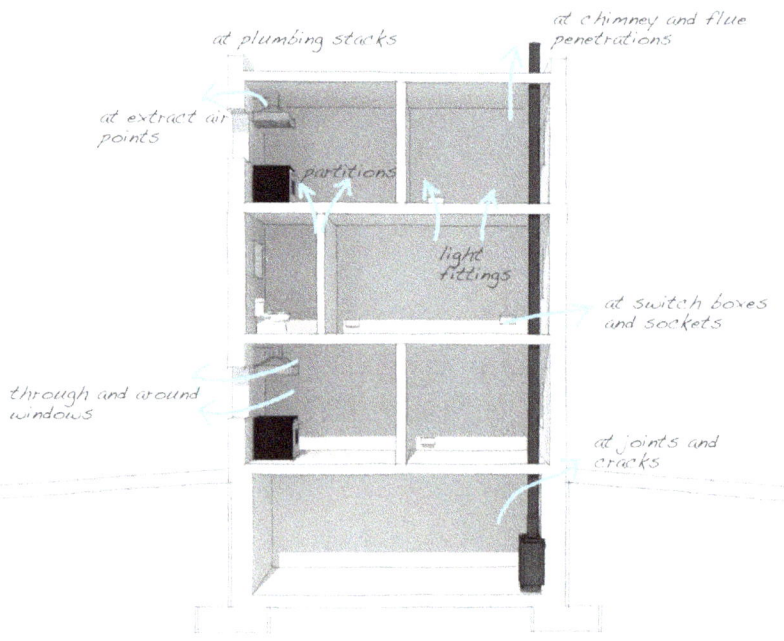

Fig 1.8 - Typical leakage paths through the building envelope

SECTION 1 - FUNCTIONAL REQUIREMENTS

For airflow to occur there must be both:
- A pressure difference between two points, and
- A continuous flow path or opening connecting the points

The general approach taken to control airflow is to attempt to seal all openings at one plan in the building enclosure. The primary plane of airtightness is called the air barrier system: an assembly of materials including every joint, seam and penetration.

Wind pressure effects (see Figure 1.8 below). Low slope roofs tend to have mostly negative (uplift) pressures, especially on the leading edge. Roofs with slopes above 25° degrees experience positive pressures on the windward face and suctions on the leeward.

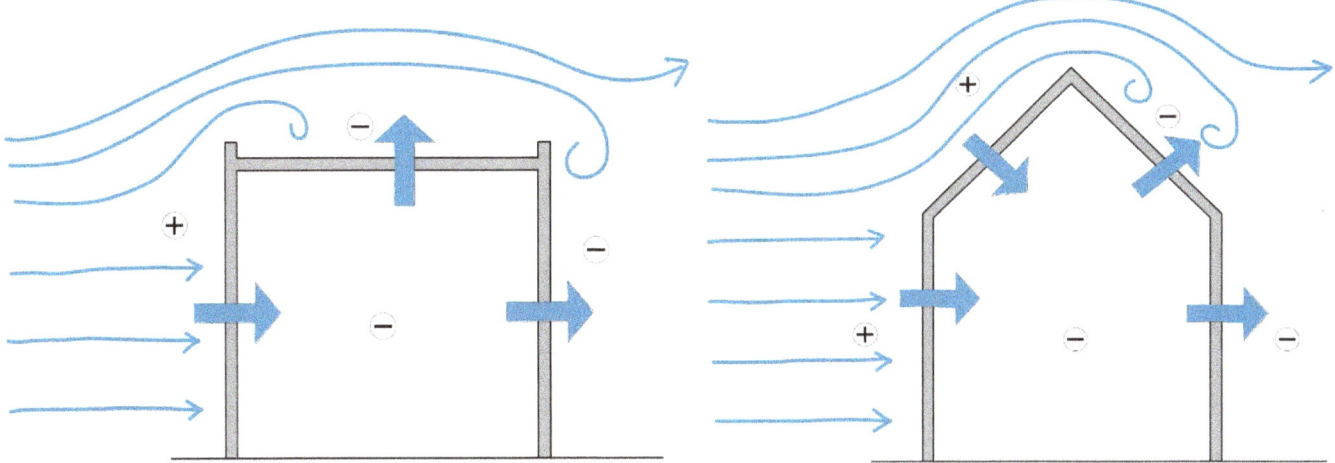

Fig 1.9 - Wind pressure effects

Stack effect pressures are generated by variations in air density with temperature. The density of warm air is less than that of cold air. Therefore hot air rises and cold air sinks. In a building, during winter, as heated air rises it 'sucks in' colder air from outside.

Bathroom exhaust fans, clothes dryers, cooker hoods all exhaust air from a building. This creates a negative pressure inside the building that can cause inward air leakage through the building enclosure.

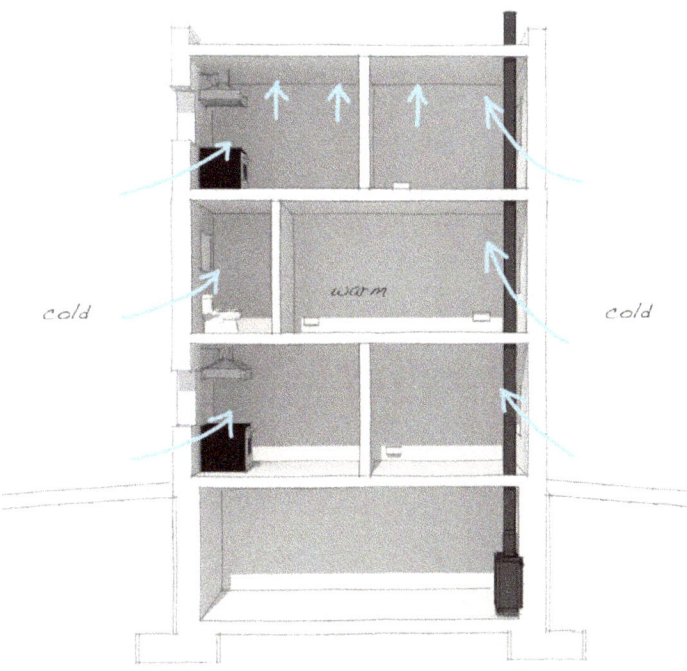

Fig 1.10 - Stack effect pressures

It is generally accepted that pollutants, such as dust mites, pet allergens, pollen, moulds, fungi, bacteria and viruses are increasing in buildings and have an increasingly negative impact on human health, such as the prevalence of asthma. Some are introduced by occupants or are brought in from the outside. However, many are a result of the built environment itself, and in the main are due to environmental conditions of humidity and temperature that have only been experienced in buildings in the very recent past.

All these pollutants generally require very high levels of humidity to thrive. They cannot thrive, if relative humidity is kept between 40% and 60%. In addition, other chemical reactions such as those involving VOCs, are more dangerous to the human body as humidity levels rise, particularly at levels over 70% RH. At levels under 40% human mucus membranes become dry and more vulnerable to irritation from chemical pollutants and small particles. People become much more sensitive to odours at low RH levels, and people wearing contact lenses can suffer irritation. Under 35% RH the effect of static on the human body is so considerable both internally and externally. For example external static shocks from walking on nylon carpets can be as high as 35,000 volts at low RH levels. Increasing RH to above 35% would automatically reduce the potential of static shock to 1,500 volts or less.

5 - ACOUSTICS

In addition to temperature and humidity, acoustic isolation is also important for comfort. As a result of the growing number of complaints about domestic noise disturbance and the potential litigation arising from these, Building Regulations have considerably improved acoustic insulation requirements since 2002.

There are a number of issues in relation to acoustics in buildings:
- sound insulation
- between dwellings
- between rooms in a building
- reverberation in rooms
- internal noise levels from: building services, outside
- noise emitted from the building

Approved Document Part E is intended to reduce the transmission of sound into, and between the rooms of residential buildings. The requirements are that dwellings, flats and rooms for residential purposes shall be designed and constructed in such a way that:

- they provide reasonable resistance to sound from other parts of the same building and from adjoining buildings; and
- that (a) internal walls between a bedroom or a room containing a WC, and other rooms; and (b) internal floors, provide reasonable resistance to sound

6 - LIGHT

Lighting in the indoor environment has three basic purposes: to enable the occupants to work and move about in safety; to enable tasks to be performed, and to make the interior look pleasant.

Buildings can be lit either naturally, by daylight received from the sky, or artificially - by electric lamps or other artificial light sources.

The quantity and quality of natural light in an interior depends on the external environment (site layout and planning) and the internal environment (size and positioning of windows, depth and shape of rooms). The primary reference in the UK for daylighting criteria is BS8206: Lighting for buildings: Part 2: Code of practice for daylighting, which treats daylight as two distinct sources of light:

- Sunlight - That part of solar radiation that reaches the earth's surface as parallel rays after selective attenuation by the atmosphere
- Skylight - That part of solar radiation that reaches the earth's surface as a result of scattering in the atmosphere.

Sunlight and skylight may therefore be considered as the direct and diffuse components of daylight.

Interior daylight is measured by the Daylight Factor (DF).

Daylight factor is defined as:

$$\text{Daylight Factor (\%)} = \frac{\text{Interior Illuminance}}{\text{Simultaneous horizontal unobstructed exterior illuminance}} \times 100$$

The Daylight Factor is a combination of three components:
- The sky component (SC) - the light received directly from the sky.
- The externally reflected component (ERC) - the light received directly by reflection from buildings and obstructions outside the room.
- The internally reflected component (IRC) - the light received from surfaces inside the room.

Estimates for the SC and ERC can be obtained from a number of sources, including: BRE Daylight Protractors, BRE Simplified Daylight Tables, Waldrum Diagrams, Fuller Moore Dot Charts. The IRC can be obtained from tabulated data.

Understanding artificial lighting requires the use of a number of terms:
- Luminous flux (F) - the amount of light emitted by a light source. Measured in lumens (lm).
- Luminous efficacy – a measure of how effectively a lamp transforms electricity into light or luminous flux: the luminous efficacy is the lamp light output in lumens per watt of electrical power consumption, (lm/W).
- Luminous intensity (I) - is the power of a light source, or illuminated surface, to emit light in a particular direction. Measured in candelas (cd).
- Illuminance (E) - the luminous flux density (spread of light) at a surface measured in lux (lx), where 1 lux = 1 lm/m2. A common minimum level for working is 200 lx, but in bright sunlight it can reach 50000lx.
- Luminance (L) - this is a measure of the ability of an area of light source, or reflecting surface, to produce the sensation of brightness.
- Colour rendering - this is the ability of a lamp to reveal the colour of a surface, compared to the colour of the surface viewed in daylight: a measure of how accurately the colour of surfaces appears under different light sources. It is expressed by a colour rendering index (Ra) of up to 100. An Ra of between 80-89 is considered very good, while one between 90-100 is regarded as excellent.
- Colour temperature - gives an indication of the appearance of the light. Lower colour temperatures mean a 'warmer' appearance. Early fluorescent lamps had a high colour temperature giving a very 'cold' appearance; but now a wide range of colour temperatures is available, including some that are similar to incandescent lamps.

7 - FIRE

Approved Document Part B2, Volume 2, Buildings Other Than Dwellings, defines the key aspects of fire safety in the construction of buildings. Some of these are:

- The building shall have a means of early warning and escape in the event of a fire.
- The internal spread of fire should be inhibited within the building by ensuring linings adequately resist the spread of flame over their surface.
- The building shall be designed and constructed so that its stability will be maintained for a reasonable period in the event of a fire.
- The building shall have a sufficient degree of fire separation within buildings and between adjoining buildings to provide fire suppression.
- Unseen spread of fire and smoke within a concealed space within the structure must be inhibited.
- External walls and roofs of a building are able to resist spread of fire from one building to another.
- The building must provide satisfactory access for fire appliances and the provision of facilities in buildings to assist firefighters.

7.1 - STRUCTURAL ELEMENTS

Although it is preferable to build new structures with non combustible materials, that is not always feasible. Many of the structural elements are combustible in some way, but we have developed suitable understanding and methods to allow use of these materials in a safe and effective manner. Timber, for example is a combustible material, but if a structural element is specified with sufficient thickness the rate of combustion of any excess timber should provide sufficient time for the building to be evacuated in the event of a fire. Masonry construction materials tend to have a good fire resistance, due to their manufacturing process being at high temperatures. Concrete however, does suffer damage in a fire as natural aggregates are used.

Steel can demonstrate a loss of strength in temperatures over 500 ºC, and it is often treated with a fire retardant coating, or covered with a material that has good fire resistance in order to protect it from fire.

7.2 - NON STRUCTURAL ELEMENTS

Internal and external finishes to a building also have an important bearing on fire resistance of an overall structure. It is key that any surfaces do not encourage the spread of fire and have a low rate of heat release or fire growth if ignited. For further information refer to the British Standards quoted in the Approved Document B2, along with the BRE Group also having a wealth of guidance and documentation.

7.3 - FIRE PROTECTION

7.3.1 - EXTERNAL WALLS

The regulations state that external walls must be constructed so that the risk of ignition from an external source and the spread of fire over their surfaces are restricted. The amount of unprotected area in the side of the building is restricted so as to limit the amount of thermal radiation that can pass through the wall. The roof is constructed so that the risk of spread of flame and fire penetration is restricted.

Materials for cladding systems and surfaces must be of limited combustibility.

Portal frame structures used for industrial or commercial means, may not need fire resistance of the structure, however, if close to a boundary may require fire resistance to prevent spread of fire between buildings.

7.3.2 - COMPARTMENTATION

The spread of fire must be restricted by providing compartmentation, where the building is sub divided by fire resisting construction. Compartmentation prevents rapid fire spread and reduces the chance of a fire becoming larger. A compartment consists of fire resisting walls and floors, and depends on a variety of factors including the availability of a sprinkler system, use of building and so on.

Approved Document B2 provides maximum dimensions of a building or compartment in non residential buildings, along with construction requirements for compartments.

7.3.3 - CAVITY BARRIERS AND FIRE STOPS

In order to restrict spread of fire or smoke in concealed places within the structure, the building regulations require the provision of cavity barriers to close cavities and voids.

A cavity barrier should be used where a pathway could be formed around a fire separating element and in extensive cavities. For example, cavity barriers must be provided around openings, at the junction between an external cavity wall and every compartment floor and compartment wall; at the junction between an internal cavity wall and every compartment floor, compartment walls or other fire resisting barrier.

The table below from the Approved Document Part B2 demonstrates the provisions for cavity barriers.

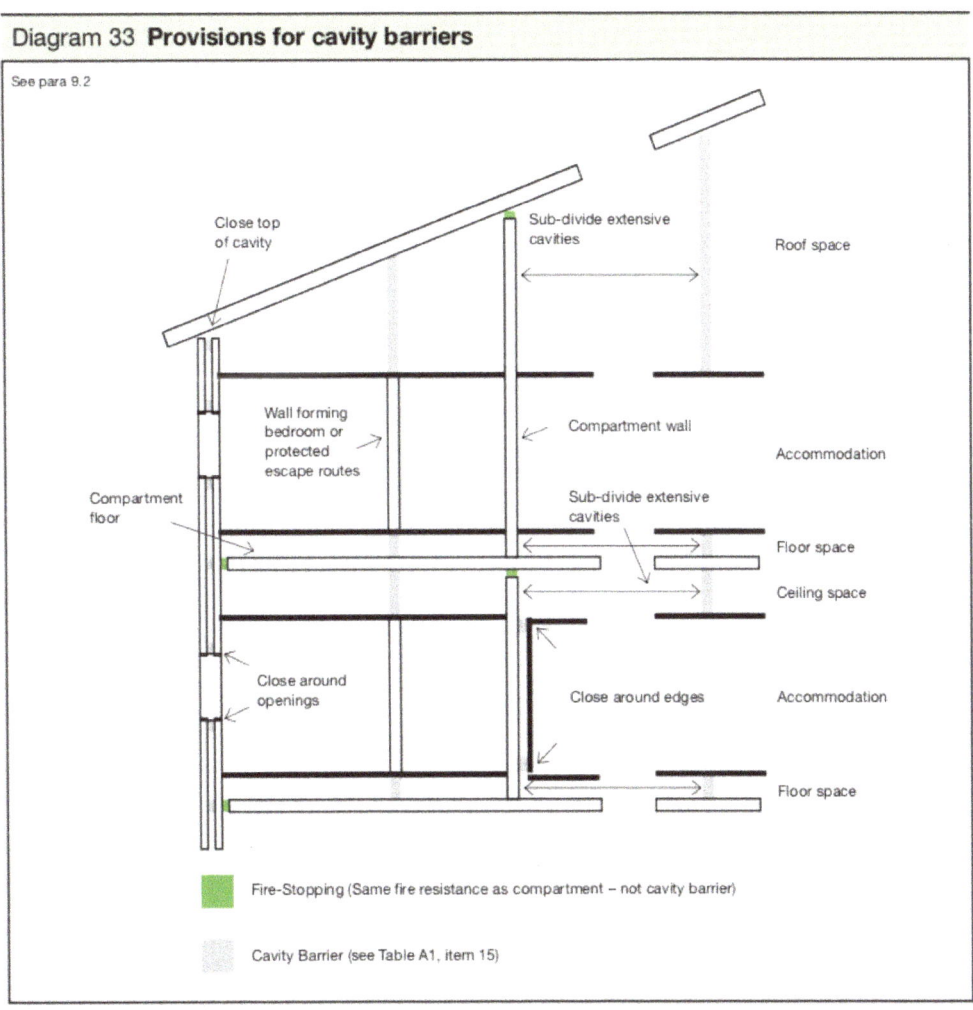

Fig 1.11 - Provisions for cavity barriers - Approved Document Part B2

A cavity barrier can be constructed with steel 0.5mm thick or above, timber at least 38mm thick, polythene sleeved mineral wool or calcium silicate and cement based gypsum boards.

The cavity barrier should be tightly fitted to a rigid construction and mechanically fixed in place.

Refer to Approved Document B2 for full details of cavity barrier requirements.

A fire stop provides protection to any opening within a fire separating element, pipework, for example. Pipes, ductwork, flues that pass through the fire separating element, should meet the provisions of Approved Document B2 in that a suitable fire stop method is used. This can include using recommended materials, proprietary seals, restricted pipe diameters, sleeving or fire dampers.

In addition to this, joints between fire separating elements should be fire-stopped, and any openings for pipes, ducts etc passing through a fire separating element should be kept to a minimum where possible.

The following tables from Approved Document B2 demonstrate fire resistance requirements for elements of structure and fire resistance periods.

Table A1 Specific provisions of test for fire resistance of elements of structure etc

Part of building	Minimum provisions when tested to the relevant part of BS 476 [1] (minutes)			Minimum provisions when tested to the relevant European standard (minutes) [9]	Method of exposure
	Loadbearing capacity [2]	Integrity	Insulation		
1. **Structural** frame, beam or column.	See Table A2	Not applicable	Not applicable	R see Table A2	Exposed faces
2. **Loadbearing wall** (which is not also a wall described in any of the following items).	See Table A2	Not applicable	Not applicable	R see Table A2	Each side separately
3. **Floors** [3]					
a. between a shop and flat above;	60 or see Table A2 (whichever is greater)	60 or see Table A2 (whichever is greater)	60 or see Table A2 (whichever is greater)	REI 60 or see Table A2 (whichever is greater)	From underside [4]
b. Any other floor – including compartment floors.	See Table A2	See Table A2	See Table A2	REI see Table A2	
4. **Roofs**					
a. any part forming an escape route;	30	30	30	REI 30	From underside [4]
b. any roof that performs the function of a floor.	See Table A2	See Table A2	See Table A2	REI see Table A2	
5. **External walls**					
a. any part less than 1000mm from any point on the relevant boundary; [5]	See Table A2	See Table A2	See Table A2	REI see Table A2	Each side separately
b. any part 1000mm or more from the relevant boundary; [5]	See Table A2	See Table A2	15	RE see Table A2 and REI 15	From inside the building
c. any part adjacent to an external escape route (see Section 5, Diagram 25).	30	30	No provision [6][7]	RE 30	From inside the building
6. **Compartment walls** separating					
a. a flat from any other part of the building (see 8.13)	60 or see Table A2 (whichever is less)	60 or see Table A2 (whichever is less)	60 or see Table A2 (whichever is less)	REI 60 or see Table A2 (whichever is less)	Each side separately
b. occupancies (see 8.18f)					
7a. **Compartment walls** (other than in item 6)	See Table A2	See Table A2	See Table A2	REI see Table A2	Each side separately
8. **Protected shafts** excluding any firefighting shaft					
a. any glazing described in Section 8, Diagram 32;	Not applicable	30	No provision [7]	E 30	Each side separately
b. any other part between the shaft and a protected lobby/corridor described in Diagram 32 above;	30	30	30	REI 30	
c. any part not described in (a) or (b) above.	See Table A2	See Table A2	See Table A2	REI see Table A2	
9. **Enclosure** (which does not form part of a compartment wall or a protected shaft) to a:					
a. protected stairway;	30	30	30 [8]	REI 30 [8]	Each side separately
b. lift shaft.	30	30	30	REI 30	

Fig 1.12 - Table A1 from Approved Document Part B2

Table A1 continued

Part of building	Minimum provisions when tested to the relevant part of BS 476 [1] (minutes)			Minimum provisions when tested to the relevant European standard (minutes) [9]	Method of exposure
	Loadbearing capacity [2]	Integrity	Insulation		
10. **Firefighting shafts**	120	120	120	REI 120	From side remote from shaft
a. construction separating firefighting shaft from rest of building;	60	60	60	REI 60	From shaft side
b. construction separating firefighting stair, firefighting lift shaft and firefighting lobby	60	60	60	REI 60	Each side separately
11. **Enclosure** (which is not a compartment wall or described in item 8) to a:					Each side separately
a. protected lobby;	30	30	30 [8]	REI 30 [8]	
b. protected corridor.	30	30	30 [8]	REI 30 [8]	
12. **Sub-division of a corridor**	30	30	30 [8]	REI 30 [8]	Each side separately
13. **Fire-resisting construction:**					
a. enclosing places of special fire hazard (see 8.12);	30	30	30	REI 30	
b. between store rooms and sales area in shops (see 5.58)	30	30	30	REI 30	Each side separately
c. fire-resisting subdivision described in Section 2, Diagram 16(b)	30	30	30	REI 30	
d. enclosing bedrooms and ancillary accomodation in care homes (see 3.48 and 3.50)	30	30	30	REI 30	
14. **Enclosure** in a flat to a protected entrance hall, or to a protected landing.	30	30	30 [8]	REI 30 [8]	Each side separately
15. **Cavity barrier**	Not applicable	30	15	E 30 and EI 15	Each side separately
16. **Ceiling** Diagram 35	Not applicable	30	30	EI 30	From underside
17. **Duct** described in paragraph 9.16e	Not applicable	30	No provision	E 30	From outside
18. **Casing** around a drainage system described in Section 10, Diagram 38	Not applicable	30	No provision	E 30	From outside
19. **Flue walls** described in Section 10, Diagram 39	Not applicable	Half the period specified in Table A2 for the compartment wall/floor	Half the period specified in Table A2 for the compartment wall/floor	EI half the period specified in Table A2 for the compartment wall/floor	From outside
16. **Fire doors**		See Table B1		See Table B1	

Notes:
1. Part 21 for loadbearing elements, Part 22 for non-loadbearing elements, Part 23 for fire-protecting suspended ceilings, and Part 24 for ventilation ducts. BS 476-8 results are acceptable for items tested or assessed before 1 January 1988.
2. Applies to loadbearing elements only (see B3.ii and Appendix E).
3. Guidance on increasing the fire resistance of existing timber floors is given in BRE Digest 208 *Increasing the fire resistance of existing timber floors* (BRE 1988).
4. A suspended ceiling should only be relied on to contribute to the fire resistance of the floor if the ceiling meets the appropriate provisions given in Table A3.
5. The guidance in Section 12 allows such walls to contain areas which need not be fire-resisting (unprotected areas).
6. Unless needed as part of a wall in item 5a or 5b.
7. Except for any limitations on glazed elements given in Table A4.
8. See Table A4 for permitted extent of uninsulated glazed elements.
9. The National classifications do not automatically equate with the equivalent classifications in the European column, therefore products cannot typically assume a European class unless they have been tested accordingly.
   'R' is the European classification of the resistance to fire performance in respect of loadbearing capacity; 'E' is the European classification of the resistance to fire performance in respect of integrity; and 'I' is the European classification of the resistance to fire performance in respect of insulation.

Table A2 Minimum periods of fire resistance

Purpose group of building	Minimum periods of fire resistance (minutes) in a:					
	Basement storey ($) including floor over		Ground or upper storey			
	Depth (m) of a lowest basement		Height (m) of top floor above ground, in a building or separated part of a building			
	More than 10	Not more than 10	Not more than 5	Not more than 18	Not more than 30	More than 30
1. Residential:						
a. Block of flats						
– not sprinklered	90	60	30*	60**†	90**	Not permitted
– sprinklered	90	60	30*	60**†	90**	120**
b. Institutional	90	60	30*	60	90	120#
c. Other residential	90	60	30*	60	90	120#
2. Office:						
– not sprinklered	90	60	30*	60	90	Not permitted
– sprinklered (2)	60	60	30*	30*	60	120#
3. Shop and commercial:						
– not sprinklered	90	60	60	60	90	Not permitted
– sprinklered (2)	60	60	30*	60	60	120#
4. Assembly and recreation:						
– not sprinklered	90	60	60	60	90	Not permitted
– sprinklered (2)	60	60	30*	60	60	120#
5. Industrial:						
– not sprinklered	120	90	60	90	120	Not permitted
– sprinklered (2)	90	60	30*	60	90	120#
6. Storage and other non-residential:						
a. any building or part not described elsewhere:						
– not sprinklered	120	90	60	90	120	Not permitted
– sprinklered (2)	90	60	30*	60	90	120#
b. car park for light vehicles:						
i. open sided car park (3)	Not applicable	Not applicable	15*+	15*+ (4)	15*+ (4)	60
ii. any other car park	90	60	30*	60	90	120#

Single storey buildings are subject to the periods under the heading "not more than 5". If they have basements, the basement storeys are subject to the period appropriate to their depth.

$ The floor over a basement (or if there is more than 1 basement, the floor over the topmost basement) should meet the provisions for the ground and upper storeys if that period is higher.

* Increased to a minimum of 60 minutes for compartment walls separating buildings.

** Reduced to 30 minutes for any floor within a flat with more than one storey, but not if the floor contributes to the support of the building.

\# Reduced to 90 minutes for elements not forming part of the structural frame.

\+ Increased to 30 minutes for elements protecting the means of escape.

† Refer to paragraph 7.9 regarding the acceptability of 30 minutes in flat conversions.

Notes:
1. Refer to Table A1 for the specific provisions of test.
2. "Sprinklered" means that the building is fitted throughout with an automatic sprinkler system in accordance with paragraph 0.16.
3. The car park should comply with the relevant provisions in the guidance on requirement B3, Section 11.
4. For the purposes of meeting the Building Regulations, the following types of steel elements are deemed to have satisfied the minimum period of fire resistance of 15 minutes when tested to the European test method;:
    i) Beams supporting concrete floors maximum $Hp/A=230m^{-1}$ operating under full design load.
    ii) Free standing columns, maximum $Hp/A=180m^{-1}$ operating under full design load.
    iii) Wind bracing and struts, maximum $Hp/A=210m^{-1}$ operating under full design load.
    Guidance is also available in BS 5950 Structural use of steelwork in building. Part 8 Code of practice for fire resistant design.

Fig 1.13 - Table A2 from Approved Document Part B2

FURTHER READING

Building Regulations Approved Documents

British Standards Institution

BRE

BRE Bookshop

Environment Agency

MCMULLAN, R (2007) Environmental Science in Building. 6th Ed. Basingstoke: Palgrave Macmillan.

DETAILING PRINCIPLES

SECTION 2

DETAILING PRINCIPLES

There is not one book, resource, or website that will ever provide a one size fits all answer to our construction detailing requirements. Every project is different, and with that, the designer is faced with a multitude of choices that need to be assessed and decisions that must be made.

The designer must consider selection of materials and components, meeting client requirements, financial restraints and budgets, aesthetic aspirations amongst many other things. It is crucial that guidance documents are consulted, manufacturer information, regulations and standards in order to present the most effective solution to the problem.

Some key sources of information are described below.

- Building Regulations Approved Documents
- British Standards
- Building Research Establishment (BRE) publications
- Trade Association publications
- Manufacturer technical guidance and literature
- Building Information Centres
- BBA - British Board of Agrement

The details in this book are intended as a guide - a base point for your own development of construction details. They shouldn't be copied as a quick solution to any construction problem - but be used as a starting point. You should question the detail.

- Is it right for your scheme, how does it integrate with the rest of the design?
- What should I change, and why?
- What elements need to be implemented from building regulations or guidance documents?
- How would this detail work in my particular region of the country?
- Can this detail be improved?

It is important to develop a critical approach, analyse the details and provide your own solution to each situation. Particular attention must be paid to junctions, due to the complexity of the geometry at these points, heat and moisture flow will not be straight through the fabric but influenced by both two and three dimensional effects. A junction is likely to contain structural elements that will have a higher thermal conductivity than the materials surrounding them. Junctions are also places where different materials meet, which can have differing properties, resulting in possibility of air gaps, movement and so on.

Beyond the guidance documents it is important to develop a key understanding of the detailing principles so that you are able to select strategies and solutions naturally, with a full understanding of the requirements and purpose of each construction detail or element. This next section looks at understanding the performance of the detail and what is required to address common functional requirements of a building.

WATER

Water can penetrate a building when there is an opening in the building assembly, there is water at the opening, and there is suitable force to push the water through the opening.

This opening can be a crack around a window or door, a gap between a roof tile or a joint between two elements of cladding. In order to stop water penetrating a building we must try to reduce the openings in the building assembly, keep water away from the openings that do occur, and neutralise the forces that can move the water through the assembly.

Reducing gaps and openings in the building assembly is about finding ways to eliminate these openings. Sealants and gaskets are a form of doing this, however a building skin shouldn't rely on this alone as sealants and gaskets will leak over time. It is better to create an overall strategy that addresses all three elements to be sure of a watertight design.

Strategies to keep water away from the building include methods such as a wash, overhang and overlap amongst others. These will be addressed individually in this chapter.

The forces that can push water through a building assembly are:

- Gravity: water will naturally move downwards
- Surface tension: causes water to cling to underside of a surface where it can run through into an opening
- Capillary action: however water can also move upwards - cracks or holes with smooth sides may act as capillary and by mechanisms of surface tension, draw in water
- Momentum: wind-blown rain possesses momentum that can move it through an opening
- Pressure differential: water will move from areas of higher pressure to areas of lower pressure

Forces	Neutralised by
Gravity	Wash and overlap
Surface tension	Overhang and drip
Capillary action	Capillary break
Absorption	Drain and weep
Momentum	Labrynth
Air pressure differentials	Rainscreen assembly

Fig 2.1 - Forces leading to moisture ingress

WASH

A wash is a slope given to a horizontal surface to drain water away from the building. A wash is used in door or window sills, sloping roof, slopes to drain, ground slopes away from a building. If the material is particularly porous it is important that the slope is steeper to allow for a faster removal of water.

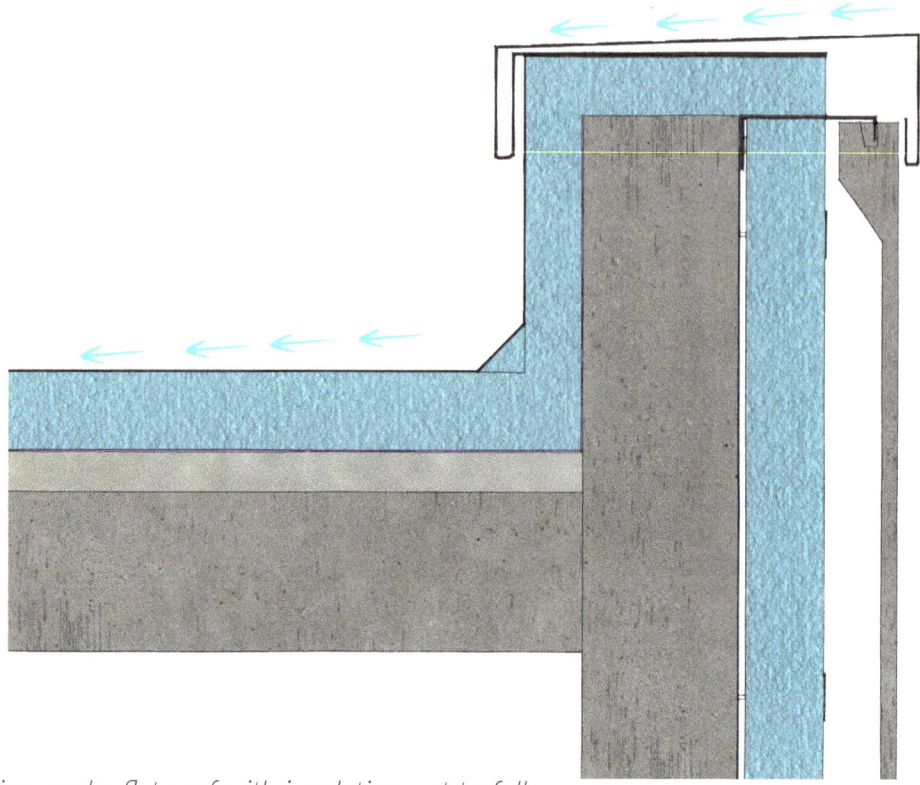

Fig 2.2 - Wash of a parapet flashing, and a flat roof with insulation cut to falls

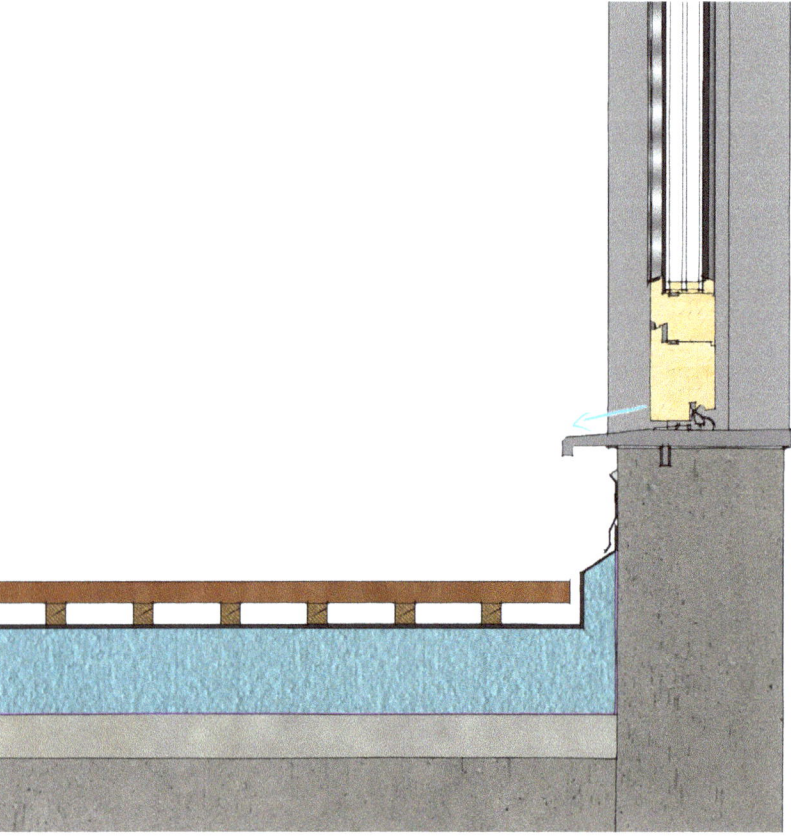

Fig 2.3 - Wash of a door threshold sill

OVERLAP

Used on a sloped or vertical plane, an overlap is where a higher element is extended over the lower element with enough distance that water cannot run behind or beneath the element. Gravity pulls the water down the sloped or vertical plan away from the overlap. An obvious example of this would be tiles on a roof. If the material is particularly porous it is important that the slope is steeper to allow for a faster removal of water.

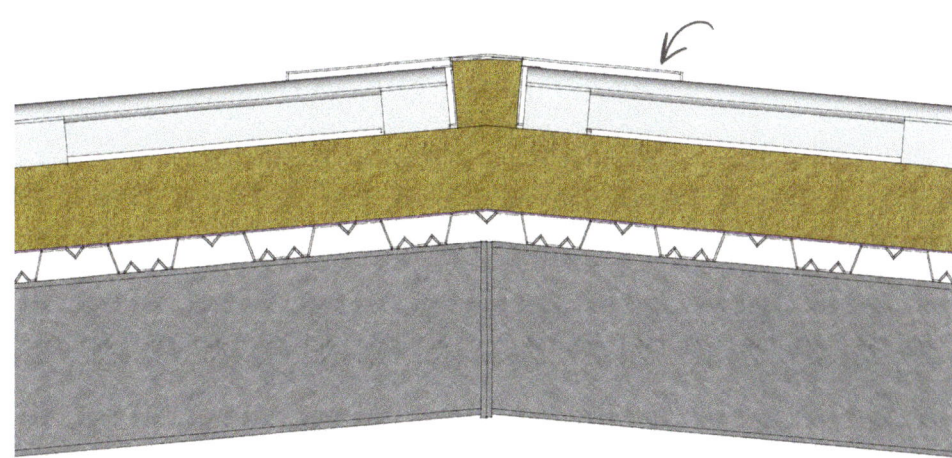

Fig 2.4 - Overlap of ridge flashing

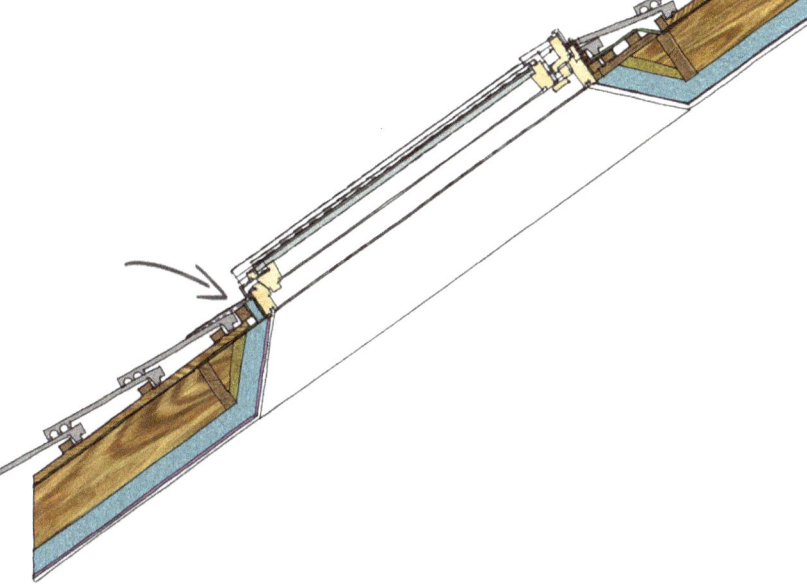

Fig 2.5 - Overlap flashing to roof light and tiles

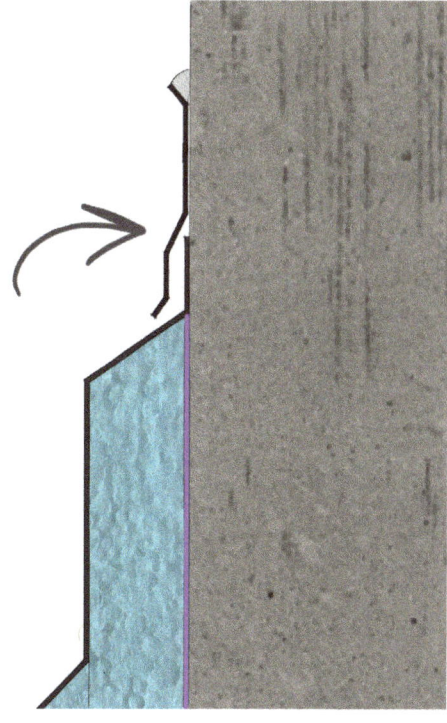

Fig 2.6 - Overlap flashing to edge detail

OVERHANG AND DRIP

Water running down a wall or element of the building assembly can be diverted from an opening by creating a projection above the opening - this is the overhang. The water is then forced by gravity to drip away from the overhang using a drip, often a groove on the underside of the overhang. An example of the overhang and drip can be seen on window sills, door sills, and coping.

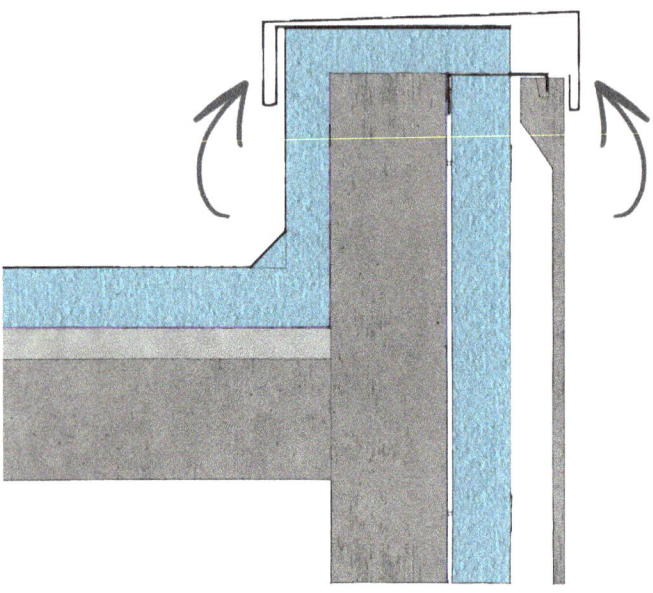

Fig 2.7 - Overhang and drip of parapet coping/flashing

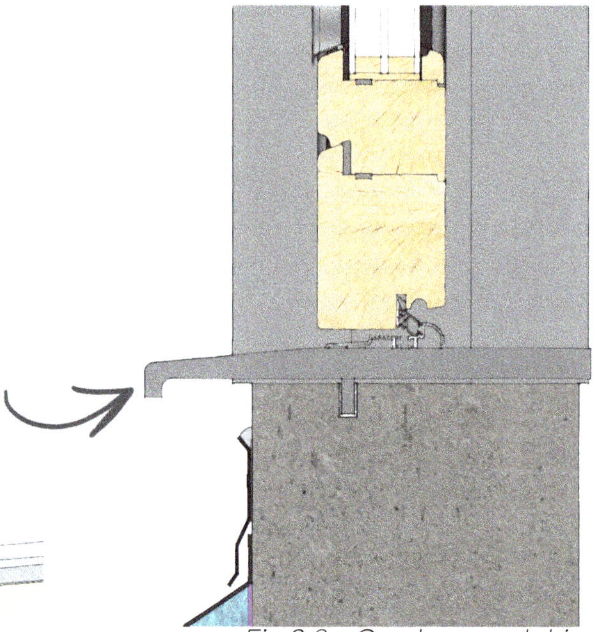

Fig 2.8 - Overhang and drip of sill

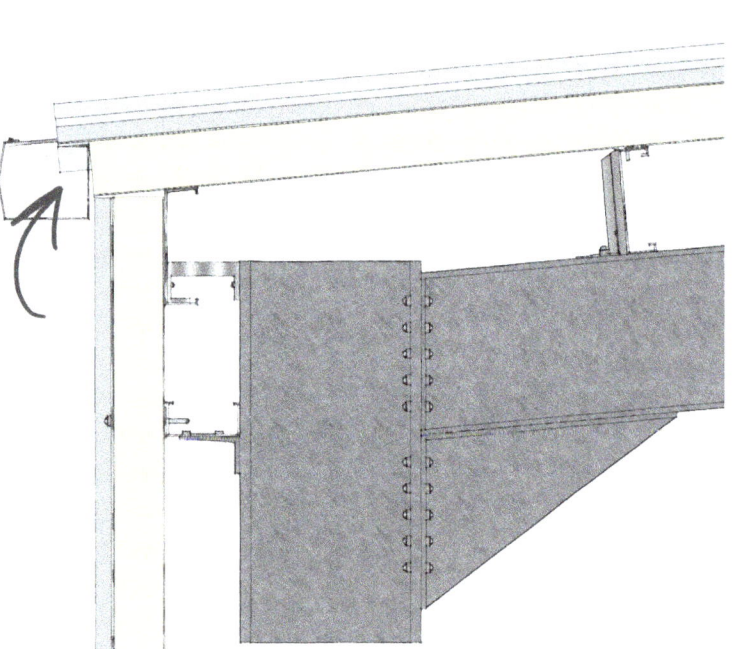

Fig 2.9 - Overhang and drip of eaves

CAPILLARY BREAK

Capillary action is the process in which water is able to pull itself upward or across a narrow crack. The crack has to be narrow for the water to be able to travel. In order to prevent capillary action, a break is provided so the water cannot bridge it.

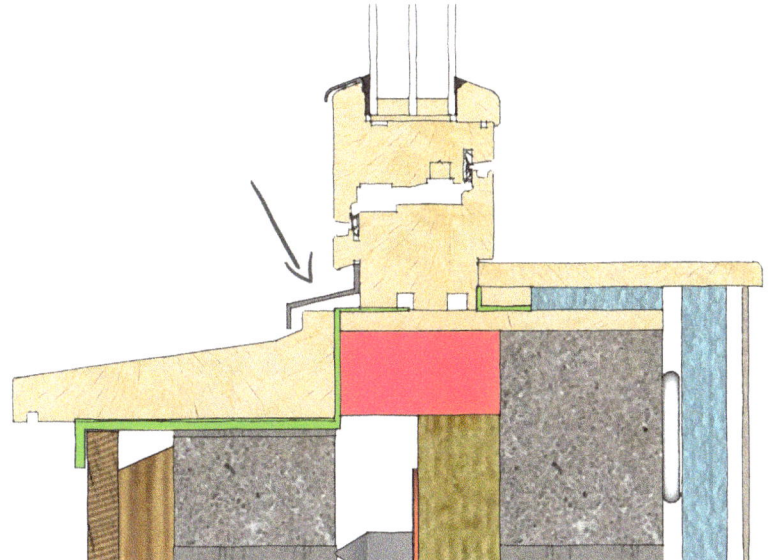

Fig 2.10 - Capillary break of window flashing

Fig 2.11 - Capillary break in vertical panel joint

DRAIN AND WEEP

In some constructions we can anticipate that water will penetrate the assembly and in this case we can detail in suitable measures. A drain and weep allows water to be conducted away from a cavity for example, and allowed to drain out of weep holes within the assembly. It can also be a suitable system to control any condensation that has built up in the construction. The drain and weep is used in masonry cavity wall construction, or a rainscreen cladding assembly.

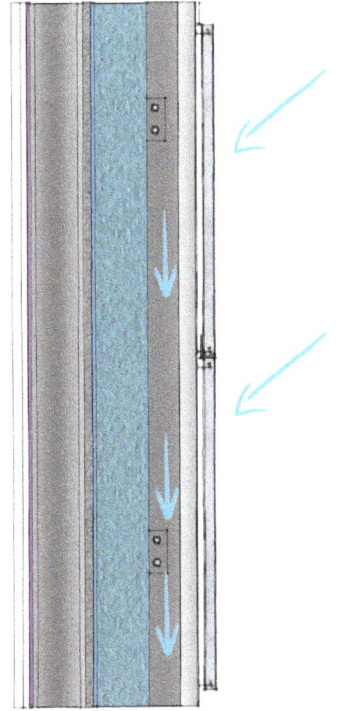

Fig 2.12 - Drain and weep of rainscreen cladding

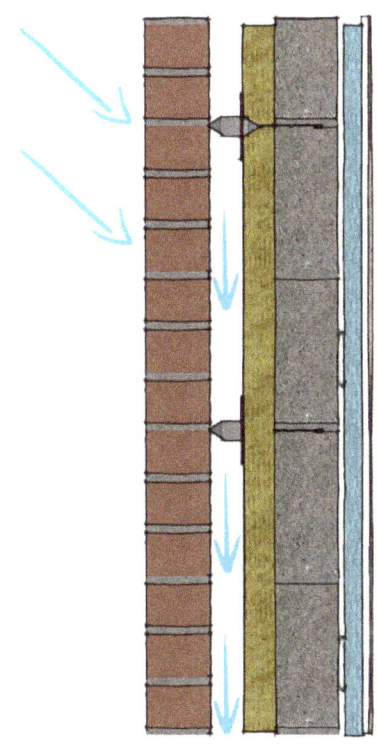

Fig 2.13 - Drain and weep of cavity wall

LABYRINTH

A labyrinth is used in a joint to stop a raindrop passing through the joint. The labyrinth is designed so that there is no straight line through the joint for anything to pass through with its own momentum.

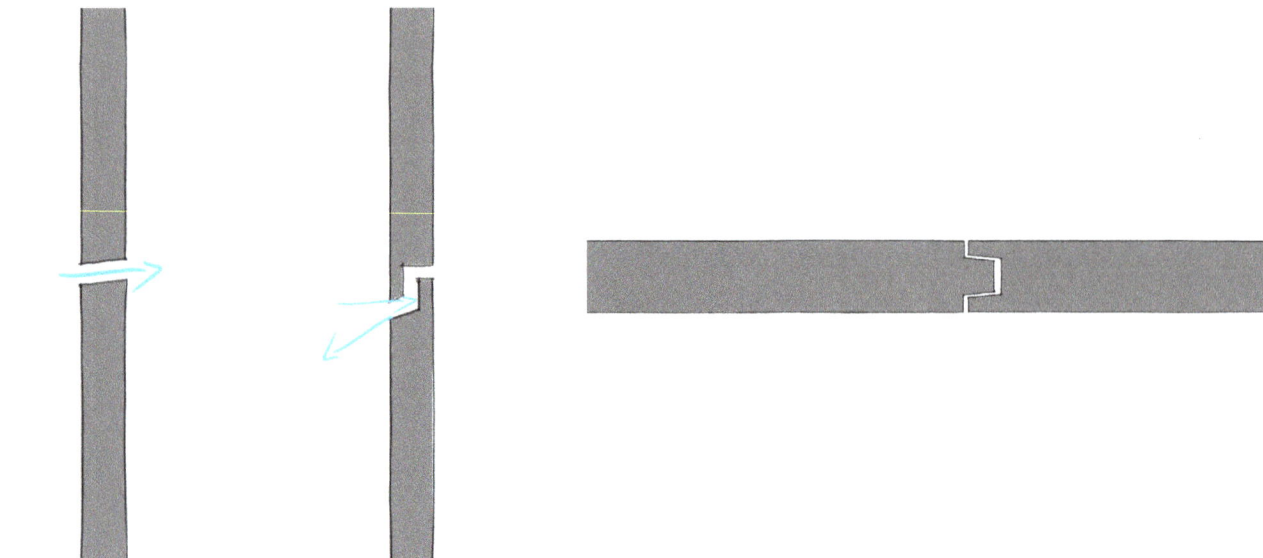

Fig 2.14 - Labyrinth in both vertical and horizontal joints between panels

WATER VAPOUR

Water vapour is always present in the air, however it can cause problems if it condenses on or within the building assembly. Condensation is caused when the moisture laden air comes into contact with a cold surface and the water vapour within the air is deposited as water onto the surface. Windows, solid walls on exposed parts of the house, cold water pipes and thermal bridges are all areas where condensation is most likely to occur. In turn, condensation is less likely to occur on double glazing or a well insulated wall because the internal temperature will be relatively high, above the dew point.

Interstitial condensation occurs within a material or porous structure. A solid wall where the inside temperature may be above the dew point but there may be a lower temperature in the wall itself.

Water vapour is often produced by activities in the house such as bathing, cleaning, drying clothes, cooking. These activities lead to condensation.

General precautions and procedures to avoid condensation include:

- the prevention of excess moisture being generated - this is largely down to the occupants.
- removal of excess moisture - in the form of suitable ventilation

There are some detailing principles that should be adopted in order to avoid water vapour condensing on or within the building assembly:

High air and fabric temperature will reduce the risk of condensation by keeping the temperature of the structure above dew point. This is best achieved with suitable thermal insulation - seen later in this chapter.

Other principles adopted to avoid water vapour condensing include the use of a vapour control layer and breather membrane.

VAPOUR CONTROL LAYER

A vapour barrier or vapour control layer is usually placed on the warm side of the insulation in order to reduce the passage of water vapour and potential problems of interstitial condensation. The VCL is a thin sheet material which reduces the diffusion of water vapour and improves the airtightness of the building fabric which in turn limits uncontrolled ventilation and leakage of warm moist air into the building assembly.

In timber and steel frame construction it is most common for the air and vapour control to be served by one membrane and air and vapour control layer (AVCL).

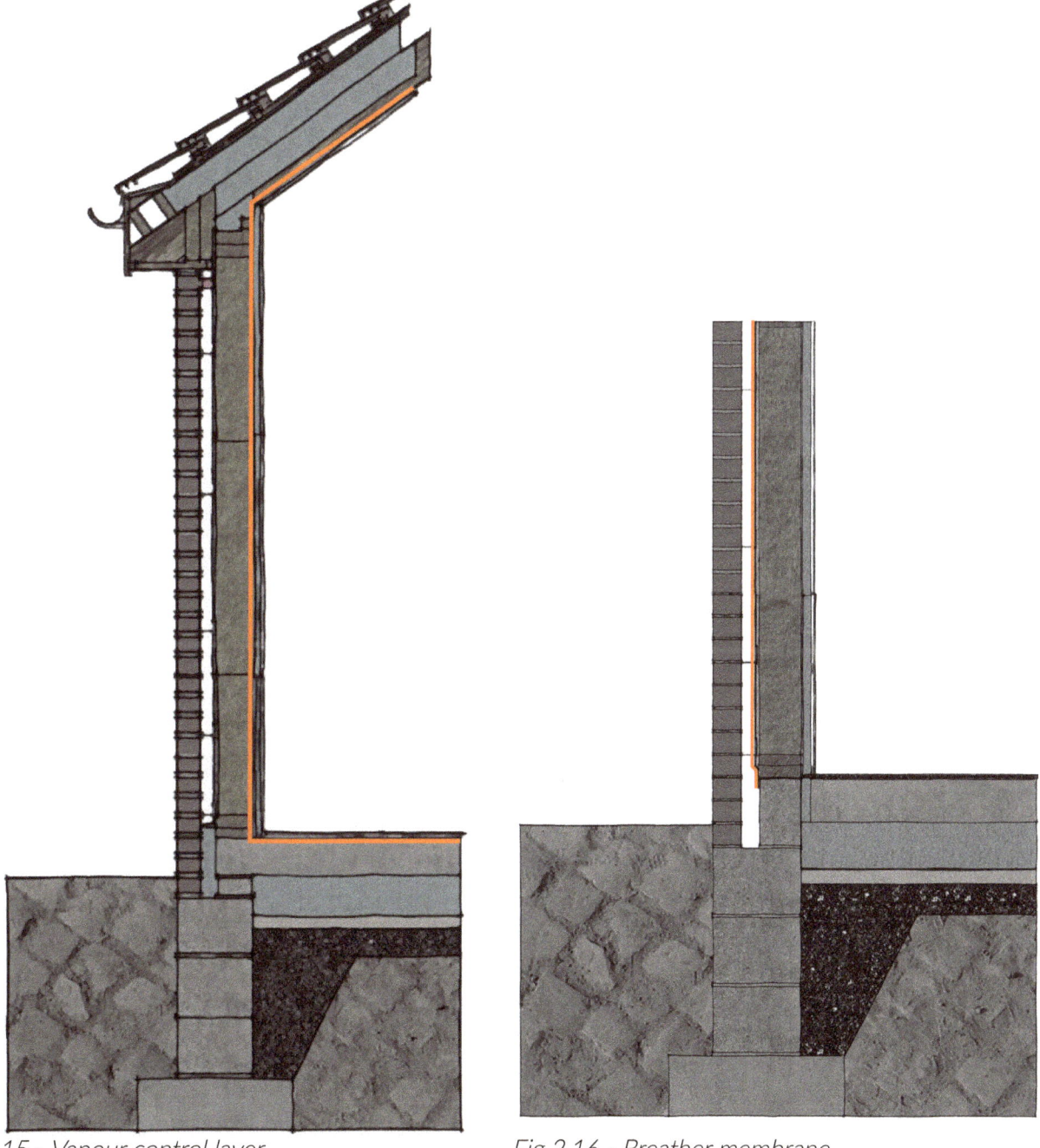

Fig 2.15 - Vapour control layer   Fig 2.16 - Breather membrane

BREATHER MEMBRANE

A breather membrane is a vapour permeable membrane, often positioned on the outside of a construction to protect vulnerable construction elements from rain during construction, and as a secondary protection throughout the life of the building. The breather membrane allows any trapped moist air within the construction to pass through and escape, while stopping any new moisture from penetrating the construction.

AIR

As we have mentioned in the previous chapter, leaking air can cause a number of problems to not only the structure but our occupants as well. An air leak within a building assembly can result in building performance problems such as:

- uncomfortable drafts
- wastes heated and cooled air which results in lost energy
- interstitial condensation resulting in damage to building fabric or reduced performance
- surface condensation resulting in mould growth, damage to finishes
- sound leaks
- transmission of heat or smoke in a fire from one part of the building to another

An air leak is an uncontrolled passage of air through an exterior wall of a building. Studies have shown that air leakage can contribute up to a third of total heat loss in a dwelling. For air leakage to occur there must be a pressure difference between the two points and a continuous flow path or opening connecting those two points.

AIR BARRIER SYSTEM

In order to reduce air leakage it is important to create an air barrier system that seals all openings at one plan in the building envelope. Great care needs to be taken when detailing junctions to ensure the air barrier remains constant.

In masonry construction the air barrier is often formed as part of the internal leaf of the cavity wall. If the inner leaf is well built with a coat of wet finish plaster, properly applied with correct detailing air tightness will be achieved. Dry-lining can also deliver air tightness, if detailed with appropriate sealing and taping, but often use of an airtight membrane is advised for improved performance in both cases.

In timber frame or steel frame construction the vapour control layer often serves as the airtightness barrier. The airtight layer is usually at or close to the inside of the building insulation envelope which also serves to prevent warm moist air from entering the building assembly.

Sealants, gaskets and weather strips are also used to ensure air tightness. Door and window openings utilise weather strips or gaskets to reduce possible air flow.

HEAT FLOW AND INSULATION

The excessive conduction of heat through a building can result in wasted energy, high heating and cooling costs, condensation leading to mould and general discomfort for the building occupants. Controlling this heat flow is crucial and this can be achieved by engaging a few detailing principles.

A thermal bridge, sometimes referred to as a cold bridge, is a weakness or discontinuity in the thermal envelope of a building. Most often seen at junctions, a thermal bridge occurs when the insulation is interrupted by a material more conductive. At these junctions heat can be lost as it is able to pass more easily through the building assembly. Thermal bridging can contribute quite significantly to overall heat losses in an otherwise well insulated dwelling. A thermal bridge can also result in condensation build up and mould growth which in turn has an effect on the building occupants. This occurs where the element that passes through the insulation layer creates a lower surface temperature and those locations, resulting in both surface and interstitial condensation.

When developing details, it is important to ensure the insulation layer remains consistent and unbroken to minimise thermal bridging. Insulation should be tightly fitted against and between construction elements to eliminate gaps and prevent slump or movement that could degrade performance.

THERMAL BREAKS AND ELIMINATING THERMAL BRIDGES

A thermal break is an insulation strip that is inserted into the building assembly where there is a risk of increased heat conduction. An example of this could be in a timber frame wall. The timber stud work will conduct heat more rapidly than the insulation between the studs. A layer of insulation is added to the inside or outside of the frame to improve the overall thermal resistance of the wall. The stud work of a timber frame wall can make up 15% of the wall, so it is worth countering this with the extra insulation. Another example of a practical use of thermal break would be in a steel frame wall, where metal conducts heat at a much higher rate. The key design aim for any junction is to ensure that there are no single elements or combination of elements that will conduct heat more rapidly through the construction. A continuous layer of thermal insulation should be designed throughout the building envelope. Heat loss can be reduced by ensuring any junctions allow the insulation within different elements to abut and/or overlap.

To avoid condensation risk there are two methods that can be considered. The first is a vapour permeable construction where the vapour permeability on materials from the warm side to the cold side of construction are increased. This allows water vapour to pass through the construction to reach a ventilated zone where it can be dispersed. The second is to install a vapour control layer on the warm side of construction to prevent the water vapour from penetrating areas of the building assembly that can cause problems. This option should always be used if there is not suitable ventilation to disperse the water vapour.

It is also worth noting that the use of two different types of insulation can cause condensation. If a rigid insulation is used with a fibrous insulation, the rigid insulation must be positioned on the warm side. If positioned the other way around, the water vapour could pass through the fibrous insulation and become trapped when it meets the rigid insulation creating a potential build up of condensation.

It is possible to read more about the risk of surface condensation in the document BRE IP 1/06 "Assessing the effects of thermal bridging at junctions and around openings" and BS 5250:2011.

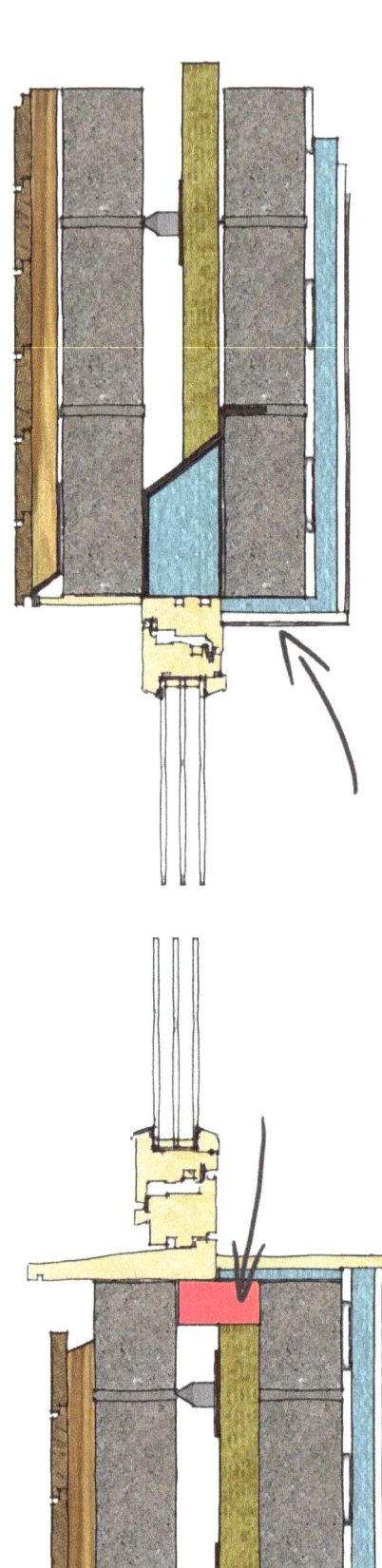

Fig 2.17 - Insulated plasterboard reveal to window head with insulated lintel

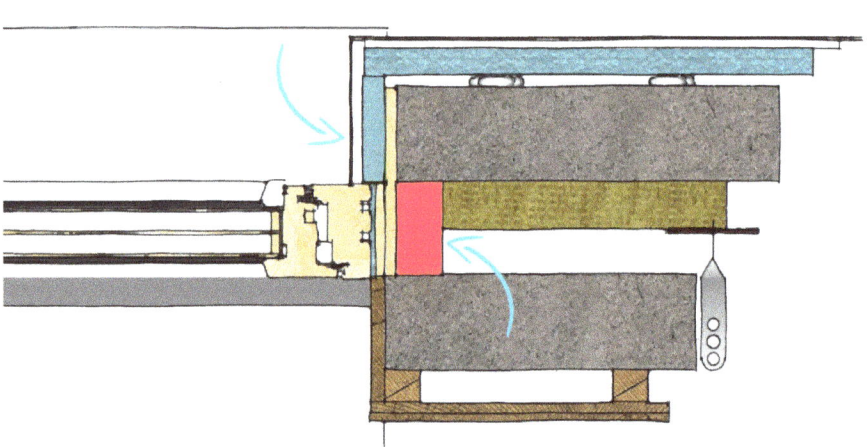

Fig 2.18 - Insulated plasterboard reveal and PU/PIR insulated cavity closer to window jamb

Fig 2.19 - Cavity closer with PU/PIR insulation core, insulation under internal window sill

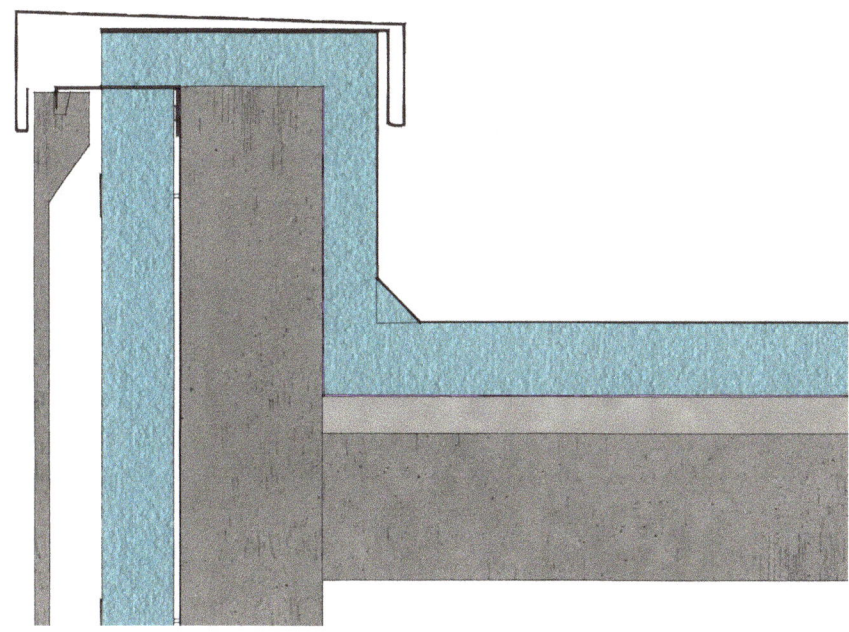

Fig 2.20 - Increased insulation around parapet

Fig 2.21 - Increased insulation at slab perimeter, with cavity insulation extending below floor insulation

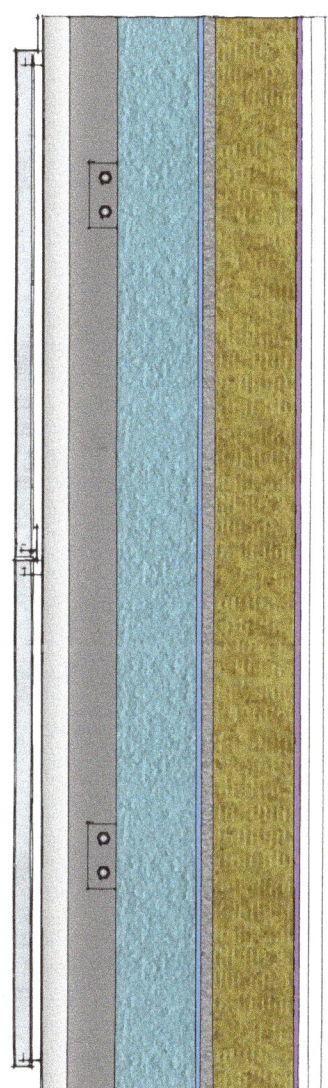

Fig 2.22 - Additional insulation on inside face of steel frame construction

Blank Page

MATERIALS

SECTION 3

SELECTING MATERIALS

There are many factors to take into consideration when selecting materials for construction, some of which are outlined below.

Structural requirements
Your structural material selection can often be dictated by the structural needs of the project, where spans and loads will naturally look to specific systems that are most suitable for the design.

Budget
Cost is always an important factor in material selection, both the initial cost of the material but also the lifetime cost. Ongoing lifetime maintenance of some lower costing materials may be less cost effective than a high cost material that is lower maintenance over its lifetime. An example of this could be ongoing maintenance of a softwood timber cladding compared to a more expensive, but durable natural stone cladding.

Location
Often the site location and orientation will play an important part in material selection. Not only should materials be chosen that relevant and appropriate for the context of the site, they also need to be suitable for the exposure, water penetration and possible pollution levels. Sourcing local materials for both environmental and aesthetic reasons should also be considered.

Construction time-frame
Working with some materials is more labour intensive than others. Therefore it is important to consider the construction time-frame, and whether it would be prudent to select prefabricated elements or materials, or whether there is the time scale available to work with more labour intensive elements. As an example, prefabricated assemblies will reduce construction times, while the use of cast in situ concrete will increase construction times due to the curing that has to be factored into the programme.

Material availability
Delivery times of materials can sometimes cause long and costly delays to a building project. Consider the availability of the key materials being chosen and whether or not they fit into the construction programme.

Lifespan requirement of the building
Some materials are considered to be far more durable, and therefore have a longer life that some other materials. Knowing the intended lifespan of the building will help inform appropriate material selection.

Maintenance
Discussions with the client should reveal whether or not an intensive maintenance programme is suitable for the project or not. These discussions should dictate material selection, with some materials requiring far more maintenance and care over their lifespan than others. For example, a softwood timber cladding will require regular maintenance, but a stone or concrete cladding will be far more self sufficient. Clients should be issued with a manual that describes necessary maintenance of the building after handover.

Environmental factors
Embodied energy, sustainability and recycling possibility are all important considerations in the selection of materials, now more than ever. Not only should you consider whether the materials have been sourced sustainably, transport requirements to get the material to site, but also its use after the life of the building and whether it can be recycled. The embodied energy of a material is the sum of all the energy inputs required for its production, from extraction to fabrication and transport, etc. It is often about finding a balance between materials that have good durability and good sustainability. Although the embodied energy of materials used to construct a building is far less than the energy used in the house over its lifetime, changes to design and standards suggest that operational expenditure is set to reduce significantly over time. The improvement of thermal insulation, and use of passive and active controls make the embodied energy component of the building more relevant.

Embodied Energy Values Used	GJ/tonne
Aluminium alloy	200
Synthetic rubber	150
Structural steel	26.8
Steel used in windows	31
Float glass	15
Softwood	13
Plasterboard	2.7
Facing bricks	11.7
Mortar	0.84
In situ concrete structure above ground	1.09
Steel reinforcement	26.8
Plywood	17
Concrete block	1.31
Wall insulation	35
Plastic	150

[Table: Adapted from Modern Construction Handbook - Andrew Watts]

Fig 3.1 - Table of embodied energy of construction materials

Aesthetic factors

There are many aspects of the aesthetic, when looking at material selection, that can be taken into account. How will the material be detailed, will the joints and connections between materials work together? What impression are you wanting to achieve with the material choice and how will it read? How will the material weather? Will it improve the look of the building or be detrimental over time? How will the material contribute to the overall feel of the building? A concrete structure will look solid and permanent, a lightweight material such as steel or glass can give more of an impression of lightness and transparency. Other considerations to note are finishes and treatments, colours and textures, and how all of these work together to create an overall cohesive design.

In this chapter we will briefly look at some of the more common materials used in commercial construction and some of their properties.

BRICK

CLASSIFICATIONS

Bricks are classified according to their use:

Common
These are used in situations where they may not be seen, they are able to carry the loads normally supported by brickwork, but have a dull texture or poor colour. They have acceptable general brick properties, but produced cheaply. They are often used on walls that will then be rendered or plastered.

Facing
Facing brick is also capable of carrying normal loads but have a better appearance and are produced in a range of colours and finishes, used in areas where they will be seen. They are more expensive to produce but have similar performance characteristics to the common brick.

Engineering Bricks
These bricks are made from selected clays and carefully produced to be able to carry heavier loads than a standard brick. They are mainly used for applications such as brick piers, engineering works, or works below ground.

Special Bricks
Special bricks are made for specific applications, such as copings, plinths, bull-nose edges and so on.

SIZES

Standard metric brick dimensions are 215mm x 102.5mm x 65mm. These dimensions are sometimes known as working dimensions or nominal sizes. The coordinating dimensions which include the mortar required on one bed, one header face and one stretcher face - 225mm x 112.5mm x 75mm.

PROPERTIES

When specifying bricks, certain performance characteristics need to be considered.

Compressive Strength
Compressive strength of bricks is measured by crushing 12 bricks individually until they fail or crumble. The average strength of the brick is measured in newton per millimetre of surface area required to crush the brick. The resistance can vary from about 3.5 N/mm2 for soft facing bricks up to 140N/mm2 for engineering bricks. This is clearly quite a range.

Water Absorption
Absorption rates in bricks can vary between 1% and 35%. The amount of water a brick will absorb is a guide to its density and therefore its strength. The level of water absorption is critical for bricks below dpc level or for dpcs. Water absorption should be a maximum of 4.5% for Class A engineering bricks or bricks used for damp proof courses, and a maximum of 7% for Class B engineering bricks. Absorption can cause problems in the bricklaying process whereby bricks with high suction rates absorb water rapidly from the mortar making repositioning difficult as work proceeds.

Thermal and moisture movement
Building materials expand and contract as a result of moisture or temperature changes. Allowance must be made for this in brickwork by using control joints. A brick wall will be constructed using movement joints at intervals according to current standards in order to allow for the movement in the material. Restrained walls should feature joints allowing 1mm of movement per 1m of brickwork, typically at 10 - 12m centres. Unrestrained walls should have movement joints at 7-8m centres. Manufacturers will offer guidance and current standards information for the positioning of movement joints. Building joints can be hidden using

careful detailing and choosing suitable locations for structural forms to adjoin, abutments, returns, recesses, downpipes and so on.

Thermal Conductivity
Generally clay bricks have high thermal conductivity and therefore a poor thermal insulation value. The thermal conductivity value varies with the type and density of the brick along with moisture content. Thermal conductivity of a clay brick with 5% moisture content typically ranges from 0.65 to 1.95 W/mK.

Fire Resistance
The fire resistance of clay brickwork is generally good - it retains its stability, integrity and insulating properties since the bricks have been fired at a higher temperature than that which normally would occur in house fires.

Appearance
Bricks are available in a wide range of colours and textures. Choice can be influenced by neighbouring buildings, local authority requirements or personal choice.

Sound Insulation
The sound insulation of brickwork is directly proportional to the density of the wall. Brickwork is a good barrier to airborne sound provided there are no voids through the mortar for the passage of sound.

For further information on bricks visit:
Brick Development Association

BLOCKS

Modern blocks in the UK are generally made from a form concrete. The blocks are larger in size than bricks and used extensively for both load bearing and non load bearing walls.

There are three general categories for concrete blocks - dense concrete, lightweight concrete and autoclaved aerated concrete (AAC). Blocks are manufactured from cement and either dense or lightweight aggregates as solid, cellular or hollow blocks. A solid block contains no formed holes or cavities. Cellular blocks contain one or more formed holes or cavities that do not completely pass through the block, whilst a hollow block has holes that pass completely through the block. Autoclaved aerated concrete blocks are made from a mixture of cement, sand or pulverised fuel ash admixtures to aerate the mix, and water. These blocks are extremely lightweight and have a density as low as 475kg/m^3 with high thermal resistance properties. They also have high water absorption characteristics.

The most common size for a concrete block is 440mm long by 215mm high. The height of the block coincides with three courses of brick in order to correspond with wall ties and bonding to brickwork. For cavity walls and internal load bearing walls 100mm thick blocks are used. 75mm thick lightweight aggregate blocks can be used for non load bearing walls.

Compressive Strength
The majority of concrete blocks have a compressive strength ranging from 2.8 to 30 N/mm^2. Aerated concrete blocks have strengths up to approximately 5.5N/mm^2.

Water Absorption
Blocks have a higher water absorption than bricks due to their porous composition and they generally contain holes or cavities in their construction. Concrete blocks that contain dense aggregates are better for below ground level use. Aerated concrete blocks are especially porous and must be protected from moisture penetration prior to their installation.

Thermal and Moisture movement
Moisture movement can be a problem with concrete blocks, particularly aerated concrete blocks and can lead to cracking due to drying shrinkage if they have been allowed to get wet prior to installation.

Thermal conductivity
Blocks have relatively good thermal resistance, in part due to their cellular or hollow construction. Thermal conductivities for blocks range from 0.70 W/mK to 1.28W/mK for dense cellular blocks, 0.11W/mK-0.20W/mK for lightweight cellular blocks and autoclaved aerated blocks.

Fire resistance
Concrete blocks offer good fire resistance with a solid 90mm un-plastered block giving up to 60 minutes fire protection, while thicker blocks can achieve up to 360 minutes fire protection.

Sound insulation
Sound insulation of concrete blocks is lower than that of bricks as they have a lower density.

For more information visit:
Concrete Block Association

CONCRETE

Concrete is a mixture of cement, aggregates and water, combined together to the correct proportions to give a strong, dense material ideal for structural components. When initially mixed, concrete is a plastic material which takes the shape of the mould or formwork. While the cement provides the setting and hardening element to the concrete, the water provides the chemical reaction with the cement allowing it to set and harden. The aggregates provide the bulk to the concrete and contribute to the overall strength. Concrete can be cast in situ (in the position it is meant to occupy in the building) or it can be cast in moulds away from its final position and moved into place when it has set. The moulds take the form of timber or steel formwork or shuttering.

Cement

Cements are manufactured in three main types - portland cements, super sulphated cements and high alumina cements. Portland cement is the most commonly used of the three types, it is available in many sub types but most common is OPC. OPC (Ordinary Portland Cement) has good setting time and strength development to suit most uses. Others include Rapid Hardening Portland Cement, which allows earlier striking of formwork, Sulphate Resisting Portland Cement which can resist sulphate salts attack which is present in some soils.

Aggregates

Aggregates form a major component of concrete - without aggregates concrete would be expensive and suffer from high amounts of drying shrinkage. Aggregates make up approximately 80% by weight of the concrete mix, with the shape and size of the particles being important factors that will influence workability and strength of the concrete. Aggregates fall into two main categories, fine aggregates made up of particles smaller than 5mm in diameter, and coarse, made up of particles larger than 5mm. They can also be classified according to their density, dense and lightweight aggregates.

Typically 20mm aggregate is used for most construction work. Lightweight aggregate concretes give a better fire resistance and thermal insulation value than concretes manufactured using a dense aggregate. However, lightweight aggregate concrete has a higher porosity and as a result does not perform so well with weather resistance and durability.

Aggregates are usually graded, ensuring that all voids between the particles are filled and that all particles are evenly coated with cement.

Strength

Concrete is strong in compression but the tensile strength of concrete is usually only 10% of the compressive strength. As a consequence steel reinforcement bars or a fabric mesh is often used as a reinforcing material. Strength is also influenced by the proportioning of the materials and the type of aggregate used.

Fire Resistance

Concrete has good fire resisting properties, with no significant loss of strength up to 250ºC. The fire resistance can be increased by using specific aggregates such as blast furnace slag, crushed bricks or lightweight aggregates.

Weather resistance

The proportioning mix of the concrete will dictate the weather resistance of the concrete. Where concrete needs to be weather and frost resistance it is important that the porosity of the concrete is minimised.

Thermal insulation

Concrete made from lightweight aggregates has an improved thermal insulation performance due to these aggregates containing more air which is a good thermal insulator.

For more information visit:
Concrete Society
BRMCA
The Concrete Centre

TIMBER

Timber is a very popular material in the construction industry due to its versatility, diversity, availability, and aesthetic properties. The material is relatively cheap, strong and can be easily converted into different shapes and sizes as required. Approximately 30% of the annual worldwide timber harvest is for use in construction with the rest going to paper production and fuel.

Commercial timber is classified into two main categories, hardwood and softwood. Hardwoods have a more complex cellular structure to softwoods and therefore present different characteristics and qualities.

Typical Hardwood	Typical Softwood
Imported:	*Imported:*
Afrormosia, Mahogany, Obeche, Sapele, Teak, Utile	Douglas Fir, Parana Pine, Pitch Pine, Redwoods, Wester Hemlock, Wester Red Cedar
Home produced:	*Home produced:*
Ash, Beech, Birch, Elm, Oak, Sycamore	European Spruce, Larch, Scots Pine, Yew

Fig 3.1 Typical hardwood and softwood
(Information from Fundamental Building Technology - see references)

Softwoods are from conifers, generally with needle shaped leaves, evergreen and growing in the northern temperate forests. Softwood examples can be seen in Figure 3.1. Softwoods are characteristically fast growing, and therefore cheaper than hardwoods. Softwoods take up about 75% of timber used in the UK construction industry. They have a lower density than hardwoods, so they are not as structurally strong, they are also less durable and tend to require preservative treatment.

Hardwoods are broad leafed deciduous trees, although the tropical varieties are evergreen. Hardwoods are strong, durable and are often used for decorative purposes. Hardwoods are generally more expensive than softwoods depending on species and dimensions of timber required.

Strength
Timber has a high strength to weight ratio, with the strength increasing in direct proportion to its density. Timber is quite elastic and can retain its original shape after deforming under a load that has then been removed. Defects in the timber, such as knots, checks and splits can affect the strength of the wood.

Timber is graded into Strength Classes. Softwoods are divided into 12 strength classes, (C14 to C50) and hardwoods into 8 strength classes (D18 to D70). This grading allows designers to specify timber fit for purpose and not over specify resulting in an increased cost and waste of material unnecessarily. The most commonly used strength classes for softwood in residential construction are C16 and C24.

TRADA have produced span tables as a guide for specifiers designing structural elements in construction. These span tables cover floors, ceilings, rafters, and so on, allowing for accurate timber sizing according to project requirements.

Thermal and moisture movement
Wood is an anisotropic material, it can take up moisture in the surrounding atmosphere which will cause it to swell or shrink when it loses the moisture again. If a timber has a high moisture content during construction, which then dries when the building is heated, it can have quite significant effects such as gaps forming, damage to finishes, or in worst cases the timber can even split or crack.

Thermal insulation
Timber is a good thermal insulator in comparison to other structural components such as steel or concrete.

Fire Resistance

Timber is a combustible material, but it is possible to provide a level of fire resistance due to the predictability of the timber. Timber has a charring rate, meaning as it burns it results in a loss of section at a predictable speed, where just a few millimetres under the burning zone the temperature of the timber will be close to normal. It is therefore able to retain its strength unlike other structural elements such as steel. Timber can be treated with surface coatings to retard the spread of fire.

Durability

Timber has a good resistance to sunlight and frost, and can be submerged in water for periods of time. However, timber is susceptible to attack from fungi, insects and marine borers. Fungal attack can be avoided if moisture content is kept below 20%. Fungal issues such as dry rot and wet rot are both related to moisture content and can cause quite significant damage.

Timbers have a grading for durability classified into five groups:
Class 1: Very durable
Class 2: Durable
Class 3: Moderately durable
Class 4: Slightly durable
Class 5: No durable

Timbers with low durability can be treated with preservatives to improve durability and reduce possibility of decay. Areas that would be particularly important are:
- where timber is in contact with ground
- where timber is used at or below the DPC level
- where the timber is encased in concrete or masonry
- where ventilation can not be provided
- where moisture content is likely to exceed 20%
- where low durability class timber is used in a high risk area
- where fungal or insect attack are high risk

Sustainability

There is a large emphasis on sustainability in timber production which has led to a number of schemes to ensure that timber is being used from sustainable sources. These schemes vary from country to country, but the UK has the FSC - the Forest Stewardship Council, and the Programme for the Endorsement of Forest Certification (PEFC). Specifiers are urged to use FSC timber wherever possible to ensure that it has come from well managed forests and is truly sustainable.

Timber has the highest sustainability credentials of all the construction materials, given that it takes up CO_2 from the air rather than produce it. It is also a great product for recycling and reclaiming, as well as being biodegradable. Chippings and sawdust from production can also be used in various boardings, such as particle board.

TIMBER PRODUCTS

There are a wide range of timber products manufactured from wood materials. Many products are manufactured from small timber sections or by-products. These include:
- Plywood
- Fibreboard
- Blackwood and laminboard
- Laminated timber
- Cross laminated timber
- Structural insulated panels
- Shingles
- Veneer

The main products we will look at are the boarding materials.

PLYWOOD

Plywood is made by laminating a series of thin timber layers or plies - they are bonded together using adhesive. The plies are crossed at 90° degrees to each other around a central core ply. They are then cured in a hot press, sanded and trimmed to the standard dimensions - usually 1200mmx2400mm. Sheet thickness ranges from 4mm to 25mm for normal construction use.

Plywood is classed according to the adhesive used and suitability to given applications.

Class1: Dry conditions (suitable for interior use)
Class 2: Humid conditions (suitable for protected applications such as behind cladding or under roof coverings.)
Class 3: Exterior conditions (exposed weather)

Plywood is used for a range of applications in the construction industry due to its strength and versatility. It is used for making structural beams such as box beams and I beams, as well as plywood panels, sheathing for timber frame, floor and roof decking, formwork amongst other things.

PARTICLEBOARD

Particle boards comprise of particles of wood, such as flakes, chips, shavings or sawdust, bonded tighter under pressure and heat to form a panel material. Particleboard can come in a range of qualities dependent on the resin used. Wood particle board is made with a resin, whereas cement particle board uses a cement binder. Wood particleboard (chipboard) is predominantly used in the furniture industry, veneered flat pack furniture is a perfect match to the qualities of chipboard. Flooring grade particle board is popular in residential construction, with heavy duty flooring and flat roof decking a structural grade moisture resistant panel would be specified.

The cement particleboards offer improved resistance to fire and water and is suitable for use both internally and externally.

OSB (ORIENTED STRAND BOARD)

OSB is manufactured from 0.5mm thick timber flakes or strands up to 75mm in width. They are formed into boards using adhesive and pressed and heated to set and form the board. OSB is similar in make up to particle board but similar in strength to plywood. OSB is used in large quantities for sheathing in timber frame housing, while the moisture resistant grade is suited to roof sarking, with the even higher grade used for flat roof decking. OSB can also be used in I Beams and heavy duty flooring. Its thickness can range from 6mm to 40mm. OSB is graded as follows:
OSB 1: General purpose, interior - dry conditions
OSB 2: Load-bearing - dry conditions
OSB 3: Load bearing - humid conditions
OSB 4: Heavy duty, load bearing - humid conditions

For more information visit:
Structural Timber Association
TRADA

METALS

Metals are categorised into ferrous and non ferrous. The term ferrous metal indicates a predominance of iron within the element. Examples of ferrous metals include steel and pig iron, and alloys of iron with other metals such as stainless steel.

Non-ferrous metals do not contain iron in appreciable amounts. Examples of non ferrous metals include aluminium, copper, lead, nickel, zinc.

A wide range of metals are used in the construction industry, ranging from structural uses, to fixings, to roof coverings and claddings. The most popular being iron, steel, aluminium, lead and zinc. Although metal has a relatively large energy input for production, this is often offset by its long life and recycling options.

Metal is a high density, high thermal conductivity material, which is generally prone to corrosion. Often alloys are used to reduce this effect.

STEEL

Structural Steel
Steel is a very common construction material. Structural steel is formed into profiles, with a specific cross section according to structural requirements and standards. The most common structural shapes in the UK are the I-Beam (an I shaped cross section) which includes the Universal Beam (UB) and the Universal Column (UC). Also the SHS structural hollow section which include square, rectangle and circular cross sections, are common structural steel shapes. Structural steel can be made by hot or cold rolling, or in some cases they can be made up of individual sections welded together.

Strength
Steel, unlike concrete, has good compressive strength as well as tensile strength - hence its consistent use in commercial and industrial construction.

Fire Resistance
Steel does not retain its strength and stiffness well when heated to high temperatures. As a result a number of fire protection measures are often taken to give suitable fire rating performance. These measures include intumescent coatings, sprayed coatings, boxing in or encasing the steel in masonry or concrete.

Corrosion
Steel can corrode after prolonged contact with water and as a result is often treated to provide water resistance. The fire resistant coatings often provide water resistance.

Steel frame construction
Light steel frame construction is an alternative to timber frame construction. The steel frame tends to be a galvanised steel channel section which is assembled off site and bolted together once in situ. Steel frame construction is covered later in this book.

Profiled Steel Sheeting
Steel sheeting, with varying profiles is often used in roof and wall cladding, particularly in a commercial and industrial setting.

Sheet Metal Coverings for Roofing
A sheet metal covering for a roof must be malleable, in order to adapt to the varying profiles of a roof. A great advantage of sheet metals for roofing and cladding is that they are durable, aesthetically pleasing and recyclable. They are however a fairly expensive option. Sheet metals will tend to have more thermal movement than other roofing materials and therefore require joints that can accommodate this movement.

ALUMINIUM

Aluminium is popular due to its durability and is lightweight compared to steel. It is used for roofing, cladding, curtain walling, structural glazing, flashings, rainwater goods, and much more.

Aluminium has a natural extremely thin aluminium oxide film on its surface, that, once scratched will immediately be produced. This makes it a durable choice for many uses in construction.

Aluminium can receive various coatings to improve either appearance or durability. Surface textures can be achieved such as polished, matt, etched and pattern rolled.

Corrosion
Aluminium is susceptible to corrosion from the alkalinity of wet cement, concrete and mortar. Therefore, it is important during construction that any aluminium is protected. Aluminium can also be affected by preservatives used to treat timber which could cause problems in conditions of high humidity. It is also susceptible to corrosion from other metals, in particular copper, so rainwater from a copper roof must not come into contact with an aluminium cladding for example.

COPPER

Copper is used in construction for roofing, and in some cases wall cladding. Copper is well known for its patina, the development of the green colour which gradually spreads when exposed to environmental conditions. In typical settings, the green patina will develop over about ten years. On wall cladding, or vertical settings however, the copper will often retain its colour due to fast water run off.

Corrosion
Copper is resistant to corrosion although it can cause staining to other materials from rainwater run off. Zinc, galvanised steel and non anodised aluminium should not be used under copper.

LEAD

Lead is used in construction for roofing, cladding and flashings, along with gutter linings. In roofing, lead is installed in continuous smooth sheets, with the joints wood cored rolled, hollow rolled, or standing seams. In wall cladding the joints are similar to roofing, but in some cases a lead faced panel can be used and fixed to the support system.

Corrosion
Lead can cause some staining to surrounding materials, which can be avoided by the use of a patination oil after the lead has been installed. Lead is generally resistant to corrosion but care must be taken to avoid a build up of condensation underneath the lead.

ZINC

Zinc is often used in roofing and cladding in the construction industry. Roll cap and standing seam roofing systems are both used, usually installed over a timber deck. In cladding, zinc can be used as interlocking tiles, held in place with fixing clips. Zinc tarnishes in the air and produces a protective oxide film - this prevents further degradation. Zinc used in a roofing system would have an expected life span of 40 years, while in a wall cladding position could last up to 60 years.

Corrosion
As mentioned previously, zinc doesn't get along very well with copper, where rainwater draining from copper discharges onto zinc. Galvanised steel above zinc can cause staining. Similar to lead, condensation build up underneath the zinc will also cause corrosion.

FLAT ROOF MATERIALS

Materials that are used in flat roof construction consist of mastic asphalt, bitumen sheet built up roofing or single ply sheeting or membranes, along with metal sheeting which we have covered previously.

MASTIC ASPHALT

Mastic asphalt is a jointless, weather proof and impermeable material with a low softening point. It is delivered onto site in the form of blocks ready to be melted before applying to the roof. The hot material is then spread over the roof in two layers which then cools and forms a hard waterproof surface. The layers tend to come to 20mm with up stands of 150mm to any masonry, roof lights or pipes. The mastic asphalt is laid over a sheathing felt to prevent any effects from structural or thermal movement, and finished with 10mm of stone chippings to protect the surface from softening under sunlight. This also prolongs the life of the mastic asphalt. If there is no parapet wall the asphalt is designed to overhang and drain into gutters. A flashing is usually positioned to drain run off from the asphalt to the gutter.

Asphalt is considered to be a relatively cheap flat roofing option, and more durable than built up bitumen sheeting, with a life of around 20 years. Mastic asphalts is derived from crude oil, and is said to cause harm to the environment in its manufacturing process. However, it is reclaimable and possible to remove from the roof and reuse.

BITUMEN FELT ROOFING

Bitumen felt or sheet roofing consists of a mat of glass or synthetic fibres impregnated with a bitumen coating which creates a water resistant sheet.

The sheets are applied to the roof surface using a hot bonding bitumen, in three layers. The first layer is partially bonded to the roof, to allow for any movement. They are laid with side laps of 75mm, which is then staggered on the following layers to avoid excess side laps on top of one another. At eaves, the sheets are lapped over the fascia to an edge trim (usually aluminium) which drains into the gutter. Any upstands to parapets or walls will need to be 150mm high, and dressed into the masonry, with a protective flashing over the top. The final layer is finished with an aggregate topping, to protect the surface from sunlight, and extend the life of the roof. A glass fibre based sheet has an expected life span of 7-15 years, while a polyester based sheet will have an expected life span of 15-25 years - the cost of the two products reflects this.

Bitumen products are not considered to be an environmentally suitable choice as they are made from crude oil, and are non recyclable.

SINGLE PLY MEMBRANES

Single ply roofing systems are becoming increasingly popular and are now a popular option for commercial and residential projects. They consist of a continuous layer between 1mm and 3mm thick that provides excellent weather protection.
They are fixed over a polyester fleece to prevent damage to the membrane, using a variety of fixing options, from bonding to mechanical fixings and in some cases loose laid. Single ply roofing systems require specialist installers as the quality of workmanship is key to the performance of the material.

The single ply systems are generally derived from petrochemicals and have poor sustainability credentials, and it is also not possible to reuse or recycle the membranes easily. The life expectancy of a single ply roofing system can be between 20-30 years.

PLASTER AND PLASTERBOARD

Plasters and plasterboards provide an internal finish to walls and ceilings. The benefits of using this method is to provide a smooth clean surface for decoration, whilst masking any background unevenness. The plaster or plasterboard can also provide an additional sound, thermal and fire resistance.

Lime plastering was introduced to Britain by the Romans. Lime plastering is used in the renovation and conservation of older buildings but modern UK practice is based on gypsum plastering. Gypsum is a naturally occurring product that is mined and factory produced. The advantage of gypsum plasters is that they are less likely to crack due to their very slight expansion on setting.

Gypsum plasters are generally applied in two coats, an undercoat and finishing coat. The undercoat tends to contain coarser aggregates than the finishing coat, with variations to suit specific site requirements. A typical thickness for an undercoat is 11mm on a wall, and 8mm for ceilings.

The finishing coat will have a finer aggregate and gives a smoother even finish. The typical thickness for a finishing coat is 2-3mm.

The type of plaster specified and its application is determined by the background surface of the wall that will be plastered. A rough textured surface such as bricks or concrete blocks has a 'key' which will allow the plaster to adhere to the wall. With smooth surfaces or surfaces that absorb water a bonding agent is required. This can be in the form of PVA applied to the wall prior to plastering, or a polymer bonding agent.

PLASTERBOARD AND DRY LINING

In recent times, wet applied plaster systems have been replaced with dry finishes. The dry finish will consist of plasterboard fixed to the background, with the joints between the boards filled, ready to receive decoration. This method is referred to as dry lining. In some cases the plasterboard receives a skim plaster finish.

Plasterboard consists of a solid gypsum core encased in strong paper liners. Plasterboard is used for dry lining or as a background for plaster, in ceilings, stud partitions and so on. The boards come in standard sizes that coordinate with timber/metal framing systems - 1200mm and 900mm wide. The standard thickness of the plasterboard is 12.5mm, 15mm and 19mm. Boards are available in moisture resistant grades suitable for use in humid conditions such as bathrooms and kitchens. It is also possible to specify fire resistant boards, or sound insulation boards. Insulated plasterboards have also been developed to improve thermal insulation properties of the external wall.

Plasterboard can be fixed to its background by steel lath, nails or screws - to timber frame or steel frame systems. The boards will be fixed directly to solid walls using a bonding of dots of plaster or adhesive. The dot and dab system has raised concerns with regard to airtightness and is now regulated to ensure improved air tightness.

Wallboard is used for a variety of applications including dry lining walls and ceilings, and has tapered or square edges. The tapered edged boards are for direct decoration, as the tapered joint allows for taping, jointing and finishing. Avoiding a wet plaster finish can keep costs down, and prevents the need for skilled plasterers. The jointing can be done by hand or by machine, and consists of applying a jointing compound, to which a jointing tape is added. The compound is then applied over the tape and feathered out.

The square edged boards tend to be skim finished in plaster.

Wallboards are available with a vapour control membrane where interstitial condensation needs to be prevented.

Gypsum used for both plasterboard and plaster is mined which can cause landscape degradation. Energy is required in production, and large amounts of waste are created on site and sent to landfill. Plasterboard is manufactured using around 50% of recycled materials, and the lining papers are usually recycled. As plaster and plasterboard is produced in the UK transportation energy is low.

For more information visit:
British Gypsum

INSULATION

Insulation is playing an increasingly vital role in building design and construction following the growing energy conscious world and knowledge of the environmental impact of the construction industry. With that, occupant comfort is at higher demand than ever before. Buildings need to be sufficiently insulated to prevent excessive amounts of heat escaping from the structure to the outside, and also to prevent excessive heat or cold from affecting the internal environment. Over the years building regulations have substantially increased with regard to thermal performance and will no doubt continue to do so.

Air is an efficient thermal insulant, and therefore most insulating materials used in construction contain large amounts of air voids. When we consider the thermal performance of a material we look at the thermal conductivity W/mK, which measures the ability of a material to conduct heat. In terms of insulation, the lower the figure, the better the performance of the insulant will be, as heat finds it more difficult to travel through the material.

As an example, a high performing new insulating material aerogel has a thermal conductivity of 0.018 W/mK while a sheet of glass can have a thermal conductivity of 1.05 W/mK.

The materials used in buildings as insulation can be grouped into organic and inorganic insulants.

INORGANIC INSULANTS

Inorganic insulants are made from naturally occurring materials, that are formed into fibre or cellular structures such as mineral wool, glass wool, exfoliated vermiculite and so on. These types of insulant are generally incombustible, they do not support the spread of flame. Inorganic insulants generally have a higher U-Value than organic insulants.

Wood wool slabs are made from wood fibres and cement. They have good load bearing properties and therefore are suitable for roof decking material.

Mineral wool is manufactured from volcanic rock to create a fibrous roll or slab of insulation. It is available in a variety of forms to be used in different settings. It can be loose for blown cavity insulation, mats for insulating lofts, batts (slabs) for cavity fill in masonry, rigid slabs for pitched roofs, weather resistant boards and more. Thermal conductivity of mineral wool is typically between 0.031 and 0.036 W/mK. Mineral wool is also used for the manufacture of fire stops to prevent fire spreading through cavities due to its good fire performance.

Glass wool is also a non combustible product, and used in similar forms as mineral wool. It can be loose for blown cavity wall insulation, rolls for roofing, batts for cavity insulation and so on. It has a typical thermal conductivity range of 0.031 to 0.040 W/mK.

Aerogel is a lightweight material with a very low density. It can be used to fully fill thin panels, or glazing units to create a high performing product. It is an expensive material but has a thermal conductivity of 0.018 W/mK.

ORGANIC INSULANTS

Some organic materials are based on hydrocarbon polymers, creating materials such as extruded polystyrene and polyurethane. Organic insulation also includes products made from natural materials such as hemp and sheep's wool or newspaper.

Expanded polystyrene (EPS) is a closed cell product with a thermal conductivity ranging from 0.033 to 0.040 W/mK. It is a combustible product and produces noxious smoke when burning, but it can be treated with a flame retardant additive. Generally seen as boards, EPS is lightweight and used in cavity walls, floors and both pitched and flat roofs.

Extruded polystyrene (XPS) is denser than EPS and therefore stronger also used in cavity wall and pitched roof insulation. It also has a high resistance to water absorption so is suitable for flooring applications below concrete slab, and on inverted roofs. Thermal conductivity ranges from 0.025 to 0.027 W/mK

Polyisocyanurate foam (PIR) is used in roof insulation, cavity walls and floor insulation. PIR is combustible but can be treated to achieve a Class 0 rating. Thermal conductivity ranges from 0.023 to 0.025 W/mK.

Polyurethane foam (PUR) is a closed cell foam, made into boards or used as a foam. It is another combustible material produces high levels of noxious fumes and smoke in a fire, although a flame resistant material is available. It is used in roofing, as well as an insulator to profiled metal sheeting. It can be injected into cavity walls but this is typically as a remedial measure and not a new build situation. PUR is often used as a spray to fill gaps around service voids and for filling small inaccessible locations. Thermal conductivity ranges from 0.019 to 0.023 W/mK for the rigid boards.

Sheep's wool is a renewable resource and comes in the form of batts. It has a low conductivity and suitable for ventilated lofts, and in timber frame construction. Care must be taken with the installation of vapour permeable breather membranes to the cold side of construction. It cannot be used in wet applications. Thermal conductivity of 0.039W/mK, although it is a renewable source with a low embodied energy it is still more expensive than standard mineral wool.

Cellulose insulation is made from shredded recycled paper. It is treated to improve its fire rating and smouldering resistance. It can be used for internal floors and loft insulation, roof voids and breathing walls - it can also be damp sprayed in between wall studs before the wall is closed. Thermal conductivity of cellulose is between 0.035 and 0.040 W/mK depending on application.

Hemp fibre insulation is a response to the demand on sustainable materials along with flax and coconut fibre insulations. Similar to cellulose it is suitable for a breathing structure. The batts can be used in ceilings and walls, wile the rolls can be used in lofts, floor and walls. The fibres receive borax treatment for fire resistance. Thermal conductivity of flat fibre insulation is 0.037W/mK, while hemp ranges between 0.038 and 0.040 W/mK, and coconut fibre is 0.045 W/mK.

Material	Thermal conductivity (W/mK)
Aerogel	0.018
Phenolic foam	0.018-0.031
Polyurethane foam	0.019-0.025
Foil faced foam	0.020
Polyisocyanurate foam	0.023-0.025
Extruded polystyrene	0.025-0.027
Expanded PVC	0.030
Mineral wool	0.031-0.040
Glass wool	0.031-0.040
Expanded polystyrene	0.033-0.040
Cellulose	0.035-0.040
Flax	0.037
Sheep's wool	0.037-0.039
Rigid foamed glass	0.037-0.048
Urea-formaldehyde foam	0.038
Hemp wool	0.040
Corkboard	0.042
Coconut fibre boards	0.045
Fibre insulation board	0.050

Fig 3.2 - Typical thermal conductivity of insulation materials (Manufacturers products may vary, information from Materials for Architects, see references.)

GLASS

There is a vast array of glass types used across the construction industry - from patterned glass to curved glass, low-e glass to toughened glass. In this section we will look at some of the more common uses for and types of glass.

The name float glass refers to the manufacture method of the glass we currently use today - where a continuous ribbon of molten glass flows across a shallow bath of molten tin. The temperature of the glass is gradually reduced as it moves along the molten tin bath until it is sufficiently solid. The glass can be controlled to create different thicknesses by the speed it is drawn through the bath, before being machine cut and stacked.

The general thickness of glass used in the construction industry is between 2-25mm, with maximum sheet sizes of 3.12m. The U-value for a standard 6mm float glass is 5.7 W/m^{2}K.

TOUGHENED GLASS

Toughened glass can be up to four to five times stronger than standard glass of the same thickness. It cannot be cut or worked so requires all cutting, drilling of holes to be completed prior to the toughening process which involves rapid heating and cooling of the glass. If broken, toughened glass will shatter into small granules that would be unlikely to cause injuries, however it will withstand considerable extremes of temperature and sudden shock temperatures.

LAMINATED GLASS

Laminated glass bonds layers of glass together with a plastic interlayer. This improves the impact resistance of the glass but also allows for other features to be incorporated such as patterned glass or curved laminates. The laminated glazing can also be used as a bullet resistant glass, as well as other specialist applications.

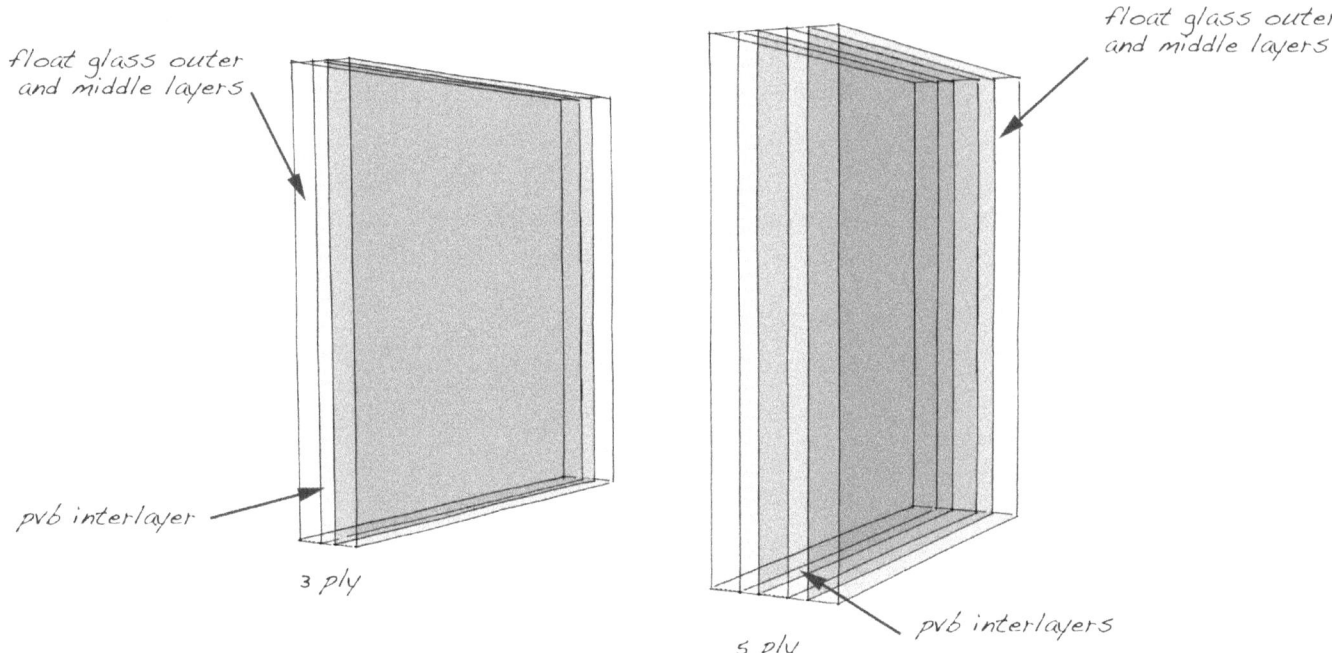

Fig 3.3 - Laminated glass types

FIRE RESISTANT GLASS

There are two types of fire resisting glass, non insulating and insulating glass. The glass can be classified in the following ways:

E30   - integrity only 30 minutes
EW30   - integrity and radiation protection 30 minutes
EI30   - integrity and insulation for 30 minutes
E30EI30   - integrity 60 minutes and insulation 30 minutes

A non insulating glass will prevent the passage of any flame, hot gases or smoke but will allow heat transfer by radiation and conduction.
Insulating glass is a laminated glass, using layers of intumescent or gel materials. When exposed to fire the materials within the glass will expand and turn opaque to prevent the passage of conductive and radiant heat. This type of laminated insulating glass has an improved fire resistance than non insulating glass, of between 30 and 120 minutes.

Of course, the integrity of any fire resistant glass will be dependant on the appropriate framing and fixings so the fire resistance looks at the complete unit, rather than just the glass alone.

DOUBLE AND TRIPLE GLAZING

In order to comply with building regulations glazing is required to achieve a certain level of performance. A single sheet of glass is unable to provide suitable levels of thermal performance. In order to reduce heat loss, multiple sheets of glazing are used with an air, partial vacuum or inert gas fill.

An optimum air gap of 16 to 20mm between two glass sheets allows for an improved thermal performance, while filling this gap with a gas such as argon, further improves performance as it has a lower thermal conductivity than air. Other gases are also used such as krypton or xenon, along with a vacuum. The table below demonstrates the performance of some typical glazing systems.

Glass System	U Value (W/m²K)
Single clear glass	5.8
Double clear glass	2.8
Double clear glass with argon fill	2.7
Double clear glass with hard low-e coating	1.7
Double clear glass with hard low-e coating and argon fill	1.5
Double clear glass with soft low-e coating	1.4
Double clear glass with soft low-e coating and argon fill	1.2
Triple clear glass with two low-e coating and two argon fills	0.8
Triple clear glass with two low-e coating and two xenon fills	0.4

Note:

Data relates to 4mm standard glass and 16mm spacing

Overall window ratings will differ considerably according to the perimeter materials and construction system

Fig 3.4 - Table showing standard U-values for glazing systems
Table adapted from Materials for Architects and Builders - Arthur Lyons

LOW-EMISSIVITY GLASS

Low-emissivity (low-e) glass reflects longer wavelength heat energy from the buildings occupants and heating systems back into the building. Any incoming solar energy is absorbed by the internal walls and re-radiated back into the room.

Low-e glass is made by coating the surface of float glass with a transparent coating. The low-e coating can reduce the U-value from 2.8 W/m²K to 1.7 W/m²K on a standard double glazing unit.

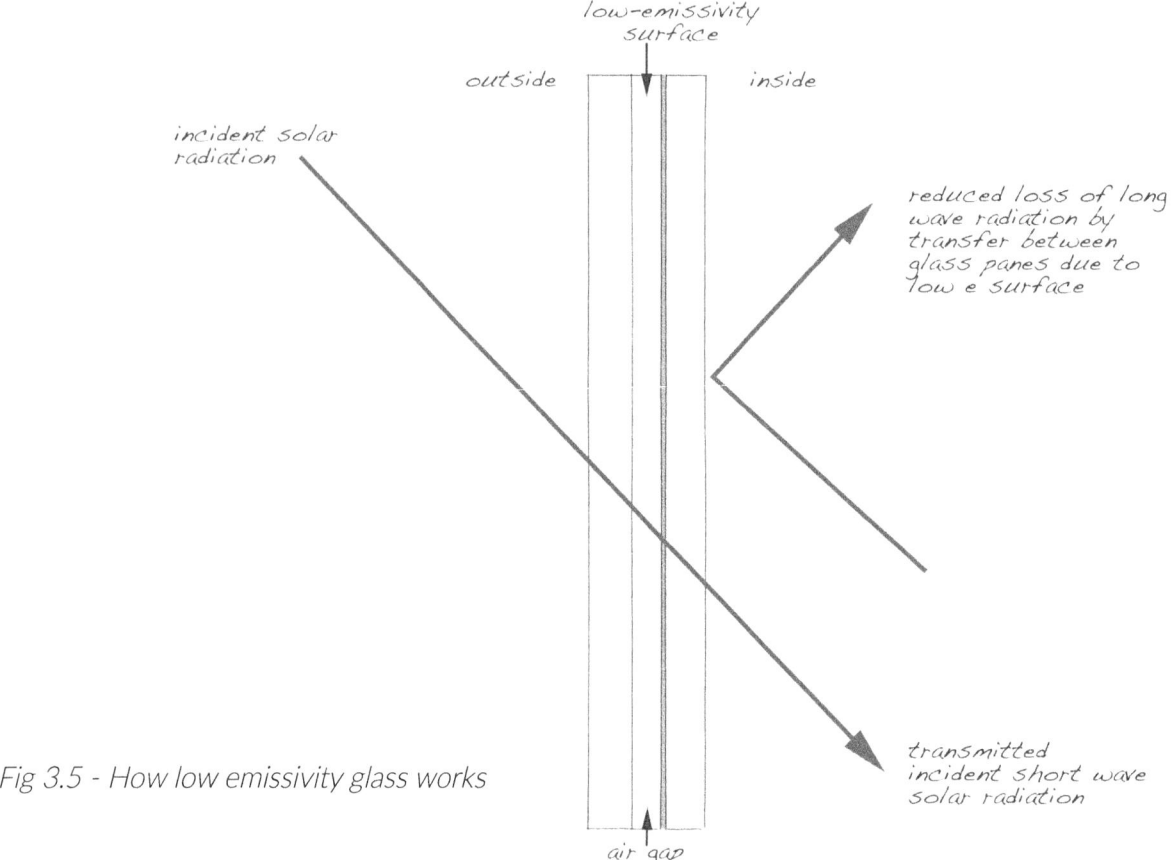

Fig 3.5 - How low emissivity glass works

SOLAR CONTROL GLASS

Solar control glass is used within an insulating glass unit. The external pane reduces solar heat gain but still allows natural light to enter the building. The pane allows sunlight to pass through the window while radiating and reflecting away a large amount of the suns heat. This produces an internal environment that stays cooler, whilst maintaining a natural bright space.

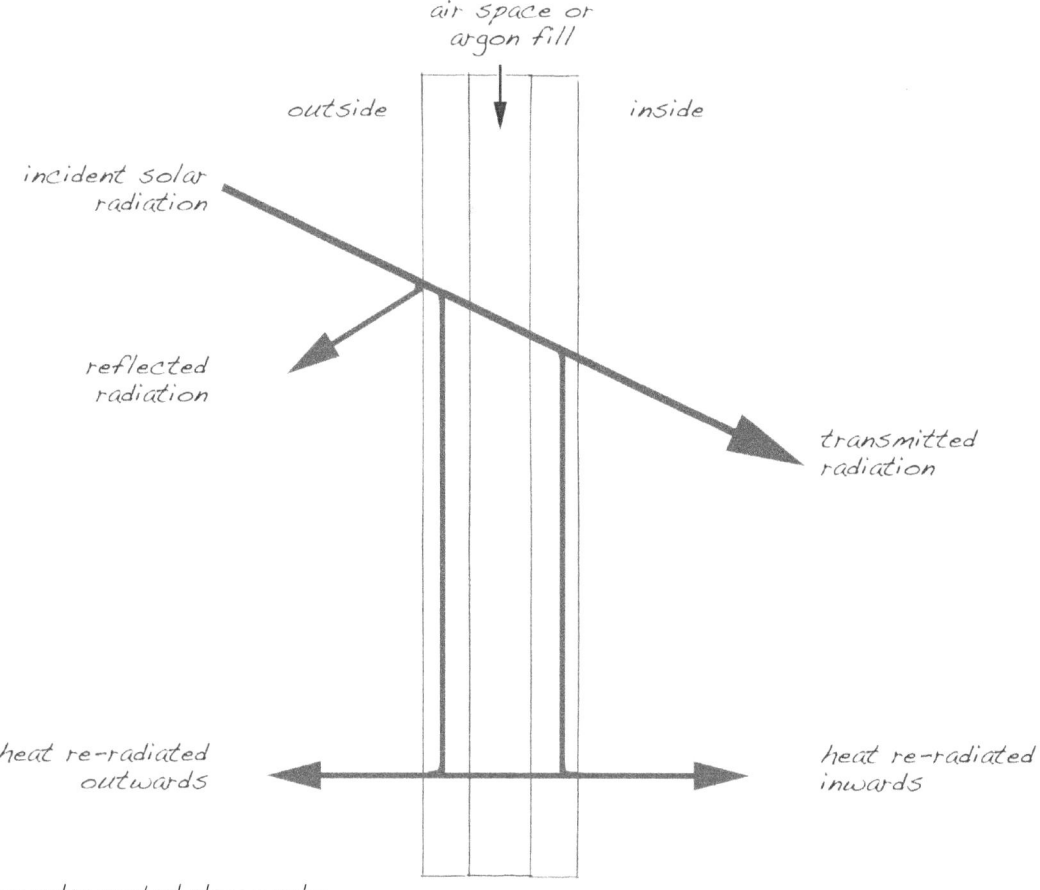

Fig 3.6 - How solar control glass works

MANIFESTATION OF GLASS

The Building Regulations Approved Document K states that transparent glazing, with which people are likely to come into contact while moving in or about a building, shall incorporate features which make it apparent. As the use of large areas of glazing has increased, it is important the presence of this glass is made clear by providing decorative features, images, logos or lines that allow building users to clearly see the glazing to avoid impact or injury. The manifestation must contrast visually with the background seen through the glass and be provided at two levels.

Manifestation should be provided at 850mm-1000mm and 1400-1600mm in any full glazing. Consult the Building Regulations Approved Document K for further guidance.

GLASS FAÇADES AND STRUCTURAL GLASS

Using glass façades and working with structural glass goes beyond the scope of this book, and will be addressed in a future publication.

FURTHER READING:

LYONS, A (2010) Materials for Architects and Builders. 4th Ed. Oxford: Elsevier.

GreenSpec

Zinc information centre

TRADA (Timber Research and Development Association)

Timber Trade Federation

Stone Federation

Glass and Glazing Federation

Copper Development Association

Concrete Centre

See also Bibliography & Further Reading

Blank page

FOUNDATIONS & FLOORS

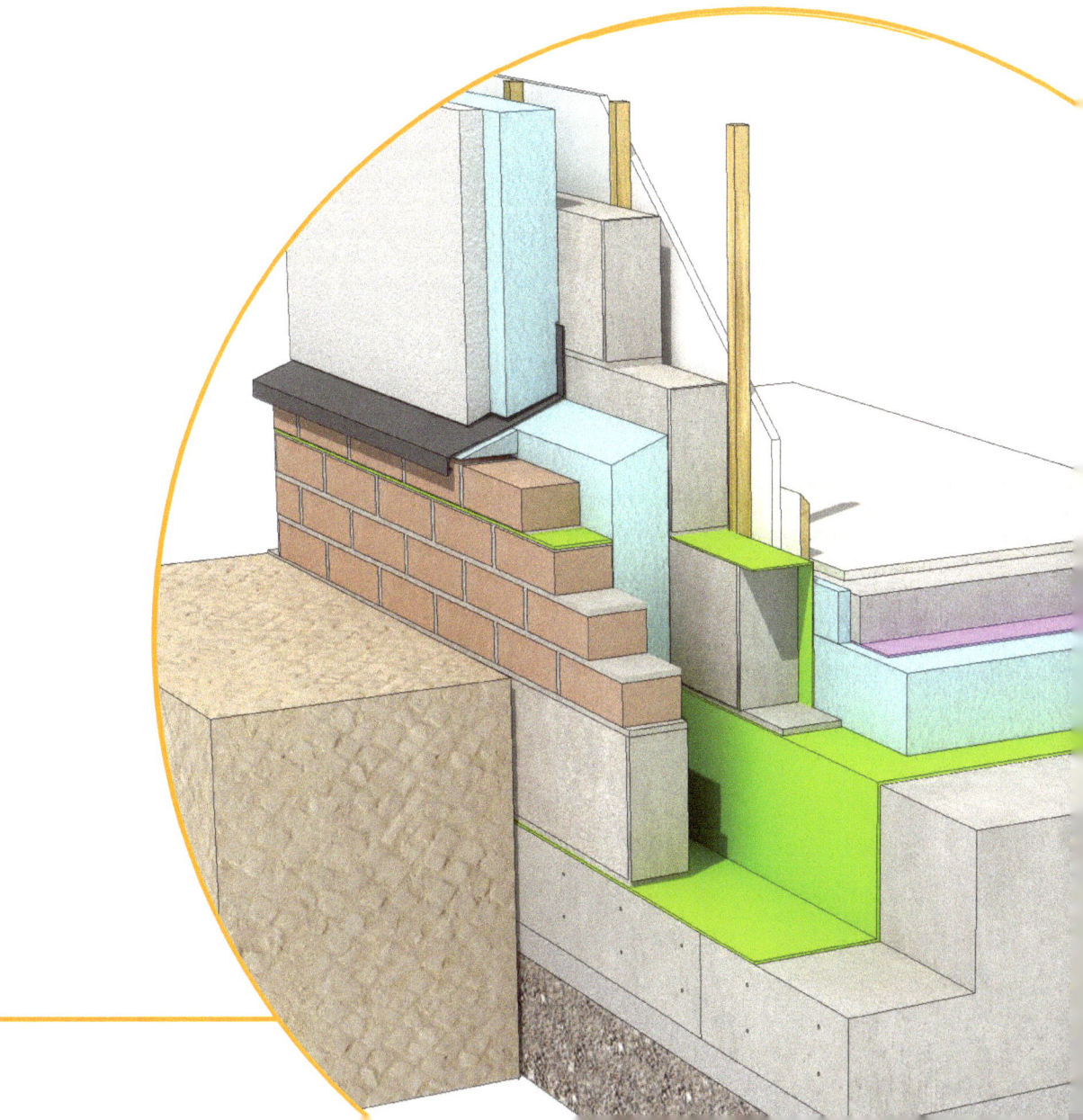

SECTION 4

INTRODUCTION TO FOUNDATION DESIGN

GROUND AND SOIL ANALYSIS

The purpose of a foundation is to support the building above, by transferring the loads of the building safely to a suitable subsoil below. There are many factors which determine the type of foundation used, such as bearing capacity of the soil, total loads of the building, safety in constructing the foundations to name a few.

Subsoils can vary from site to site, with some having a good bearing capacity like granite, while others have a poor bearing capacity like soft clay which are unable to support any significant load.

The role of the foundation is to transmit the loads of the building down to a suitable level where the subsoil has a safe bearing capacity and therefore strong enough to support the building. The first step in selecting a suitable foundation, is of course to study the soil present on the site. This can be in the form of a site study of boreholes and trial pits where samples are taken for analysis. Desktop studies can also be useful in providing data based on geological maps, soil reports and so on.

SOIL TYPES

Topsoil usually consists of a mixture of solid particles, water and air. It usually contains organic remains of decayed vegetation close to the surface. Top soil is not suitable for supporting foundations and is stripped from the immediate site, and retained for landscaping the surrounding site.

Subsoils can be categorised into five main types. In addition to solid rock, there is gravel, sands, silts, clays and peats. The subsoil sits below the topsoil and supports the load of the building. Generally soils with larger particles are free draining, while soils with smaller particles retain moisture.

The following table demonstrates typical bearing capacities of common subsoils we find in the UK.

Groud Type	Bearing Capacity (kN/m^2)	Notes
Granite		
Limestone		
Sandstone	600 - 10,000	These sub-soils provide good support to foundations. They generally require pneumatic or hydraulic tools for excavation
Slate		
Hard Chalk		
Compact Sands	100 - 600	Sub-soils provide good support. They do not require special tools for excavation, only standard machinery.
Gravels		
Firm and stiff clays	150 - 600	Wider foundations may be required than sands and gravels. Excavation can be done by hand or machine.
Sandy Clays		
Loose sand		
Soft silt	<150	Easy to excavate but generally will require specially designed foundations
Soft Clay		

Fig 4.1 - Typical subsoil bearing capacity

Rock
Rock generally has a very high bearing capacity and is in most cases a suitable surface on which to build. The drawbacks of building on a site where there is a rock subsoil is difficult excavation and levelling works which has an effect on cost. Some rocks like soft sandstones, chalks, soft limestones have a variable bearing capacity and can experience swelling and softening on exposure to water. Where these types of rock are present they can be protected with a layer of concrete.

Gravel and sands
This category of soils is broadly classified as particles from 0.06mm upwards that tend to move independently of one another when a load is applied to them. They are termed as non cohesive coarse grained soils. Although some movement occurs and voids can form between particles, these types of soils can provide a suitable base for construction. These soils do not tend to display changes in volume when moisture content in the soil fluctuates.

Silts and Clays
These soils are fine grained cohesive soils that have a considerable change in volume when exposed to moisture content changes. When silts and clays have a high water content, in wet weather, the soil swells, whilst when it is dry and the moisture content is low the soil shrinks. These changes usually occur where moisture content fluctuates, up to around 1m below ground. Beyond this, it is usually possible to find a satisfactory bearing.

Peats
Peats are considered to be unsuitable for building due to the changes in volume that occurs when the organic matter in the soil decays. Peats are also subject to compression when loaded. Where peats or soils with a large amount of organic matter are present, the soil will be excavated.

FROST HEAVE
If the water table is high, and close to the surface, some soils will expand when frozen. This is due to ice crystals forming in the soil and causing it to expand - creating frost heave. In the UK the ground is rarely frozen at depths of more than 600-700mm which should be sufficiently deep for most foundations in these types of soil.

CONTAMINATED GROUND
The presence of any contaminant in the ground must be established prior to starting works. Desktop studies can establish previous uses of the site along with any existing soil reports. On site soil testing will allow for the soil present on the site to be laboratory tested. Contaminated land can consist of liquid, solid or gas contaminants. These can be due to the site being used for industrial and manufacturing works, landfills, mines, power stations, printing works, sewage works to name but a few.

The presence of a contaminant on the site will raise the question whether the build is viable, but will present a few options to treat the problem:

- Remove the contaminated material to another site by license
- Provide an impervious layer between the contaminated ground the building
- A biological treatment to neutralise the contaminant

TYPES OF FOUNDATION

Foundation selection is determined by a number of factors. Unlike residential construction, most commercial buildings consist of a framed structure which have concentrated loads through the columns which are passed on to the foundations. These framed buildings often require a deeper foundation in order to transfer the loads to a subsoil with a suitable bearing capacity.

Considerations when selecting a foundation:
- Bearing capacity of the ground
- Depth of strata
- Loads from the building
- Building structure
- Basement requirements
- Ease and safety of constructing the foundation

Foundations are usually made of reinforced concrete.

Shallow Foundation: A shallow foundation is one that transfers the loads of the structure close to the ground floor level of the building, such as a strip foundation or raft foundation. This type of foundation tends to be suitable for lighter loads.

Deep Foundations: Deep foundations transfer the loads to a subsoil much further down than the shallow foundation, using pad or pile foundations. They tend to incorporate reinforcement in the concrete.

In commercial construction the main types of foundations used are:

- Strip foundations
- Raft foundations
- Pad foundations
- Pile foundations
- Specialist foundations - underpinning or deep piled rafts for example

pad foundation

raft foundation

pile foundation

Fig 4.2 - Types of foundation

STRIP FOUNDATIONS

Strip foundations consist of a single strip of concrete which provides a firm and level base for the construction of the walls above. Strip foundations spread the load from walls of brick, masonry or concrete to the subsoil. The foundation depth depends on the strength of material, foundation loads and bearing capacity of the subsoil.

It is common place that a strip foundation will be trench filled with concrete (in some cases reinforced), meaning the trench is dug to a minimum level of 1m below ground, and filled with concrete to within 150mm of ground level. This increases the cost of concrete, but reduces the cost of labour and materials of a bricklayer constructing the foundation wall below ground. It is also safer to avoid the need for the bricklayer to work in the excavation trench. Strip foundations are also positioned under load bearing internal walls.

Strip foundations are more commonly used in residential and low rise construction, they are suitable for supporting a continuous load, like a wall, rather than the point loading of a column.

Standard calculation for a strip foundation:

$$\text{Minimum width of strip} = \frac{\text{total loading of building per metre kN/m}}{\text{safe bearing capacity of subsoil kN/m}^2}$$

The Building Regulations provide tables of minimum widths relative to subsoil type, condition, bearing capacity and loads to assist with design.

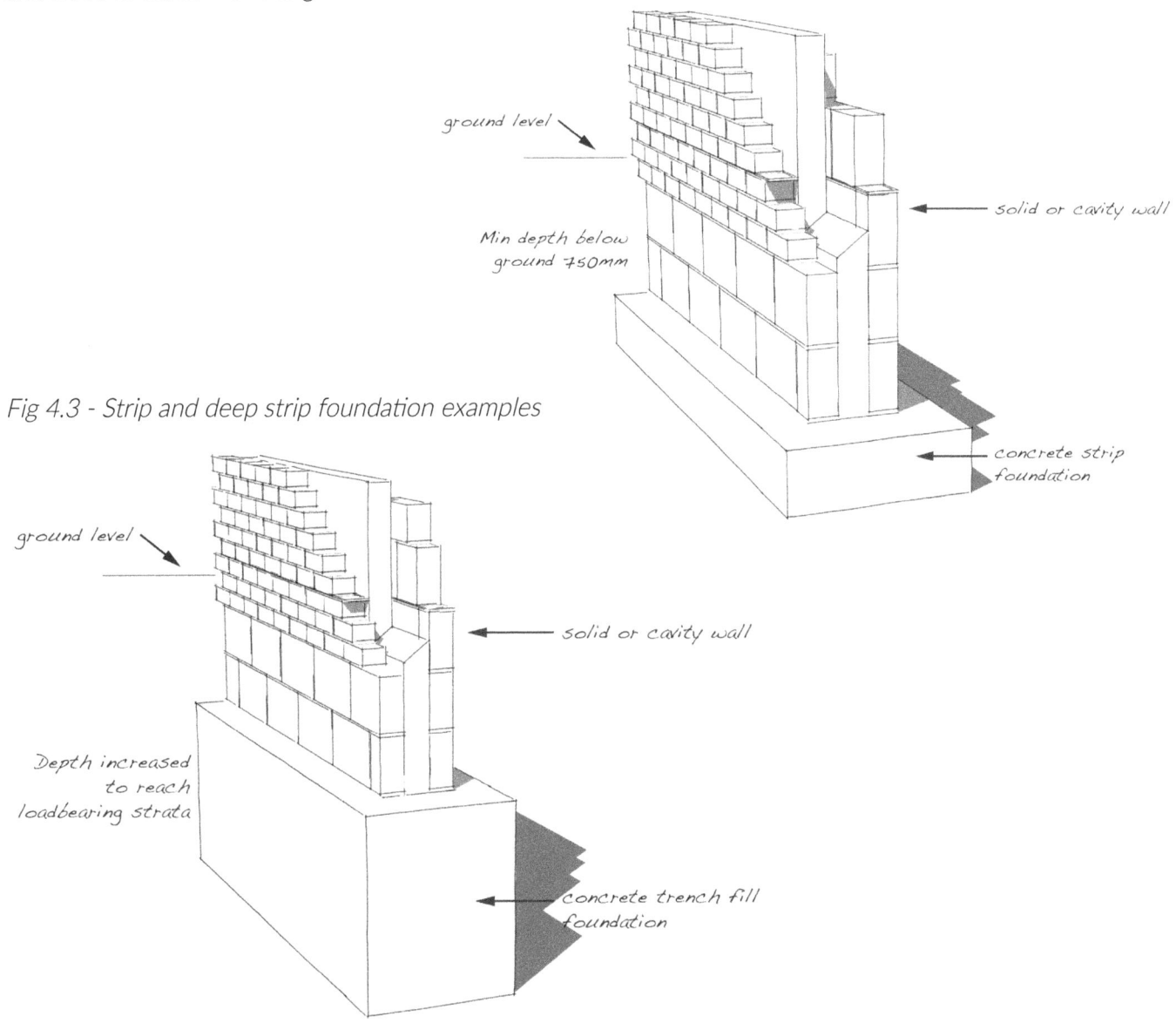

Fig 4.3 - Strip and deep strip foundation examples

RAFT FOUNDATIONS

Raft foundations are a continuous slab which extends beneath the whole building and sometimes beyond, made from reinforced concrete. The loading of the building is therefore spread over the whole area of the building, therefore there is little if any settlement. Raft foundations can be used where there is compressible ground such as soft clay, where alternative foundation options would not be suitable without excessive excavations.

There are three main types of raft foundation:
- Flat slab raft
- Beam and slab raft
- Cellular raft or buoyant raft

Flat slab raft
The flat slab raft is of uniform thickness and uses reinforcement to the top and base of the slab. These types of rafts are used for smaller buildings where the loads are comparatively low, for example bungalows or small houses. A flat slab raft is poured on a blinding layer of 50mm concrete which provides a level and stable base. The reinforcing cage is then positioned on the blinding before the concrete raft slab is poured, and levelled. The waterproof membrane was traditionally positioned under the slab, but it is more common now to position the damp proof membrane over the insulation. Insulation is usually placed on top of the structural slab, as rigid boards, with a screed topping to finish. A concrete raft is usually a minimum of 150mm thick.

Beam and slab raft
In areas of the slab that require additional strength, the perimeter of the slab, load bearing internal walls or structural columns, the raft is thickened below any load bearing wall with mass concrete to increase strength. The edge beam of the raft can often include a toe which allows for a brickwork cladding to hide the concrete above ground level. This is known as a beam and slab raft. This allows an increased strength to the raft to support heavier loads, without the cost of thickening the entire raft to accommodate the loads. The beams can be either upstand or down stand beams, which spread the load onto the slab, and in turn transmit the loads evenly onto the subsoil below.

Cellular or Buoyant Raft
When the raft foundation is required to support more significant loads, or there is a risk of settlement a cellular raft is often specified. This consists of top and bottom slabs with cross ribs in both directions to create a cellular structure. This type of structure spreads the loads of the building evenly and avoids differential settlement. In some cases the cellular raft is the full depth of a basement level, allowing the voids between the cross ribs to be utilised as car parking, storage or plant.

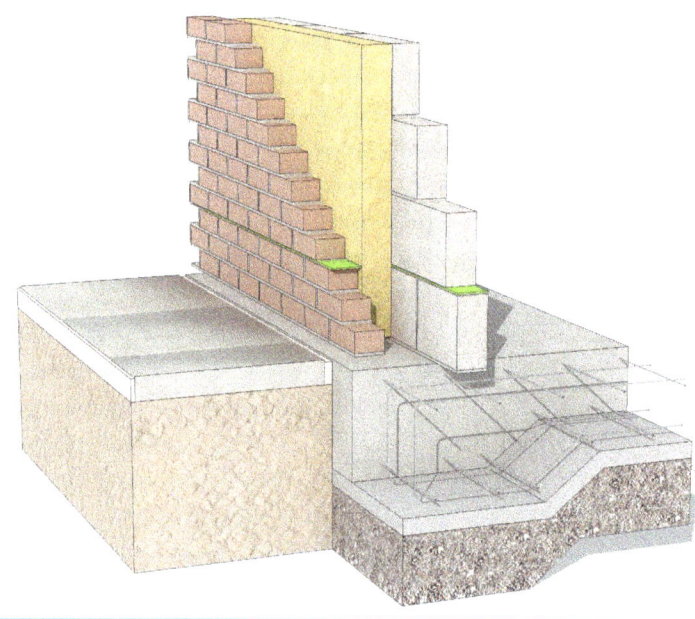

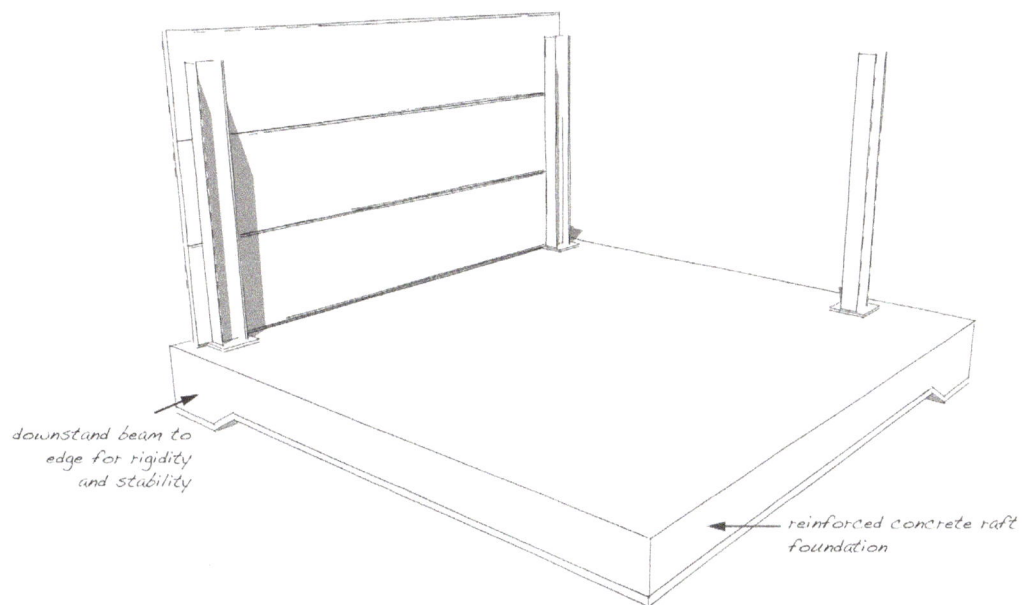

Fig 4.4 - Raft foundation example

PAD FOUNDATIONS

Pad foundations are often specified for a framed structure, where loads from the building are exerted onto the foundations in the form of concentrated point loads. Pad foundations are generally square pads of reinforced concrete, to a depth determined by the anticipated moments and shear forces, along with the bearing capacity of the subsoil. In some cases, where foundations are close to boundaries or other obstacles, the pads can be designed into different shapes, as long as the column loading is central to avoid rotation or punching through.

The fixing of the steel or concrete column to the pad foundation can vary considerably in different situations. If the pad is to support a steel column, holding down bolts are usually cast into the concrete pad. Pads can also be used where there is a requirement to support heavy manufacturing machinery.

Pad foundations can also be used to support load bearing walls, where reinforced concrete ground beams span between the pads that then support the load bearing wall above.

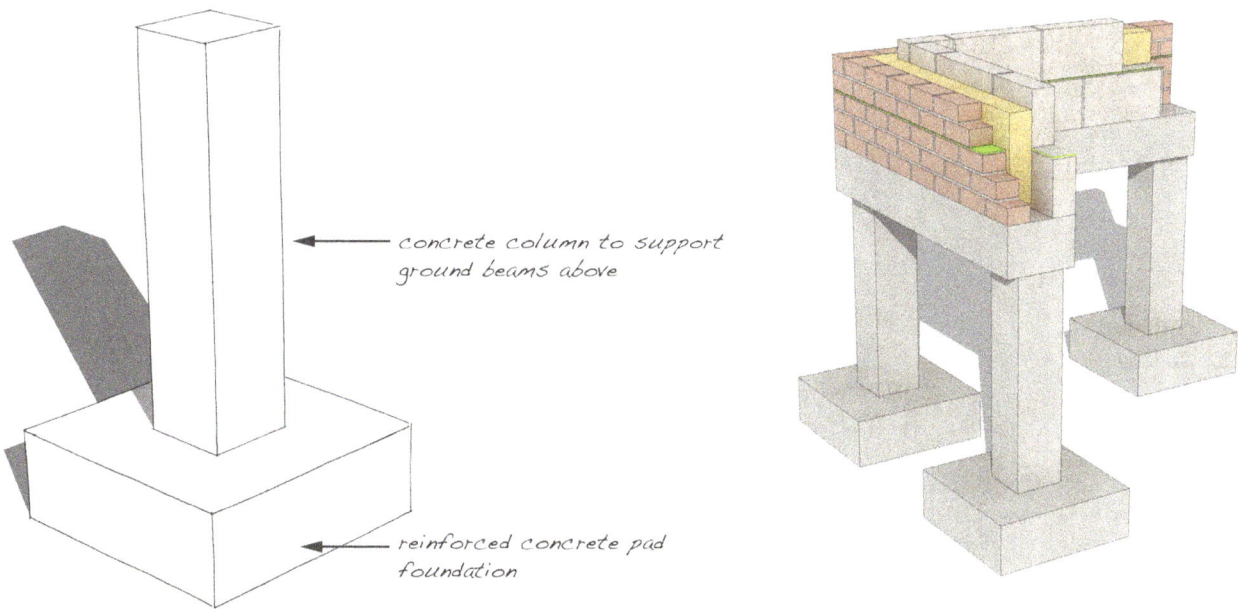

Fig 4.5 - Pad foundation examples

PILE FOUNDATIONS

Pile foundations are columns, usually concrete, cast deep into the ground to carry the load of the building to a firm strata. They use a combination of friction along the sides and end bearing at the pile or point base. Pile foundations are a common form of foundation construction in modern framed buildings and commercial structures.

There are many different types of pile foundation, but they can be classified into two main categories, displacement piles and replacement piles.

Displacement Piles - these precast sections or full piles that are forced into the ground using a driving rig or jack. Alternatively a number of shell sections or casings are driven into the ground, concrete is then poured into the void as the casings are removed. The soil is not removed during the process of displacement piles, and therefore a greater friction is present between the pile and surrounding ground. This pile system generates little waste and is not weather dependent during installation.

Replacement Piles - are formed by removing the soil and replacing it with a load bearing pile, usually concrete. The hoes are bored, and to prevent the hole caving in, a casing is often used to keep the shape. Replacement piles are considered end bearing whereby the loads of the building are bearing on the bottom area of the pile.

Pile Connections
Once the pile has been installed, a suitable surface needs to be created to carry the load of the structure above. Pile caps, usually formed of reinforced concrete create a loading platform that allows the loads to be safely transmitted from the building to the piles below. The pile cap can be positioned over an individual pile or a collection of piles.

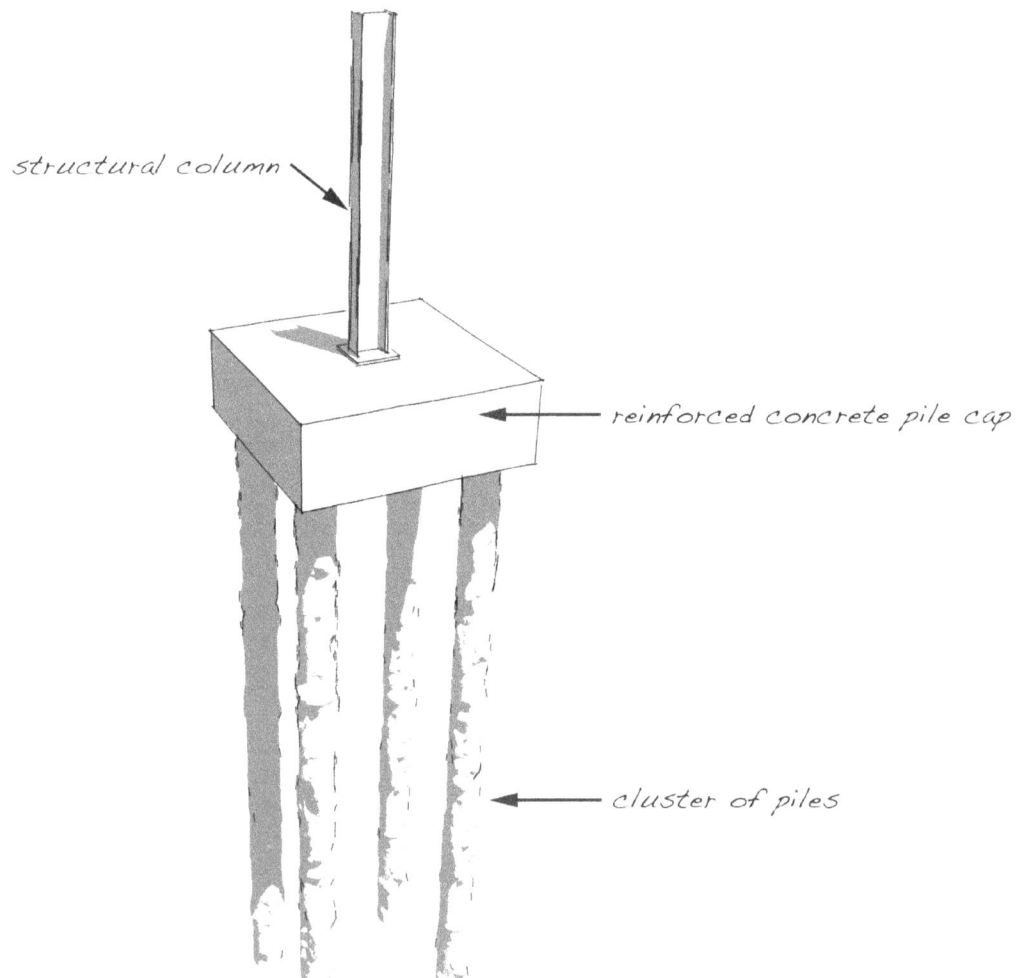

Fig 4.6 - Pile foundation example

Foundation Type	Advantages	Disadvantages	Suitable application
Raft Foundation	Economic as foundation and floor slab are combined.	Not most appropriate option for point loading, would require specific treatment.	Situations of poor ground, for lightweight structures. Ground with poor bearing capacity
	Shallow excavation	Edge erosion is possible if not prepared correctly.	
	Can adapt to poor ground conditions		
Pad Foundation	Minimal excavation as the foundation is shallow	If used for high point loads can become very large.	Suitable for framed buildings if the bearing capacity close to the ground is good.
	Pad shape can be adapted to suit tight spaces and sites.	Limited to dealing with point loads.	
	Size means that this type of foundation can be economical.		
Bored Pile Foundation (large diameter)	Appropriate for buildings with heavy loads	Require consistent soil conditions	Used for large buildings with heavy loads
	Large diameter allows for fewer piles to be used	Large plant required for the excavation	
	No need for permanent support		
Driven Pile Foundation	Provide element of ground consolidation	Can be issues if there are problems with ground stability	Sites with poor general ground conditions.
	Suitable for varying ground conditions	Difficult to install if there is demolition debris in the ground	
	Manufactured off site ensures quality		

Fig 4.7 - Factors affecting foundation selection
Table adapted from Construction Technology 2: Industrial & Commercial Building - Mike Riley & Alison Cotgrave

G01 FOUNDATION DETAILS

SIMPLE STRIP FOUNDATION

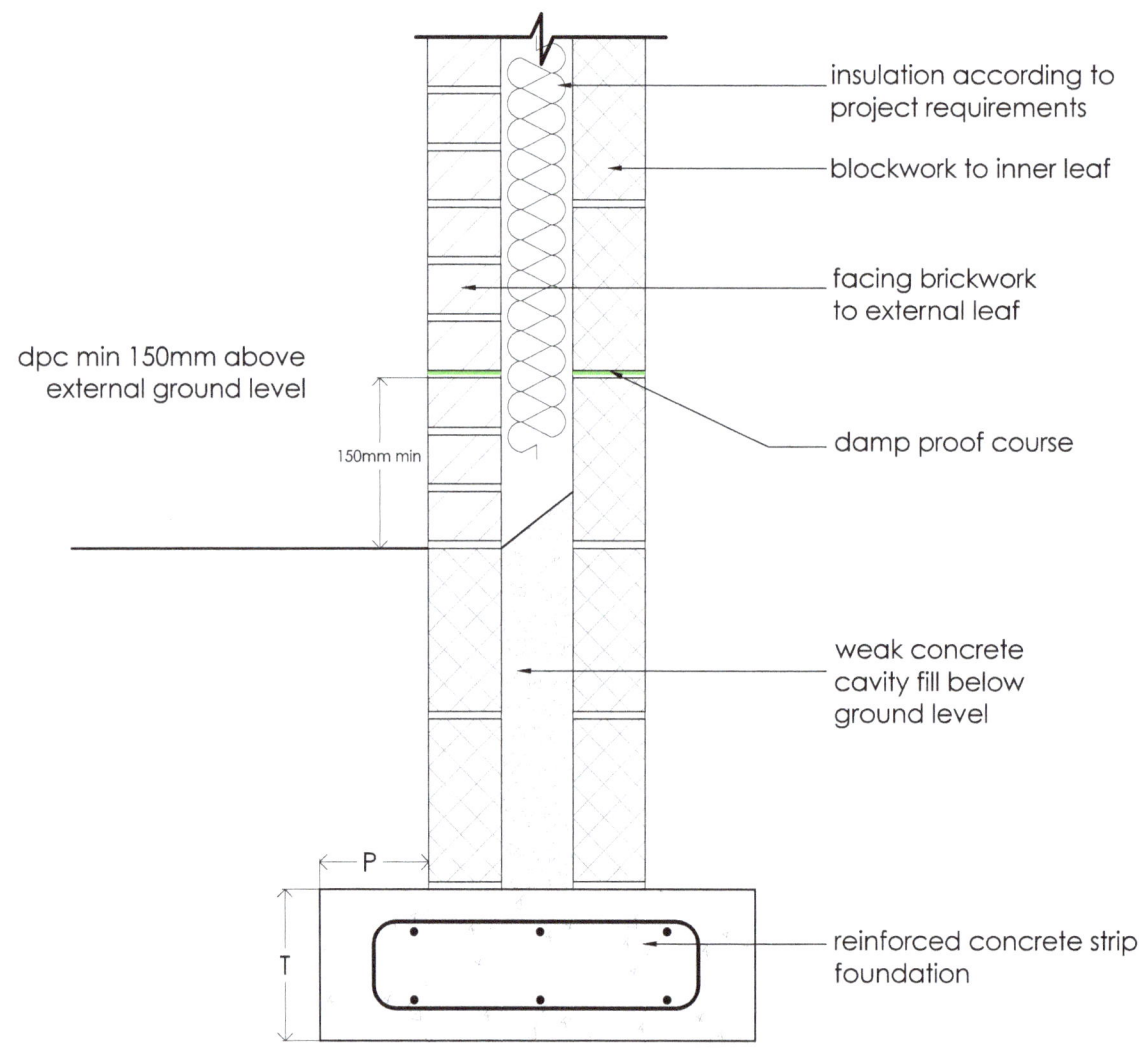

2D Detail G01 - Simple strip foundation

Notes:
T should be more than P, and P should be more than 150mm. In coarse soils depth below ground should be min 500mm. In clay soils min 750mm below ground depending on shrinkability - always check with local building control and structural engineer. Reinforcing bars indicative.

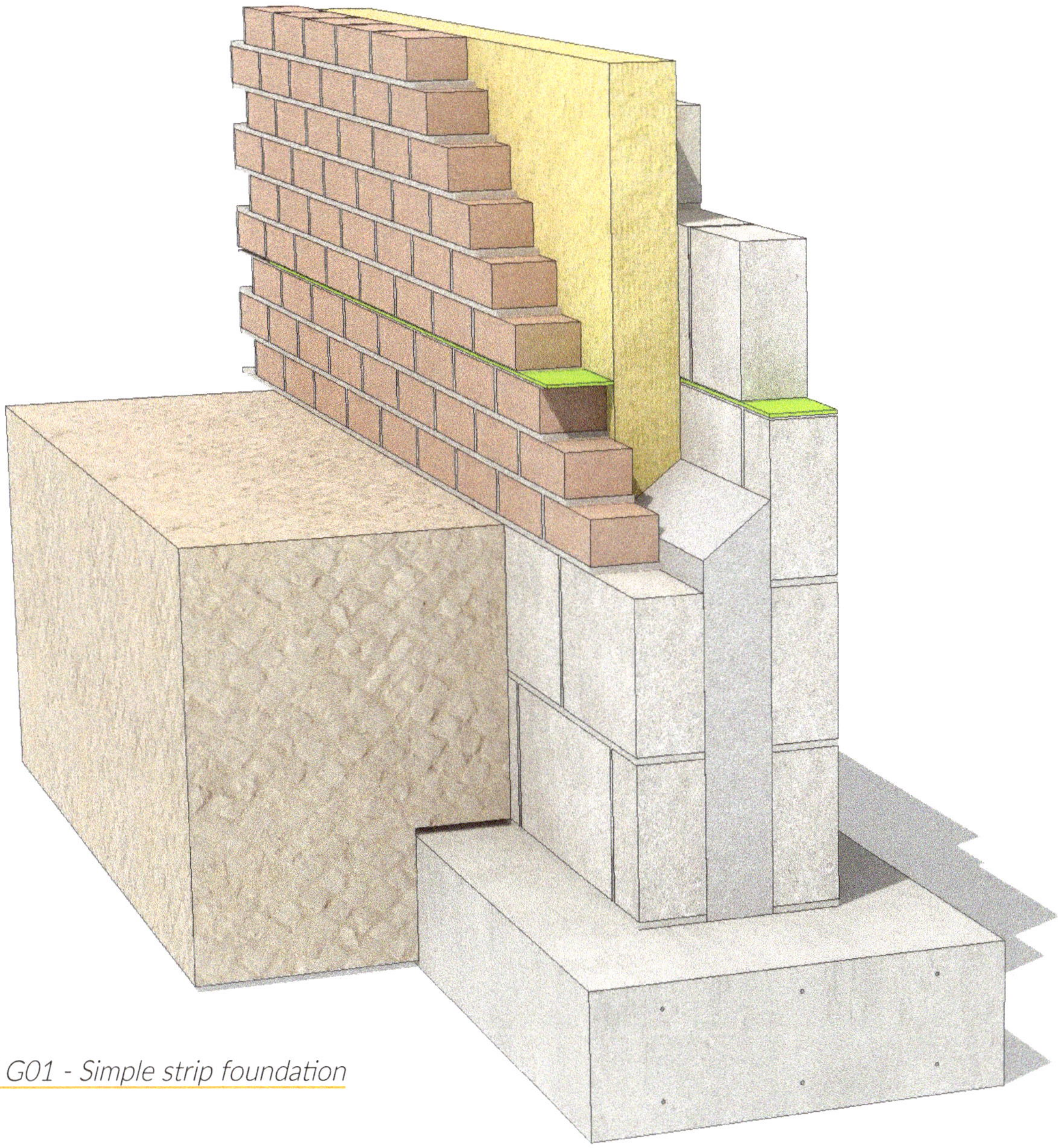

3D Detail G01 - Simple strip foundation

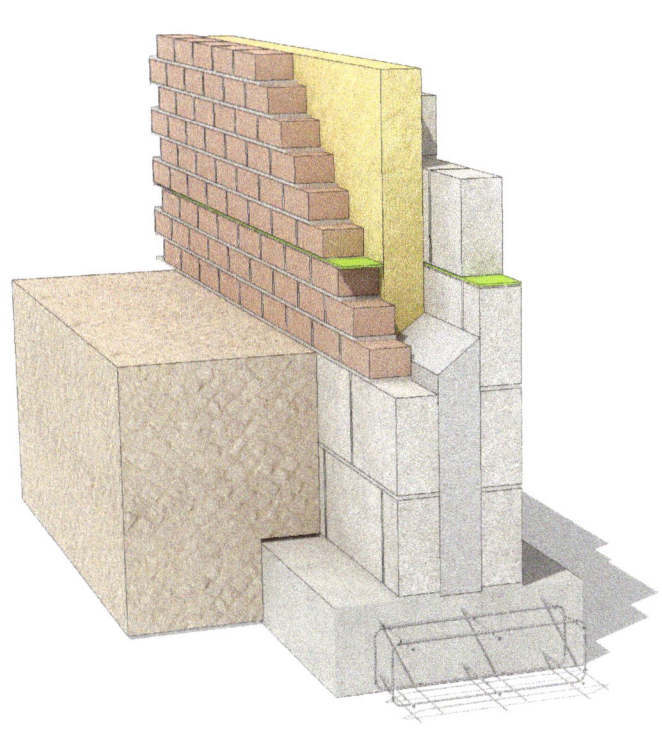

G02

DEEP STRIP OR MASS/TRENCH FILL FOUNDATION

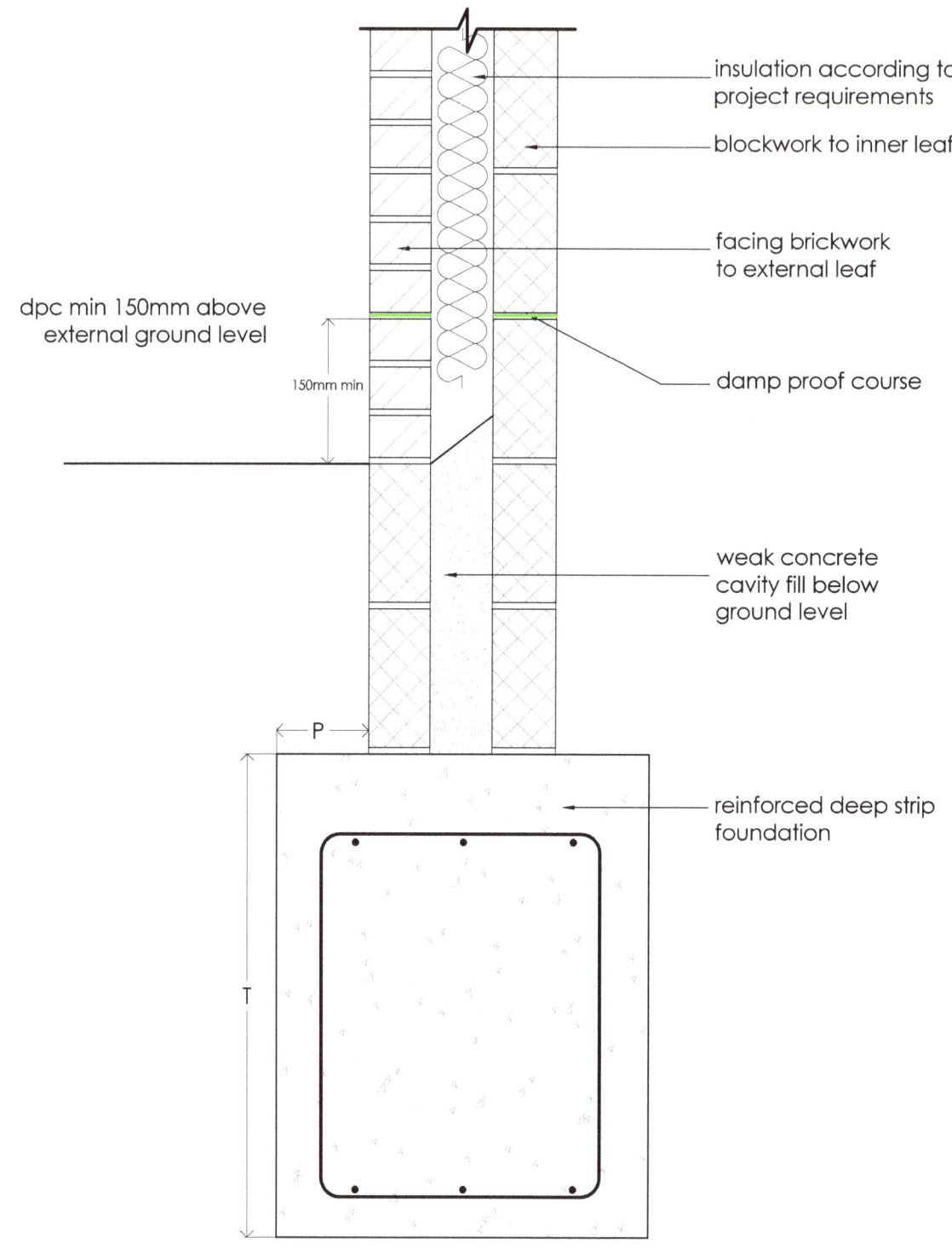

2D Detail G02 - Deep strip or mass/trench fill foundation

Notes:
Depth increased to load bearing strata or where soil is unaffected by changes in moisture content. Depth of T 750mm minimum in clay soils. Reinforcing bars indicative.

3D Detail G02 - Deep strip or mass/trench fill foundation

G03

SIMPLE RAFT FOUNDATION

- cavity infill wall
- damp proof course
- concrete perimeter paving to protect edges of raft from weathering and frost
- 150mm min
- min 1000mm
- raft foundation with reinforcement running in both directions
- 50mm concrete blinding creates level surface and seals the platform
- well compacted hardcore

Notes:
This type of raft foundation is suited to buildings with light loads and where ground is weak. Insulation and floor build up not shown.

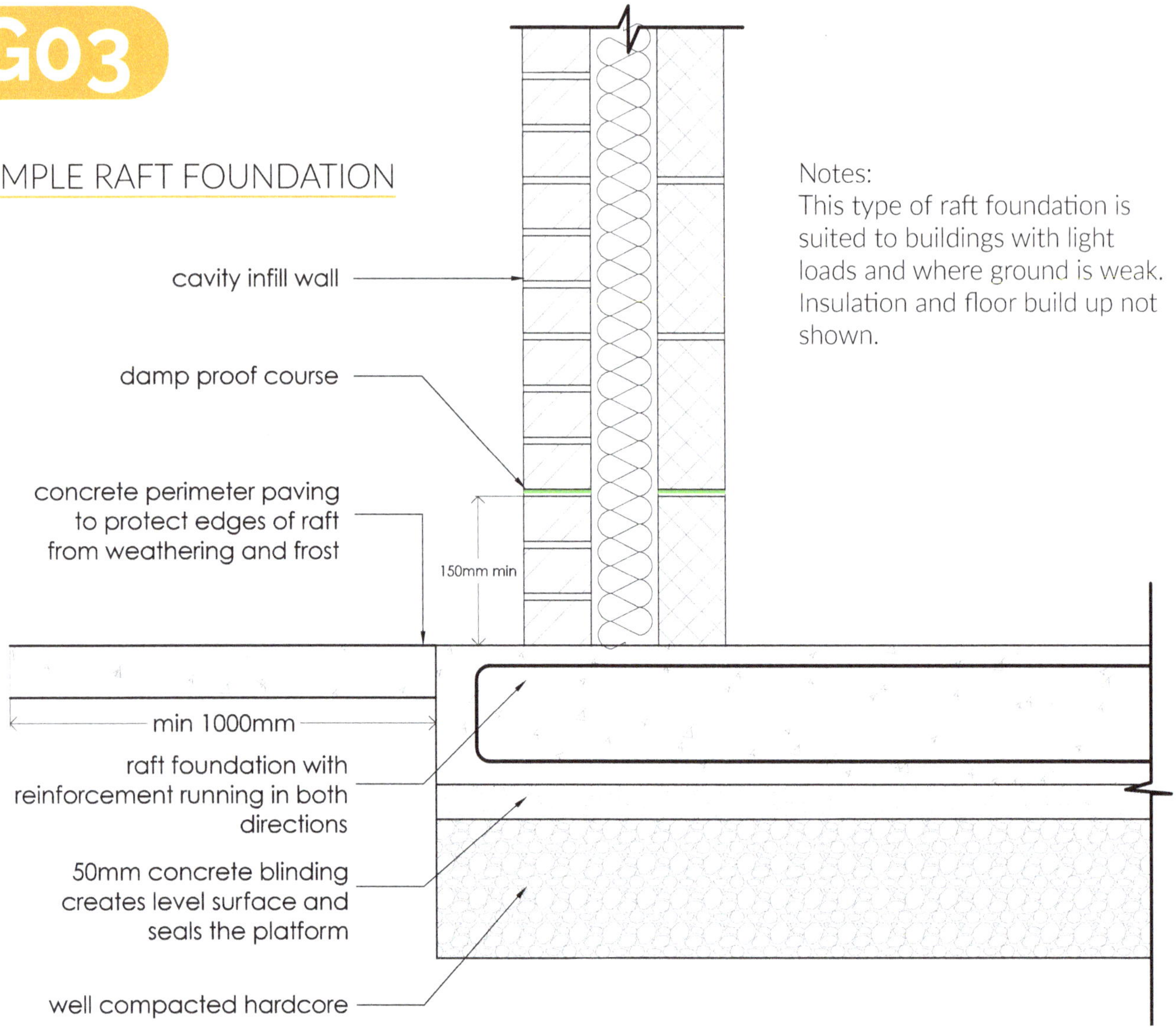

2D Detail G03 - Simple raft foundation

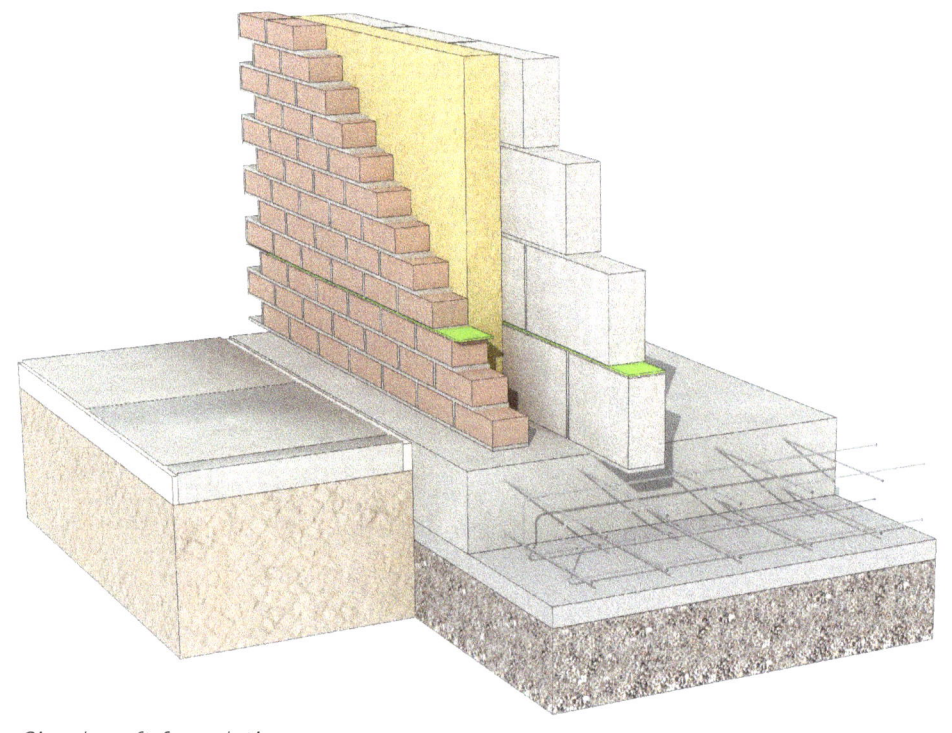

3D Detail G03 - Simple raft foundation

SECTION 4 - FOUNDATIONS AND FLOORS

G04

SIMPLE RAFT FOUNDATION WITH DOWNSTAND BEAM

- cavity infill wall
- damp proof course
- concrete perimeter paving to protect edges of raft from weathering and frost
- 150mm min
- min 1000mm
- raft foundation with reinforcement running in both directions, downstand beams add stability to the foundation
- 50mm concrete blinding creates level surface and seals the platform
- well compacted hardcore

Notes:
Downstand beam also known as edge thickening. Depth can vary, according to requirements. Downstand beams also specified under load bearing internal walls. Floor build up not shown.

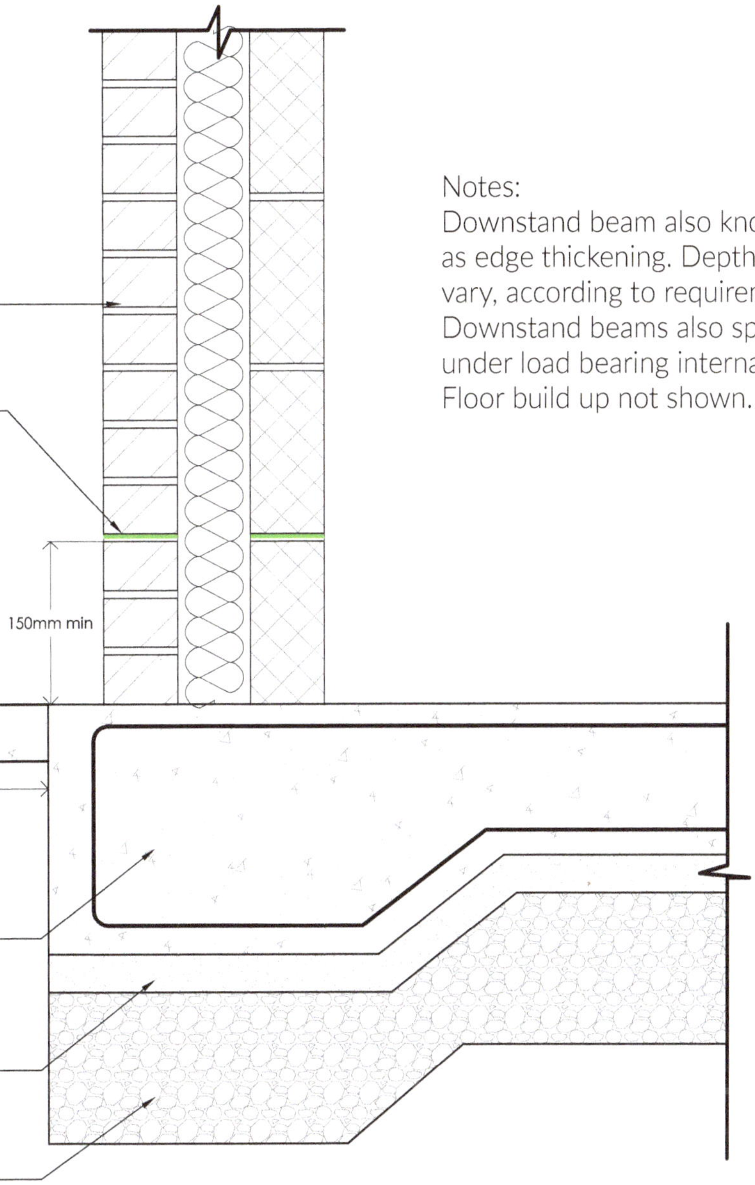

2D Detail G04 - Simple raft foundation with downstand beam

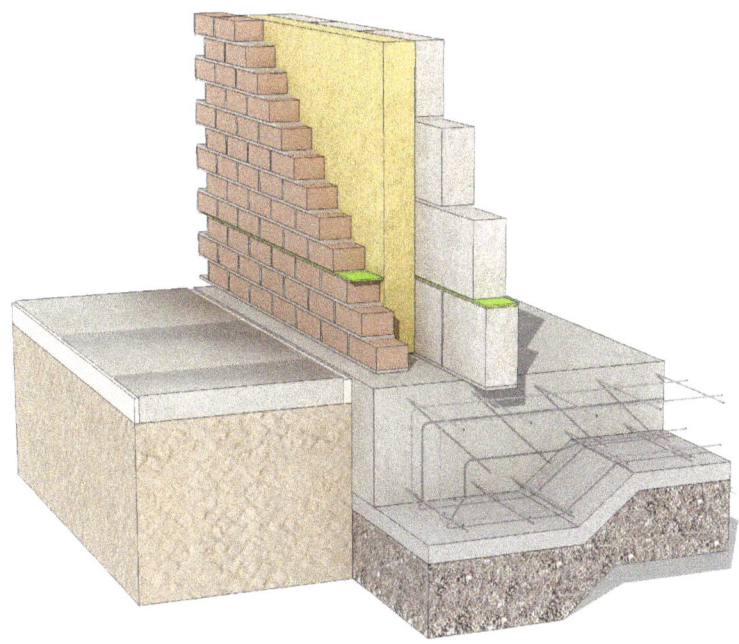

3D Detail G04 - Simple raft foundation with downstand beam

G05

SIMPLE RAFT FOUNDATION WITH DOWNSTAND AND TOE

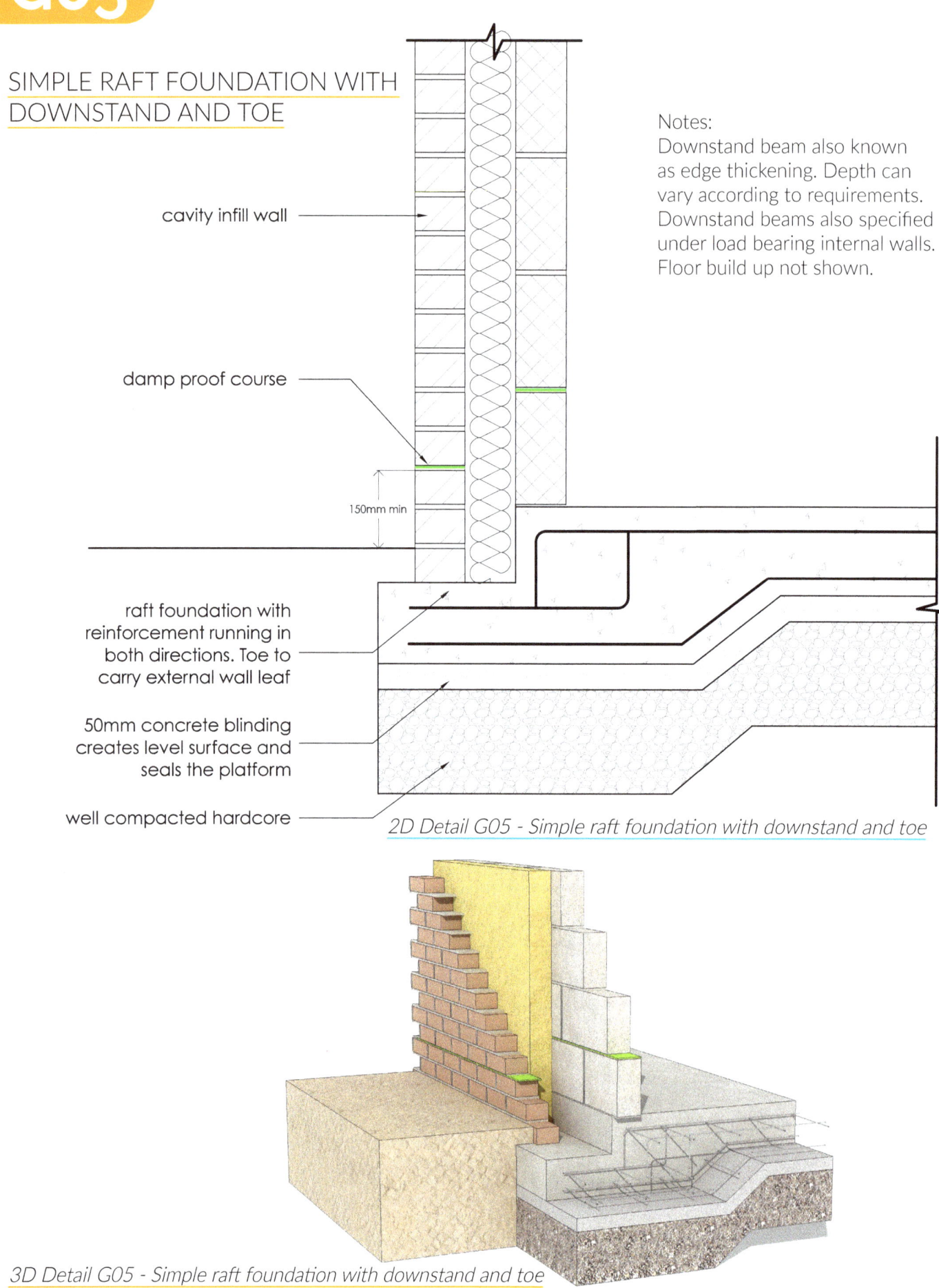

Notes:
Downstand beam also known as edge thickening. Depth can vary according to requirements. Downstand beams also specified under load bearing internal walls. Floor build up not shown.

Labels:
- cavity infill wall
- damp proof course
- 150mm min
- raft foundation with reinforcement running in both directions. Toe to carry external wall leaf
- 50mm concrete blinding creates level surface and seals the platform
- well compacted hardcore

2D Detail G05 - Simple raft foundation with downstand and toe

3D Detail G05 - Simple raft foundation with downstand and toe

SECTION 4 - FOUNDATIONS AND FLOORS

G06

SIMPLE REINFORCED PAD FOUNDATION

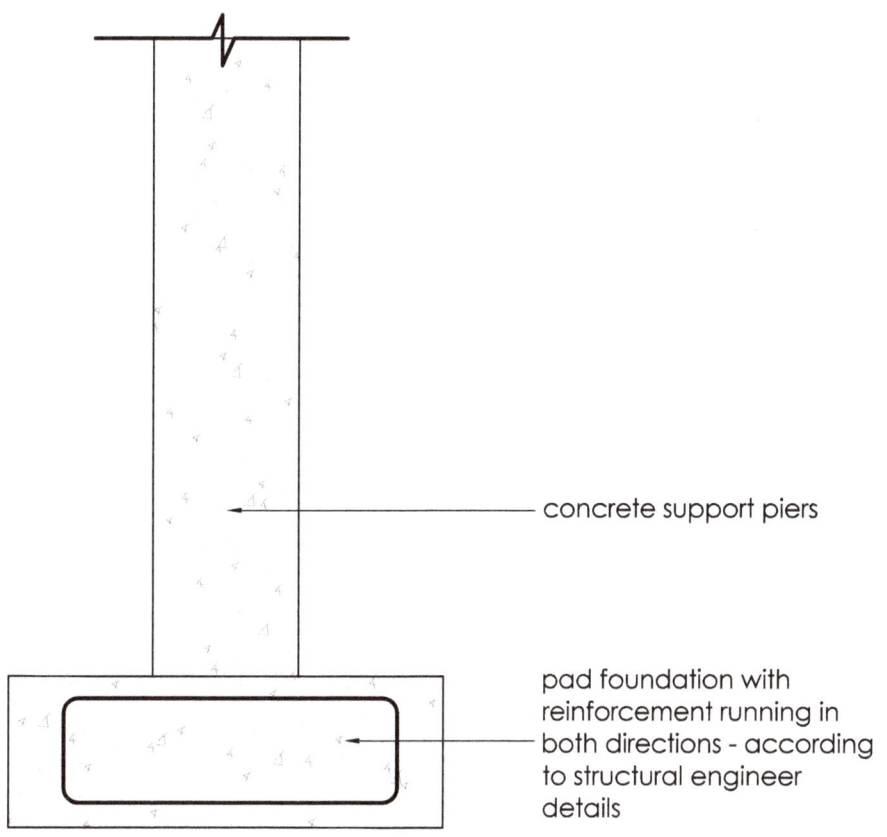

2D Detail G06 - Simple reinforced pad foundation

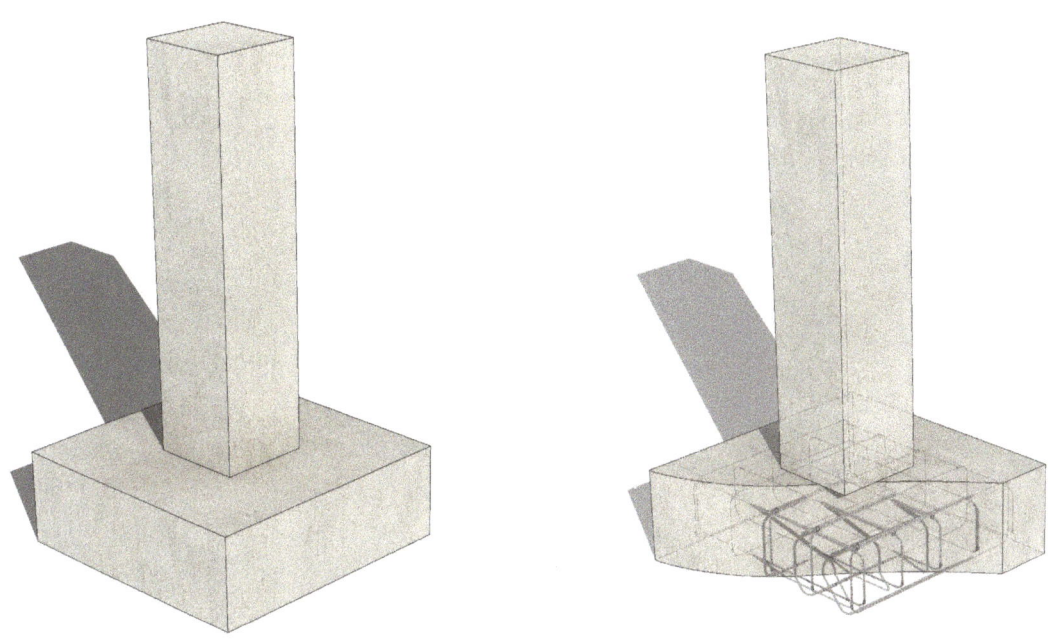

3D Detail G06 - Simple reinforced pad foundation

G07

PAD FOUNDATION WITH SUPPORT PIERS AND GROUND BEAM

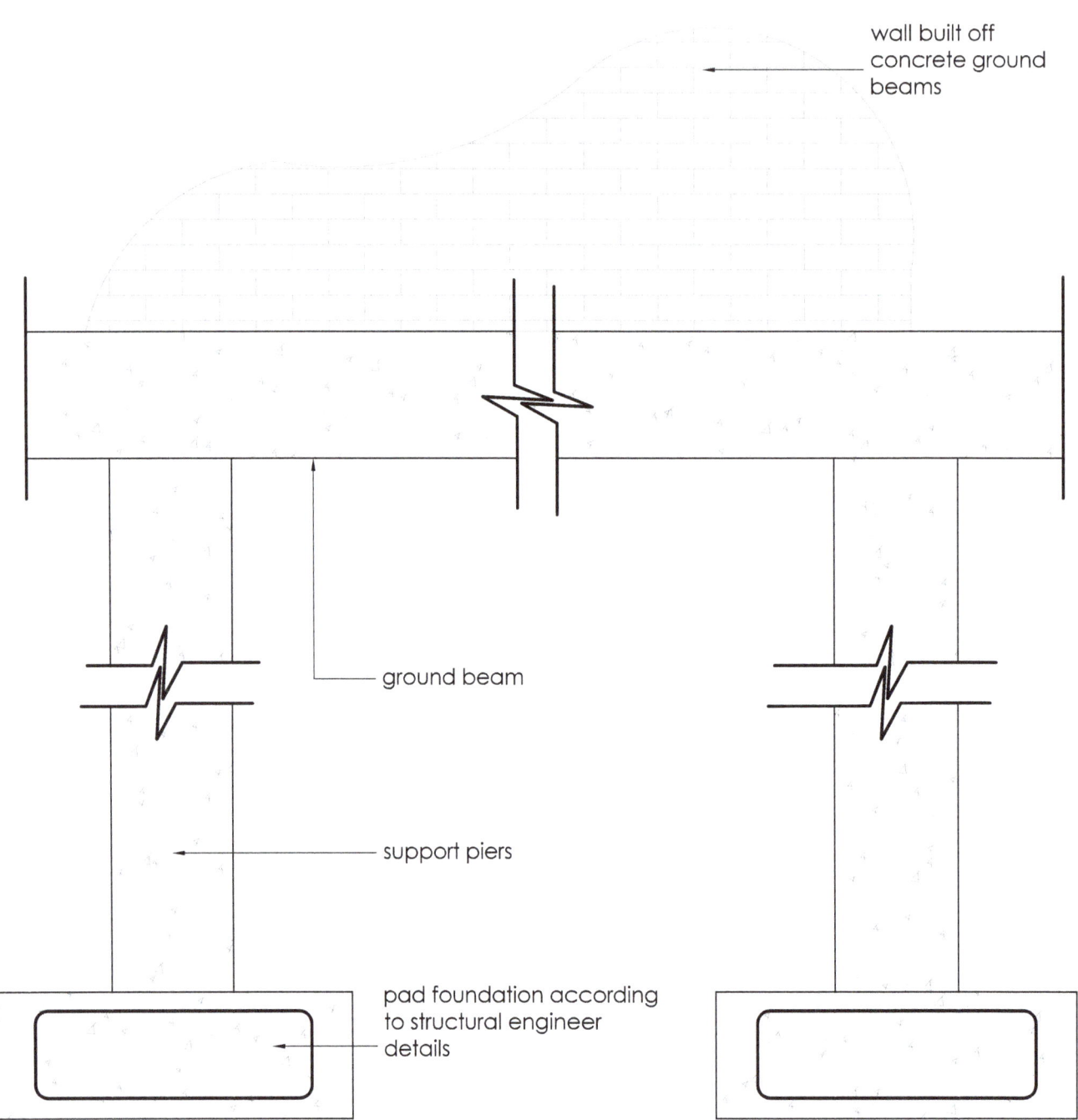

2D Detail G07 - Pad foundation with support piers and ground beam

Notes:
Pads positioned at suitable load bearing strata. Ground beams at or just below ground level.

3D Detail G07 - Pad foundation with support piers and ground beam

G08

PAD FOUNDATION WITH GROUND BEAM

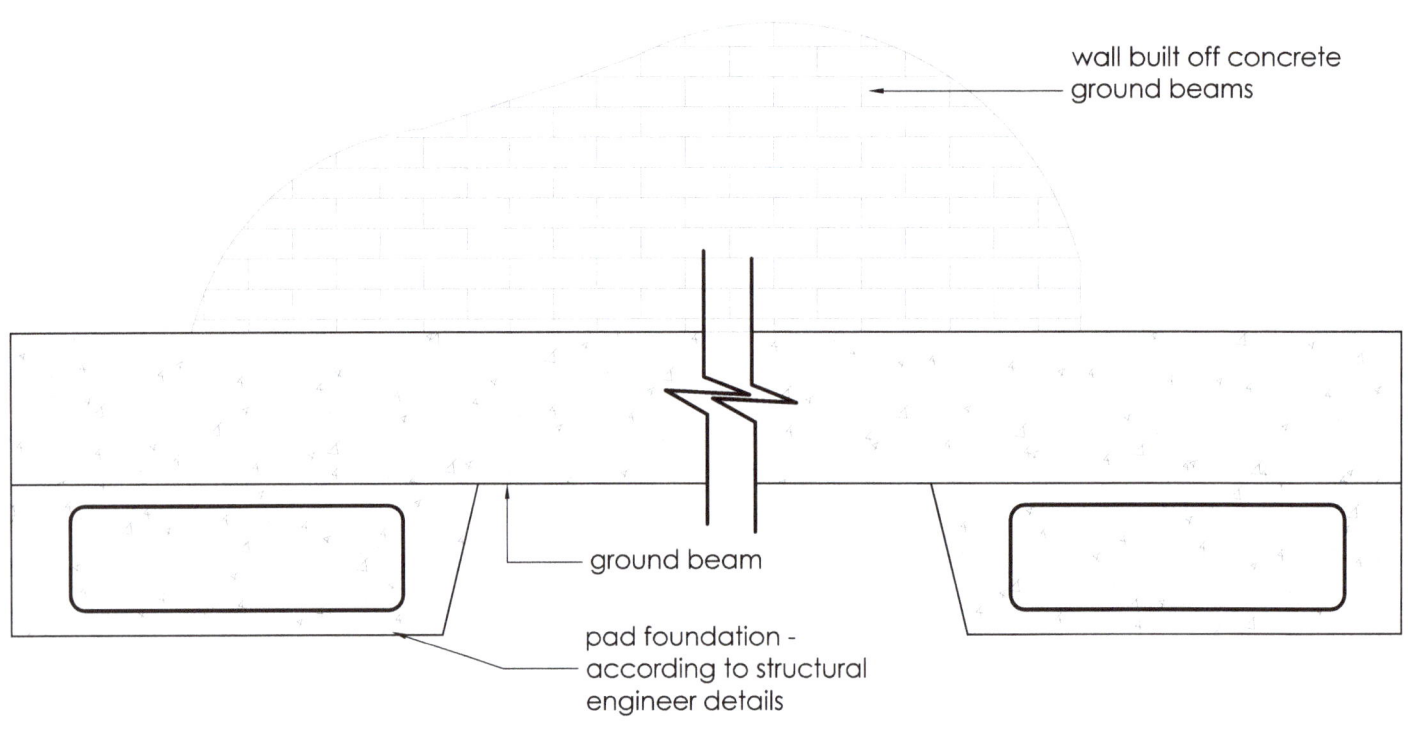

2D Detail G08 - Pad foundation with ground beam

Notes:
Pads positioned at suitable load bearing strata. Ground beams at or just below ground level.

3D Detail G08 - Pad foundation with ground beam

G09

PILE FOUNDATION WITH GROUND BEAM

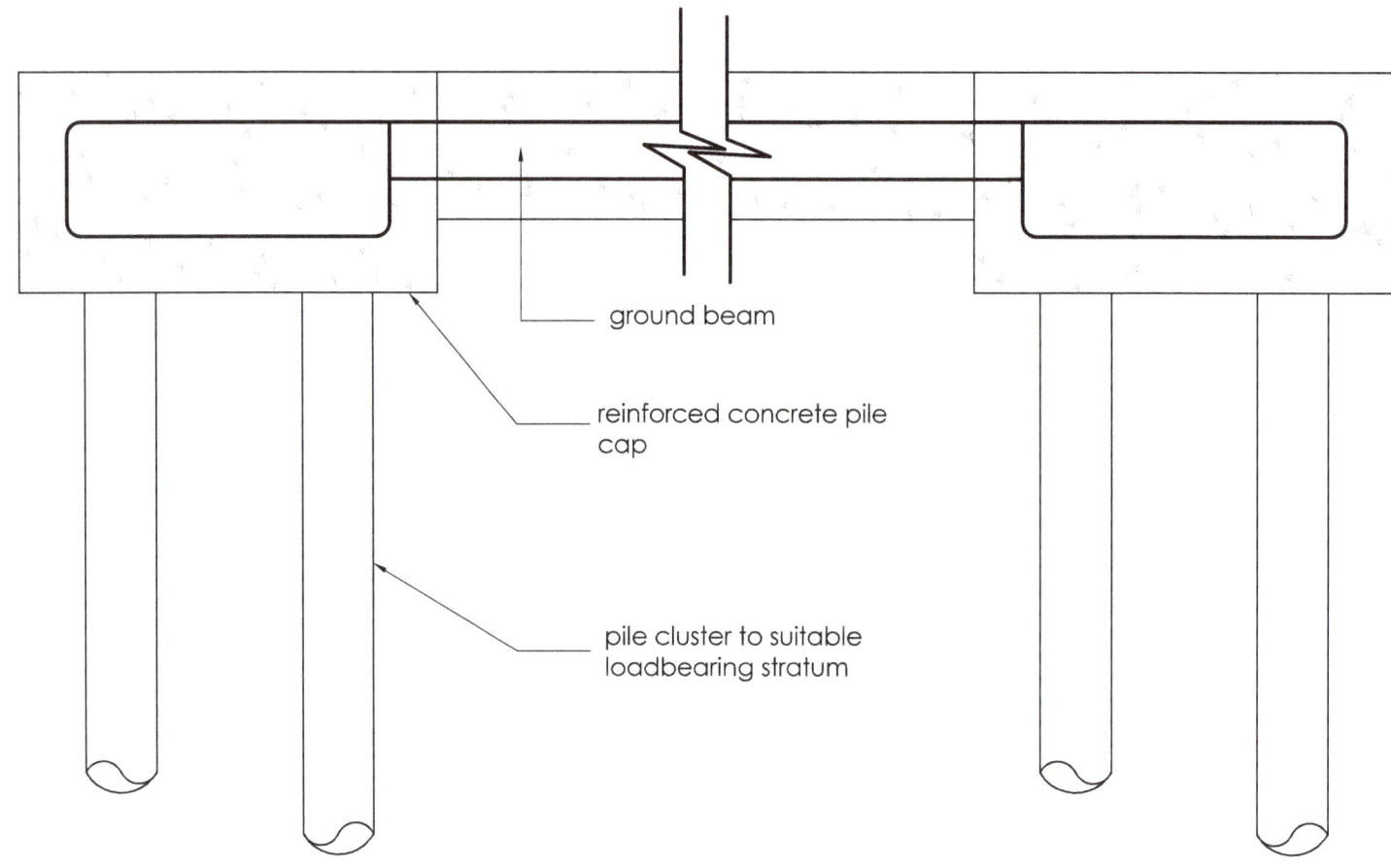

2D Detail G09 - Pile foundation with ground beam

Notes:
Pile clusters topped with reinforced concrete pile caps. Reinforced ground beams at or just below ground level.

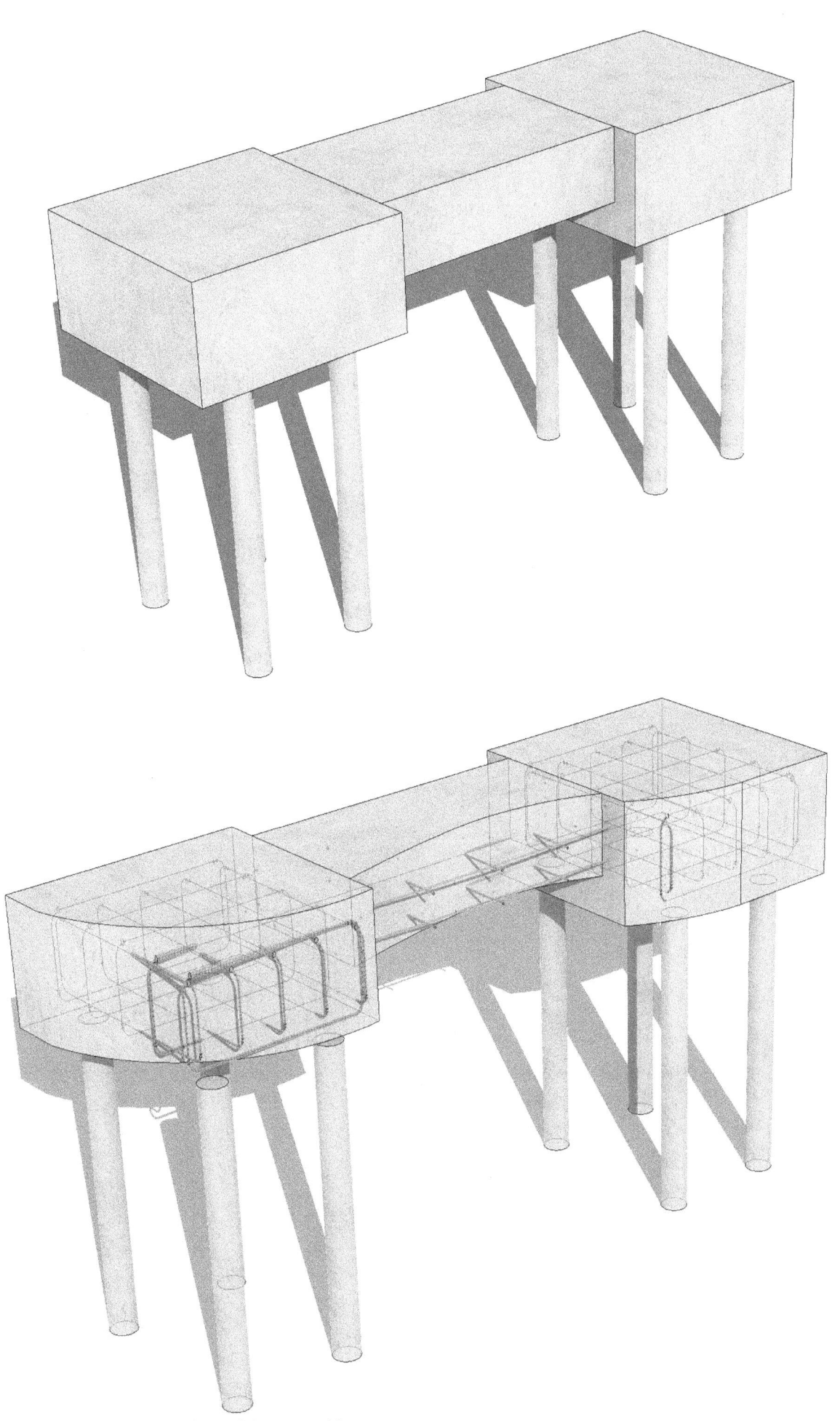

3D Detail G09 - Pile foundation with ground beam

G10

PRECAST CONCRETE COLUMN CONNECTION TO FOUNDATION

reinforced concrete column

concrete column submerged into foundation with in situ concrete or grout

leveling shims

in situ concrete foundation

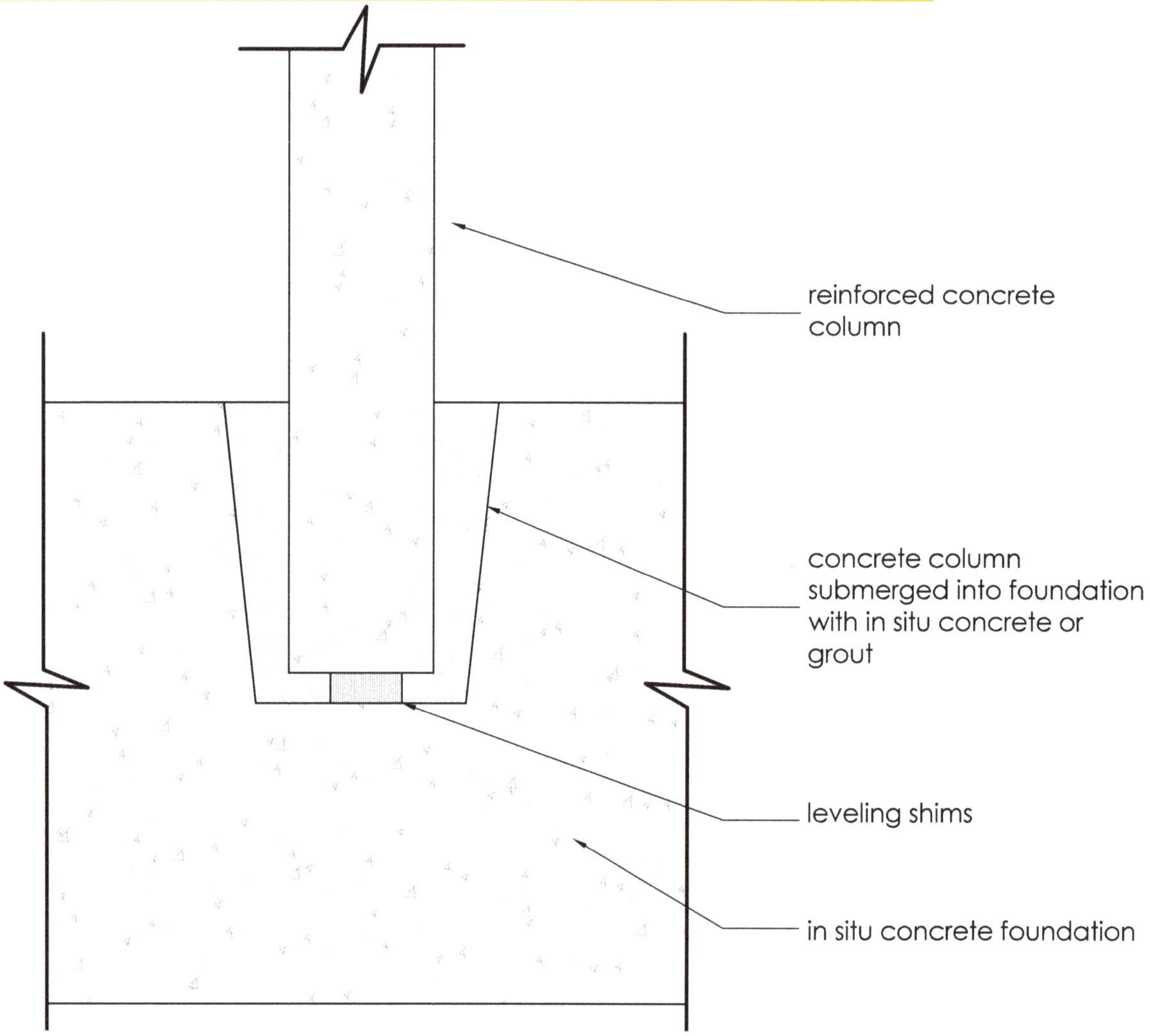

2D Detail G10 - Precast concrete column connection to foundation

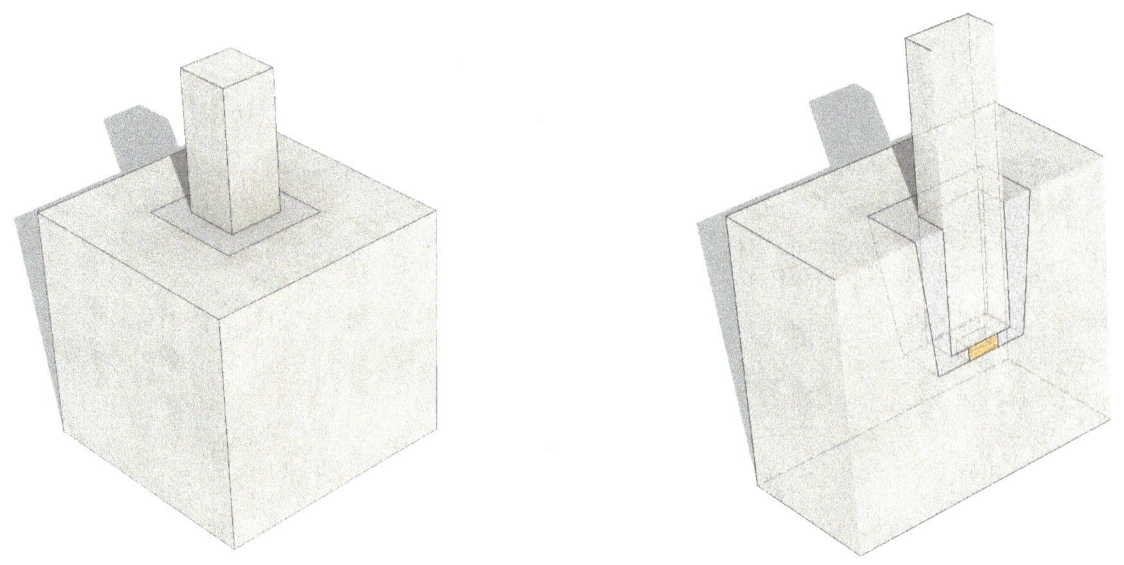

3D Detail G10 - Precast concrete column connection to foundation

SECTION 4 – FOUNDATIONS AND FLOORS

G11

PRECAST CONCRETE COLUMN CONNECTION TO FOUNDATION - ALTERNATIVE

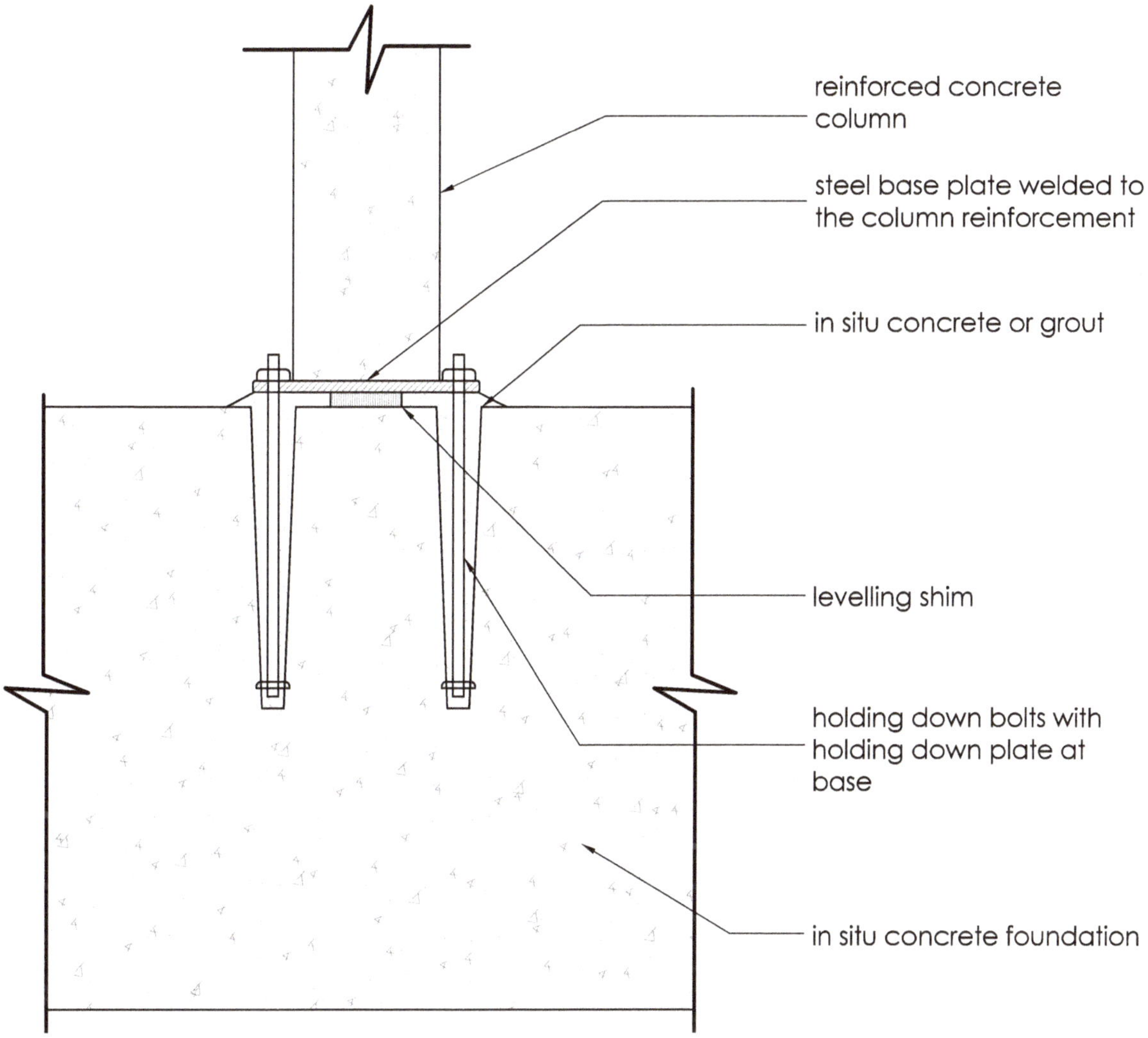

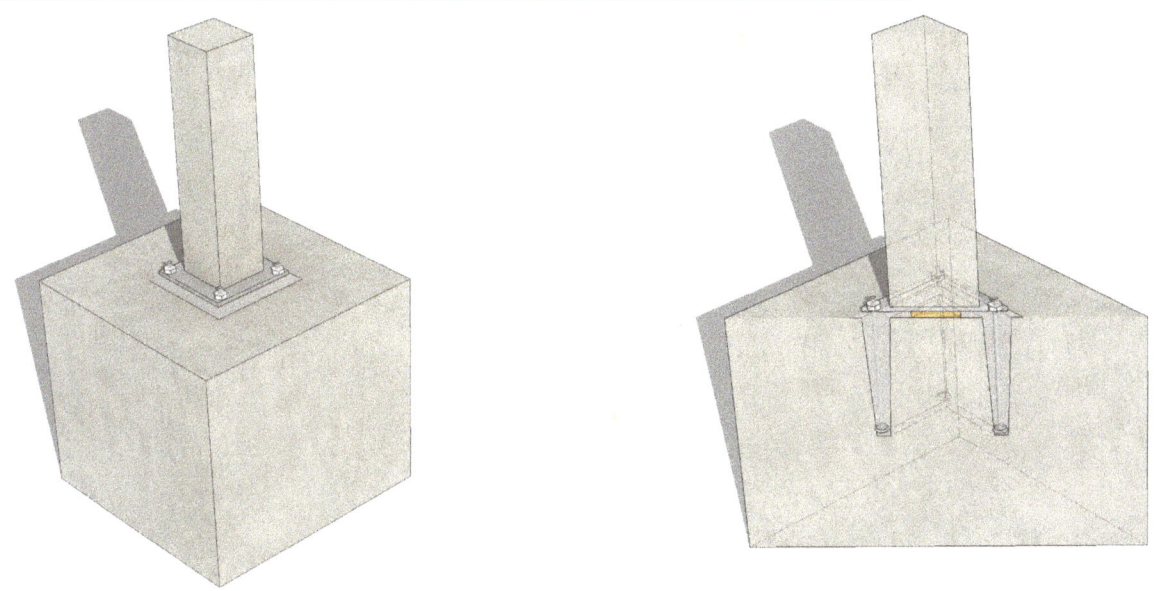

2D Detail G11 - Precast concrete column connection to foundation - alternative

- reinforced concrete column
- steel base plate welded to the column reinforcement
- in situ concrete or grout
- levelling shim
- holding down bolts with holding down plate at base
- in situ concrete foundation

3D Detail G11 - Precast concrete column connection to foundation - alternative

G12

STEEL COLUMN CONNECTION TO FOUNDATION

- universal steel column
- in situ concrete or grout
- levelling shim
- holding down bolts with holding down plate at base
- in situ concrete foundation

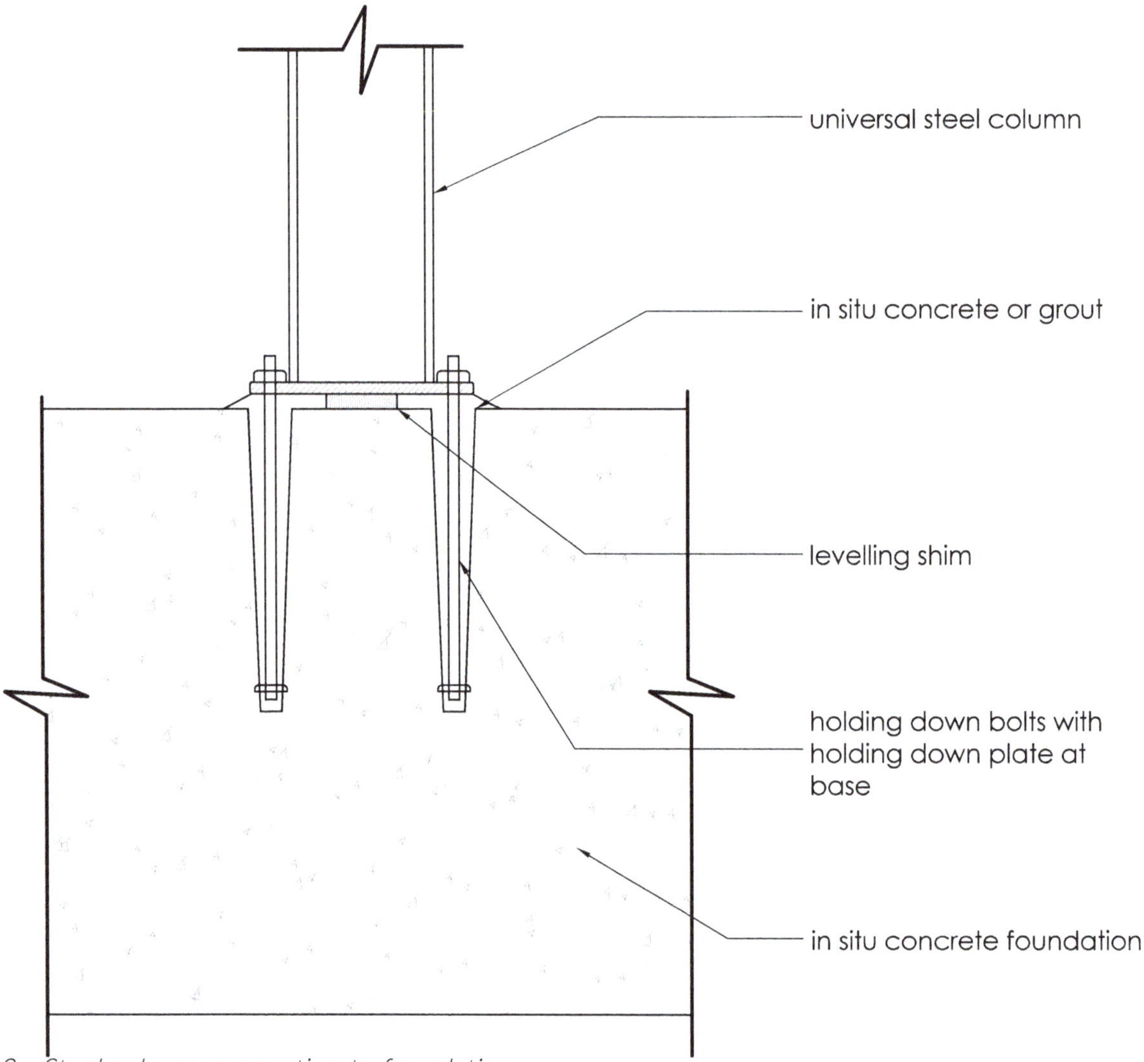

2D Detail G12 - Steel column connection to foundation

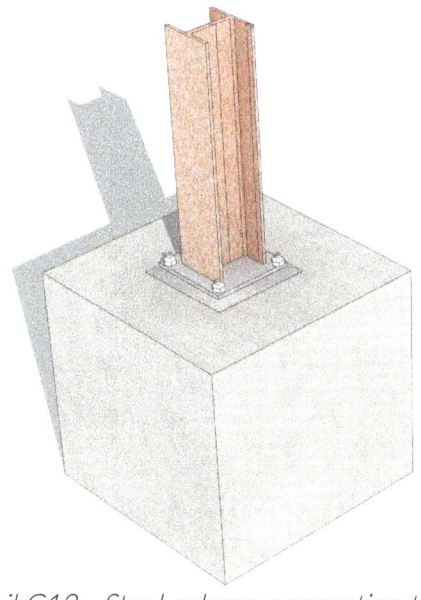
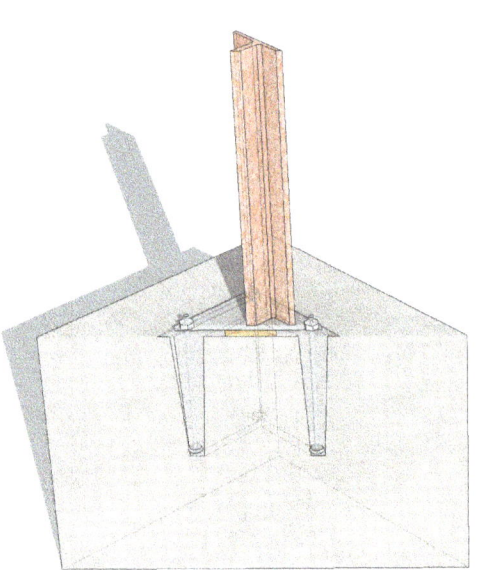

3D Detail G12 - Steel column connection to foundation

SECTION 4 - FOUNDATIONS AND FLOORS

Blank Page

FLOORS

In this section we give an overview to some of the more basic forms of floor construction. There are many more options to consider, like Termodeck and floors that incorporate both passive and active cooling along with other forward thinking technologies that go beyond the scope of this book.

GROUND FLOORS

The design of commercial and industrial ground floors differ from residential and domestic construction, due to the significant difference in the size and loadings of a commercial or industrial structure. Generally speaking, ground floor construction is limited to concrete and steel in most cases, although occasionally suspended timber floors can be seen in timber frame three storey or less construction. Suspended timber floors are covered in Understanding Architectural Details Residential Construction and will not be covered in this book.

Ground floors generally fall into two main categories; suspended floors and ground supported (or ground bearing) floors. A ground supported floor is a solid concrete floor construction that is in constant contact with, and supported by the ground below. A suspended floor is formed from elements, concrete or steel usually, that span between supports. The suspended floor does not use the ground for support, but the surrounding walls and structure that transfer the floor loads to the foundations, and strata below.

FUNCTIONAL REQUIREMENTS AND FACTORS AFFECTING SELECTION OF FLOOR TYPE

The nature of the site, requirements of the building, quality of construction, budget and speed of construction can all determine the selection of ground floor structure. No matter the solution, all floors must fulfil the same functional requirements.

Structural stability
The ground floor structure of a commercial or industrial building must be strong and stable enough to support any dead load of the floor along with any anticipated imposed loads of the occupants, activities, furniture and equipment. It is worth considering that in industrial buildings it is possible that there will be vibration from machinery, rolling loads such as forklift trucks that will place quite a considerable demand on the ground floor structure. In these cases, a reinforced concrete ground supported structure would be specified which would distribute the loads effectively into the ground below. Although suspended floors are uncommon in industrial buildings, commercial buildings often have basements, or car parking below ground level, as such the ground level floor is often suspended.

The floor must also have sufficient stiffness to remain stable under loading from the occupants, activities carried out, equipment and so on, whilst also accommodating any services in the floor depth, or below or above the floor itself.

Resistance to weather and moisture
The Building Regulations Part C states that the floor must provide resistance to the passage of moisture through ground floors to the inside of the building. Ground floors can be subject to high levels of water pressure, in particular when basements are created beneath the structure. It is important that a detailed solution is produced to prevent the passage of moisture into the building.

Thermal insulation
As with all elements of the main fabric of the building a ground floor must provide sufficient resistance to the transfer of heat, where there is a temperature difference on the opposite side of the floor. The levels of

insulation required is dependent on structure and the size of the building. In large buildings, areas of the floor close to the perimeter suffer greater heat loss than areas in the centre of the building. For this reason, it can be seen that the perimeter of the building is insulated to a higher level than the central part of the building, which has considerable financial savings.

A suspended floor generally has the same heat loss levels over the element and is insulated in a uniform manner. If the suspended floor is separating an area that is unheated, like car parking, it will require more insulation than if it is separating a heated area, like basement storage for example.

Durability
Industrial buildings in particular require durable materials to be specified for ground floor constructions due to the activities carried out, along with some possibilities of the use of corrosive materials. The floor must provide a good life span and be designed in accordance with the future use of the building.

Selection
Factors which will inform the design and specification of a ground floor include:
- The type of building to be constructed
- The proposed use of the building
- Proposed loadings of the building
- Nature of the site
- Surface finishes required to the floors
- Budget and financial restraints

It is worth considering that the nature of a commercial building is often quite different to that of an industrial building, and requirements of the ground floors in these two types of structures can be quite different.

SOLID CONCRETE GROUND FLOOR

As mentioned previously, the loads on a non domestic floor can be considerable, particularly industrial usage. A ground supported floor will be able to distribute the loads through the contact area of heavy loads.

The different types of loading that can be expected on a floor are:
- Rolling loads - from wheeled vehicles such as fork lift trucks. These type of loads have an impact on the surface of the floor. When a rolling load is anticipated, a thick slab is specified with a concrete of a good strength grade.
- Point loads - these can be from heavy machinery, the legs of racking or storage units which can result in a failure of the floor. If this type of loading is anticipated a thicker slab will be selected.
- Uniformly distributed loads - these are from situations where the floor is used for direct storage, so items will be stacked on the floor in a uniform manner (without the point loading of racking legs).

A solid concrete floor consists of the following elements - from the base:

- Hardcore
- Blinding (if required)
- Damp proof membrane
- Insulation
- Concrete slab
- Surface finish

The arrangement of the elements can vary, particularly the position of the damp proof membrane and the insulation.

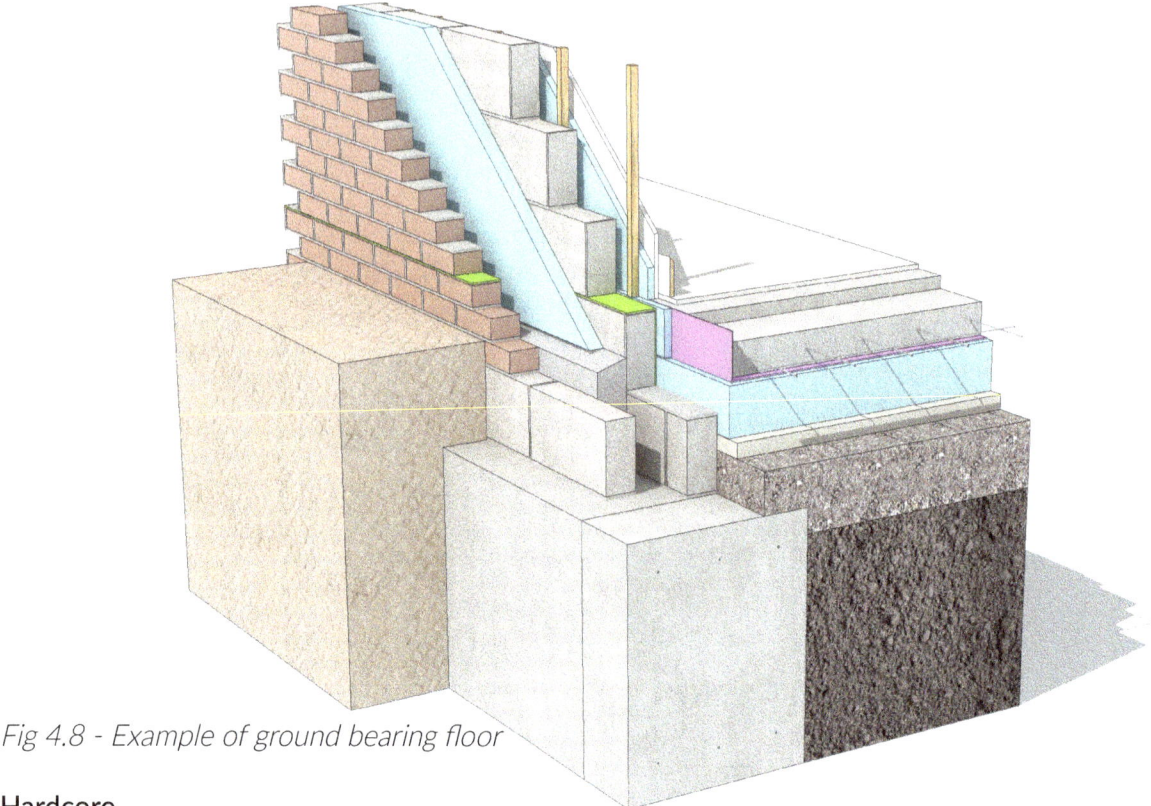

Fig 4.8 - Example of ground bearing floor

Hardcore
The hardcore is a layer of mixed material used to infill the space below the slab, to bring the ground to a suitable level with an even surface. The material used for hardcore can be graded crushed bricks, stone or concrete, sometimes reclaimed from site. The hardcore does not absorb moisture and provides a solid base for the ground structure, usually at a thickness of 150mm-300mm deep laid in layers. The maximum depth allowed by the Building Regulations Part C is 600mm - any depth required that is greater would be more suited to a suspended floor system. Approved Document Part C also recommends that no hardcore laid under a solid ground floor should contain water soluble sulphates or other harmful matter in such quantities that it could cause damage to the floor.
The hardcore is compacted down using a vibrating plate to minimise risk of settlement and movement later on.

Blinding
A blinding layer of 50mm sand was common to create an even base with a suitable surface for the damp proof membrane to avoid punctures from the hardcore below. The sand would also stop the concrete from seeping through the gaps in the hardcore. Blinding consists of a layer of 25-50mm sand, or 50-75mm layer of weak concrete if a surface for reinforced concrete is required. These days, hardcore is well graded, meaning the concrete is unable to drip through, and there are less likely to be punctures to the damp proof membrane so the sand blinding layer is sometimes omitted.

Damp proof membrane (DPM)
In order to avoid penetration of moisture into the building, a damp proof membrane is required according to Building Regulations Approved Document Part C, to protect the structure from the passage of moisture, and where necessary protect from the passage of harmful gases such as radon and methane.

Some concrete used in industrial and commercial construction can be inherently waterproof, but not always. The membrane is usually made of 0.25mm polythene or polyethylene sheets, which must be impermeable to water in both liquid and vapour form. The sheets are lapped and jointed around 150mm-300mm. The membrane is lapped up the walls to the damp proof course in order to provide a continuous layer of protection against any moisture penetration.

The position of the DPM will vary according to the requirements of the construction. When a DPM is positioned under the concrete, it is protected from damage and the concrete remains dry. If a rigid impermeable insulation is specified, it is prudent to position the DPM on the warm side (internal) of the insulation in order to avoid interstitial condensation. If underfloor heating is used, the DPM should be positioned under the concrete slab.

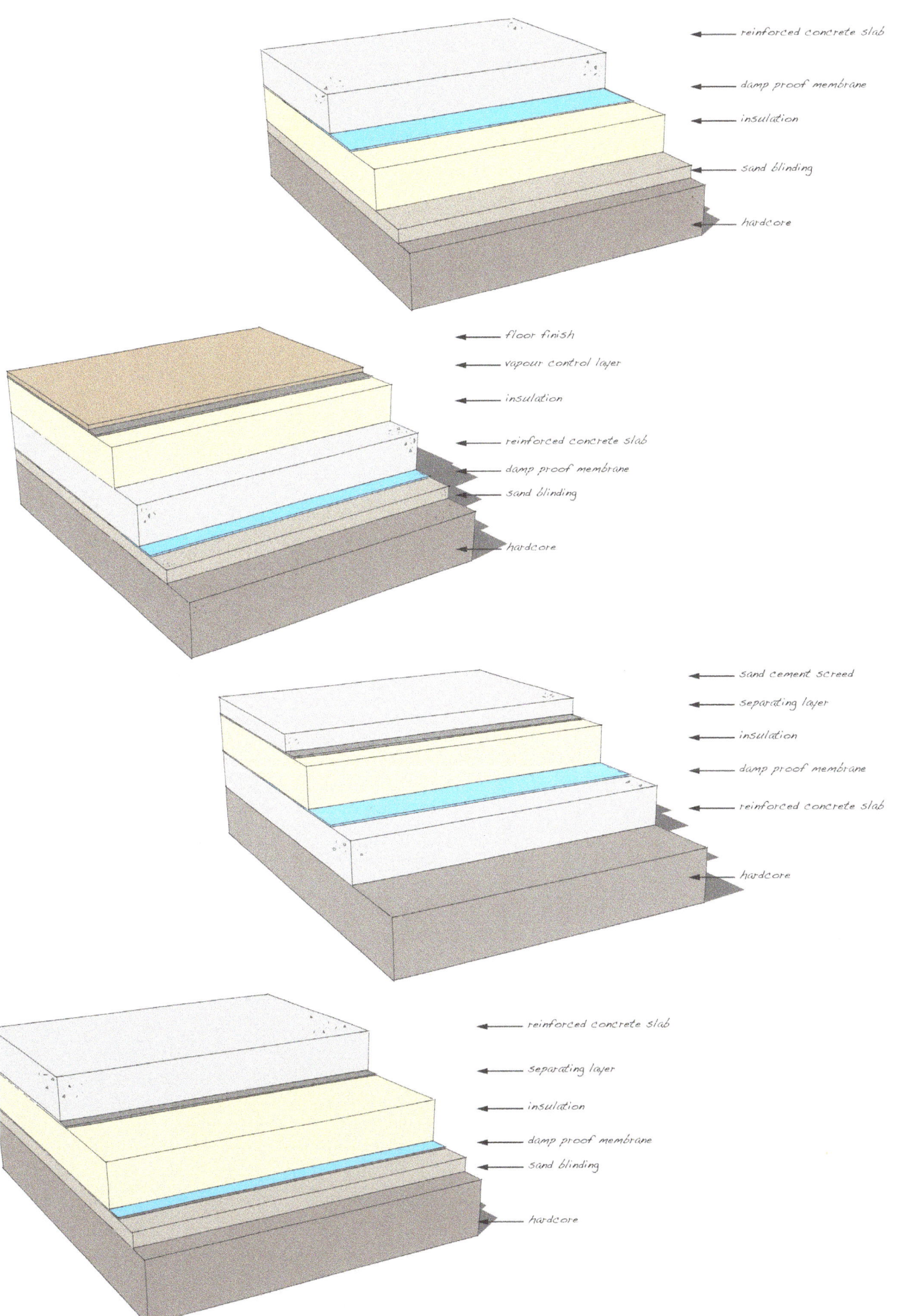

Fig 4.9 - Example of damp proof membrane positions

Concrete Slab
The concrete slab will be cast in situ, the thickness will vary according to loading requirements, and will be reinforced as required. A slab thickness of a minimum 150mm will be used.

Insulation
All floors need to comply with the current Building Regulations Part L where the limiting fabric heat loss or U-value must not be greater than $0.25W/m^2K$.

Insulation can be situated above or below the concrete slab. When positioned below the slab the concrete retains the heat using thermal mass and omits the heat back into the building when the temperature drops. This type of system requires an insulation board with a high compressive strength as it not only needs to support the general loadings of the building occupants and activities, but it also must support the weight of the slab.

Insulation can also be positioned above the concrete slab, the building will heat up more quickly, and the insulation will not need to be as strong.

Any insulation specified in floor construction must have a good load bearing capacity and suitable for flooring applications. It is also important that the insulation to the floor and wall overlap in order to avoid cold bridges where heat may escape from the building.

In buildings with large floor areas it is sometimes not necessary to insulate the entire floor, and instead only insulate the perimeter, where heat loss is most likely to occur by cold bridging.

SUSPENDED GROUND FLOOR
A suspended concrete floor at ground level can be necessary where a basement or additional storeys sit below the external ground level. In terms of construction, the ground floor essentially becomes an intermediate or upper floor, with the construction assembly resembling that of any standard suspended concrete floor at upper levels.

Suspended floors at ground level can also be specified where the ground slopes, has poor bearing capacity or has the potential to change its volume, i.e. swell and shrink according to moisture content or site conditions.

UPPER FLOORS
Many factors affect the selection of an upper floor assembly, but the primary function is to provide a sound, level surface that is capable of supporting all of the imposed and dead loads. The floor must provide adequate fire protection, along with good sound and thermal performance, but speed of construction and economic factors also play a part.

The functional requirements of the upper floors include:

Structural stability
The floor is required to carry all of the dead and imposed loads of the structure and furniture as well as anticipate any future uses of the building according to the requirements of the Building Regulations. Although deflection is allowed, it must not adversely affect the strength and stability of the building. The floor must also be durable for the proposed use and require minimal maintenance.

Thermal performance
The floor must be designed to avoid any cold bridges, so a good continuous thermal insulation is important. Upper floors are susceptible to heat loss and air leakage in services penetrations that have not been sealed correctly.

Fire Safety
Building Regulations Approved Document Part B provides guidance with regard to fire safety. The key requirement is to provide safe escape of people from buildings in case of fire (rather than protecting the

building itself).

UPPER FLOORS - FOR CONCRETE FRAME

Cast in situ concrete slab

A cast in situ concrete slab floor can take many forms including a beam and slab floor, waffle grid, drop beam and flat slab. These types of floors are specified when a cast in situ structural frame is being used. The floor slab is poured at the same time to create an integrated system. Solid concrete floors are usually only specified up to four storeys, it is a heavy construction and therefore requires significant structure in order to support it.

One of the most common of these is the beam and slab floor which is an economical option for use with reinforced concrete frame construction. This type of floor sees the beams of the slab spanning in two directions between the structural grid. It usually takes the form of a square grid which allows for a minimum

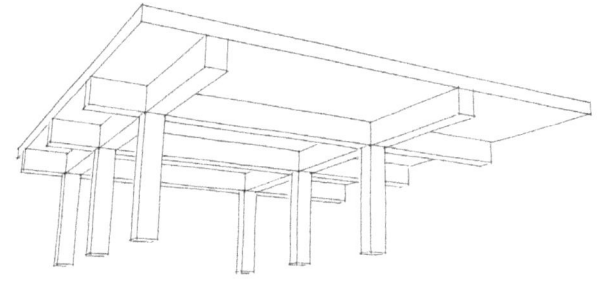

Fig 4.10 - Grid beam and slab floor

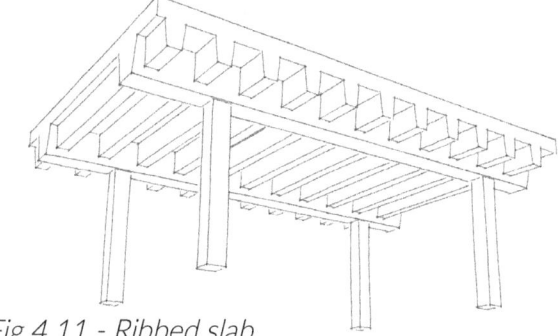

Fig 4.11 - Ribbed slab

A waffle grid slab floor allows for a greater span between beams and is cast in a grid that gives a waffle like appearance from the underside. This type of floor is suitable to support heavy loads while maintaining a wide column grid.

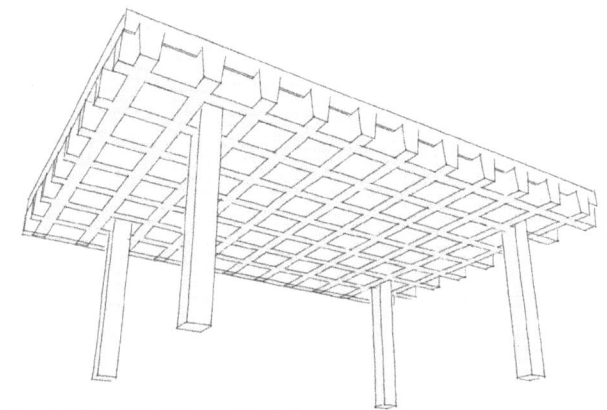

Fig 4.12 - Waffle grid slab

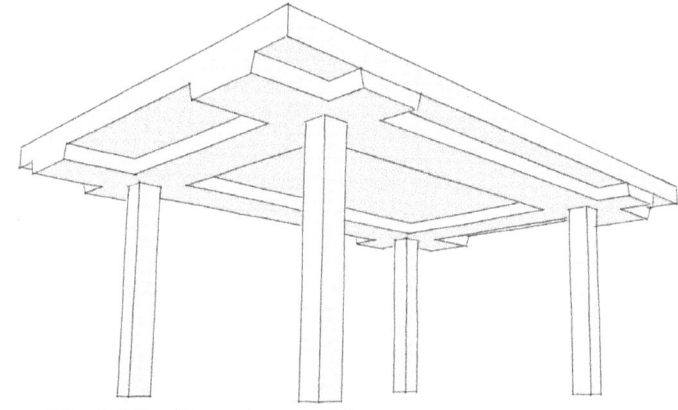

Fig 4.13 - Drop beam slab

The drop beam slab uses a shallow but wide beam between columns that allows for an overall shallow depth of construction. It is used predominantly in square grid structures where wide unobstructed areas are required. It is considered to be quite an expensive option due to the additional reinforcement required.

Finally the flat slab floor construction maintains a uniform thickness throughout with areas spanning between the column grid heavily reinforced. This form of construction allows for reduced overall floor thickness which provides benefits in multi storey buildings, but is also an expensive option due to additional reinforcement required.

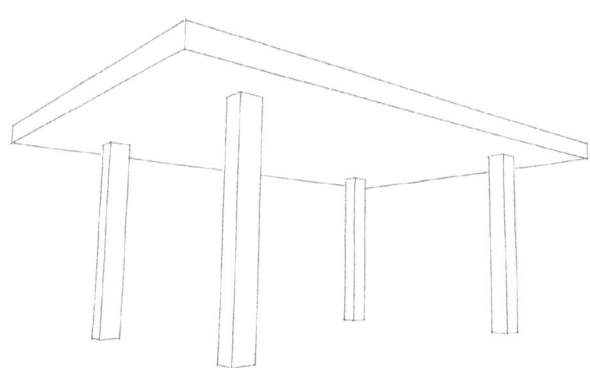

Fig 4.14 - Flat slab

All of the above methods of construction can be used with the reinforced cast in situ method of construction or using hollow, beam or plank floor systems. It is worth mentioning that consideration should be taken to the overall thickness of the floor construction and the requirements of services such as air conditioning, lighting, heating, fire fighting services on the ceilings. The services can significantly increase the overall floor thickness of each storey, thus increasing cost. In some cases it may be beneficial to chose a more expensive, slimmer floor construction, which will allow an overall reduced thickness in floor, thus saving in the overall height of the construction.

The formwork required for the construction of cast in situ concrete floors, along with the curing time generally creates a time consuming process and delays building progress. For this (and other) reasons precast concrete floor systems are often used in multi storey constructions. Some precast units contain hollow cores which can allow for services to pass through, thus negating the need for suspended ceilings.

PRECAST CONCRETE FLOOR SYSTEMS

Precast concrete floors have overcome many of the disadvantages of cast in situ concrete slabs. Precast concrete floor systems consist of planks, beams, t beams or infill blocks that require little or no temporary support systems during construction. The beams are topped with a structural screed once installed. The selection of a precast concrete floor system takes into account many factors, including:

- maximum span
- nature of support
- weight of the concrete unit
- thickness of the concrete unit
- thermal insulation performance
- sound insulation
- fire performance
- speed of construction
- requirement of temporary support

BEAM AND BLOCK FLOORING

Sometimes known as precast T beam flooring, this construction is generally used to span small distances and taken small loads, commonly seen in more residential construction. Beams in the shape of a T are placed at specified centres, built into the walls or bearing on structural beams. Concrete blocks, either solid or hollow are then placed between the beams in rows, with a structural concrete topping added to spread the load. The underside of the floor can be plastered or a suspended ceiling can be installed. The infill blocks can also be made of extruded polystyrene providing a lightweight solution with good thermal insulation properties, allowing fast construction with minimum health and safety issues.

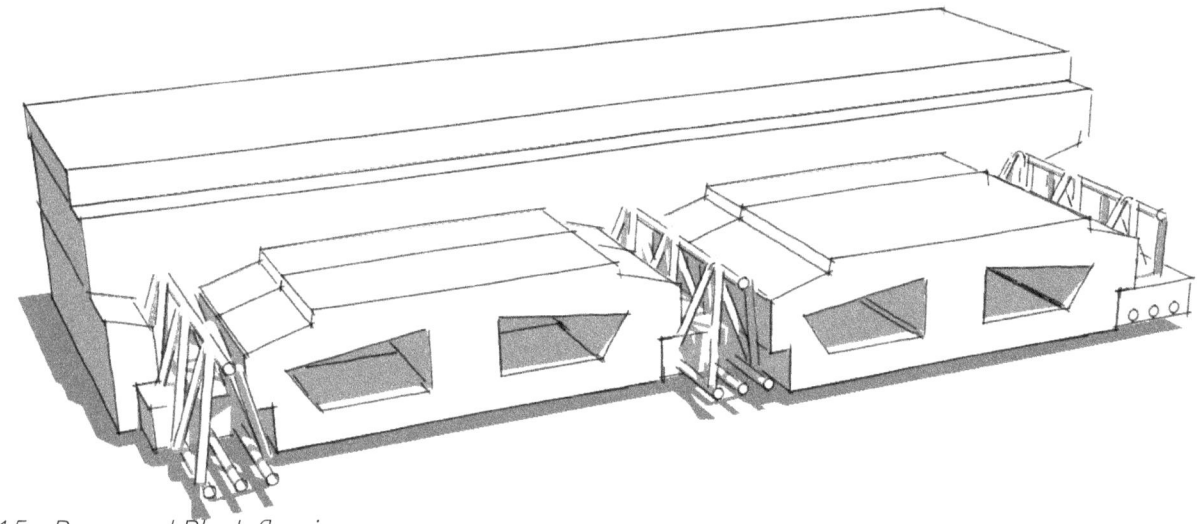

Fig 4.15 - Beam and Block flooring

HOLLOW BEAM FLOOR UNITS

Reinforced hollow concrete beams are usually between 350mm and 1200mm wide and depth can vary from 130mm to over 300mm. The beams can span up to 10m long. They are placed side by side with their ends supported by load bearing masonry walls or structural frame. The beams are not strong enough to fully support potential imposed loads, so a structural concrete topping is levelled over the beams usually to a thickness of 50mm.

The use of a hollow beam floor unit can see a reduction of up to 50% in the volume of concrete used compared to a cast in situ floor.

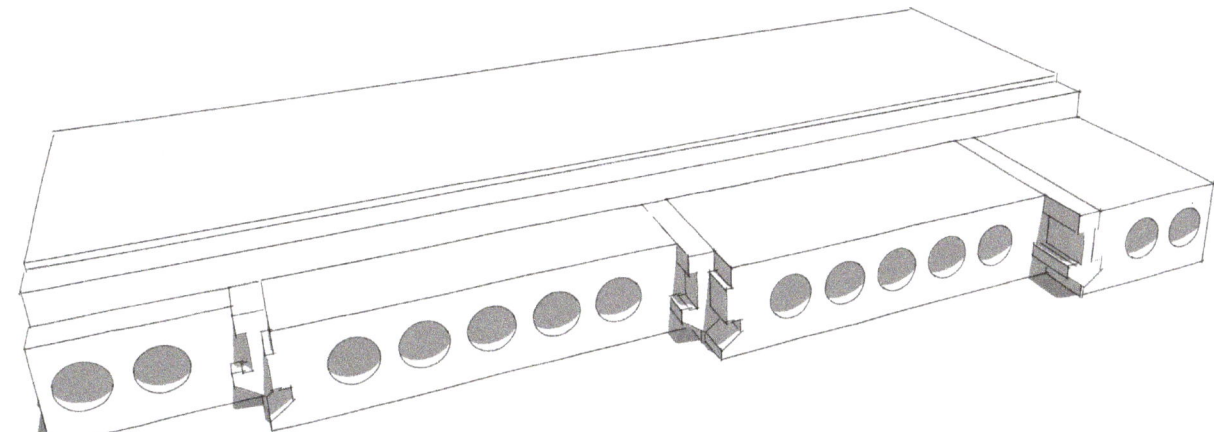

Fig 4.16 - Hollow beam floor units

PRECAST CONCRETE PLANK FLOOR UNITS

Precast plank units are thin prestressed planks that span up to 9.5m. They are generally finished with a concrete topping. Prestressed units are popular because the units are thin and therefore the weight can be reduced for large span applications. The drawback of using precast units is the potential lead in time for delivery and difficulty of lifting the units into position.

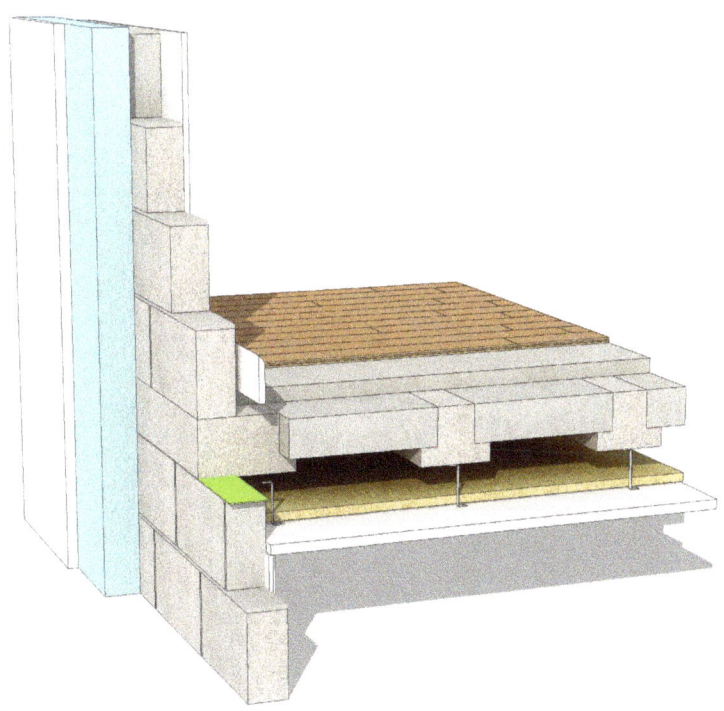

Simple beam and block floor

UPPER FLOORS - FOR STEEL FRAME STRUCTURES

STEEL DECK AND CONCRETE FLOOR

The most common form of floor system for steel frame structures is the use of cold rolled steel decks that provide a permanent formwork for a concrete topping which often incorporates a form of reinforcement.

A steel frame is often constructed in one operation, which when attempting to lift and position large concrete plank floor units can provide difficulty. This is why the steel deck is a popular option, as it is easier to handle, and creates a permanent formwork for the reinforcement and concrete.

This form of construction is fast, given the lightweight sheets which are easily fixed in place. The concrete topping provides fire protection to the steel deck, with the underside coated in a suitable material, the decking can be manufactured with intumescent properties, or a protective suspended ceiling can also be used.

The steel sheets are fitted to the steel structural floor beams, with the reinforcement mesh laid over the decking. The concrete is then poured onto the deck. This form of floor construction is not often used with masonry wall, timber frame or concrete frame construction.

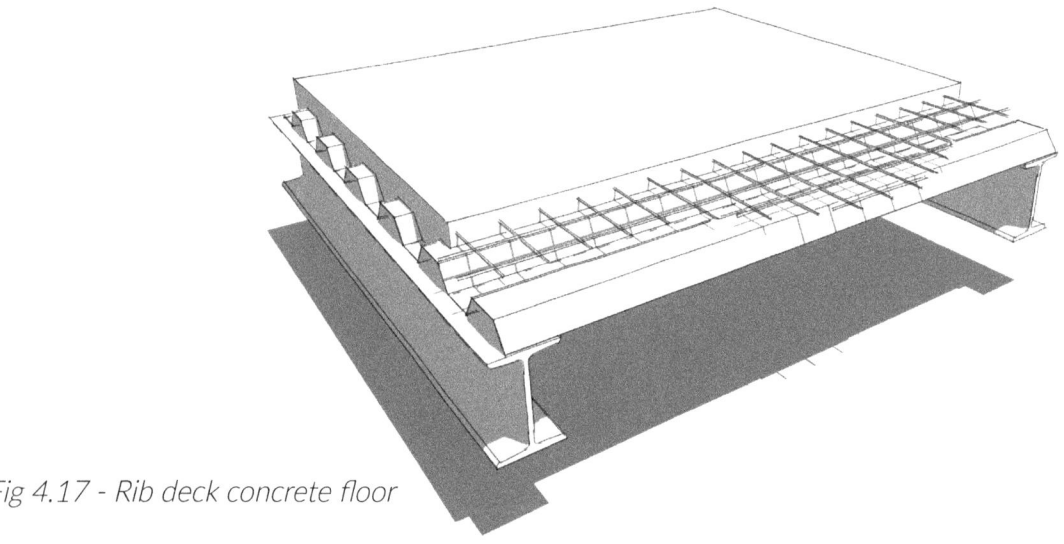

Fig 4.17 - Rib deck concrete floor

PRECAST HOLLOW FLOOR BEAMS

Precast hollow floor beams are usually between 350mm and 1200mm wide and depth can vary from 130mm to over 300mm. The beams can span up to 10m long. They are placed side by side with their ends supported by the steel structural frame, they are usually supported by steel shelf angles which are welded or bolted to the beam. By fixing the concrete unit within the depth of the steel beam the floor depth is kept to a minimum.

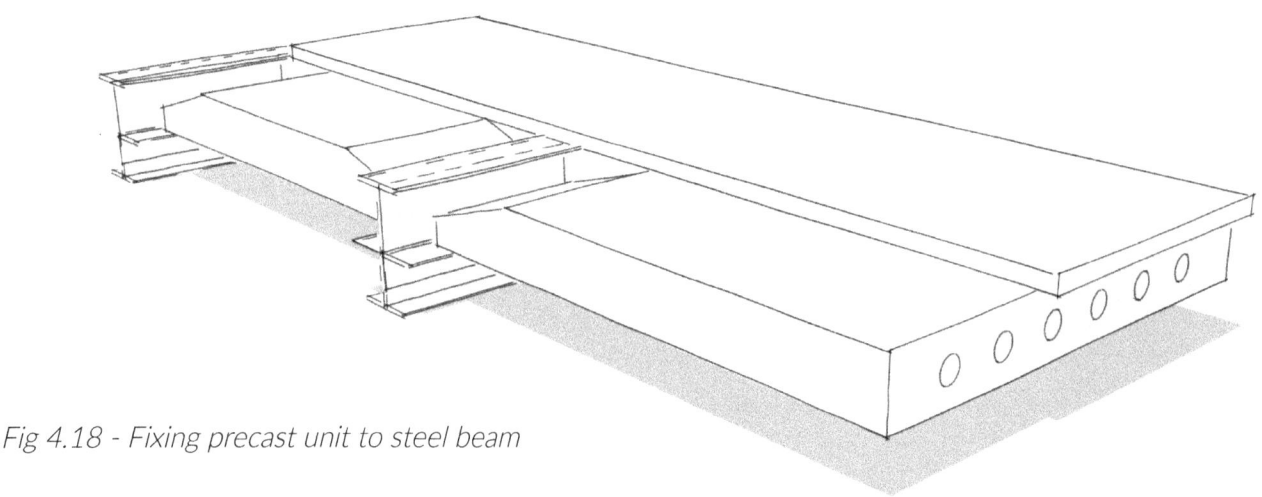

Fig 4.18 - Fixing precast unit to steel beam

The beams are then finished with a structural concrete topping where heavier loads are anticipated or a levelling screed where there will be lighter loading. A raised access floor can also be installed over the beams.

PRESTRESSED CONCRETE FLOOR UNITS

Precast plank units are thin prestressed planks that span up to 9.5m. They are positioned on top of the structural beams and are generally finished with a concrete topping. Prestressed units are popular because the units are thin and therefore the weight can be reduced for large span applications. The drawback of using precast units is the potential lead in time for delivery and difficulty of lifting the units into position.

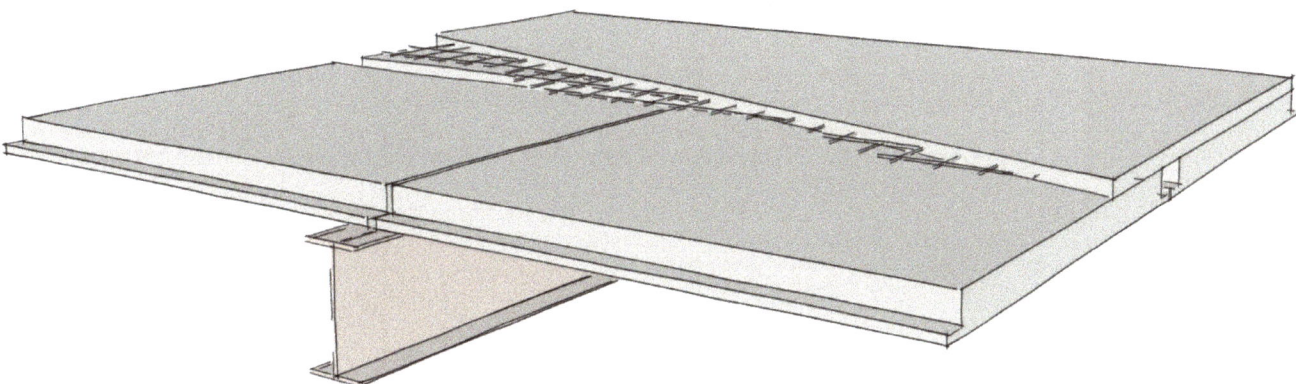

Fig 4.19 - Prestressed concrete floor units

PRECAST BEAM AND BLOCK

Sometimes known as precast T beam flooring, this construction is generally used to span small distances and takes small loads, commonly seen in more residential construction. Beams in the shape of a T are placed at specified centres, bearing on structural beams. Concrete blocks, either solid or hollow are then placed between the beams in rows. The beams are reinforced with steal that protrudes from the top, which acts in conjunction with a structural concrete topping added to spread the load. The underside of the floor can be plastered or a suspended ceiling can be installed.

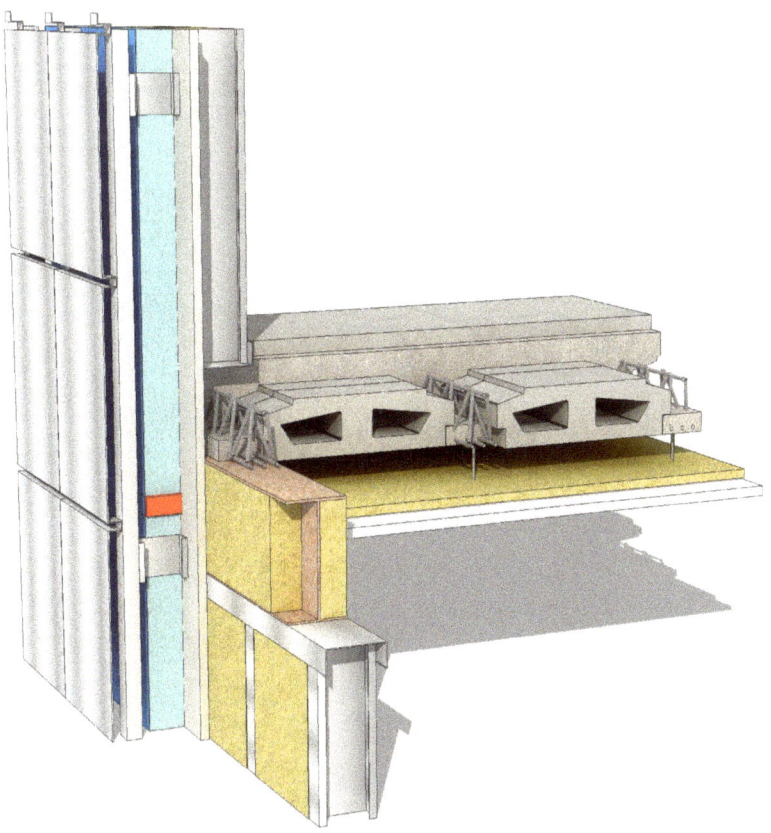

FLOOR DETAILS

F01
GROUND BEARING CONCRETE FLOOR, INSULATION BELOW SLAB

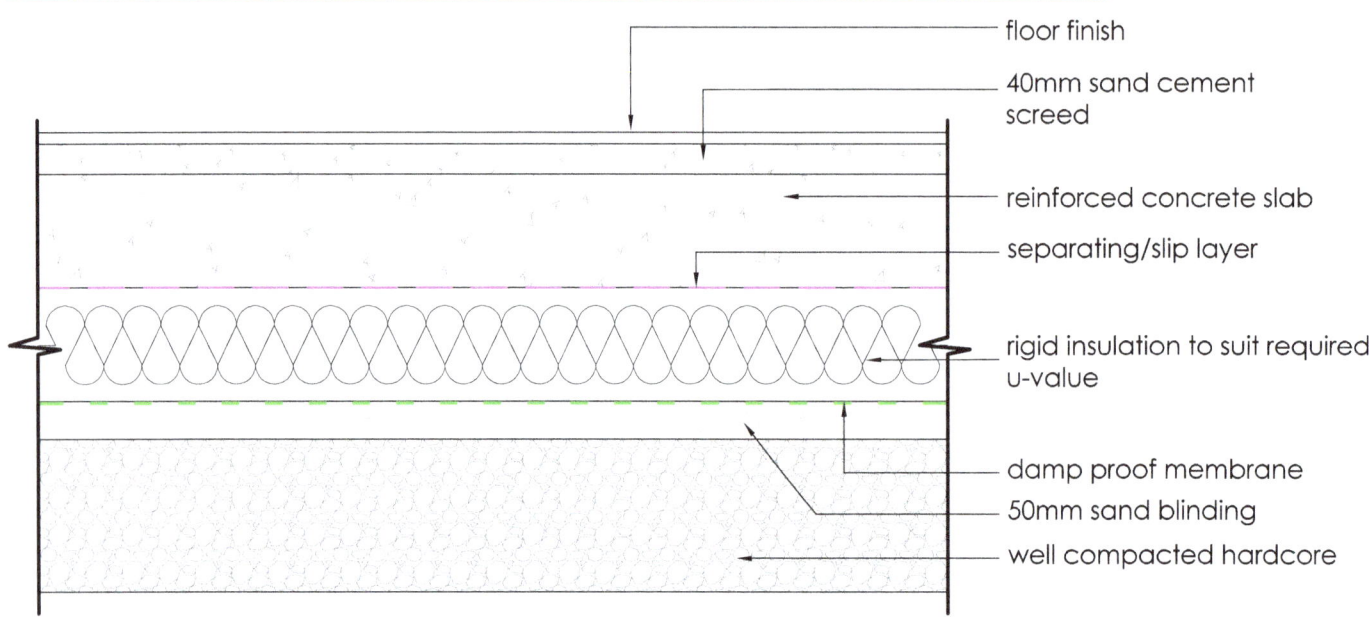

2D Detail F01 - Ground bearing concrete floor, insulation below slab

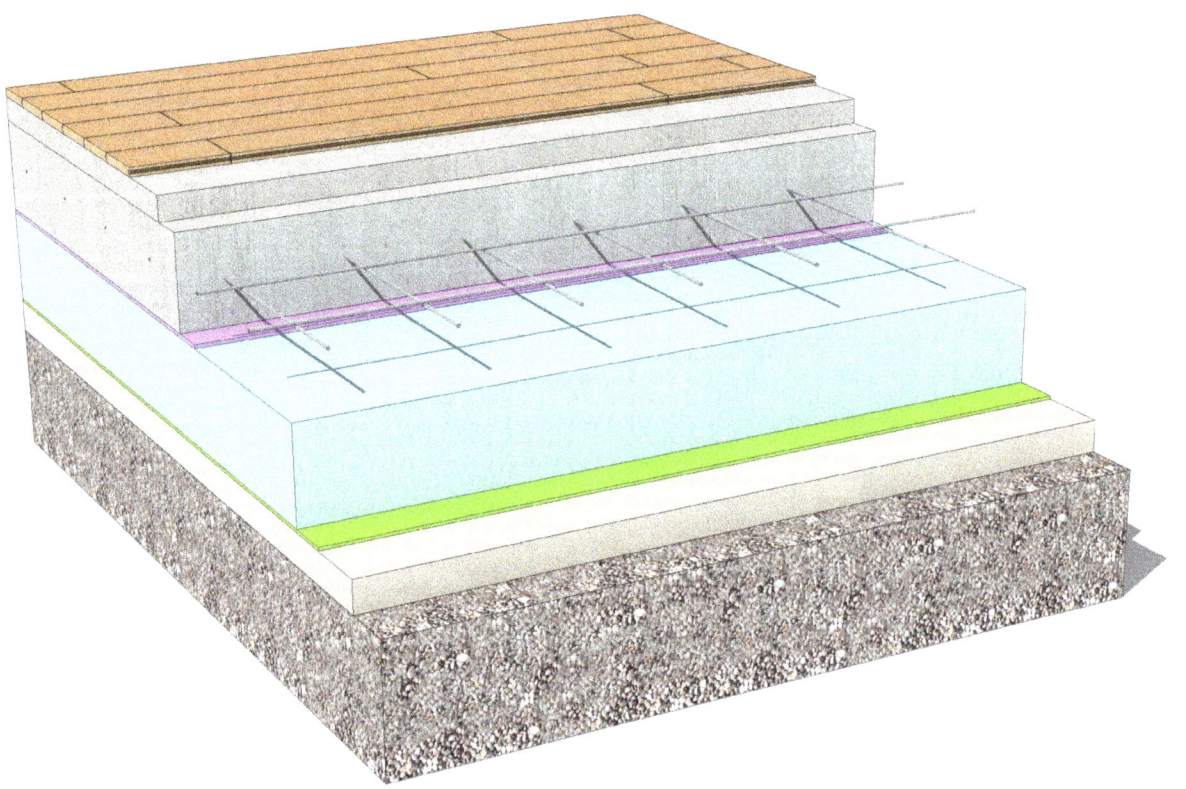

3D Detail F01 - Ground bearing concrete floor, insulation below slab

Notes:
Separating/slip layer provides vapour control and prevent concrete seeping into the cracks between insulation boards when concrete is being poured.

F02

GROUND BEARING CONCRETE FLOOR, INSULATION ABOVE SLAB

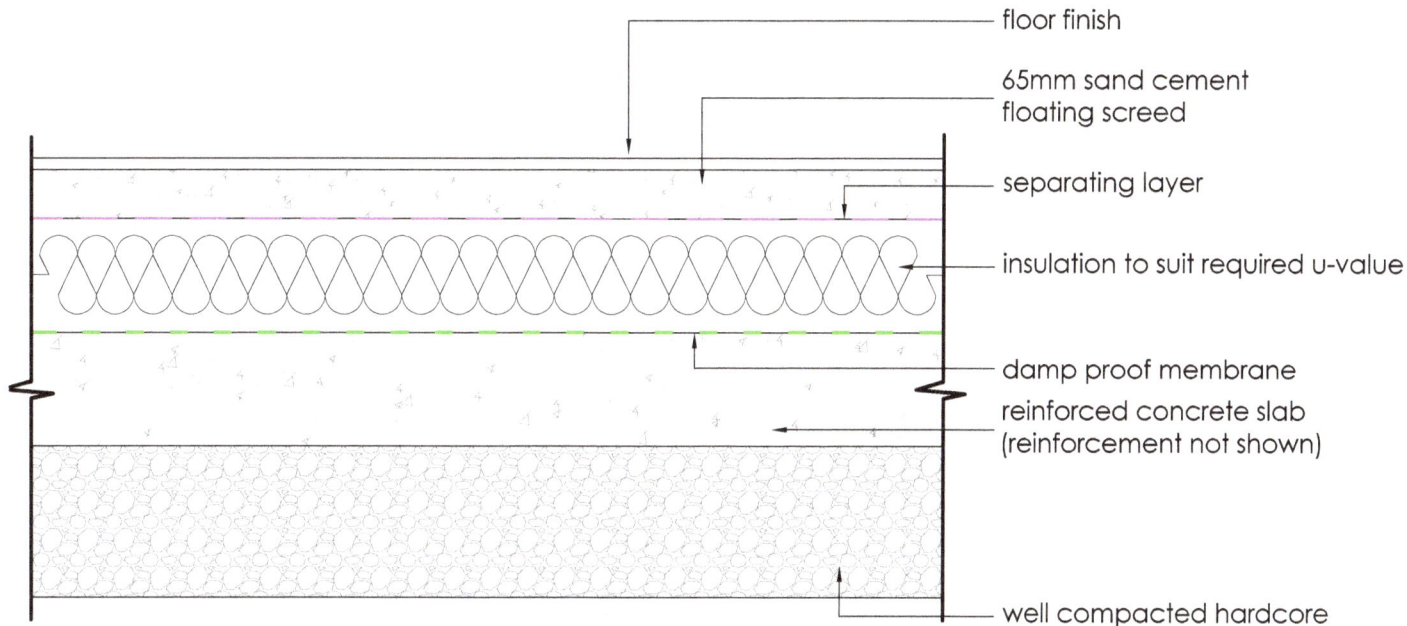

2D Detail F02 - Ground bearing concrete floor, insulation above slab

3D Detail F02 - Ground bearing concrete floor, insulation above slab

Notes:
Separating/slip layer provides vapour control and prevent concrete seeping into the cracks between insulation boards when concrete is being poured. Sand blinding not necessary when dpm is not on hardcore.

F03

GROUND BEARING CONCRETE FLOOR, INSULATION ABOVE SLAB

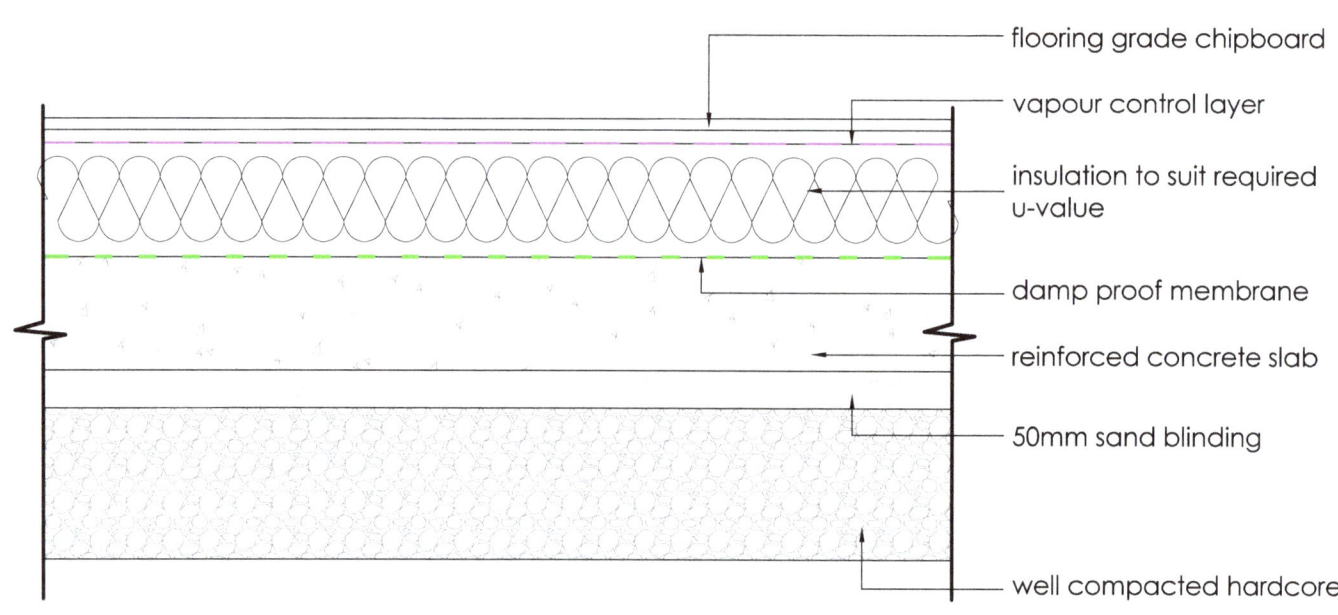

2D Detail F03 - Ground bearing concrete floor, insulation above slab

Notes:
Vapour control layer required with timber floors. If a vapour barrier is not used the moist air can penetrate through to form condensation on top of the DPM.

3D Detail F03- Ground bearing concrete floor, insulation above slab

F04

GROUND BEARING CONCRETE FLOOR, STRIP FOUNDATION

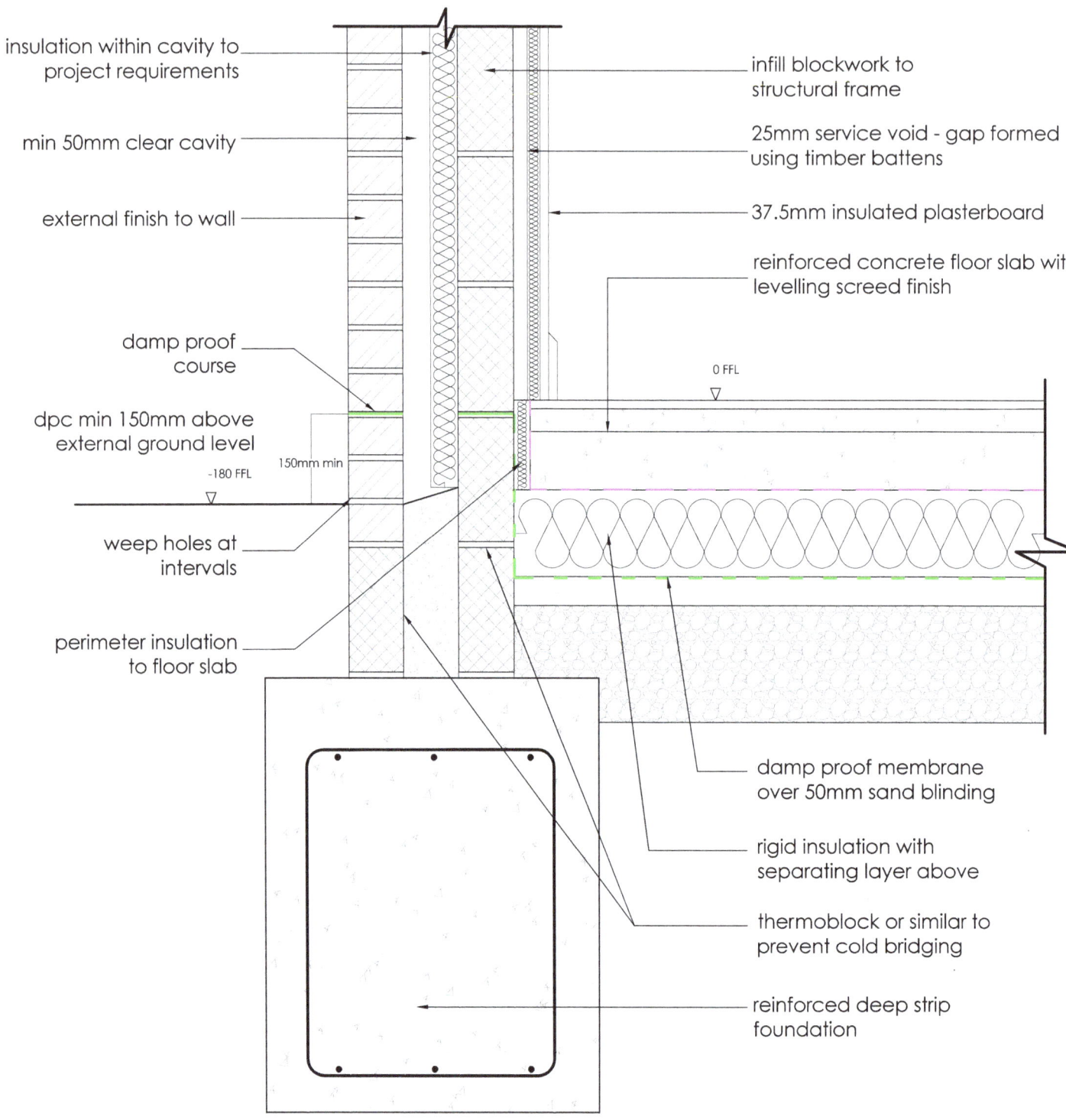

2D Detail F04 - Ground bearing concrete floor, strip foundation

Notes:
Minimum 20mm perimeter insulation placed vertically around the edge of the floor slab. Wall insulation must extend at least 150mm below top of perimeter insulation upstand.

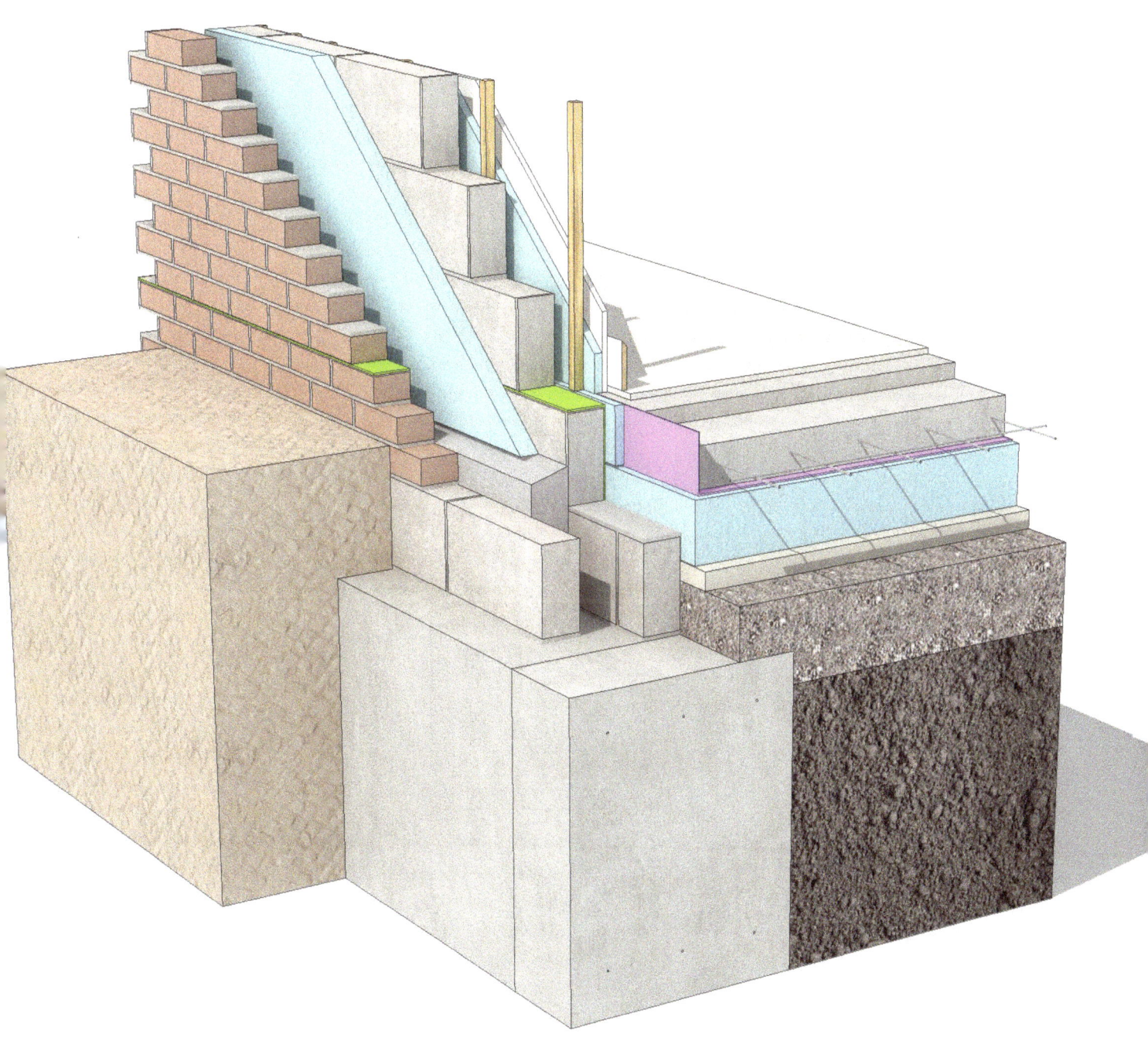

3D Detail F04- Ground bearing concrete floor, strip foundation

F05

GROUND BEARING CONCRETE FLOOR, RAFT FOUNDATION

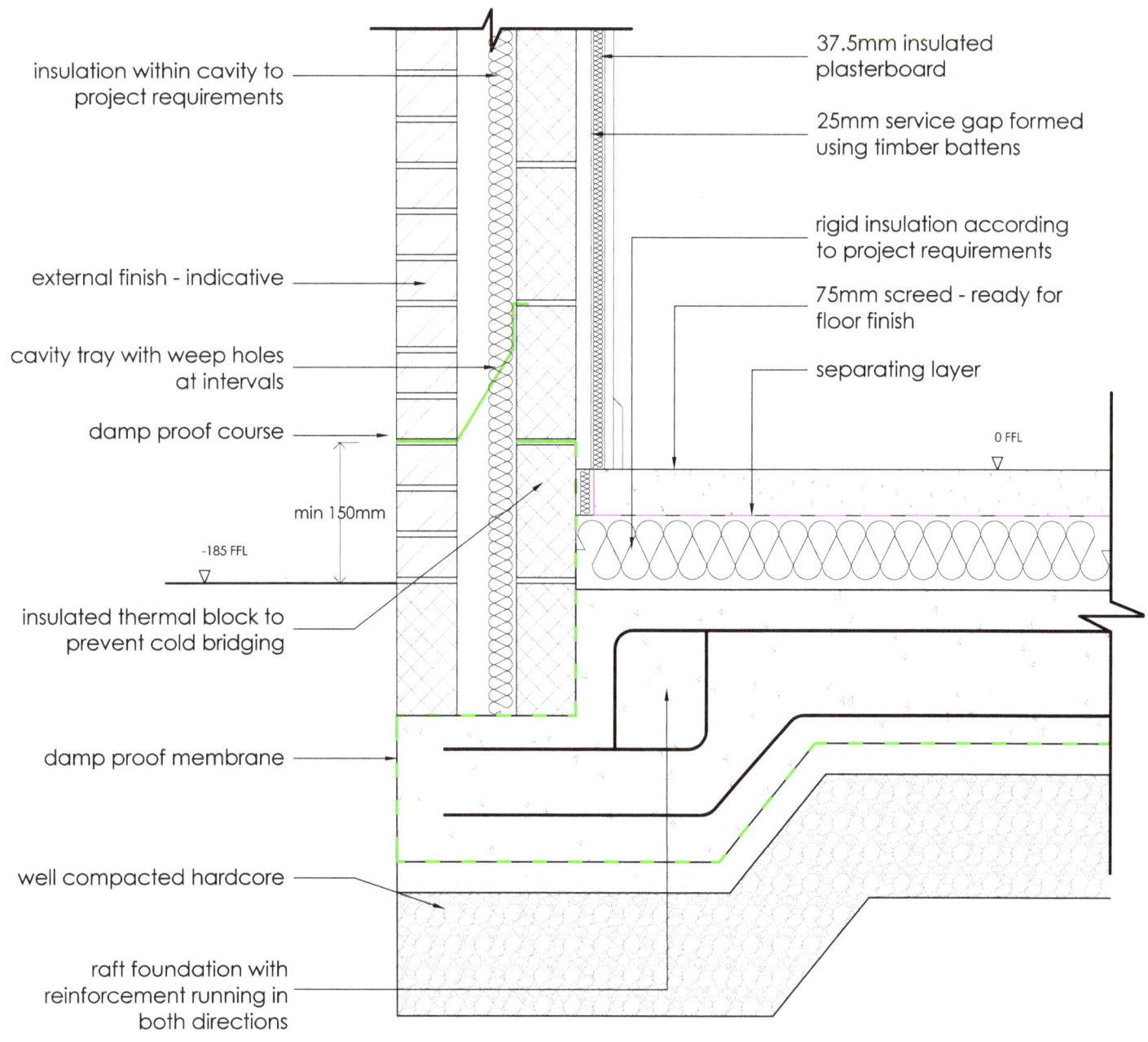

2D Detail F05 - Ground bearing concrete floor, raft foundation

Notes:
Minimum 20mm perimeter insulation placed vertically around the edge of the floor screed. Wall insulation must extend at least 150mm below top of perimeter insulation upstand. Downstand beams add stability to the foundation with toe cast into slab to carry infill walling/ cladding to hide concrete slab.

SECTION 4 - FOUNDATIONS AND FLOORS

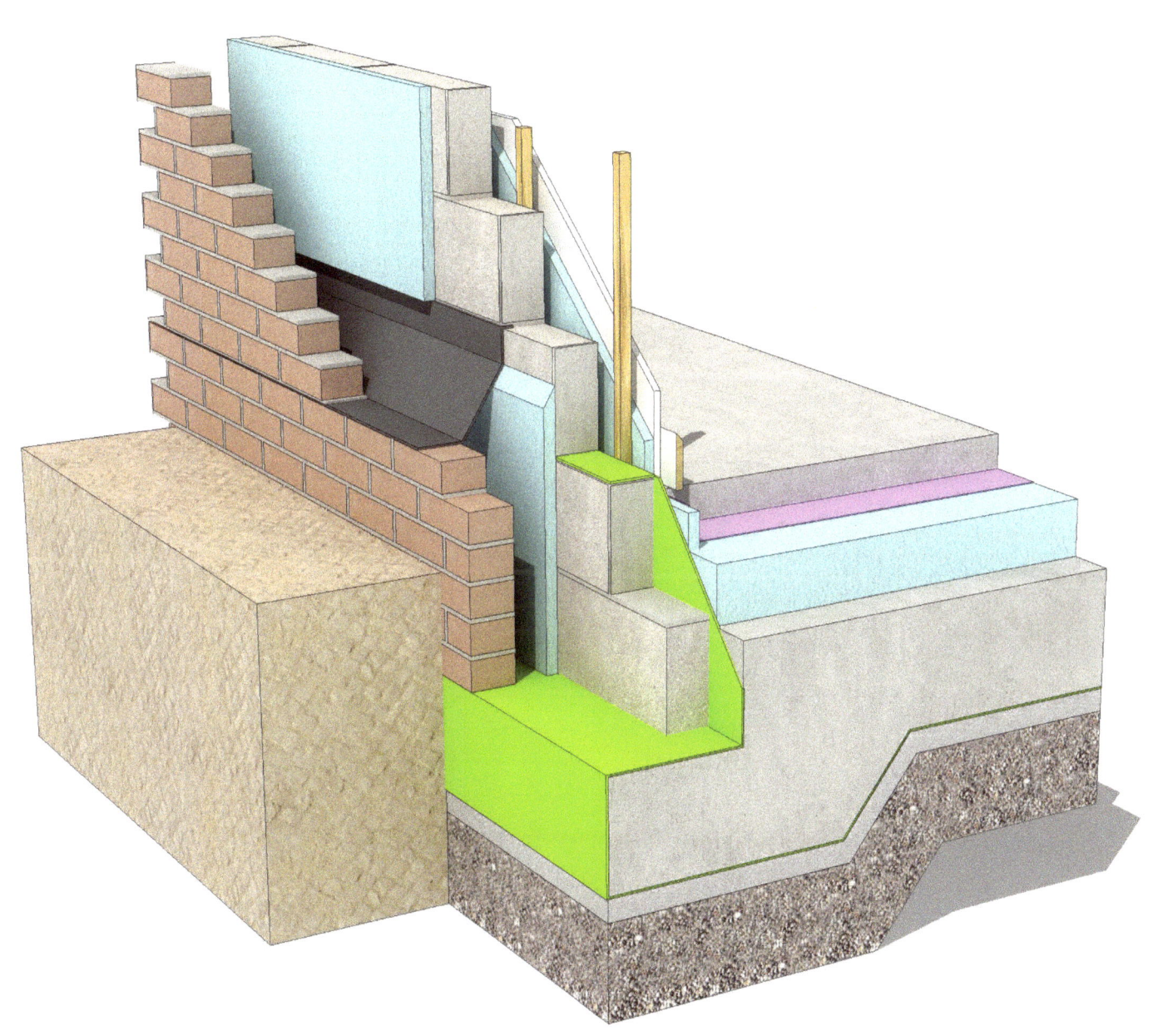

3D Detail F05- Ground bearing concrete floor, raft foundation

F06

GROUND BEARING CONCRETE FLOOR, RAFT FOUNDATION - ALTERNATIVE

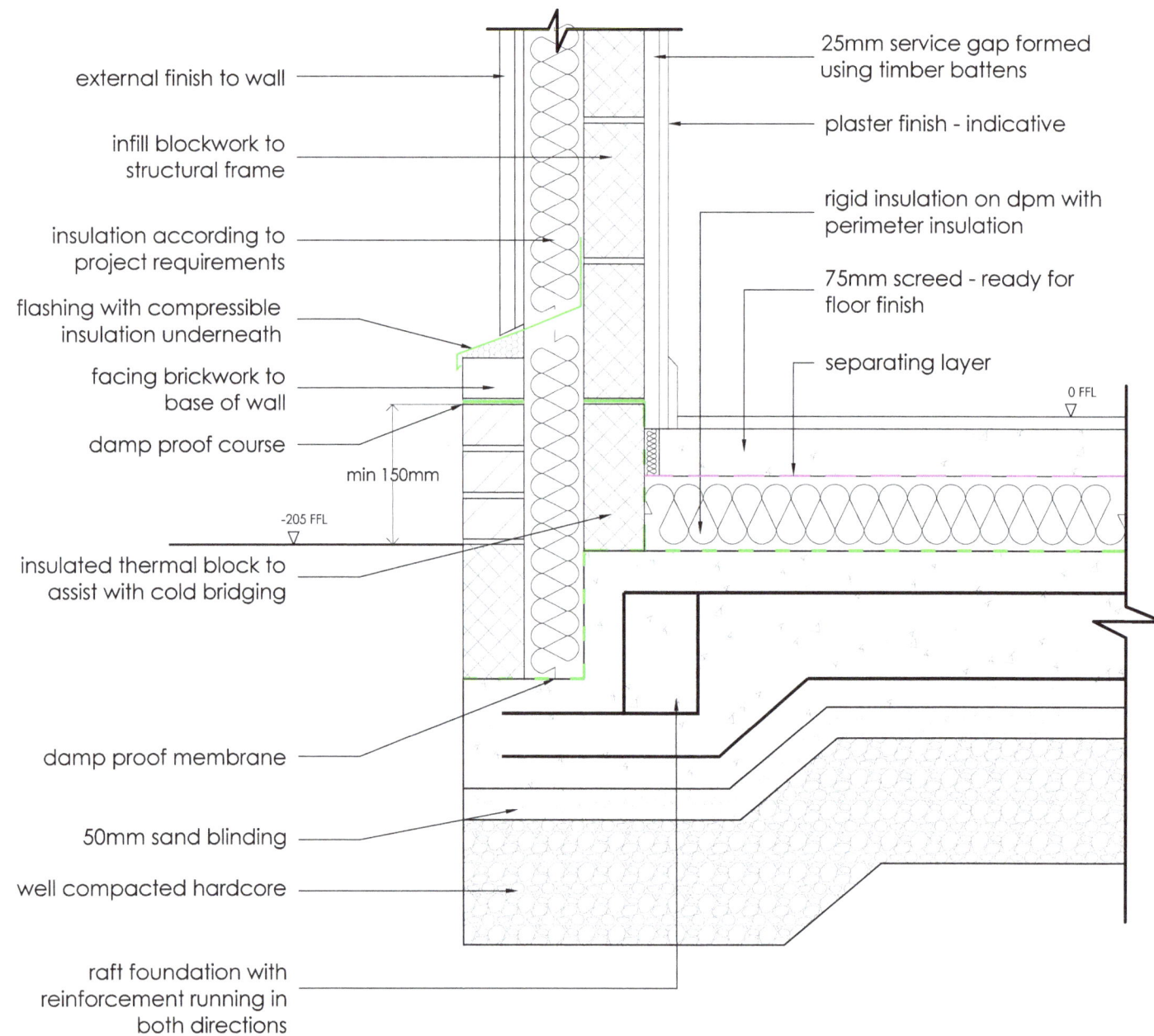

2D Detail F06 - Ground bearing concrete floor, raft foundation - alternative

Notes:
Minimum 20mm perimeter insulation placed vertically around the edge of the floor screed. Wall insulation must extend at least 150mm below top of perimeter insulation upstand. Downstand beams add stability to the foundation with toe cast into slab to carry infill walling/ cladding to hide concrete slab.

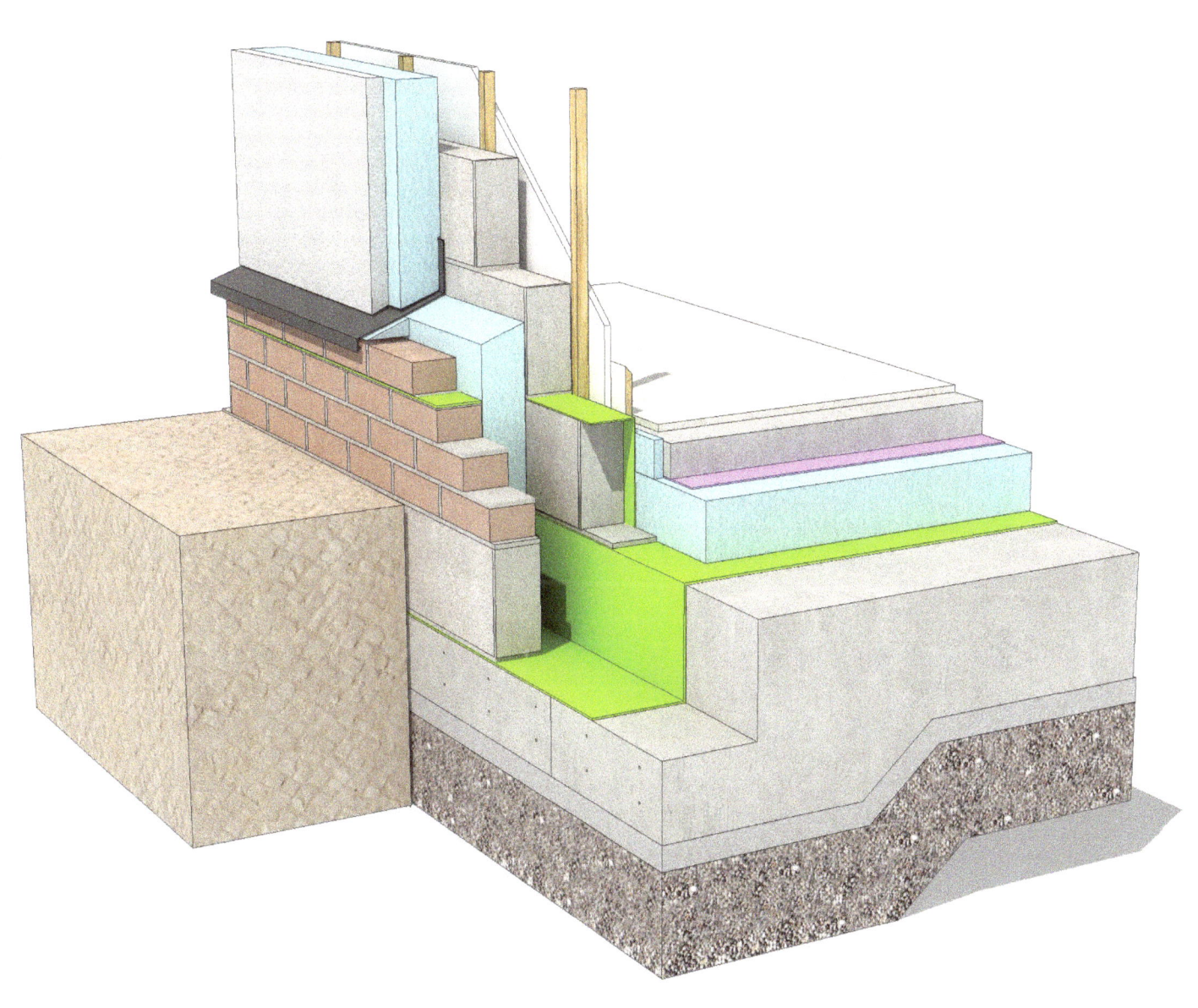

3D Detail F06- Ground bearing concrete floor, raft foundation - alternative

F07

SOLID CONCRETE GROUND BEARING SLAB - TIMBER FLOOR ON BATTENS

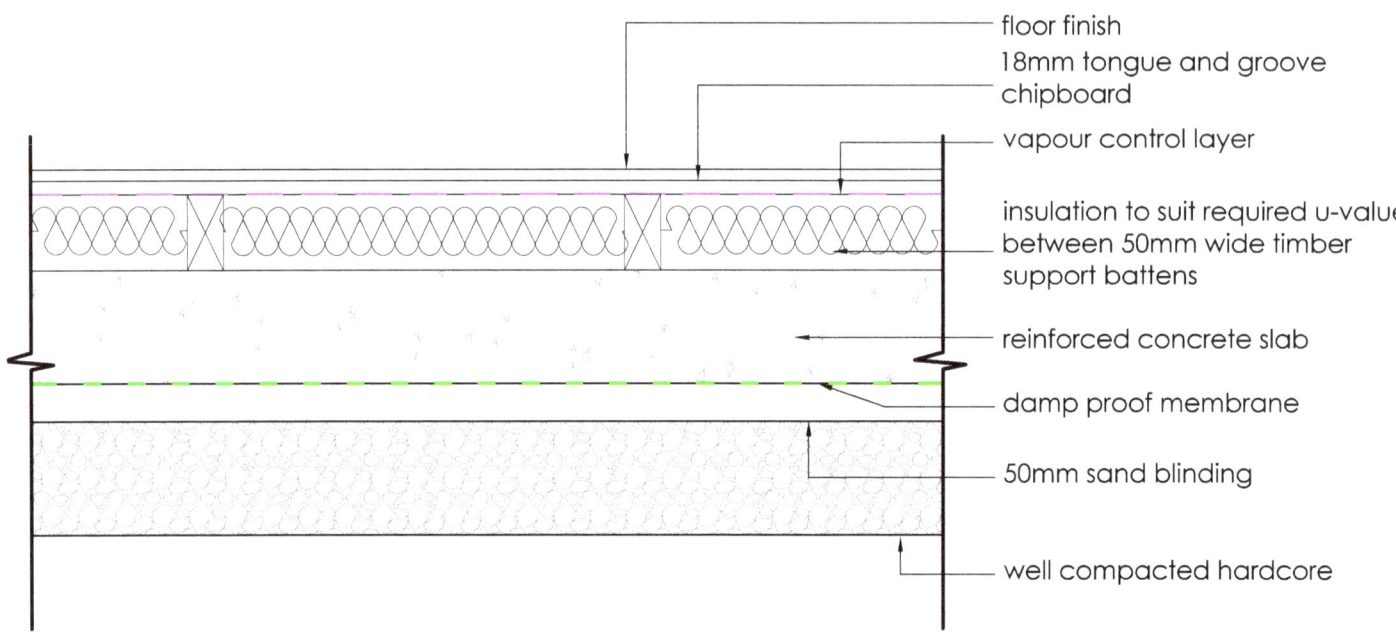

2D Detail F07 - Solid concrete ground bearing slab - timber floor on battens

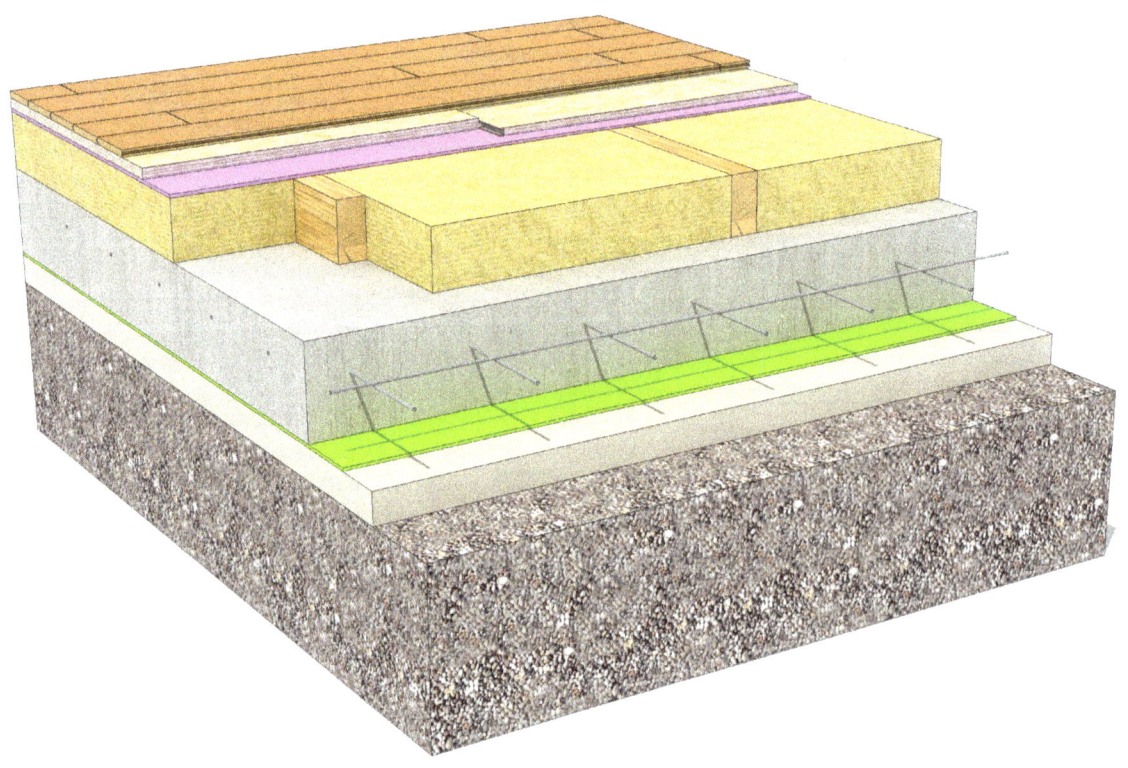

3D Detail F07 - Solid concrete ground bearing slab - timber floor on battens

Notes:
Battens to be same thickness as insulation to ensure they are flush with the insulation boards, unless underfloor heating is specified.

SECTION 4 - FOUNDATIONS AND FLOORS

F08

SOLID CONCRETE GROUND BEARING SLAB - SCREED FINISH WITH UNDERFLOOR HEATING

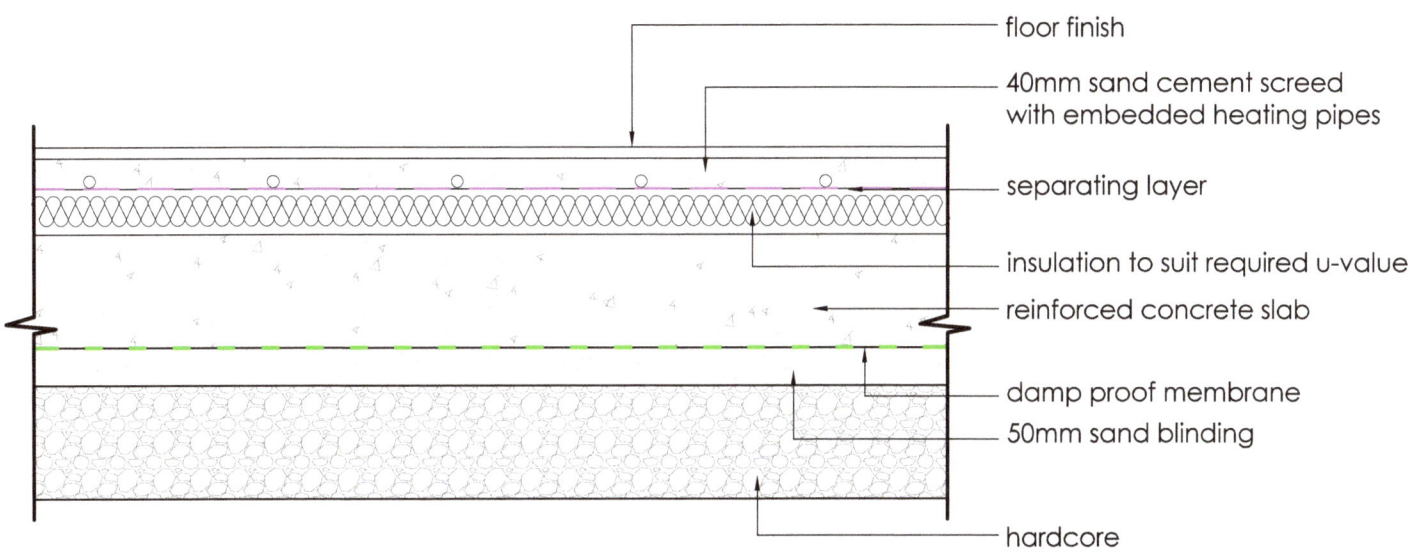

2D Detail F08 - Solid concrete ground bearing slab - screed finish with underfloor heating

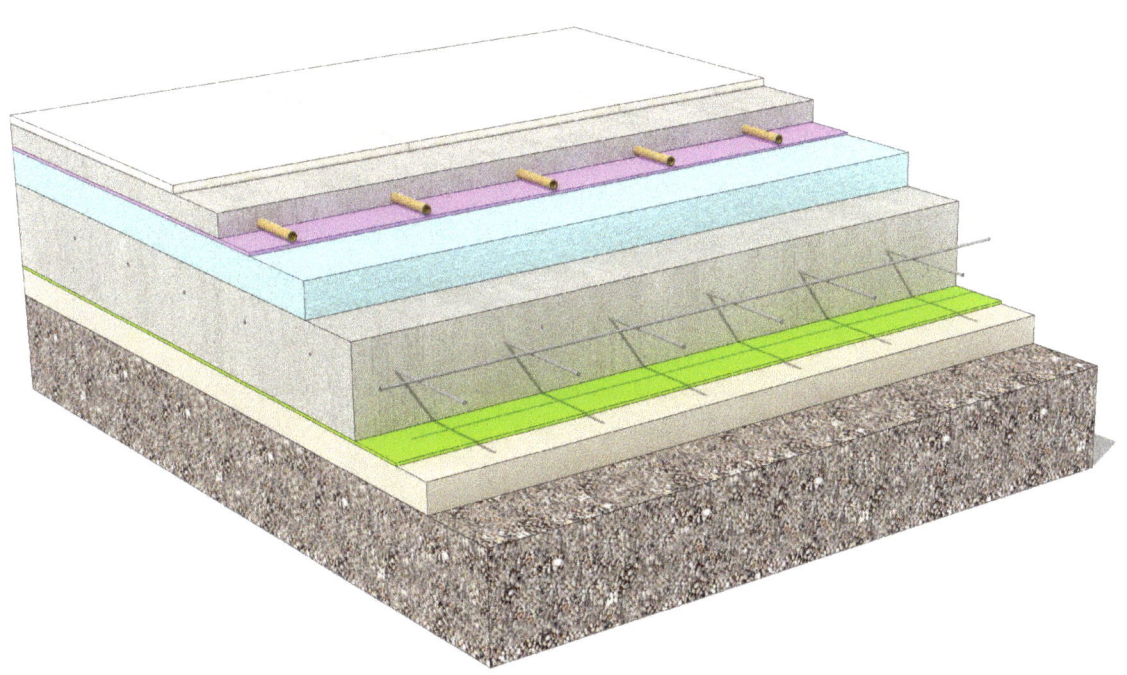

3D Detail F08 - Solid concrete ground bearing slab - screed finish with underfloor heating

F09

CAST IN SITU REINFORCED CONCRETE FLOOR - RAISED ACCESS FLOOR

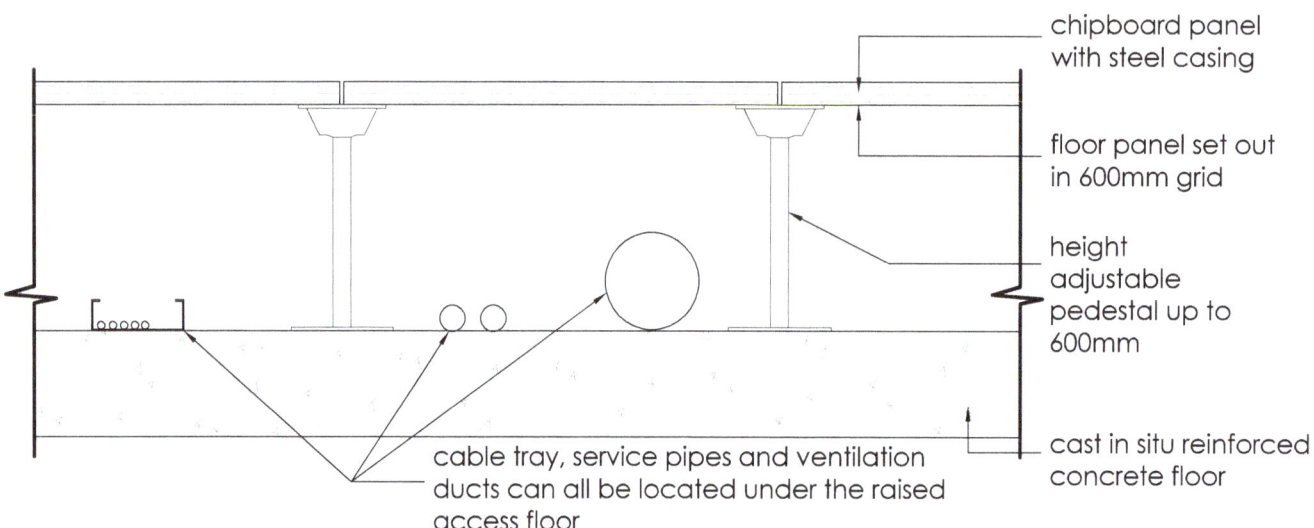

2D Detail F09 - Cast in situ reinforced concrete floor - raised access floor

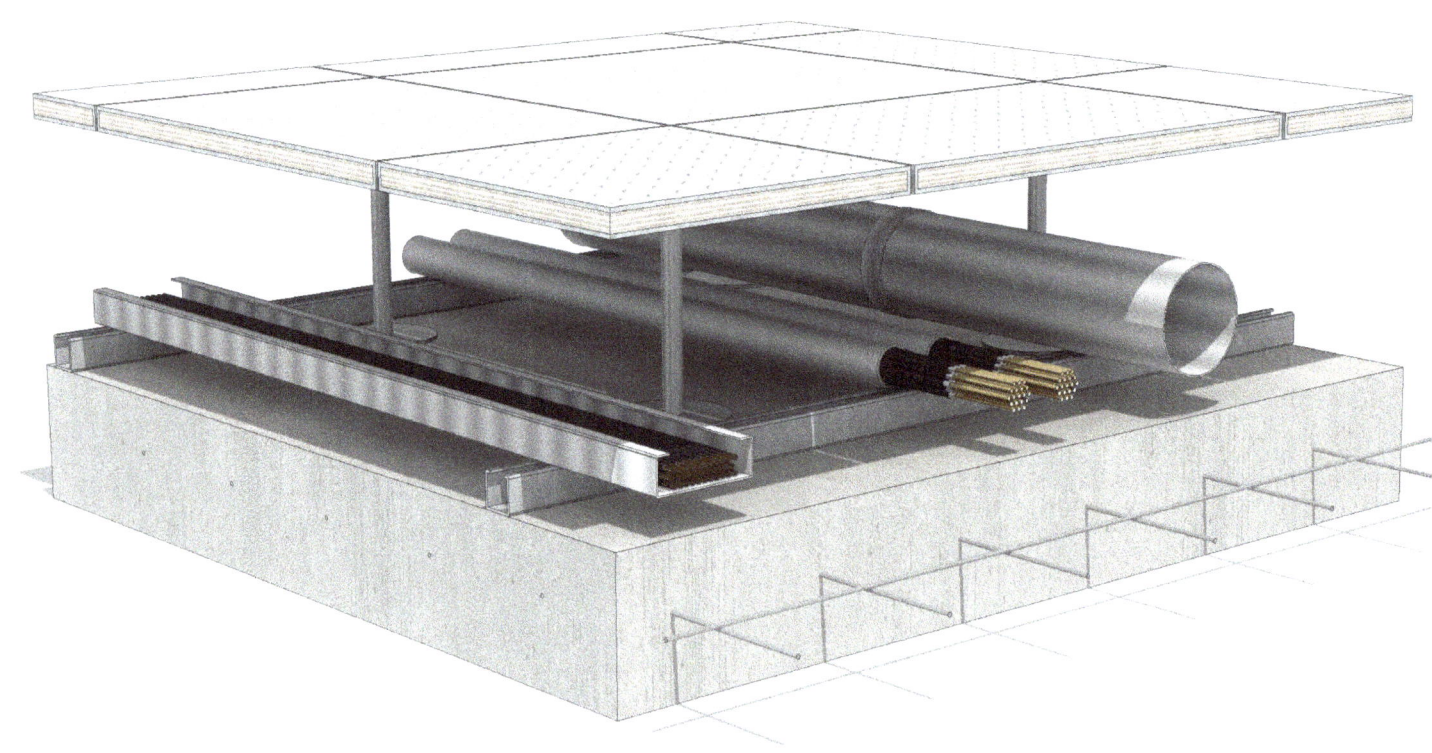

3D Detail F09 - Cast in situ reinforced concrete floor - raised access floor

SECTION 4 - FOUNDATIONS AND FLOORS

Blank Page

F10

GROUND BEARING CONCRETE FLOOR, TYPICAL INTERNAL LOAD BEARING WALL

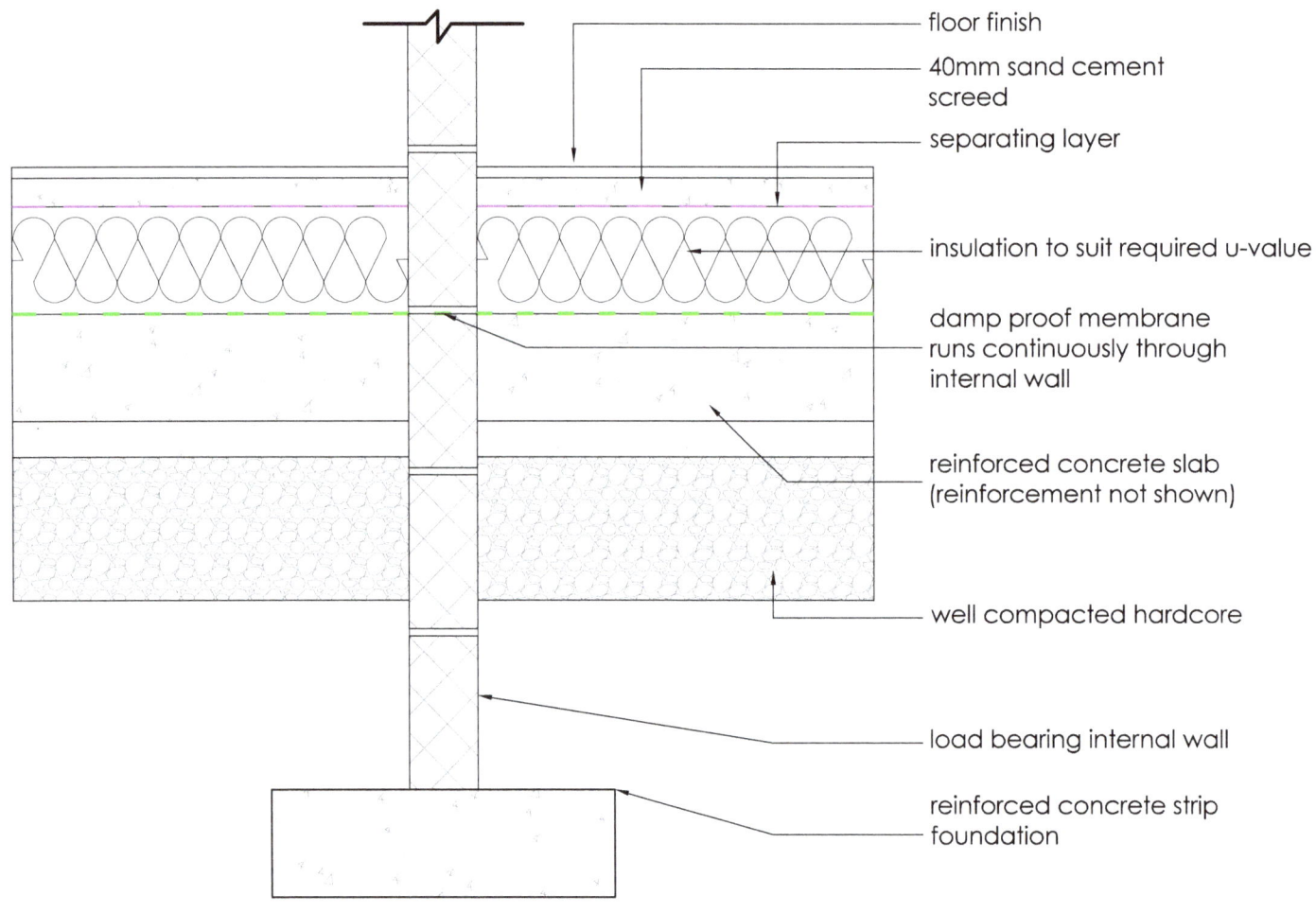

2D Detail F10 - Ground bearing concrete floor, typical internal load bearing wall

SECTION 4 - FOUNDATIONS AND FLOORS

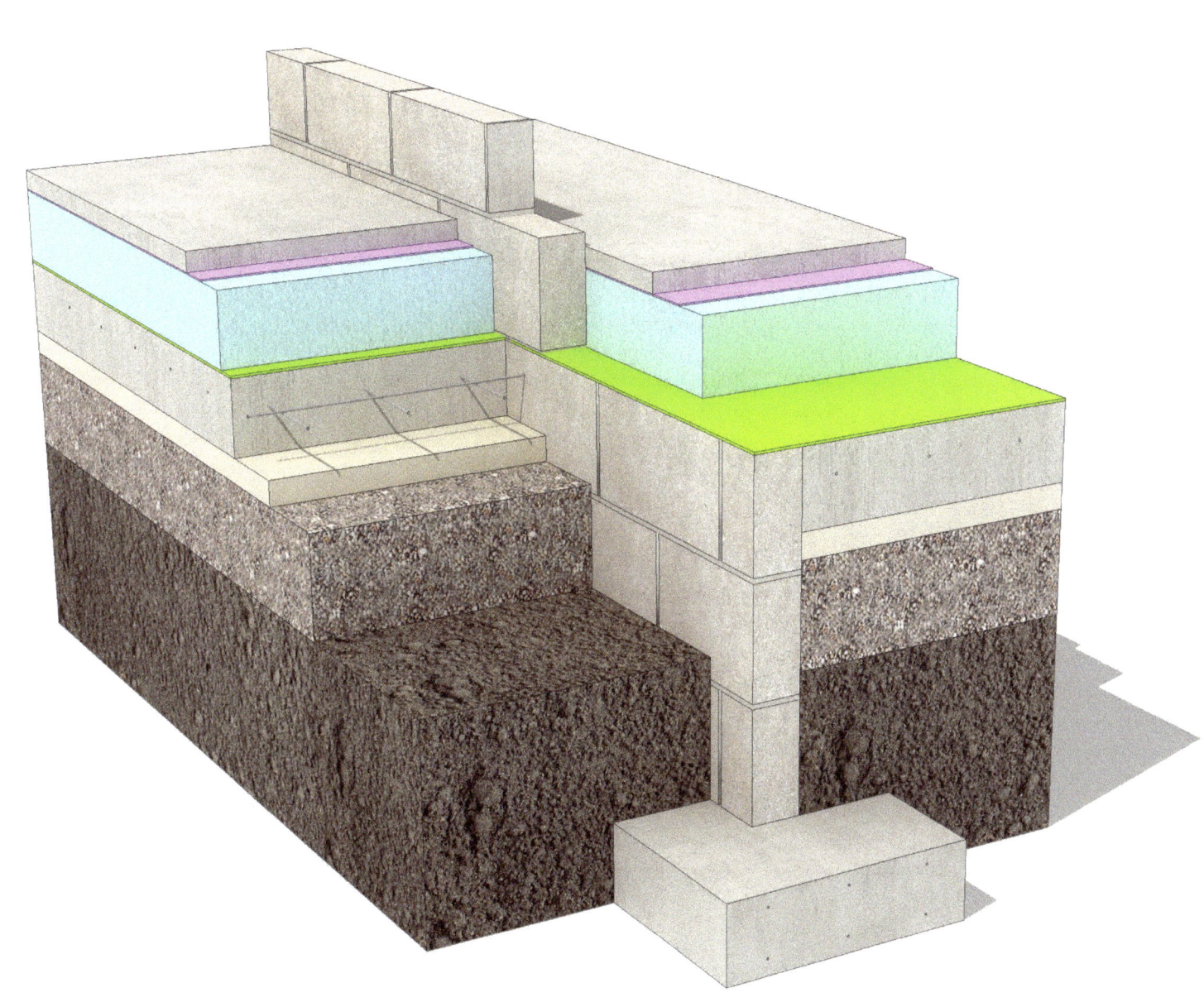

3D Detail F10 - Ground bearing concrete floor, typical internal load bearing wall

F11

GROUND BEARING CONCRETE FLOOR, TYPICAL INTERNAL LIGHT LOAD BEARING WALL

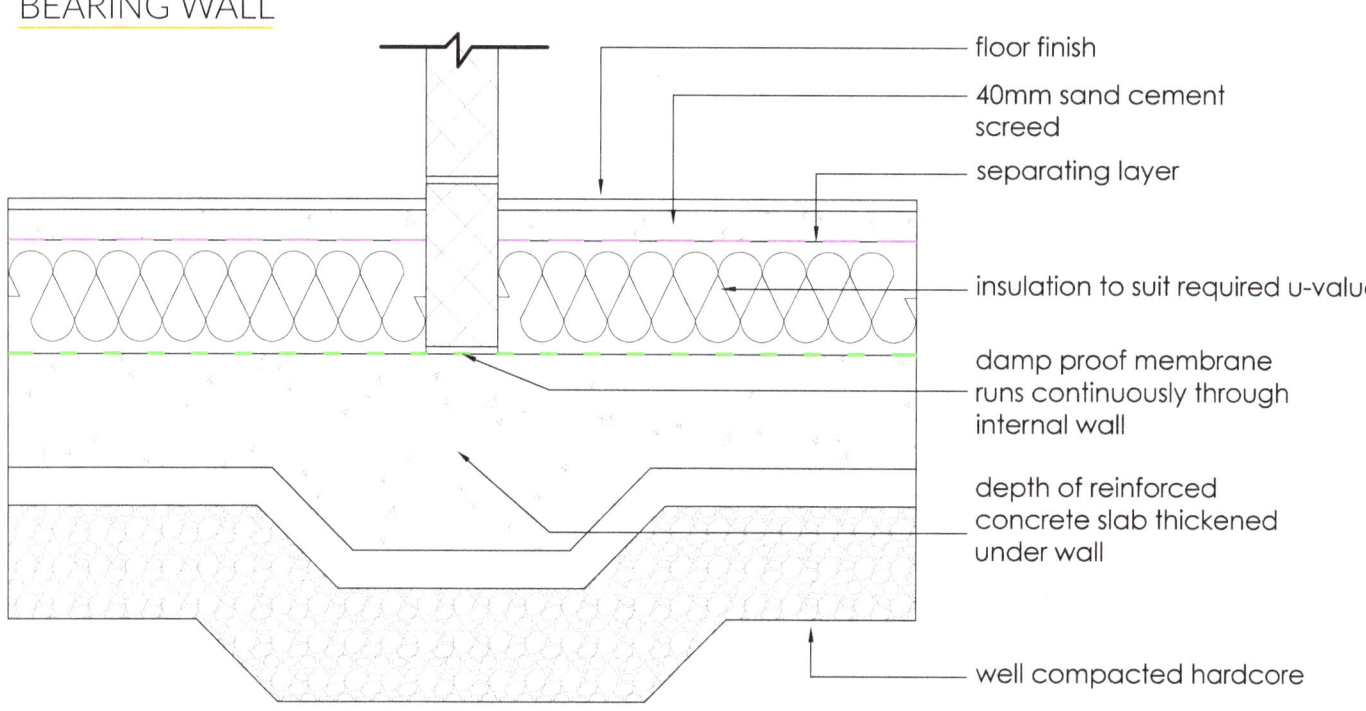

2D Detail F11 - Ground bearing concrete floor, typical internal light load bearing wall

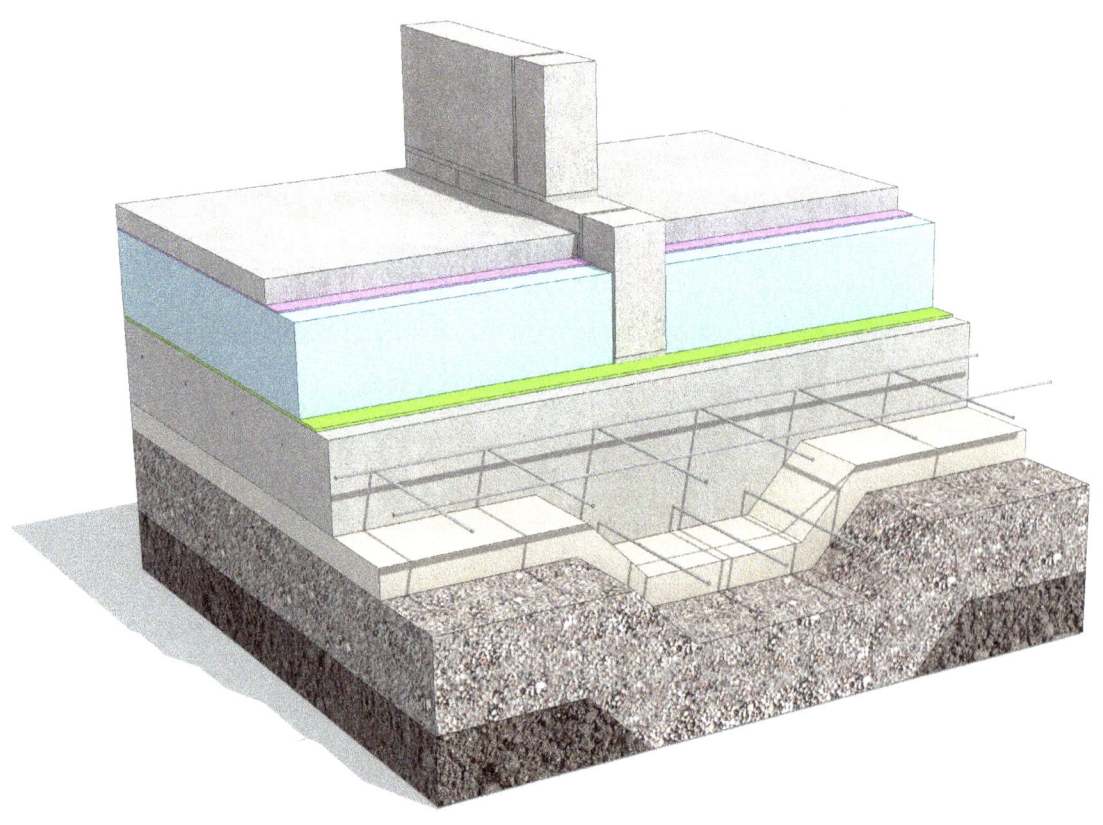

3D Detail F11 - Ground bearing concrete floor, typical internal light load bearing wall

F12

GROUND BEARING CONCRETE FLOOR, TYPICAL INTERNAL NON LOAD BEARING WALL

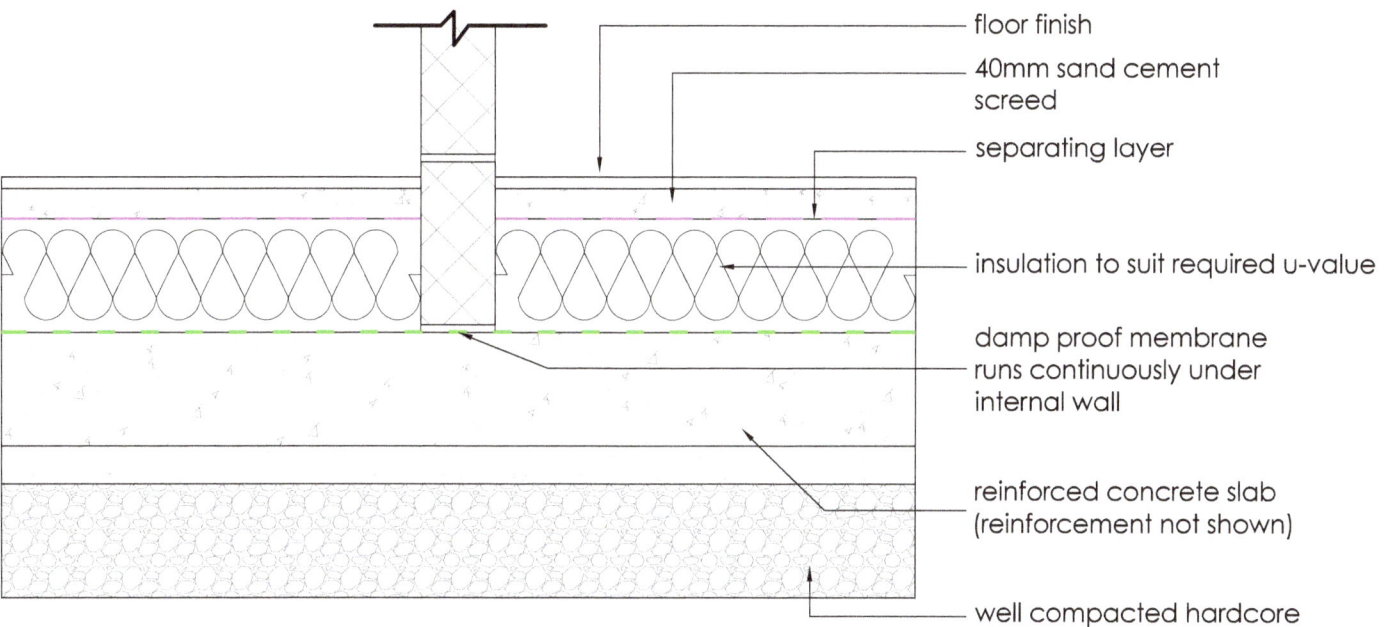

2D Detail F12 - Ground bearing concrete floor, typical internal non load bearing wall

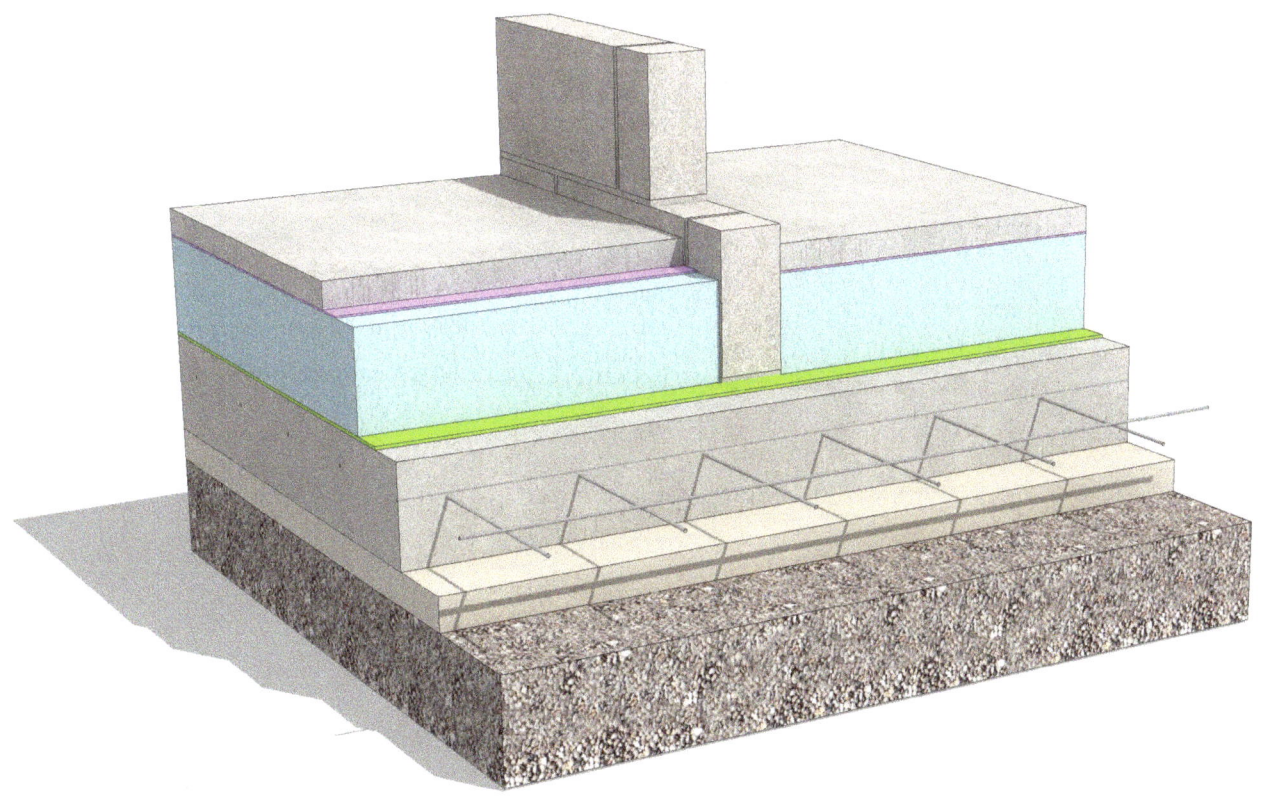

3D Detail F12 - Ground bearing concrete floor, typical internal non load bearing wall

F13

SUSPENDED CONCRETE FLOOR, BEAM AND BLOCK, SCREED FINISH

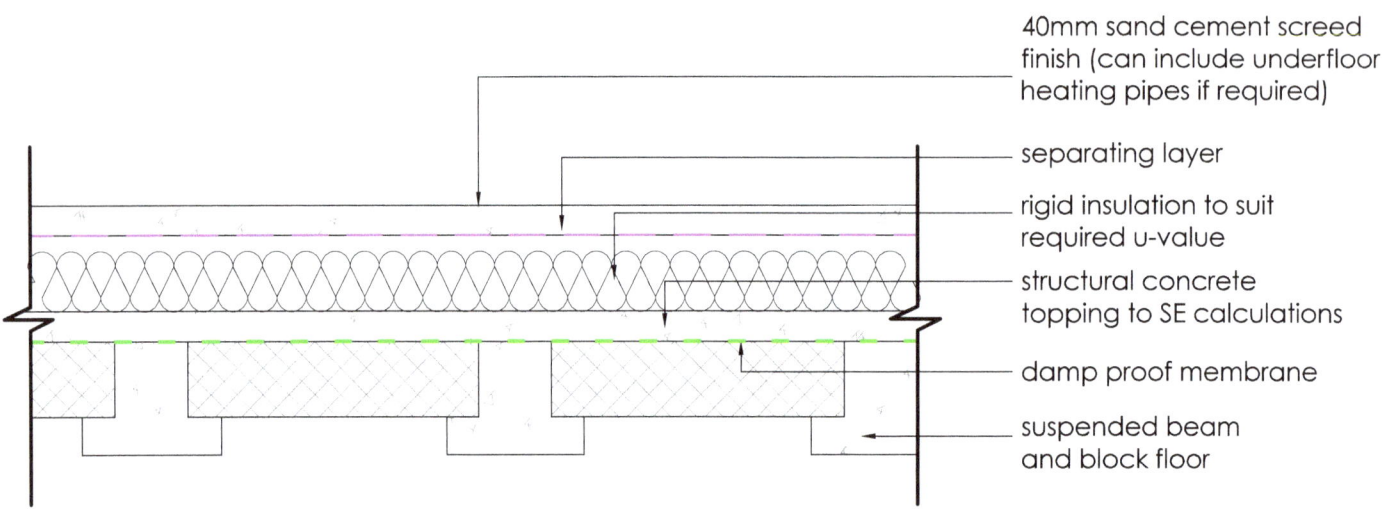

2D Detail F13 - Suspended concrete floor, beam and block, screed finish

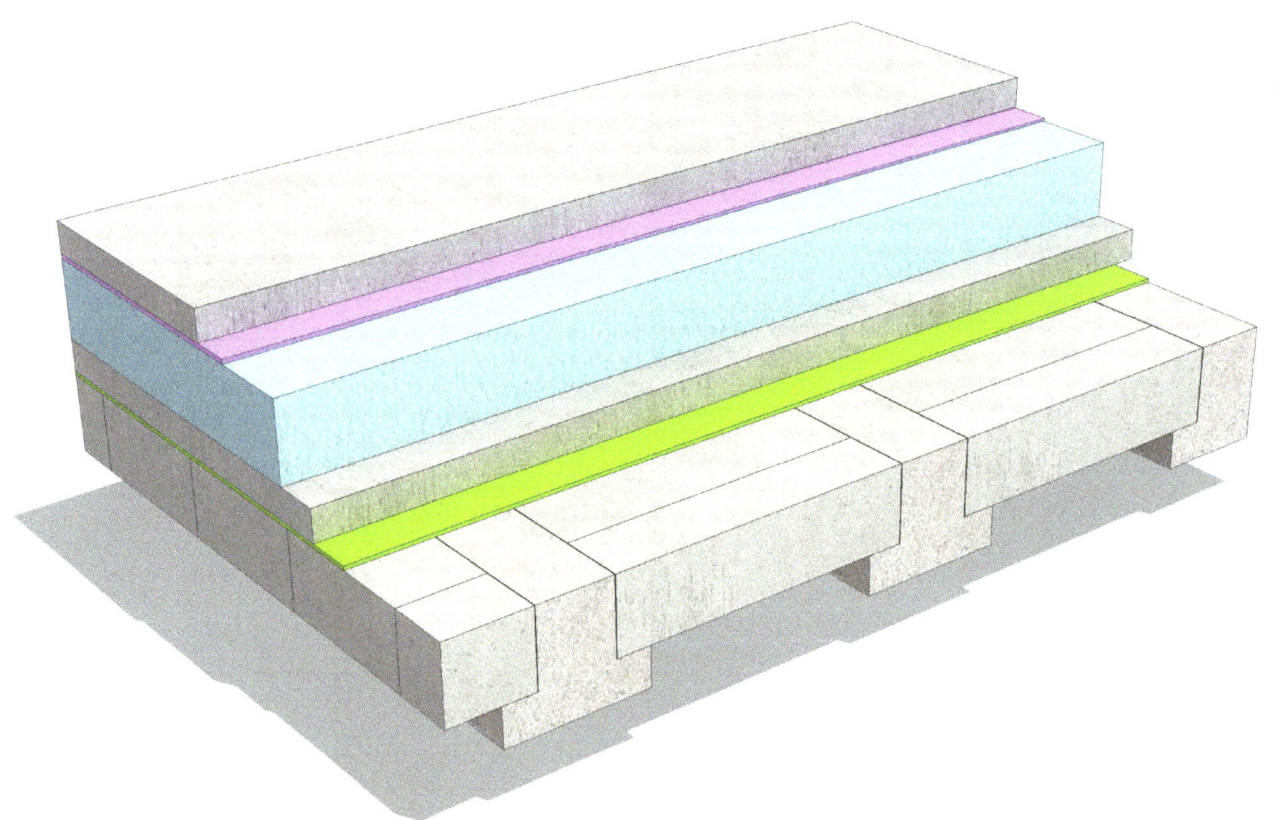

3D Detail F13- Suspended concrete floor, beam and block, screed finish

F14

SUSPENDED CONCRETE FLOOR, BEAM AND BLOCK, TIMBER FLOOR FINISH

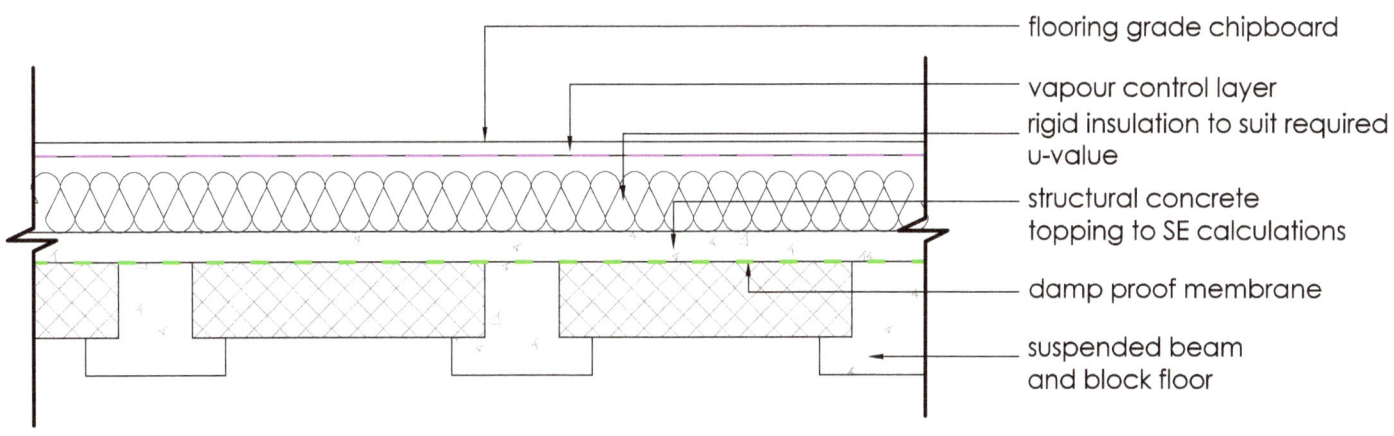

2D Detail F14 - Suspended concrete floor, beam and block, timber floor finish

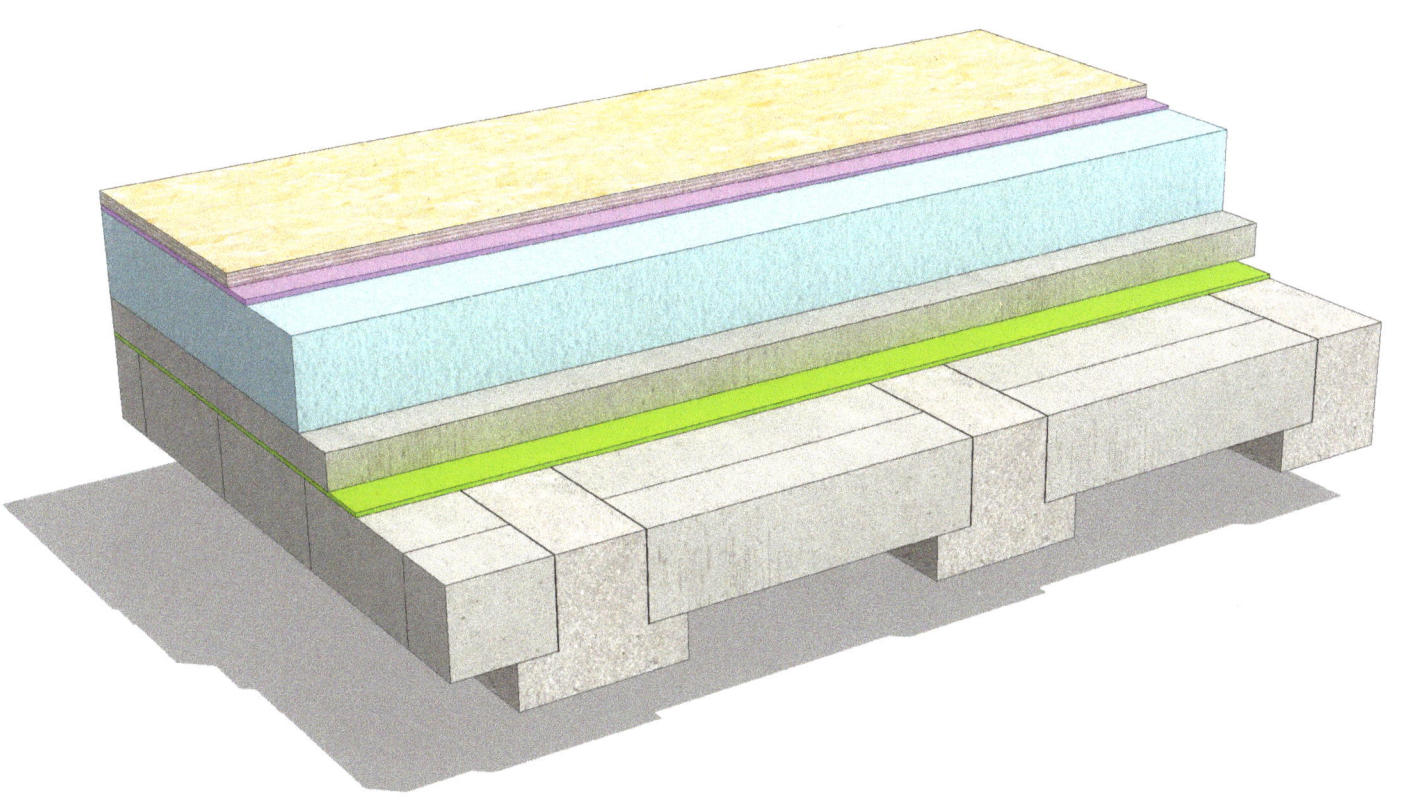

3D Detail F14 - Suspended concrete floor, beam and block, timber floor finish

F15

SUSPENDED CONCRETE FLOOR, BEAM AND EPS BLOCK

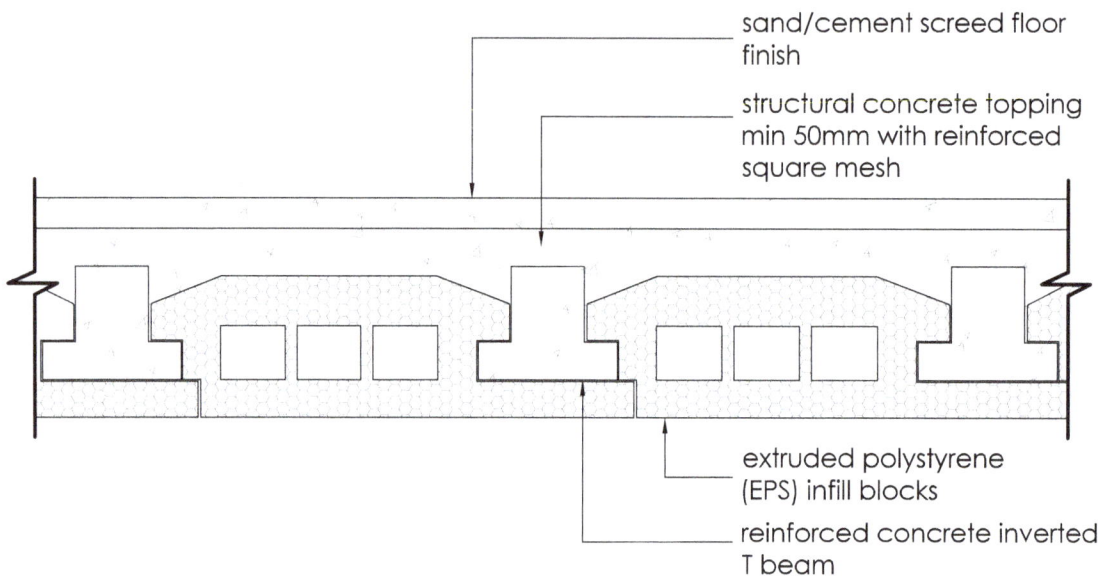

- sand/cement screed floor finish
- structural concrete topping min 50mm with reinforced square mesh
- extruded polystyrene (EPS) infill blocks
- reinforced concrete inverted T beam

Notes:
Levelling screed or separating layer depending on requirement. Infill block dimensions 200mm deep by 1200mm long

2D Detail F15 - Suspended concrete floor, beam and EPS block

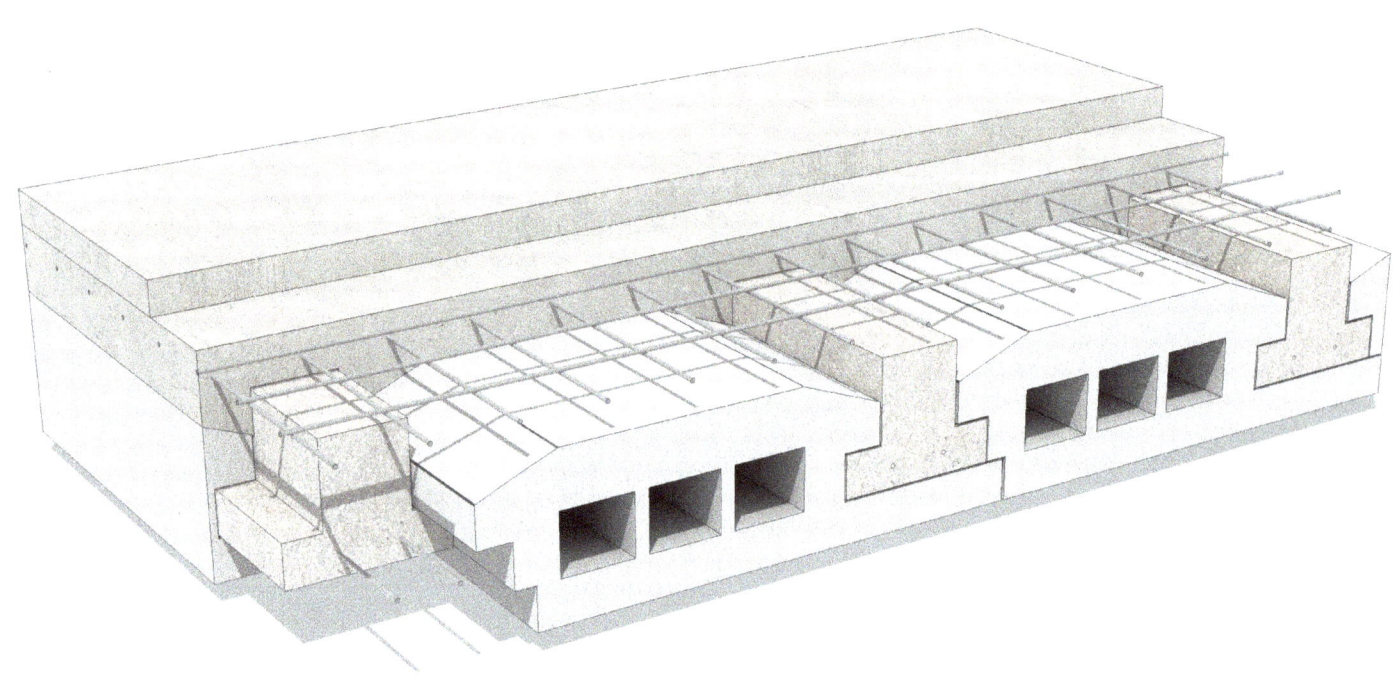

3D Detail F15- Suspended concrete floor, beam and EPS block

F16

SUSPENDED CONCRETE FLOOR, PRECAST BEAM AND HOLLOW FILLER BLOCK

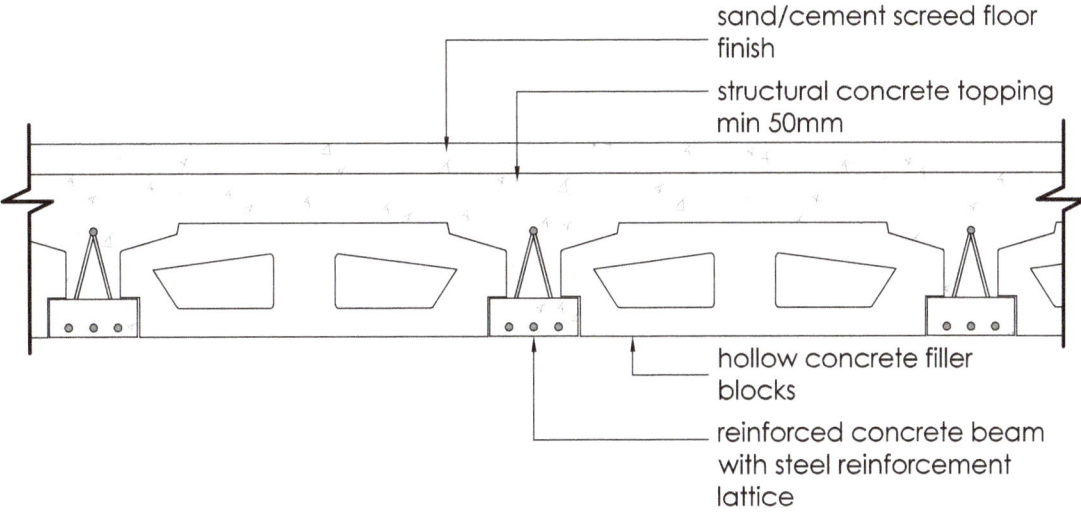

Notes:
Block dimensions 440mm wide by 225mm deep and 150mm high

2D Detail F16 - Suspended concrete floor, precast beam and hollow filler block

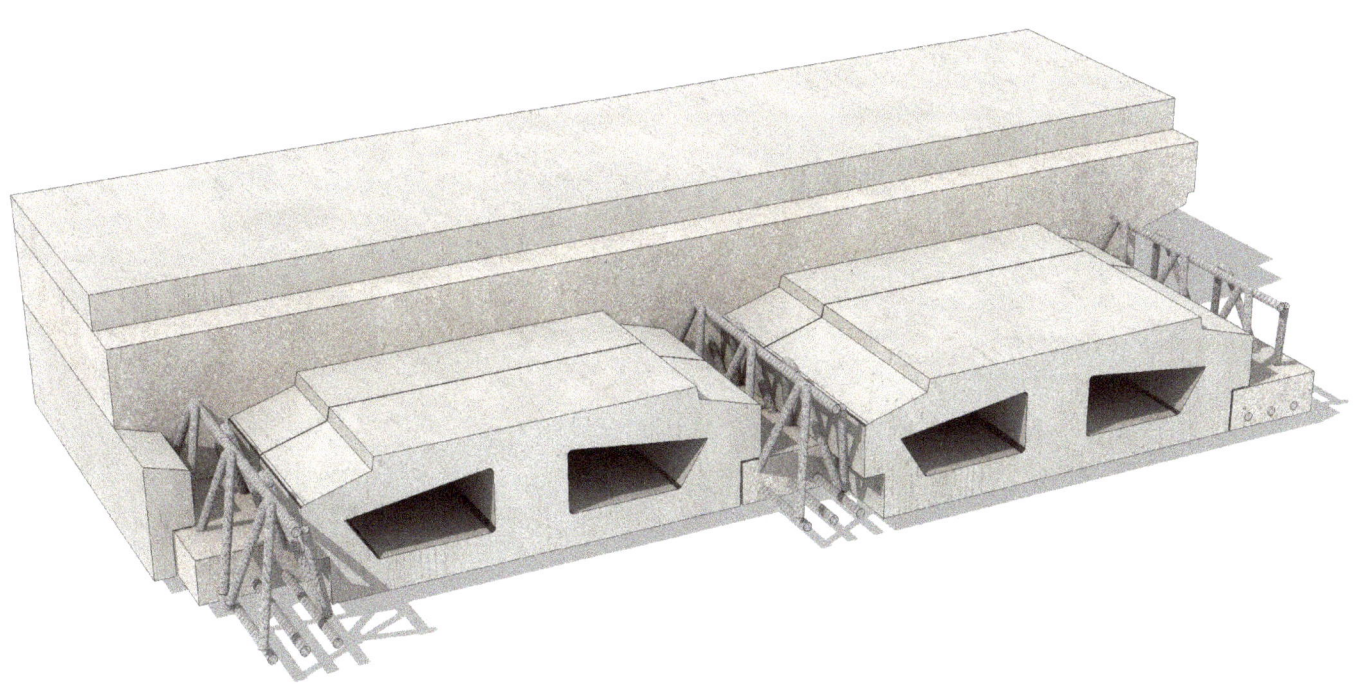

3D Detail F16 - Suspended concrete floor, precast beam and hollow filler block

F17

SUSPENDED CONCRETE FLOOR, PRECAST HOLLOW FLOOR UNIT

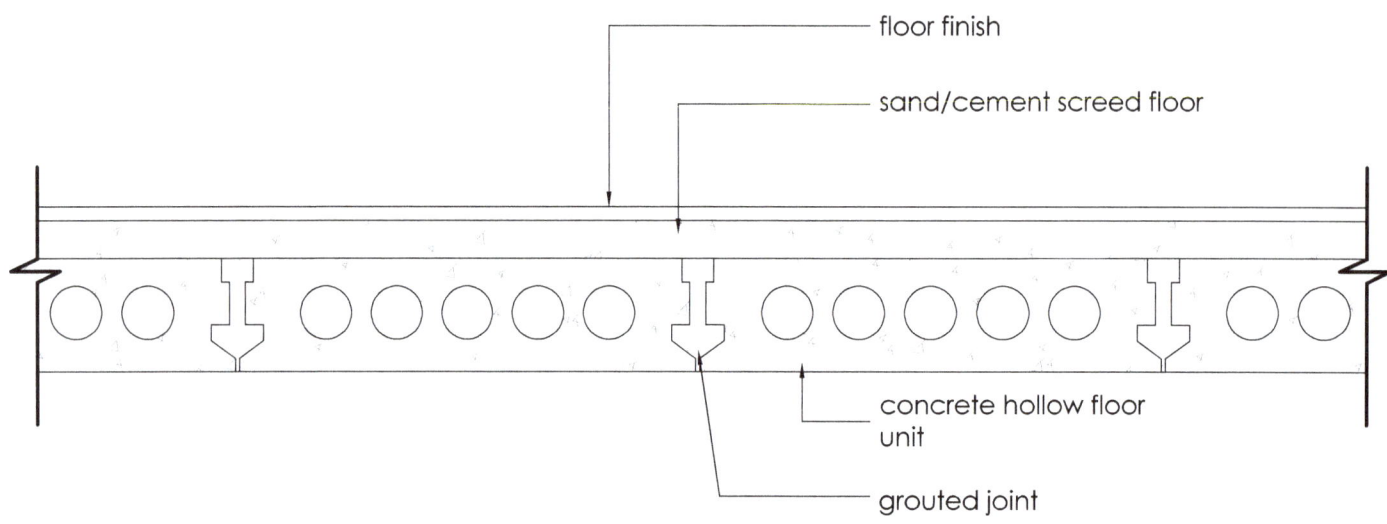

2D Detail F17 - Suspended concrete floor, precast hollow floor unit

Notes:
Levelling screed or separating layer depending on requirement. Infill block dimensions 200mm deep by 1200mm long. Underside can be left exposed or a suspended ceiling fitted.

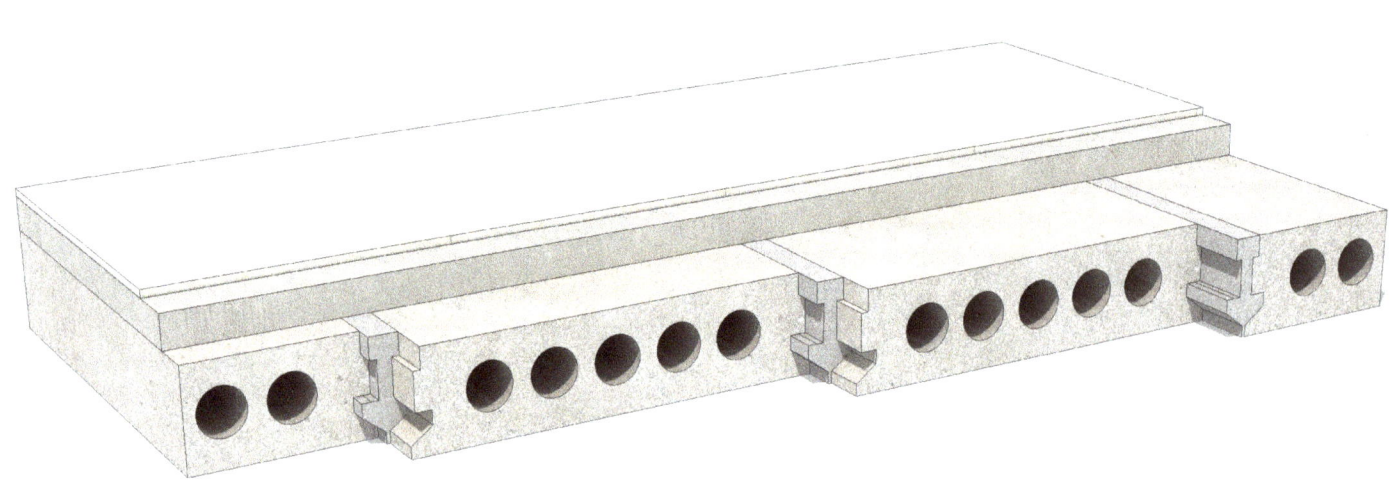

3D Detail F17 - Suspended concrete floor, precast hollow floor unit

SECTION 4 - FOUNDATIONS AND FLOORS

Blank Page

F18

SUSPENDED CONCRETE FLOOR, BEAM AND BLOCK, GROUND FLOOR

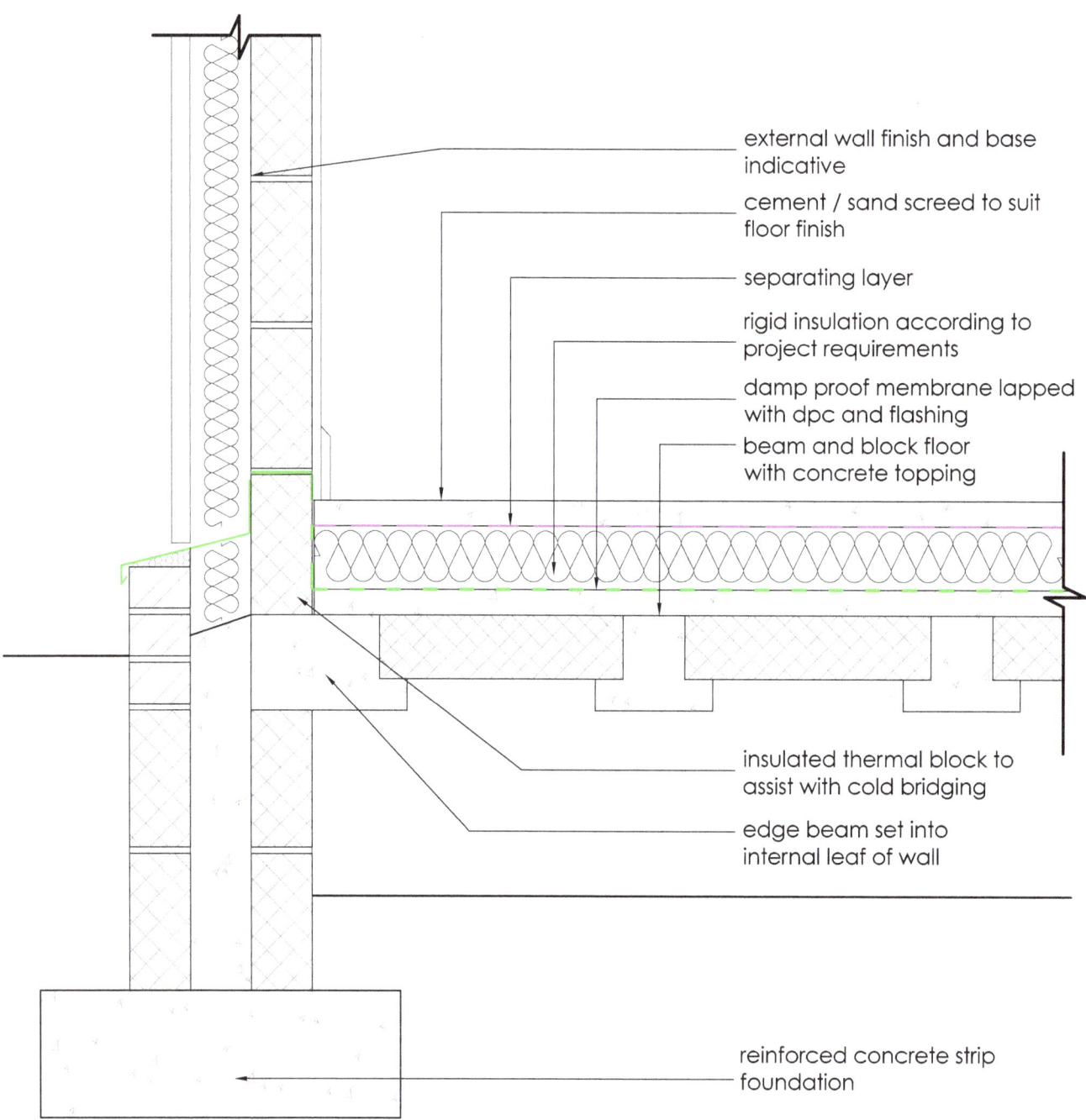

2D Detail F18 - Suspended concrete floor, beam and block, ground floor

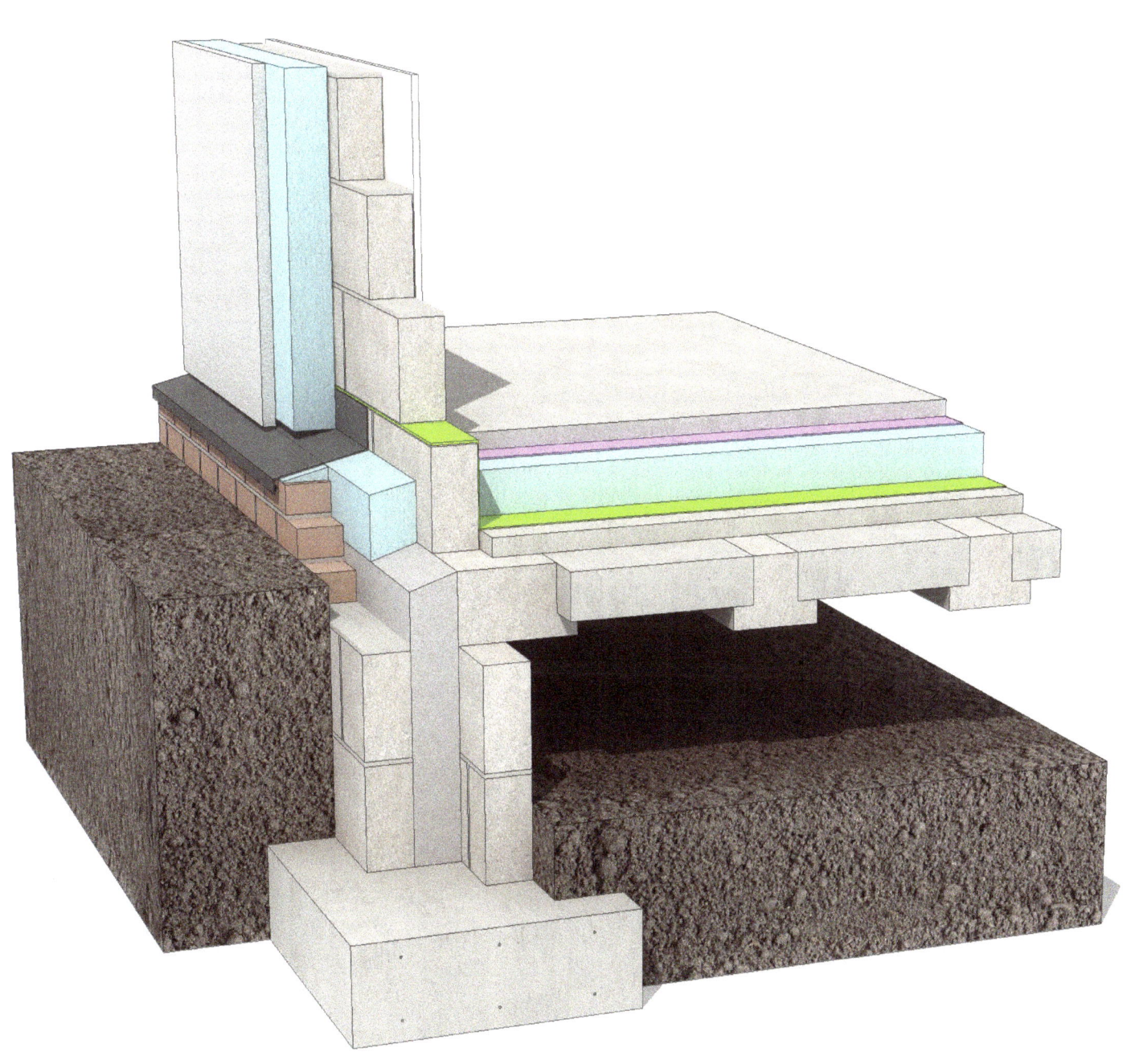

3D Detail F18- Suspended concrete floor, beam and block, ground floor

F19

SUSPENDED CONCRETE FLOOR, BEAM AND BLOCK, BEAMS PARALLEL WITH WALL, UPPER FLOOR

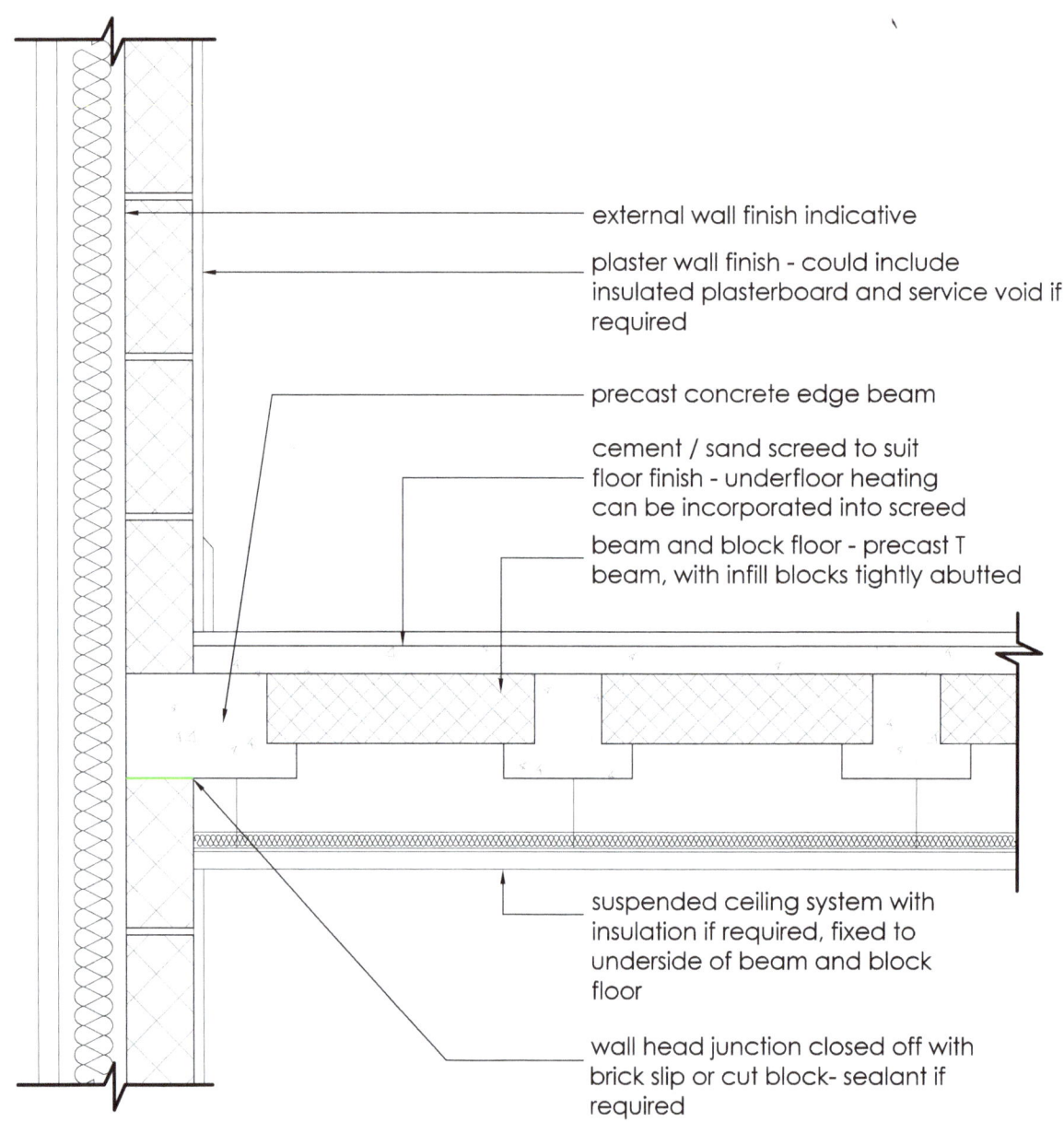

- external wall finish indicative
- plaster wall finish - could include insulated plasterboard and service void if required
- precast concrete edge beam
- cement / sand screed to suit floor finish - underfloor heating can be incorporated into screed
- beam and block floor - precast T beam, with infill blocks tightly abutted
- suspended ceiling system with insulation if required, fixed to underside of beam and block floor
- wall head junction closed off with brick slip or cut block - sealant if required

Notes:
Topping to beam and block floor can vary depending on project requirements. A structural concrete topping may be necessary, or a simple screed levelling finish. This example shows a masonry infill wall to concrete frame.

2D Detail F19 - Suspended concrete floor, beam and block, beams parallel with wall, upper floor

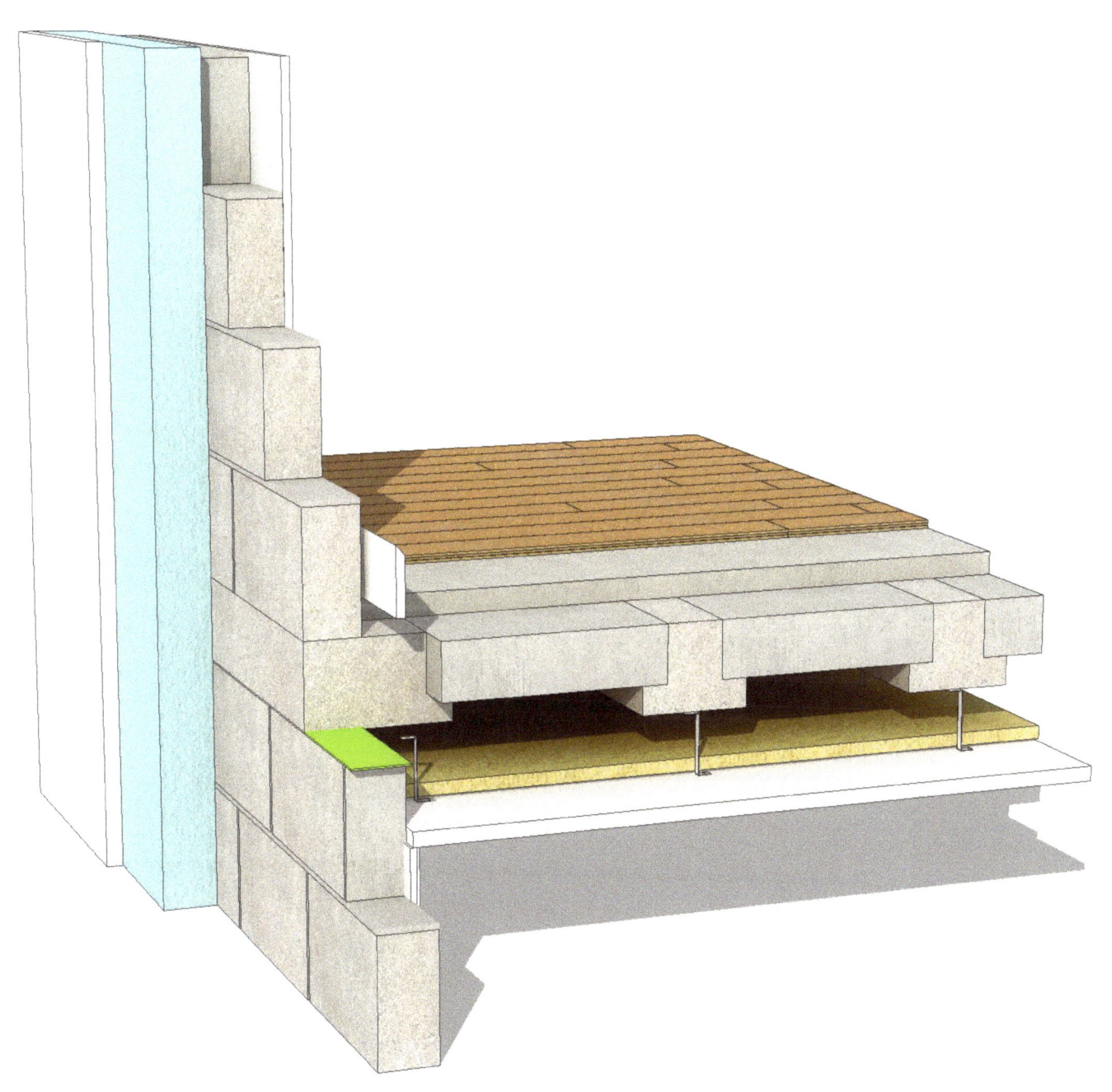

3D Detail F19- Suspended concrete floor, beam and block, beams parallel with wall, upper floor

F20

SUSPENDED CONCRETE FLOOR, PRECAST HOLLOW BEAM AND BLOCK, UPPER FLOOR

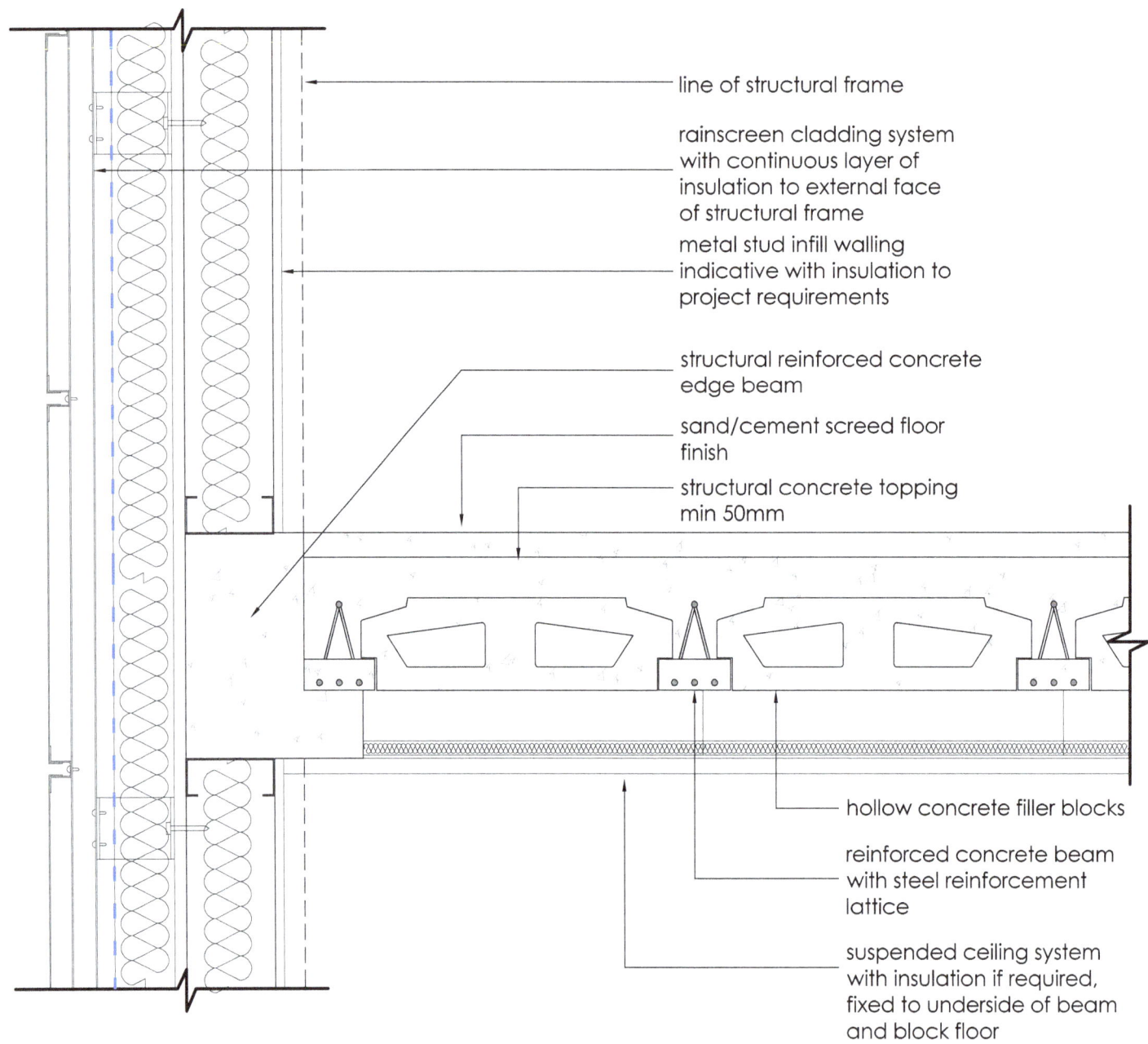

Notes:
This example shows alternative infill and frame option. Concrete frame with steel frame infill and rainscreen cladding finish to wall.

2D Detail F20 - Suspended concrete floor, precast hollow beam and block, upper floor

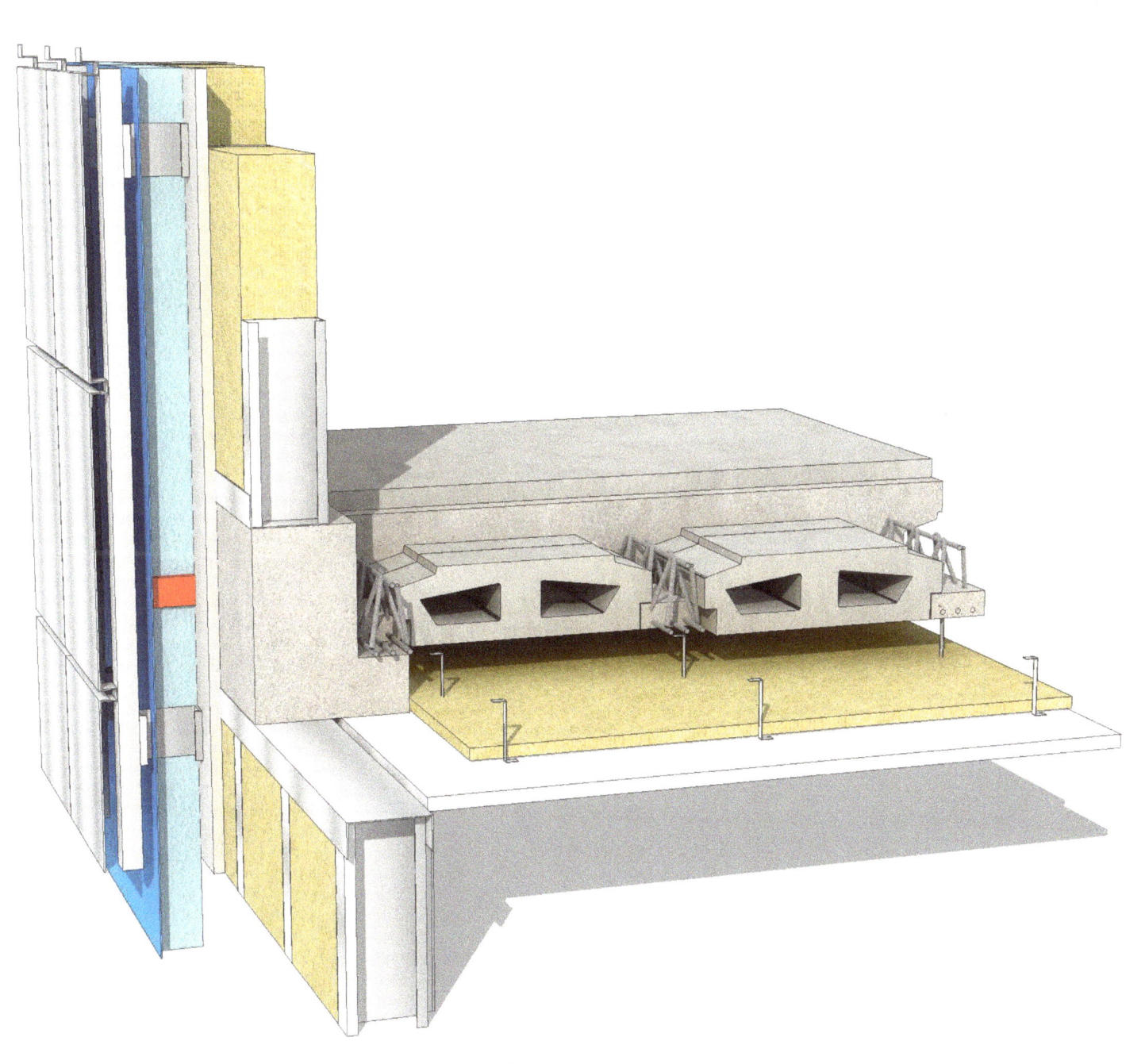

3D Detail F20- Suspended concrete floor, precast hollow beam and block, upper floor

F21

SUSPENDED CONCRETE FLOOR, PRECAST CONCRETE PLANK SYSTEM

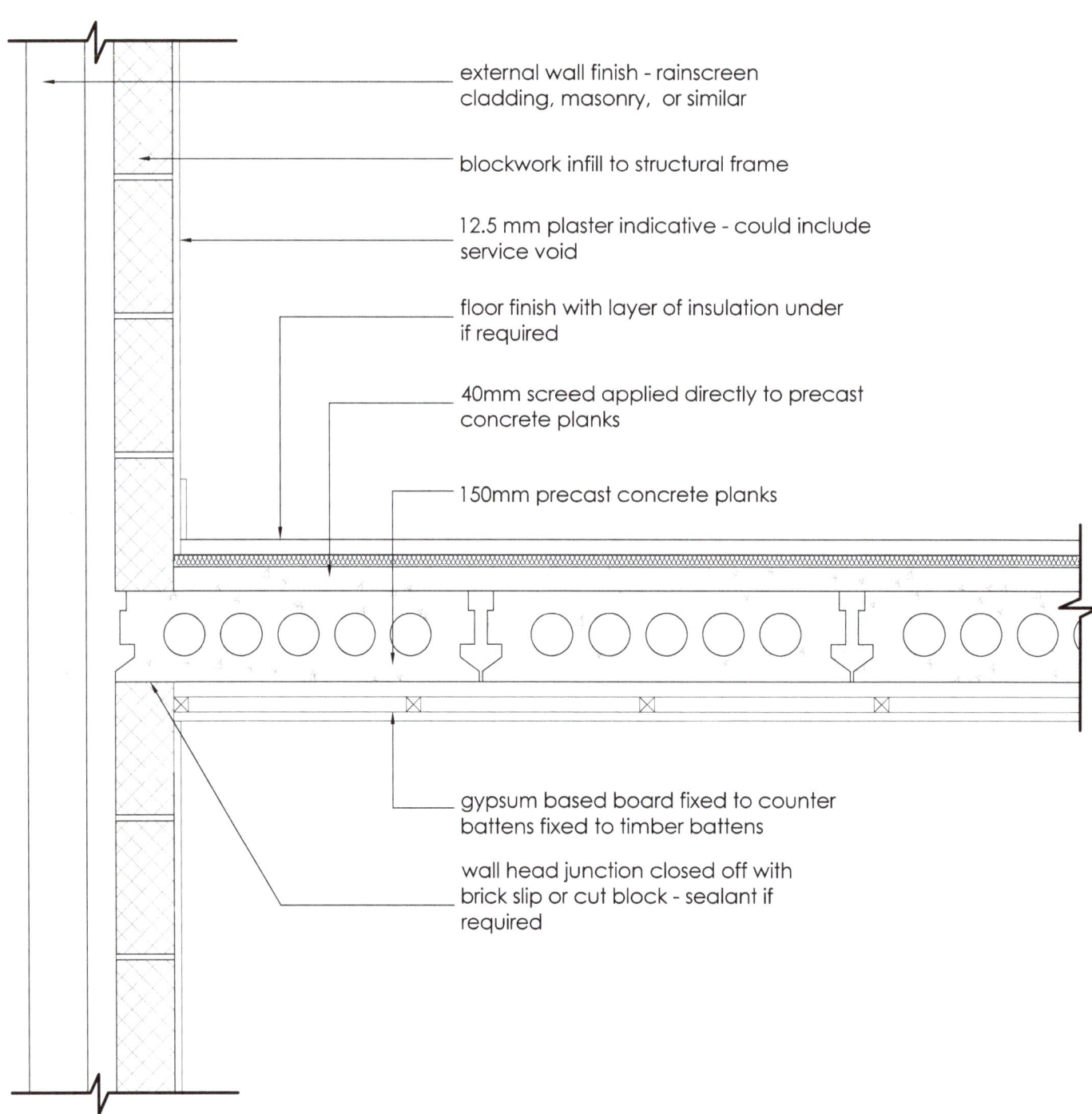

2D Detail F21 - Suspended concrete floor, precast concrete plank system

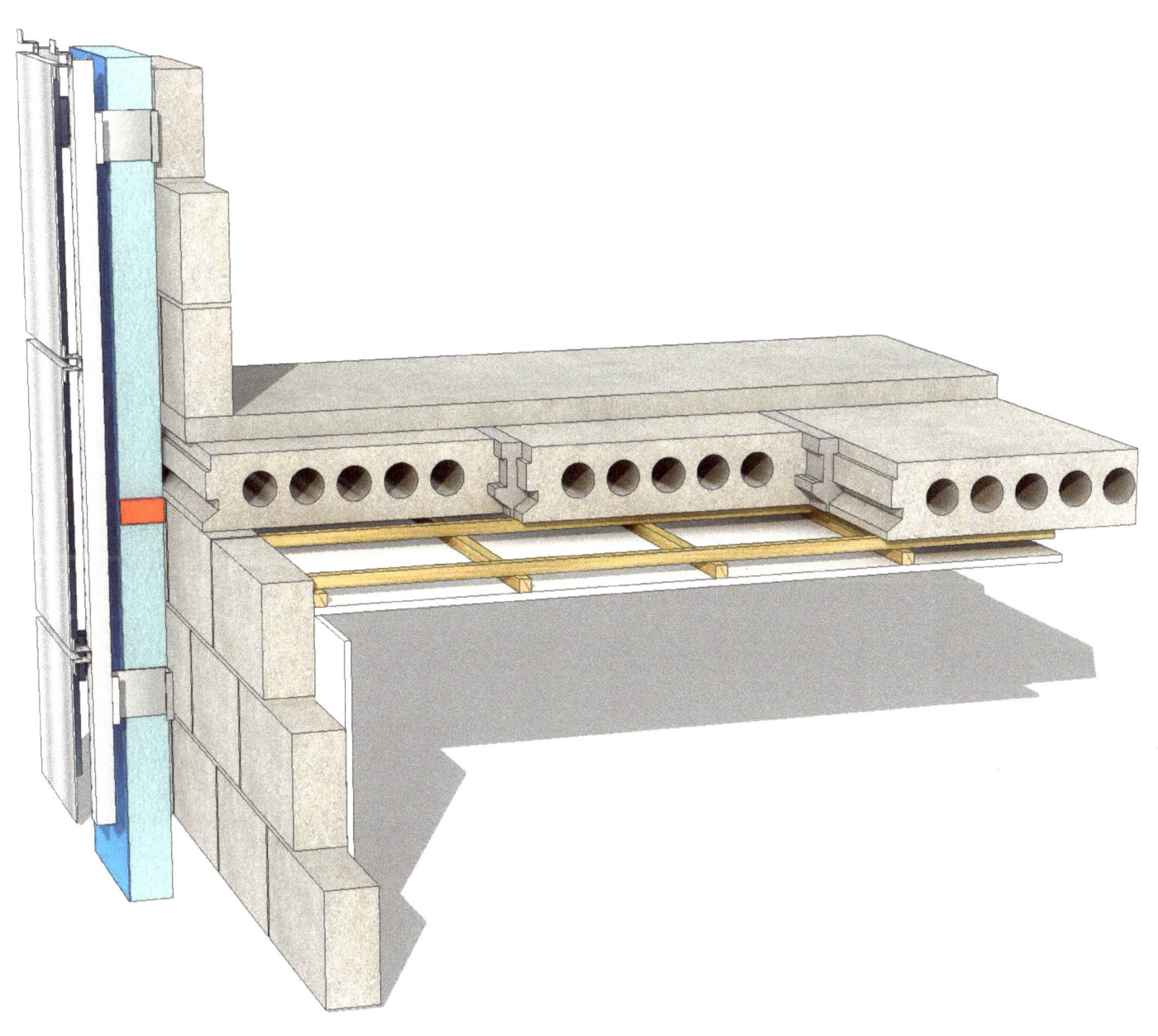

3D Detail F21- Suspended concrete floor, precast concrete plank system

F22

CAST IN SITU REINFORCED CONCRETE UPPER FLOOR

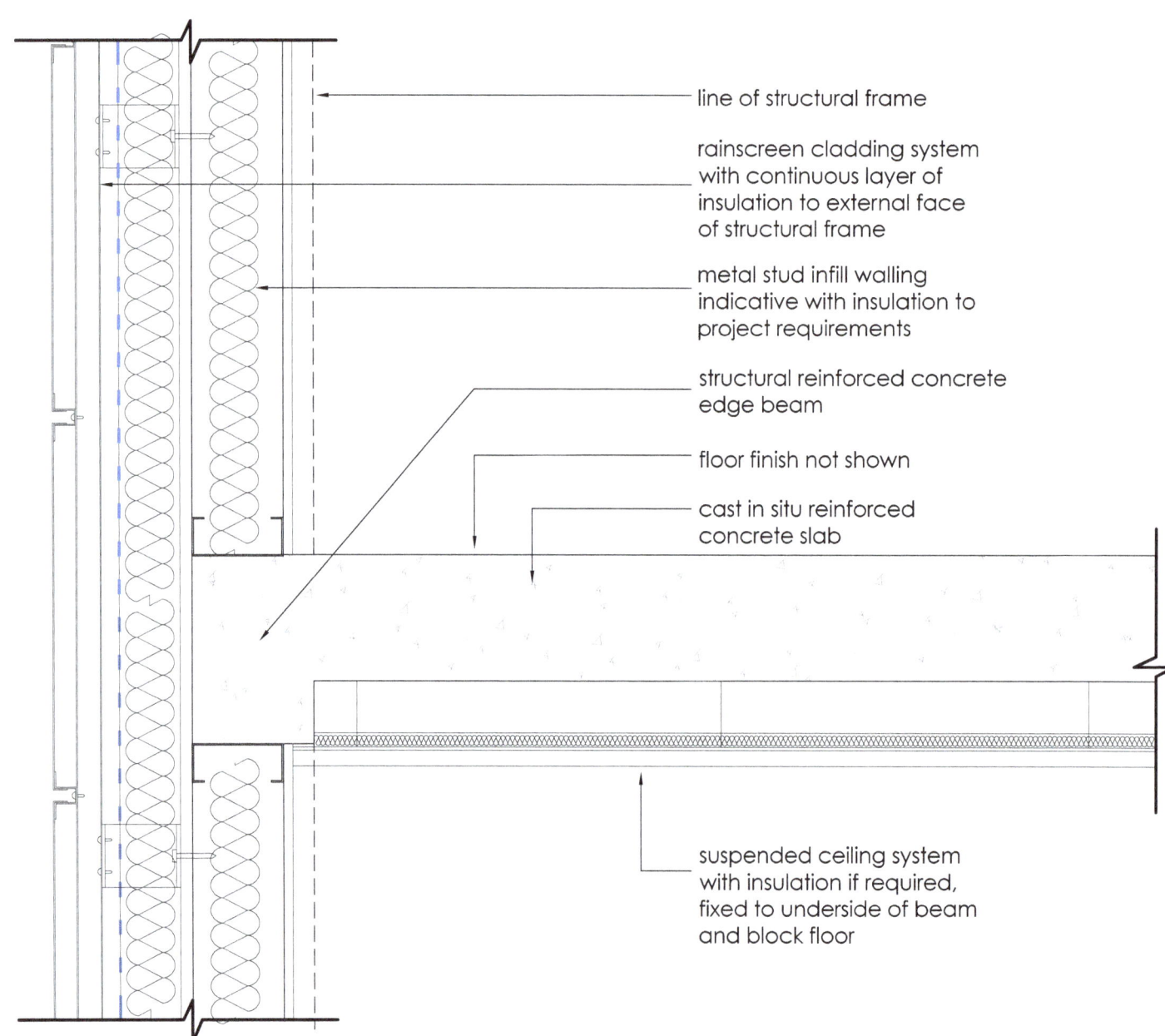

2D Detail F22 - Cast in situ reinforced concrete upper floor

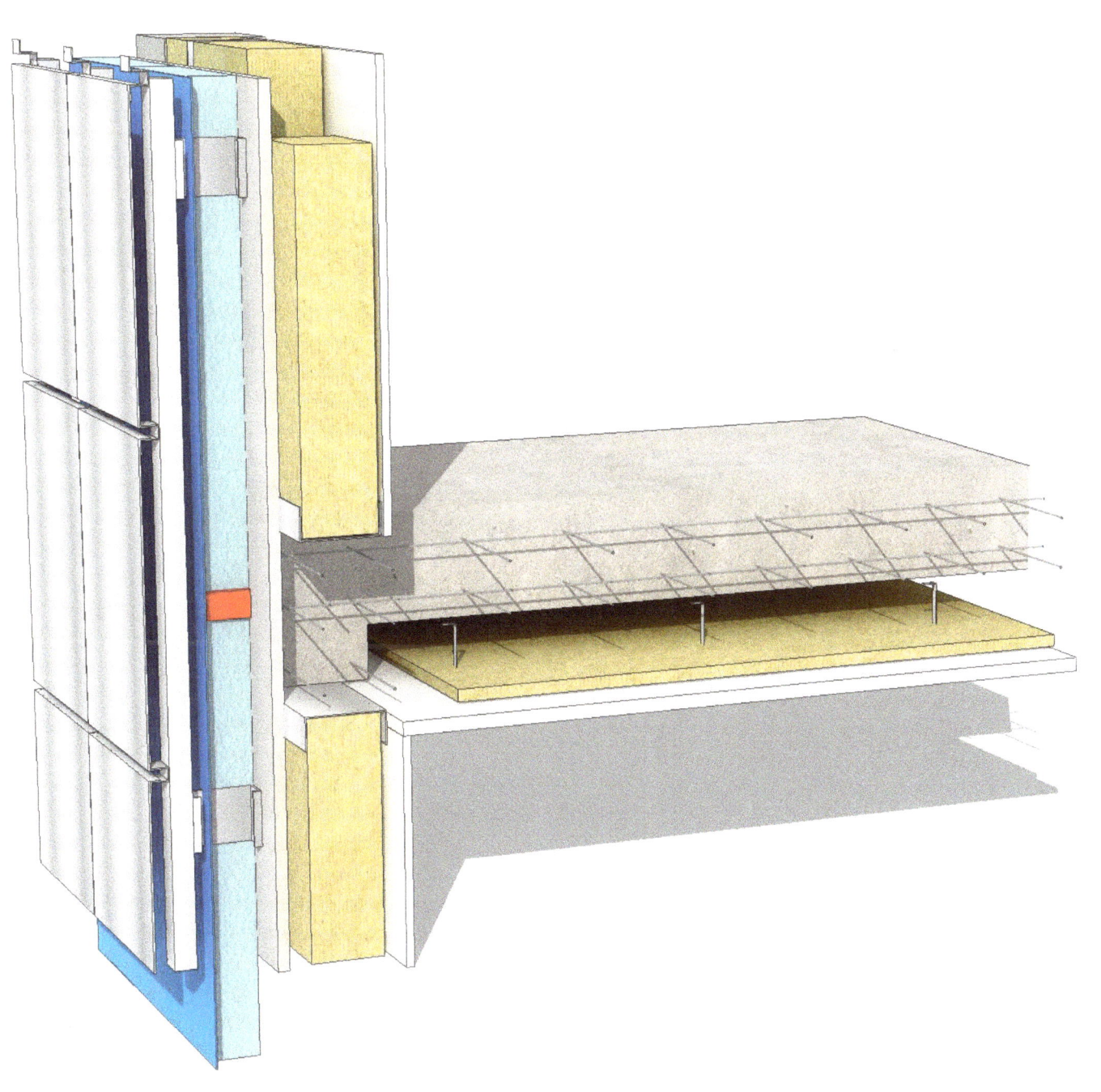

3D Detail F22- Cast in situ reinforced concrete floor

F23

FLOOR FINISH OPTIONS

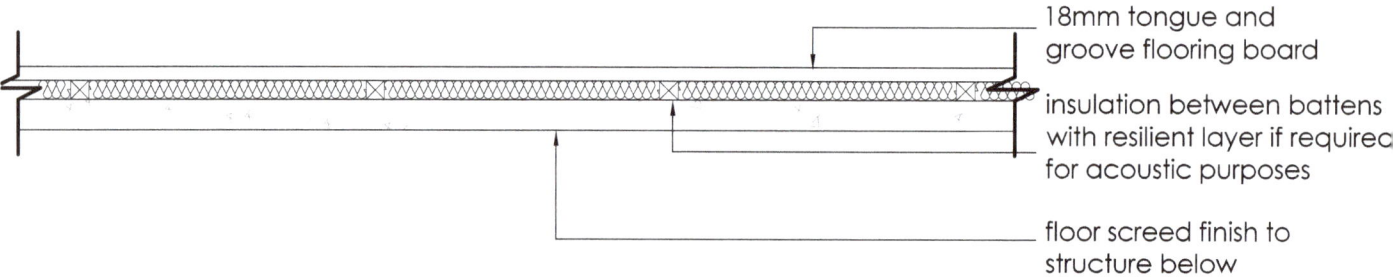

2D Detail F23 - Timber floor finish on battens

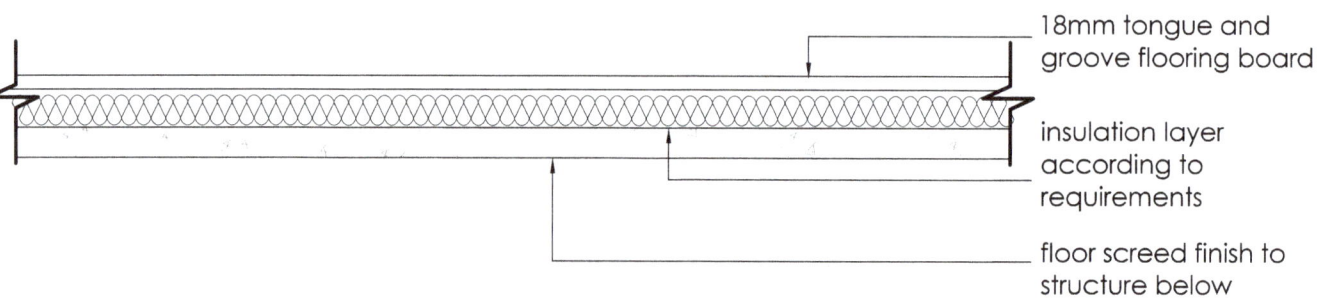

2D Detail F24 - Insulated floating floor

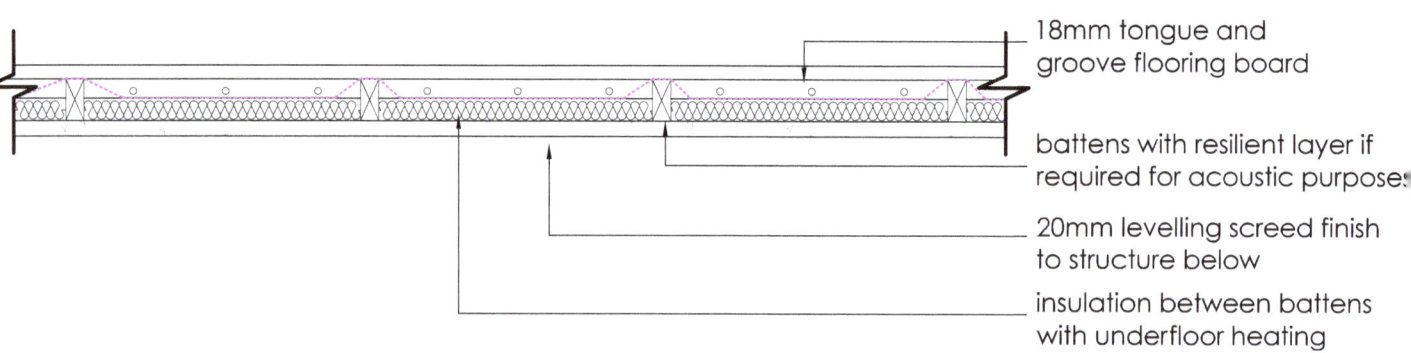

2D Detail F25 - Insulated floor with underfloor heating, intermittent heating applications

Notes:
This type of underfloor heating is suited to applications where fast response is required.

SECTION 4 - FOUNDATIONS AND FLOORS

3D Detail F23- Timber floor finish on battens

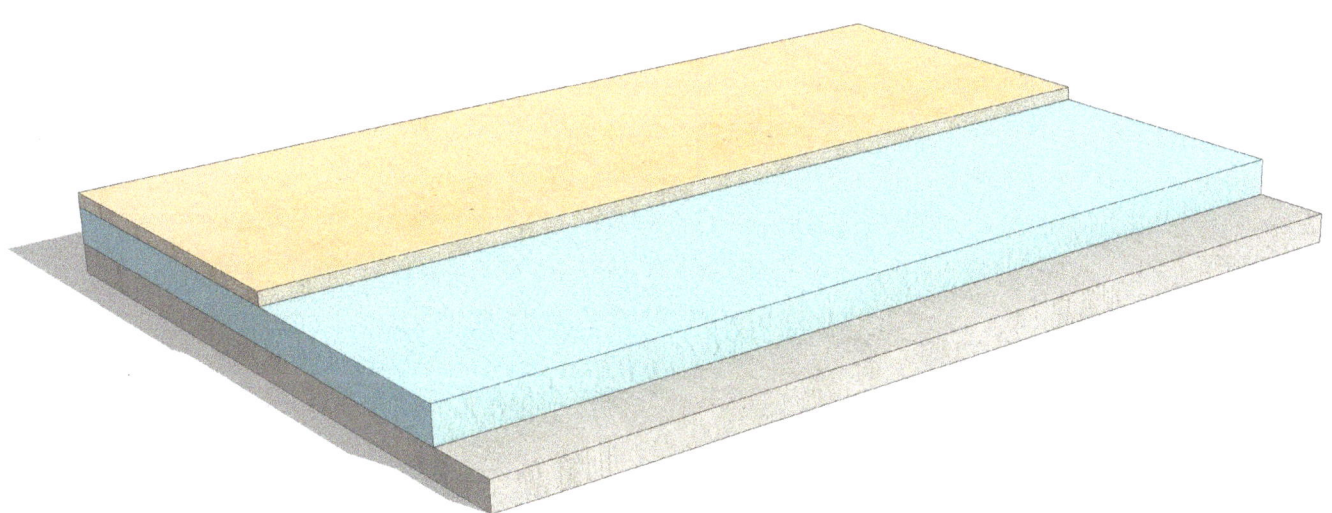

3D Detail F24- Insulated floating floor

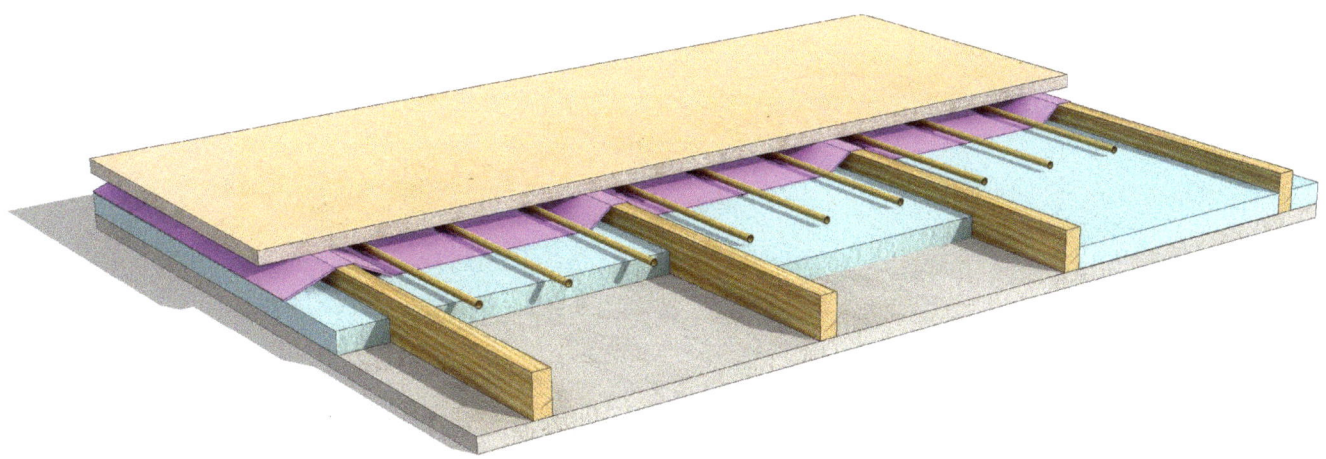

3D Detail F25- Insulated floor with underfloor heating, intermittent heating applications

F26

SUSPENDED FLOOR, STEEL DECK AND CONCRETE FLOOR COMPOSITE

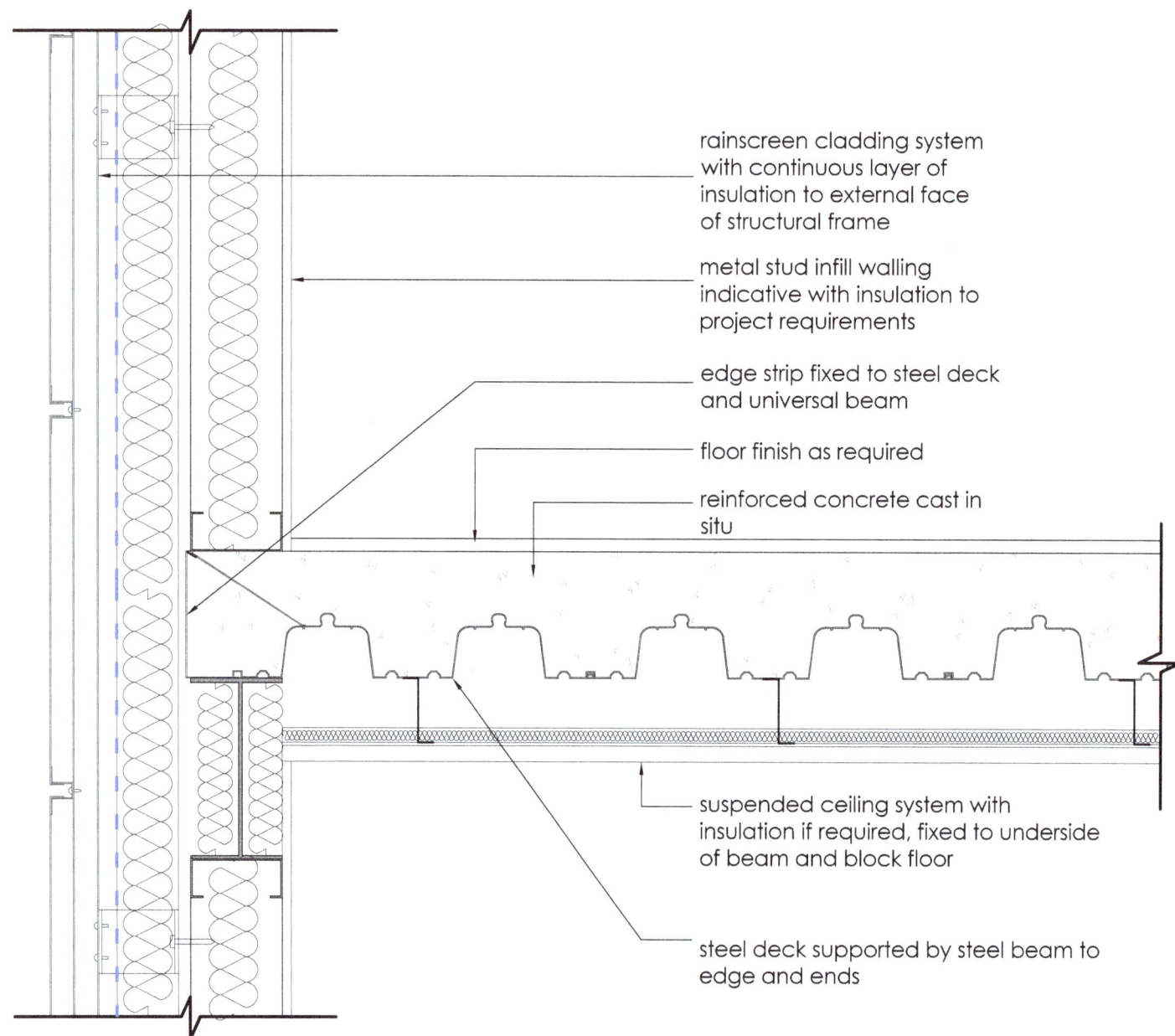

2D Detail F26 - Suspended floor, steel deck and concrete floor composite

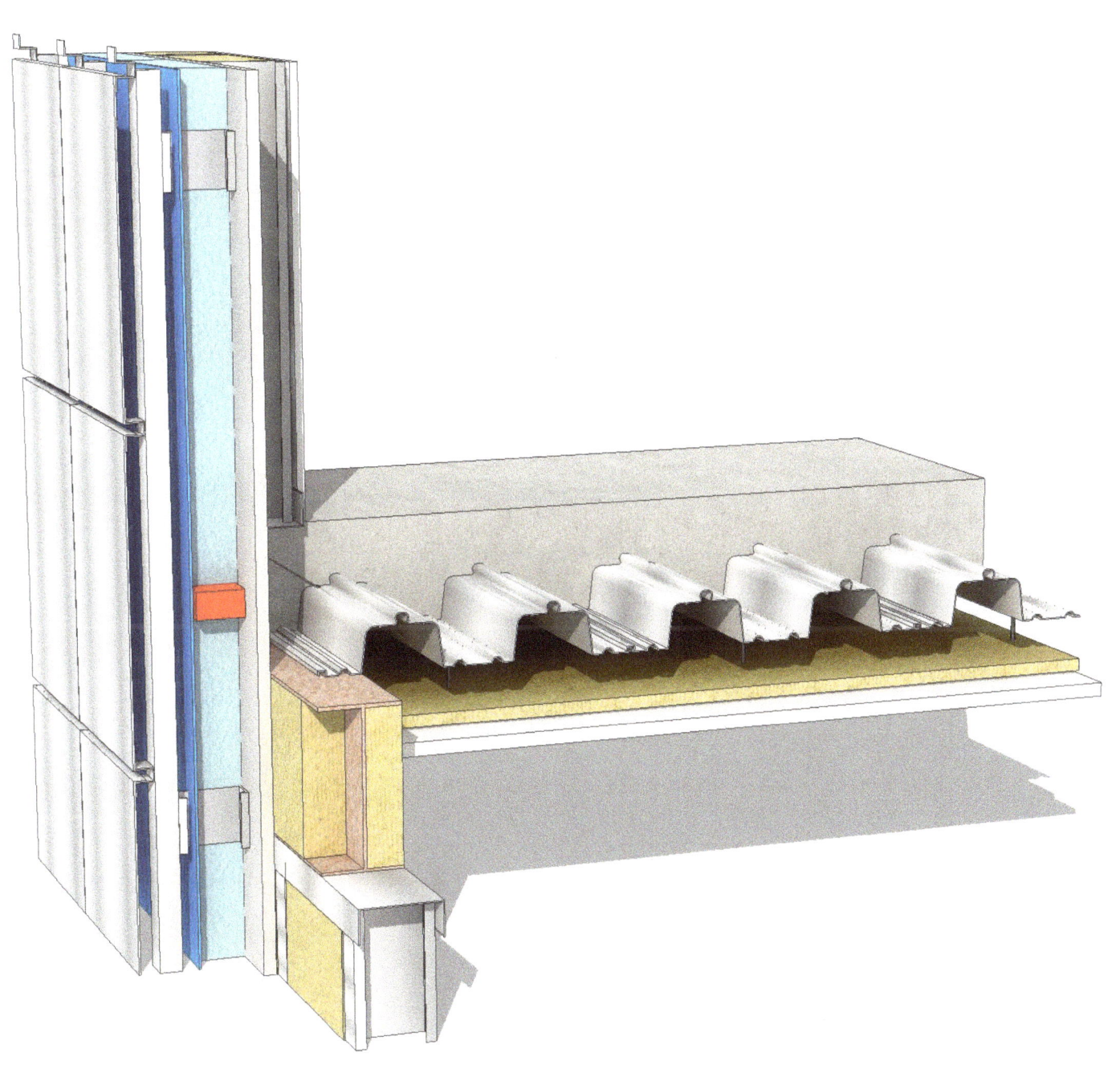

3D Detail F26- Suspended floor, steel deck and concrete floor composite

F27

SUSPENDED FLOOR, PRECAST HOLLOW FLOOR BEAM JUNCTION

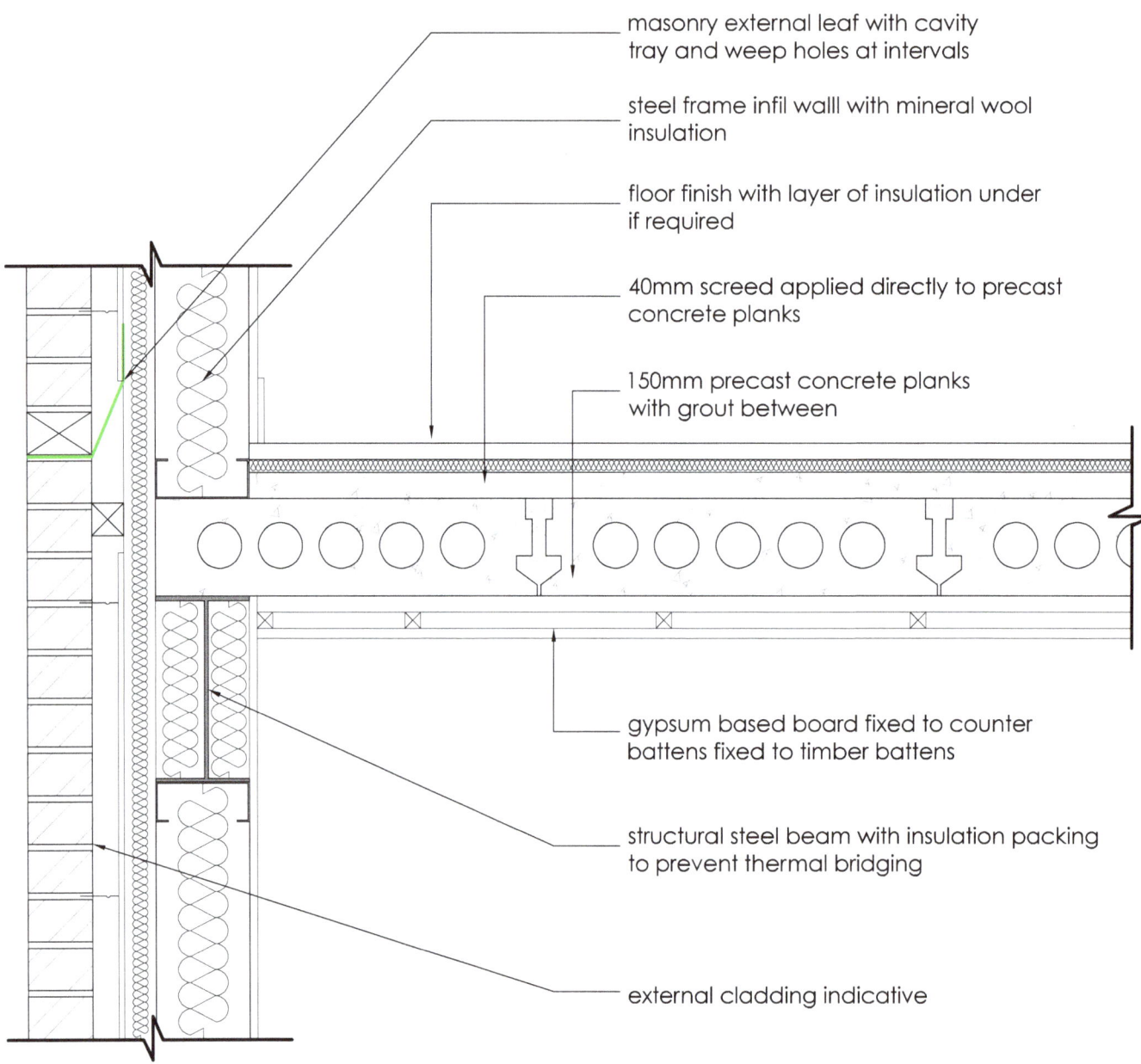

Notes:
For more information on external wall details, see Walls and Cladding section

2D Detail F27 - Suspended floor, precast hollow floor beam junction

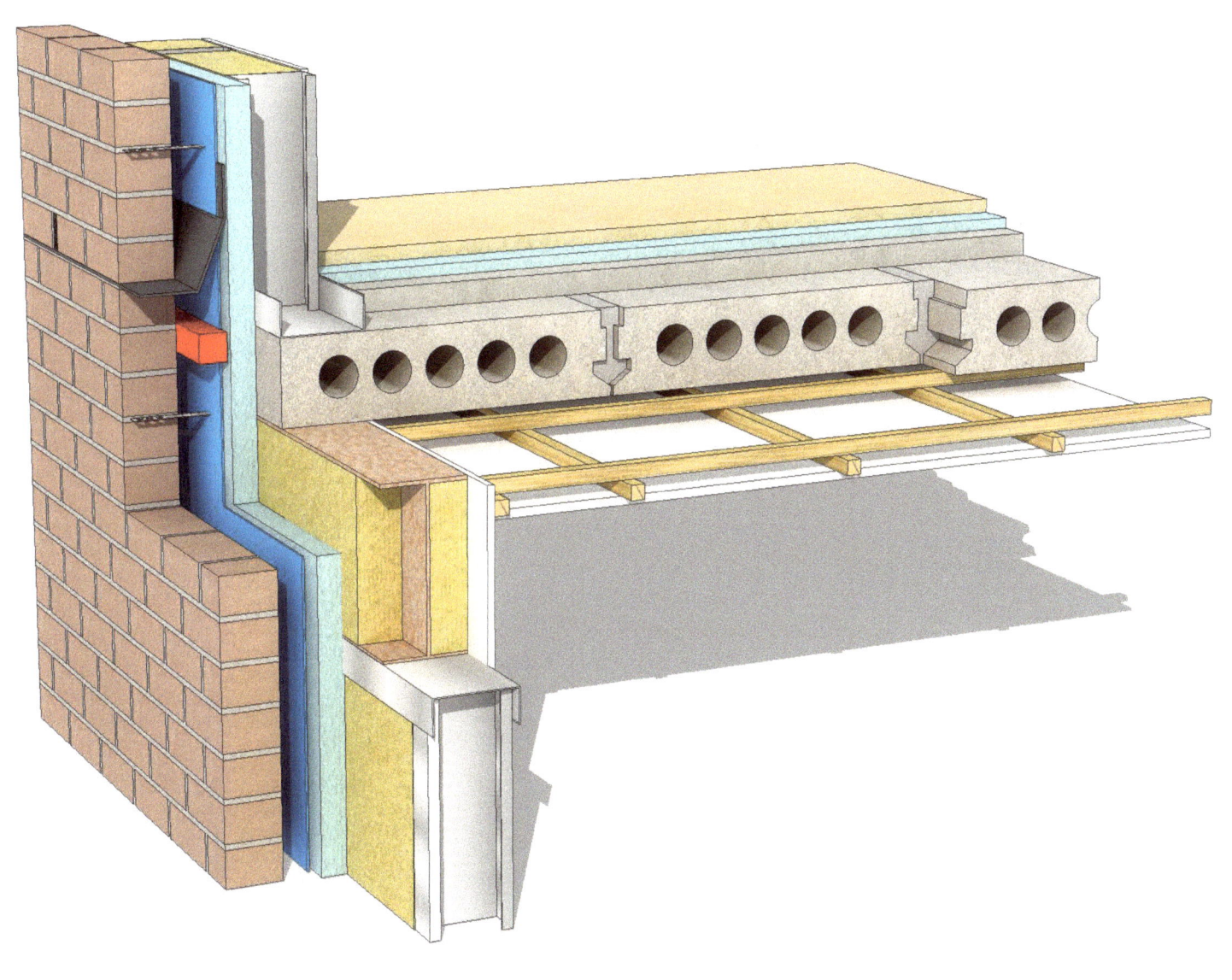

3D Detail F27- Suspended floor, precast hollow floor beam junction

F28

SUSPENDED FLOOR, PRECAST HOLLOW FLOOR BEAM

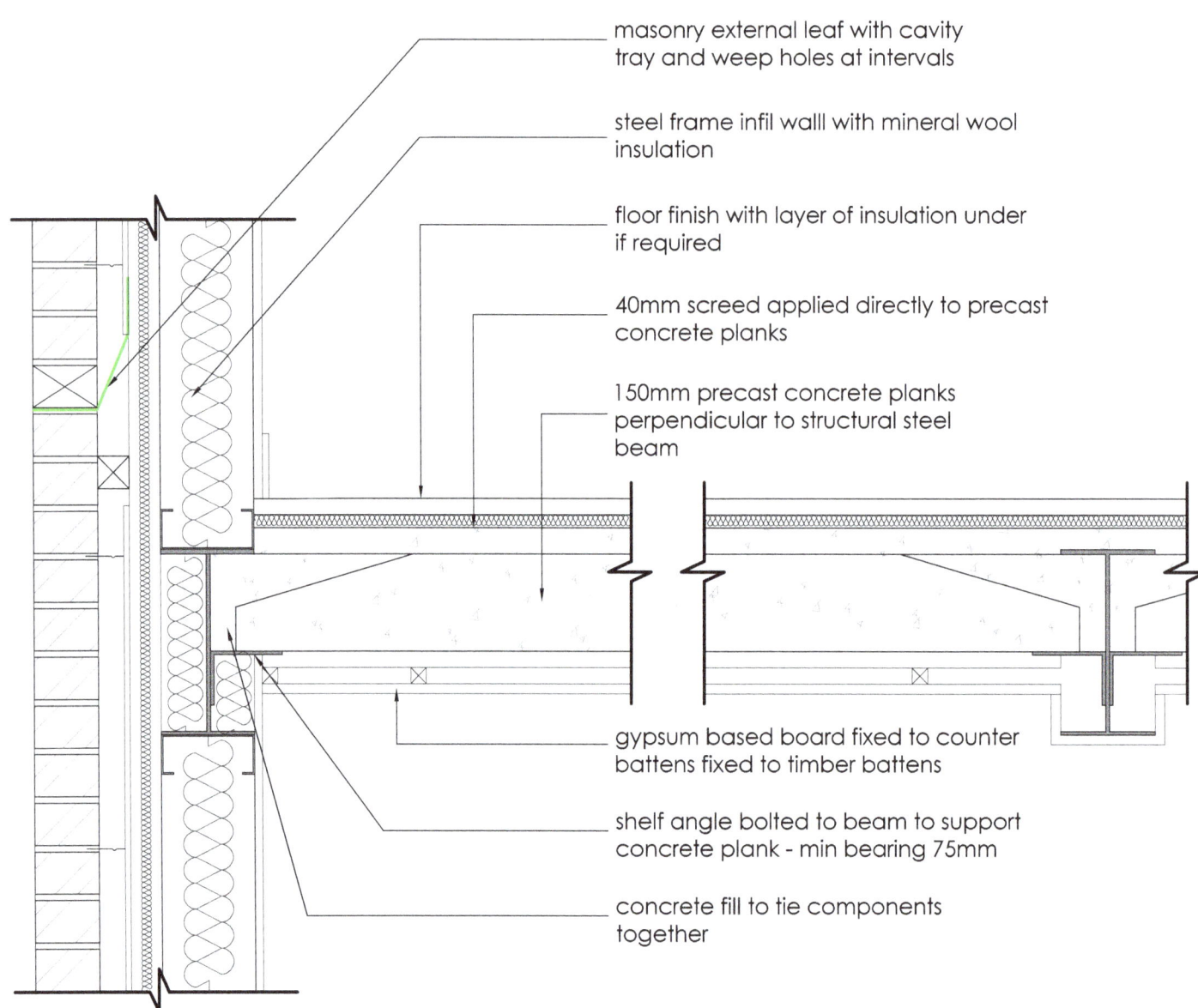

2D Detail F28 - Suspended floor, precast hollow floor beam

Notes:
Alternative detail - units within floor depth at right angle with steel beam.
Other suspended ceiling types could be specified.

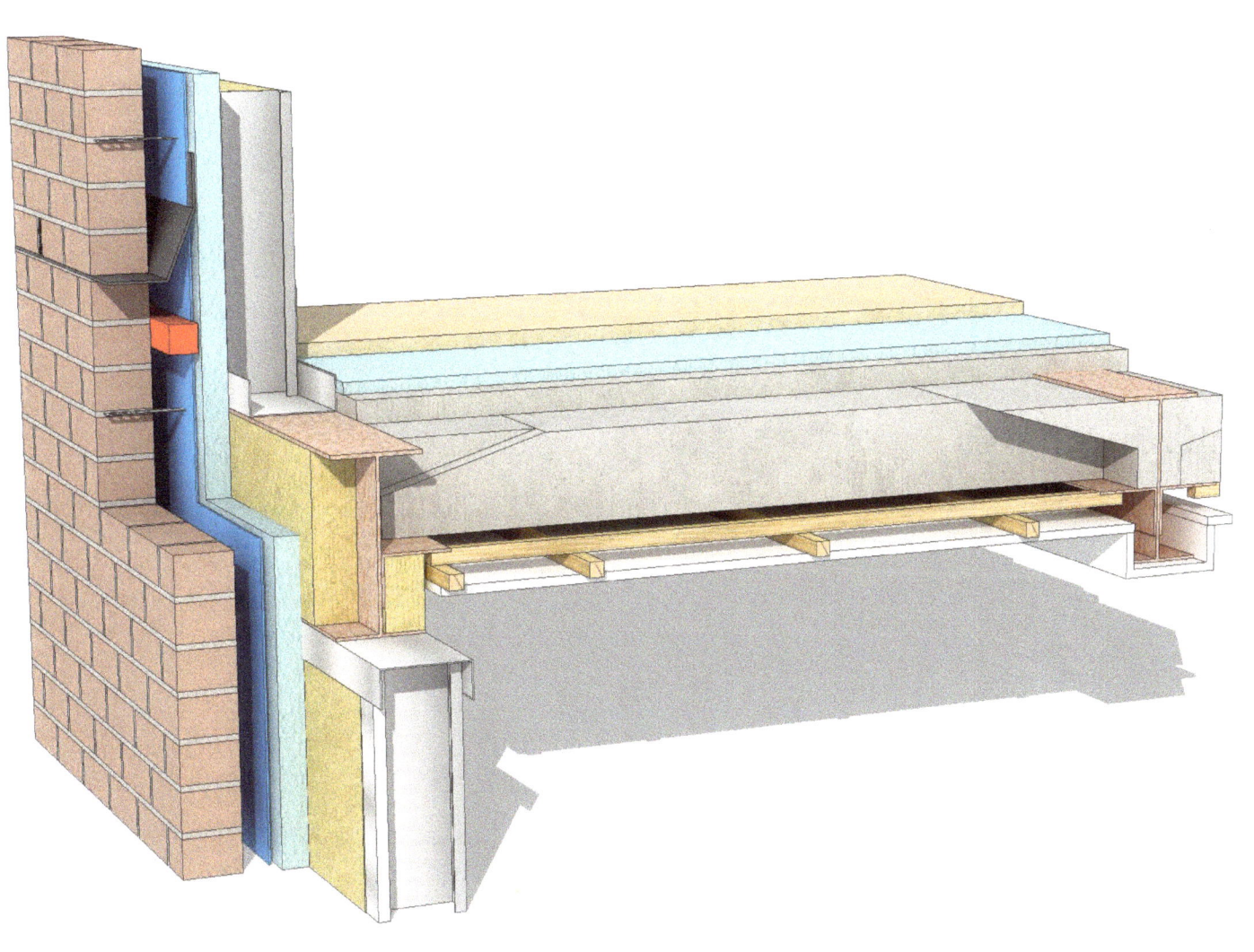

3D Detail F28- Suspended floor, precast hollow floor beam

F29

SUSPENDED FLOOR, PRECAST BEAM AND HOLLOW BLOCK JUNCTION

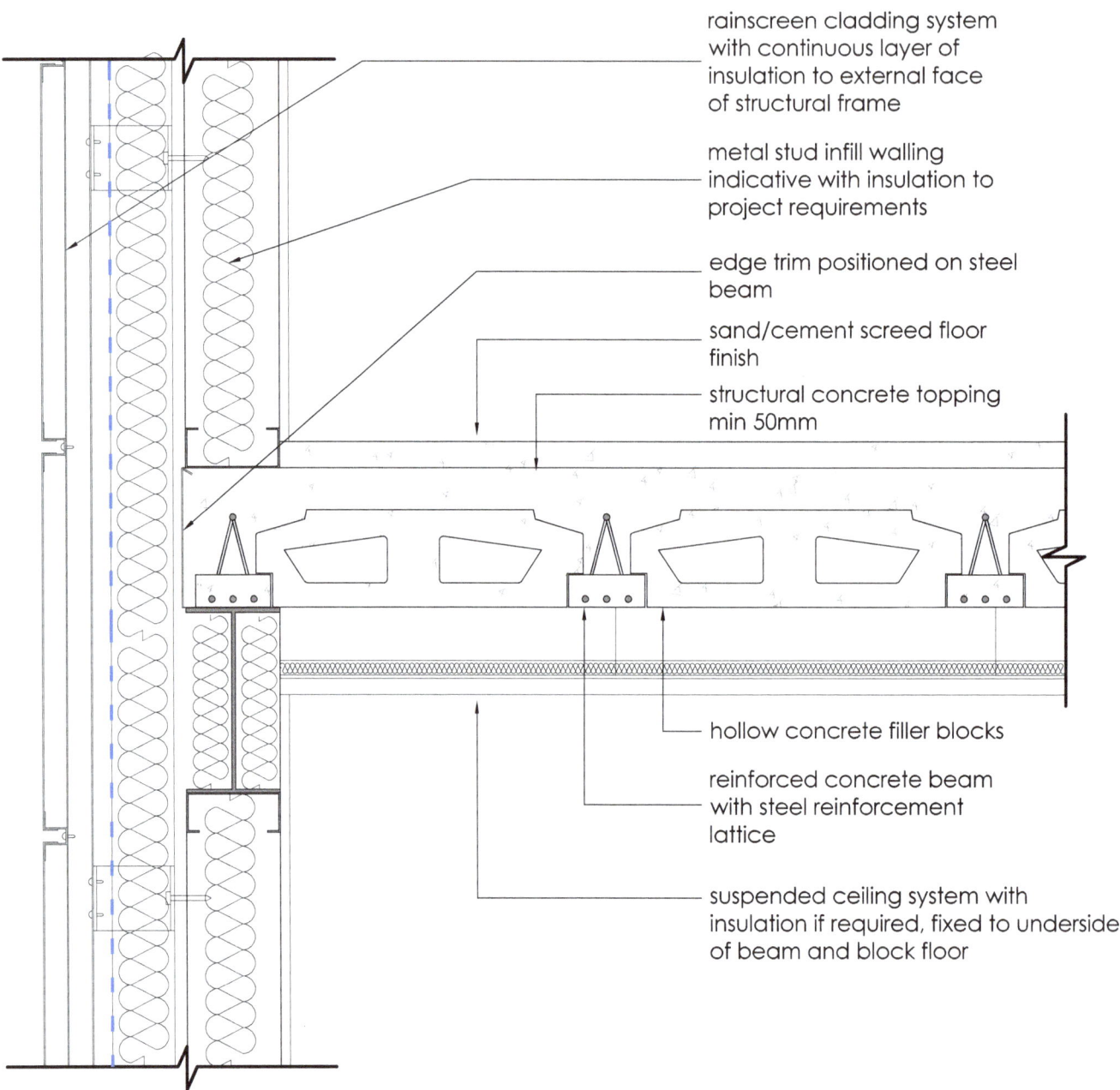

2D Detail F29 - Suspended floor, precast beam and hollow block junction

SECTION 4 - FOUNDATIONS AND FLOORS

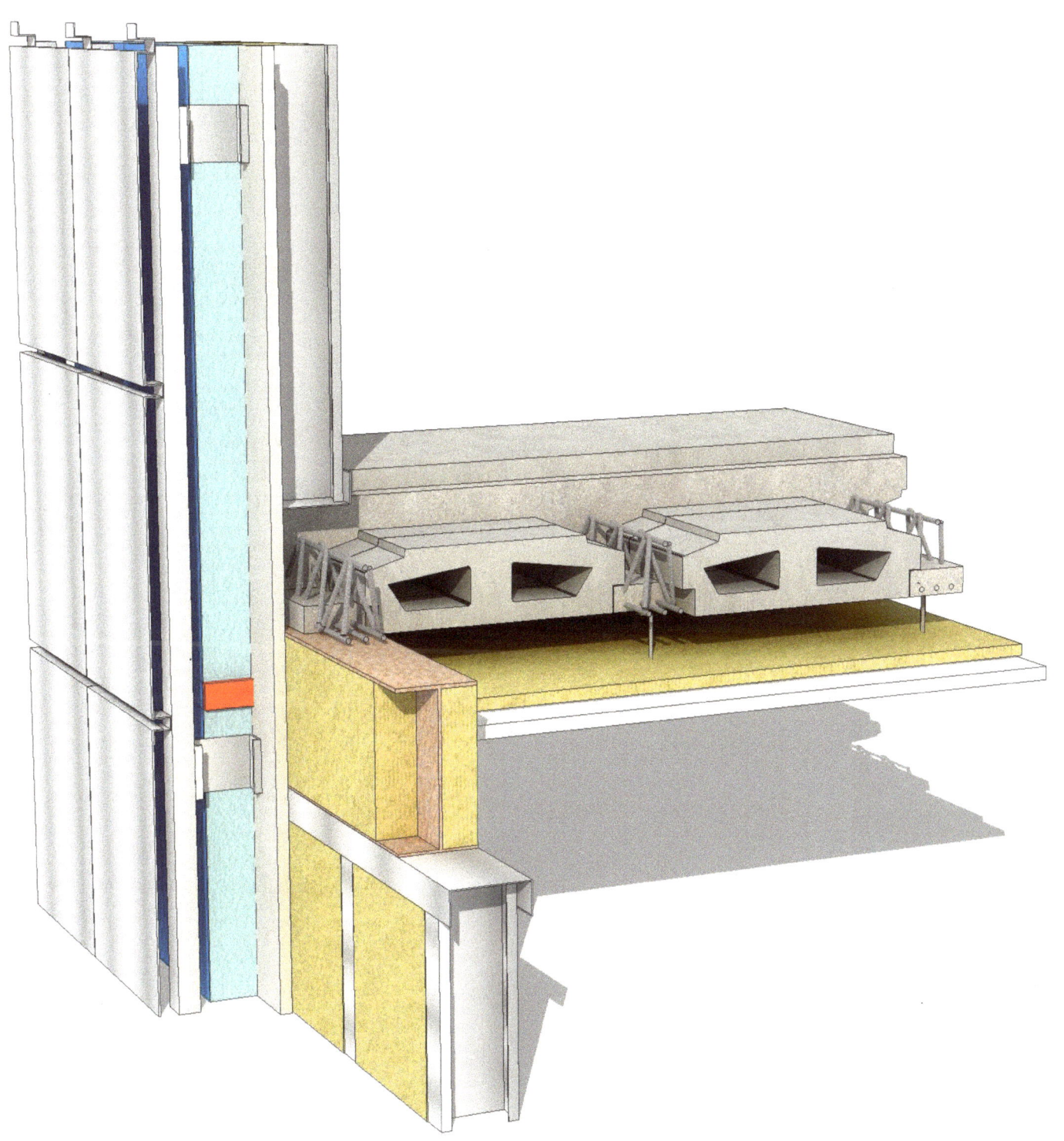

3D Detail F29- Suspended floor, precast beam and hollow block junction

Blank Page

BASEMENTS

SECTION 5

BASEMENTS

In the general context of buildings a basement can be described as a storey which is below the ground storey, and therefore below ground level. Basement construction can provide valuable space for commercial uses, storage or car parks, along with many other uses. They have good acoustic attenuation with the concrete walls surrounding them providing good sound insulation. In some cases, where ground has a poor bearing capacity it is sometimes necessary to excavate which naturally creates an area to construct the substructure, and a basement area.

The basement requires careful design in order to achieve the correct level of waterproofing for the internal environment.

The design of basements is well established and achievable provided design guidance is implemented. The structural wall of a basement below ground is essentially a retaining wall which have to resist both the pressures of surrounding soil and groundwater, along with transmitting the loads of the structure above to the foundations.

DESIGN PRINCIPLES

The general principle of basement design is to assess the risk of water reaching the below ground structure and to select the appropriate form of construction to achieve the required internal environment.

The designer needs to consider the requirements of the client and the potential use of the basement along with the associated requirements in terms of building regulations and standards. The designer then needs to carry out an appropriate site investigation to establish the ground conditions and most suitable construction method to suit these conditions. See Figure 5.1.

The process can be divided into four main steps:
- Establish basement usage
- Collect site information
- Determine form of construction
- Establish waterproofing method

There are some measures that can be taken to minimise the risk in basement design, which are listed below.

Initial considerations
- Initial and future use of basement
- Initial and future ground water conditions
- Orientation of the building in relation to ground water
- Current and future daylighting and ventilation requirements
- Shape of construction/space to facilitate simple detailing and waterproofing
- Location and access on site to ease construction
- Avoidance of penetrating waterproof membrane with services wherever possible

Grade of construction	Use of basement	Conditions required	Moisture exclusion	Suggested type of construction
Grade 1 - Basic Utility	Car parking, plant room	15-32°C temperature with >65% humidity, some seepage and some damp patches may occur	Acceptable wet seepage and visible damp patches	Type B. Reinforced concrete designed in accordance with BS8110
Grade 2 - Improved Utility	Workshop, retail storage, electrical plant room	<15°C storage, up to 42°C for plant rooms, 35-5% relative humidity, no water penetration or seepage, but moisture vapour is tolerable	Wet seepage or damp patches unacceptable	Type A internal tanking system. Type B to BS 8007 watertight concrete
Grade 3 - Habitable space	Offices, residential use, kitchens, restaurants, leisure centre	18-29°C temperature depending on use with 40-60% humidity, dry environment, tightly controlled	Wet seepage or damp patches unacceptable. Internal environment controlled to achieved required temp and humidity	Type A internal tanking system. Type B to BS 8007 monolithic concrete structure. Type C drained cavity system to BS 8110
Grade 4 - Special	Archive storage of books or documents, computer rooms	13-22°C temperature, controlled environment, totally dry with 35-50% relative humidity	Active measures to tightly control both temperature and humidity, with any seepage and visible dampness unacceptable.	Type A internal tanking system. Type B to BS 8007 monolithic concrete structure, combined with vapour proof membrane. Type C Drained cavity system, ventilated wall cavity and vapour barrier to inner skin and floor

Fig. 5.1 - Table of basement grades adapted from BS8102

Site Investigation
Geotechnical investigation to demonstrate current and anticipated future ground water regime
Soil testing to establish surface loading and lateral earth pressures
Presence of contamination / gases

Detail design
- Construction and waterproofing to suit ground conditions and use
- Structural and waterproofing design to be in accordance with best practice recommendations
- Access for future maintenance and alterations
- Specialist advice if required

Health and Safety
- Excavation requirements
- Working in excavation
- Working from height
- Temporary stability of walls
- Craning of large basement parts

TYPES OF CONSTRUCTION

There are three main methods for waterproofing a basement as set out in British Standard BS 8102:2009 - Code of practice for protection of below ground structures against water from the ground.

TYPE A - BARRIER PROTECTION

A Type A basement structure uses an impervious material applied to either internally or externally, to prevent the passage of moisture to the inside of the basement. If the membrane is applied to the external face of the wall, the structure is also protected as hydrostatic pressure will keep the membrane in place. The membrane must be protected, usually in the form of a slim brick protective wall with a weak concrete mix in the cavity between the wall and the membrane. If the membrane is not protected it can become damaged during backfilling or other site works. If there are any defects, it is difficult to gain access to an external tanking system, and for this reason, sometimes an internal tanking system is specified.

In some cases, it is not possible to apply the membrane externally, due to poor working space around the perimeter of the basement. In this situation an internal tanking membrane can be specified. An internal membrane is applied to the inside face of the basement wall, but is at risk of damage from internal fixings and hydrostatic pressure forcing the membrane away from the wall. For these reasons, the internal membrane is protected by a leaf of blockwork which both protects it from fixings, but braces the membrane to the external wall.

This form of construction does not incorporate an integral water protection, and therefore completely relies on the performance of the waterproof membrane.

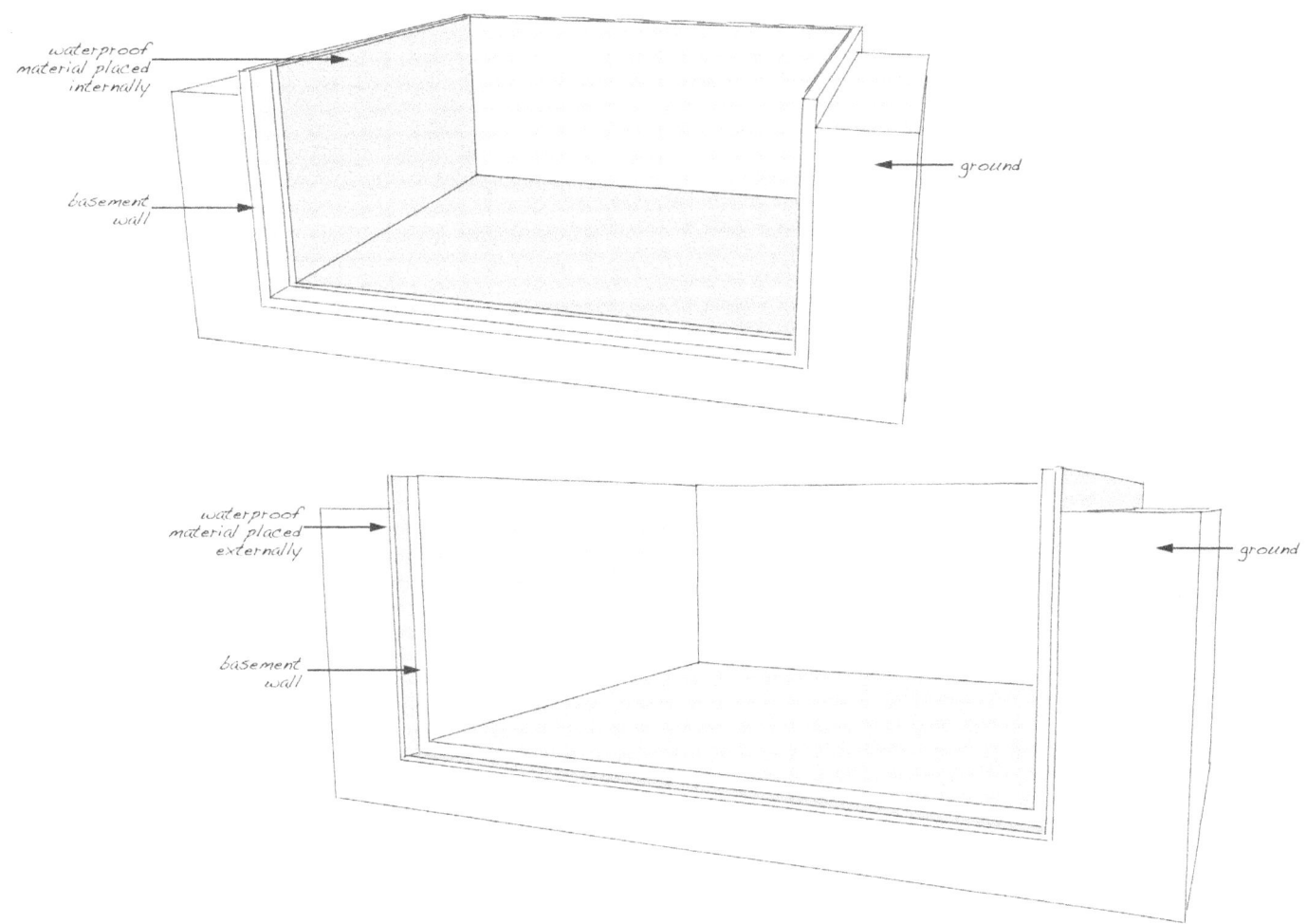

Fig. 5.2 - Type A - Barrier protection

Suitable materials to form a tanking membrane are:
- mastic asphalt tanking
- bonded sheet membranes (fibre reinforced bituminous felt, polythene sheet)
- liquid applied membranes (epoxy resin compounds)
- geosynthetic clay liners (bentonite impregnated matting)
- cementitious slurries and layer coats

The chosen membrane can be installed in a number of ways:
- on the exterior face of walls and floors [external]
- on an external source of support [reversed]
- within the construction [sandwiched]
- on the interior face of walls [internal]

Type A tanking systems rely on the formation of adequate joints where sheet systems are used, along with prevention of damage to the membrane during construction and a suitable bond to the substrate.

If installed in a location with a high water table, any defects in the tanking system will allow water to penetrate the structure and enter the basement as free water. If this is no removed the basement will fill to the level of the water table.

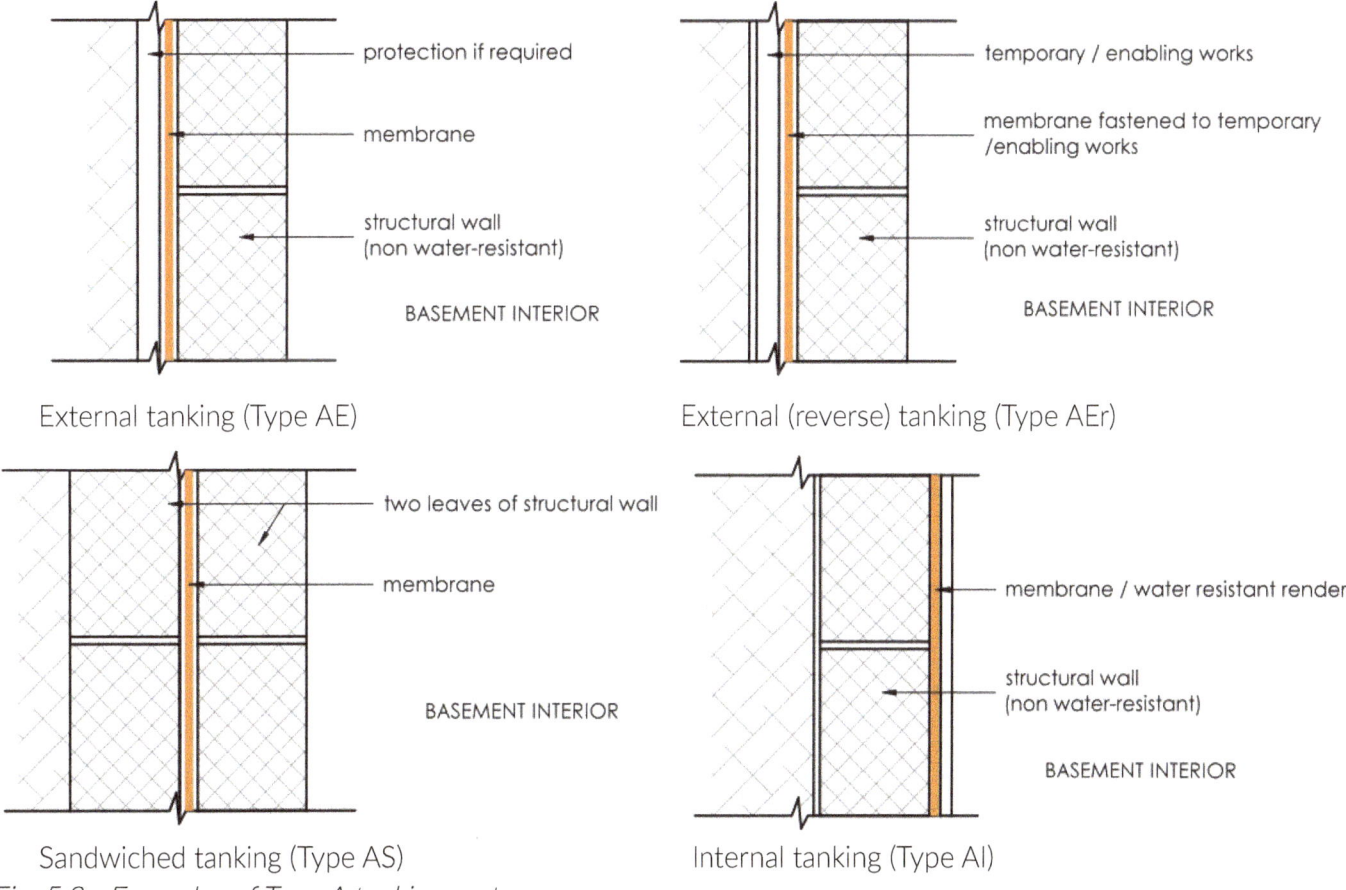

Fig. 5.3 - Examples of Type A tanking systems

External: Providing site conditions permit, external tanking is the preferred option of Type A construction. External water pressure forces the membrane against the structure, thus creating a song resistance. External tanking can be considered to be reliable on a medium term, however, access for repairs and maintenance can be difficult. It can be expensive to install and require specialist contractors.

Reverse: This method applies the tanking membrane to a surface (often piling support or temporary/enabling works) prior to construction of the main structural elements against it. For example, in constructing a floor level tanking, the concrete blinding layer will be positioned, followed by the membrane which is then protected by a layer of screed, before the concrete slab is cast on top. The membrane will be taken well beyond the edge of the slab to allow for a suitable lap joint to be formed with the wall.

Sandwiched: Should external tanking be unsuitable, it is suggested sandwiched tanking to be used. This method places the membrane to a structural masonry wall (or floor), and fully supported by a loading coat, (concrete slab for floors and blockwork for walls) which will prevent it from being detached and pushed away from the surface by external pressures.

Internal: Internal tanking is applied to the inside of a structural wall, however, it is susceptible to hydrostatic pressure, and as such must be fixed using mechanical anchorage or in some cases a non structural inner skin.

TYPE B - STRUCTURALLY INTEGRAL PROTECTION

A Type B protection requires the structure itself to be water resistant. This is usually in the form of pre stressed or reinforced concrete, with carefully detailed joints to incorporate waterstops. Without the addition of a separate membrane this form of construction is not as effective in resistance of water vapour as Type A or Type C. In some cases, Type B protection is incorporated with Type A or Type C construction.

Most Type B designs are carried out in accordance with BS8007 and BS8110, which give guidance on grades of concrete and steel spacing. Type B construction is reliant on the design and construction of the basement as an integral shell, using concrete of low permeability and the appropriate joint details.

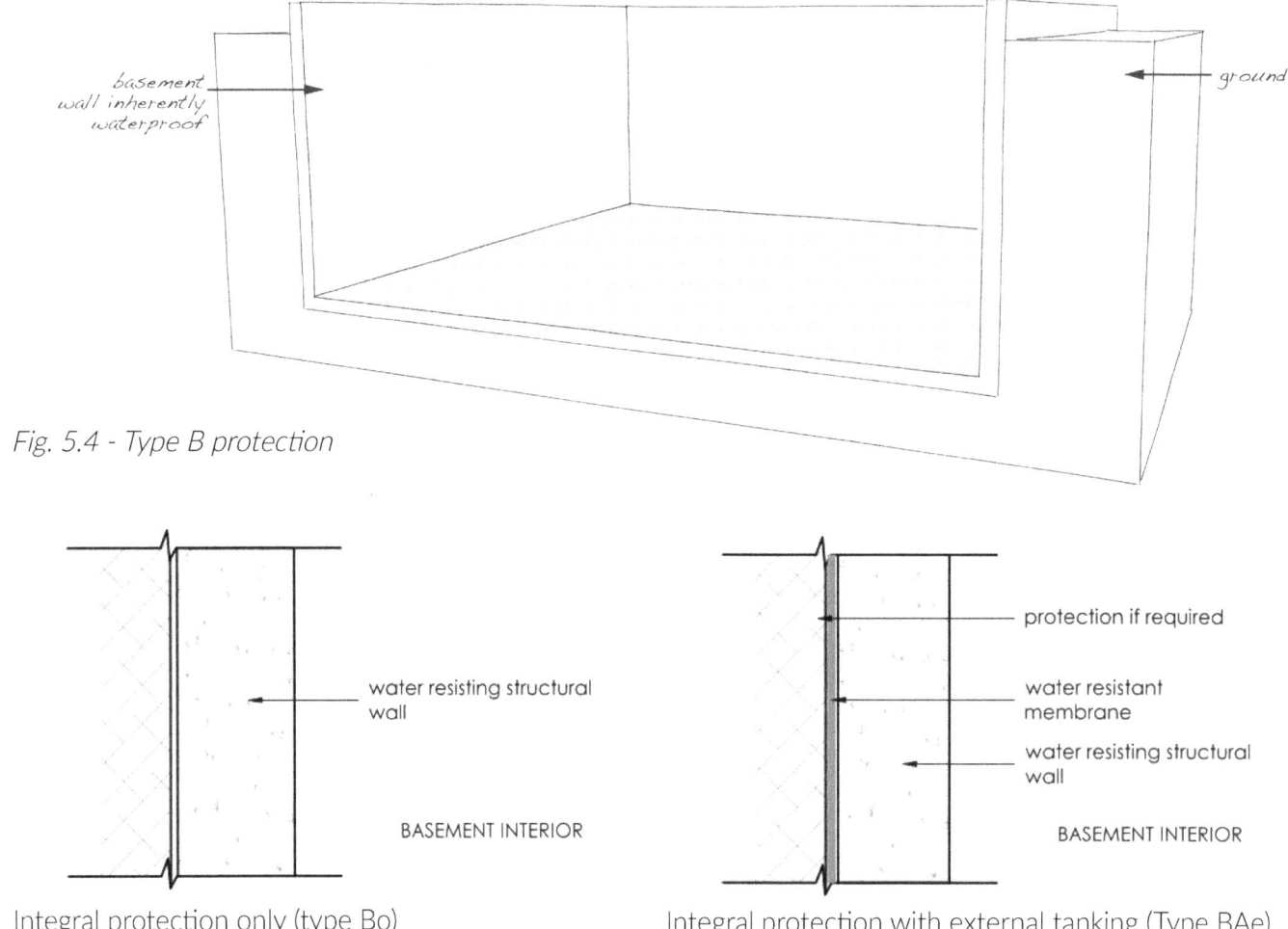

Fig. 5.4 - Type B protection

Integral protection only (type Bo)   Integral protection with external tanking (Type BAe)

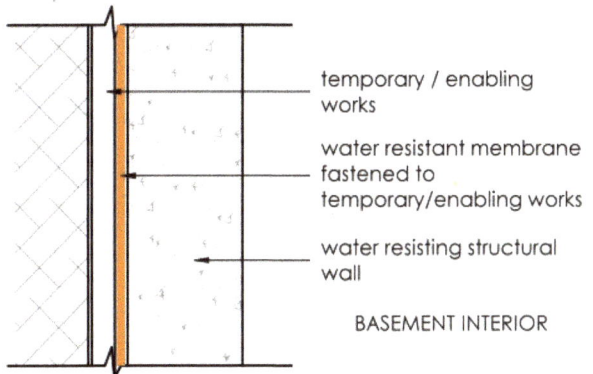

Integral protection with external reverse tanking (Type BAer)

Integral protection with internal tanking (Type BAI)

Fig. 5.5 - Type B protection types and examples

TYPE C - DRAINED PROTECTION

Type C protection incorporates a drainage cavity within the structure which collects any water that passes through, and removes it to a pump drainage system. In this type of construction it is critical that the cavity remains clear and free flowing and not to be overloaded.

The structural wall can be made up of concrete (reinforced, prestressed or plain) or masonry, but the construction must provide enough resistance to water to ensure that the cavity only receives a restricted amount of water or dampness. The cavity should not be used to conceal large leaks. Potential hazards can include failure of drains or mechanical pumps, and blockage of the cavity.

Type C structures tend to be selected when there is a free draining site with a low water table. Types A and B can often be incorporated into a Type C construction.

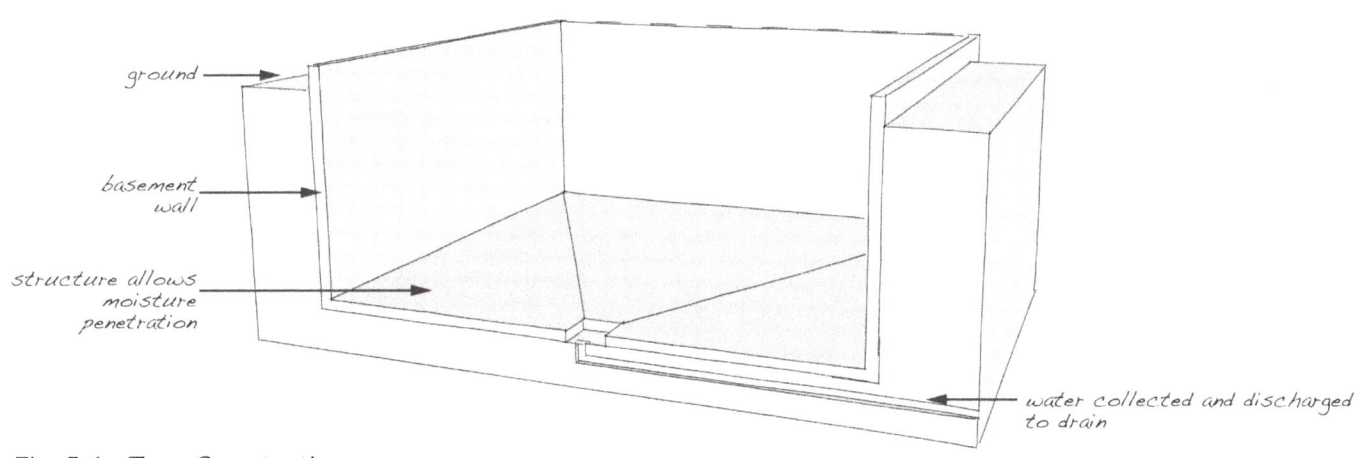

Fig. 5.6 - Type C protection

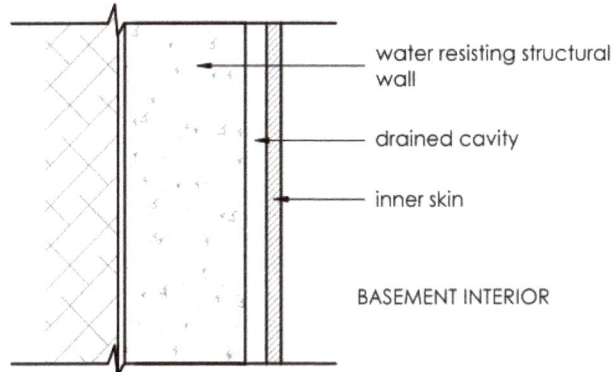

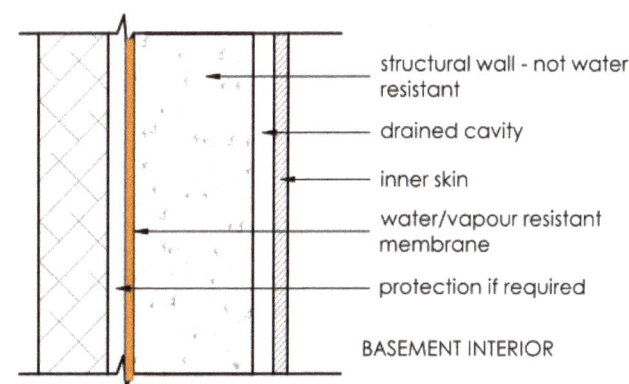

Drained cavity with integral protection (Type CBo)

Drained cavity with external tanking (Type CAe)

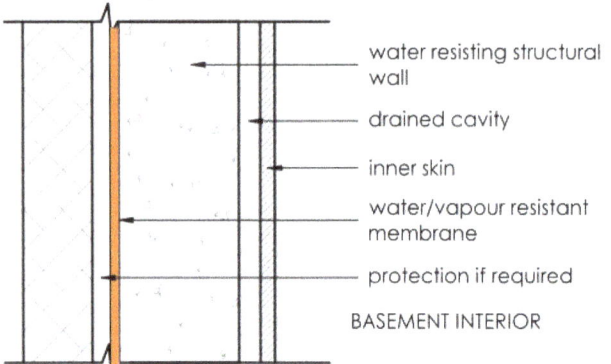
Drained cavity with integral protection and external tanking (Type CBae)

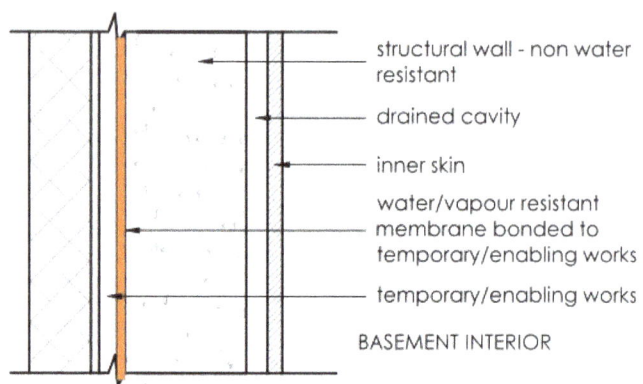
Drained cavity with external reverse tanking (Type CAer)

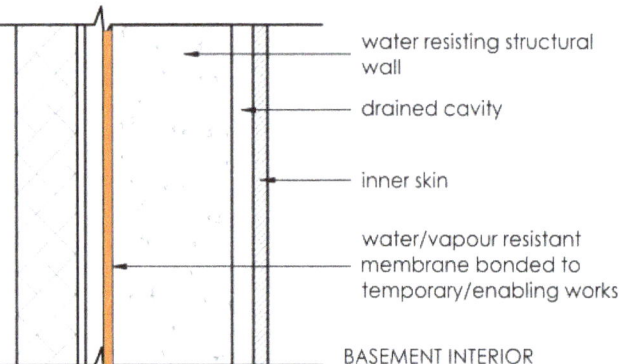
Drained cavity with integral protection and external reverse tanking (Type CBAer)

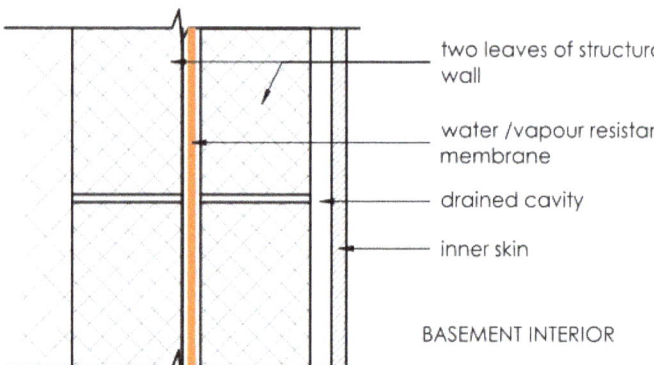
Drained cavity with sandwiched tanking (Type CAs)

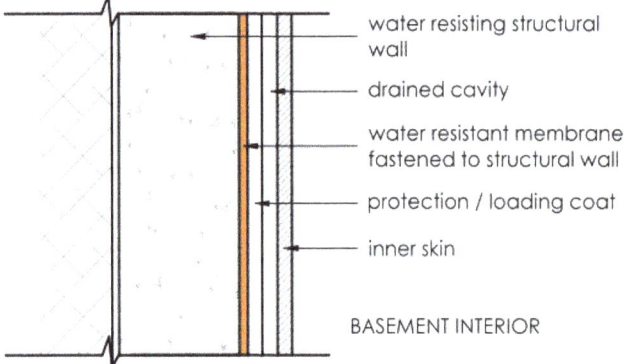
Drained cavity with integral protection and internal tanking (Type CBAi)

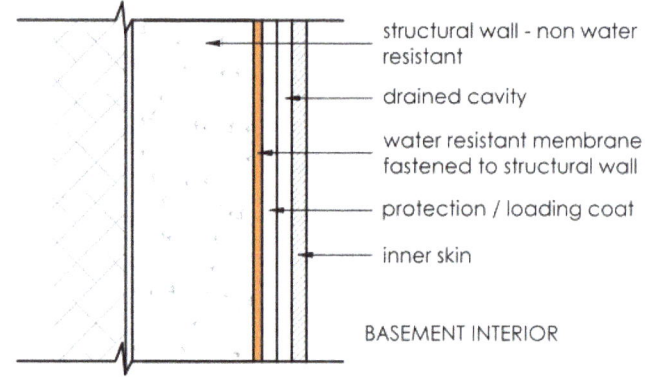
Drained cavity with internal tanking (Type CAi)

Fig. 5.7 - Type C protection examples

CONSTRUCTION METHODS

Concrete is the most common and suitable material to use in the construction of a new basement. Benefits of concrete in basement construction include cost and availability of material, concrete has an inherent resistance to water along with good durability under ground. The method chosen will be dependent on various factors particular to each individual project some of which include access for both labour and mechanical equipment such as cranes, cost, and type of construction required according to the site water table and use of structure.

Masonry construction or concrete blockwork
Cavity walls constructed with dense concrete blockwork with each leave a minimum of 100mm is a form of

basement wall construction. The cavity is grouted with strong mortar as constructed, and can sometimes contain reinforcing bars to tie to the basement slab. This type of construction is suitable for Type A waterproofing protection, although masonry walls are often used in Type C basement construction as an internal lining to create the drained cavity in the basement wall.

This form of construction is only seen in residential basement construction in the UK these days, although concrete is more common in residential basement construction now.

Cast in situ concrete

Cast in situ concrete is suited to all types of basement construction. Reinforced concrete walls can be cast in situ using formwork. These types of basements need initial temporary support to surrounding soil, which can be removed once the walls are at a suitable strength. Care must be taken when using cast in situ concrete in basement construction to ensure all joints are carefully detailed to ensure no water seepage at these points.

The walls are cast with steel reinforcement bars to control cracking in the structure, with particular care taken at corner junctions.

A waterstop is a barrier to prevent the penetration of water through construction joints and movement joints. They are made with PVC or rubber, and can accommodate any movement in the joint. PVC waterstops are fixed to the formwork prior to pouring the concrete and run the entire length of the join on the external face of the concrete. Rubber stops are often cast into the concrete in the middle of the joint rather than the external face.

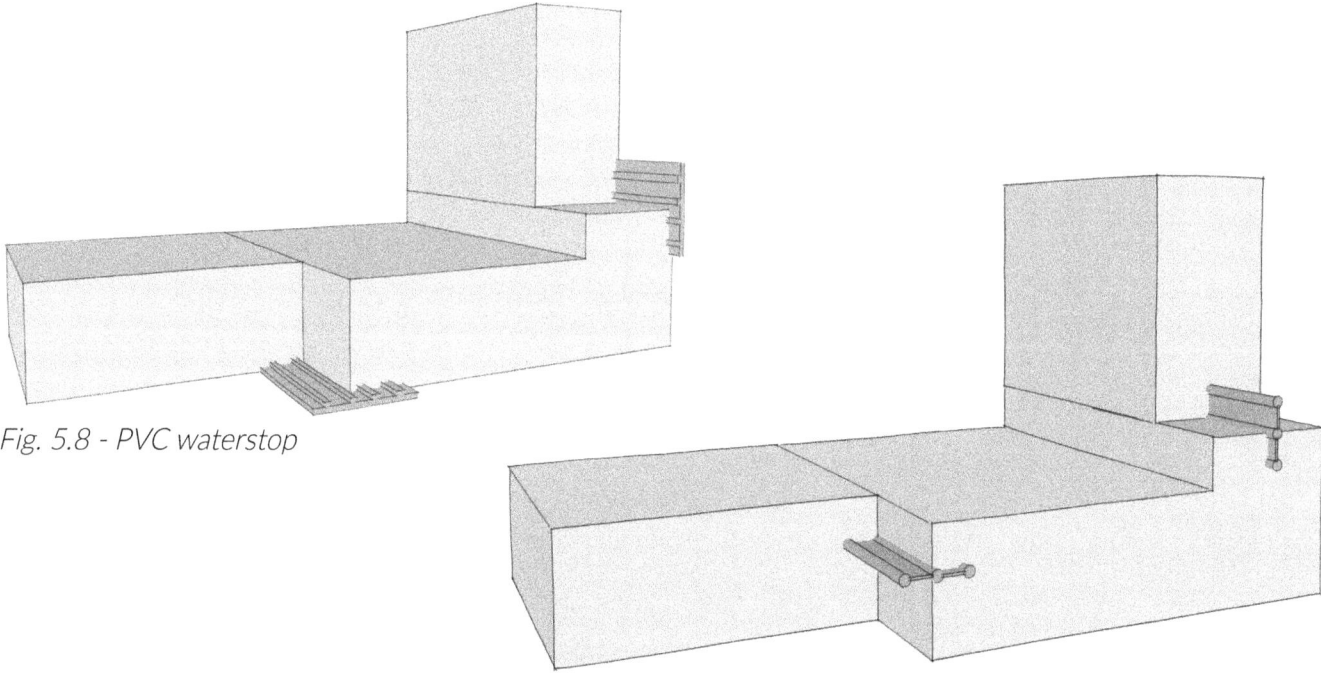

Fig. 5.8 - PVC waterstop

Fig. 5.9 - Rubber waterstop

A rubber waterstop is cast into the concrete wall, and runs the length of the joint.

Water Resisting Concrete

The inherent water resistance of concrete can be further improved by the introduction of admixtures. This provides further protection from water ingress, although very small levels of water vapour can pass through the concrete which are unlikely to cause problems. This type of concrete is available from specialist suppliers allowing the construction of Type B basements.

Precast reinforced concrete

A more recent development in basement construction is the use of precast concrete modular units. These are factory constructed with voids which are filled with polystyrene insulation. The units slot together on site with a membrane fixed to the external face which is then backfilled. This type of construction is becoming increasing popular and can be used as a Type A, B or C method with careful design. They are particularly suited to basements that have a high number of repeated standardised elements.

Insulating Concrete Formwork (ICF)
ICF systems use thin walled expanded polystyrene blocks to create a formwork wall. The formwork is then filled with concrete and then left in place to act as the insulation to the structure. The polystyrene is a suitable background for waterproofing barriers. This method of construction is suitable for new build basements, being simple, inexpensive and effective.

Contiguous / Secant Piles
In this type of basement construction, the perimeter of the proposed basement sees piles installed adjacent to one another extending to a depth lower than the lowest point of the completed basement. Once the piles are in position they will prevent the surrounding soil from falling into the excavation area. Soil is excavated creating the void of the basement, bracing is positioned (usually in the form of steel work) to resist the lateral forces of the surrounding ground.

The basement is then constructed using reinforced concrete with a waterproofing system suitable for the site and project requirements.

The secant pile method is similar, but instead of the pile being installed side by side, the piles are installed overlapping or interlocking into one another. This reduces the possibility of gaps between the units. The basement is excavated in the same way as the contiguous piles. The main difference is that the secant pile has an increased strength and increased moisture exclusion. The secant pile is a more modern form of basement construction, and is more popular today.

Other methods include steel sheet piling and diaphragm walls but these methods go beyond the scope of this book.

BASEMENT FOUNDATIONS

Wherever possible the simplest form of foundation is adopted in order to avoid complex details which are difficult to build and thus at risk of water penetration. Different types of basements lend themselves to particular foundation types, with differing variations according to site conditions and project requirements. If a more complicated foundation option is chosen, it is likely the waterproofing solution will be internal, whereas a simpler foundation form will allow for a wider variety of waterproofing solutions.

Strip foundation and ground beams
Where shallow basements are constructed, a simple strip foundation is often used where access is good. If the ground conditions are poor, a ground beam may be used to support the masonry walls, with piles supporting the beam at regular intervals.

Raft foundation
A raft foundation acts as both the foundation and structural basement floor. This option is a simpler option as the floor and foundation is a single unit, thus allowing for a less complicated waterproofing system. This type of foundation can be used for deep basements, with the external walls constructed from masonry, with a series of structural columns, or the walls constructed from concrete.

Concrete box construction
The concrete box construction is a monolithic structure where the floor slab acts as a raft foundation and the perimeter walls act as retaining walls to resist both the ground pressure and water penetration.

Piled walls
In this form of basement, the piles act as foundation elements for the superstructure, with additional independent pad or pile foundations to provide support to any internal columns.

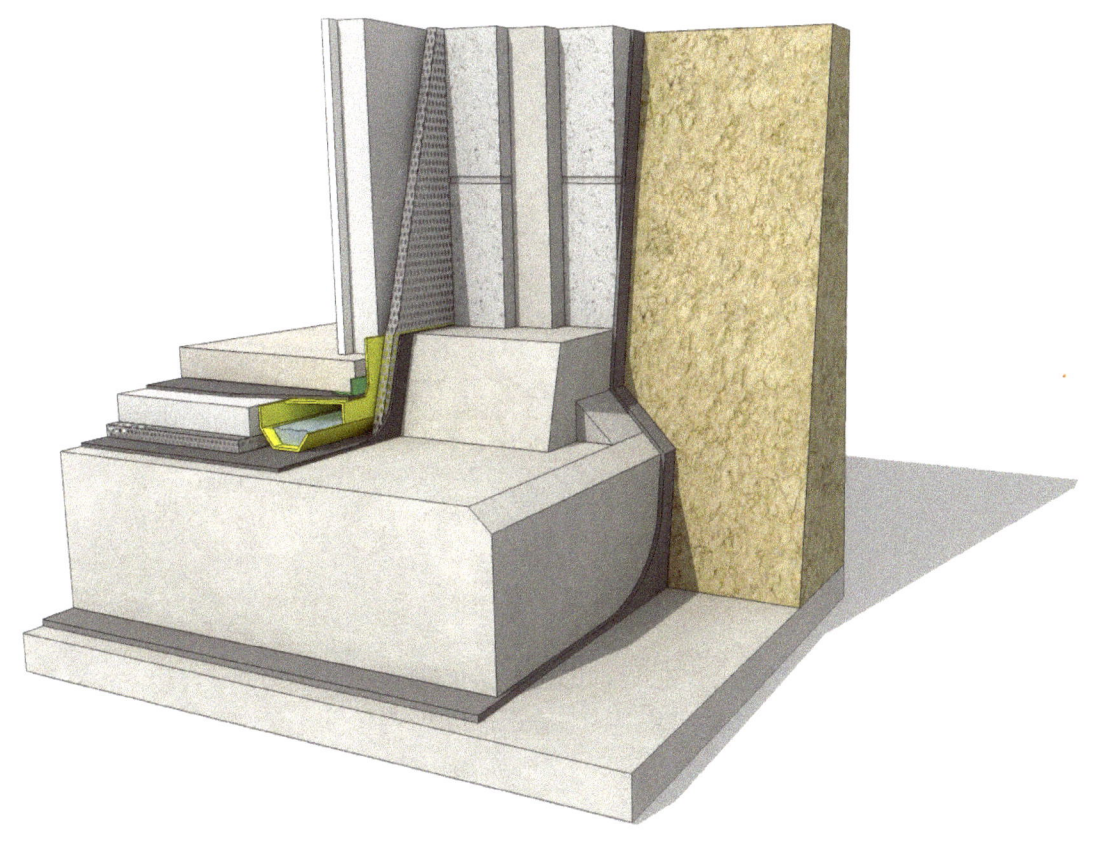
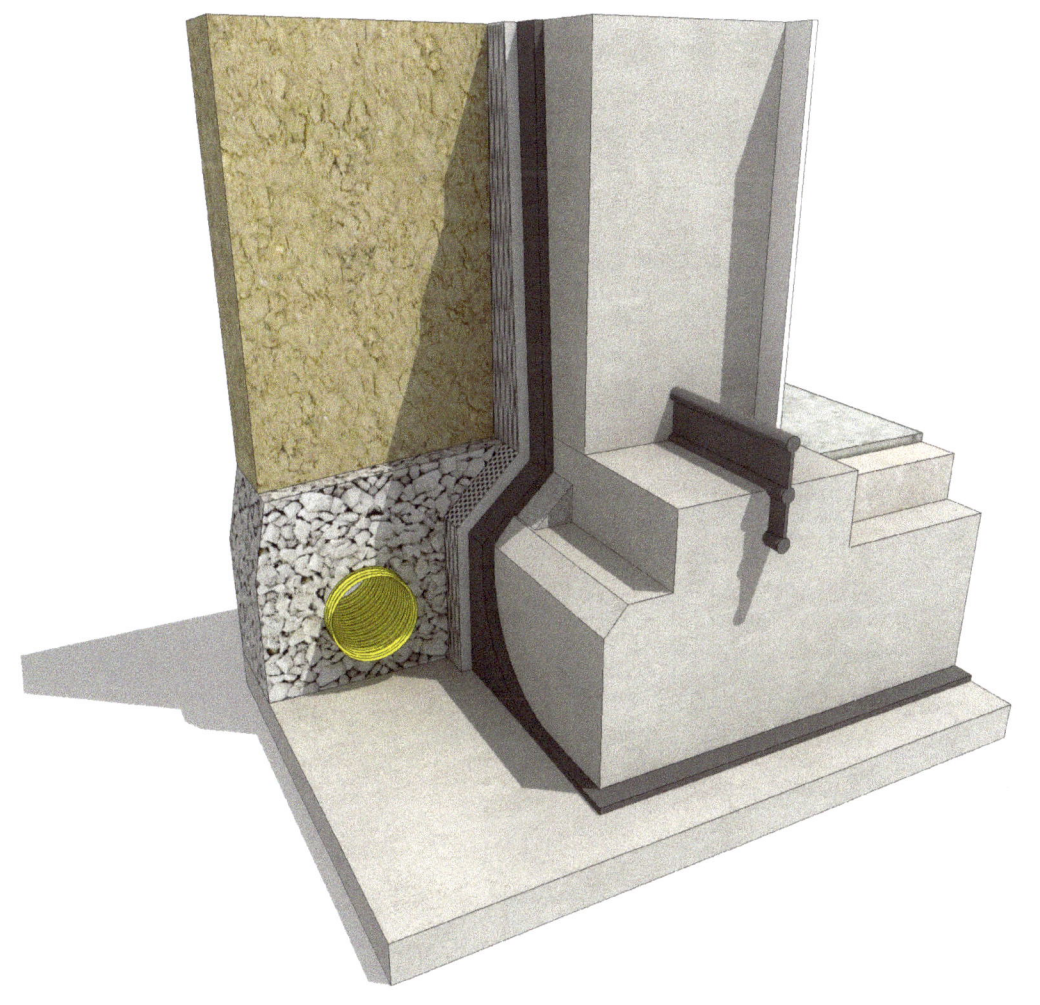

BASEMENT DETAILS

B01
EXTERNAL TANKING (WITH OR WITHOUT INTEGRAL PROTECTION)

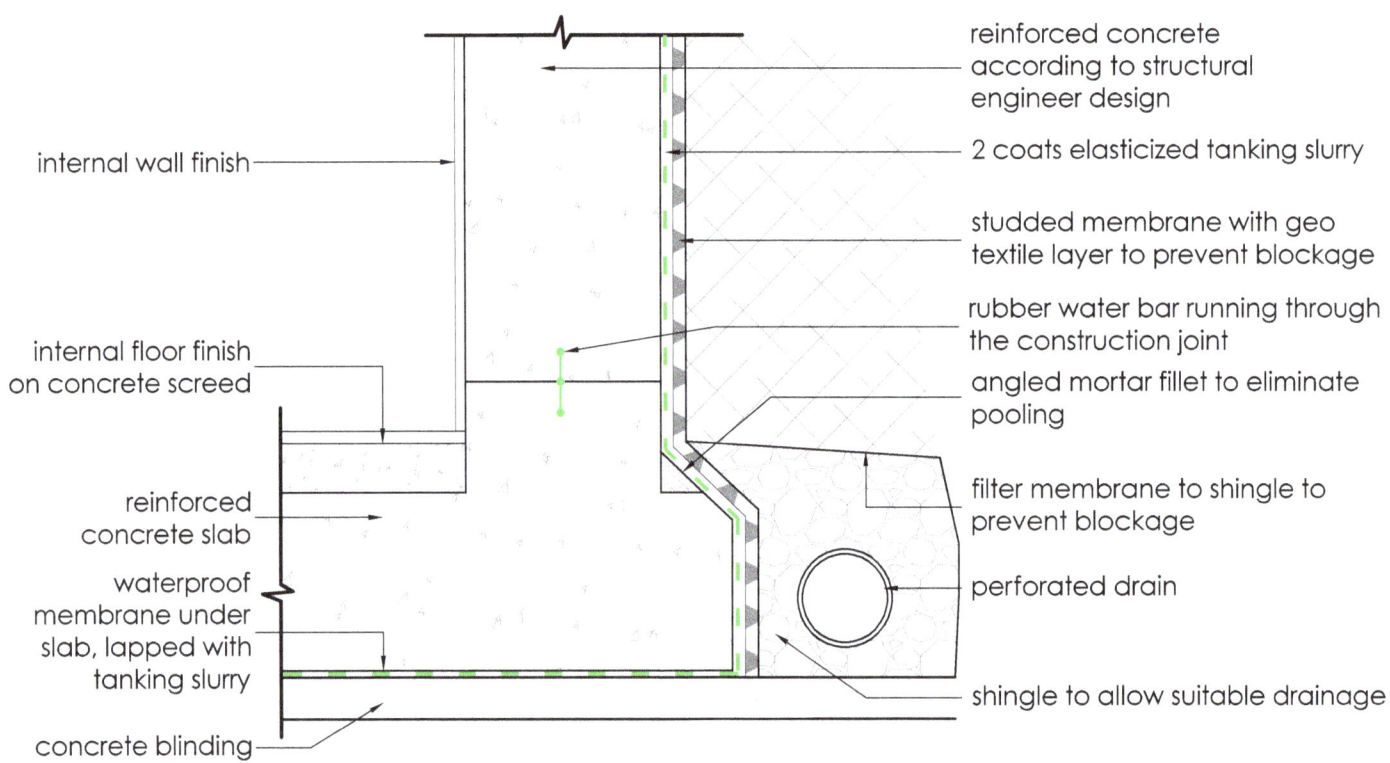

2D Detail B01 - External tanking, (with or without integral protection)

Notes:
This form of construction could be specified with water resisting concrete or standard water permeable concrete - depending on project requirements. Reinforcing bars not shown.
With integral protection: Type Bae
Without integral protection: Type Ae
Type Ae is most suited to small scale basements

SECTION 5 - BASEMENTS

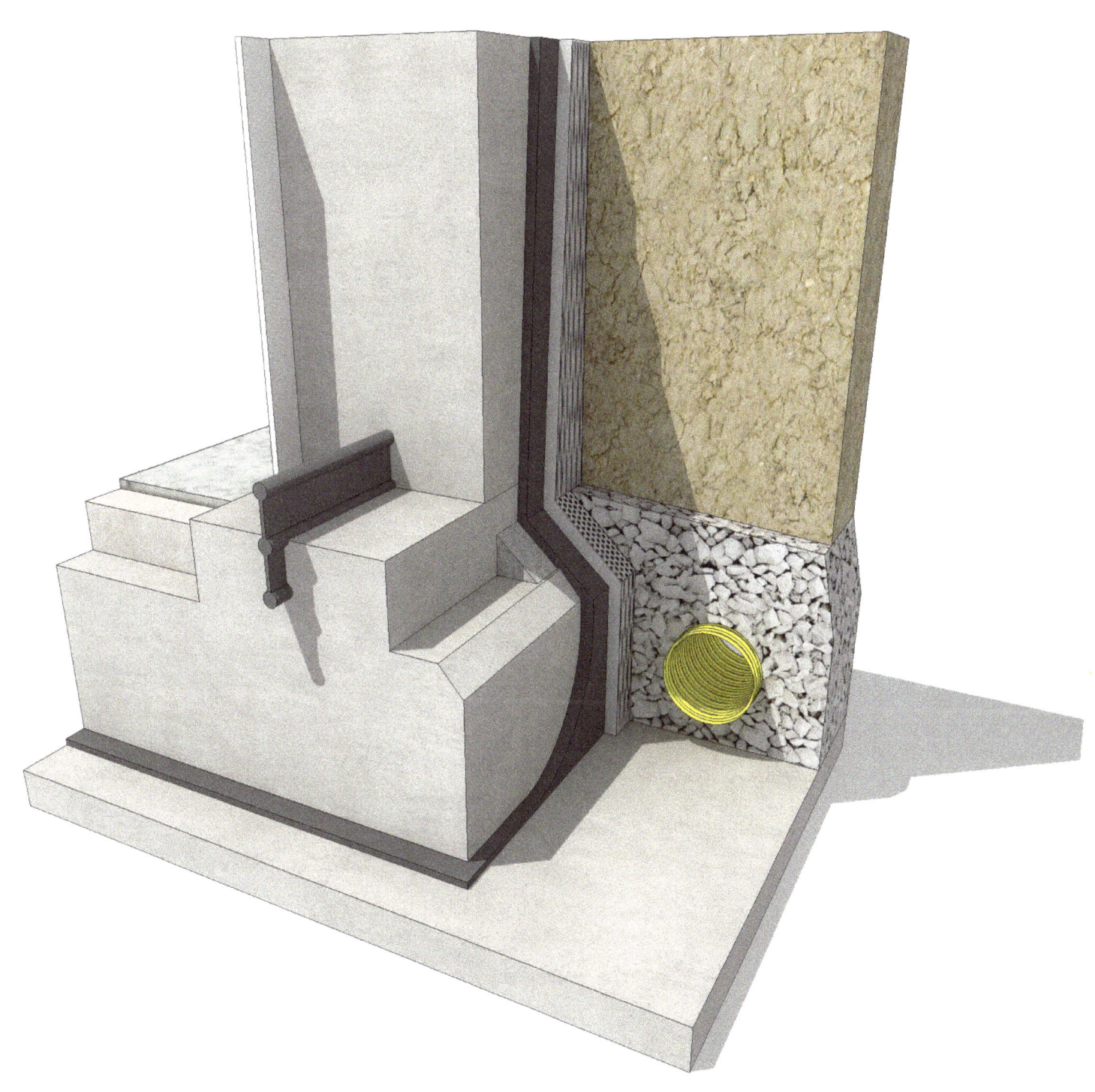

3D Detail B01 - External tanking, (with or without integral protection)

B02

EXTERNAL TANKING, EXTERNAL INSULATION (WITH OR WITHOUT INTEGRAL PROTECTION)

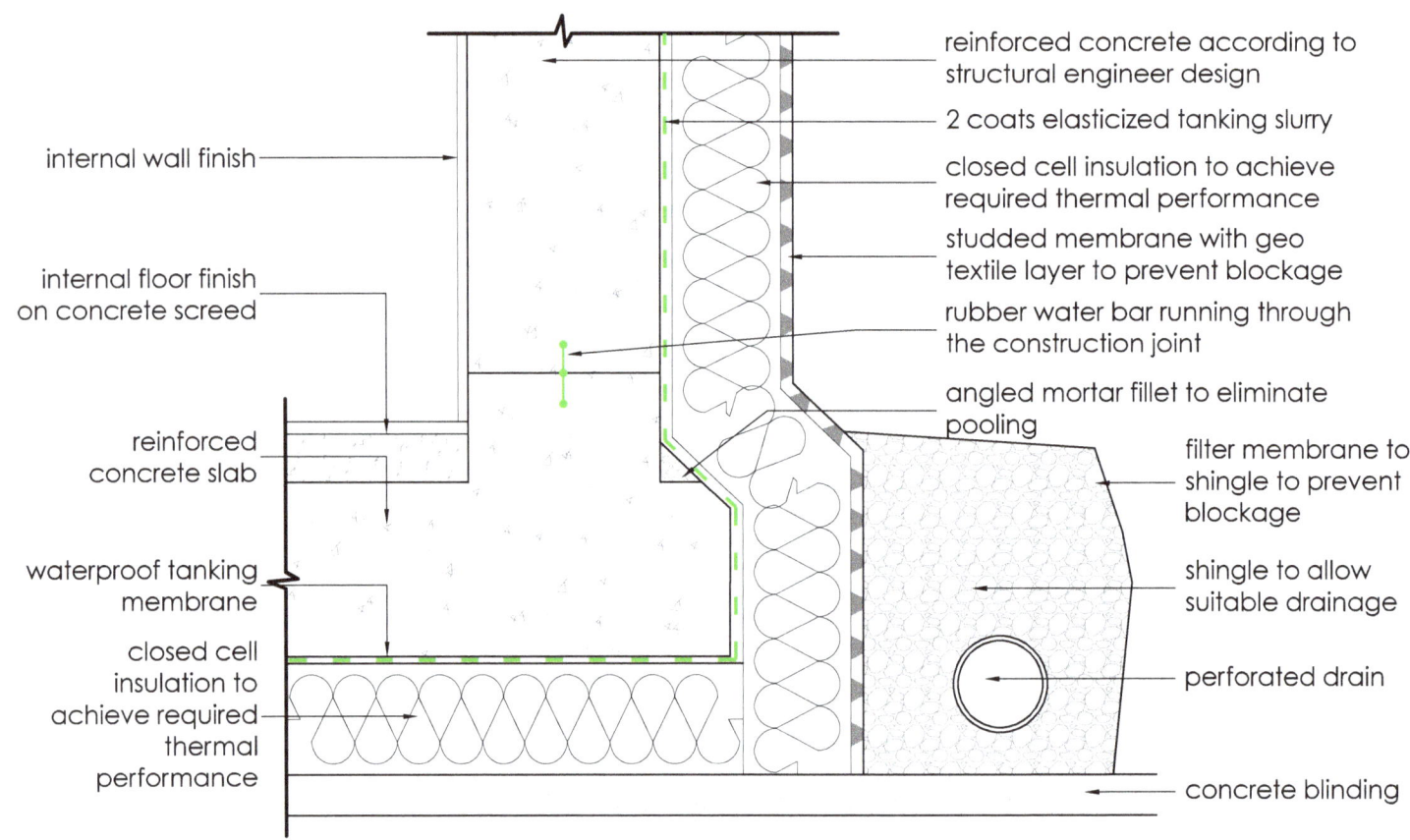

2D Detail B02 - External tanking, external insulation (with or without integral protection)

Notes:
This form of construction could be specified with water resisting concrete or standard water permeable concrete - depending on project requirements. Reinforcing bars not shown.
With integral protection: Type Bae
Without integral protection: Type Ae
Type Ae is most suited to small scale basements

SECTION 5 - BASEMENTS

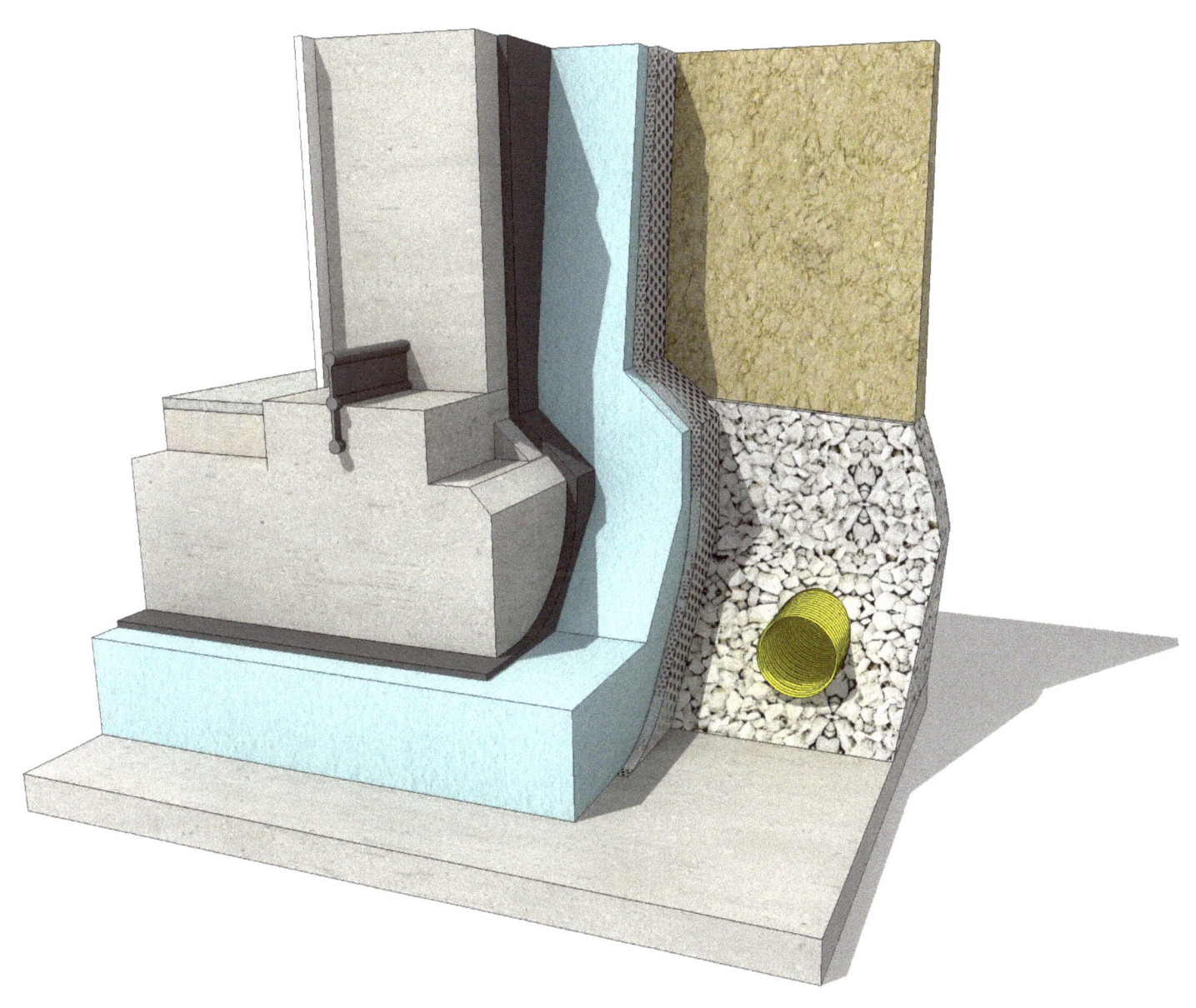

3D Detail B02 - External tanking, external insulation (with or without integral protection)

B03

SANDWICH TANKING, (WITH OR WITHOUT INTEGRAL PROTECTION)

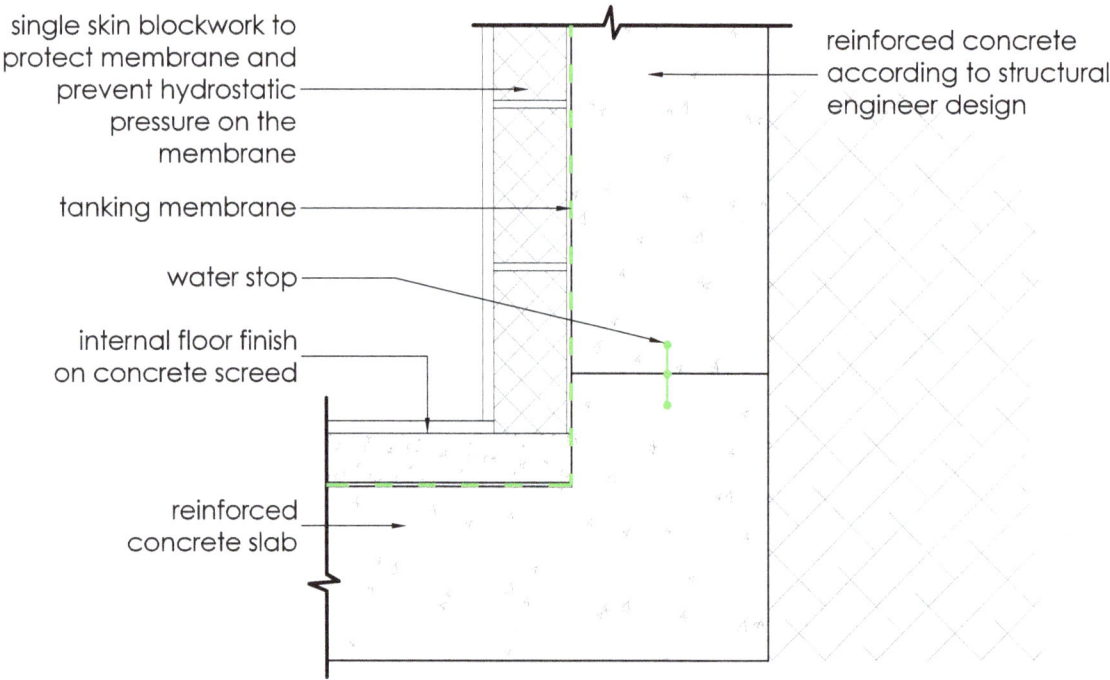

2D Detail B03 - Sandwich tanking, (with or without integral protection)

Notes:
This form of construction could be specified with water resisting concrete or standard water permeable concrete - depending on project requirements. This is a non insulated basement.
Reinforcing bars not shown.
With integral protection: Type Bas
Without integral protection: Type As
Type BAs is most suited to larger scale basement structures and deep basements

SECTION 5 - BASEMENTS

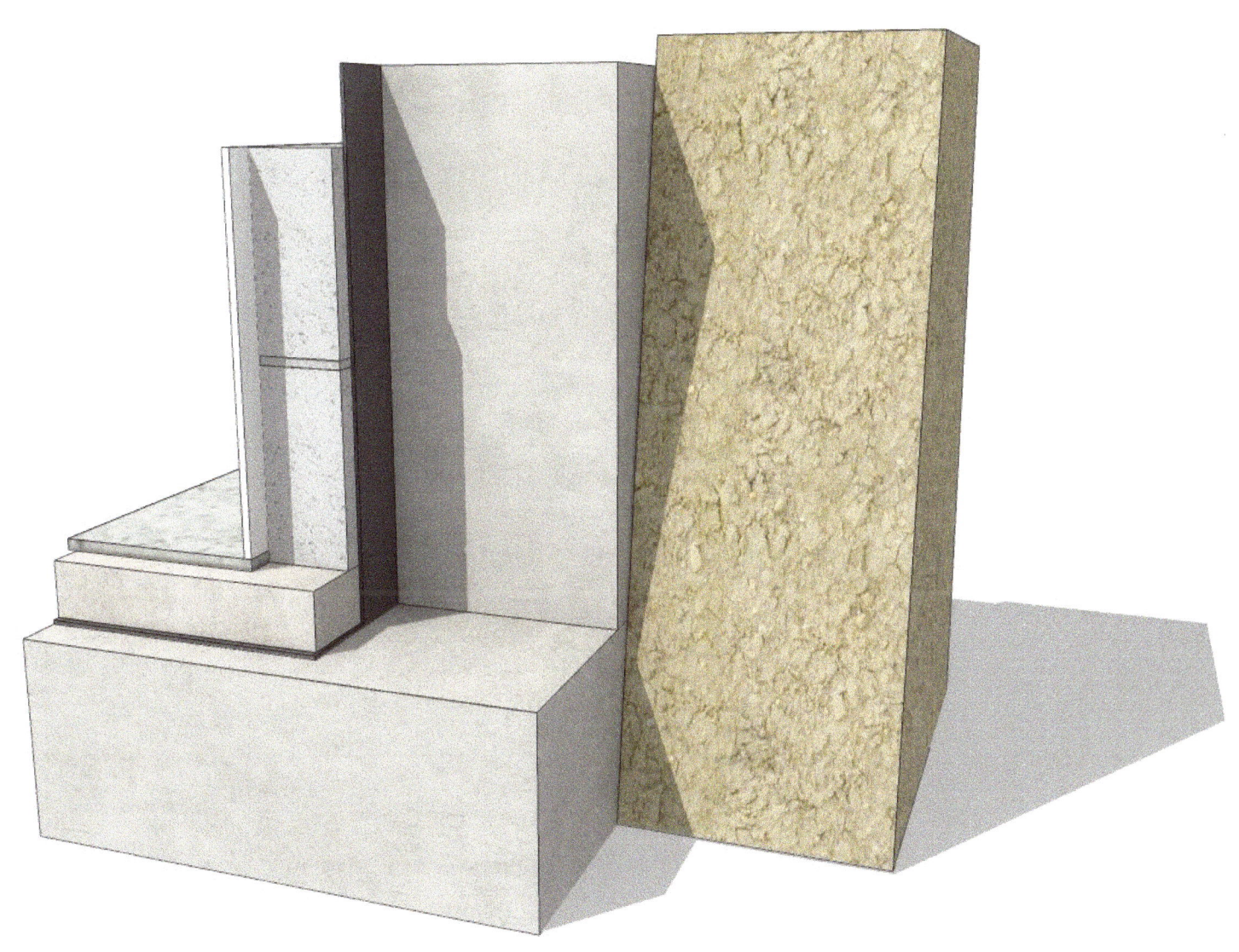

3D Detail B03 - Sandwich tanking, (with or without integral protection)

B04

EXTERNAL TANKING, INSULATED CONCRETE FORMWORK CONSTRUCTION

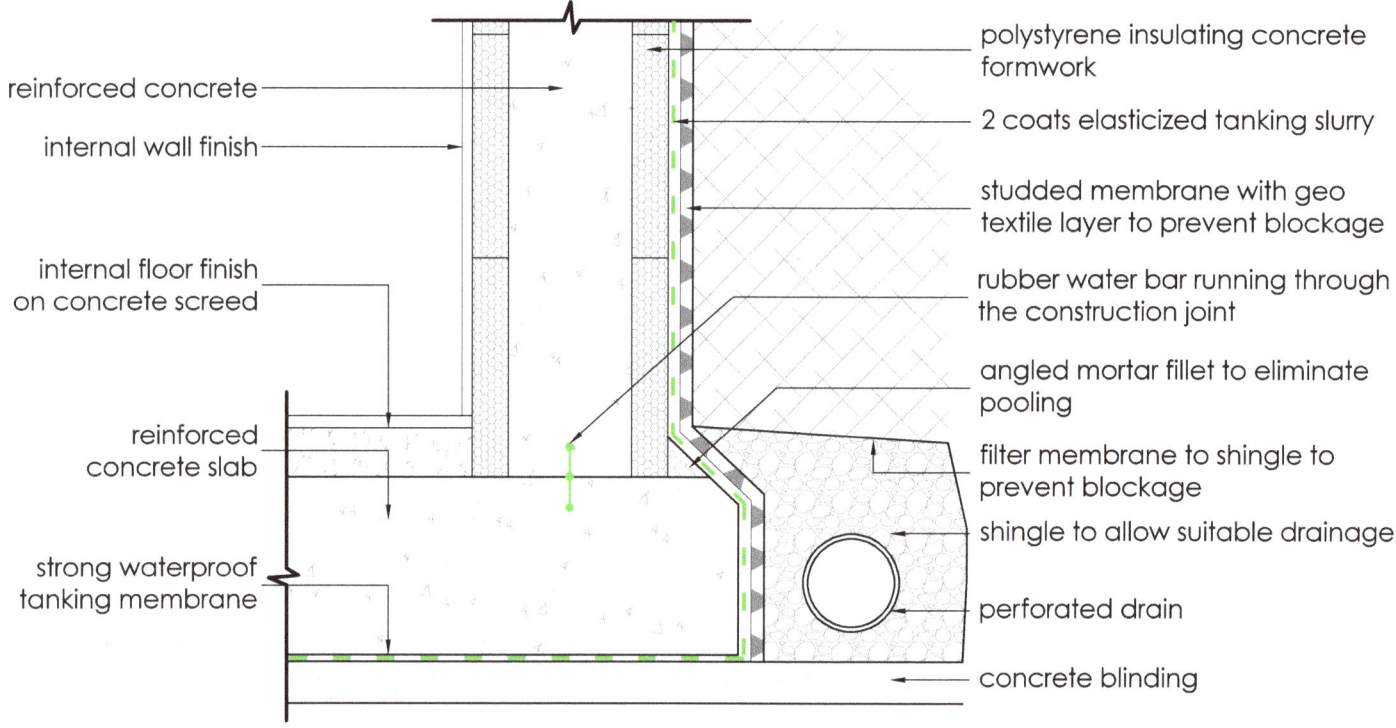

2D Detail B04 - External tanking, insulated concrete formwork construction

Notes:
This form of construction could be specified with water resisting concrete or standard water permeable concrete - depending on project requirements.
Reinforcing bars not shown.
Type Ae
Most suited to smaller scale basement construction with access for laying EPS formwork.

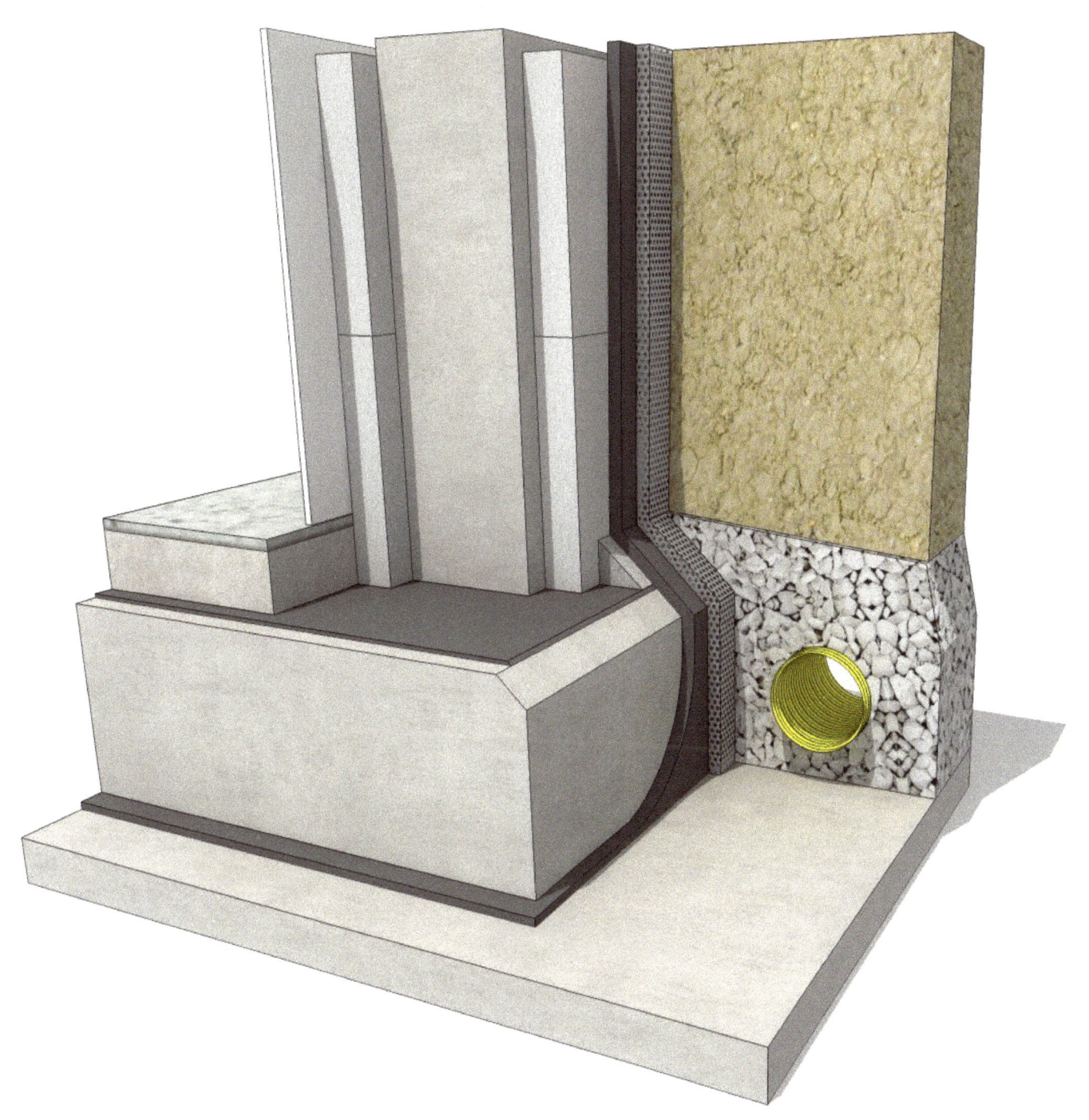

3D Detail B04 - External tanking, insulated concrete formwork construction

B05

EXTERNAL TANKING, BLOCKWORK BASEMENT WALL CONSTRUCTION

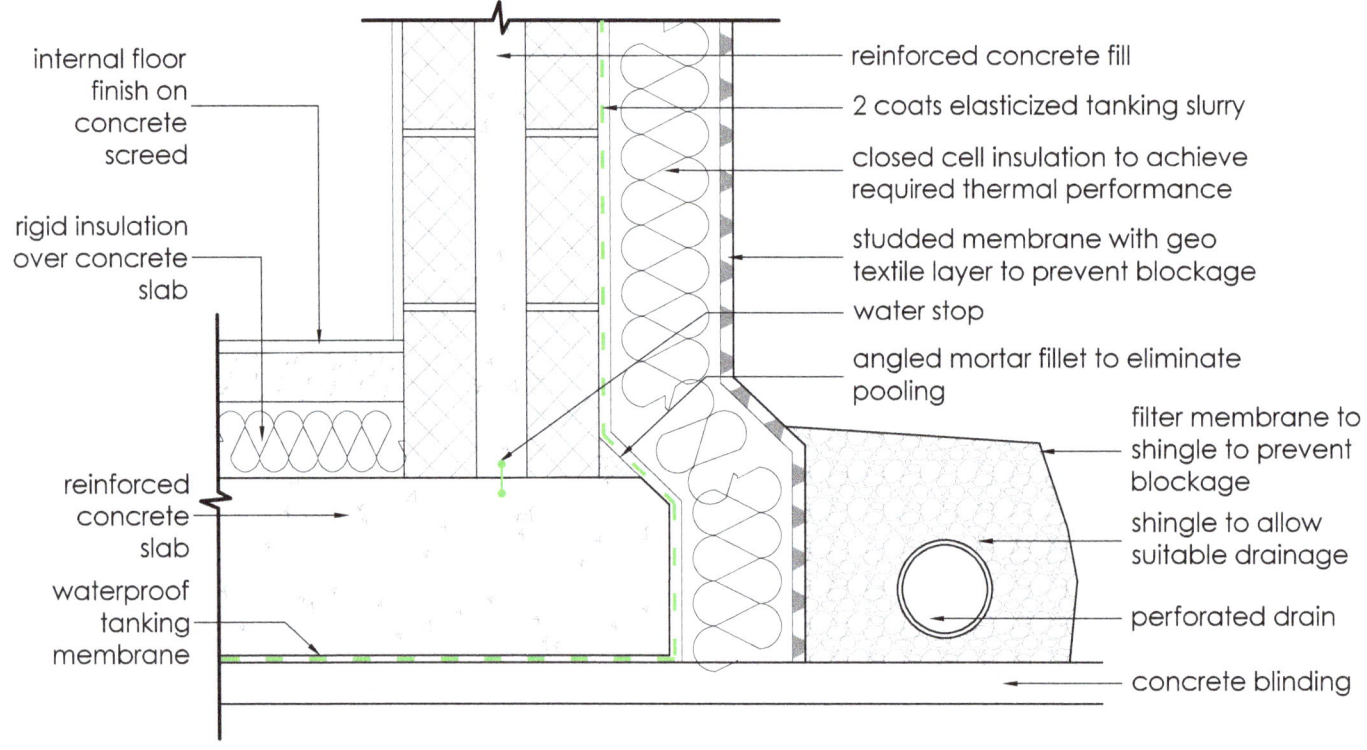

2D Detail B05 - External tanking, blockwork basement wall construction

Notes:
Reinforcing bars not shown.
Type Ae
Masonry basement walling is most suited for shallow basements with good access for block laying.

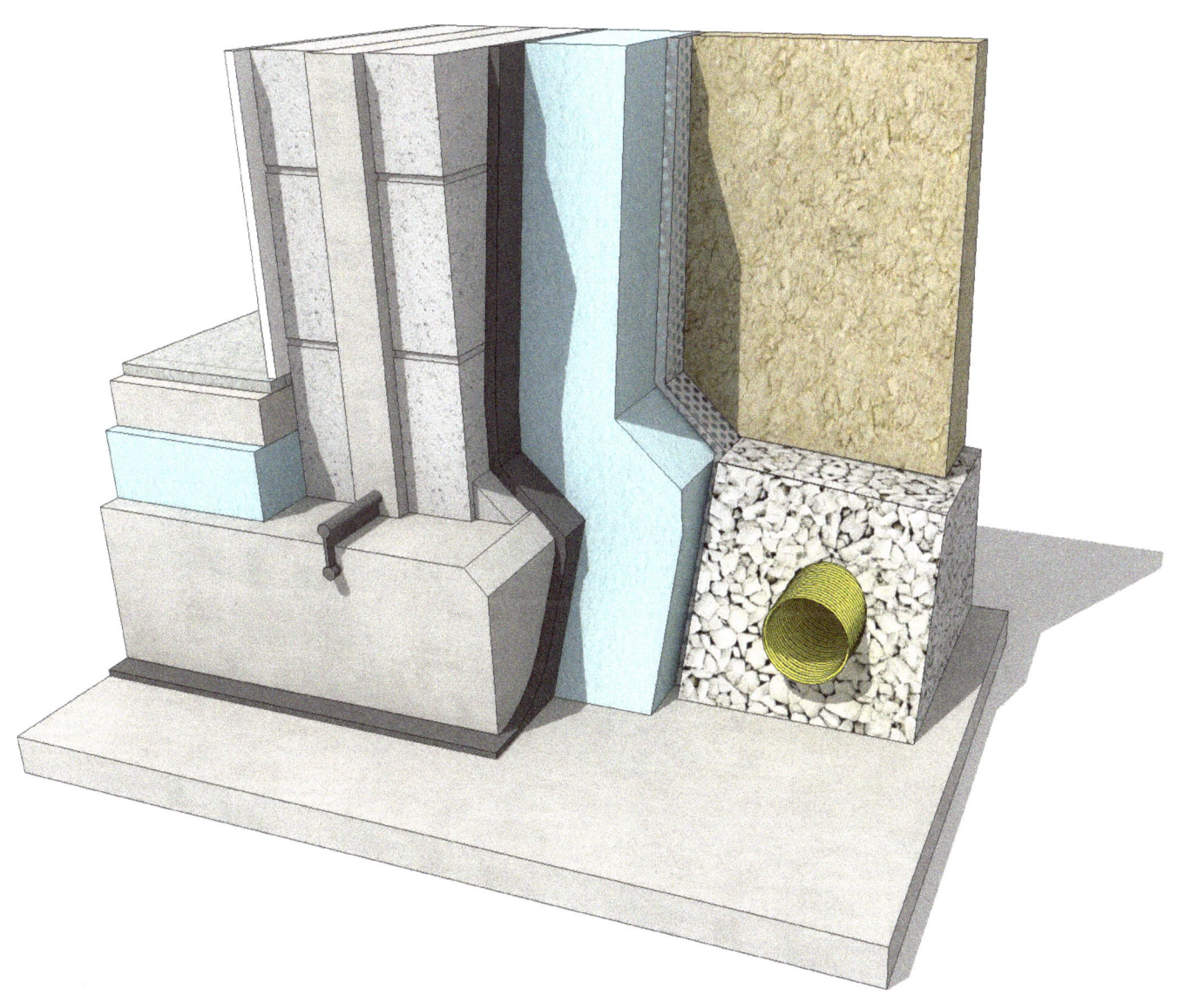

3D Detail B05 - External tanking, blockwork basement wall construction

B06

DRAINED CAVITY, WATERTIGHT REINFORCED CONCRETE

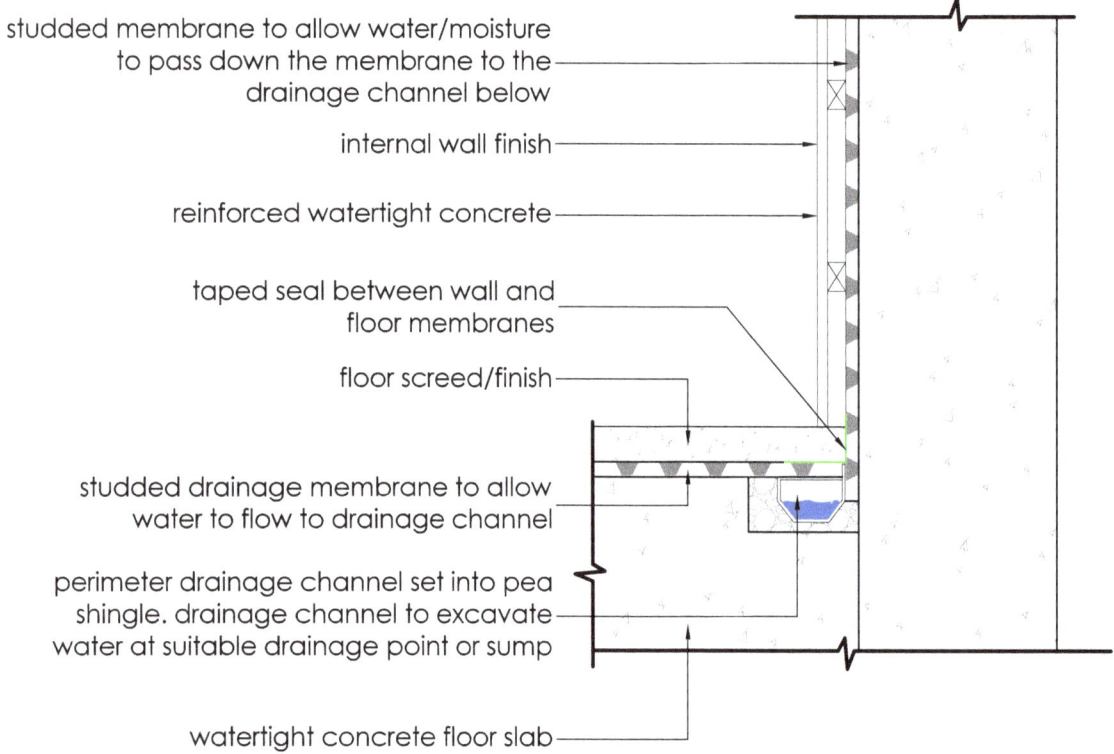

2D Detail B06 - Drained cavity, watertight reinforced concrete construction

Notes:
This detail demonstrates an uninsulated design. This construction can be used with non watertight concrete for a reduced protection. Reinforcing bars not shown.
With integral protection: Type BC
Without integral protection: Type C

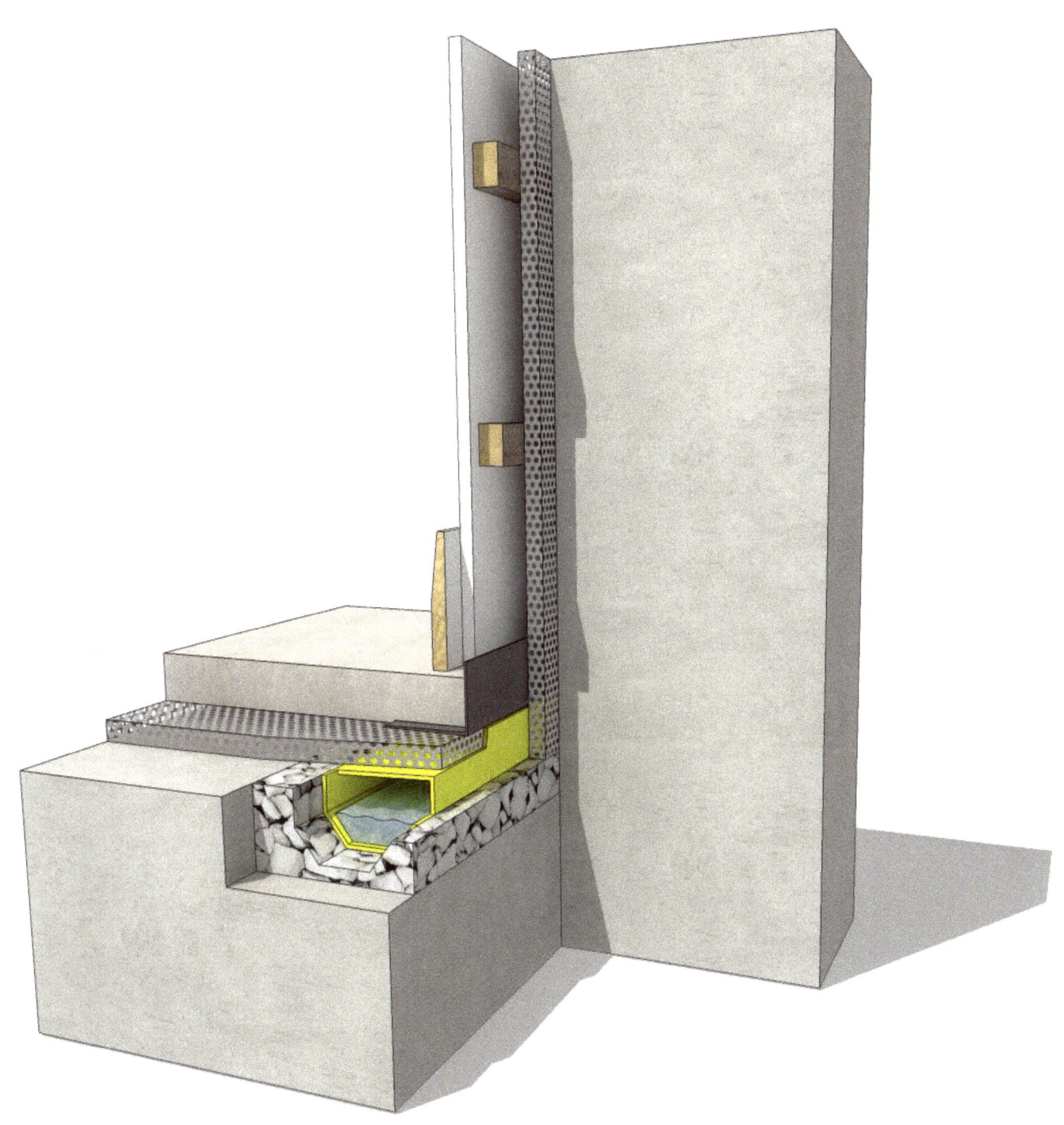

3D Detail B06 - Drained cavity, watertight reinforced concrete construction

B07

DRAINED CAVITY, EXTERNAL TANKING

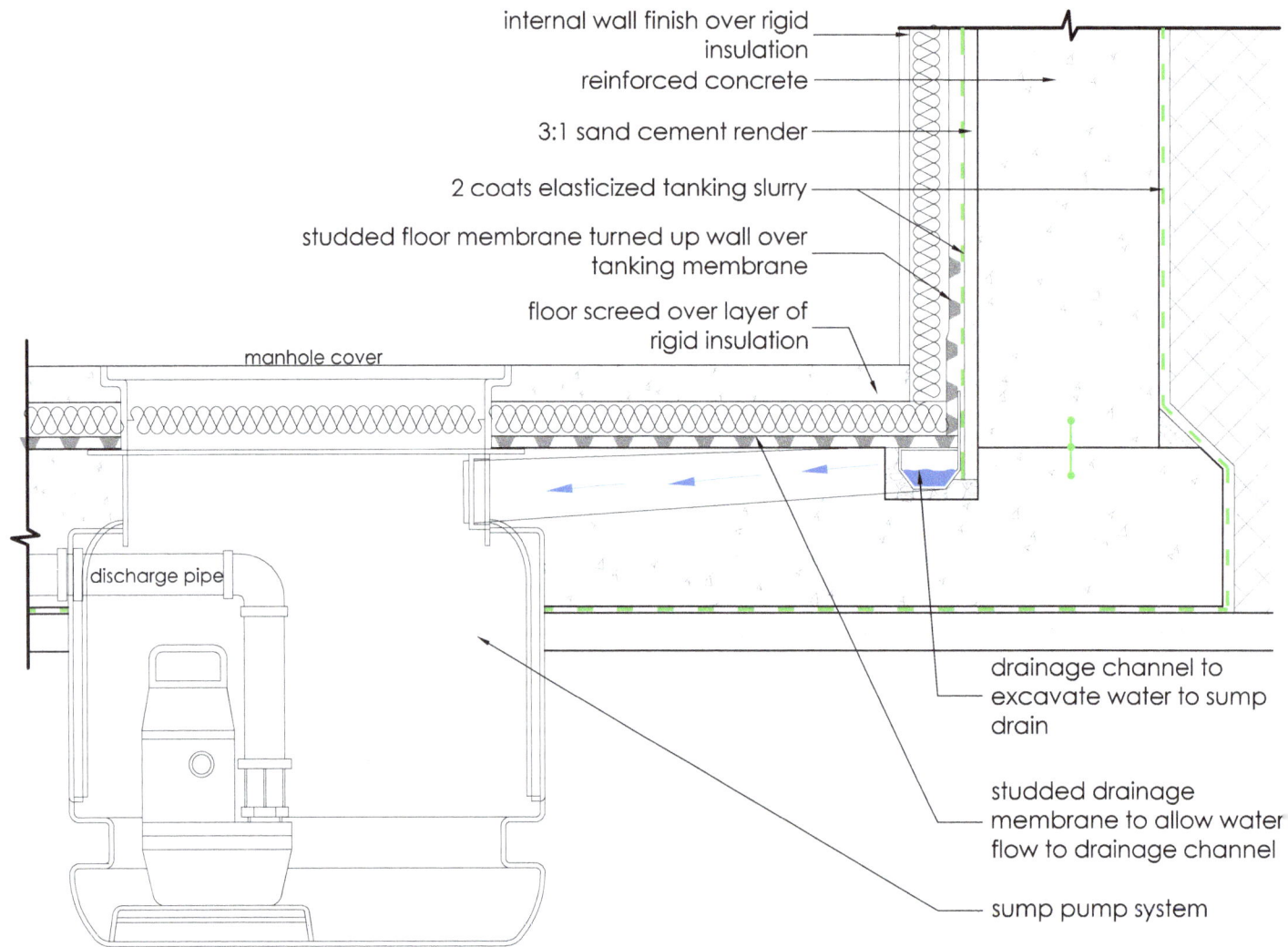

2D Detail B07 - Drained cavity, external tanking

Notes:
Type CAe. Reinforcing bars not shown. Watertight concrete could be used in high risk situations, which would make the construction Type CBAe.
This form of construction has flexible use, external tanking and drained cavity minimise moisture penetration.

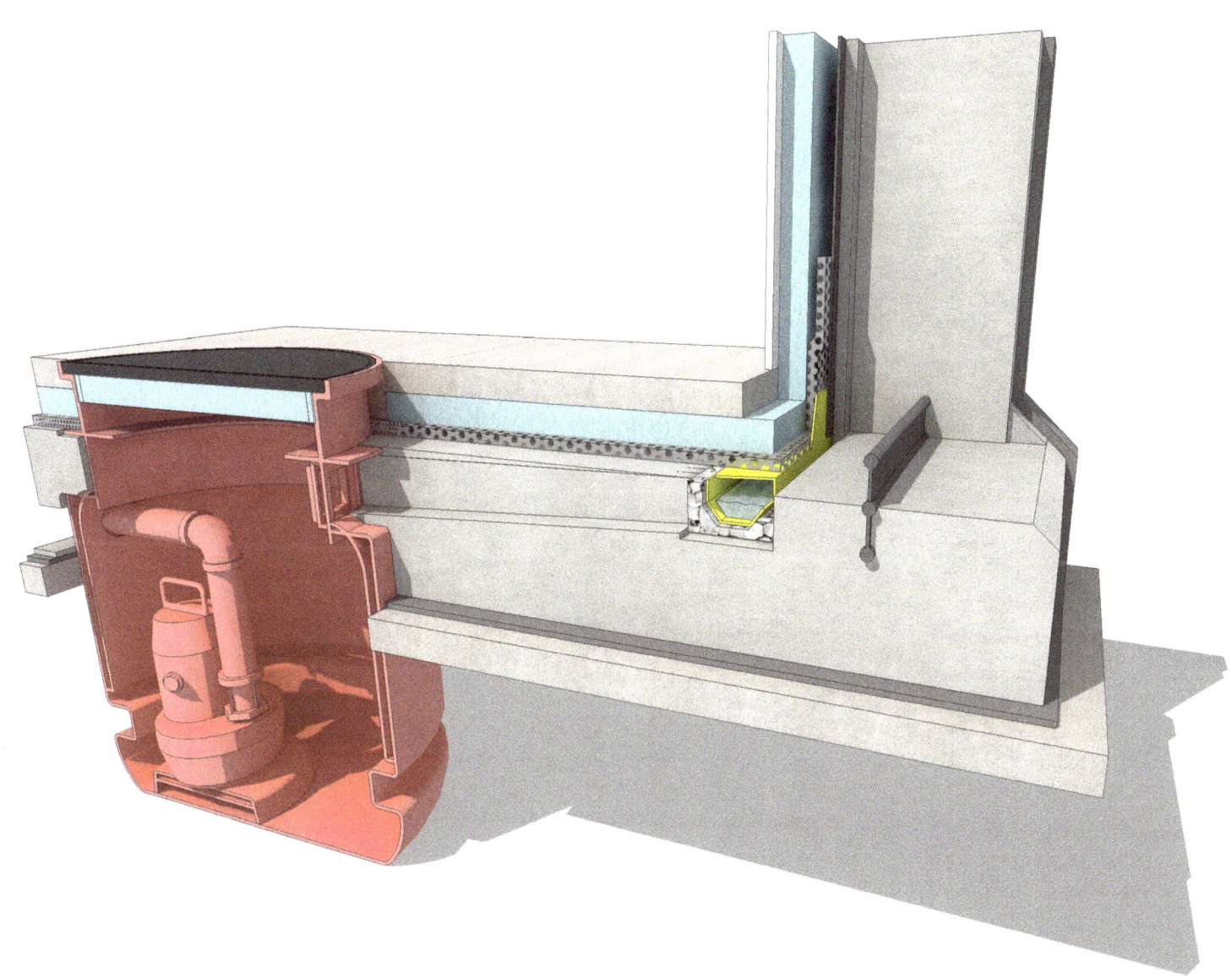

3D Detail B07 - Drained cavity, external tanking

B08

DRAINED CAVITY, BLOCKWORK CONSTRUCTION, INTERNAL INSULATION

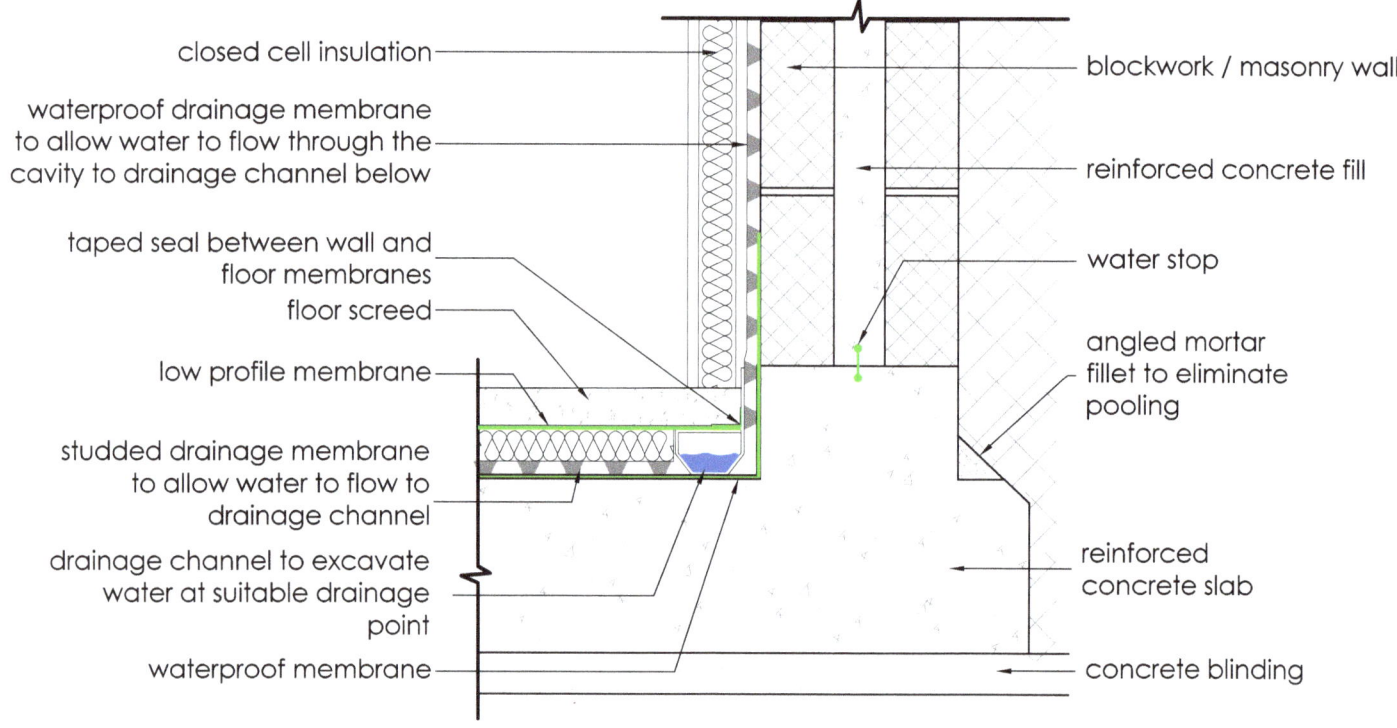

2D Detail B08 - Drained cavity, blockwork construction, internal insulation

Notes:
Type C. Reinforcing bars not shown.
Suitable for smaller scale construction, requires good access for block laying.

3D Detail B08 - Drained cavity, blockwork construction, internal insulation

B09

SOFFIT DETAIL

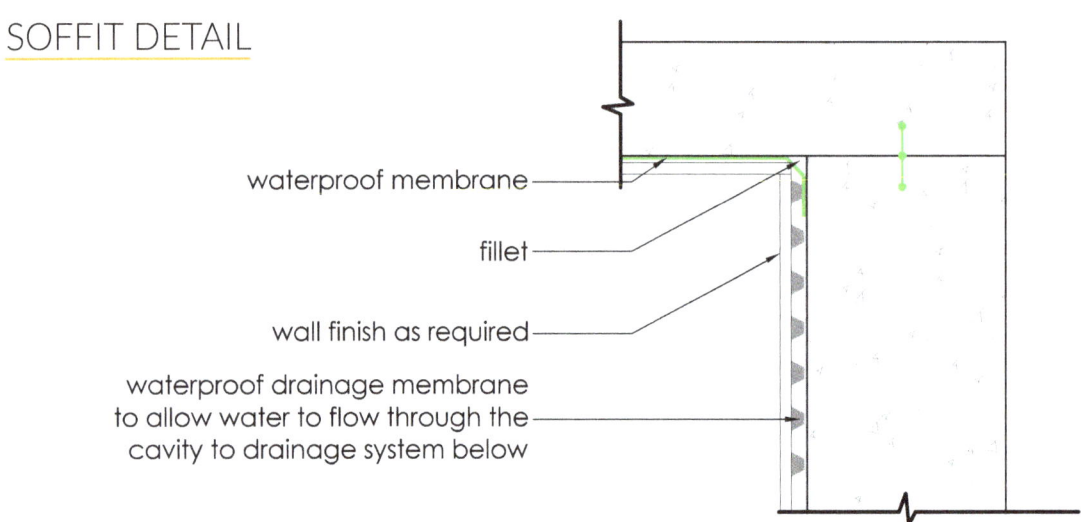

2D Detail B09 - Soffit detail

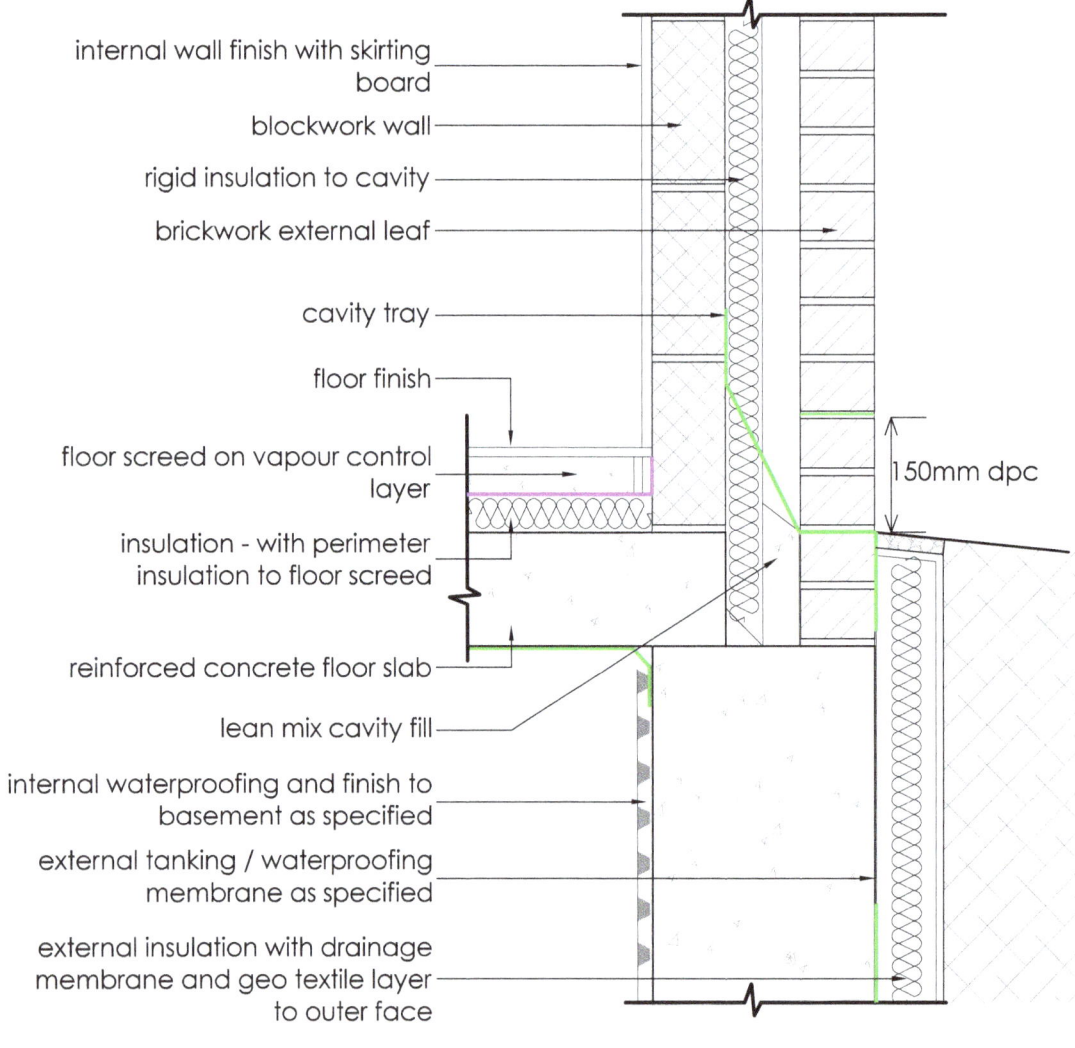

2D Detail B10 - Wall head detail

SECTION 5 - BASEMENTS

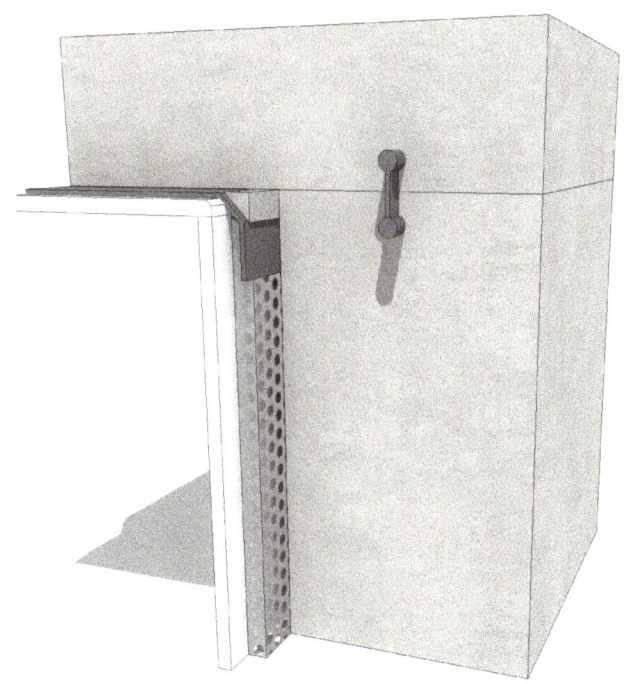

3D Detail B09 - Soffit detail

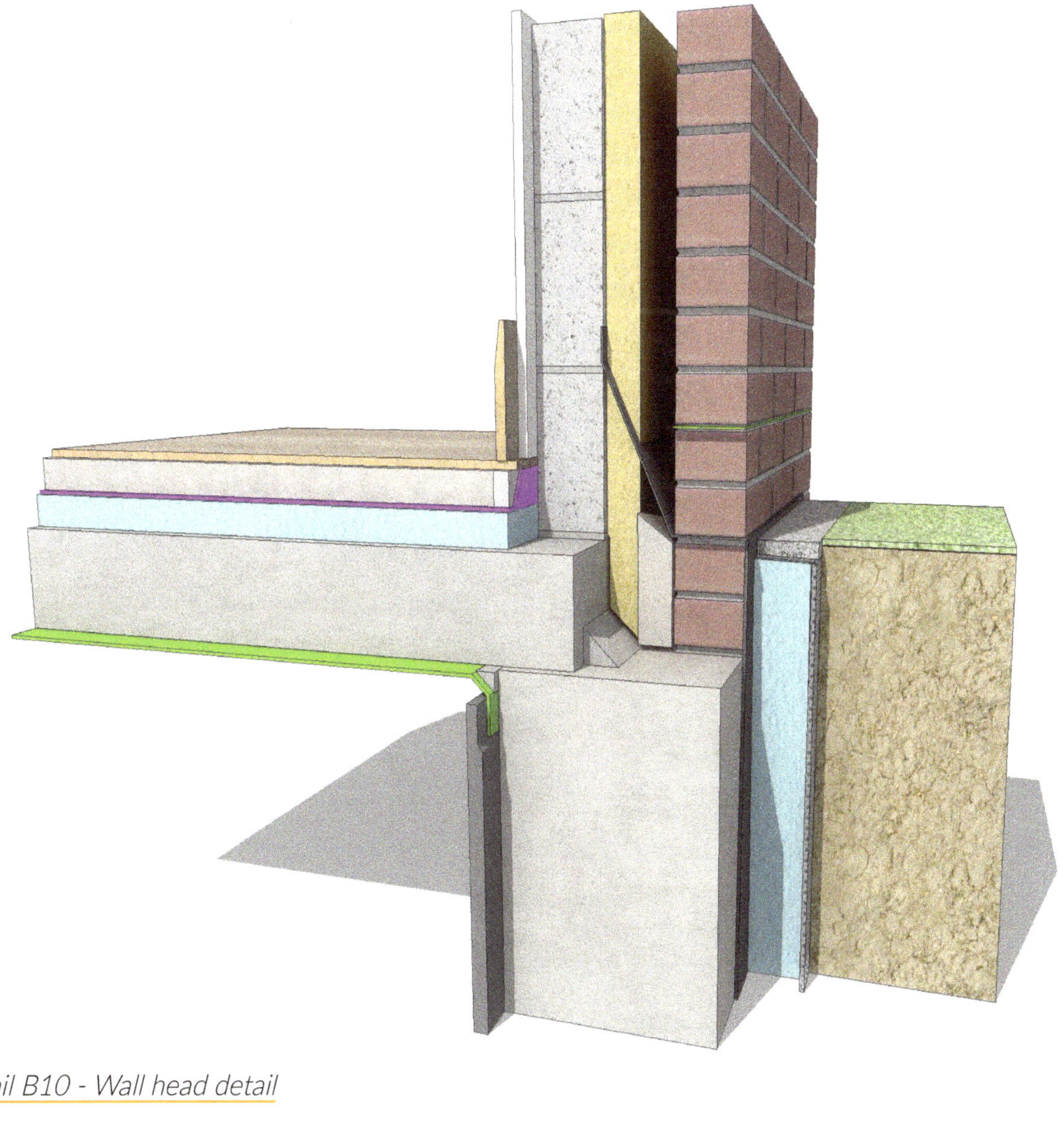

3D Detail B10 - Wall head detail

Blank Page

FRAMES

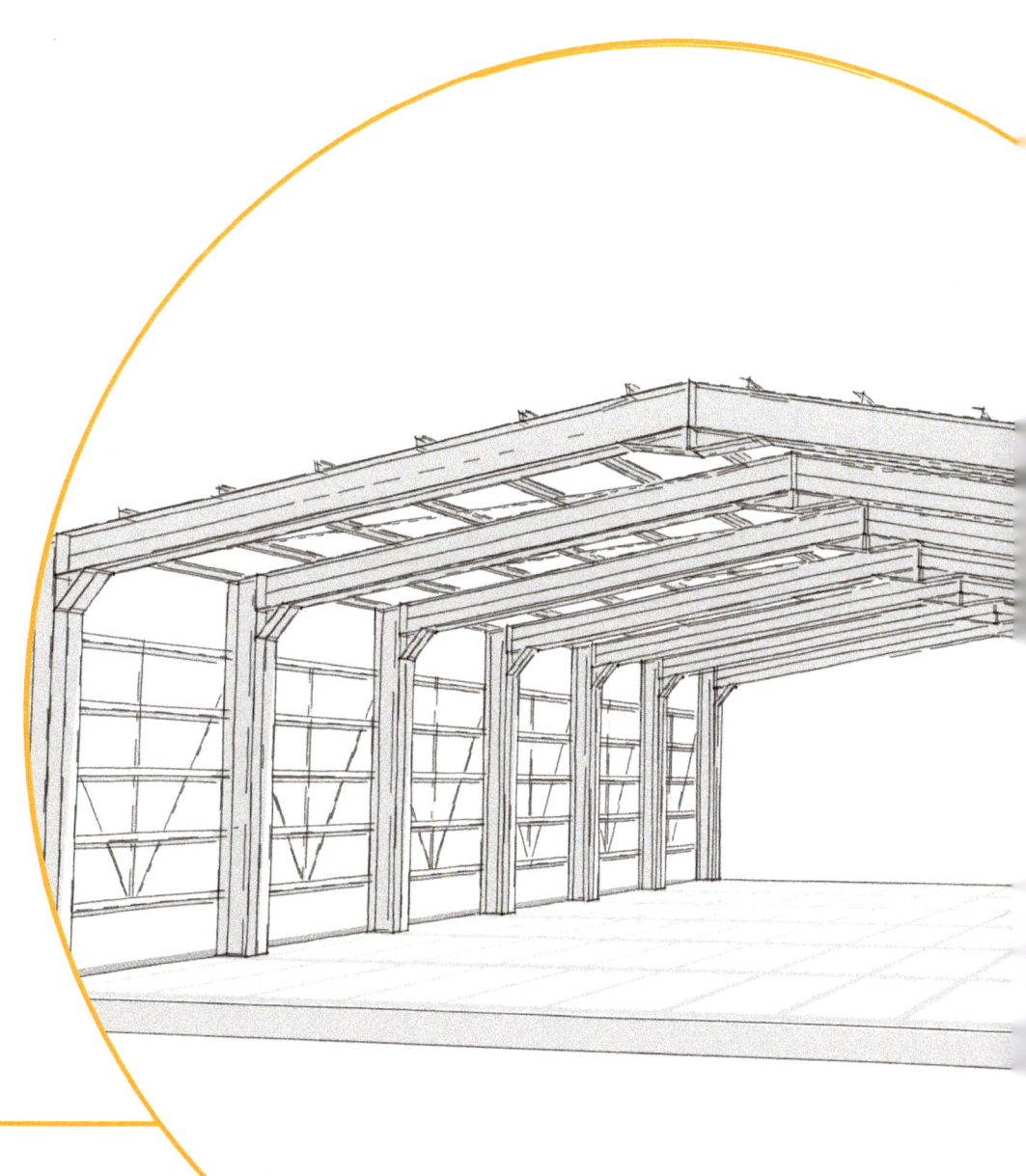

SECTION 6

FRAMES

Framed structures are used in most multi storey commercial buildings and indeed single storey industrial buildings. The use of a structural frame allows the provision of large usable floor spaces with minimum space taken up by structure.

The structural frame transfers the loads of the structure and imposed loads to the foundations. The frame supports the external walling and weatherproofing, the roof, the internal walls, floors, and any fixtures and fittings.

Frames can fall into four main categories:
- Plane Frame
- Portal Frame
- Space Frame
- Skeleton Frame

Plane Frame
A plane frame, often seen as a truss or girder, is flat two dimensional plane, with a series of connected rigid triangles forming a structural member. These types of frames are used mostly in roof construction, they require lateral bracing to resist wind loads.

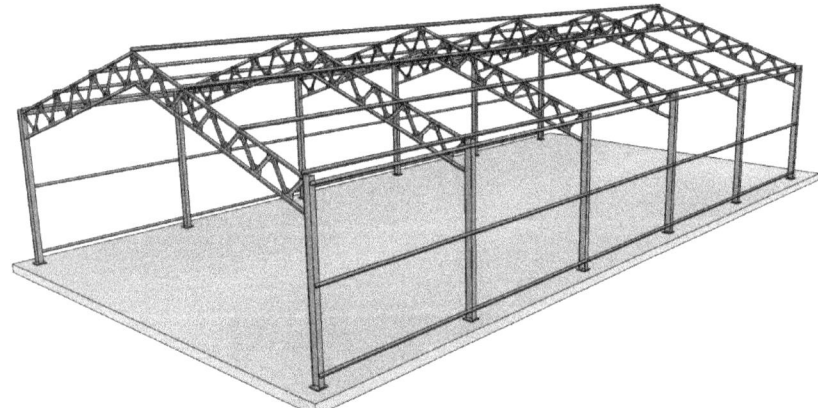

Fig. 6.1 - Steel frame structure with lattice beams in roof construction

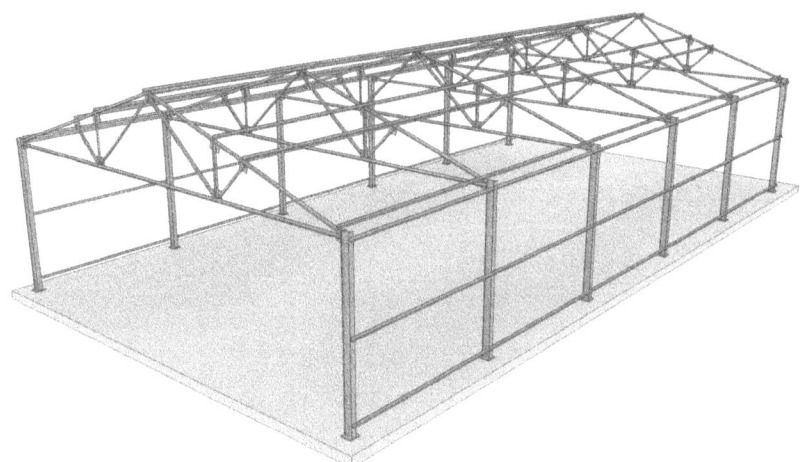

Fig. 6.2 - Steel frame structure with lattice truss in roof construction

Portal Frame

A portal frame consists of a vertical column and horizontal or inclined beam to create a strong rigid two dimensional unit. If they are spanning short distances the connections can be welded or bolted, but for longer spans pin connections are used to allow movement and help redistribute the loads. A portal frame requires bracing horizontally.

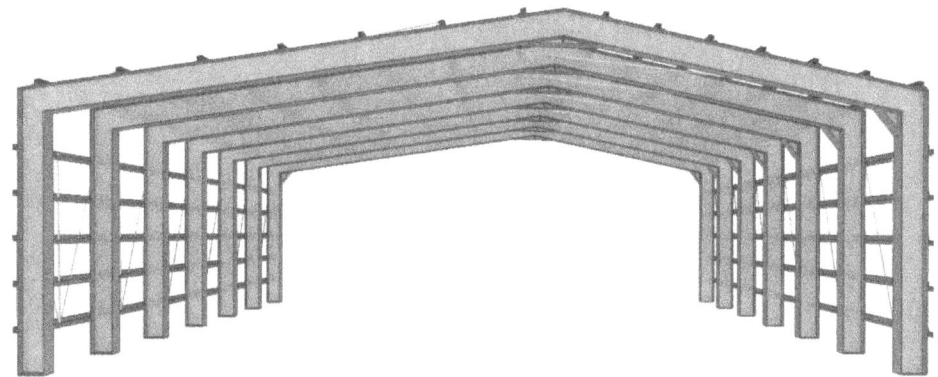

Fig. 6.3 - Portal frame structure

Space Frame

A space frame spans in two directions and can be seen in lightweight roof structures such as geodesic domes, along with buildings that require a large uninterrupted floor area.

Skeleton Frame

A skeleton frame is a series of rectangular frames placed at right angles to one another. This type of frame transfers the loads from one member to another to reach the foundations. Skeleton frames can be constructed using a range of materials, including concrete cast in situ, precast concrete, steel and timber. The most common materials used are concrete and steel, or a combination of the two.

A number of considerations will determine material selection for a skeleton frame structure, including:
- Type of site conditions
- Proposed use of the building (space needs etc)
- Functional requirements (sound resistance, thermal performance, fire resistance, etc)
- Material costs
- Speed and ease of construction
- Maintenance costs of building

There are various factors that will determine the framing system used for any building project. The main considerations are site costs, construction costs and maintenance costs.

Fig. 6.4 - Skeleton frame

CONCRETE FRAMES

The design of structural frames is the prerogative of the structural engineer, but we will touch on the different types of concrete frame structures that are used in construction today.

BENEFITS OF CONCRETE FRAMED BUILDINGS

Concrete offers a wide range of frame options. It is said that a in situ concrete framed building takes no longer to construct than a steel framed building, using sophisticated formwork systems, post tensioning and precast elements. Concrete offers high thermal mass which can regulate temperate swings and reduce operational costs. The inherent fire resistance of concrete means that generally the material requires no further fire protection. Given the intrinsic mass of concrete, it performs well according to acoustic requirements. Building with concrete allows for simple edge and junction details that aid in ensuring an airtight structure, an essential part of the Building Regulations Document Part L.

Demolished concrete is 100% recyclable and often can be reused.

The types of structural frames can be demonstrated as:
- Flat slab
- Ribbed slab
- Waffle slab
- Beam and slab
- Deep beam and slab
- Hybrid concrete frame
- Precast concrete frame
- Crosswall

We will briefly look at these different types of concrete frame.

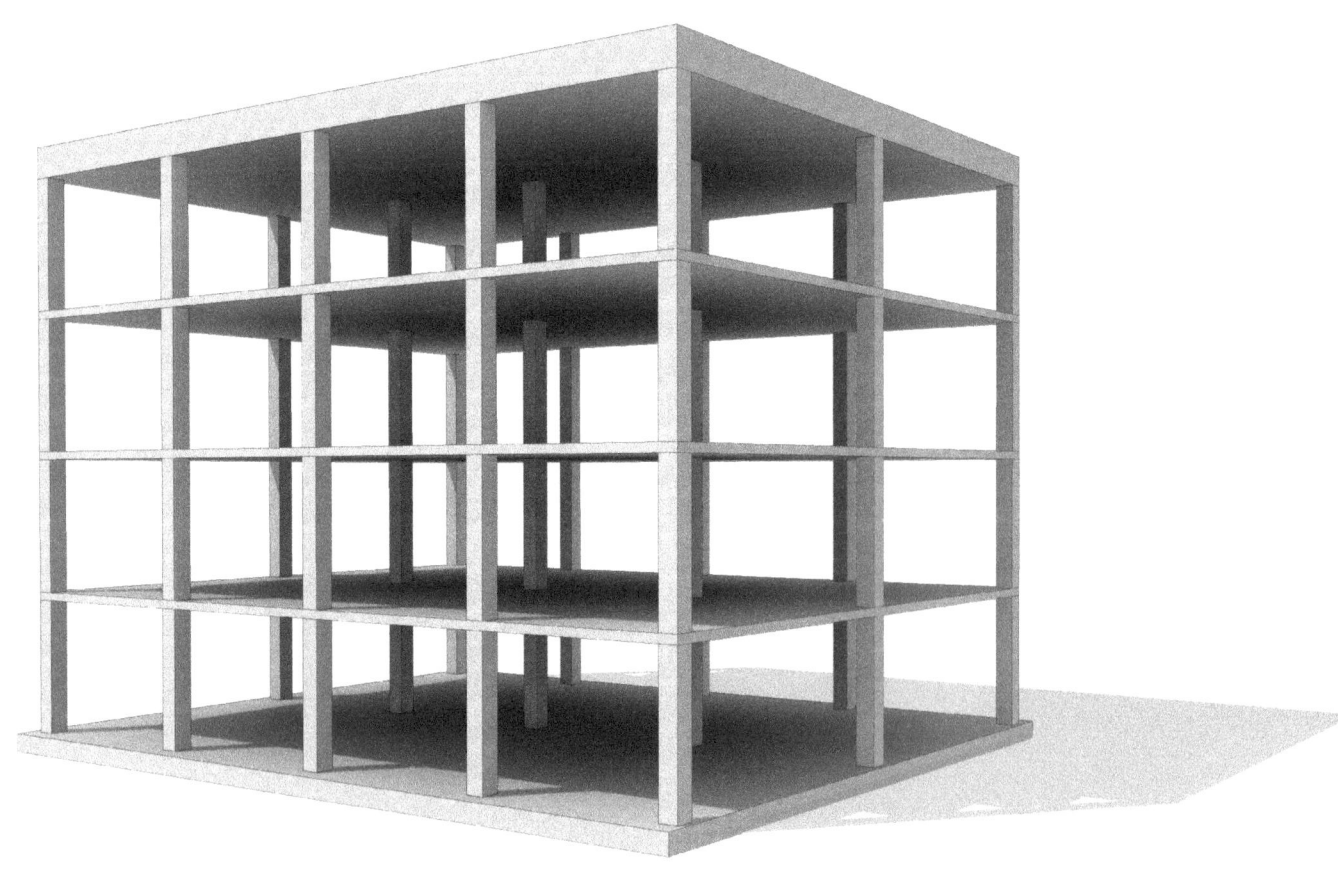

Flat Slab - In situ

Flat slab construction is often seen in modern construction due to its versatility, fast construction and flexibility in column grids.

The flat slab can be designed to have a high quality finish to the underside (soffit) to allow for an exposed surface, and thus making use of the buildings inherent thermal mass.

Used in:
- Residential
- Commercial
- Hospitals
- Laboratories
- Hotels

Benefits:
- Cost
- Speed
- Flexibility
- Sound control
- Fire resistance
- Robustness
- Thermal mass
- Durable finishes

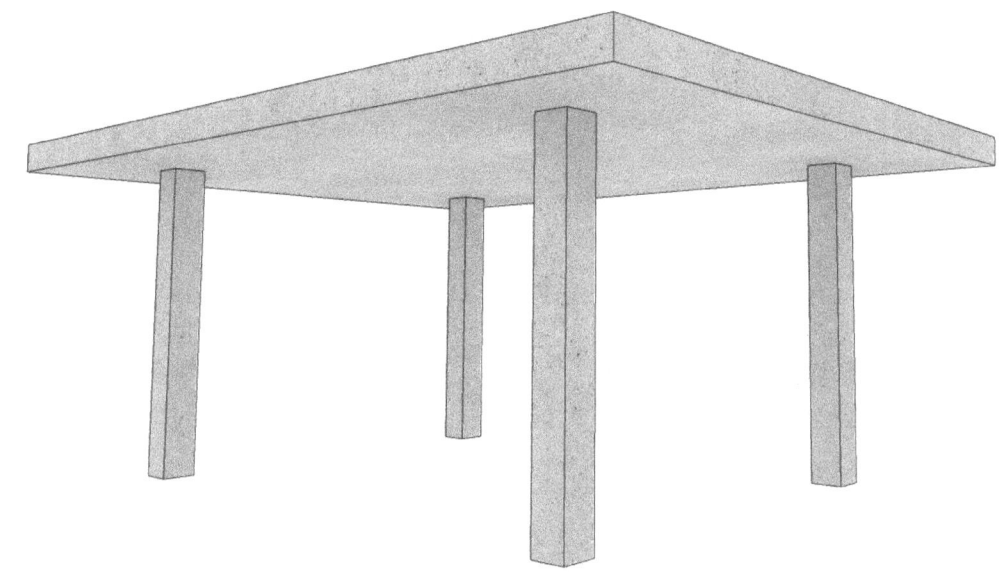

Fig. 6.5 - Flat slab construction

Ribbed and Waffle Slab - In situ

These types of slab allow for a lighter construction than the flat slab, therefore reducing loading requirements of the foundations. A ribbed slab is made up of beams running between the main columns, with smaller beams running perpendicular to these. They have a thin top concrete slab. This form of slab is overall deeper than the simple flat slab.
The waffle slab is similar to the ribbed slab, tends to be a bit deeper and has beams spanning in both directions.

This form of construction is slower than the flat slab, and require moulds for the slabs that need to be sourced prior to starting on site. These slabs can also be exposed to the underside allowing benefits of thermal mass.

Used in:
- Vibration relevant projects
- Hospitals
- Laboratories

Benefits:
- Lightweight
- Flexibility
- Relatively slim floor depth
- Robust
- Good vibration characteristics
- Thermal mass
- Service integration
- Durable
- Fire resistance

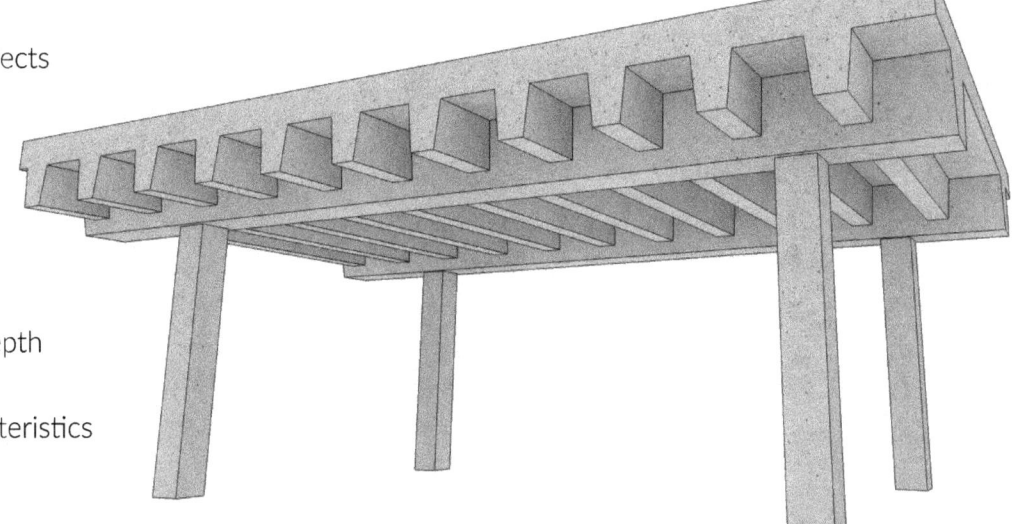

Fig. 6.6 - Ribbed slab construction

Beam and slab - In situ

The beam and slab frame construction uses a simple slab, with beams spanning between columns. The beams can be wide or deep, depending on requirements. This form of construction is used when large spans are required or perhaps a flat slab is not suitable. Commonly seen in retail and storage situations, it is a common form of construction. Beam and slab is however slow on site, due to the formwork required.

Used in:
- Heavily loaded slabs
- Long spans

Benefits:
- Flexibility
- Sound control
- Fire resistance
- Robust
- Thermal mass

Fig. 6.7 - Beam and slab construction

Hybrid Concrete Construction - In situ and precast

Hybrid concrete construction combines precast concrete units with in-situ concrete, producing a robust and durable construction that is fast to construct and benefits from an excellent finish.

Combinations can include:
- Precast columns and edge beams with a cast in situ floor slab
- Precast columns and floor units with a cast in situ beam
- Cast in situ column and beam with precast floor units
- ...and many more

A great benefit of this form of concrete frame is of course the speed of construction, due to the fact many elements can be factory made off site.

Used in:
- Offices
- Schools
- Car parks
- Retail
- Sporting stadiums

Benefits:
- Cost
- Speed
- Accuracy of prefabricated elements
- Sound control
- Fire resistance
- Robust
- Thermal mass
- Durable
- Safety

Precast Concrete Frames - precast

Precast concrete frames are becoming more popular in recent times after they fell out of favour in the 1960's due to structural failures in the connections. Most of the problems have since been resolved and precast frames are gaining traction.

Precast concrete frames come with the benefit of speed of construction and a good finish. They are best specified when a large amount of repetition is required in order to reduce the amount of moulds required for prefabrication.

Precast frames are often designed by specialist contractors who would take particular care on junction design. Precast columns are connected to foundations using one of two methods. For lighter loads, a pocket can be formed in the foundation that allows the precast column to be positioned within the pocket, then grouted to fix its position once levelled. Alternatively the column can be fixed to the foundation by welding a base plate to the column which can then be fixed to the foundation using holding down bolts.
Connections between column to column or beam to beam have many configurations, but the key is to maintain continuity within the joint. This is achieved with a selection of dowel joints, lapped reinforcement bars, along with the use of reinforced in situ concrete.

Used in:
- Residential
- Hotels
- Car parks
- Shopping centres
- Commercial
- Student accommodation
- Prisons

Benefits:
- Speed on site
- Accuracy of prefabricated elements
- Sound control
- Fire resistance
- Robustness
- Thermal mass
- Durable finishes
- Safety
- Minimal deliveries

Crosswall - Precast

Crosswall is a precast system often used where there is a repetitive cellular plan, such as hotels, housing, student accommodation. All of the elements are precast, such as walls and slabs, including stairs, which are delivered to site and craned into position. The wall panels can have finishes applied after positioning, or they can be prefabricated sandwich panels with the finish forming part of the panel itself along with insulation incorporated into the panel.

The construction on site of the crosswall system is fast, due to the use of prefabricated units, and the repetitive nature of the plan. The units are craned directly into possible from the delivery vehicle, thus avoiding the need for on site storage. Once in position, the joints are grouted between the elements.

Used in:
- Residential
- Housing
- Hotels and hostels
- Student accommodation
- Prisons

Benefits:
- Speed
- Accuracy of prefabrication
- Sound control
- Fire resistance
- Robustness
- Thermal mass
- Durable
- Safety
- Minimal deliveries

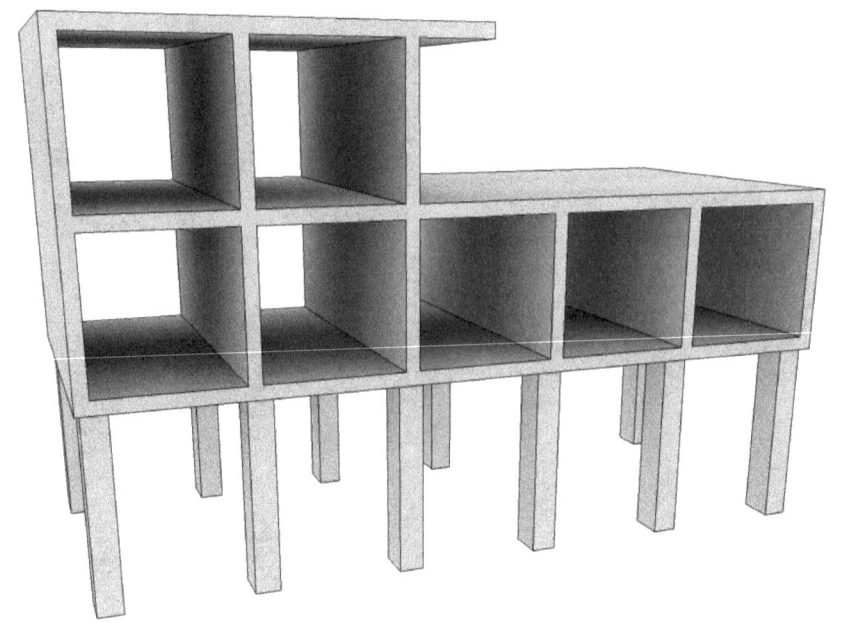

Fig. 6.8 - Crosswall construction

Wind bracing

It is common in concrete multi storey frames to provide a rigid access/service core, that contains lifts, stairs and other services. This core will be constructed of reinforced solid concrete walls, providing a stiff column that runs vertically through the structure strengthening the frame against any wind pressures. The core will also assist with carrying some of the loads through the building.

STEEL FRAMES

Structural steel frames are a popular choice, and frequently used in construction of both large scale and mid scale buildings. The advantages of steel frame construction is the speed of erection of the pre-prepared steel work, accuracy allows for smaller tolerances which assists with the fixing of cladding materials. Material and labour costs are often considered to be lower than the concrete frame alternatives, and steel is suitable for reclaiming, recycling and reusing at the end of the building's life.

The design, fabrication, supply and erection of steel frame structures is generally carried out by a specialist sub-contractor. The structural design is complex, and will be carried out in accordance with Eurocode 3: Design of steel structures BS EN 1993. Other guidance includes BS4 and BS EN 10067 and the Handbook of Structural Steelwork by the British Constructional Steelwork Association and the Steel Construction Institute.

Structural Steel Sections
The types of standard hot rolled sections are listed below:

- Universal Beams - Sections with tapered or parallel flanges
- Rolled Steel Joists - Small size beams that are used for lintels and small frames, with tapered flanges
- Universal Columns - Sections with parallel flanges designated in the same manner as universal beams.
- Channels - Rolled with tapered flanges, these are used for trimming and bracing or as a substitute for joist sections.
- Angles - These have parallel flanges, used for light framing or for bracing.
- T Bars - Used similarly to angles, they can have a short or long stalk

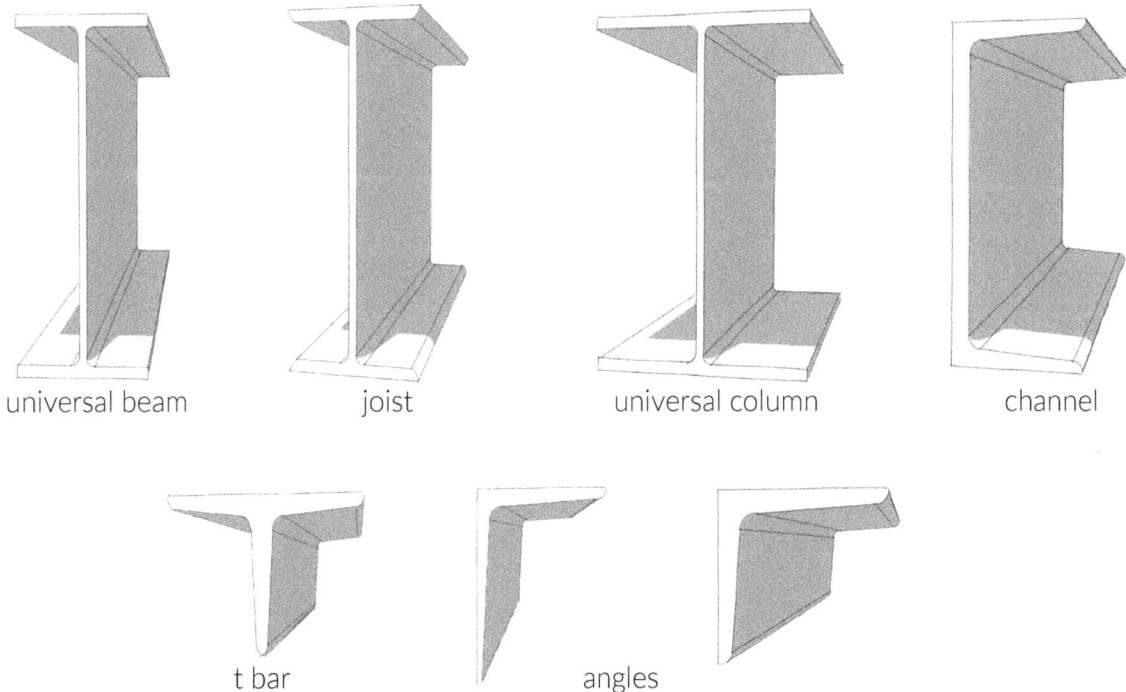

Fig. 6.9 - Types of steel sections

Cold rolled sections are also used, typically seen in lightweight situations, such as prefabricated construction or modular units. Zed and Sigma sections are used widely instead of steel angles for truss purlins.

Type of frame

The conventional steel frame is a skeleton frame format, with beams and columns supporting the imposed and dead loads of the floors, walls and roof, and wind pressures. The frame is often braced to prevent racking, which is when the structure is unable to resist window forces and distorts due to these lateral forces. Cross bracing is introduced between the structural members to ensure a right angled connection of the frame. The bracing will be designed according to the requirements of the structure and anticipated loads on the building. A service core is often used to provide a solid concrete core that assists with bracing by acting as a solid vertical cantilever which takes the wind forces.

As mentioned previously, the design of the steel frame is usually carried out by specialists and goes beyond the scope of this book.

Connections

Connections between the steel sections is usually either a bolted connection or welded connection. Welding tends to be carried out off site, due to the health and safety risks associated with welding in site conditions. A welded connection also requires inspection which can be more difficult on site.

Connecting the structural steelwork to the foundations can take two forms, a base plate or a gusset base. The steel column has a relatively small area that needs to be attached the foundation base, so a steel base plate is welded to the base of the column to spread the load of the column onto the foundation, and to provide a means of fixing with holding down bolts. The gusset base comprises of additional angled plates that further spread the load to the base plate.

Both types of connection are fixed to the concrete foundation using holding down bolts that have been cast into the foundation.

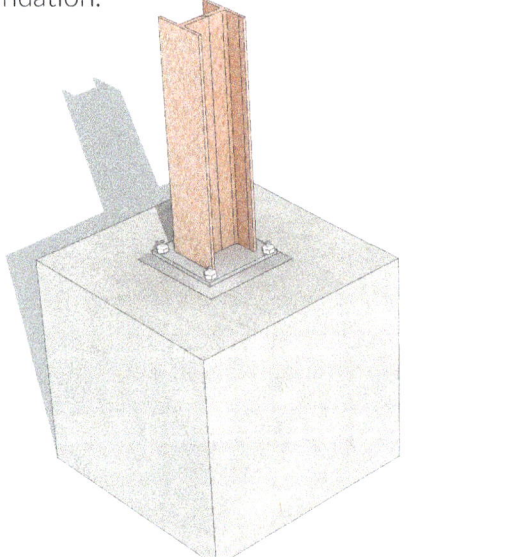
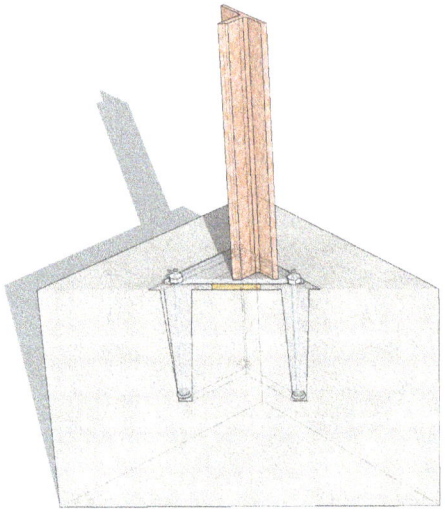

Fig. 6.10 - Base connection of steel frame to concrete foundation, complete and section

Fire

The Building Regulations Approved Document Part B provides minimum fire resistance periods for steel structures and components. Steel loses a lot of its strength when subjected to high temperatures and at 550°C would begin to deform and sag, and no longer support its load. Therefore the regulations require a casing to structural steel members to protect the structure from potential damage from the intense heat of a fire.

Although traditional methods used to include casting concrete around the steel members, and also encasing the steel in brickwork - nowadays it is more common to use more lightweight systems such as:
- Spray coatings
- Board casings
- Preformed casings
- Plaster and lath

SINGLE STOREY FRAMES / PORTAL FRAME / LONG SPAN FRAMES

Large single storey buildings such as warehouses, industrial or commercial units, use structural frames to enable a considerable floor space and relatively large floor to ceiling heights. This form of building can often be divided into three types, a short span, mid span and long span building. These commercial buildings are often constructed from a standard selection of parts, which is then fitted out according to specific requirements. The longer span frame structure can be seen in many forms but the most popular is the portal frame. We will briefly touch on the other forms of frame in this chapter, but focus mainly on the portal frame construction.

Types of frame used for long span buildings:

Plane Frame
A plane frame is a frame which is constructed in one flat plane, usually a truss or a girder. They are usually a series of triangles which allows for minimal use of materials and a lightweight structure. This type of frame is often used in short span roofs, ranging up to 10m in span. A truss is considered to have a pitched profile, while a lattice girder has a parallel top and bottom boom.

Space Frame
The space frame is similar to the plane frame but spans in two directions. They are also used in roof structures and allow for a much larger span.

Structural Frame
The structural frame is used for large single storey buildings providing good floor to ceiling heights and large floor spaces. The portal frame falls in this category.

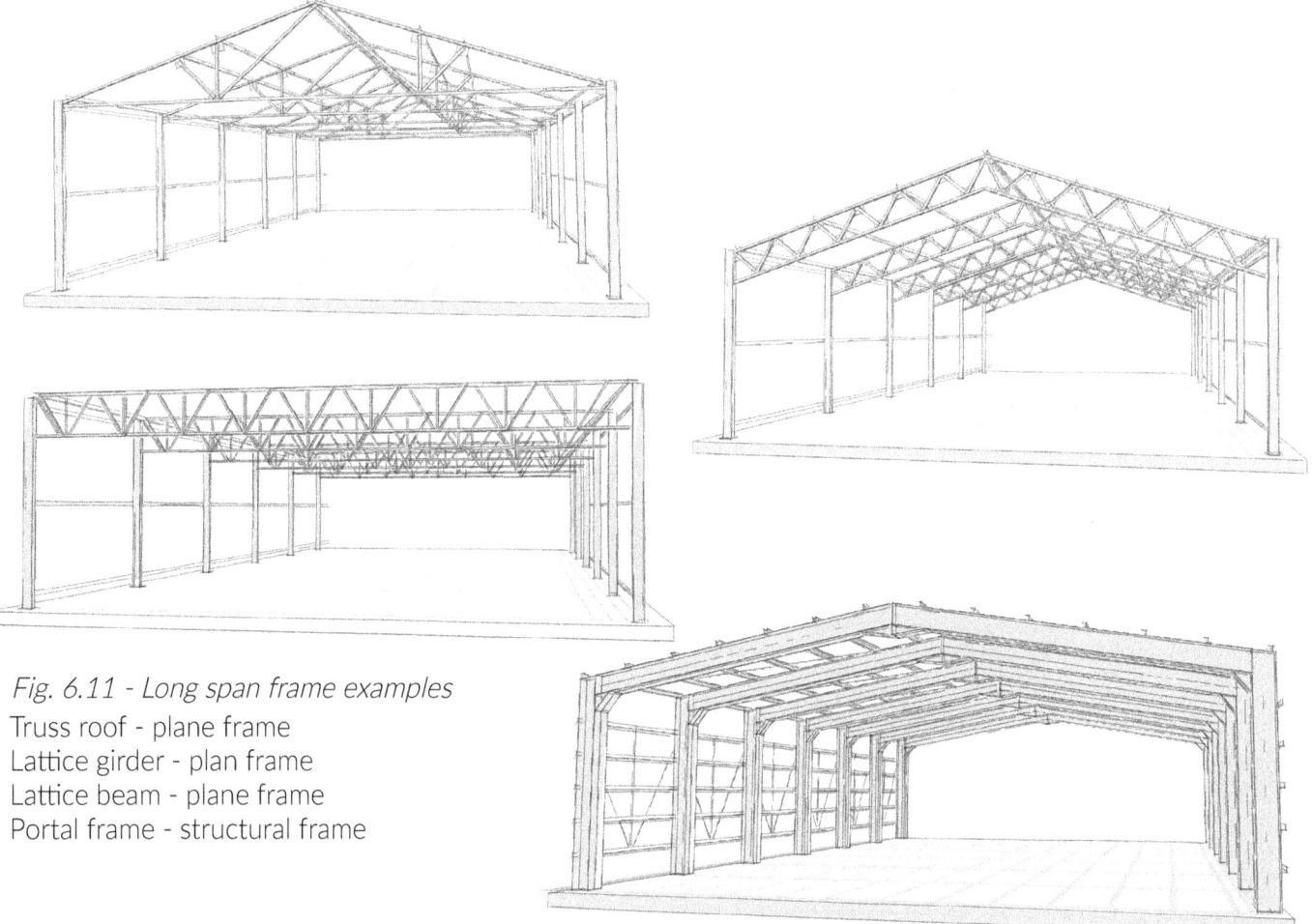

Fig. 6.11 - Long span frame examples
Truss roof - plane frame
Lattice girder - plan frame
Lattice beam - plane frame
Portal frame - structural frame

PORTAL FRAME

This form of construction is easy to build, cost effective, and a very practical solution to long span building requirements. The frame is typically made from steel, laminated timber or reinforced concrete - the most common material being steel. The structure can be formed as a rigid frame, a two-pin frame or a three-pin frame. The steel portal frame can span distances of 10m to 60m, with the portal units at centres between 4.5m and 7.5m. A portal frame with a span of up to 15m is considered to be a short span, between 16m and 35m is defined as a medium span and frames with spans up to 60m are long span.

The frame is constructed using supporting steel columns, which have connections to the steel rafters, these are then linked together with purlins. The roof pitch is set as low as possible to minimise the spread at the knee of the portal frame (the point between the rafter and the column of the portal). The apex or ridge on a short or medium span portal frame will often be made on site, with a rigid bolted connection. Long span portal frames may have a pin jointed connection at the ridge in order to permit some movement between the rafters of the frame, which are pin jointed at the foundation bases. The foundations tend to be simple reinforced concrete isolated base or pad foundations to suit the loading requirements and site conditions.

The structure itself does not often provide sufficient rigidity and will be stiffened with additional bracing, which depends on the scale of the structure and specific design requirements. In many medium and long span frames the connection between the rafters and column include a haunch which deepens the connection, thus making it stiffer.

Purlins are fixed across the rafters, and sheeting rails fixed to the columns to provide support and fixing for the roofing and wall cladding materials along with insulation. The most common form is the Zed and Sigma sections as a fixing point for the external units.

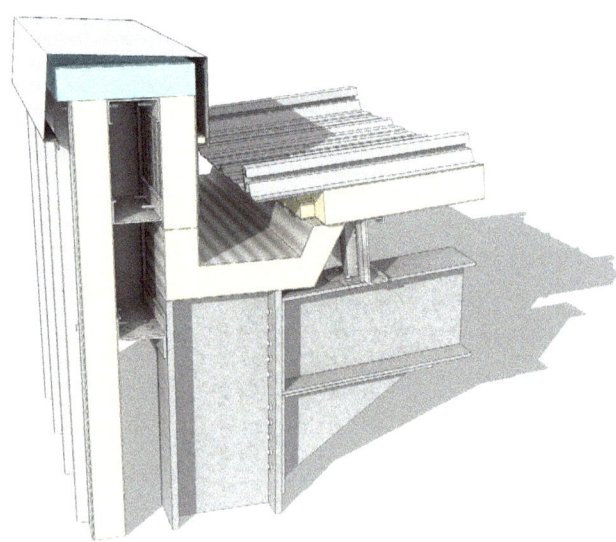

LIGHTWEIGHT CLADDING FOR PORTAL FRAME STRUCTURES

The cladding to a portal frame must:
- provide sufficient strength to support imposed wind and snow loadings
- resist weather penetration
- be lightweight
- have good fire resisting qualities and resistance to the spread of flame
- be durable and require minimal maintenance
- provide suitable thermal insulation to any habitable space or area requiring space heating

A wide variety of steel and aluminium cladding is available for portal frame applications, which are often treated by galvanisation or plastic coatings. The insulation is also varied, with rigid board insulation used in a composite panel or flexible glass fibre insulation built up into layers. Some agricultural and industrial structures will not require insulation, and in this case the cladding acts purely as a weather resistant envelope.

The lightweight cladding of portal frames are considered non load bearing only supporting their own weight and any wind or snow loads. The choice of cladding will depend on factors such as aesthetic requirements, planning conditions, long term and short term costs and personal preference. In many cases it is common to use a masonry cavity wall to the lower portion of the external wall, with the upper portion of the wall as lightweight cladding. This is due to the masonry base being more hard wearing and less susceptible to any impact damage than the lightweight alternative.

Cladding materials
Profiled steel sheeting has a good strength to weight ratio but can suffer fast corrosion is left unprotected. It is usually zinc coated with a galvanising process to ensure its durability. The profiles on the sheets improve the overall strength.

In single skin form the steel sheet is fixed directly to the purlins or sheeting rails without any thermal insulation. This is a very cheap form of construction and only seen on buildings that do not need to be heated such as warehouses and stores.

Profiled aluminium sheeting has a longer life expectancy than steel and as a result is a more expensive option. It is also available in a variety of profiles and systems.

Fibre cement sheets are corrugated and usually finished in a grey colour traditionally seen in industrial and agricultural settings.

The main types of cladding system that incorporate insulation are:

Built up system with liner sheets
This system contains an external and internal cladding sheet which are separated by spacer rails and insulation. The spacers are fixed to the cladding rails that span between the columns of the portal frame.

Built up system with liner trays
A U-shaped tray spans between the columns of the portal frame with rigid board insulation set within the liner tray and the external cladding is then fixed to the outer flanges of the liner tray. The trays are bolted to the structure.

Composite panel system
The build up systems have been largely superseded by the composite panel, which consists of two profiled or smooth sheets of aluminium or steel, which are bonded either side of a rigid insulation core. The composite panel is faster to install and a more cost effective solution.

For the detail examples we will focus on a portal frame system that incorporates a composite cladding.

PORTAL FRAME DETAILS

P01
WALL TO FLOOR JUNCTION WITH MASONRY WALL

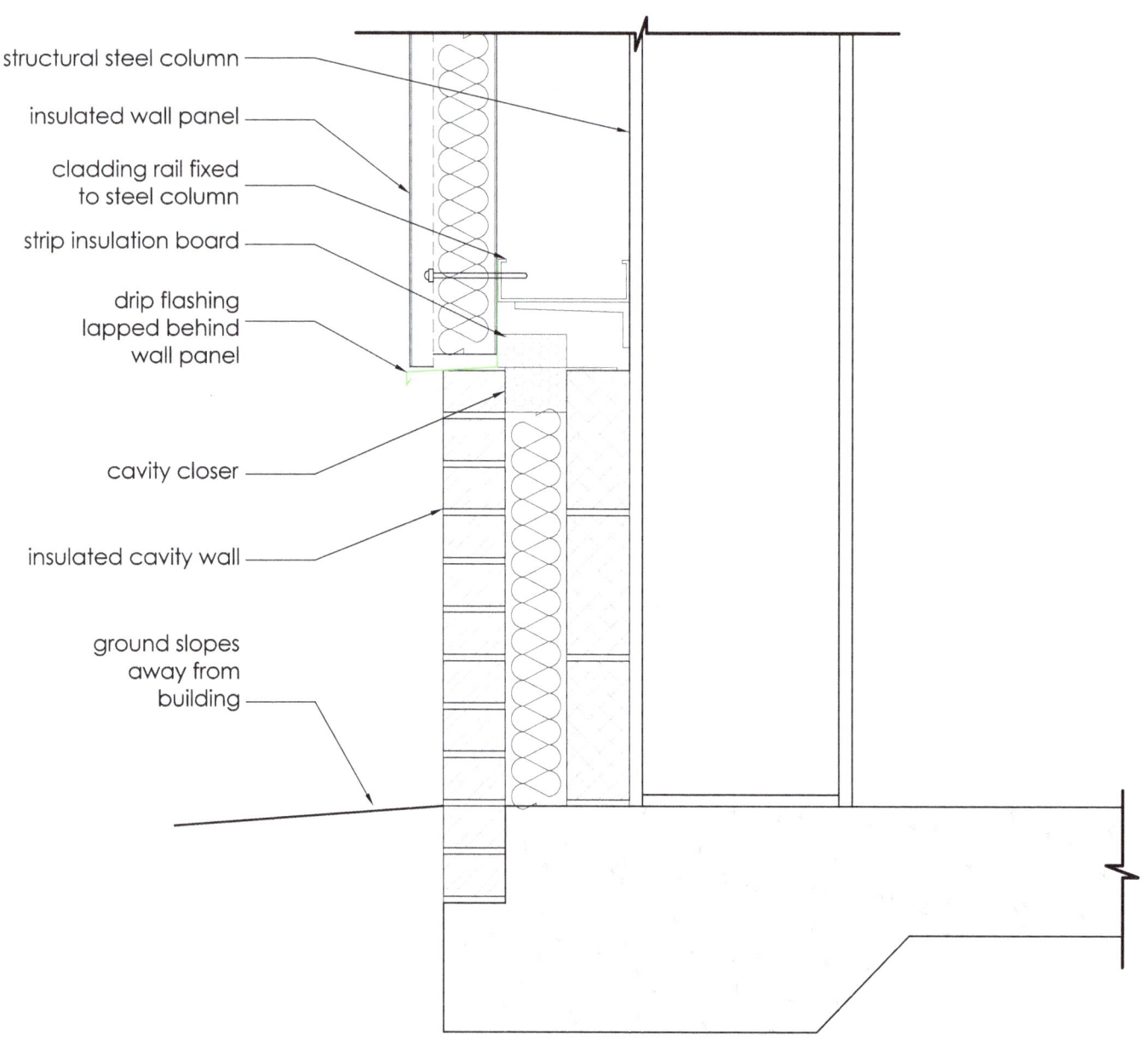

2D Detail P01 - Wall to floor junction with masonry wall

SECTION 6 - FRAMES

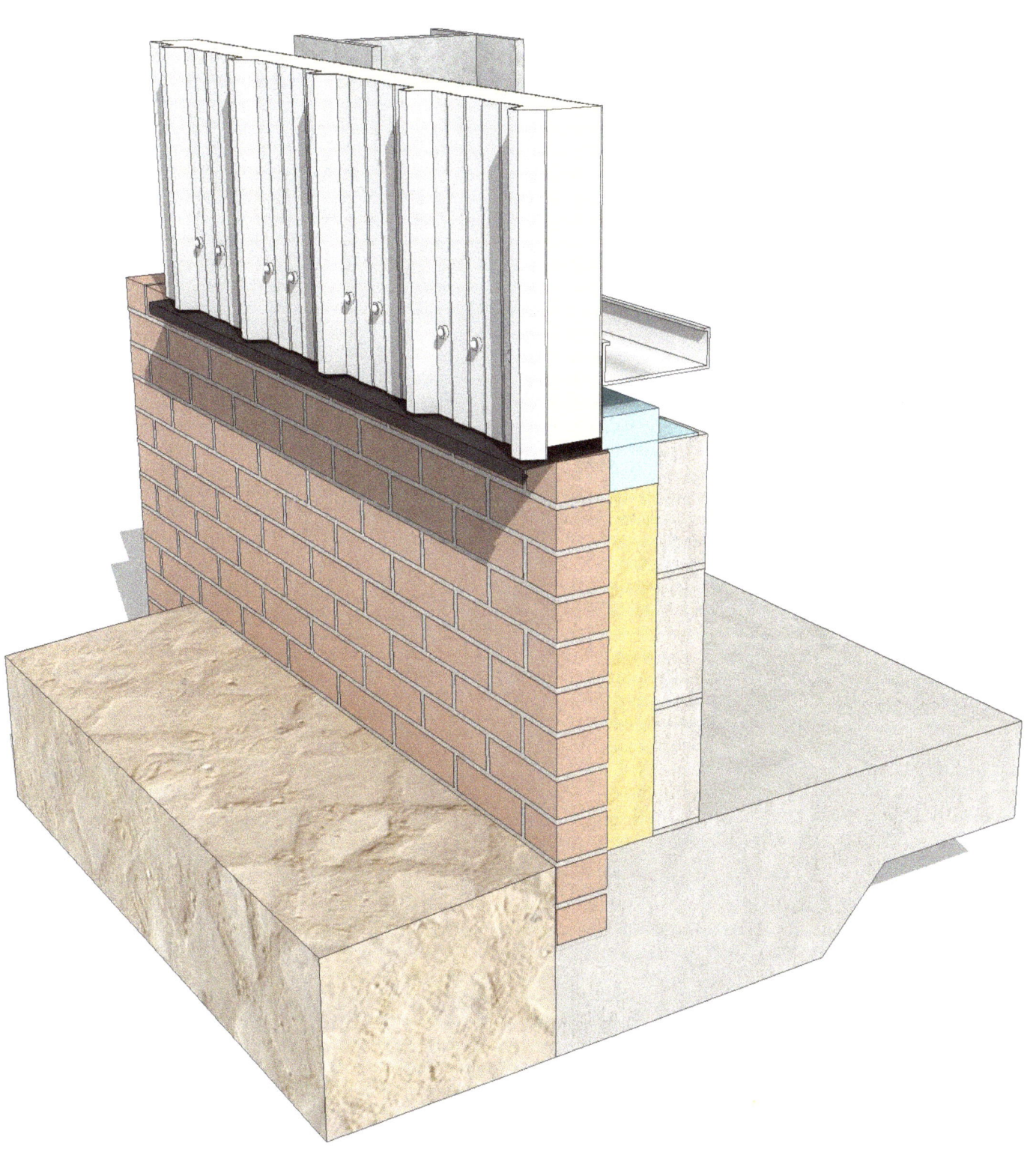

3D Detail P01 - Wall to floor junction with masonry wall

P02

WALL TO FLOOR JUNCTION DRIP DETAIL

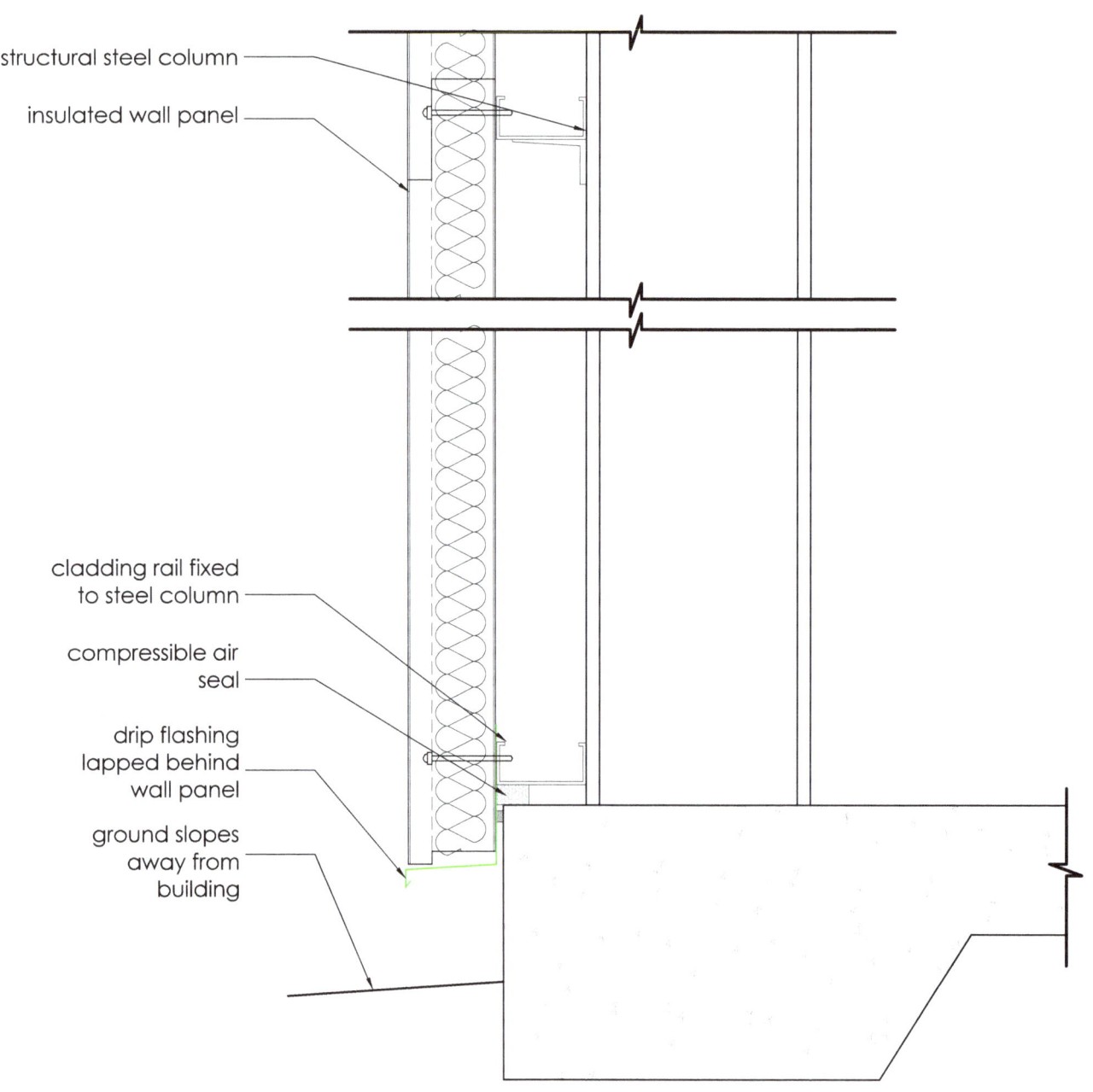

2D Detail P02 - Wall to floor junction drip detail

SECTION 6 - FRAMES

3D Detail P02 - Wall to floor junction drip detail

P03

WALL TO FLOOR JUNCTION FLUSH DRIP DETAIL

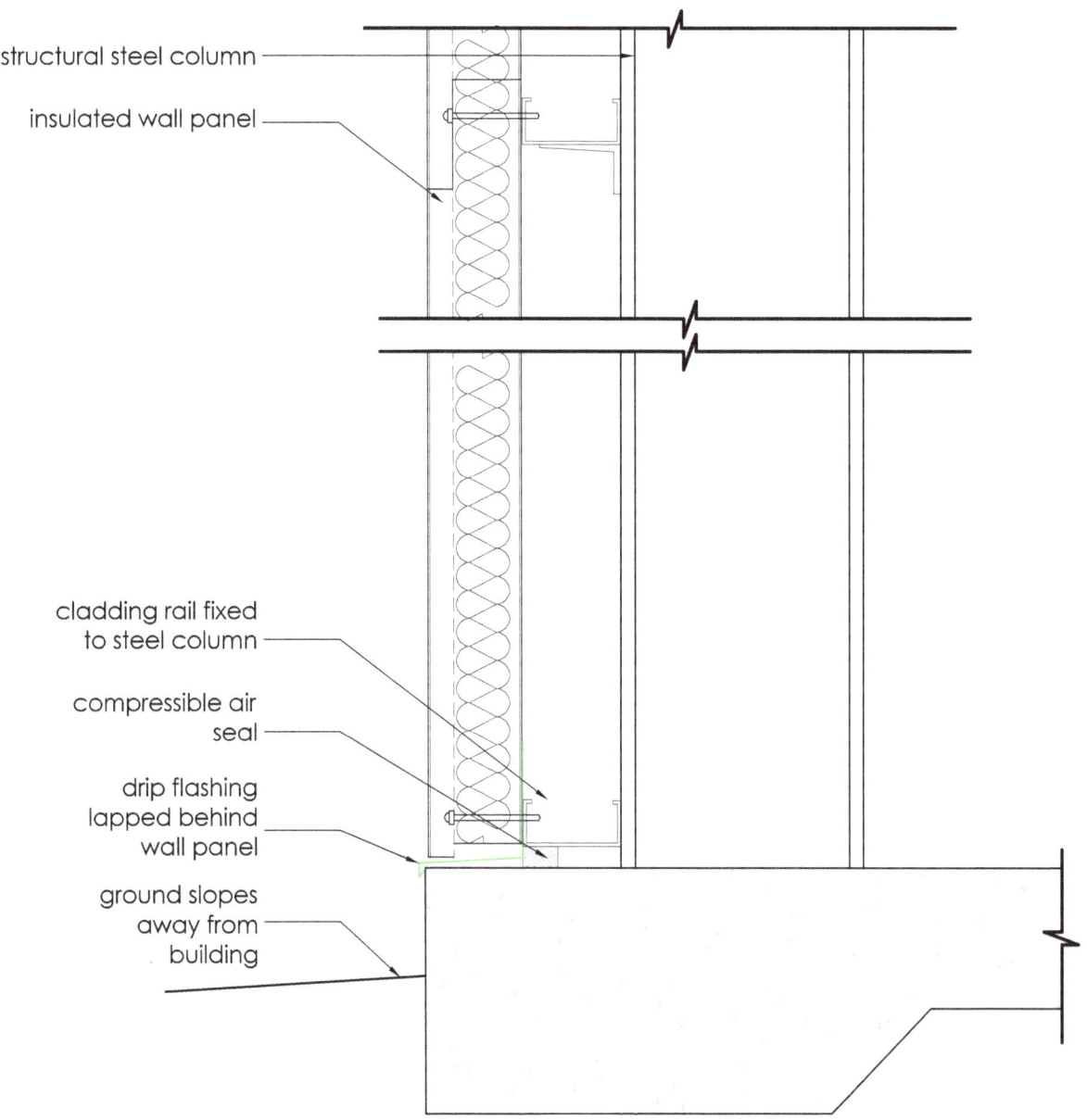

2D Detail P03 - Wall to floor junction flush drip detail

SECTION 6 - FRAMES

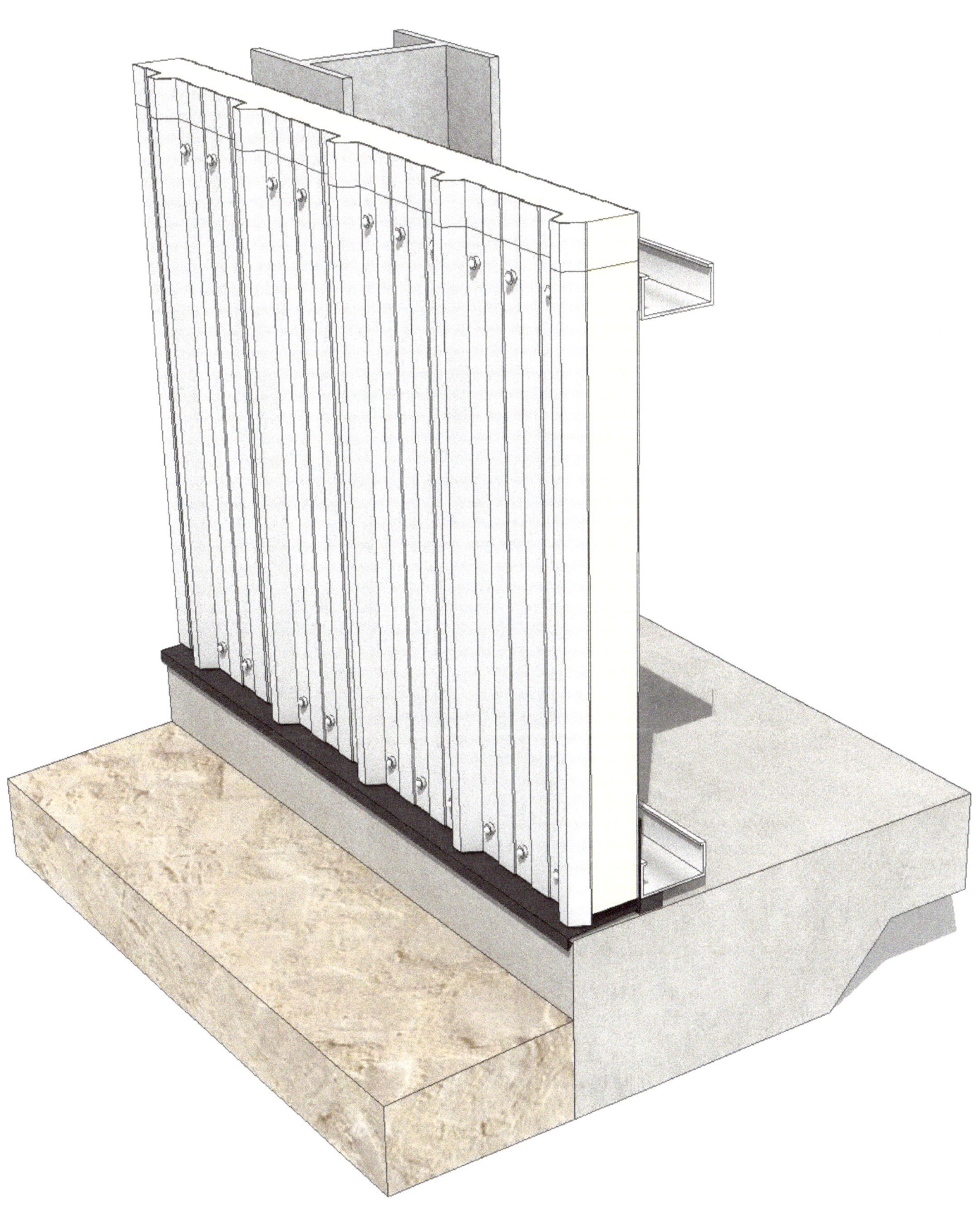

3D Detail P03 - Wall to floor junction flush drip detail

P04

WINDOW HEAD AND SILL DETAIL

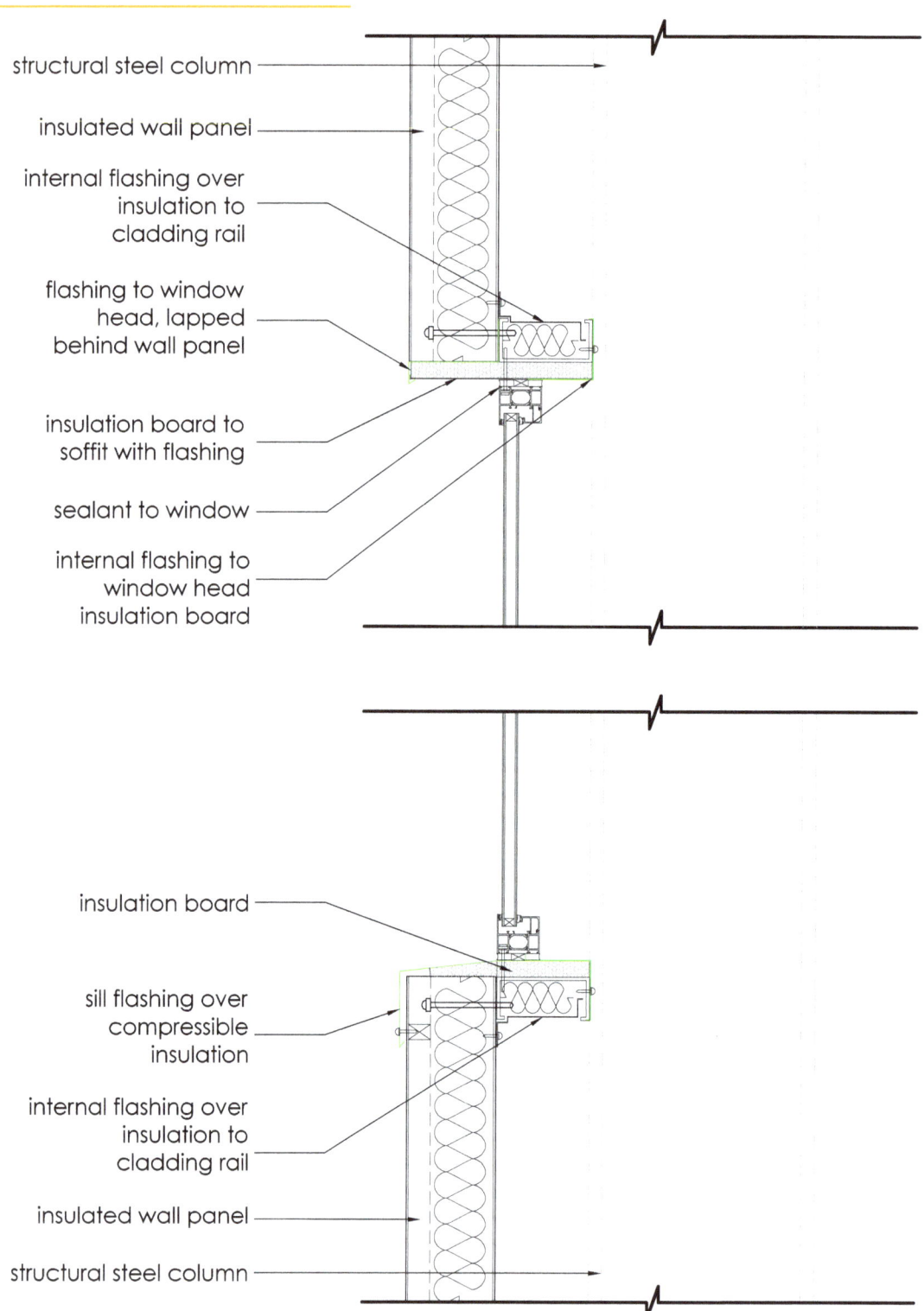

2D Detail P04 - Window head and sill detail

SECTION 6 - FRAMES

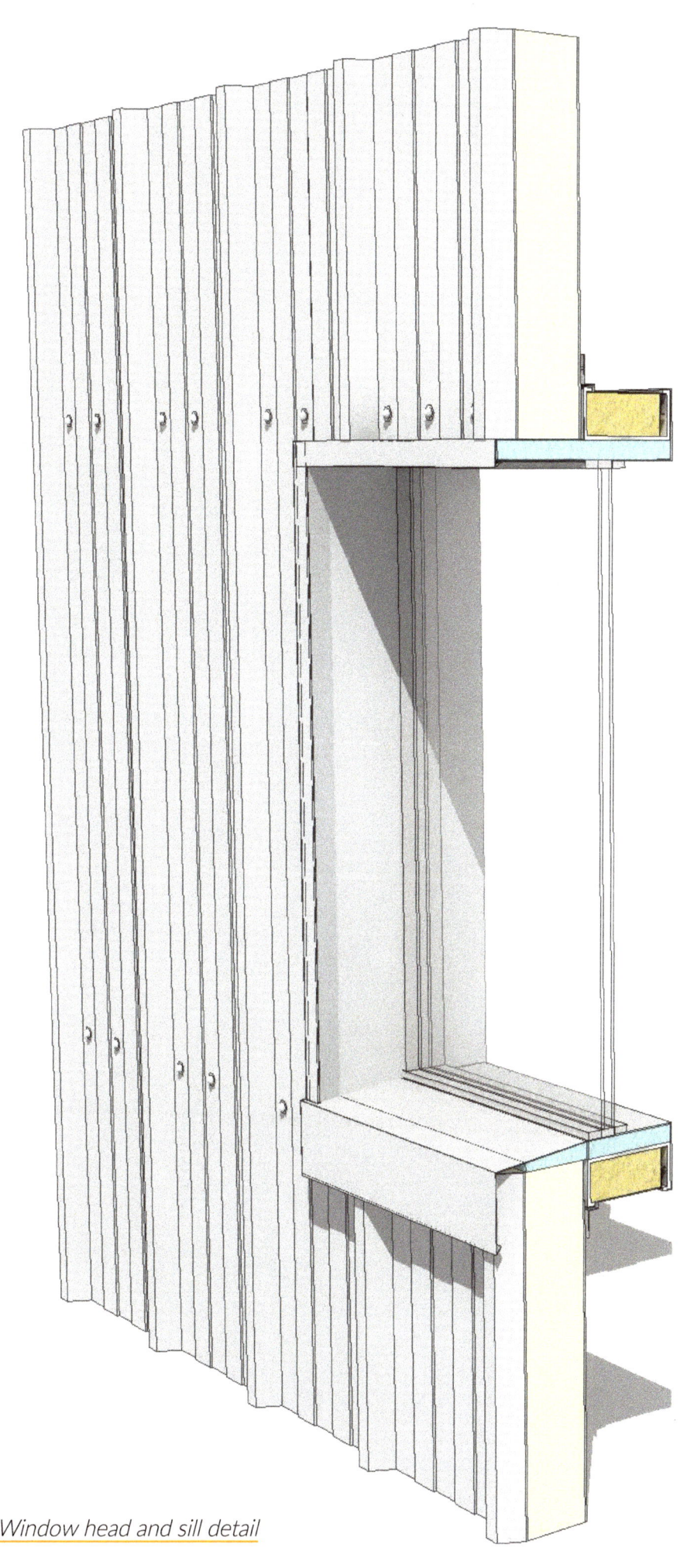

3D Detail P04 - Window head and sill detail

P05

WINDOW JAMB DETAIL

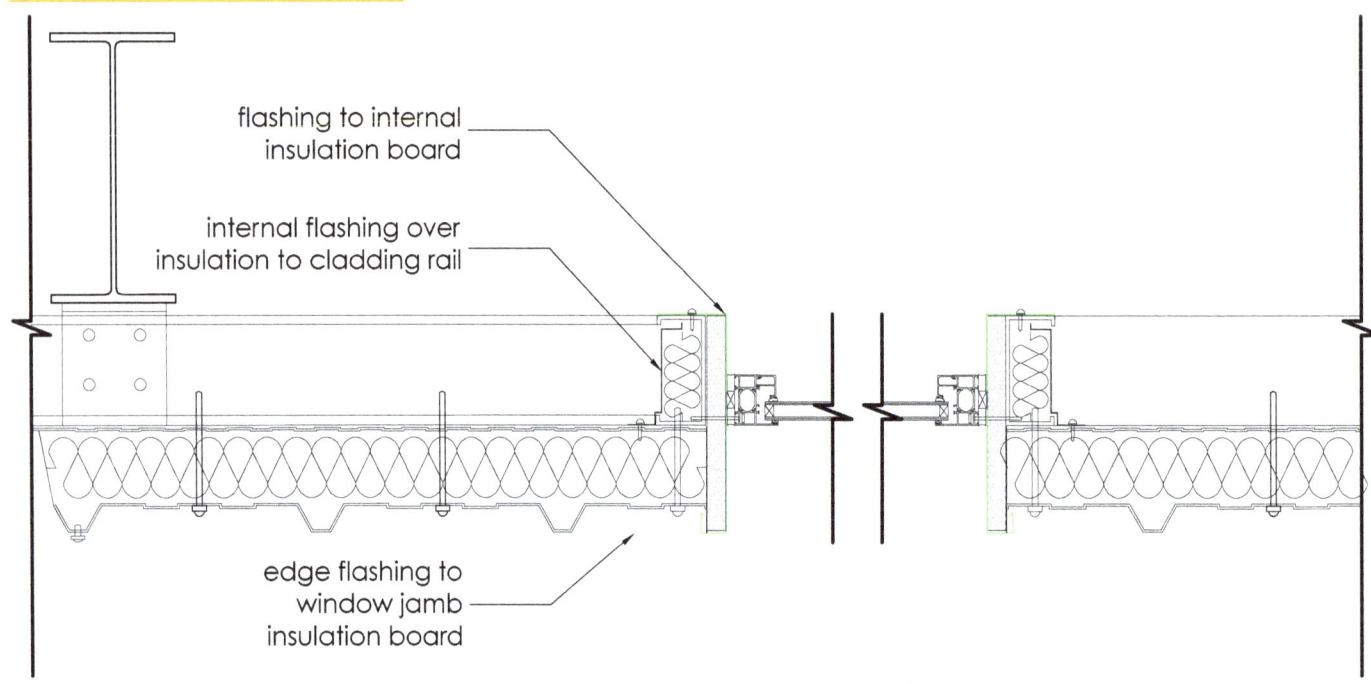

2D Detail P05 - Window jamb detail - plan

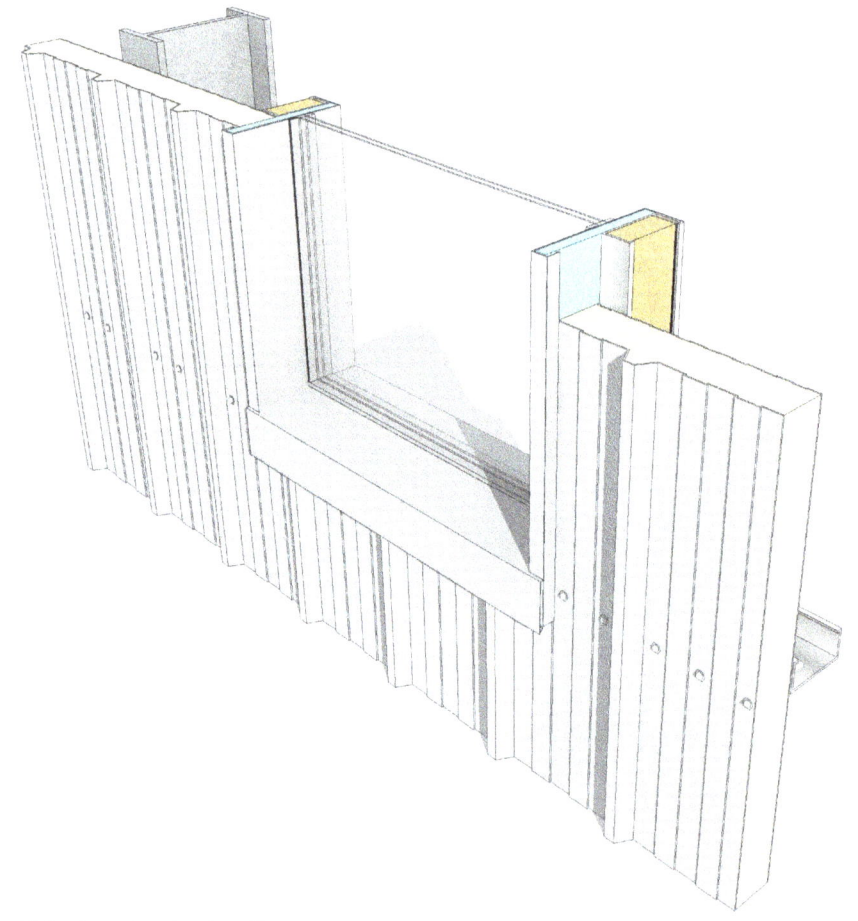

3D Detail P05 - Window jamb detail

SECTION 6 - FRAMES

P06

EXTERNAL CORNER DETAIL - PLAN

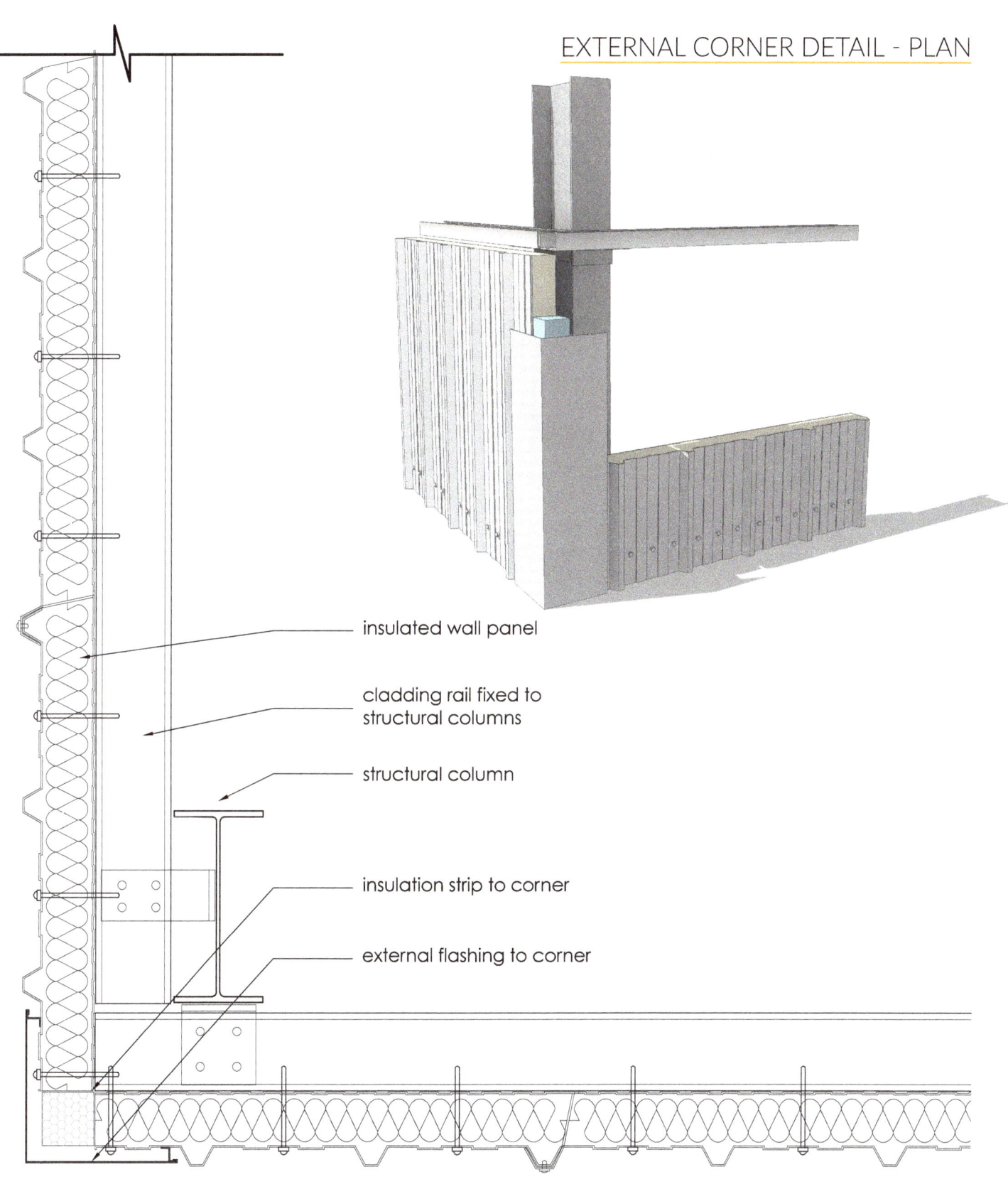

- insulated wall panel
- cladding rail fixed to structural columns
- structural column
- insulation strip to corner
- external flashing to corner

2D Detail P06 - External corner detail - plan

3D Detail P06 - External corner detail

P07

DOOR HEAD DETAIL

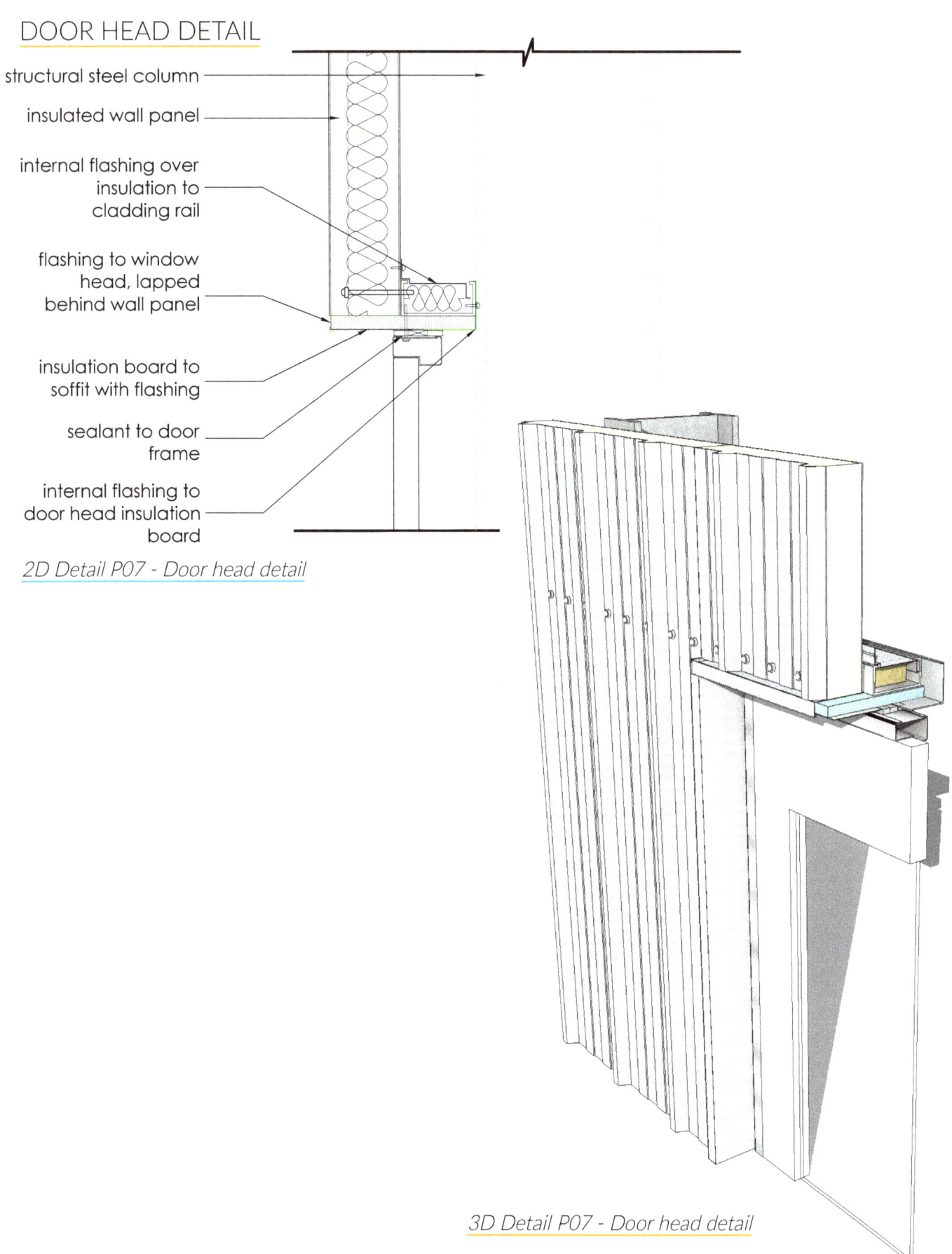

- structural steel column
- insulated wall panel
- internal flashing over insulation to cladding rail
- flashing to window head, lapped behind wall panel
- insulation board to soffit with flashing
- sealant to door frame
- internal flashing to door head insulation board

2D Detail P07 - Door head detail

3D Detail P07 - Door head detail

SECTION 6 - FRAMES

P08

DOOR JAMB DETAIL - PLAN

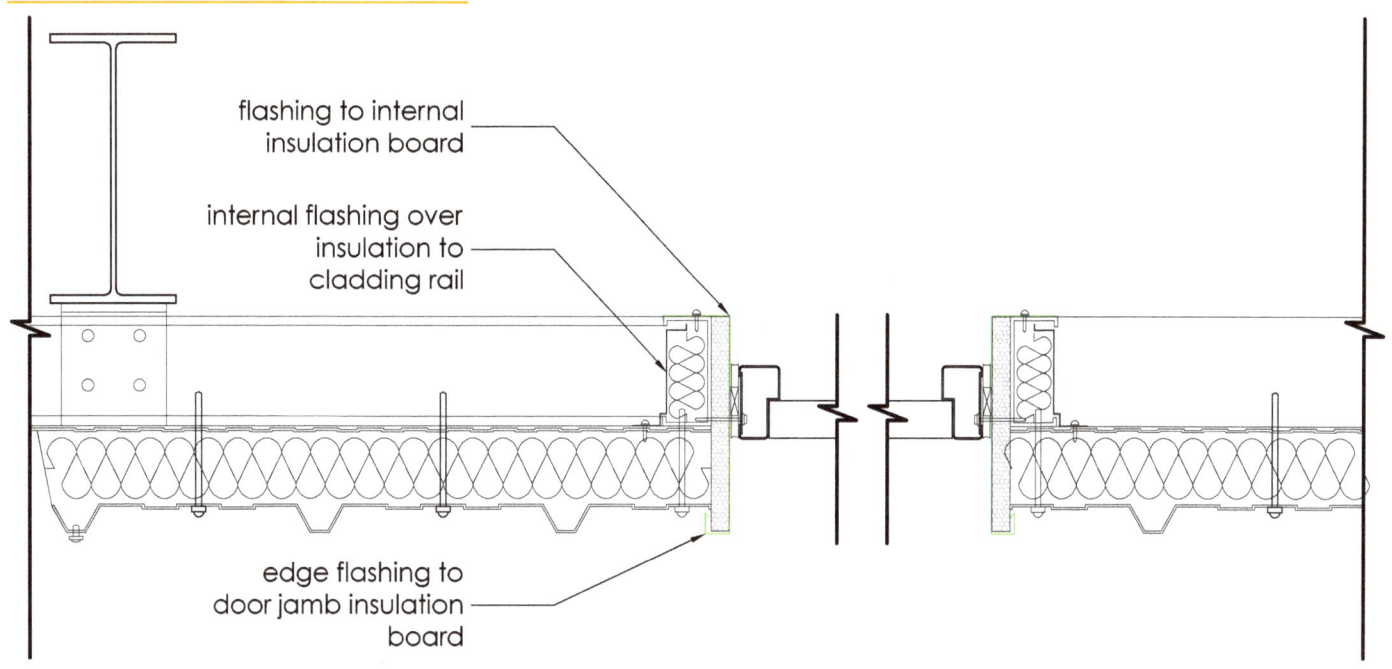

2D Detail P08 - Door jamb detail - plan

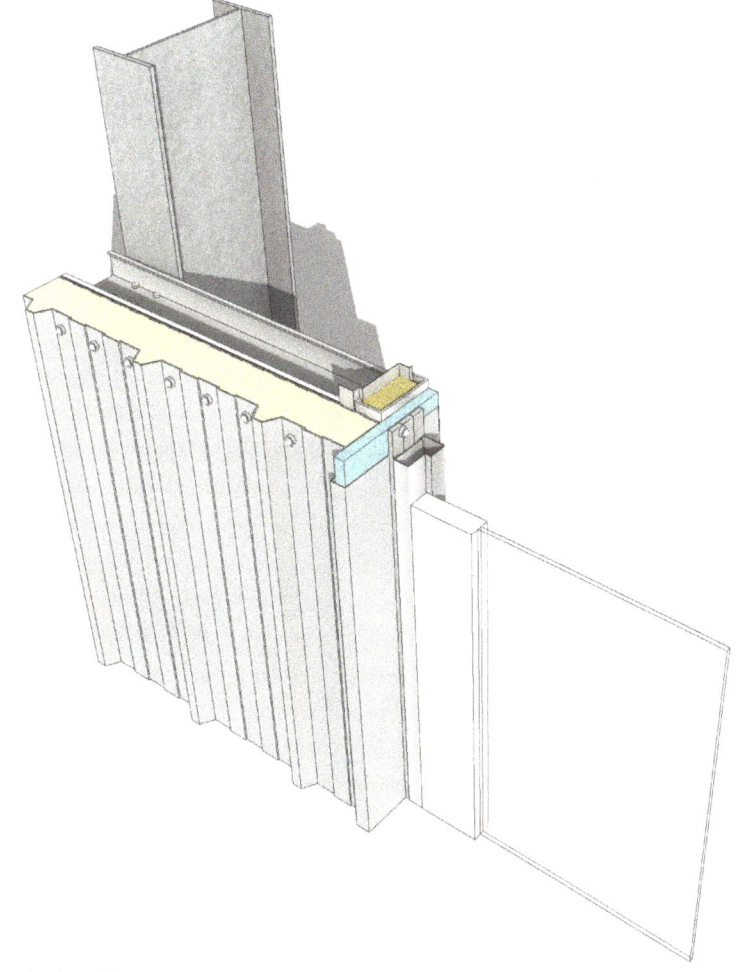

3D Detail P08 - Door jamb detail

P09

RIDGE DETAIL

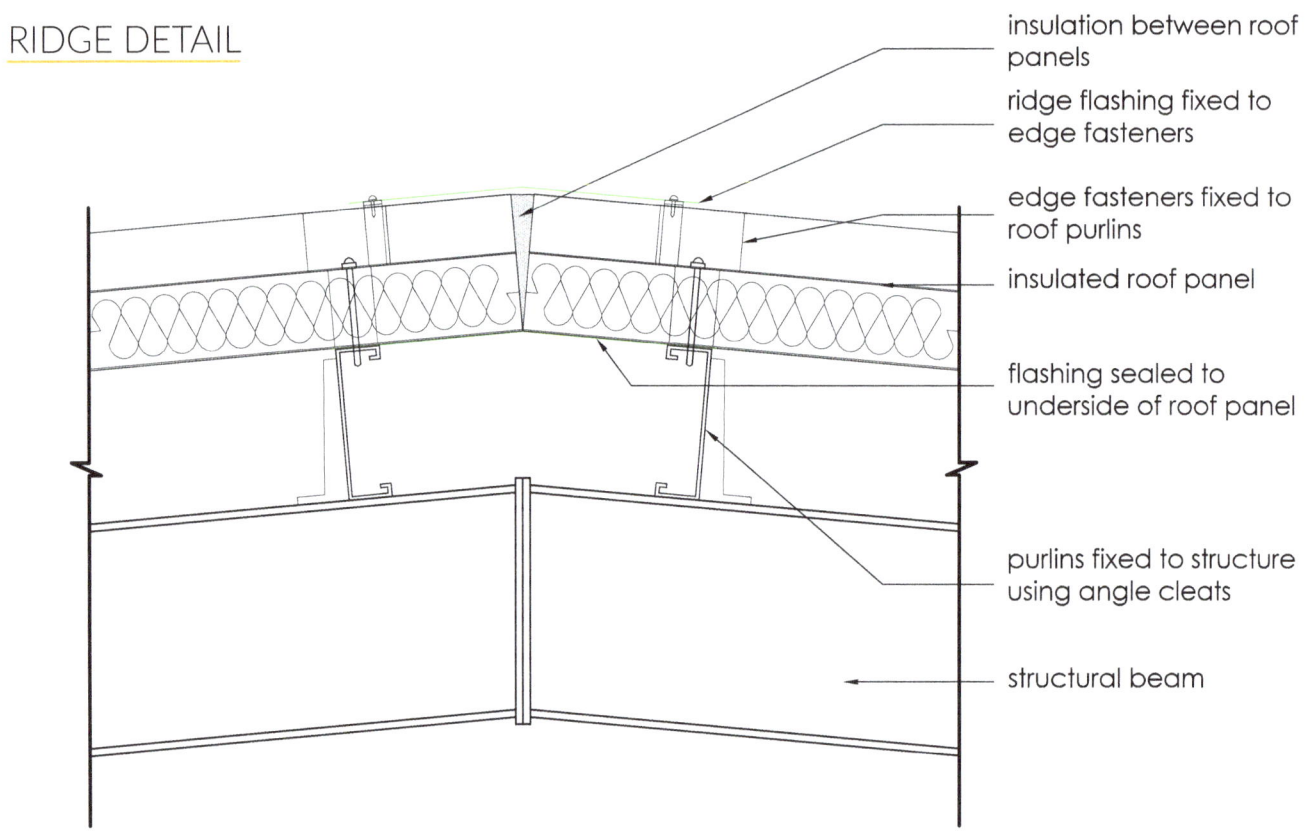

2D Detail P09 - Ridge detail

- insulation between roof panels
- ridge flashing fixed to edge fasteners
- edge fasteners fixed to roof purlins
- insulated roof panel
- flashing sealed to underside of roof panel
- purlins fixed to structure using angle cleats
- structural beam

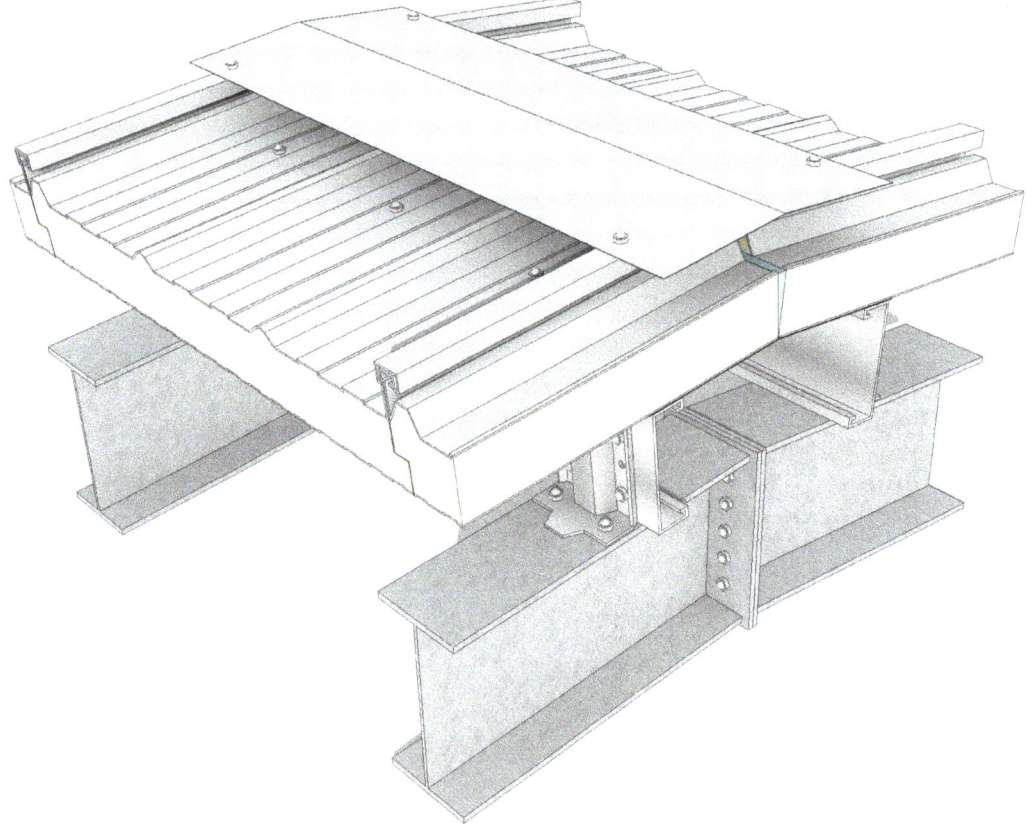

3D Detail P09 - Ridge detail

SECTION 6 - FRAMES

P10

EAVES DETAIL

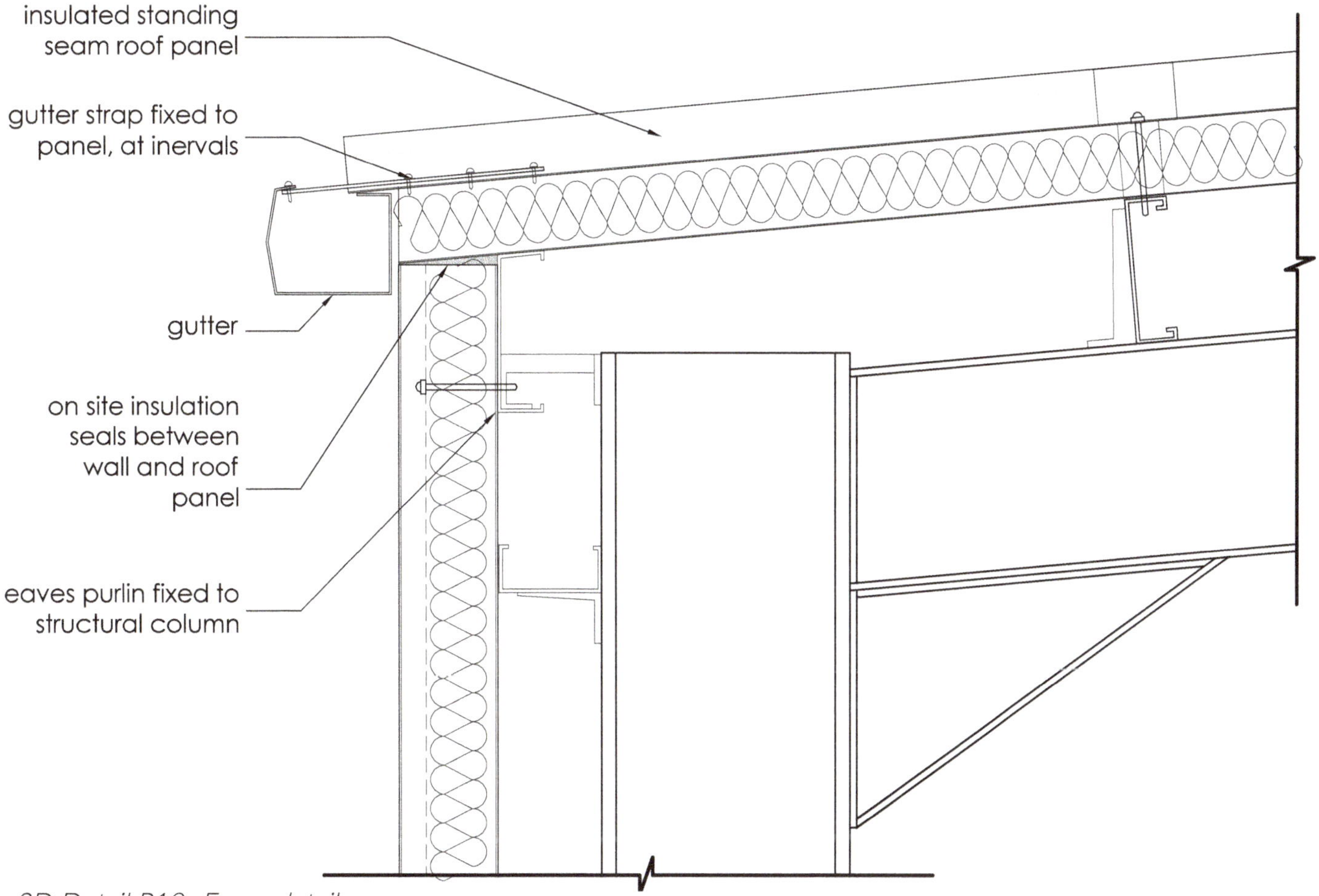

- insulated standing seam roof panel
- gutter strap fixed to panel, at inervals
- gutter
- on site insulation seals between wall and roof panel
- eaves purlin fixed to structural column

2D Detail P10- Eaves detail

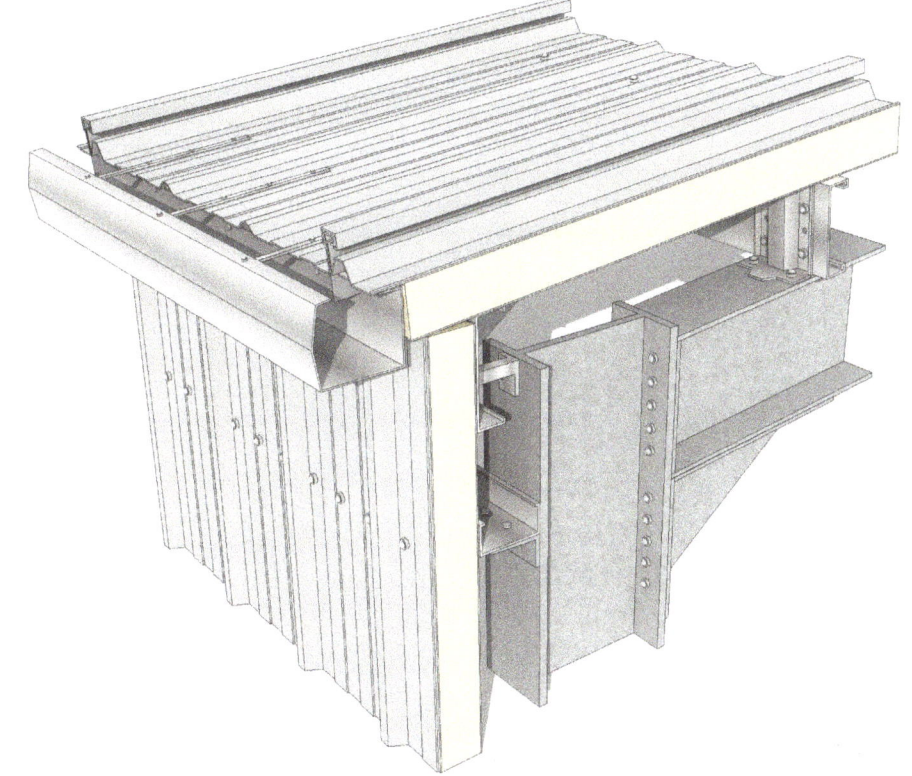

3D Detail P10 - Eaves detail

P11

EAVES DETAIL WITH INTEGRATED GUTTER

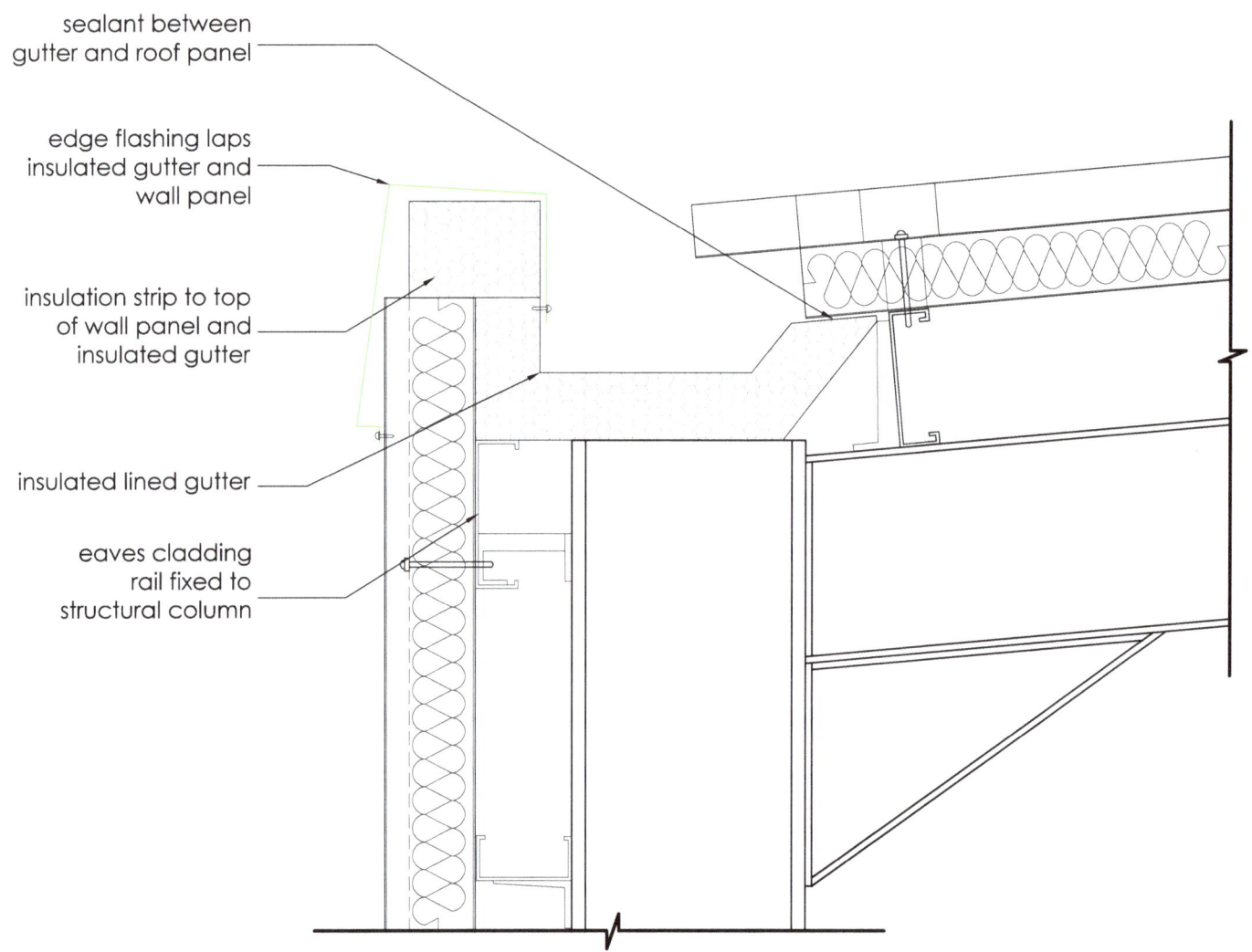

2D Detail P11 - Eaves detail with integrated gutter

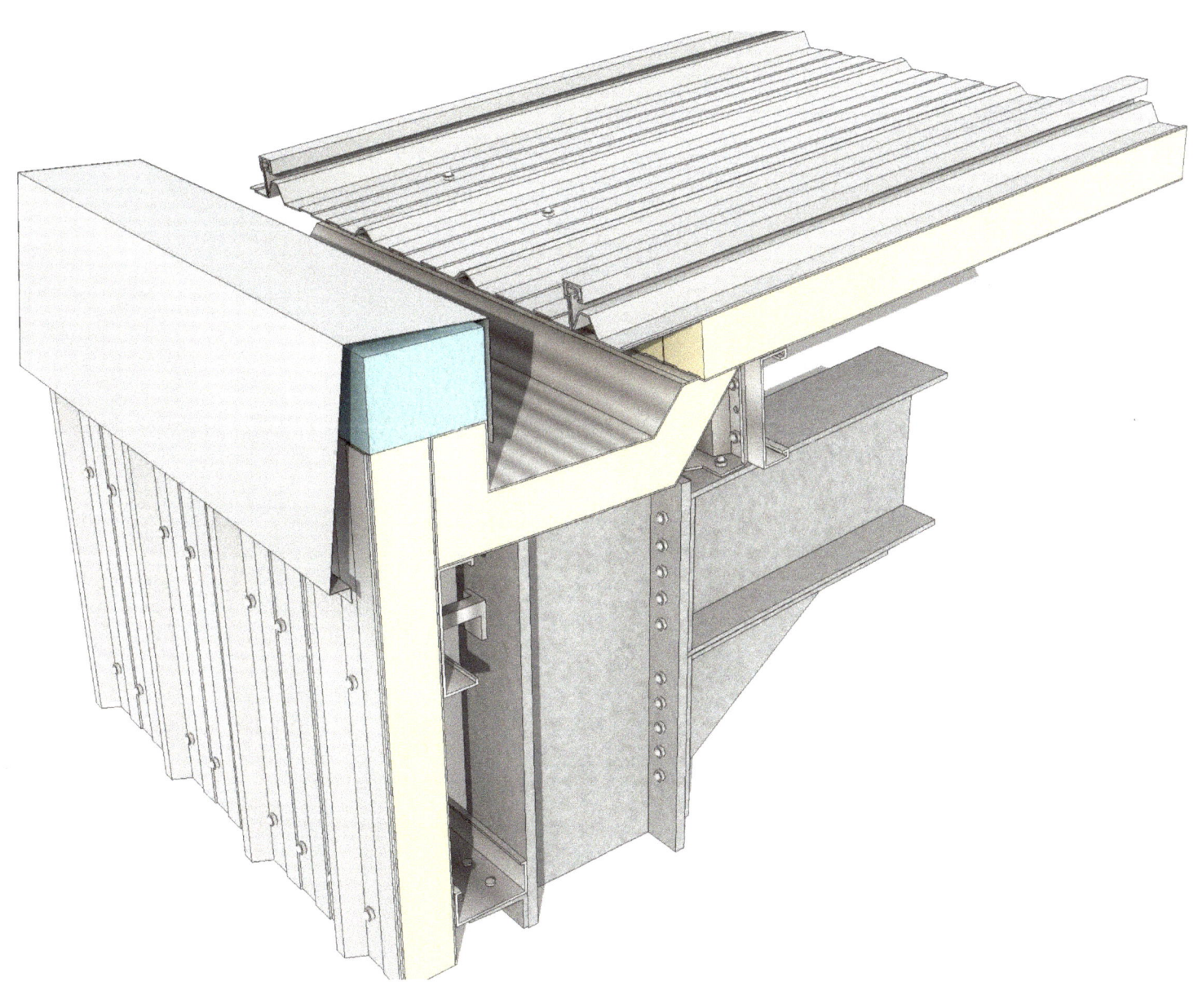

3D Detail P11 - Eaves detail with integrated gutter

P12

PARAPET DETAIL

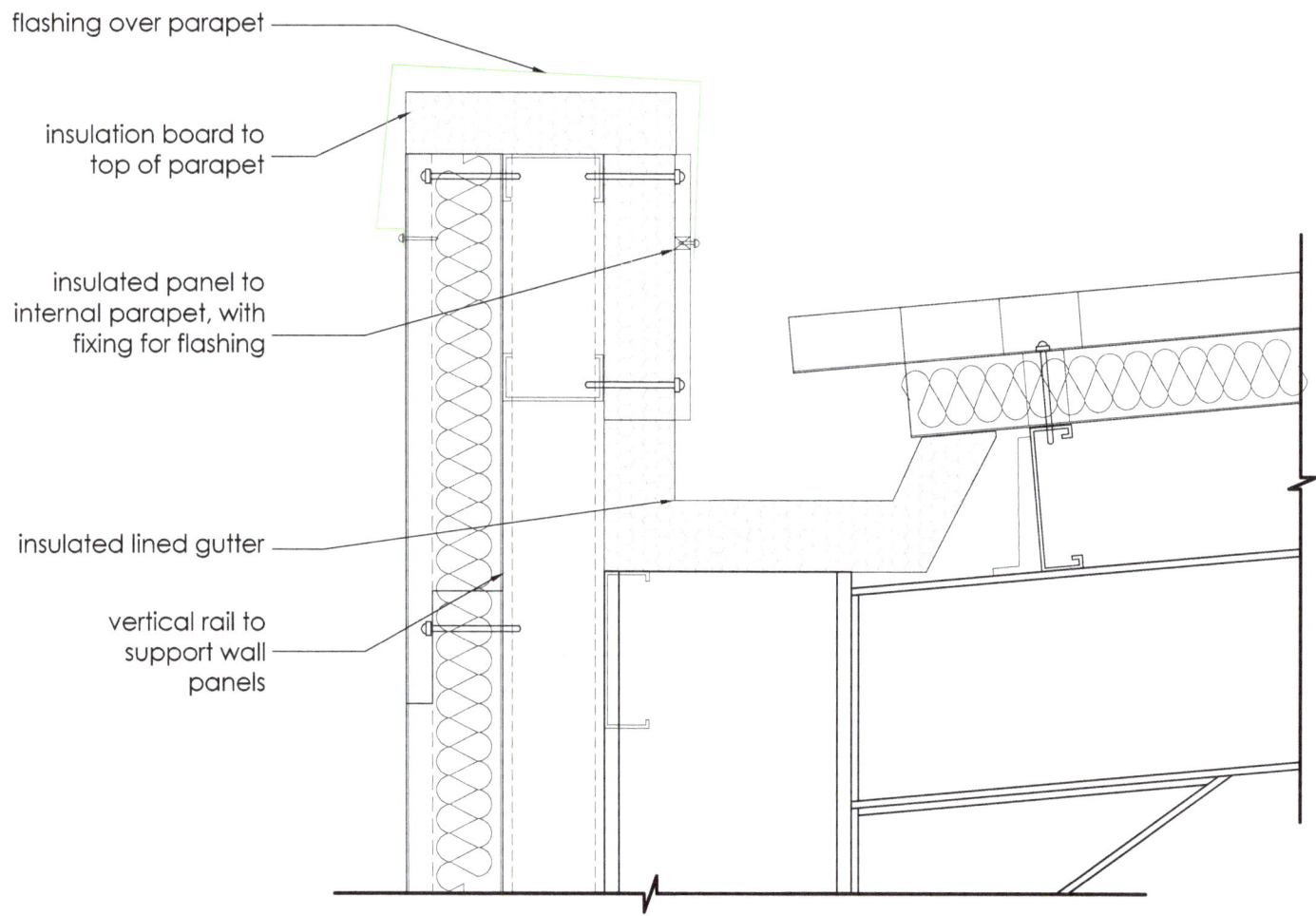

2D Detail P12 - Parapet detail

SECTION 6 - FRAMES

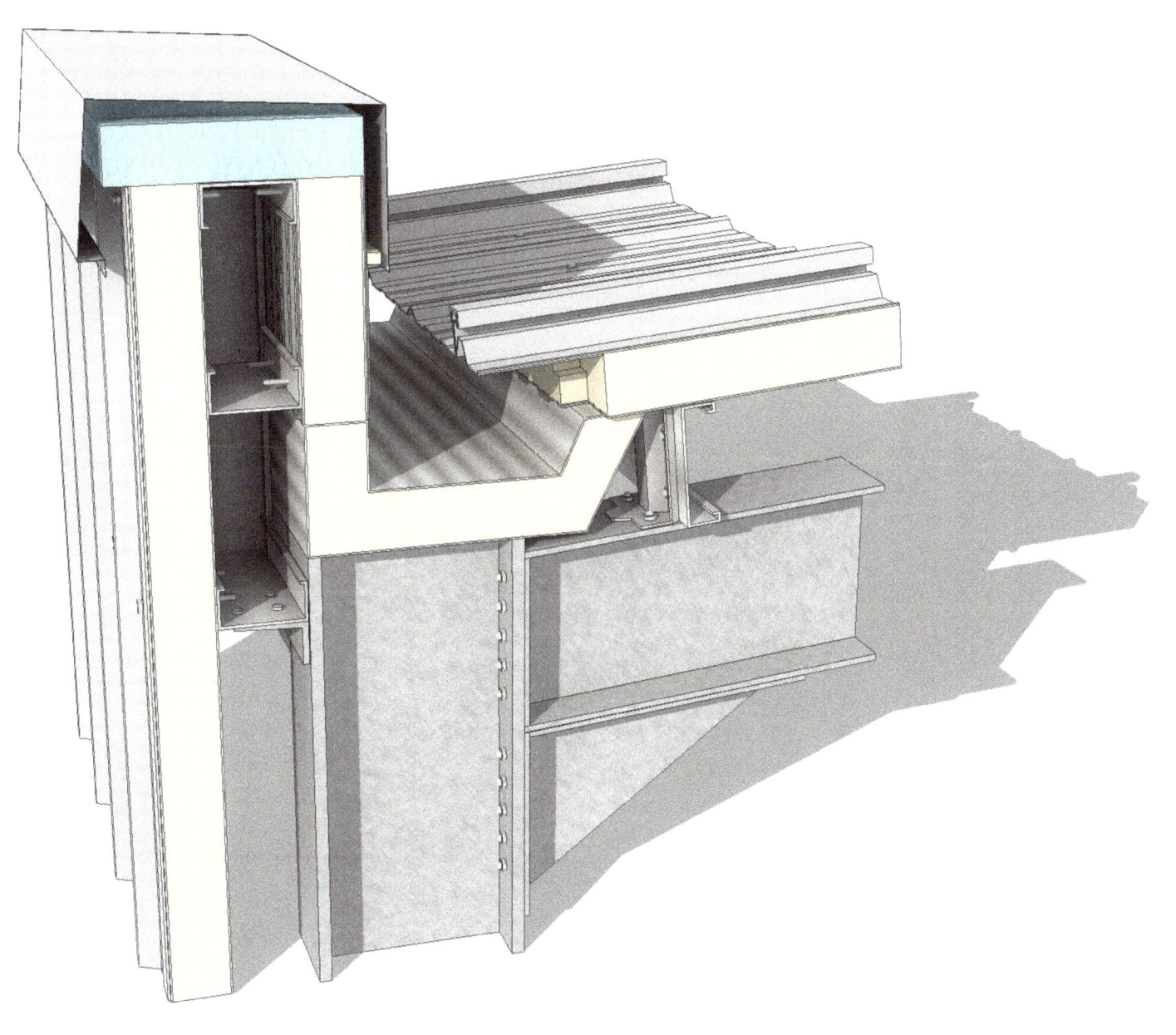

3D Detail P12 - Parapet detail

P13

MONO-RIDGE DETAIL

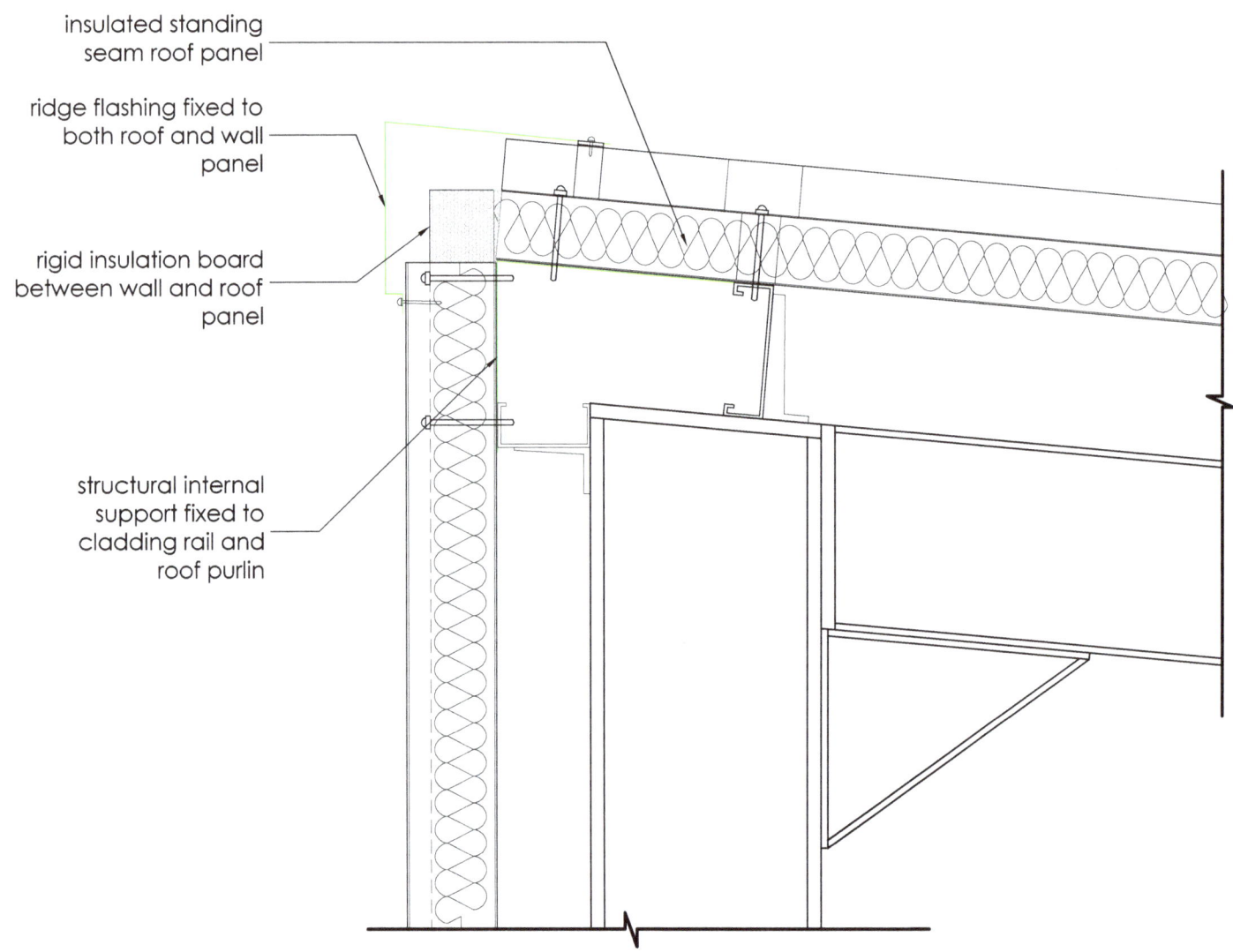

2D Detail P13 - Mono-ridge detail

SECTION 6 - FRAMES

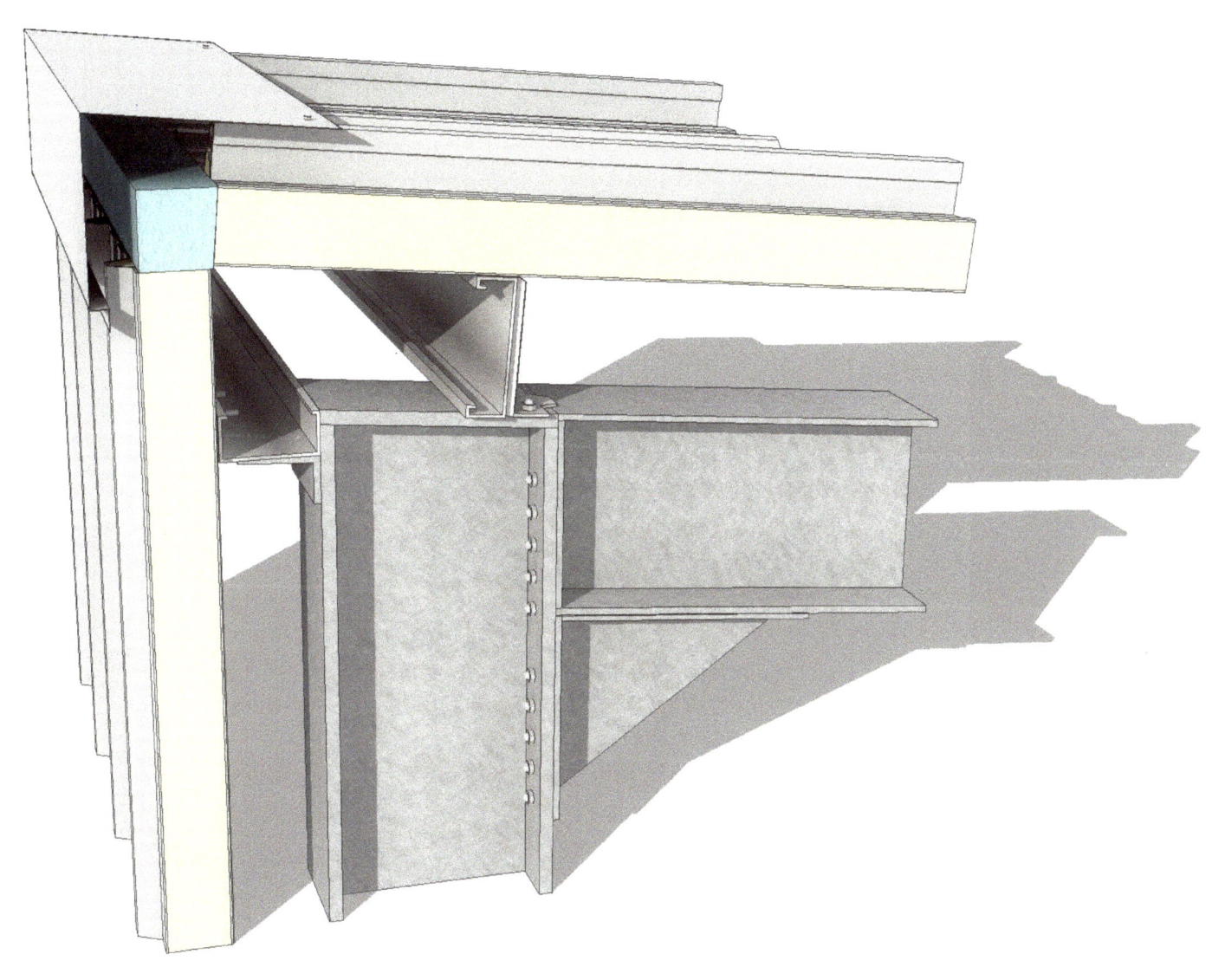

3D Detail P13 - Mono-ridge detail

P14

VERGE DETAIL

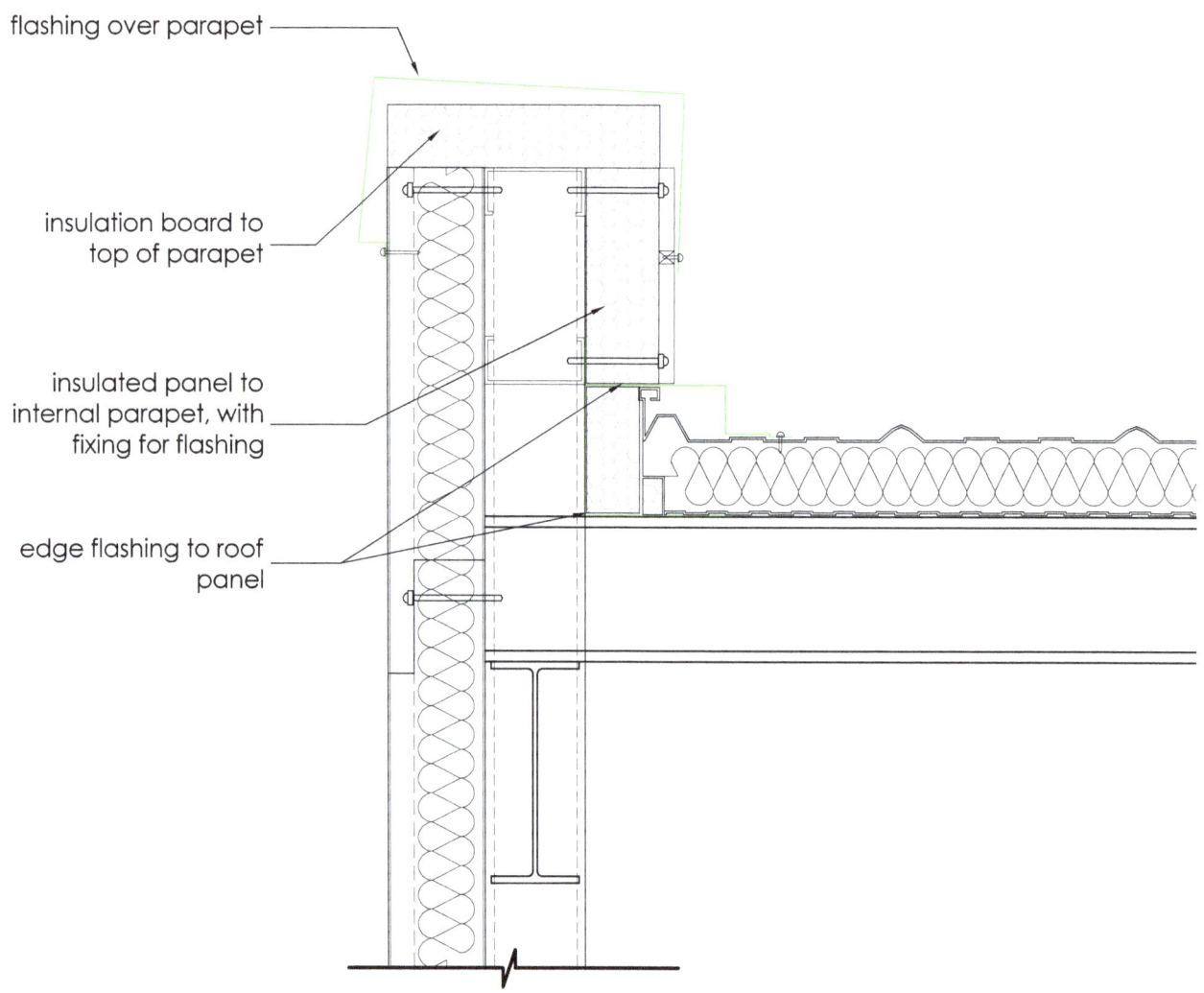

2D Detail P14 - Verge detail

SECTION 6 - FRAMES

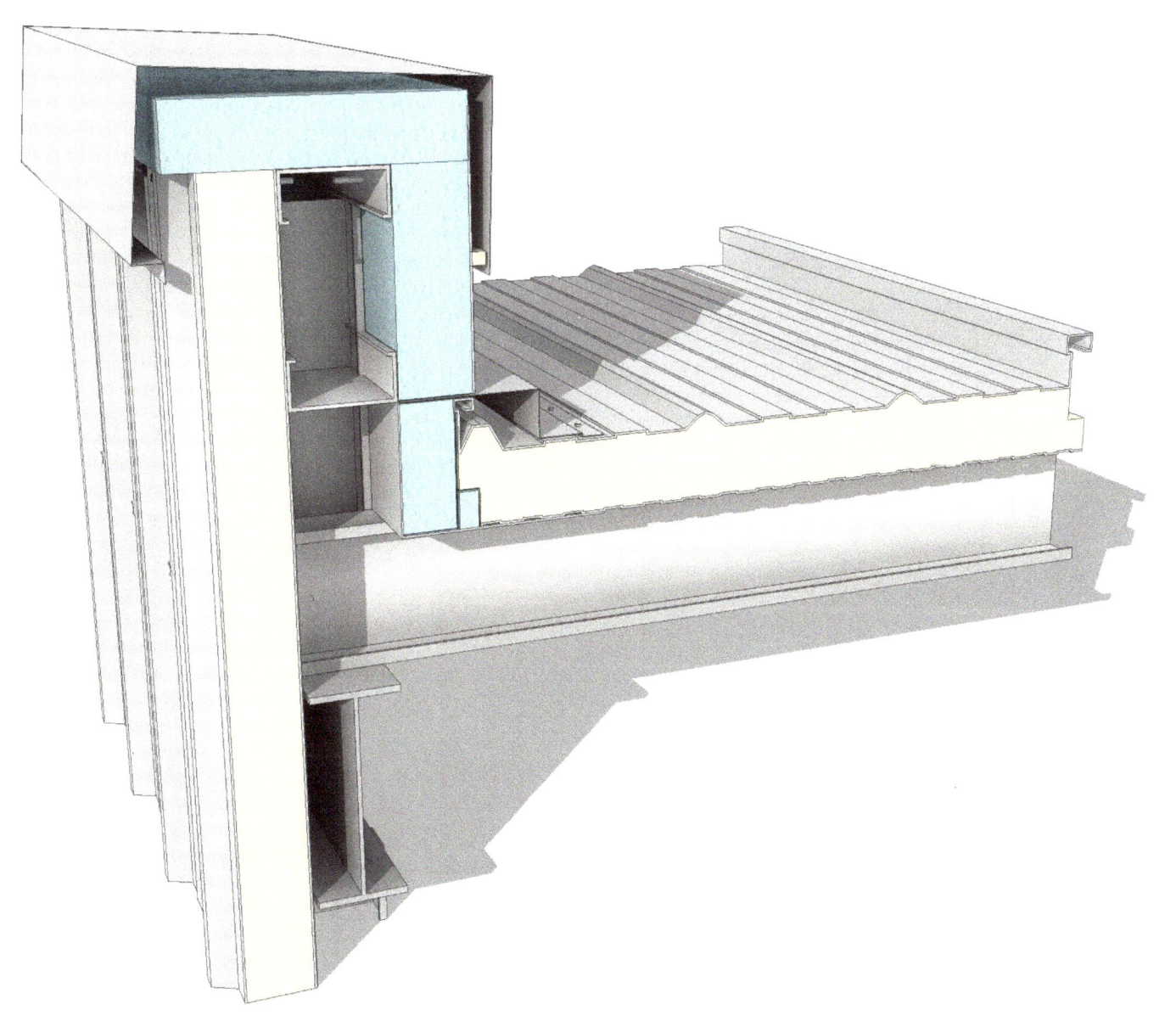
3D Detail P14 - Verge detail

Blank Page

WALLS AND CLADDING SYSTEMS

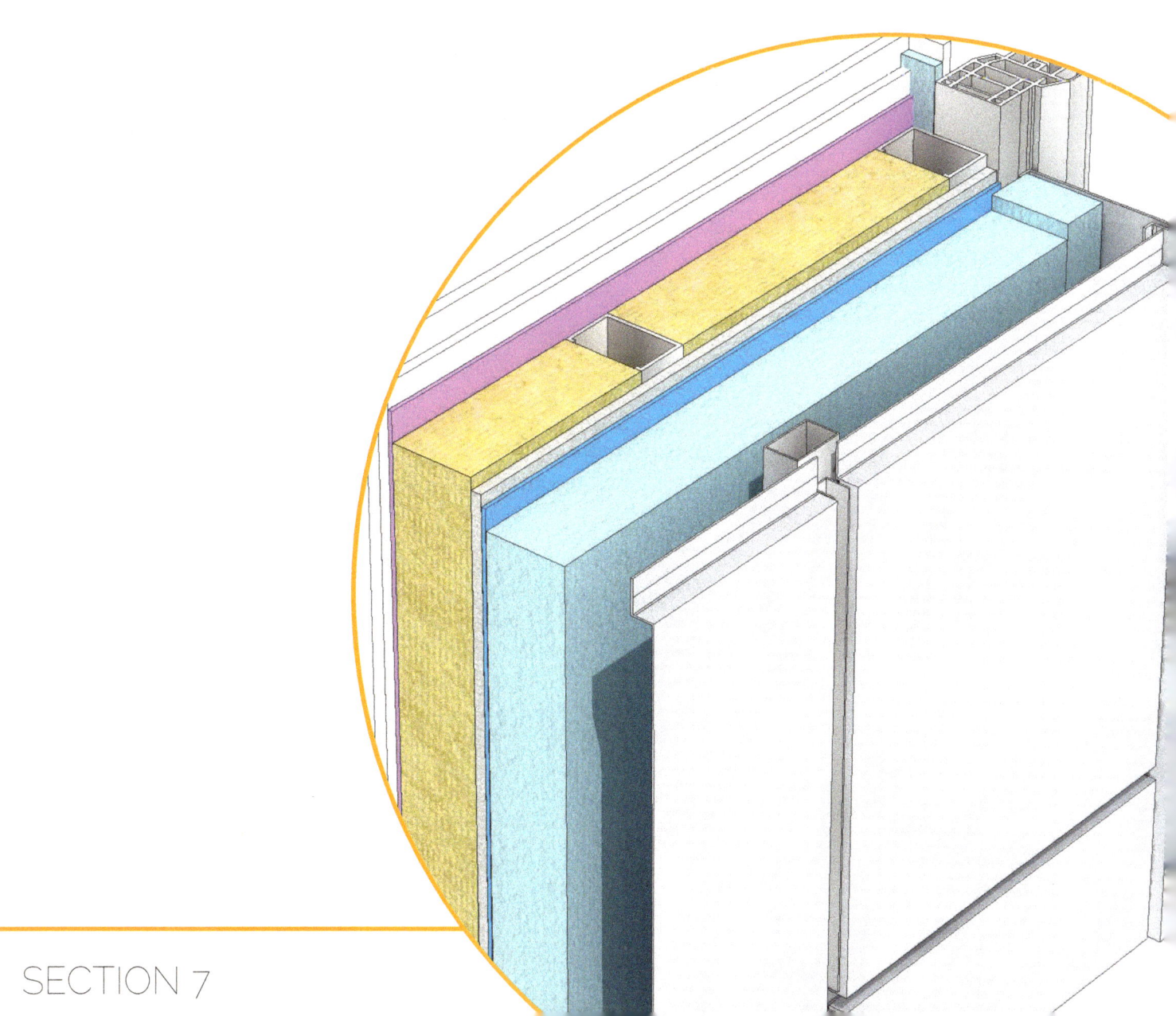

SECTION 7

INTRODUCTION TO WALLS AND CLADDING SYSTEMS

There are a wide variety of walling and cladding systems available for commercial and industrial structures, with many factors determining what construction method is chosen. The walls of any high rise or commercial structures must fulfil a set of performance criteria, and the cladding and walling options of today meet those standards. These functional requirements include:

Strength and stability
The cladding system should be able to support its own weight between fixings or framing members. It should also have sufficient strength to resist wind forces, and allow for differential movement between the wall system and the structural frame.

Protection from weather and moisture
The walling system must resist rain penetration, and wind penetration.

Thermal insulation
A building must achieve certain thermal comfort standards, and the cladding system will have an impact on these standards. It is important that the building provides adequate thermal insulation, but also avoids excessive solar heat gain. When working with structural frames, another key design factor is the avoidance of thermal bridging.

Sound insulation
The walling system must resist sound transmission, both impact sound and airborne sound.

Resistance to fire
Main considerations with cladding systems is the spread of fire across surface materials, and within concealed spaces such as cavities and voids in construction. Cavity barriers and cavity stops must be specified as a barrier where applicable to prevent the spread of smoke and flames. The regulations state that cavity barriers must be provided to close the edges of cavities, including around openings, and any junction between an external or internal cavity wall and every compartment floor and compartment wall. They must also be provided to sub divide any cavity, including any roof space so that the distance between cavity barriers does not exceed dimensions given in the regulations.

There are a wide variety of cavity barriers, stops and closers on the market to fulfil the requirements of the building regulations. The requirements for resistance to fire in high rise and commercial applications is intricate and requires thoughtful design. For advice on fire protection, seek guidance from the Approved Documents, specifically Part B, and a certified fire consultant.

Ventilation
With walling and cladding systems often being completely sealed units, it is more common to incorporate mechanical ventilation systems to provide a regular change of air required for human comfort. Open plan spaces and the use of atriums often assist with the movement of air, along with stack ventilation designs.

Durability
A wall finish of brick or masonry will require little lifetime maintenance, whereas a finish of glass requires regular cleaning. The selection of a walling system will need to consider the maintenance requirements and costs, along with the safety precautions required for said maintenance.

CLADDING CATEGORIES

The structural frame allow for the possibility of numerous variations in the form and appearance of buildings, with a vast variety of materials and finishes constantly changing and progressing. Wall and cladding systems can be categorised in a number of ways. For this book, I have narrowed down the systems into five main areas:

- Solid wall systems
- Cladding façades and cladding panels
- Rain screen panels
- Glazed curtain walling
- Infill walling

Over this chapter we will explore these different walling methods, some in more detail than others.

SOLID WALL SYSTEMS

A concrete frame building can often be constructed using a solid wall system, usually made of concrete, but in some cases masonry is also used. The solid walls are either left un-clad as the final outer finish, or used as a backing wall for fixings for cladding systems.

Fig 7.1 - Solid concrete wall system

Concrete in situ

Concrete cast in situ is a very flexible material in terms of the shapes and finishes that can be achieved. It is only restricted by the formwork that can be created and the amount of concrete that can be poured at one time. Concrete cast in situ with a concrete frame structure can be used as a facade that leaves the cast concrete as a surface finish. The use of concrete load bearing walls has been popular for many years, and as the requirement for improved thermal performance came into place, insulation was often positioned on the inside of the concrete walls. Positioning the insulation inside of the structure does work, but it prevents the use of the concrete's inherent thermal mass for night time cooling.

A more recent development is to set the thermal insulation within the depth of the construction, allowing the benefits of the thermal mass to be gained, along with the face of the concrete being exposed both externally and internally if desired. This method is sometimes referred to as diaphragm walling. Both options can be adopted, depending on the requirements of the building in terms of insulation and night time cooling, along with aesthetic requirements. If insulation is incorporated into the concrete structure, continuity of the insulation must be maintained at openings to avoid thermal bridging.

Concrete cast in situ can have a range of finishes, either using the formwork to create the finish, or by implementing methods such as acid etching, sand blasting, tooling and polishing.

Precast Concrete

Precast concrete can also be used as a solid load bearing wall in a frame construction. Precast units can be formed as load bearing units, or as cladding panels that are fixed to the structural frame. The precast load bearing panels are storey height, and jointed with the floor slab, usually with insulation positioned within the panel or on the internal face. The precast unit can have a decorative finish on the external side, and be left 'bare faced' or it can form the backing wall to cladding systems such as rain screen, where the thermal insulation will be set on the outside of the concrete, with the rain screen cladding system positioned over the insulation.

As with the cast in situ concrete, precast units can also be finished with varying methods, including acid etching, polishing, sand blasting or tooling.

Masonry

Most load bearing solid wall systems use concrete as the primary material, with masonry walling being used mainly in residential settings. However, in recent times masonry walling is being implemented either as brick or blockwork walls that are load bearing on larger scale projects.

There are a number of arrangements that can be specified including:
- Solid brick walls, these must be relatively deep in order to prevent rainwater penetration, usually 315mm or 1.5 bricks, with insulation positioned on the inside face.
- Solid blockwork wall, with insulation positioned on the inside face of the wall. The blockwork outer face can be rendered or used as a backing for another suitable finish.
- Brick cavity wall, with the cavity for draining any water penetration, along with the positioning of the insulation.
- Stone or block cavity wall, similar to the brick cavity wall, but with the outer leaf in stonework.

Masonry can also be used as infill to a structural frame, providing a backing for any cladding systems. This is usually blockwork as the backing wall will not be seen and therefore does not need to have any aesthetic value.

CLADDING FAÇADES AND CLADDING PANELS:

This is quite a wide category, covering anything from a facing applied to a solid backing wall, to composite panels.

Cladding to a building can be described as components that are attached to the primary structure of a building to form a non load bearing external surface. A cladding will fulfil many duties, above just creating a weather protective barrier to the building.

Fig 7.3 - Composite cladding system

A cladding system will be selected based on a number of requirements, such as:
- The building's end use
- The required internal and external conditions
- The necessary durability of the system and maintenance requirements
- Planning requirements and the local context of the building
- Building regulation requirements
- Budget
- Appearance

Cladding systems can be formed using many materials including:
- stone
- concrete
- ceramic
- timber
- glass
- various metals
- plastic
- amongst others

There are certainly too many types of cladding to cover in this book, so we will briefly look at some of the available options.

Concrete cladding panels

Precast concrete cladding panels offer a variation of finishes and sizes, being factory made to suit the designers needs. Sometimes incorporating an insulation layer, the precast units can be self supporting, and stacked together or interlocked up to about 10m with lateral support provided by the structural frame. Concrete cladding is also available as a rainscreen option (which we will look at later) and fixed to a backing wall using fixing brackets or onto a stainless steel frame.

Panels can span large distances, i.e. storey to storey, or indeed be much smaller panels.
Selection of the panel type would take into account some of the following:

- Structural frame spacing, determining the span of the panels
- Weight of panels required
- Method of jointing panels
- Finish or facing requirements
- Weather conditions and exposure of the building and site

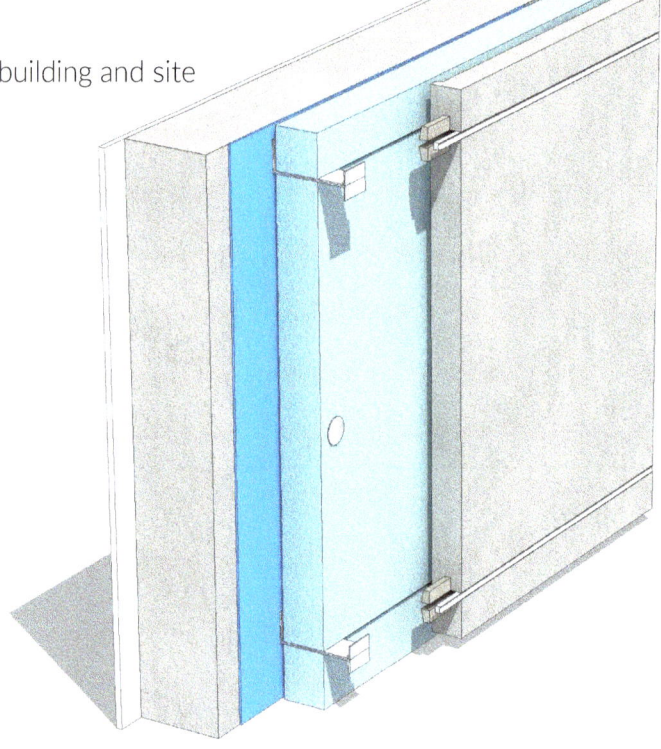

Fig 7.4 - Concrete cladding system

Facings - stone, ceramic, glass

A facing can be described as a relatively thin non structural cladding of stone, ceramic, glass (amongst others) that is fixed to the face of a solid background wall or to the structural frame as a decorative finish to the building.

These types of facings can come in many different shapes, sizes and finishes, and can be applied to the building in a number of ways.

Stone Facings

Stone facings can be a relatively expensive option. Granite, limestone, slate, sandstone and marble (although this is not common) can be used, and range in thickness from about 30mm to 75mm depending on material and position on the building. The size of the facing is usually restricted to 1.5m, which is the maximum practical size that can be obtained from the quarry.

The finishes for stone facings can include rubbed, honed, polished and flamed finishes for different stone types allowing again for greater variety and visual interest.

Fixing
The facings require support fixings but also restraint fixings that will aid with the resistance of wind pressure and suction forces that act on the wall. Any facing design will require movement joints, both horizontally and vertically to accommodate any structural movements. The facings must also be resistant to the penetration of any rainwater.

The facing is fixed to the structure with a cavity between the facing itself and the supporting wall or frame. The cavity fulfils a number of functions, including providing space for the fixing system, allow for structural movement. The cavity is not especially wide at about 10 to 20mm, but will be completely free of any element.

The fixings can include load bearing fixings in the form of stainless steel angles or corbel plates that carry the weight of the facing, restraint fixings that hook into grooves at the edges of the slabs or sometimes a combination of the two. The facings can also be face fixed to the background wall, where each slab is bedded in mortar behind the slab and is secured in place using bolts. The holes that are drilled into the facing for the fixing is then filled with a small piece of stone that matches the facing itself.

The joints between the facings must be sealed to prevent the penetration of rainwater, this can be done with mortar or sealants depending on the stone and requirement. A closed joint system such as this will act in a similar way to a cavity wall and require ventilation at the top and bottom of the void to allow any moisture to dry.

Sheet metal cladding
Profiled metal cladding is covered in the portal frame section of this book, and is often used for industrial or

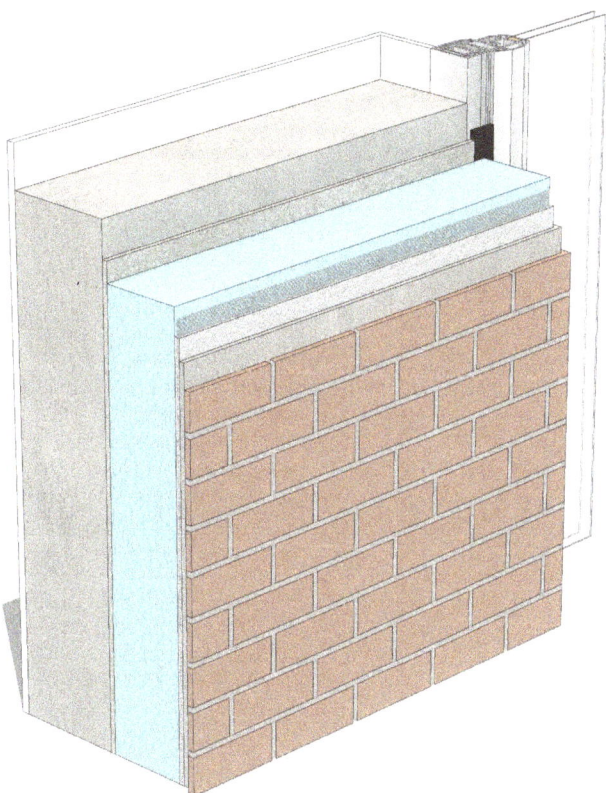

Fig 7.5 - Brick slip cladding system

agricultural buildings. However, sheet metal cladding is popular in more commercial construction settings.

Sheet metal cladding is usually supported by a timber substrate, usually plywood, which is fixed to a backing wall. The timber substrate is ventilated on its internal face to ensure any moisture can escape. Sheet metal cladding is popular due to its ability to follow complex geometries and achieve shapes, folds and curves that other cladding finishes cannot. It can also be used to cover a roof and wall as one continuous facade.

Two methods of sheet metal cladding are a standing seam system or tiled shingles. In both applications the typical build up from the backing wall would include insulation fixed to the backing wall, breather membrane or water resistant layer, ventilation cavity between fixing battens, timber substrate (plywood) and the sheet metal finish.

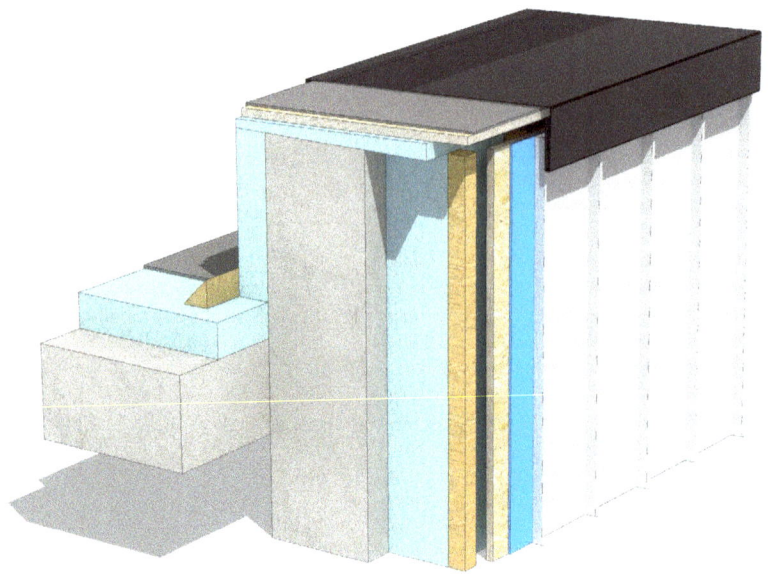

Fig 7.6 - Sheet metal cladding system

Composite cladding panels

Composite panels consist of a metal outer skin (usually steel or aluminium) bonded to a core of insulation. This panel can be used as a final cladding finish to a building or as a substrate to fix a facade to. Available in a range of different sizes, colours and finishes composite panels are a popular option. Manufacturers have developed their own fixing methods according to the panels they have developed, all of which will provide a certain amount of movement for structural and thermal expansion, while maintaining a weather resistant facade.

The composite panels allow for excellent U-values, joints that meet air leakage requirements, fast construction times along with many other benefits.

Panels are fixed to a metal frame structure fixed to the main concrete or steel frame. The panels are fixed to the frame using mechanical fixings that are then covered with a capping system, or the fixing is hidden in the interlocking joint. Panels can also be supported on horizontal rails, and interlock either side with one another.

Render cladding systems

Insulated render systems provide a number of colour and texture finishes to the external envelope of the building. Insulation is fixed to a substrate, with a mesh and base coat applied to the insulation layer, followed by a top primer and decorate finish. The system can also be used on steel frame structures, using a light gauge steel frame fixed to the structural frame.

Insulated render systems offer great flexibility, and can fulfil a number of requirements dependant on the project and site.

It is also possible to install brick slips, ceramic tiles and stone onto the same external wall insulation systems.

Fig 7.7 - Render cladding system

RAINSCREEN CLADDING:

Rainscreen cladding provides an outer layer to the building that screens the rain down its surface. The joints of the system are often left open, to allow any excess moisture to pass through, and be drained down the cavity. The backing wall or frame is usually fitted with insulation with a water resistant layer to provide the weather protection. Rainscreen cladding systems are popular and can be seen in a variety of shapes, sizes and materials including timber, ceramic tiles, terracotta, render, metal, laminates to name a few. It is worth seeking out some manufacturers literature to get a true sense of the options available.

Rainscreen cladding systems were developed when standard cladding joints were being penetrated by water due to the outside air pressure being greater than pressure inside the joint. The rainscreen system allows water to enter the joint but ensures the air pressure in the void is the same as the air pressure outside. The main functions of a rainscreen system are to provide a decorative weather resistant layer for the waterproofing system behind, to provide a protective layer to the thermal insulation fixed to the face of the structure and suitably drain any excess moisture down the cavity and away from the building.

The void behind the cavity has the potential to spread smoke and flame, therefore cavity barriers must be installed in accordance with the Building Regulations.

Metal rainscreen
A metal rainscreen system allows wind blown rain water to pass through the joints between panels and drain away down the cavity. The panels are installed on a metal frame system, fixed to the concrete or steel structural frame. Behind the cavity sits the waterproofed thermal insulation. The backing wall is not visible from the outside so is usually constructed of an economic material.
The metal panels can be visually striking with crisp lines. Most systems tend to avoid having visible fixings by using a hook on system or slot system. Different manufacturers have developed a variety of fixing and installation options that allow for a number of configurations.

When working with openings to the rainscreen, in order to avoid staining sills are usually formed to direct rainwater to the sides of the opening and down the joints between panels, rather than directly down the face of the panel below.

Masonry rainscreen
As with the stone facings we explored earlier, the masonry cladding can be designed as a rainscreen if desired. The panels are individually supported but the rainscreen fixing system, with the joints remaining open to allow rainwater to pass through the facing and drain down the cavity.

Terracotta rainscreen cladding is a more recent development and proving popular. The panels are fixed to a vertical or horizontal framing system. The panels are available in a variety of colours and textures. The panels remain relatively lightweight due to their hollow extruded profile.

As well as terracotta panels, it is also possible to use terracotta shingles which are fixed to horizontal rails. Finishing trims are usually made from folded aluminium or rolled steel channels.

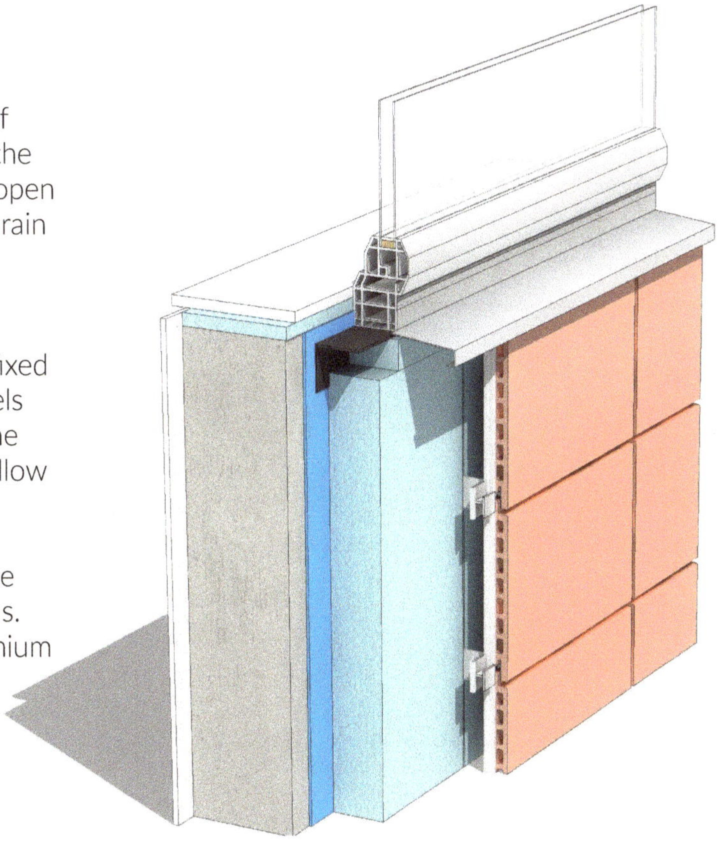

Fig 7.8 - Rainscreen cladding system

Concrete rainscreen

Small precast concrete panels can be used as a rainscreen system. The fixings are similar to those used in stone cladding fixed to a carrier frame that is attached to the main structure. The backing wall will have a layer of waterproof insulation followed by a void for the draining of any moisture. The concrete panels are available in a number of sizes and finishes to create an array of textures and interest.

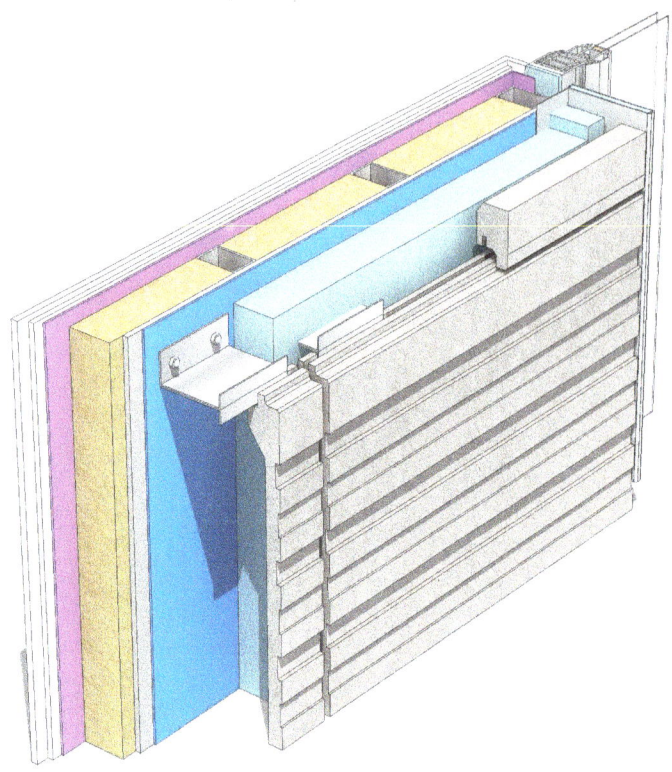

Fig 7.9 - Concrete rainscreen cladding system

Timber cladding systems

Timber cladding can be used in commercial settings much the same way it is used in residential. The timber cladding boards are fixed to battens that are fixed to a backing wall. The cladding often allows moisture to penetrate the outer face, and will therefore have a void for ventilation, behind the cladding. The insulation and waterproofing layer will be fixed to the backing wall.

Timber cladding is available in many forms, both vertical and horizontal as well as panel systems.

GLASS WALLING SYSTEMS

There are a number of glass systems used in construction today to create a continuous glazed wall with dramatic effect and daylight levels.

Some of the different types of glass façades include:
- Bolted glazing
- Cable supported glazing
- Stick glazing
- Truss supported glazing
- Fin supported glazing
- Suspended glazing
- Panel system glazing

Glass walling systems are varied, with a vast number of systems available, the details of which go beyond the scope of this book, and will be addressed in a future issue.

INFILL WALLING

Infill panels sit between the structural frame of a building, they are generally lightweight panels that are not load bearing. The infill panels can be glazed to allow light into a building, and as such are suited to buildings that do not require thermal insulation. An issue with infill walling is thermal bridging where the structural members are exposed. The infill walling systems are more suited to climates that do not require high levels of thermal insulation.

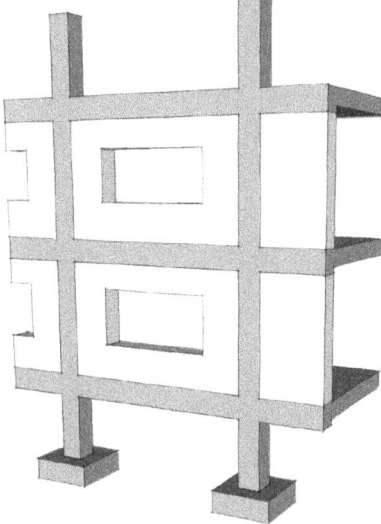

Infill wall example

GREEN WALLS

Also known as living walls, a green wall is a cladding system that creates a building facade that is completely covered in vegetation.
Gaining in popularity in recent years, green walls can be seen on façades of museums, shops, offices and many other commercial buildings.

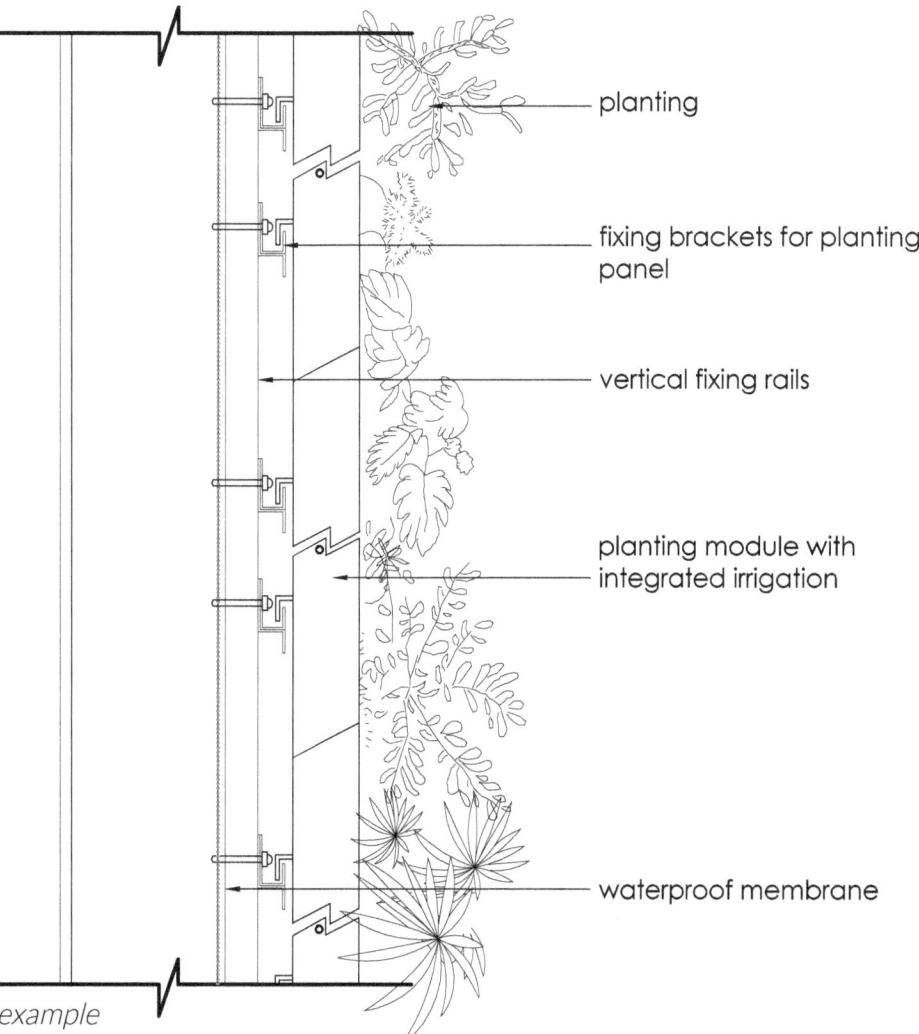

Fig 7.10 Green wall system example

TYPES OF GREEN WALL

There are three main types of living walls.

CLIMBING FAÇADES

These walls use trailing or climbing plants established in the ground or troughs or pots, that are trained to climb a framework, or trail from above. These are considered the simplest method to introduce a green wall into a design. Frames can be made using wires, trellises, mesh frames or steel cables. It can take some years to for the plants to grow to achieve the desired coverage and density.

SUBSTRATE OR SOIL BASED MODULAR SYSTEMS

The modular system employs a cassette type element that is filled with a soil that the plant draws its nutrients from. They typically use a moulded trough or container that is built on or attached to an existing wall. These units tend to be grown off site until ready for installation where the modules are then fixed to a supporting structure. The advantage of using a soil based system is the substrate will allow water retention which means irrigation systems can be quite simple in their design. The modular system enables replacement of individual panels as required. The drawback of the soil based system is the weight of the substrate can apply additional loadings to the structure compared with other solutions.

HYDROPONIC MODULAR SYSTEMS

Plants do not require soil to grow, and this system takes advantage of this fact by providing a mineral rich water to the plants which are grown in panels with specialist felt pockets for the plants. This creates a lightweight modular system that is irrigated with the water drops across the facade. These systems can be complex, with computer operated irrigation systems to ensure the plants never dry out.

Benefits

Green walls offer many advantages and benefits to a building, some of which are listed below:

- Improvement in atmosphere due to the ability to suppress dust particles, and the absorption of CO2.
- Improved ecosystem biodiversity by introducing new plants to encourage a variety of insects and bird life.
- Rainwater harvesting for irrigation to the green wall, eliminates the requirement for fresh water supply.
- Green walls can reduce the local heat gains in cities by providing cooling of trapped air and reducing reflected heat.
- The green wall can help regulate internal temperatures in the building and reduce cooling requirements in the summer.
- Green walls can reduce heat loss from a building in winter
- The vegetation on a green wall can help with noise absorption.
- Green walls are considered to be an aesthetic addition to a building design and improve peoples health and well being.
- It is possible to introduce food growing in urban environments that have limited space with the use of green walls.

Disadvantages

- Green walls can be expensive to install, and require specialist input from an early stage to ensure correct design and implementation.
- Irrigation systems are key to maintaining the life of the wall, and if a system should fail, the vegetation can dry out very quickly.
- Maintenance and access are a major consideration and potential cost to installing a green wall, one that the client should be made aware of.
- Roots and tendrils can break through waterproof barriers and seals, so careful detailing is key to ensure the structural integrity of the building.
- Leaves, other vegetation matter can block rainwater pipes and gutters, and must be monitored.

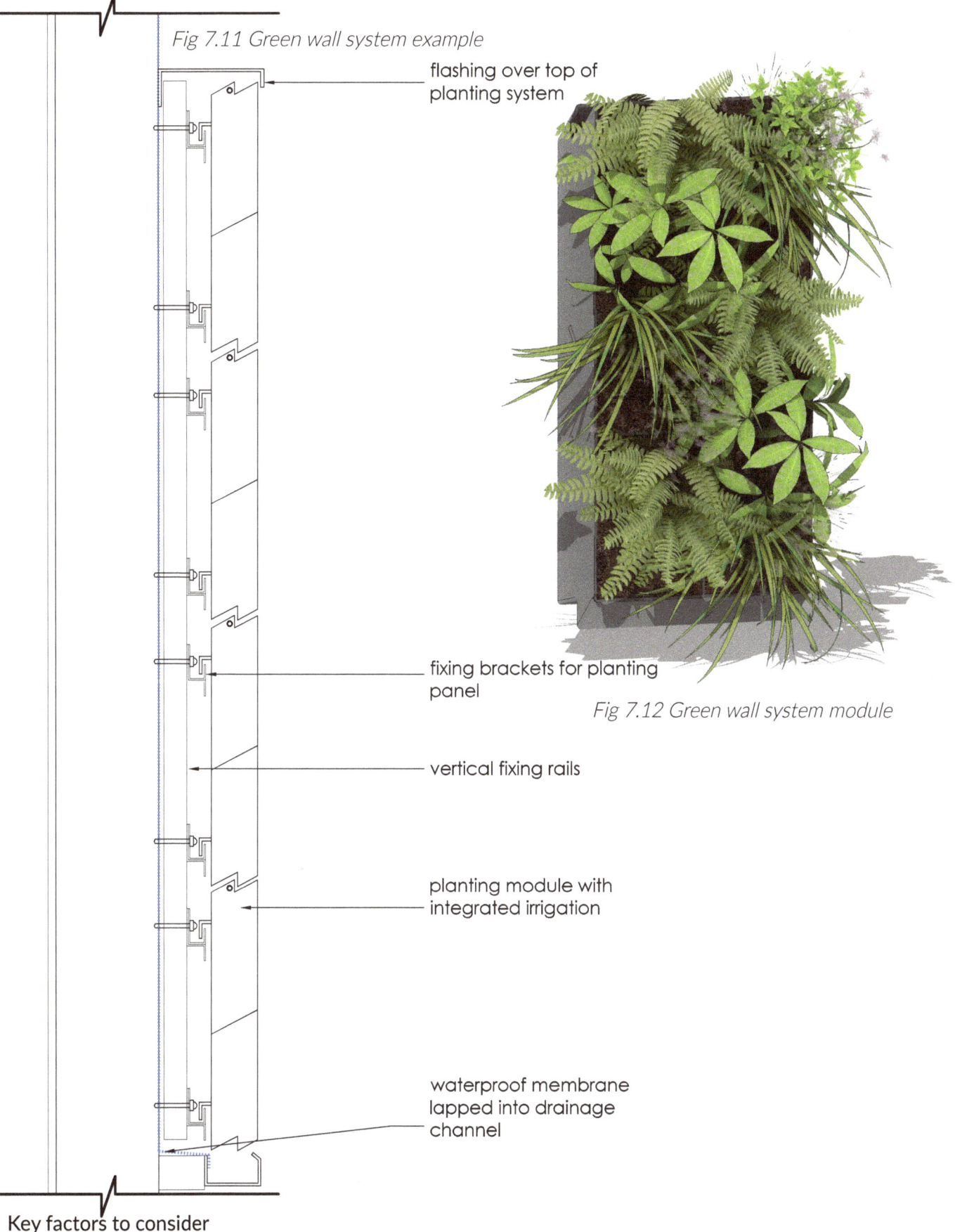

Fig 7.11 Green wall system example

flashing over top of planting system

fixing brackets for planting panel

Fig 7.12 Green wall system module

vertical fixing rails

planting module with integrated irrigation

waterproof membrane lapped into drainage channel

Key factors to consider
- Structural requirements and loading to the structure
- Plant selection is key based on a number of factors including local climate, exposure, light levels, client requirements.
- Plants should be chosen that require similar irrigation
- Maintenance required including pruning, feeding and replacement.
- Access to services for the wall such as water and power are essential and should be considered at early stage of design to ensure they are within the scope of the budget.

WALL DETAILS

CONCRETE CLADDING PANEL, CONCRETE BACKING WALL

- stainless steel support bracket fixed to substrate
- substrate - blockwork infill / concrete wall etc. (internal finishes not shown)
- insulation mechanically fixed to substrate
- concrete cladding panel
- joint sealant with backing rod

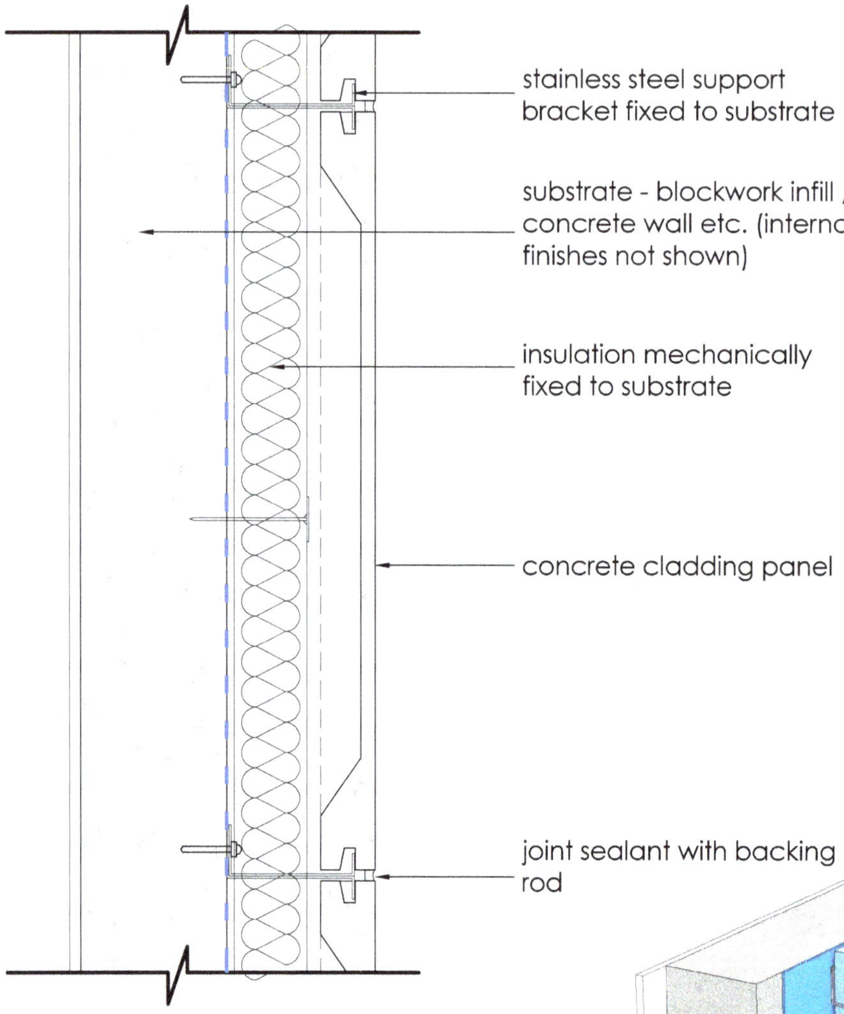

2D Detail W01 - Concrete cladding panel, concrete backing wall

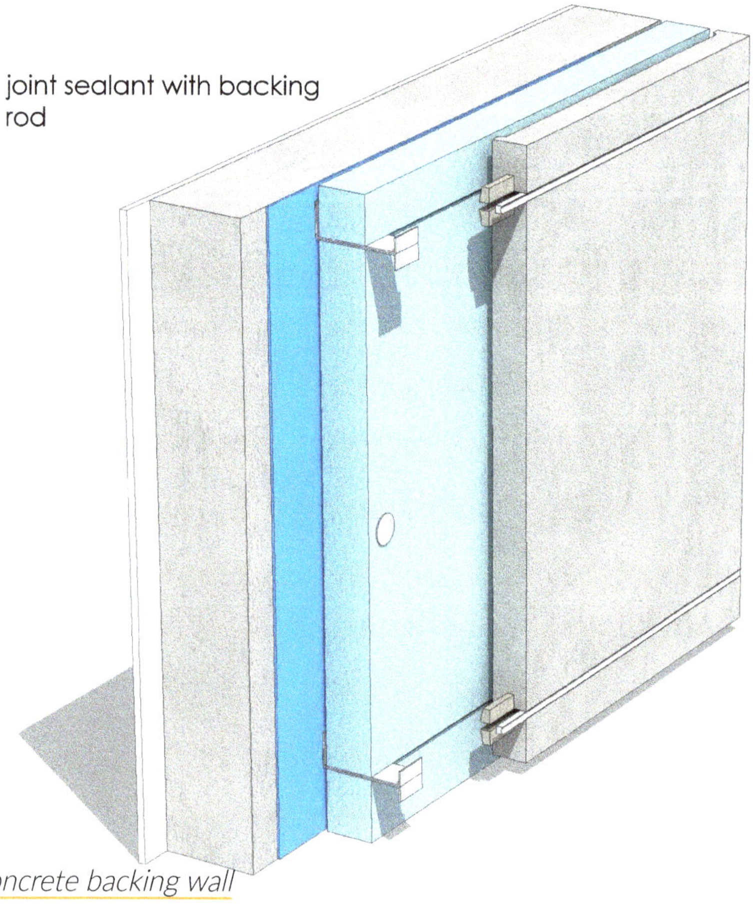

3D Detail W01 - Concrete cladding panel, concrete backing wall

W02

CONCRETE CLADDING PANEL, BASE DETAIL

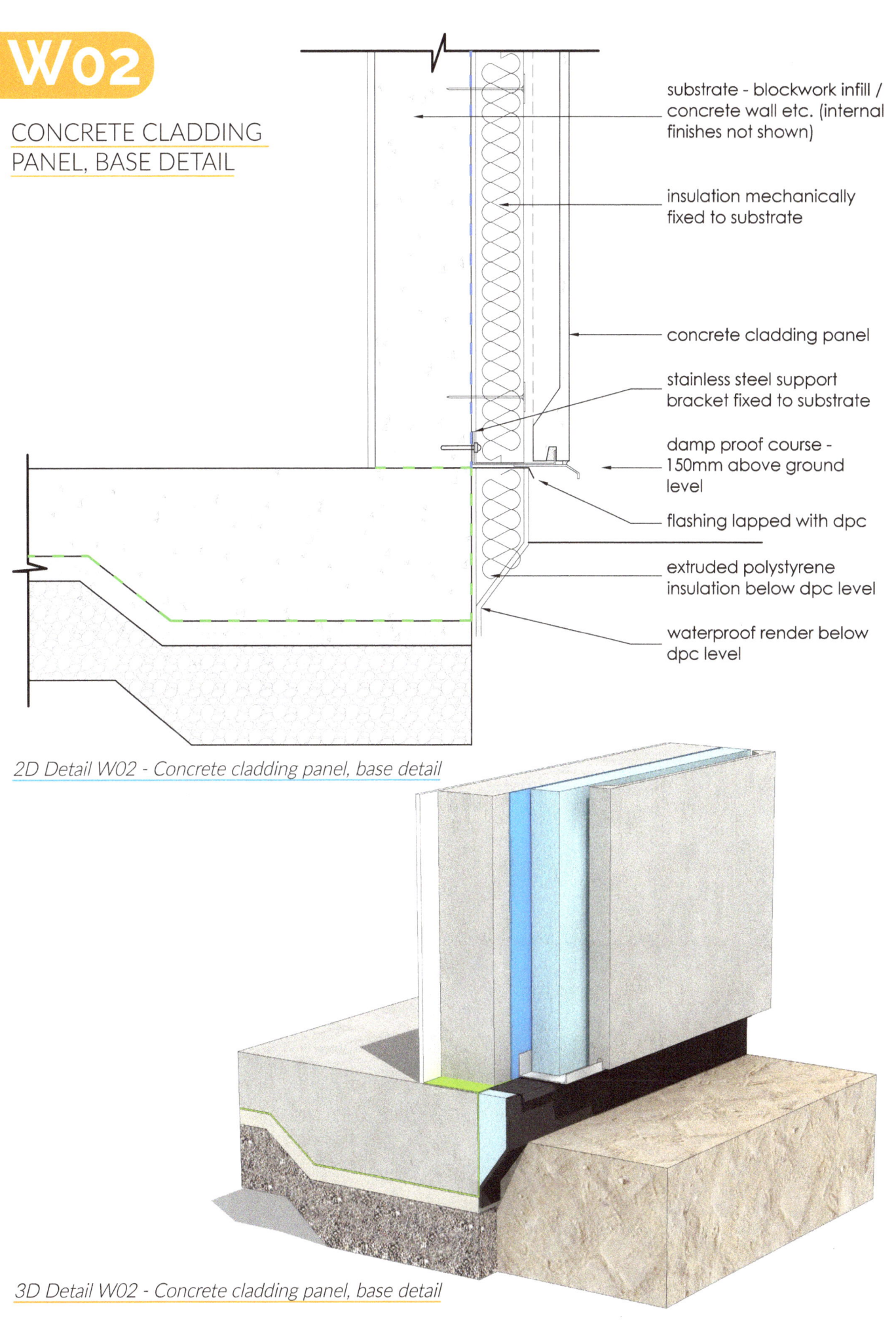

2D Detail W02 - Concrete cladding panel, base detail

3D Detail W02 - Concrete cladding panel, base detail

W03

CONCRETE CLADDING PANEL, WINDOW HEAD DETAIL

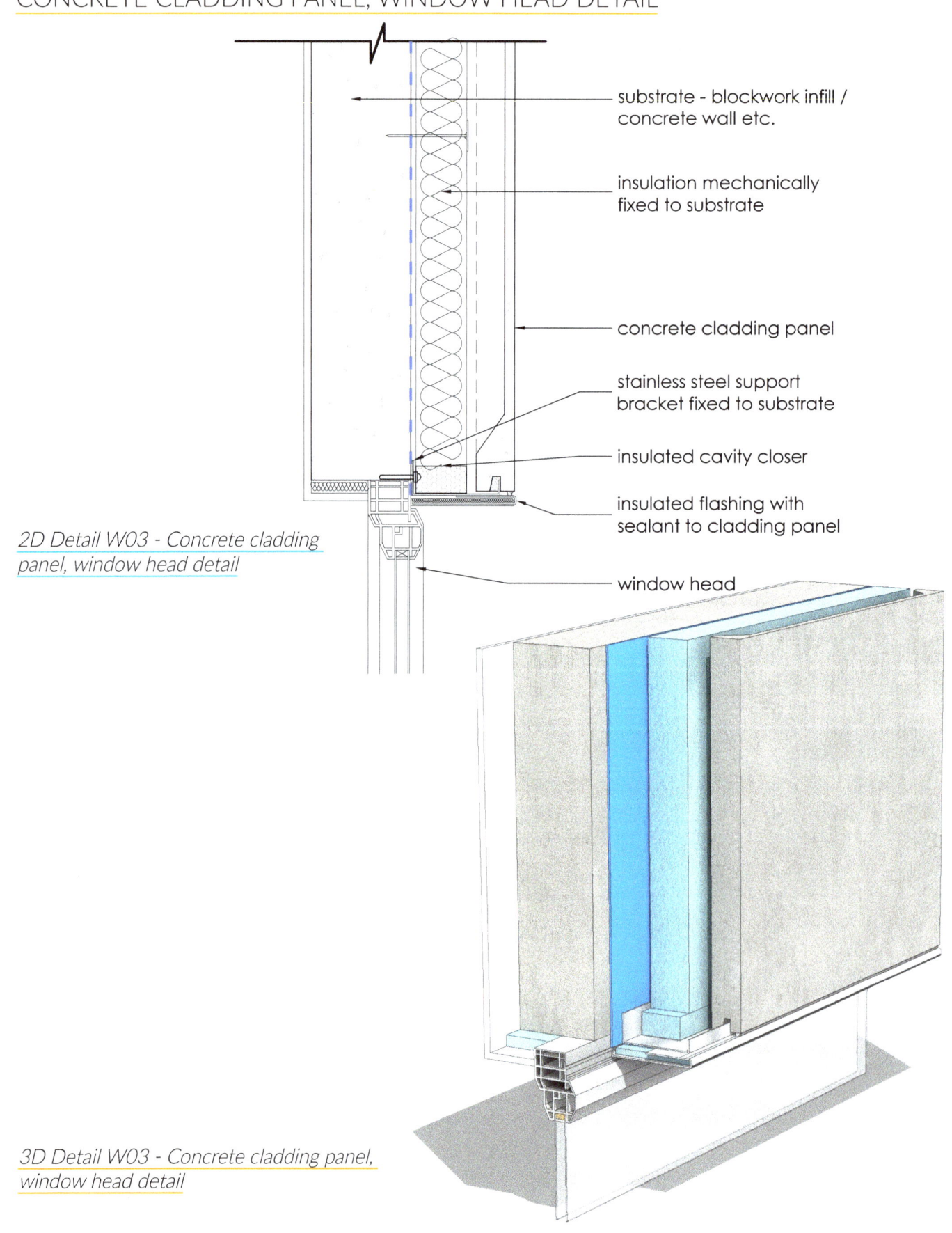

2D Detail W03 - Concrete cladding panel, window head detail

3D Detail W03 - Concrete cladding panel, window head detail

CONCRETE CLADDING PANEL, WINDOW SILL DETAIL

- sill overhang
- sealant strip
- insulation under sill
- insulated cavity closer
- stainless steel support bracket fixed to substrate
- insulation mechanically fixed to substrate
- concrete cladding panel

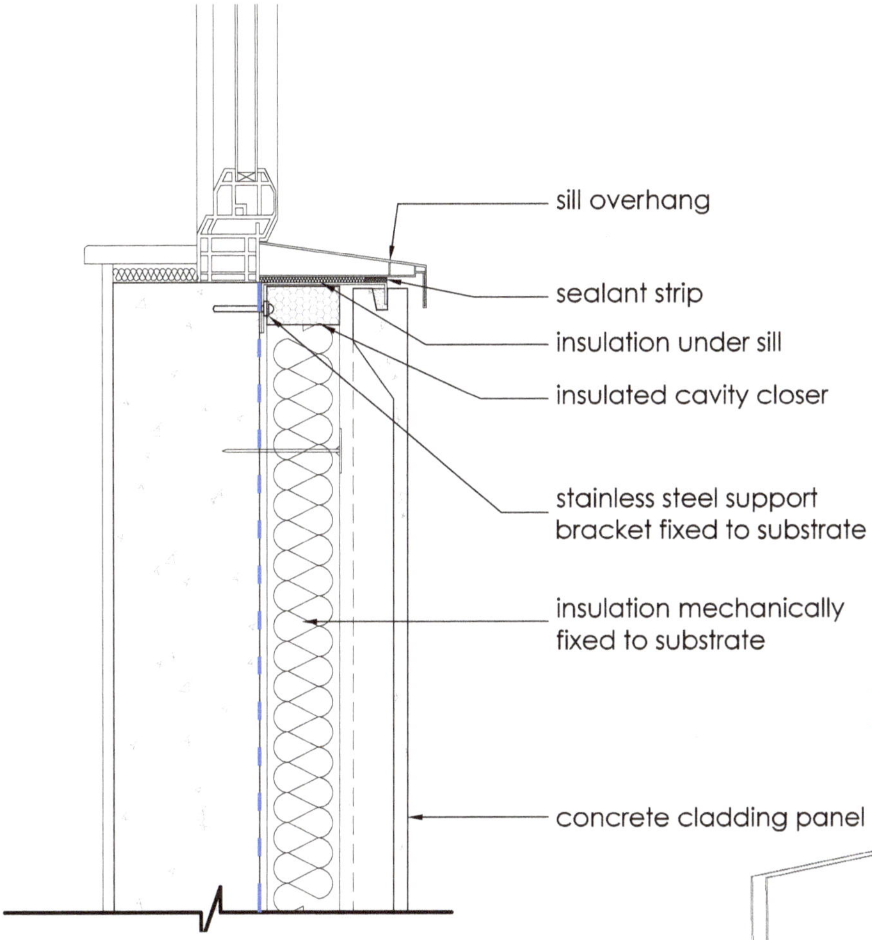

2D Detail W04 - Concrete cladding panel, window sill detail

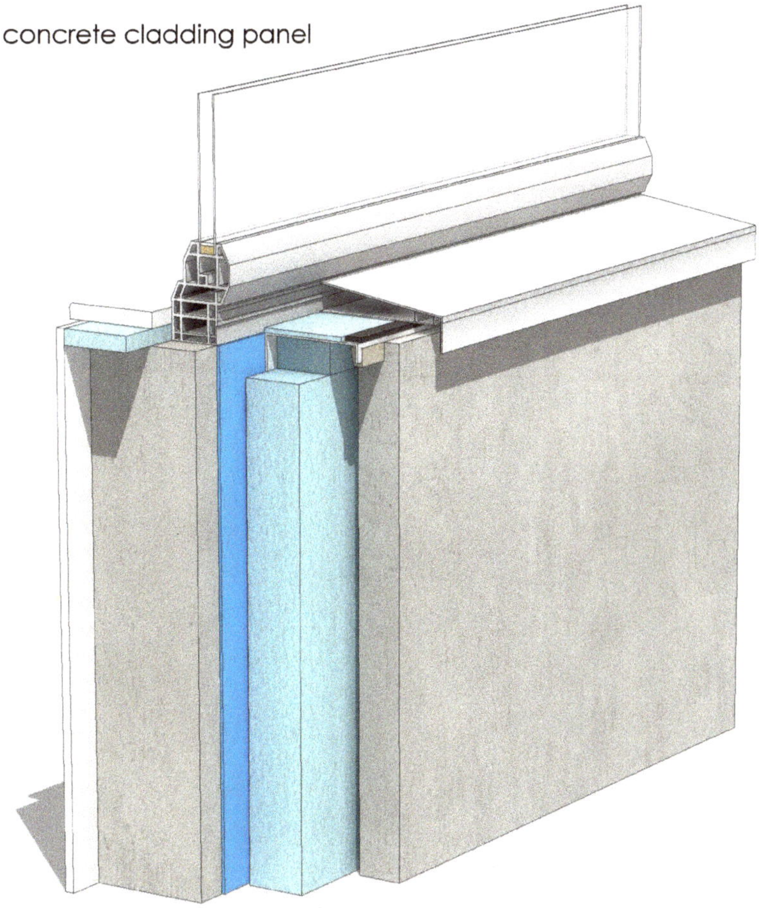

3D Detail W04 - Concrete cladding panel, window sill detail

CONCRETE CLADDING PANEL, WINDOW JAMB DETAIL (PLAN)

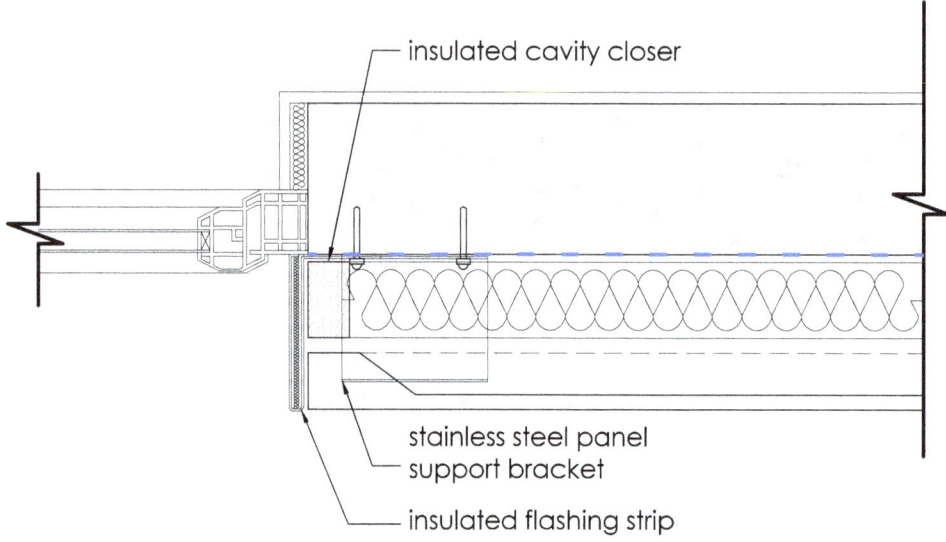

2D Detail W05 - Concrete cladding panel, window jamb detail (plan)

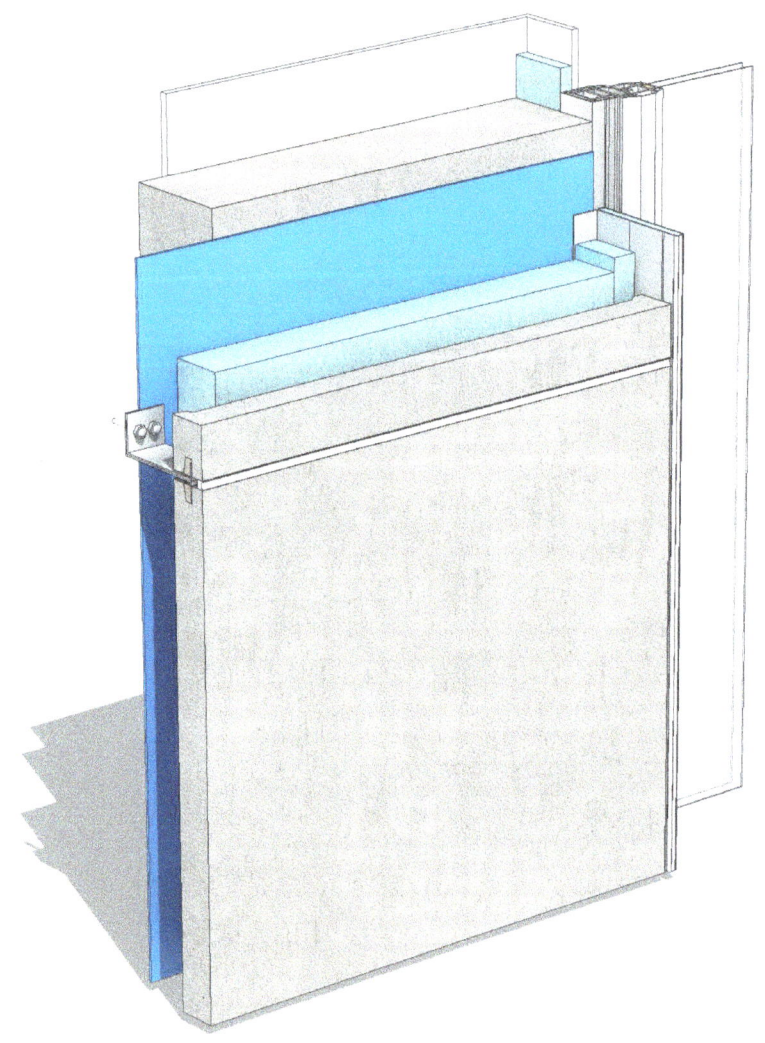

3D Detail W05 - Concrete cladding panel, window jamb detail

SECTION 7 - WALLS

W06

CONCRETE CLADDING PANEL, PARAPET DETAIL

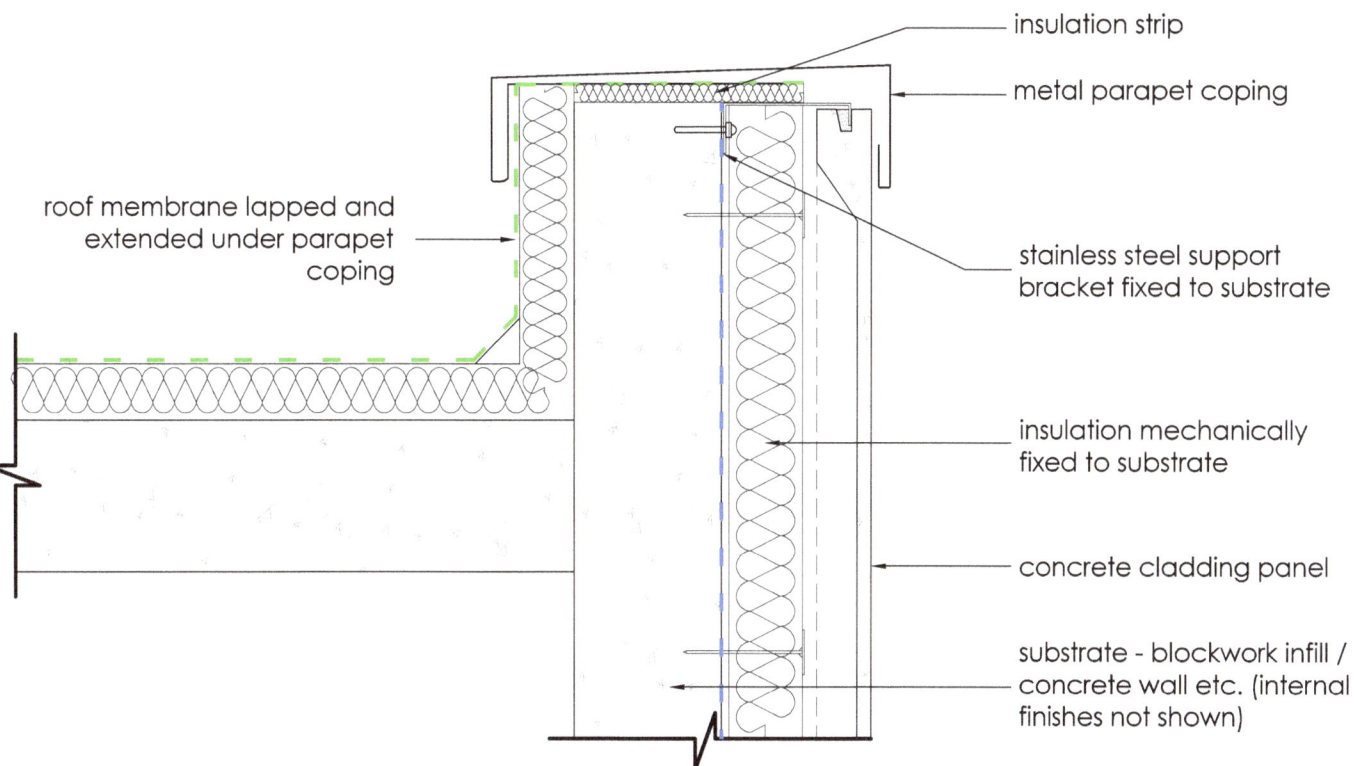

2D Detail W06 - Concrete cladding panel, parapet detail

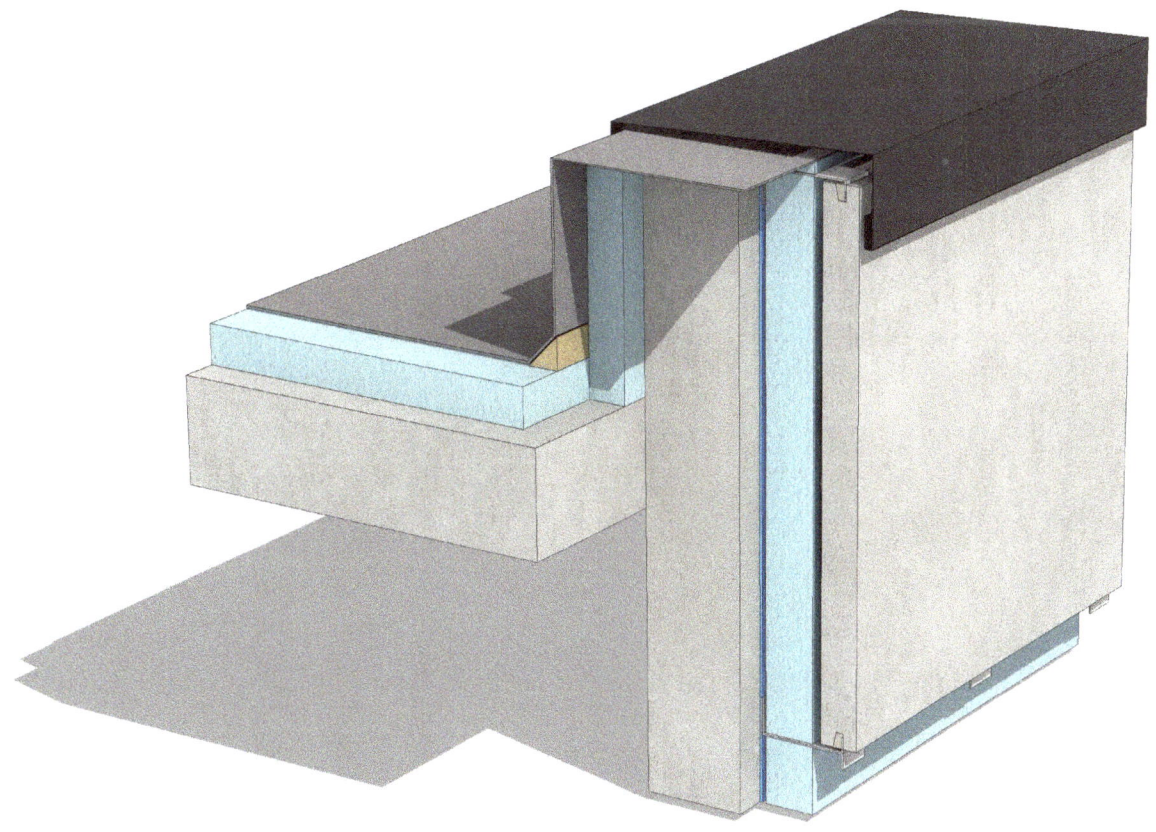

3D Detail W06 - Concrete cladding panel, parapet detail

W07

SHEET METAL STANDING SEAM

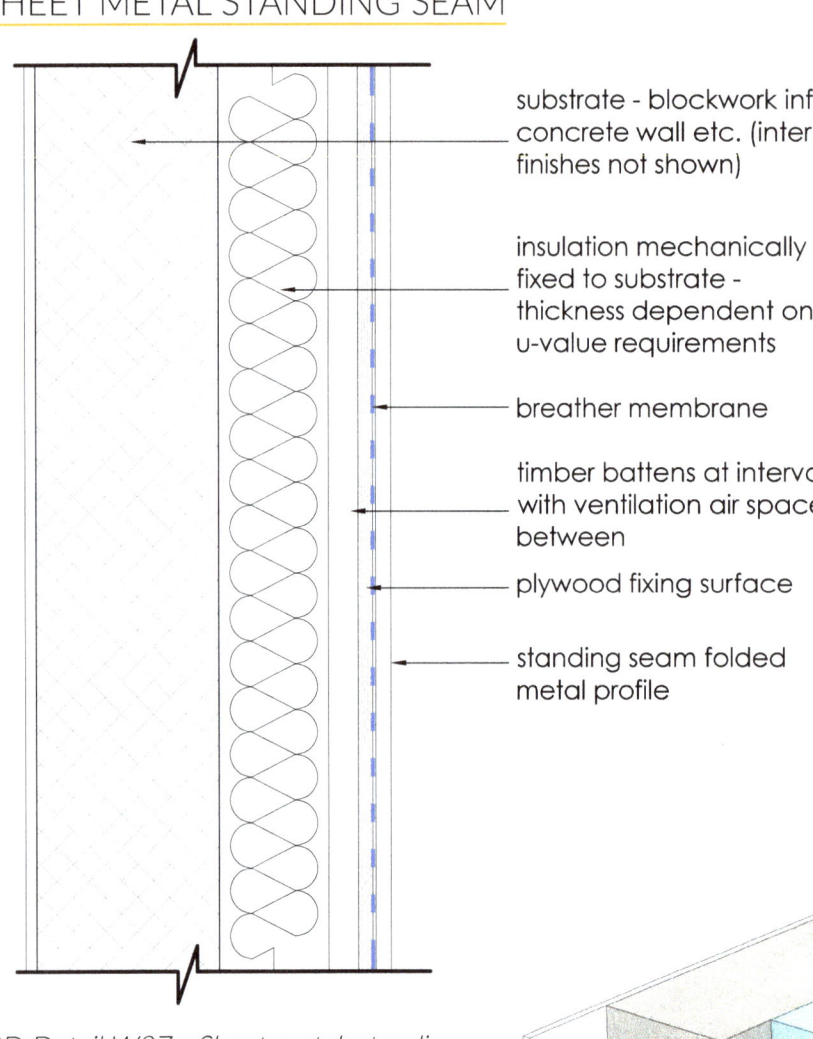

- substrate - blockwork infill / concrete wall etc. (internal finishes not shown)
- insulation mechanically fixed to substrate - thickness dependent on u-value requirements
- breather membrane
- timber battens at intervals with ventilation air space between
- plywood fixing surface
- standing seam folded metal profile

2D Detail W07 - Sheet metal, standing seam

3D Detail W07 - Sheet metal, standing seam

SECTION 7 - WALLS

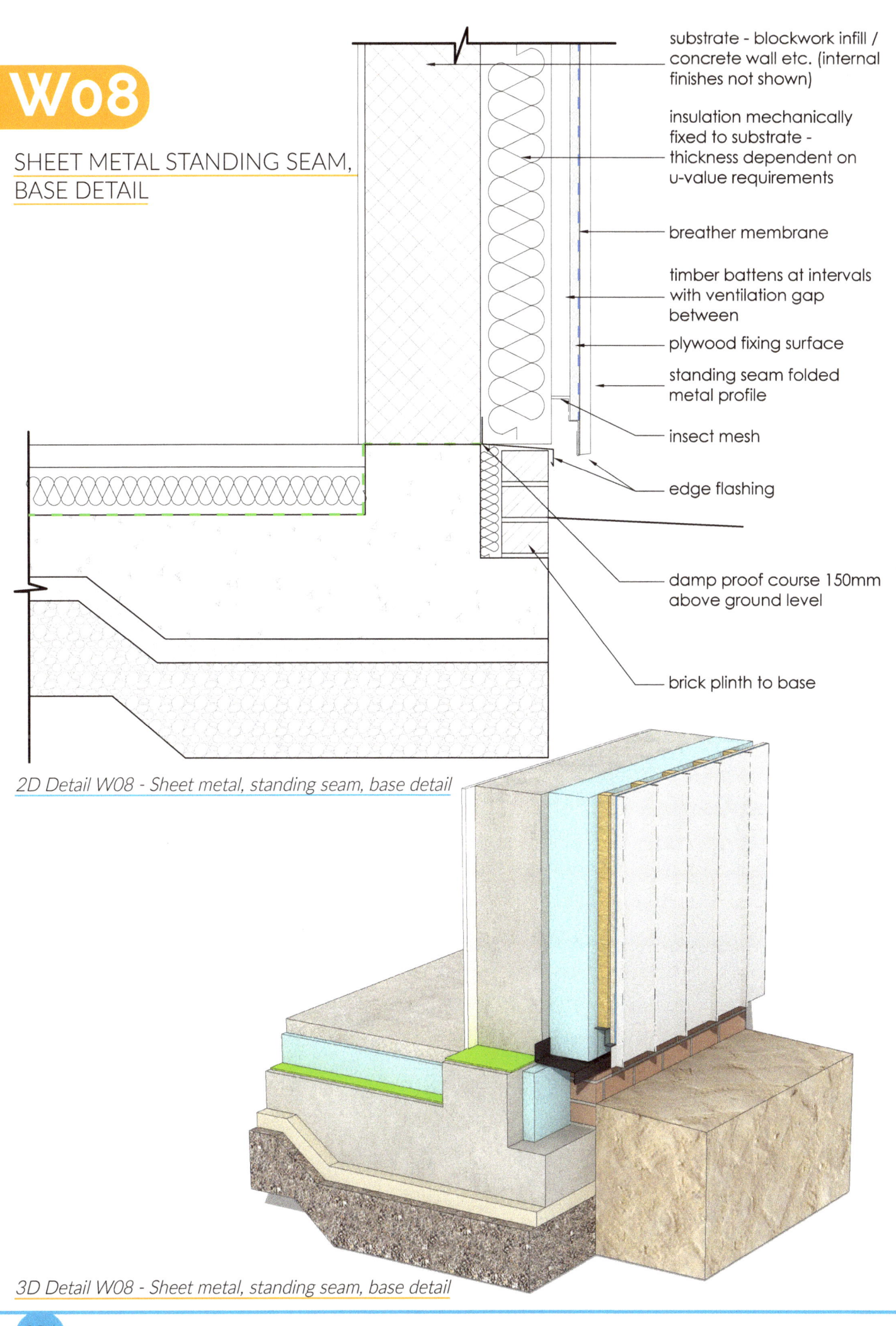

W08

SHEET METAL STANDING SEAM, BASE DETAIL

2D Detail W08 - Sheet metal, standing seam, base detail

3D Detail W08 - Sheet metal, standing seam, base detail

W09

SHEET METAL STANDING SEAM, WINDOW HEAD DETAIL

- substrate - blockwork infill / concrete wall etc.
- insulation mechanically fixed to substrate - thickness dependent on u-value requirements
- breather membrane
- timber battens at intervals with ventilation gap between
- plywood fixing surface
- standing seam folded metal profile
- folded metal profile with perforated ventilation gap
- plywood fixing surface
- insulated packing strip

2D Detail W09 - Sheet metal, standing seam, window head detail

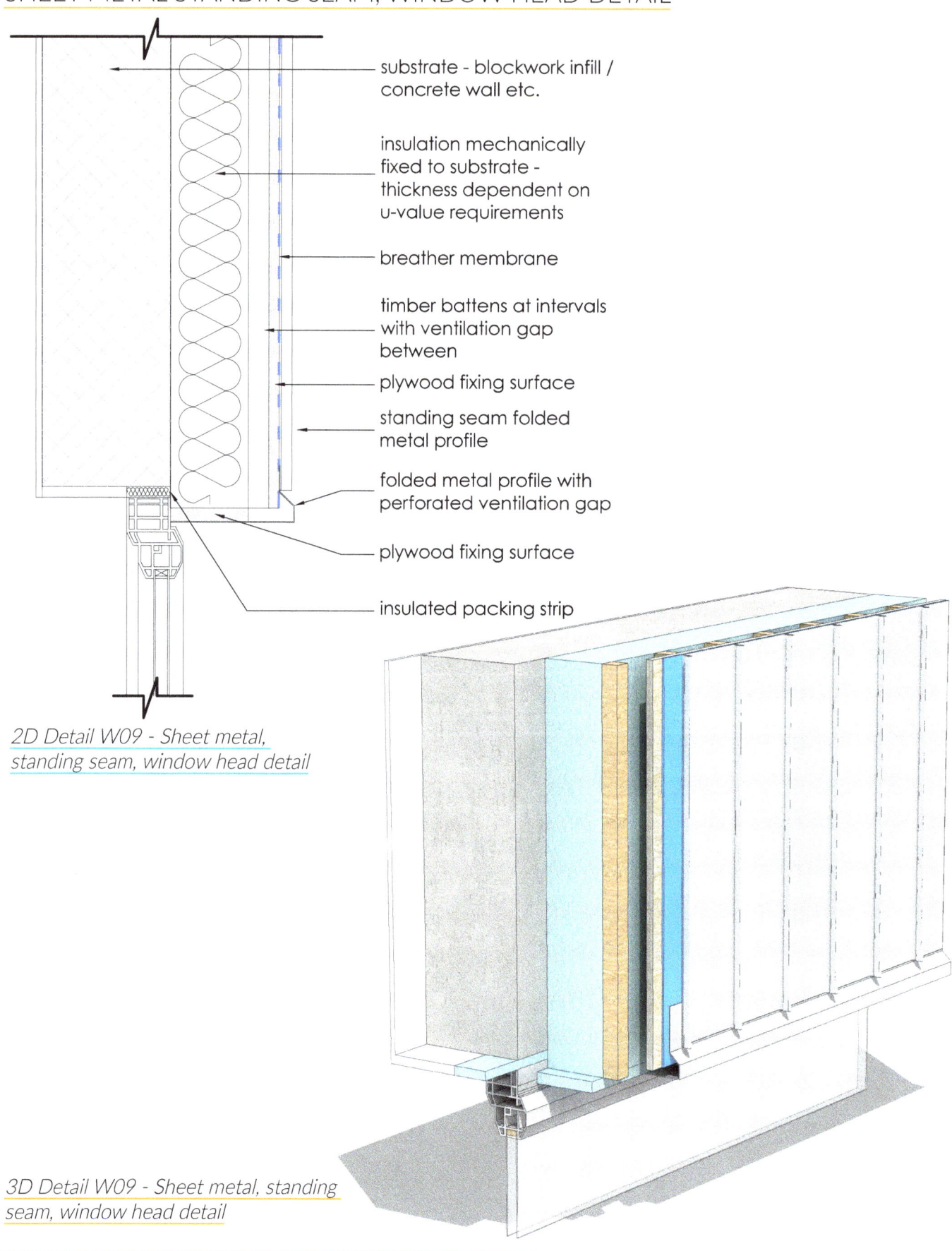

3D Detail W09 - Sheet metal, standing seam, window head detail

W10

SHEET METAL STANDING SEAM, WINDOW SILL DETAIL

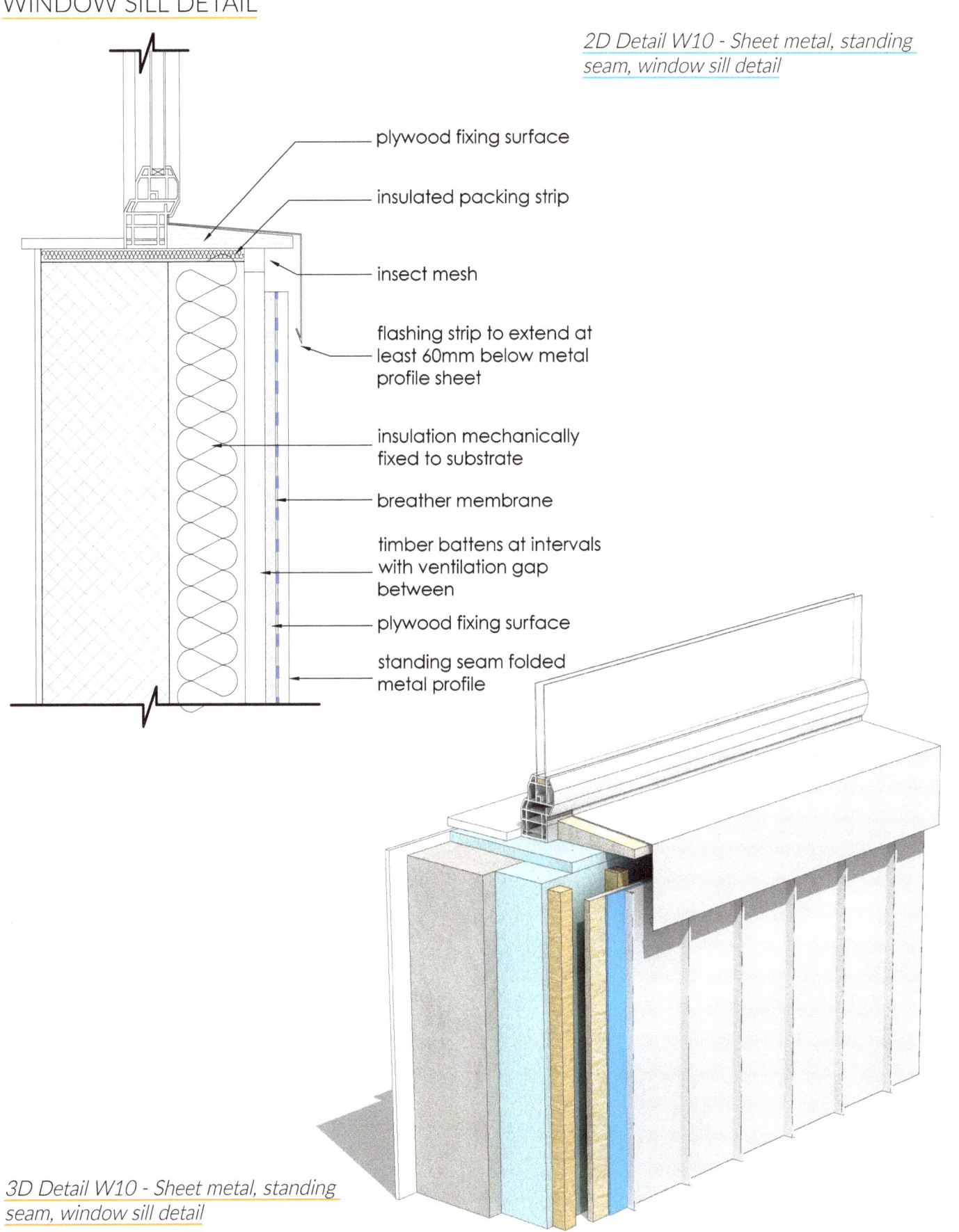

2D Detail W10 - Sheet metal, standing seam, window sill detail

- plywood fixing surface
- insulated packing strip
- insect mesh
- flashing strip to extend at least 60mm below metal profile sheet
- insulation mechanically fixed to substrate
- breather membrane
- timber battens at intervals with ventilation gap between
- plywood fixing surface
- standing seam folded metal profile

3D Detail W10 - Sheet metal, standing seam, window sill detail

W11

SHEET METAL STANDING SEAM, WINDOW JAMB DETAIL (PLAN)

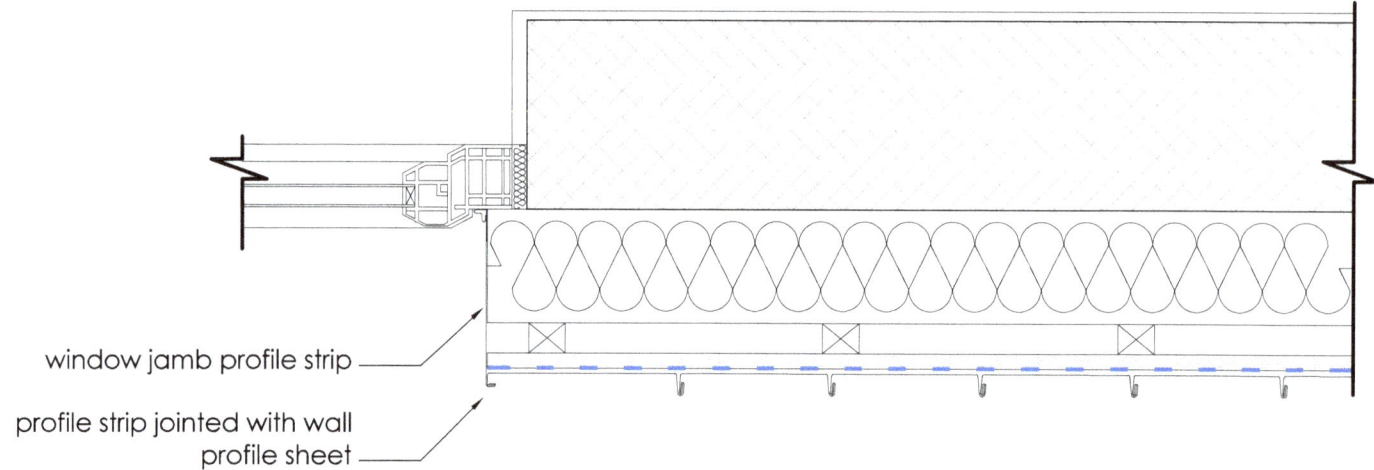

- window jamb profile strip
- profile strip jointed with wall profile sheet

2D Detail W11 - Sheet metal, standing seam, window jamb detail (plan)

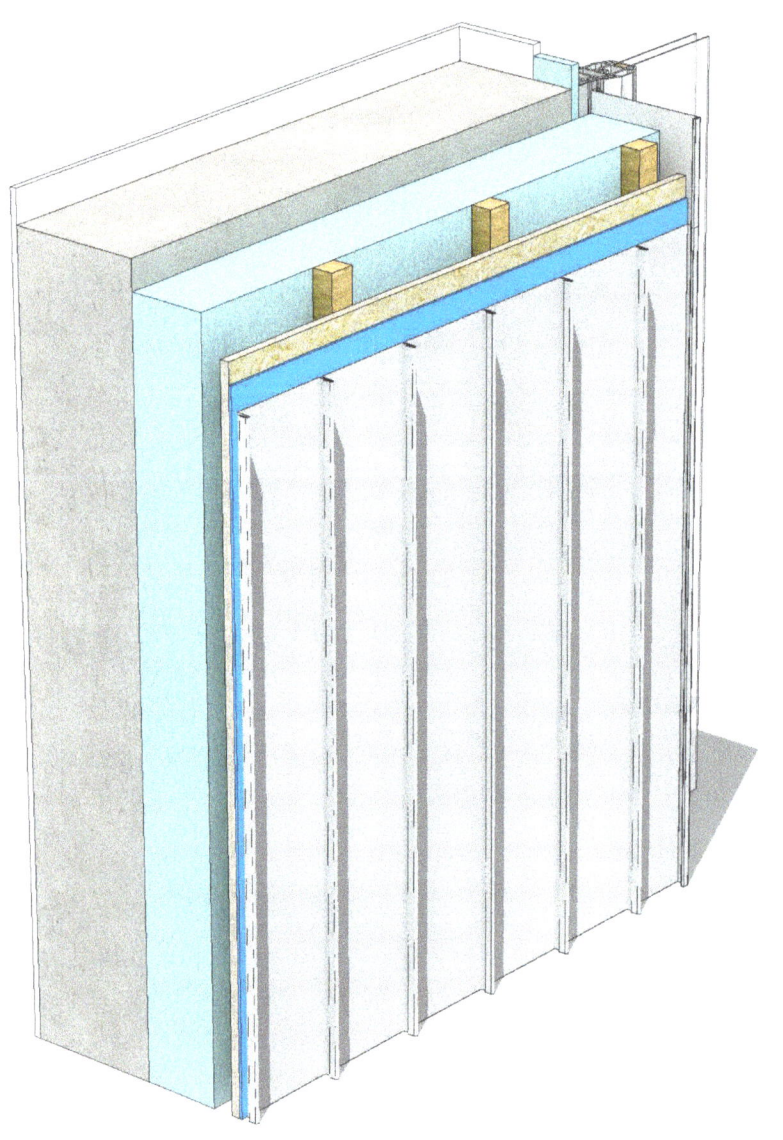

3D Detail W11 - Sheet metal, standing seam, window jamb detail

W12

SHEET METAL STANDING SEAM, PARAPET DETAIL

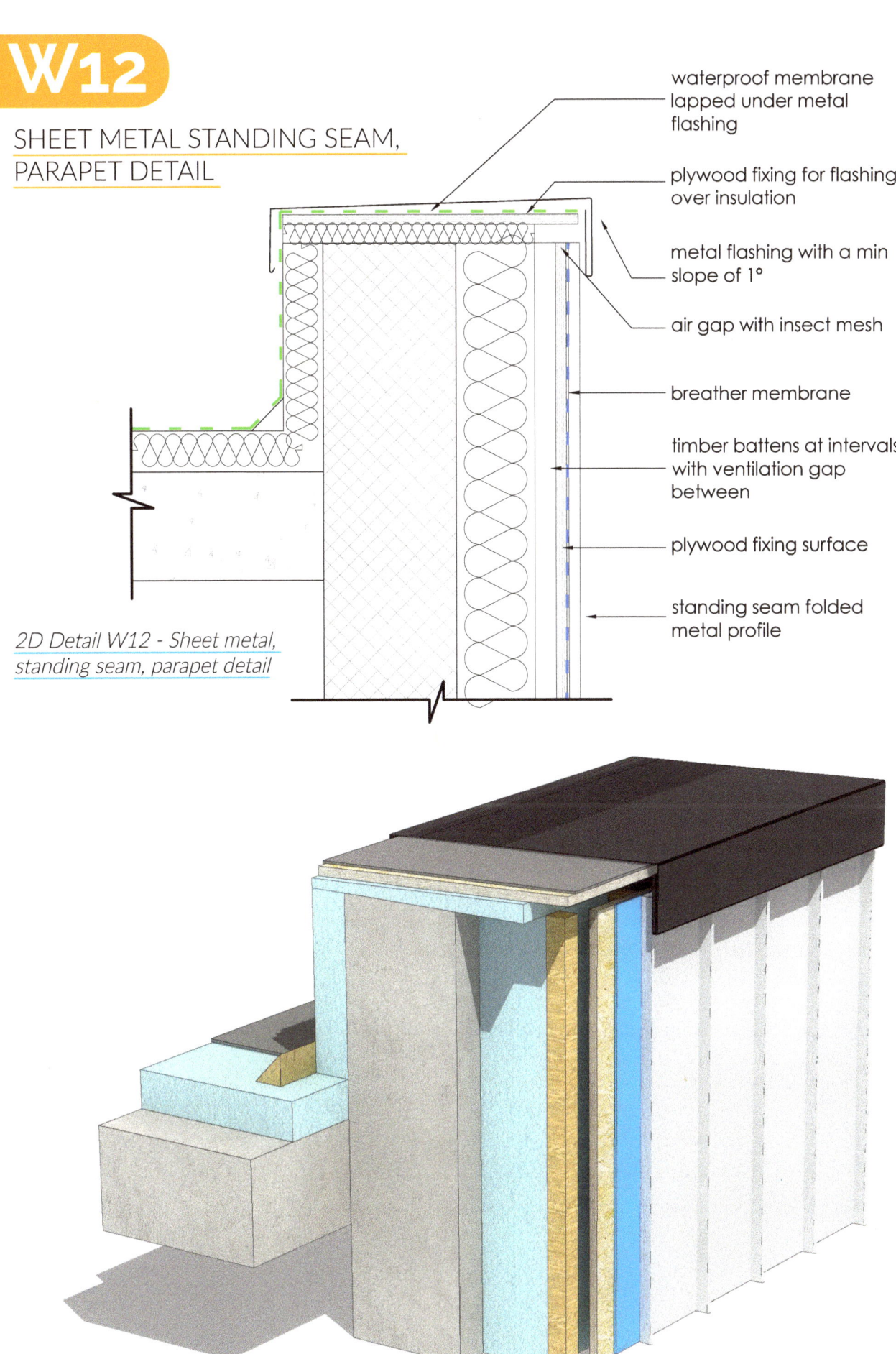

2D Detail W12 - Sheet metal, standing seam, parapet detail

- waterproof membrane lapped under metal flashing
- plywood fixing for flashing over insulation
- metal flashing with a min slope of 1°
- air gap with insect mesh
- breather membrane
- timber battens at intervals with ventilation gap between
- plywood fixing surface
- standing seam folded metal profile

3D Detail W12 - Sheet metal, standing seam, parapet detail

W13

SHEET METAL STANDING SEAM, LIGHT GAUGE STEEL FRAME (LGSF) BACKING WALL

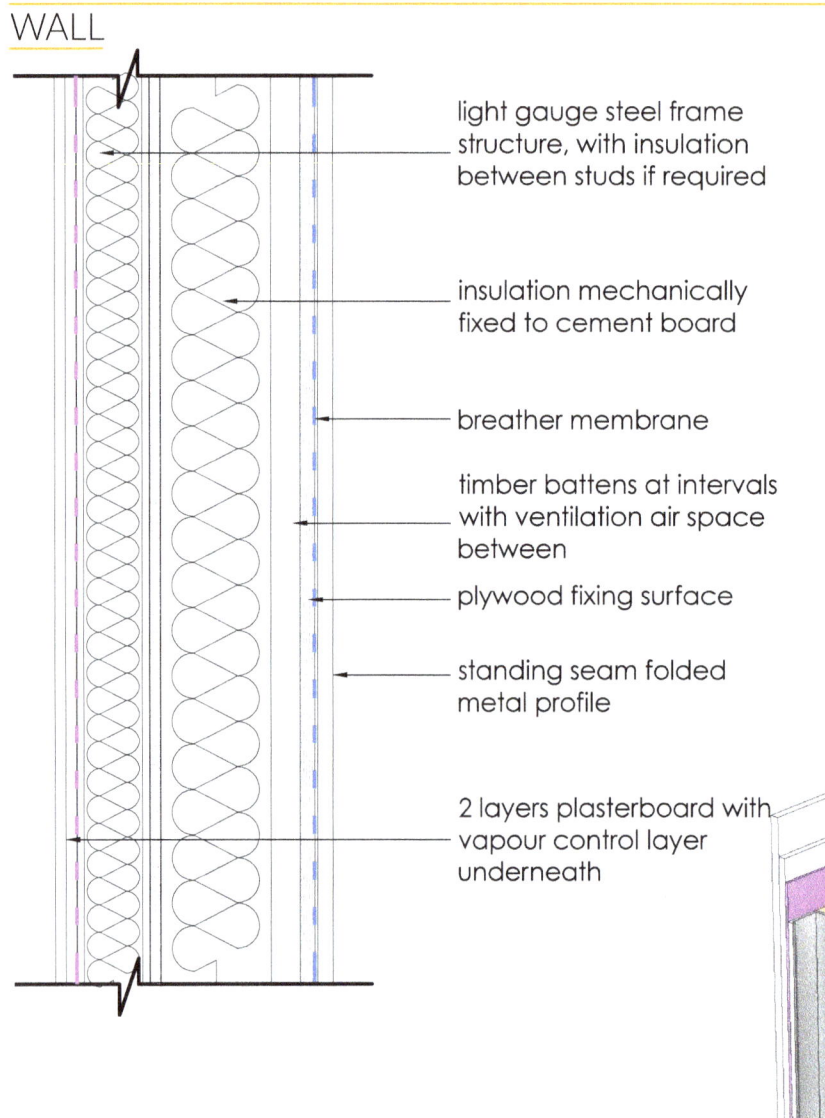

- light gauge steel frame structure, with insulation between studs if required
- insulation mechanically fixed to cement board
- breather membrane
- timber battens at intervals with ventilation air space between
- plywood fixing surface
- standing seam folded metal profile
- 2 layers plasterboard with vapour control layer underneath

2D Detail W13 - Sheet metal standing seam, lgsf

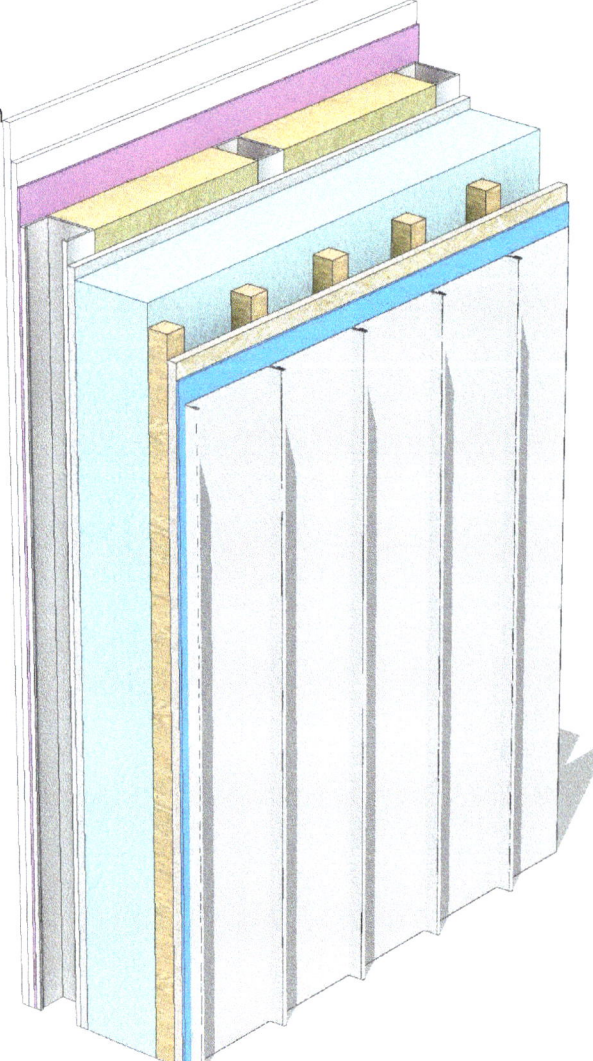

3D Detail W13 - Sheet metal standing seam, lgsf

SECTION 7 - WALLS

W14

SHEET METAL STANDING SEAM, LGSF, BASE DETAIL

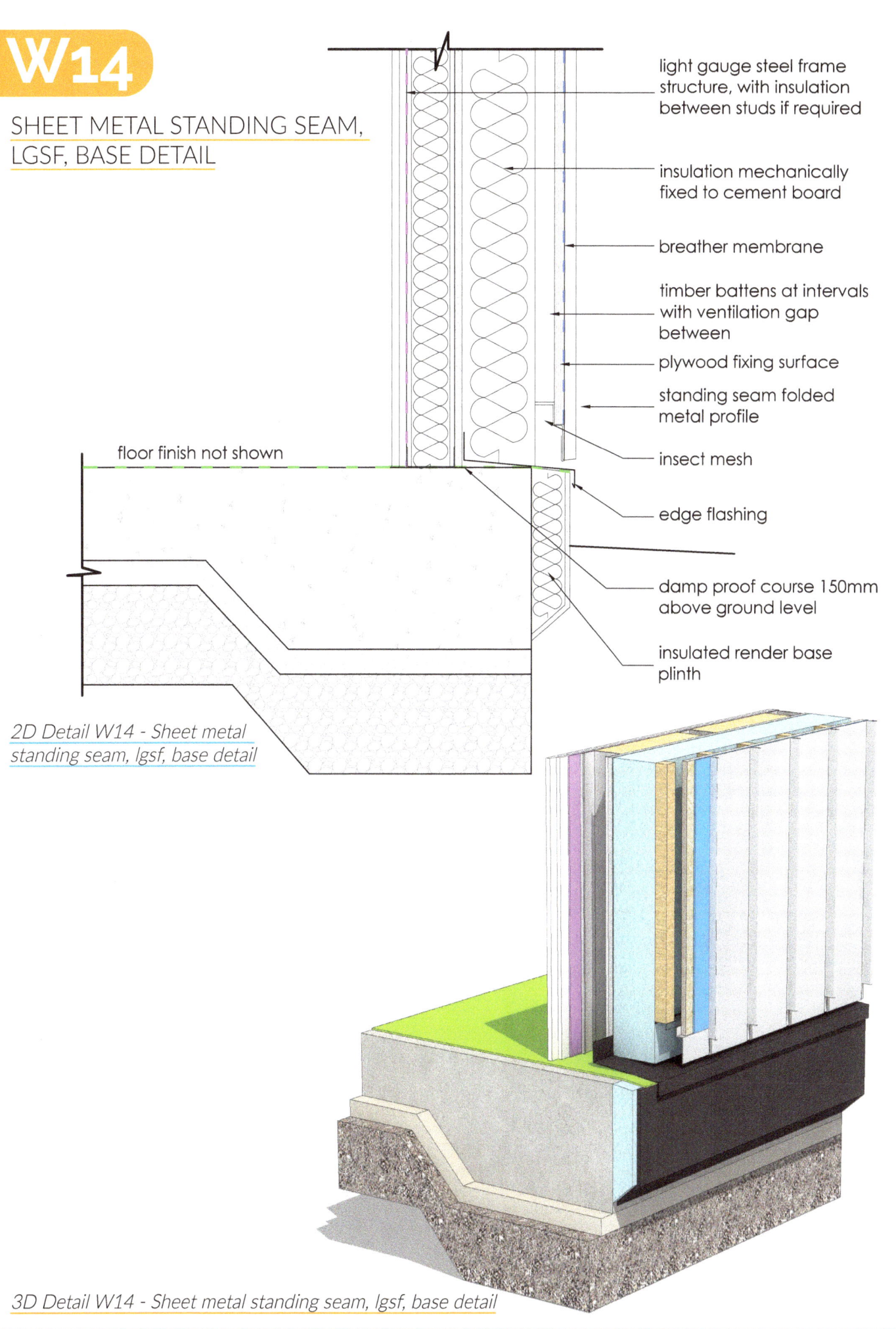

- light gauge steel frame structure, with insulation between studs if required
- insulation mechanically fixed to cement board
- breather membrane
- timber battens at intervals with ventilation gap between
- plywood fixing surface
- standing seam folded metal profile
- insect mesh
- edge flashing
- damp proof course 150mm above ground level
- insulated render base plinth

2D Detail W14 - Sheet metal standing seam, lgsf, base detail

3D Detail W14 - Sheet metal standing seam, lgsf, base detail

W15

SHEET METAL STANDING SEAM, LGSF, WINDOW HEAD DETAIL

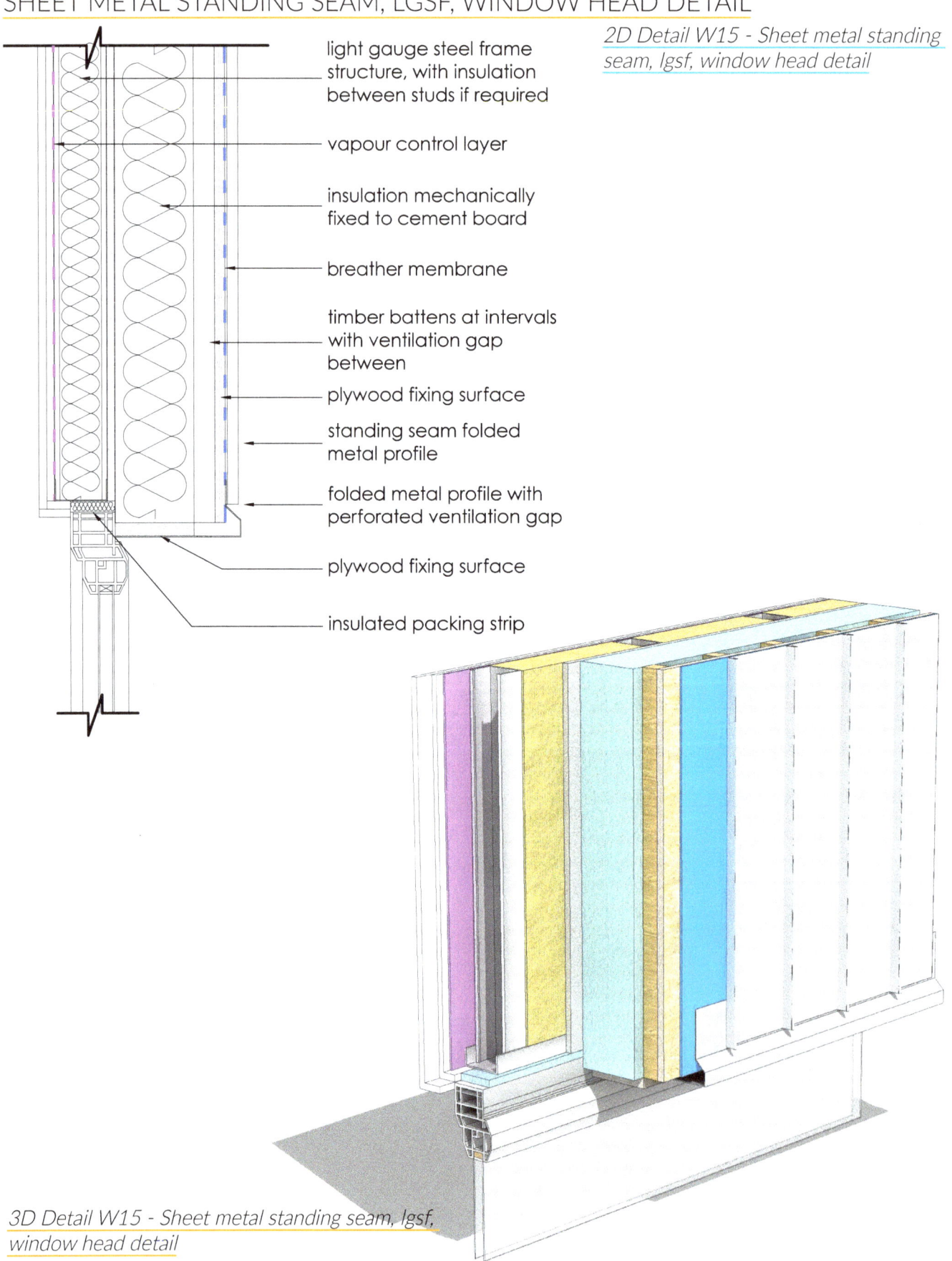

- light gauge steel frame structure, with insulation between studs if required
- vapour control layer
- insulation mechanically fixed to cement board
- breather membrane
- timber battens at intervals with ventilation gap between
- plywood fixing surface
- standing seam folded metal profile
- folded metal profile with perforated ventilation gap
- plywood fixing surface
- insulated packing strip

2D Detail W15 - Sheet metal standing seam, lgsf, window head detail

3D Detail W15 - Sheet metal standing seam, lgsf, window head detail

SECTION 7 - WALLS

W16

SHEET METAL STANDING SEAM, LGSF, WINDOW SILL DETAIL

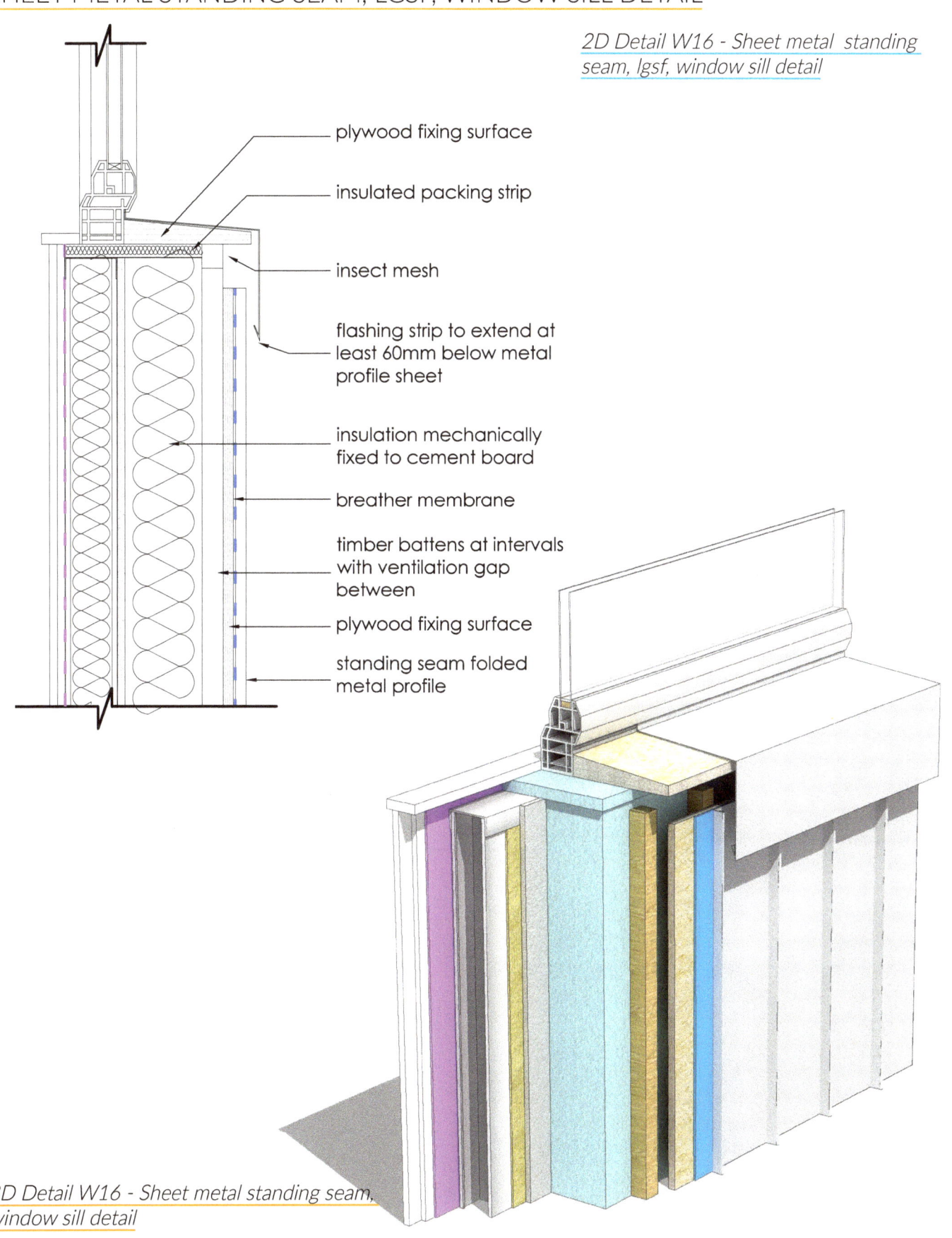

2D Detail W16 - Sheet metal standing seam, lgsf, window sill detail

- plywood fixing surface
- insulated packing strip
- insect mesh
- flashing strip to extend at least 60mm below metal profile sheet
- insulation mechanically fixed to cement board
- breather membrane
- timber battens at intervals with ventilation gap between
- plywood fixing surface
- standing seam folded metal profile

3D Detail W16 - Sheet metal standing seam, window sill detail

SHEET METAL STANDING SEAM, LGSF, WINDOW JAMB DETAIL (PLAN)

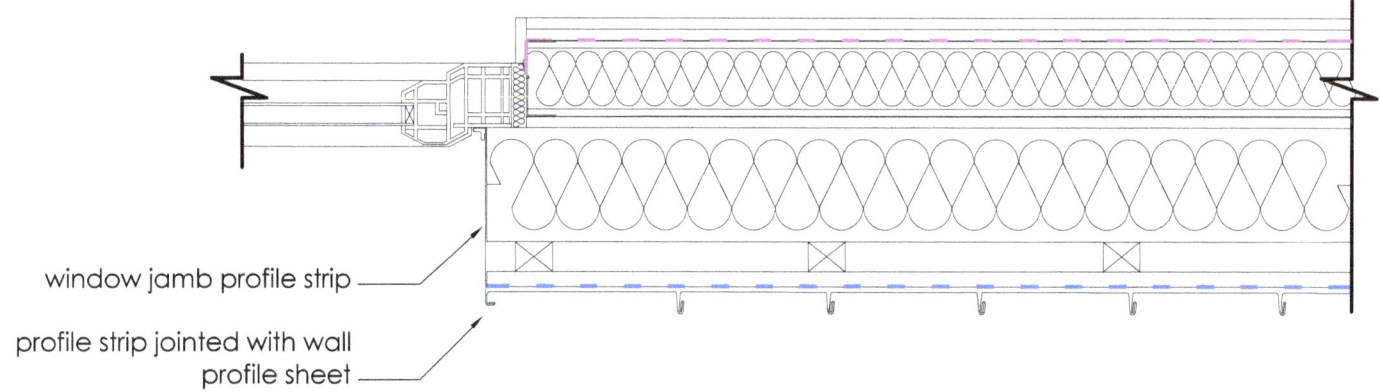

- window jamb profile strip
- profile strip jointed with wall profile sheet

2D Detail W17 - Sheet metal standing seam, lgsf, window jamb detail (plan)

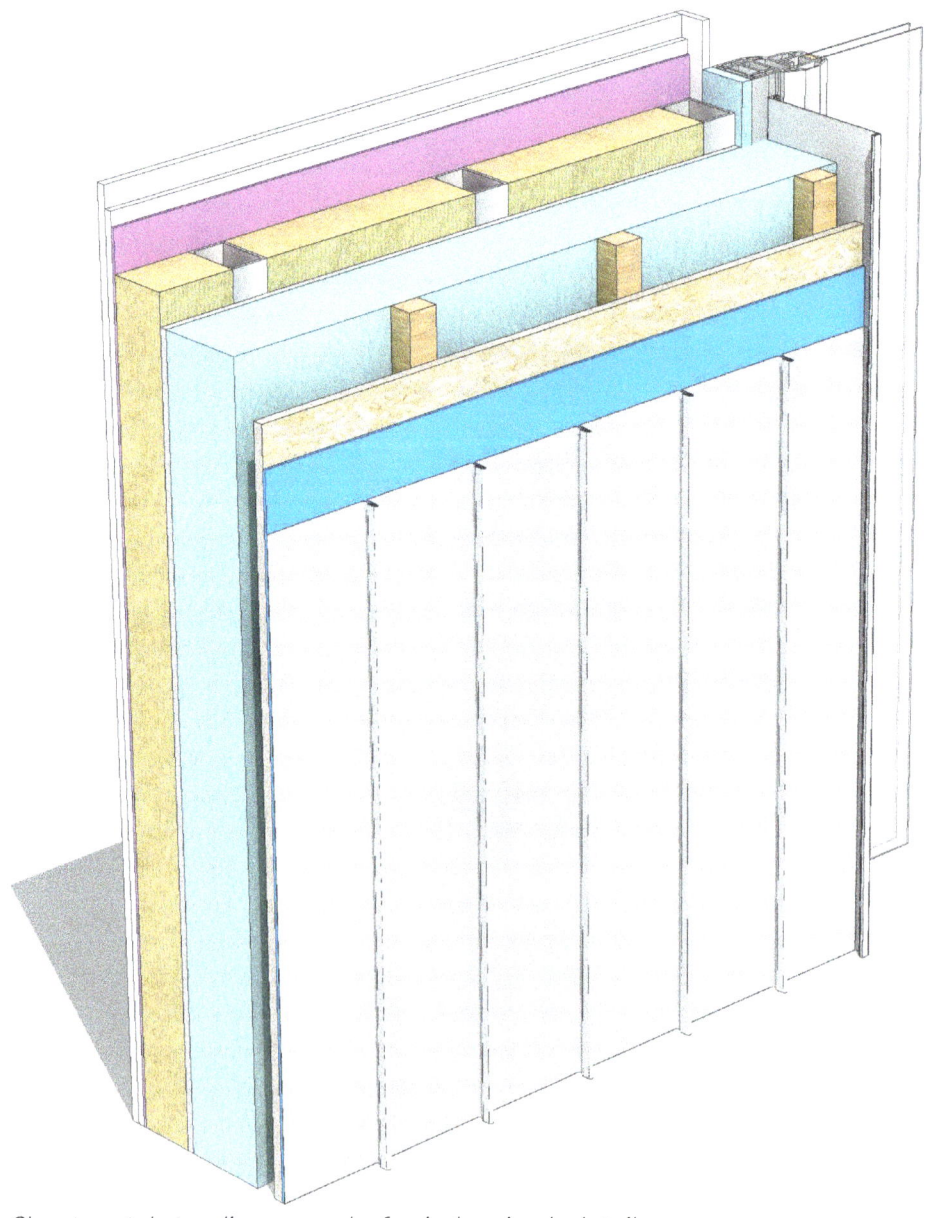

3D Detail W17 - Sheet metal standing seam, lgsf, window jamb detail

W18

SHEET METAL STANDING SEAM, LGSF, PARAPET DETAIL

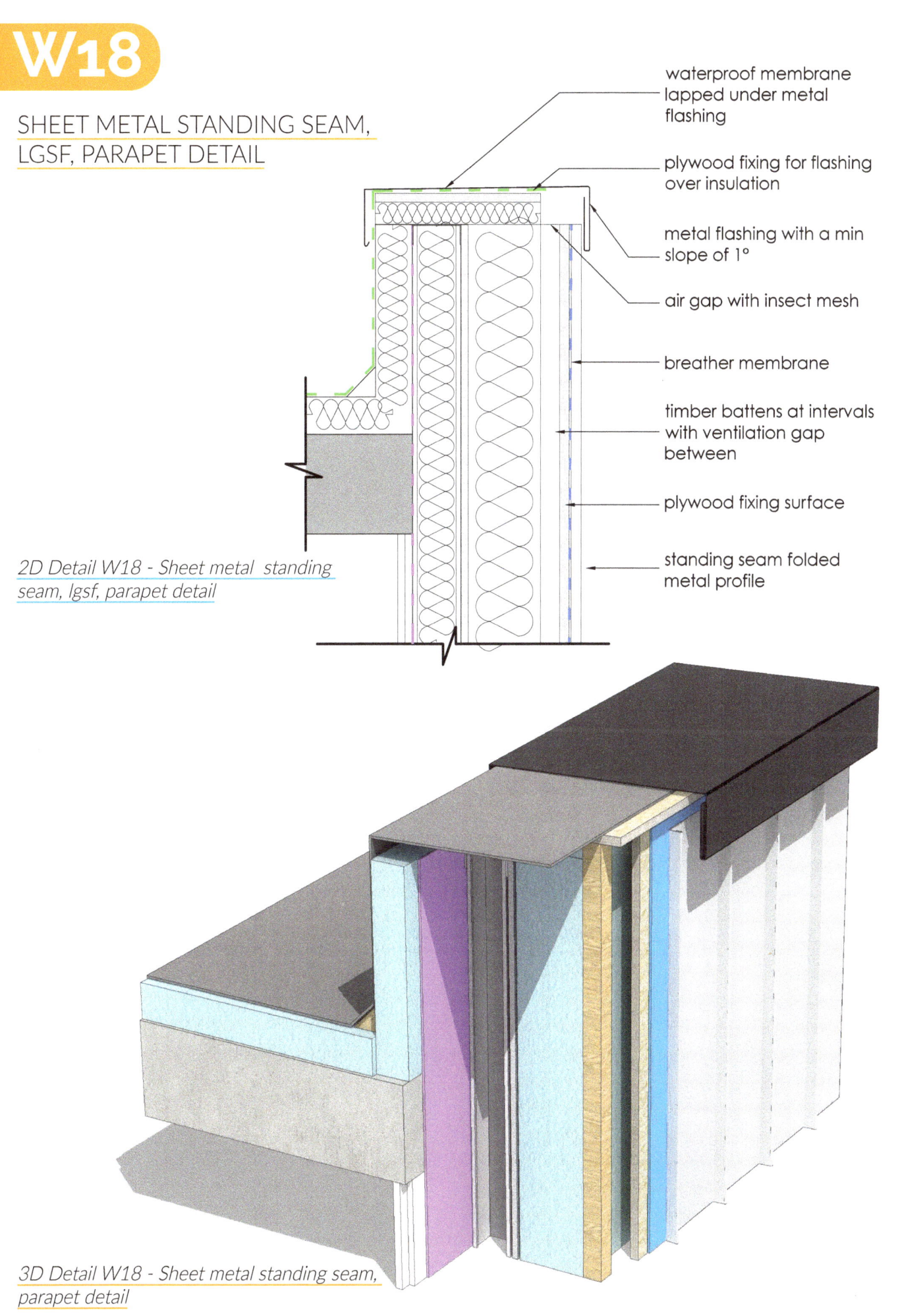

2D Detail W18 - Sheet metal standing seam, lgsf, parapet detail

3D Detail W18 - Sheet metal standing seam, parapet detail

W19

COMPOSITE CLADDING PANEL, LGSF

2D Detail W19 - Composite cladding panel, lgsf

- light gauge steel frame wall - insulation if required
- composite panel fixed to cladding rail - sealant between panels
- vertical cladding rail supporting the cladding panel at vertical joints

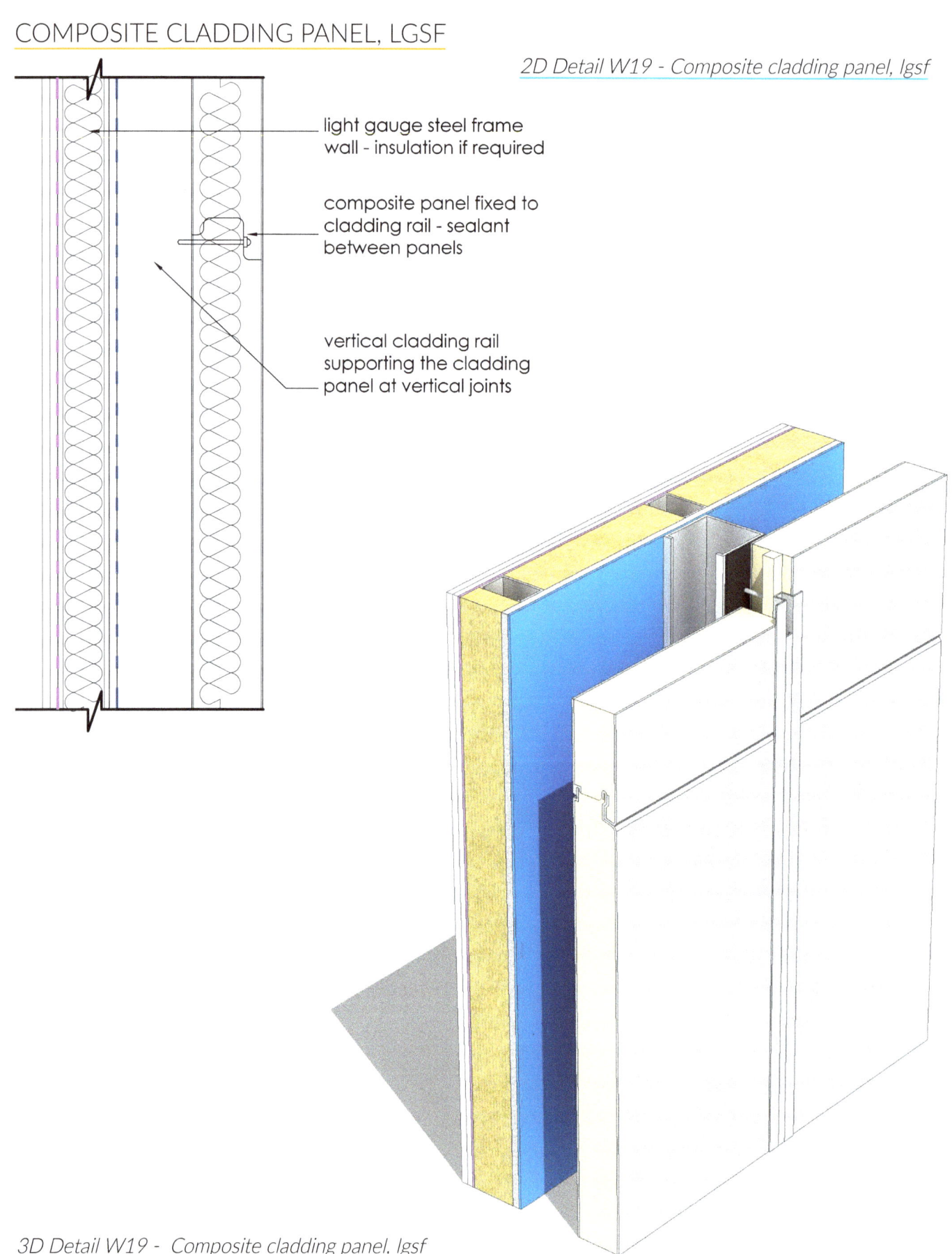

3D Detail W19 - Composite cladding panel, lgsf

SECTION 7 - WALLS

W20

COMPOSITE CLADDING PANEL, LGSF, BASE DETAIL

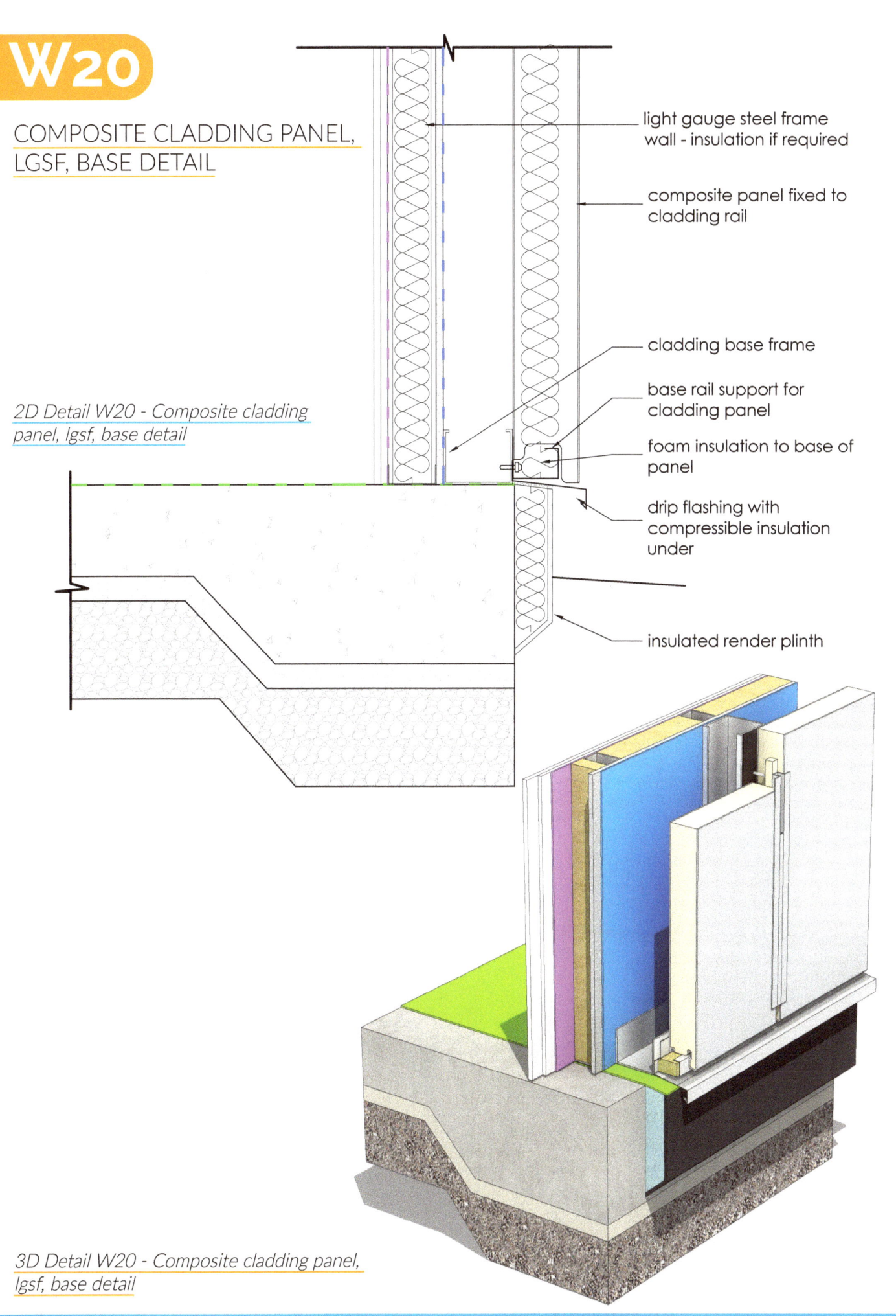

2D Detail W20 - Composite cladding panel, lgsf, base detail

3D Detail W20 - Composite cladding panel, lgsf, base detail

- light gauge steel frame wall - insulation if required
- composite panel fixed to cladding rail
- cladding base frame
- base rail support for cladding panel
- foam insulation to base of panel
- drip flashing with compressible insulation under
- insulated render plinth

W21

COMPOSITE CLADDING PANEL, LGSF, WINDOW HEAD DETAIL

2D Detail W21 - Composite cladding panel, lgsf, window head detail

- light gauge steel frame wall - insulation if required
- composite panel fixed to cladding rail
- window fixed to cladding rail with air seal
- foam insulation at base of panel

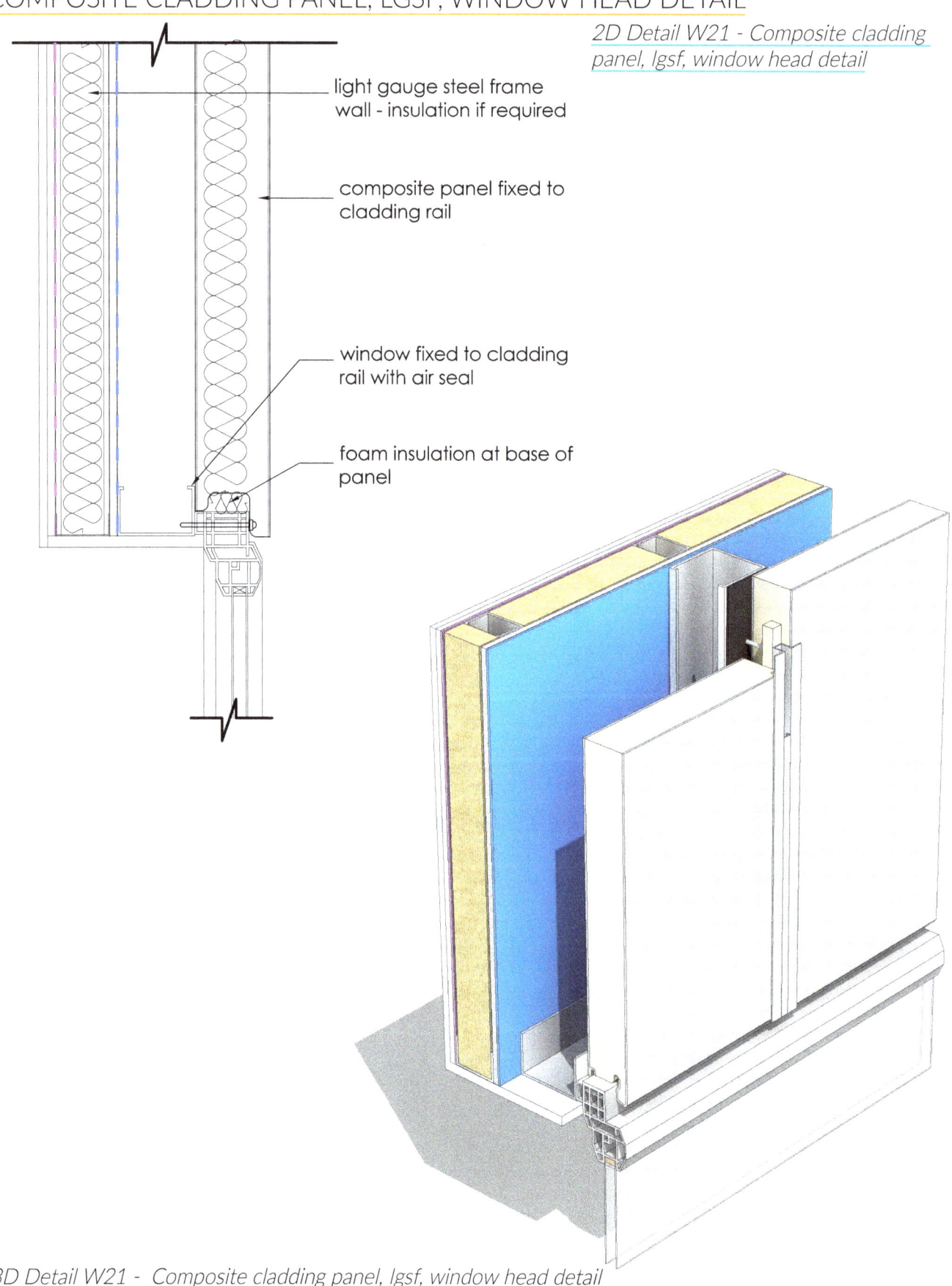

3D Detail W21 - Composite cladding panel, lgsf, window head detail

SECTION 7 - WALLS

W22

COMPOSITE CLADDING PANEL, LGSF, WINDOW SILL DETAIL

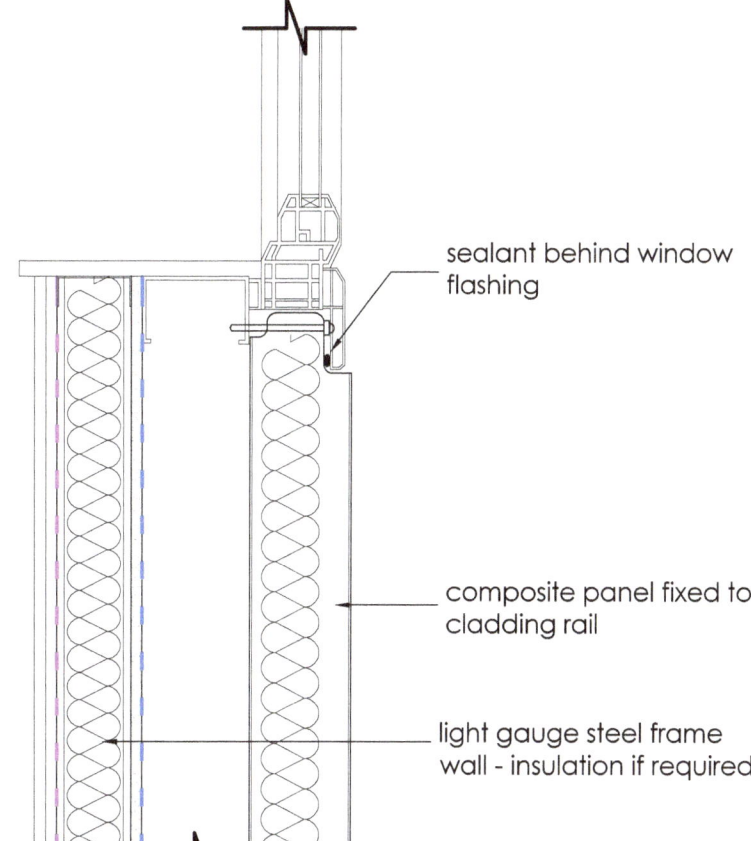

2D Detail W22 - Composite cladding panel, lgsf, window sill detail

3D Detail W22 - Composite cladding panel, lgsf, window sill detail

W23

COMPOSITE CLADDING PANEL, LGSF, WINDOW JAMB DETAIL

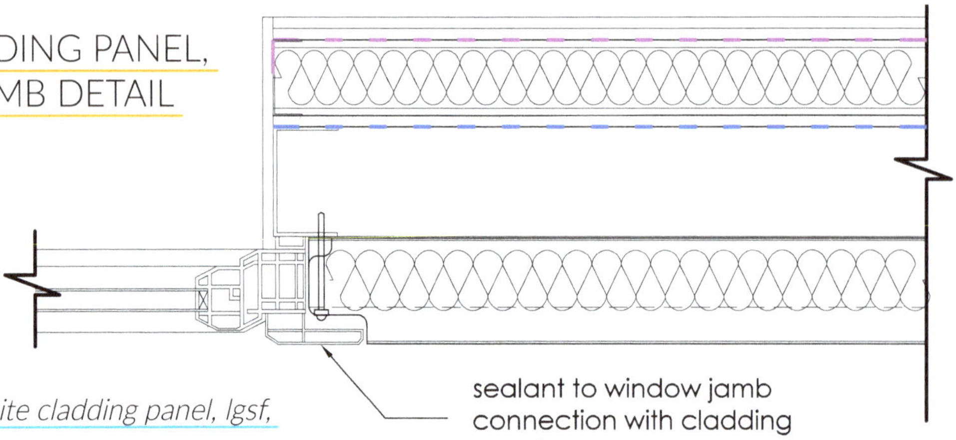

2D Detail W23 - Composite cladding panel, lgsf, window jamb detail (plan)

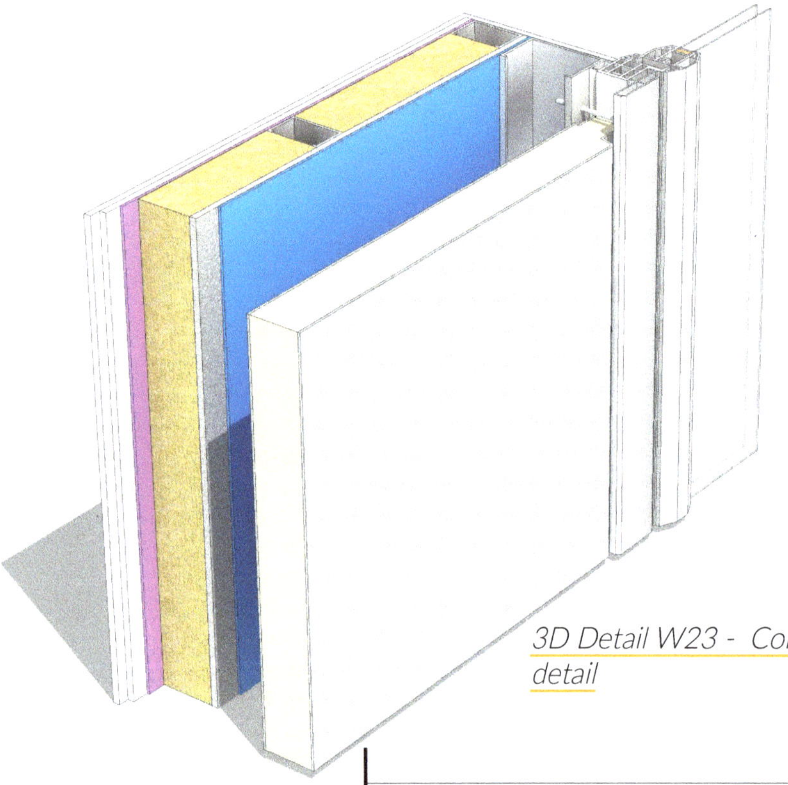

sealant to window jamb connection with cladding panel

3D Detail W23 - Composite cladding panel, lgsf, window jamb detail

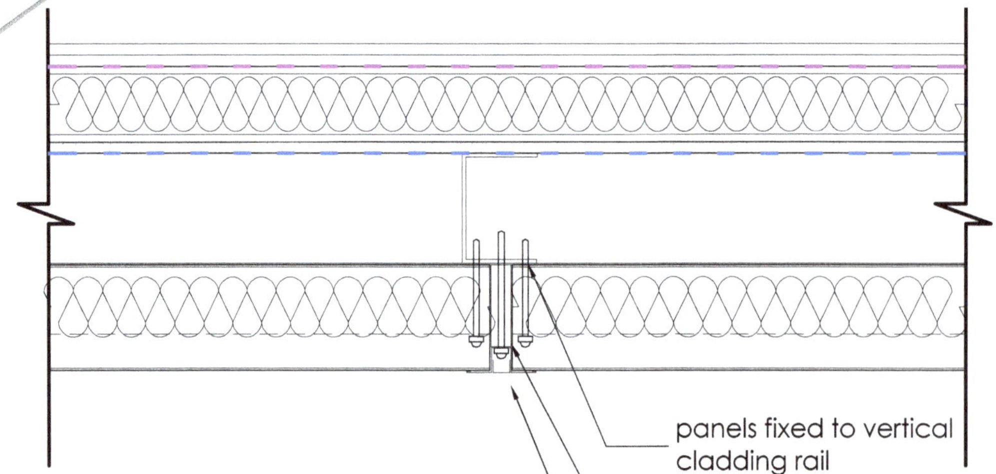

2D Detail W24 - Composite cladding panel, lgsf, panel joint detail

panels fixed to vertical cladding rail

insulation fixed inside joint with top hat extrusion

joint finished with fixing cap

SECTION 7 - WALLS

W25

COMPOSITE CLADDING PANEL, LGSF, PARAPET DETAIL

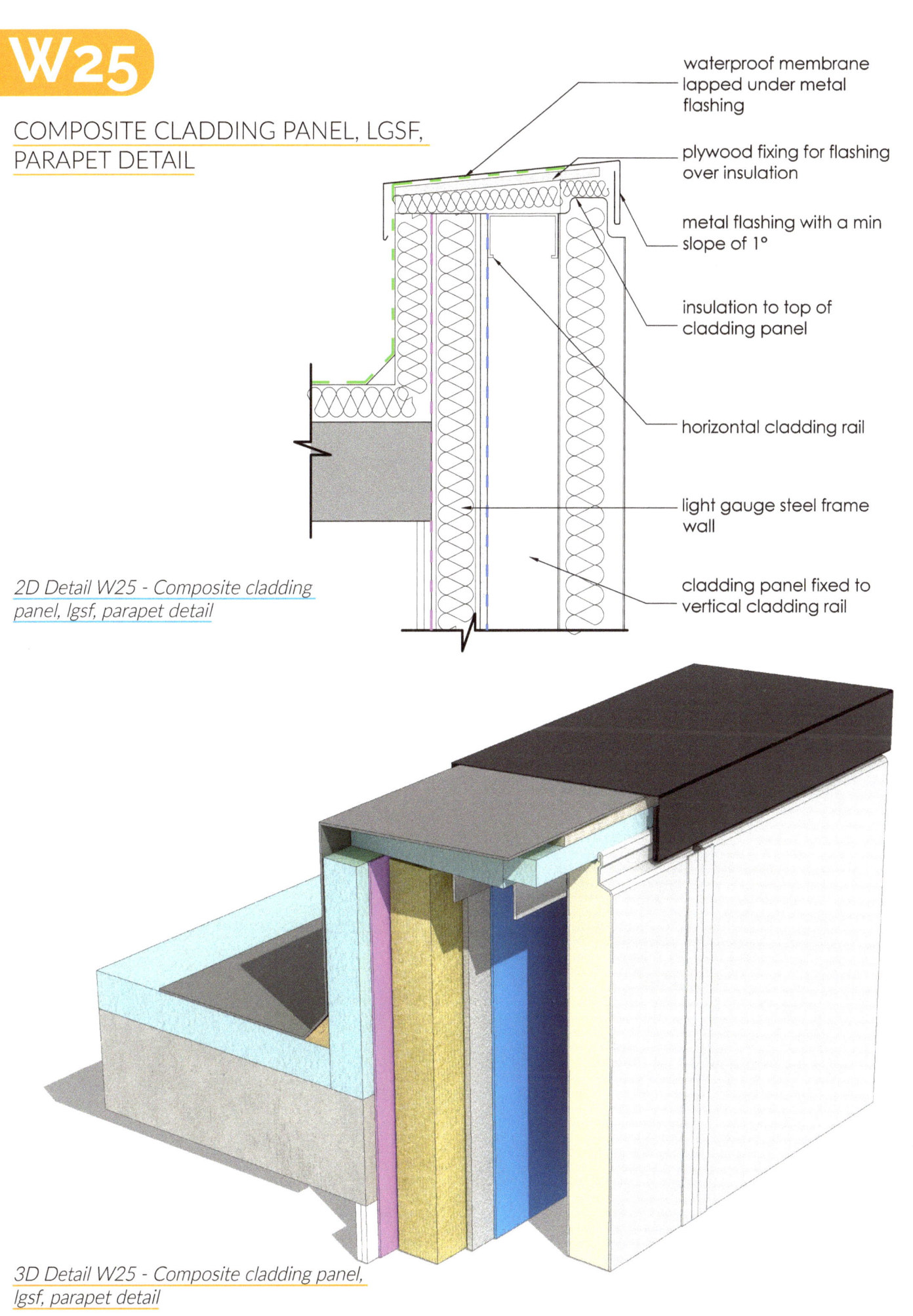

2D Detail W25 - Composite cladding panel, lgsf, parapet detail

3D Detail W25 - Composite cladding panel, lgsf, parapet detail

W26

INSULATED RENDER, LGSF

- light gauge steel frame structure, with insulation between studs if required
- cement particle board fixed to steel frame
- breather membrane
- insulation mechanically fixed to vertical spacer rails fixed to cement particle board
- basecoat render with reinforced mesh
- top coat primer and render finish to required texture

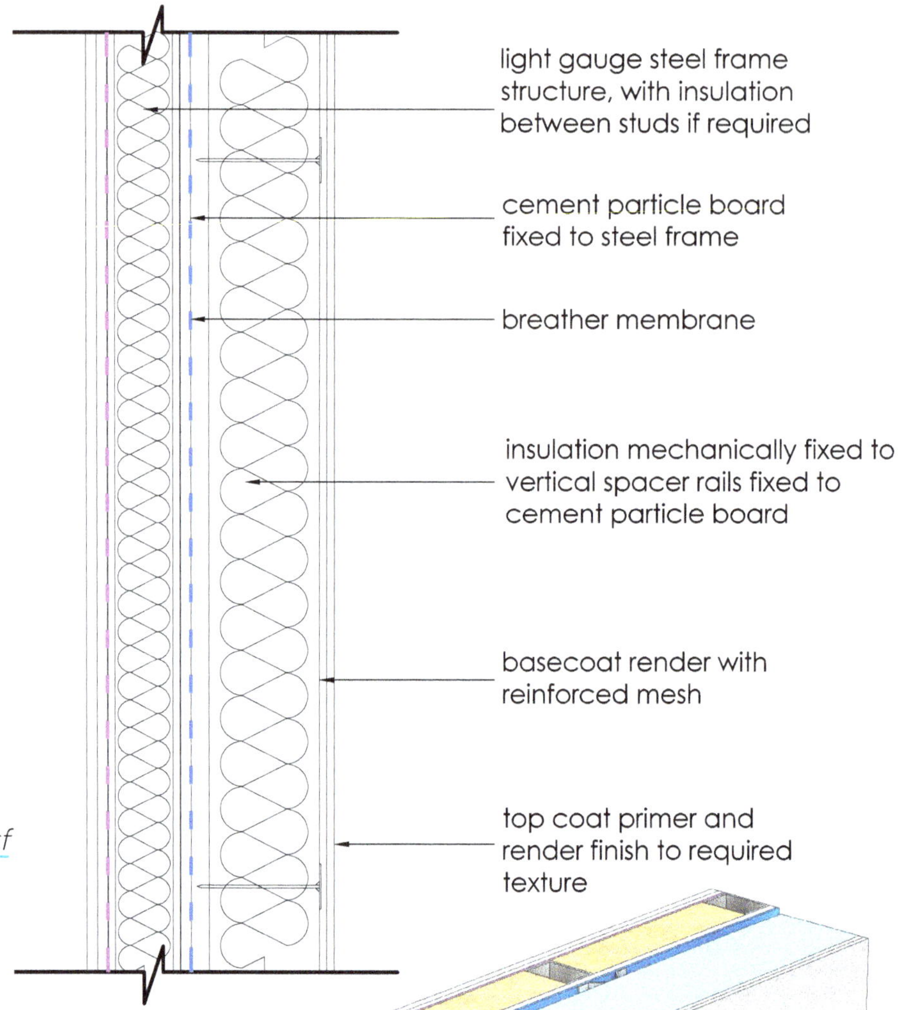

2D Detail W26 - Insulated render, lgsf

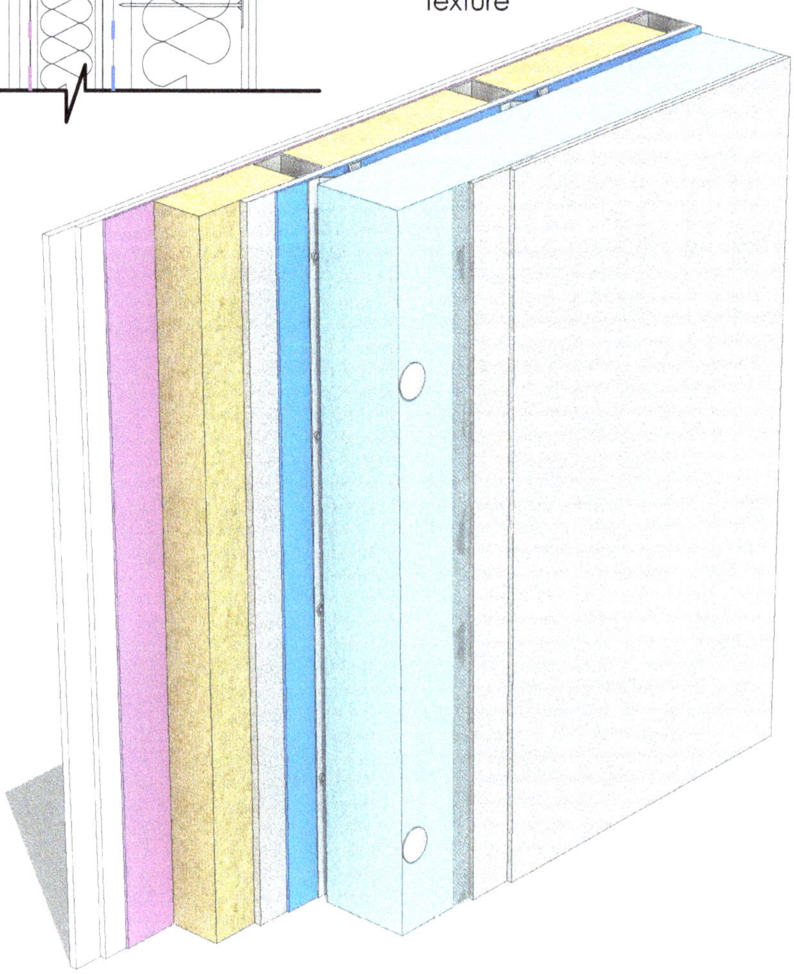

3D Detail W26 - Insulated render, lgsf

SECTION 7 - WALLS

W27
INSULATED RENDER, LGSF, BASE DETAIL

- vapour control layer
- light gauge steel frame structure, with insulation between studs if required
- insulation mechanically fixed to vertical spacer rails fixed to cement particle board
- damp proof course - 150mm above ground level
- cement particle board fixed to steel frame
- breather membrane
- basecoat render with reinforced mesh
- top coat primer and render finish to required texture
- base track with insect mesh fixed to cement board
- flashing fixed to cement board with breather membrane lapped over
- compressible insulation under flashing
- brick plinth with rigid insulation behind

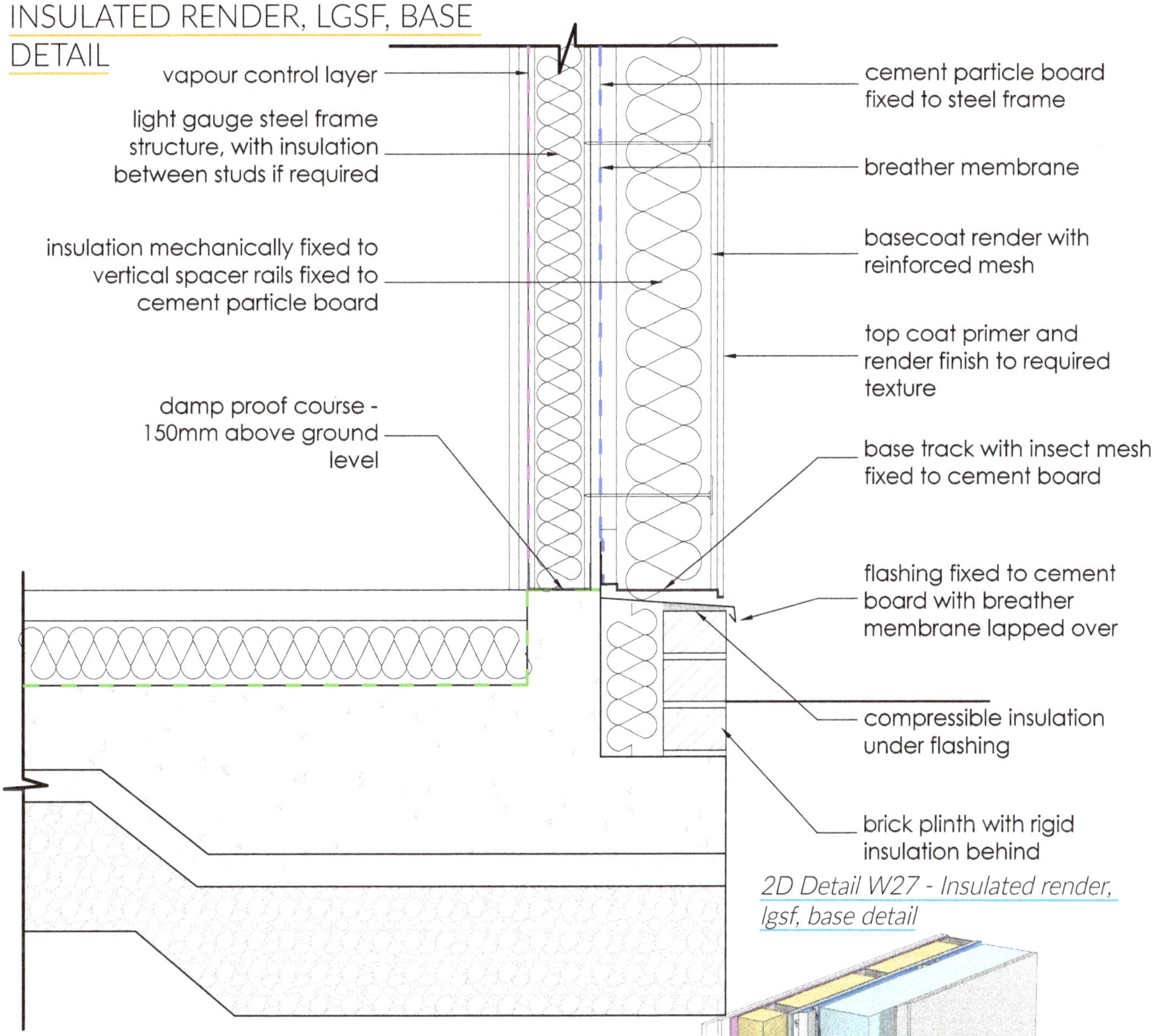

2D Detail W27 - Insulated render, lgsf, base detail

Notes:
There are numerous configurations for a base detail to insulated render systems, this detail demonstrates just one of those options.

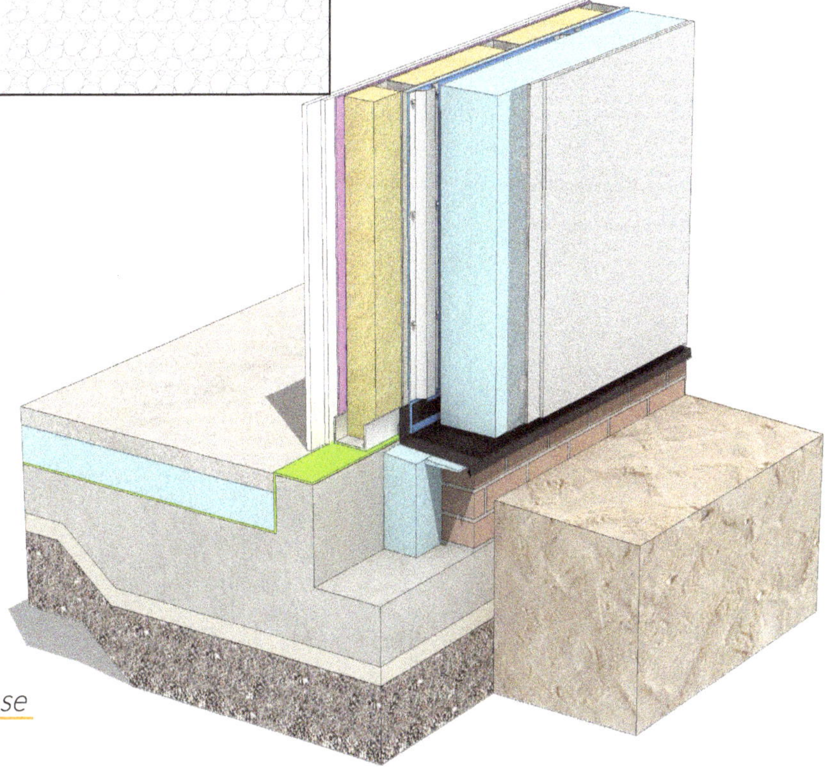

3D Detail W27 - Insulated render, lgsf, base detail

W28

INSULATED RENDER, LGSF, WINDOW HEAD DETAIL

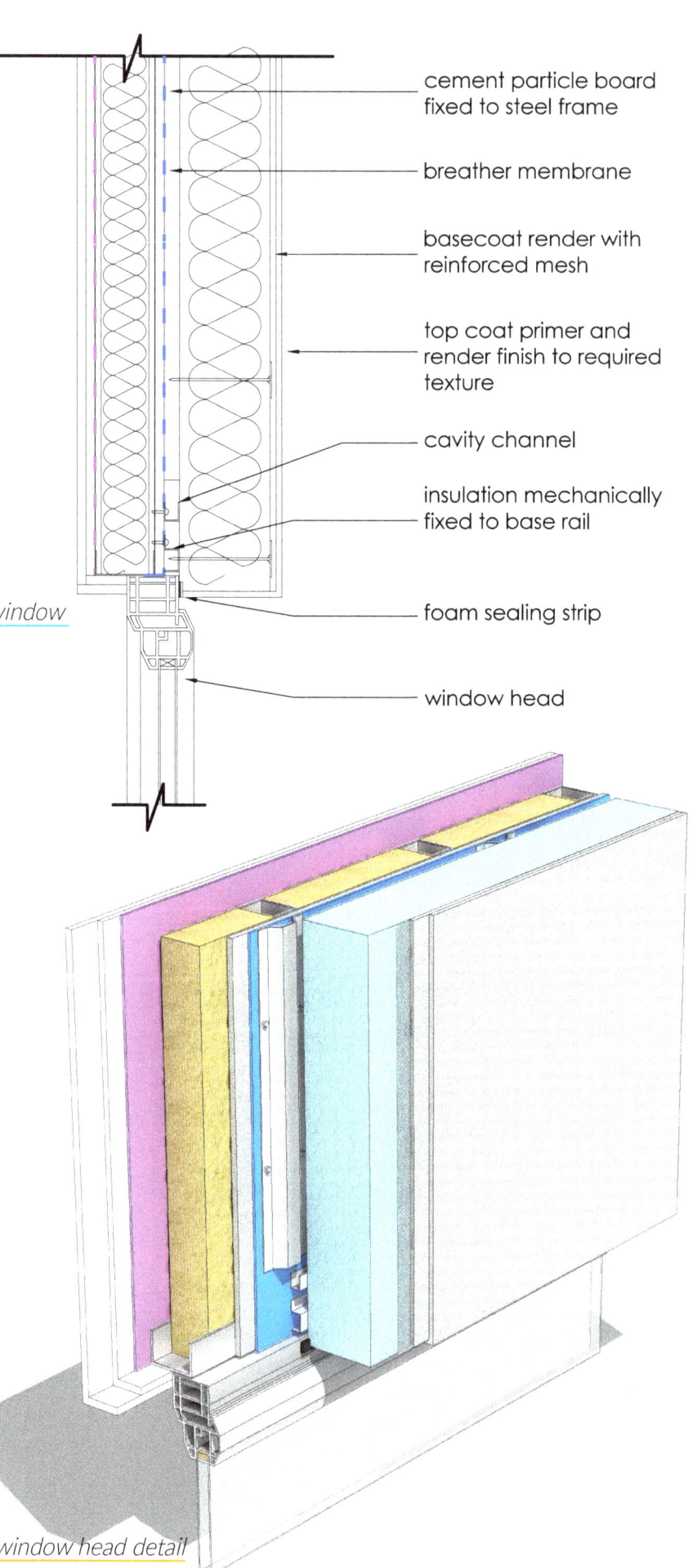

2D Detail W28 - Insulated render, lgsf, window head detail

3D Detail W28 - Insulated render, lgsf, window head detail

SECTION 7 - WALLS

W29

INSULATED RENDER, LGSF, WINDOW SILL DETAIL

2D Detail W29 - Insulated render, lgsf, window sill detail

- sill overhang min 50mm
- foam insulating sealing strip
- top fixing rail
- insulation mechanically fixed to vertical spacer rails
- basecoat render with reinforced mesh
- top coat primer and render finish to required texture

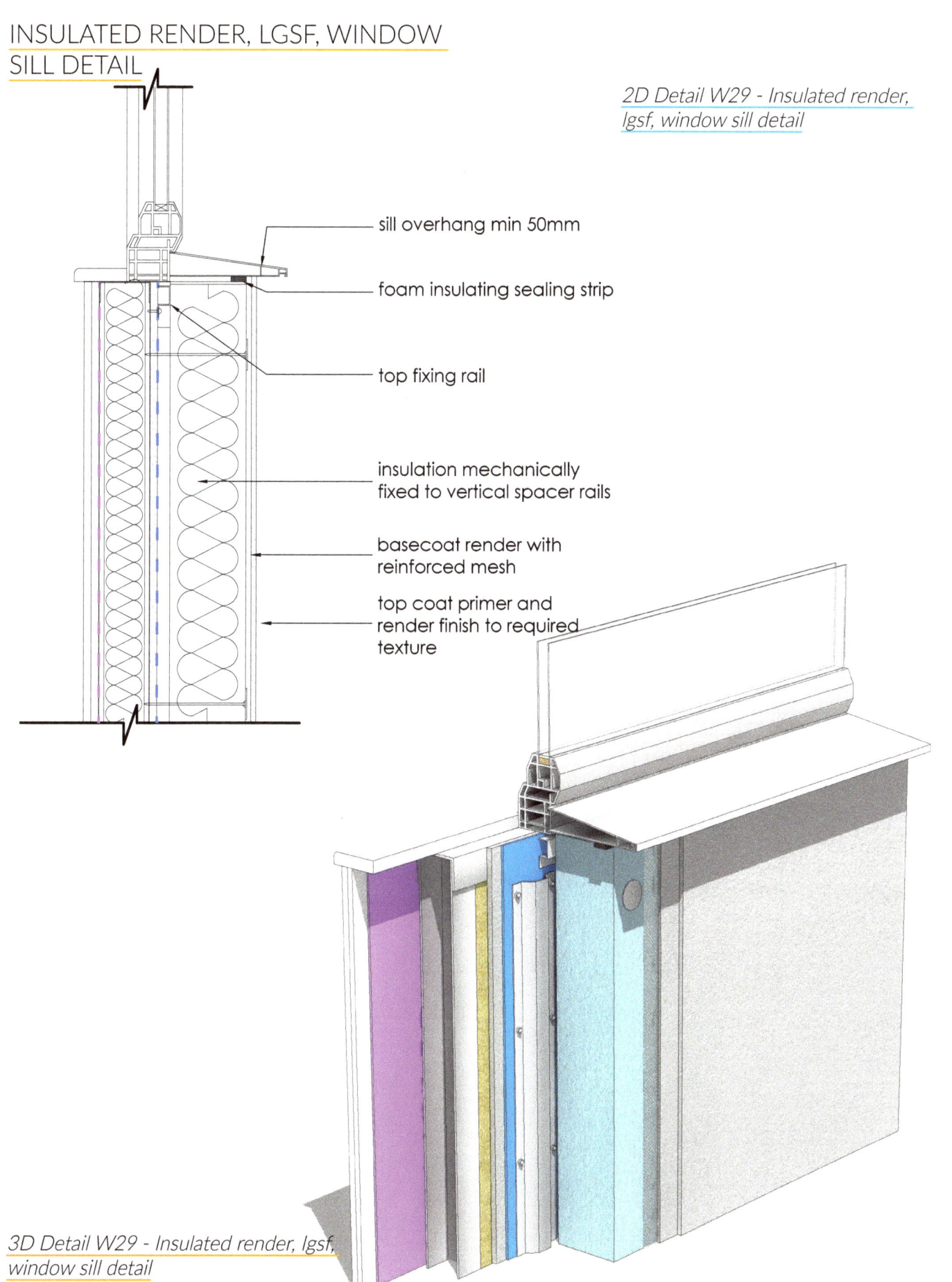

3D Detail W29 - Insulated render, lgsf, window sill detail

W30

INSULATED RENDER, LGSF, WINDOW JAMB DETAIL (PLAN)

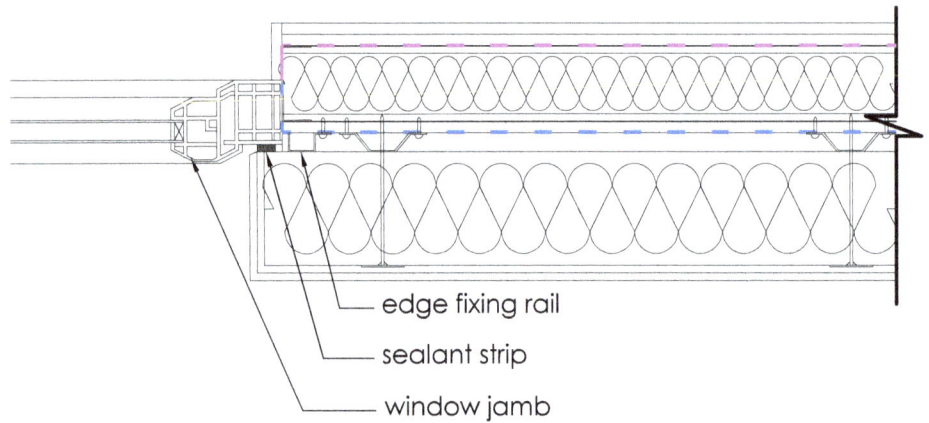

- edge fixing rail
- sealant strip
- window jamb

2D Detail W30 - Insulated render, lgsf, window jamb detail (plan)

3D Detail W30 - Insulated render, lgsf, window jamb detail

SECTION 7 - WALLS

W31

INSULATED RENDER, LGSF, PARAPET DETAIL

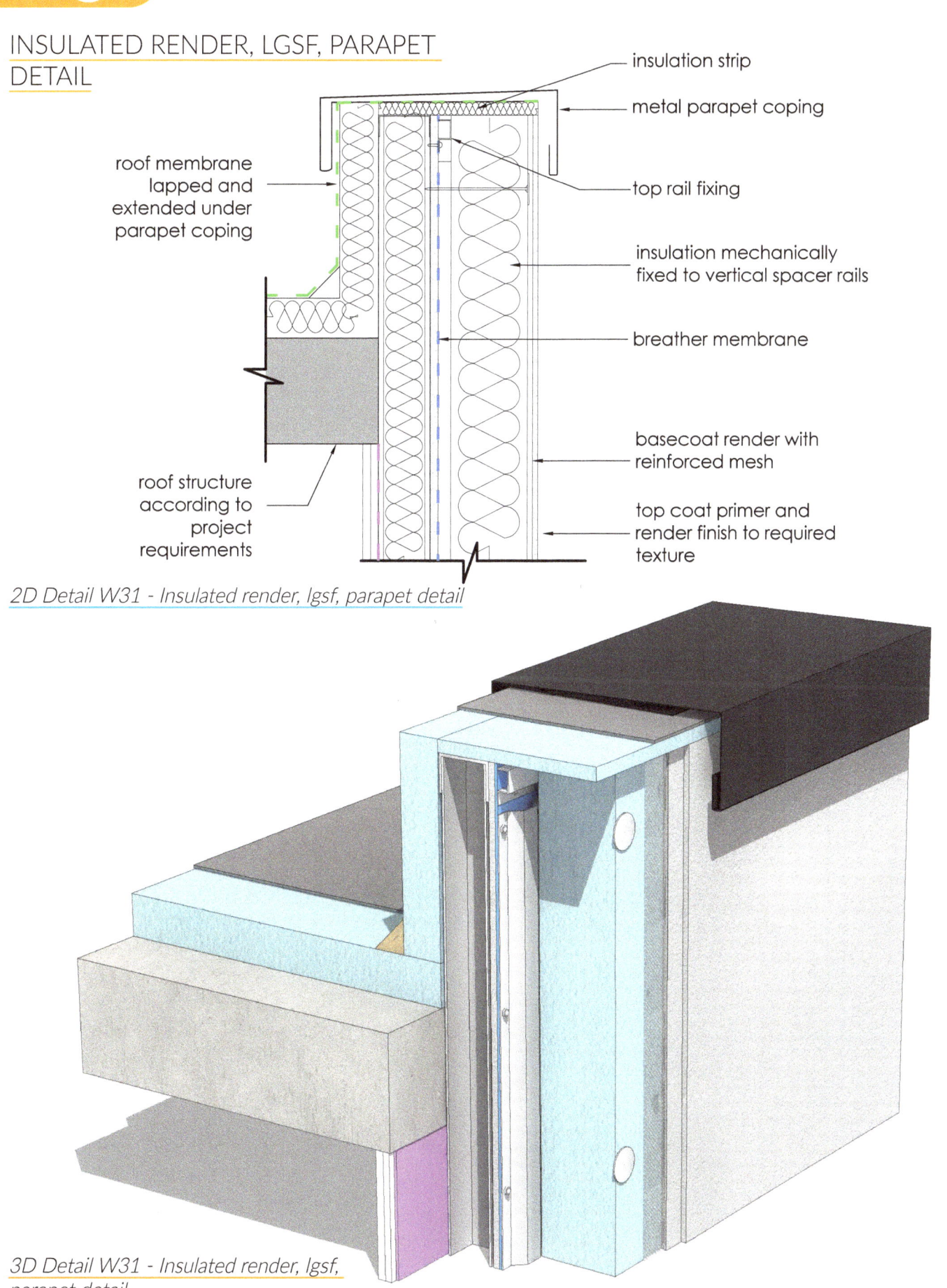

2D Detail W31 - Insulated render, lgsf, parapet detail

3D Detail W31 - Insulated render, lgsf, parapet detail

W32

INSULATED BRICK SLIPS, CONCRETE BACKING WALL

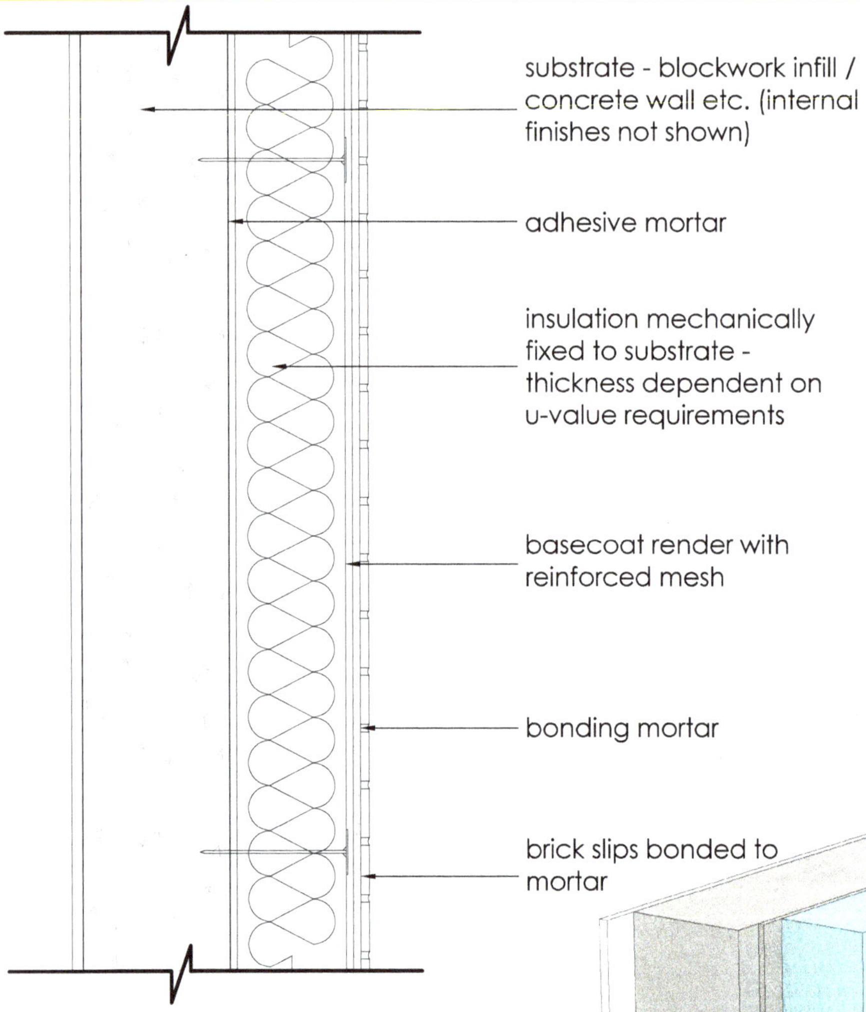

2D Detail W32 - Brick slips, concrete backing wall

- substrate - blockwork infill / concrete wall etc. (internal finishes not shown)
- adhesive mortar
- insulation mechanically fixed to substrate - thickness dependent on u-value requirements
- basecoat render with reinforced mesh
- bonding mortar
- brick slips bonded to mortar

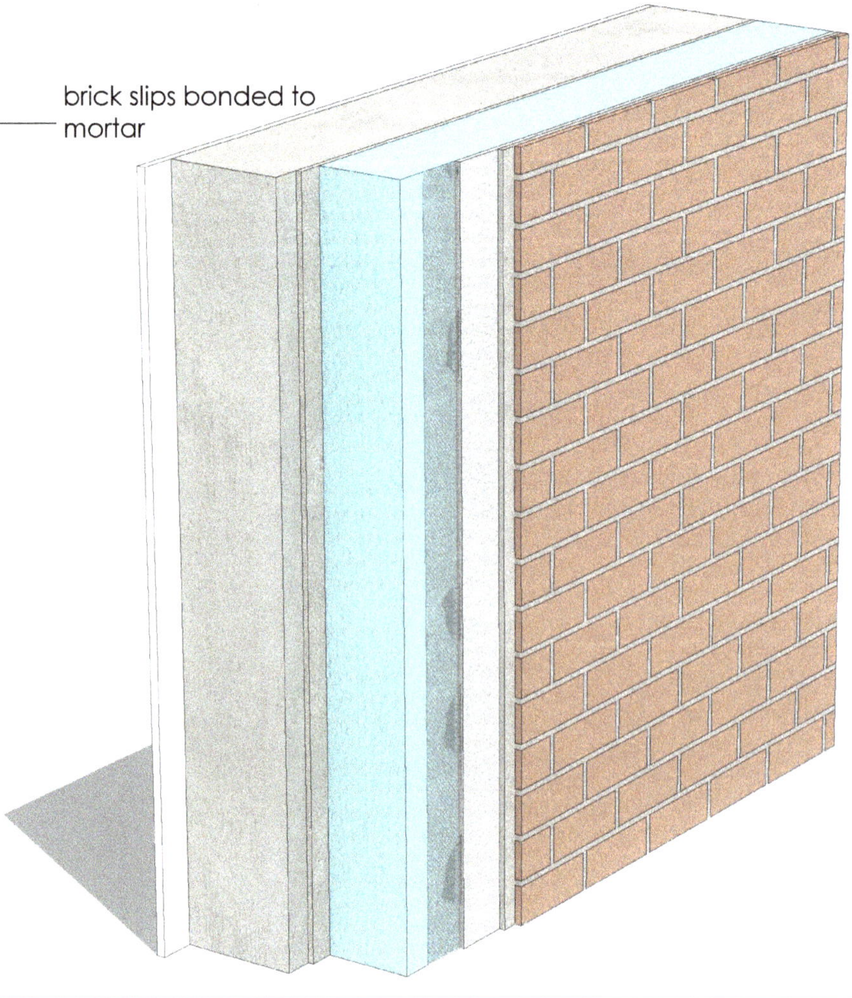

3D Detail W32 - Brick slips, concrete backing wall

SECTION 7 - WALLS

W33

INSULATED BRICK SLIPS, LGSF, BASE DETAIL

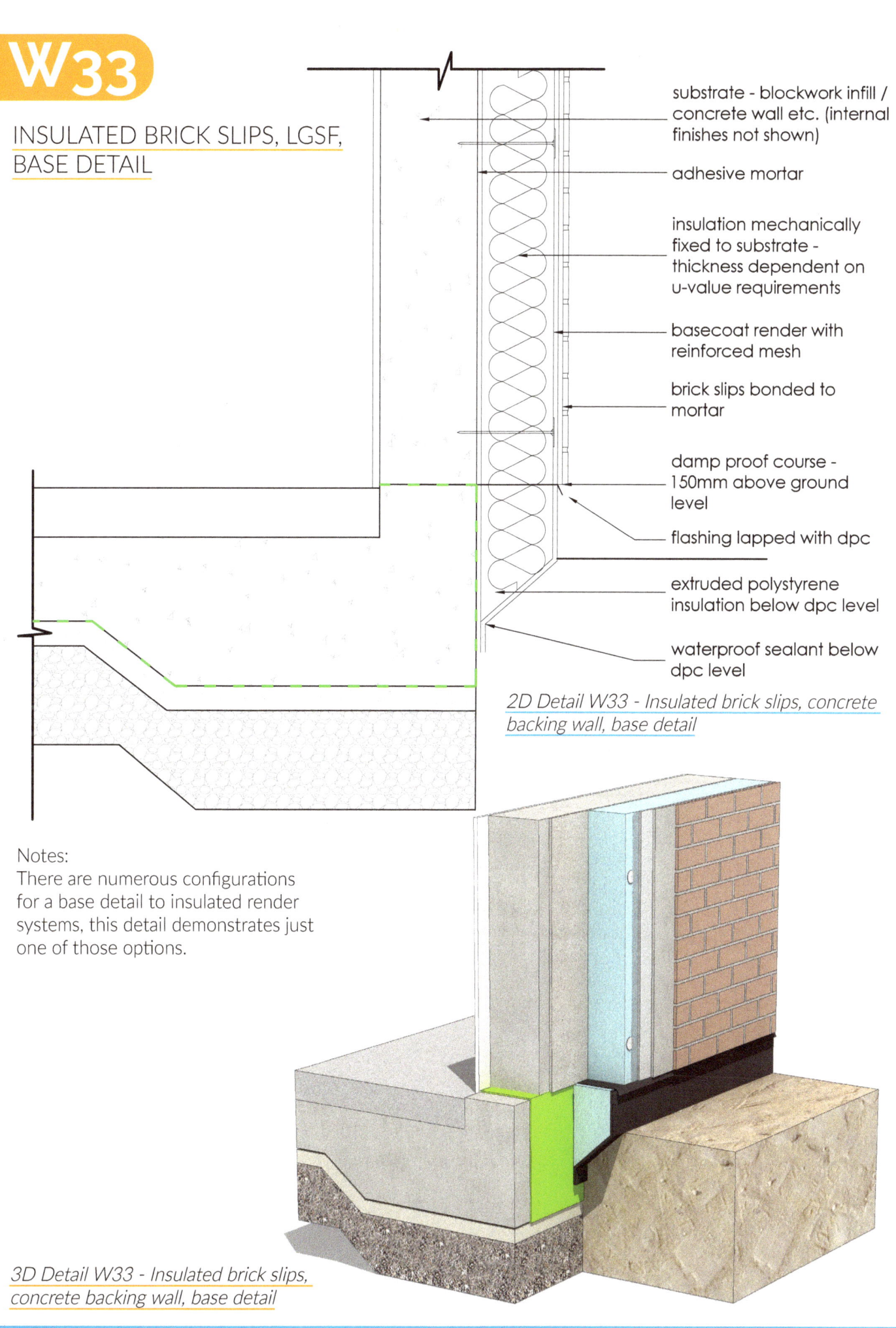

- substrate - blockwork infill / concrete wall etc. (internal finishes not shown)
- adhesive mortar
- insulation mechanically fixed to substrate - thickness dependent on u-value requirements
- basecoat render with reinforced mesh
- brick slips bonded to mortar
- damp proof course - 150mm above ground level
- flashing lapped with dpc
- extruded polystyrene insulation below dpc level
- waterproof sealant below dpc level

2D Detail W33 - Insulated brick slips, concrete backing wall, base detail

Notes:
There are numerous configurations for a base detail to insulated render systems, this detail demonstrates just one of those options.

3D Detail W33 - Insulated brick slips, concrete backing wall, base detail

W34

INSULATED BRICK SLIPS, WINDOW HEAD DETAIL

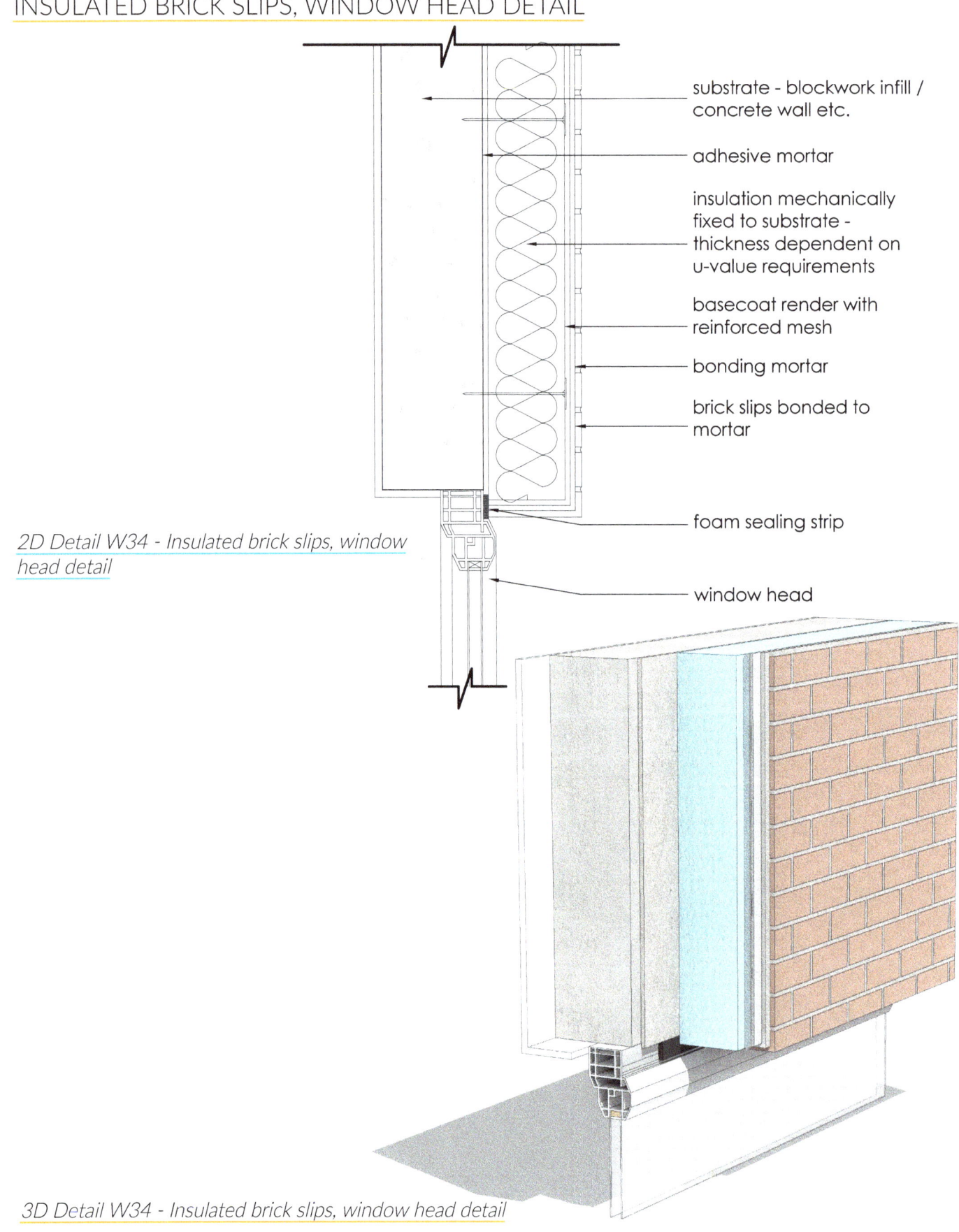

2D Detail W34 - Insulated brick slips, window head detail

3D Detail W34 - Insulated brick slips, window head detail

SECTION 7 - WALLS

W35

INSULATED BRICK SLIPS, WINDOW SILL DETAIL

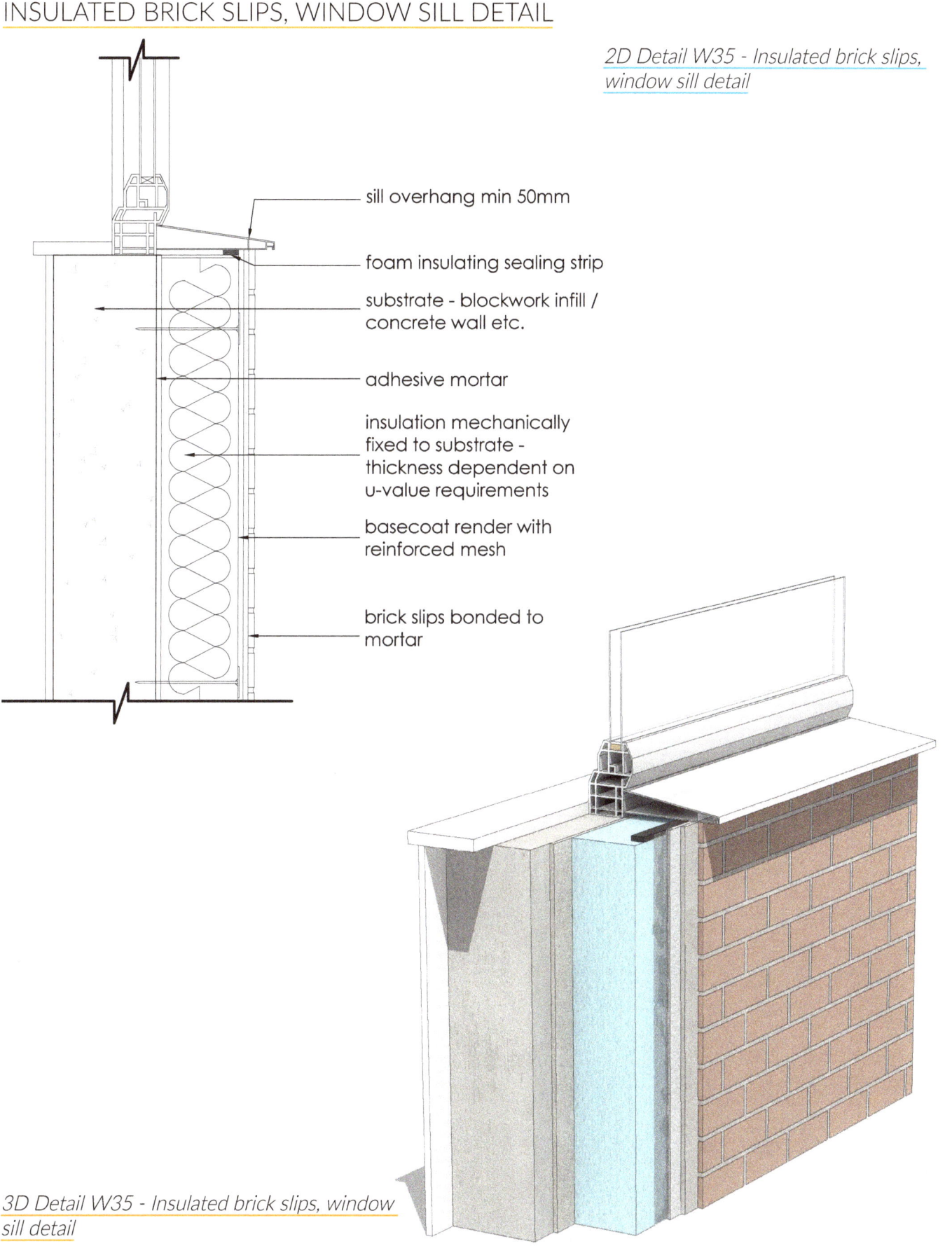

2D Detail W35 - Insulated brick slips, window sill detail

- sill overhang min 50mm
- foam insulating sealing strip
- substrate - blockwork infill / concrete wall etc.
- adhesive mortar
- insulation mechanically fixed to substrate - thickness dependent on u-value requirements
- basecoat render with reinforced mesh
- brick slips bonded to mortar

3D Detail W35 - Insulated brick slips, window sill detail

W36

INSULATED BRICK SLIPS, WINDOW JAMB DETAIL (PLAN)

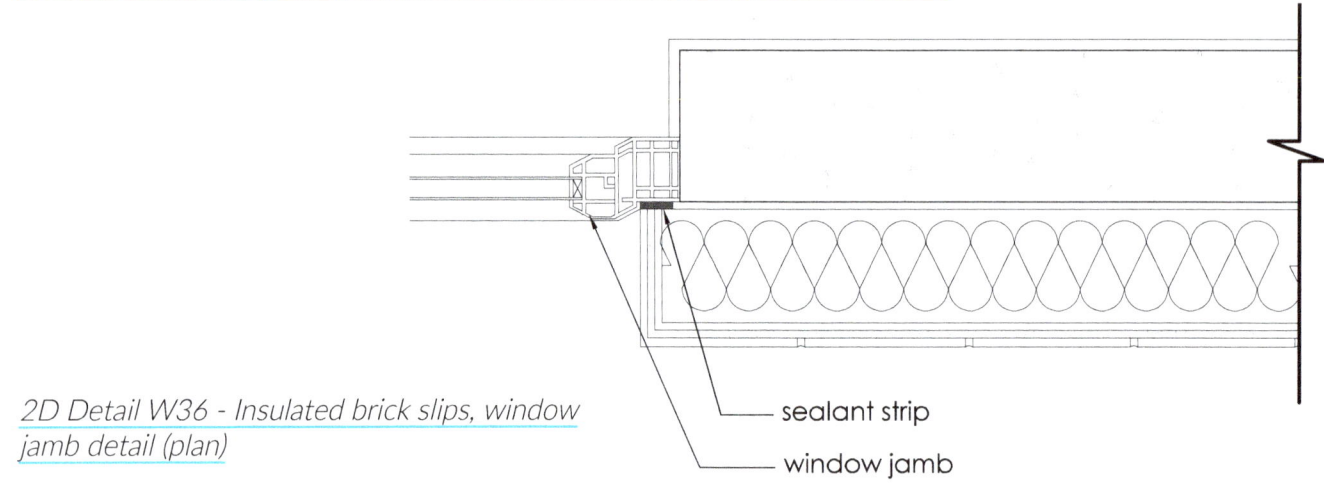

2D Detail W36 - Insulated brick slips, window jamb detail (plan)

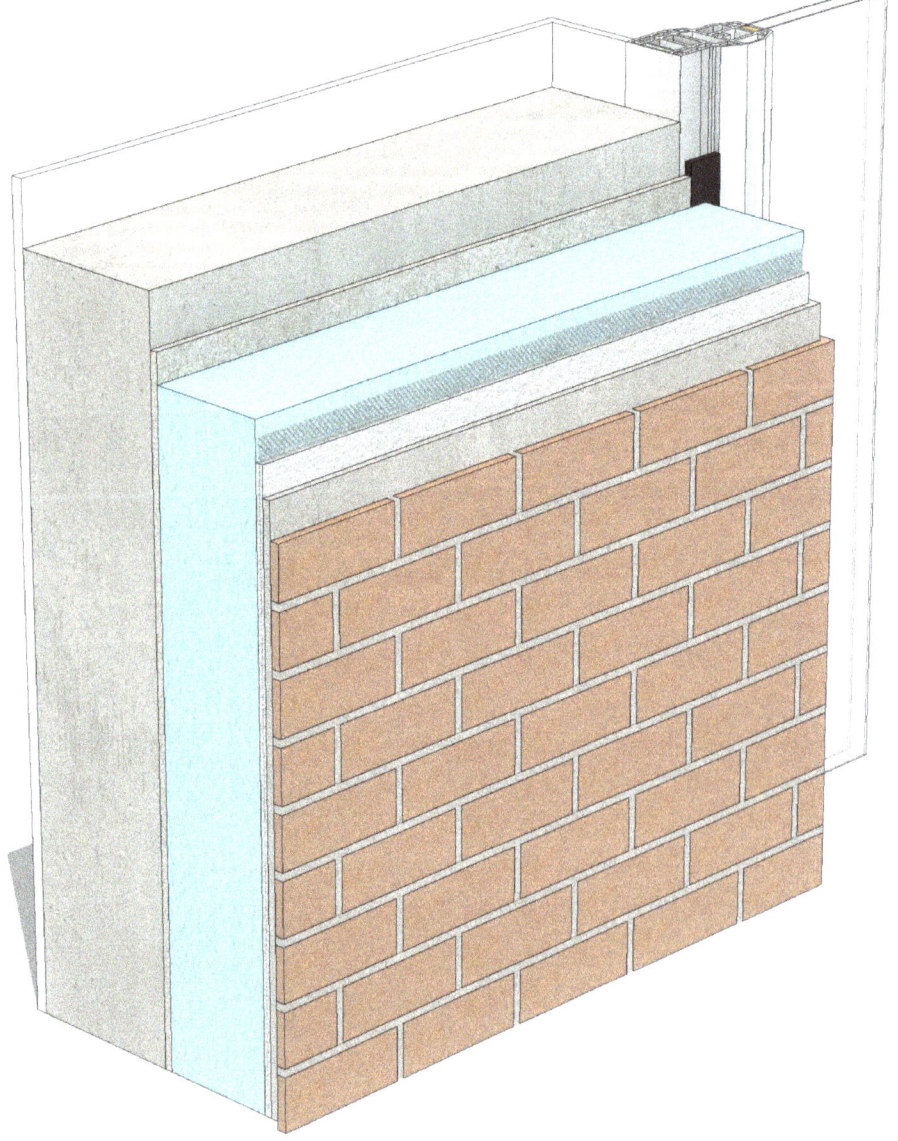

3D Detail W36 - Insulated brick slips, window jamb detail

SECTION 7 - WALLS

W37

INSULATED BRICK SLIPS, PARAPET DETAIL

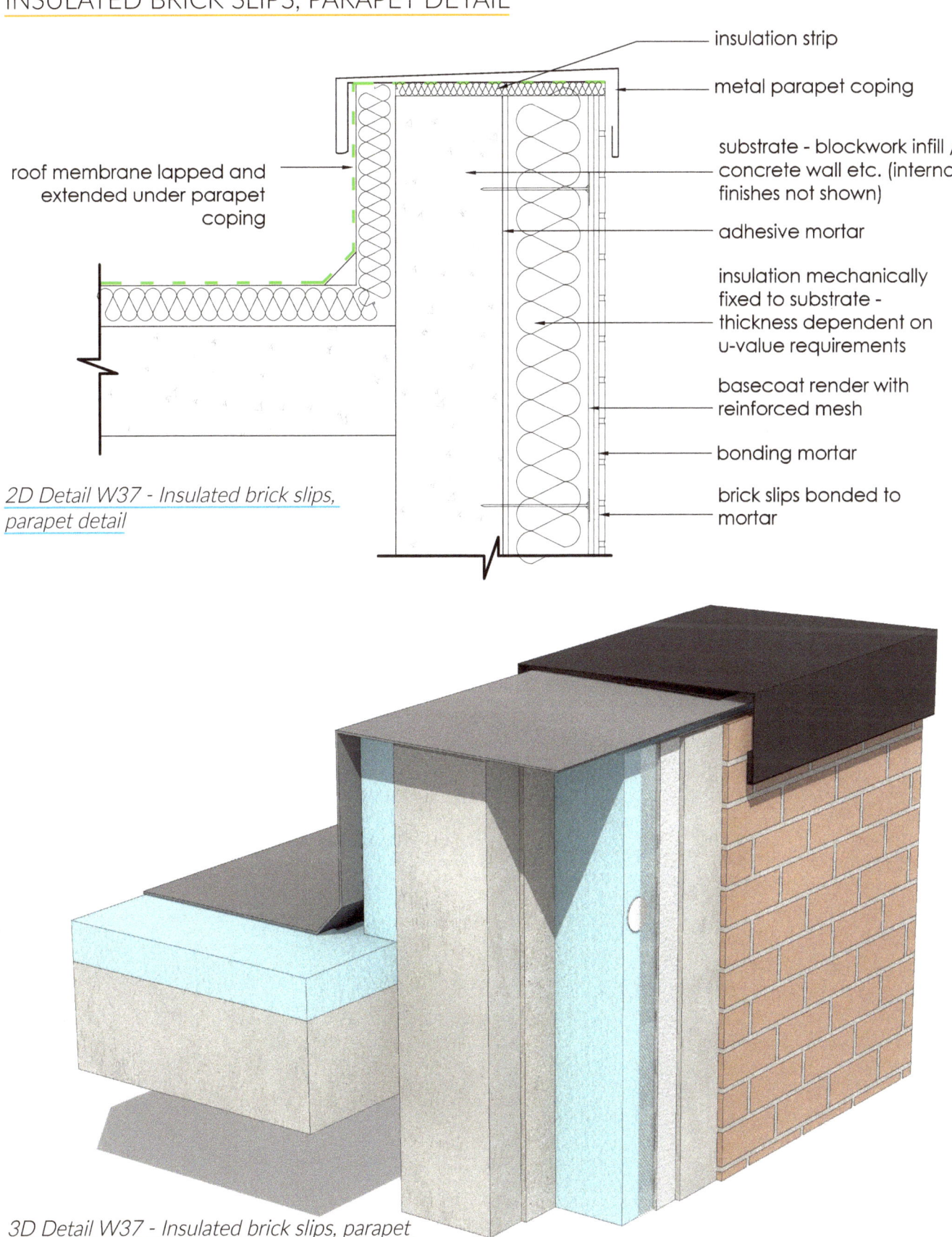

2D Detail W37 - Insulated brick slips, parapet detail

3D Detail W37 - Insulated brick slips, parapet detail

W38

TERRACOTTA RAINSCREEN CLADDING, CONCRETE BACKING WALL

- substrate - blockwork infill / concrete wall etc. (internal finishes not shown)
- insulation - thickness dependent on u-value requirements
- breather membrane
- vertical cladding rails
- fixing clips positioned on vertical cladding rails securing terracotta panels in place
- terracotta rainscreen cladding

2D Detail W38 - Terracotta rainscreen cladding, concrete backing wall

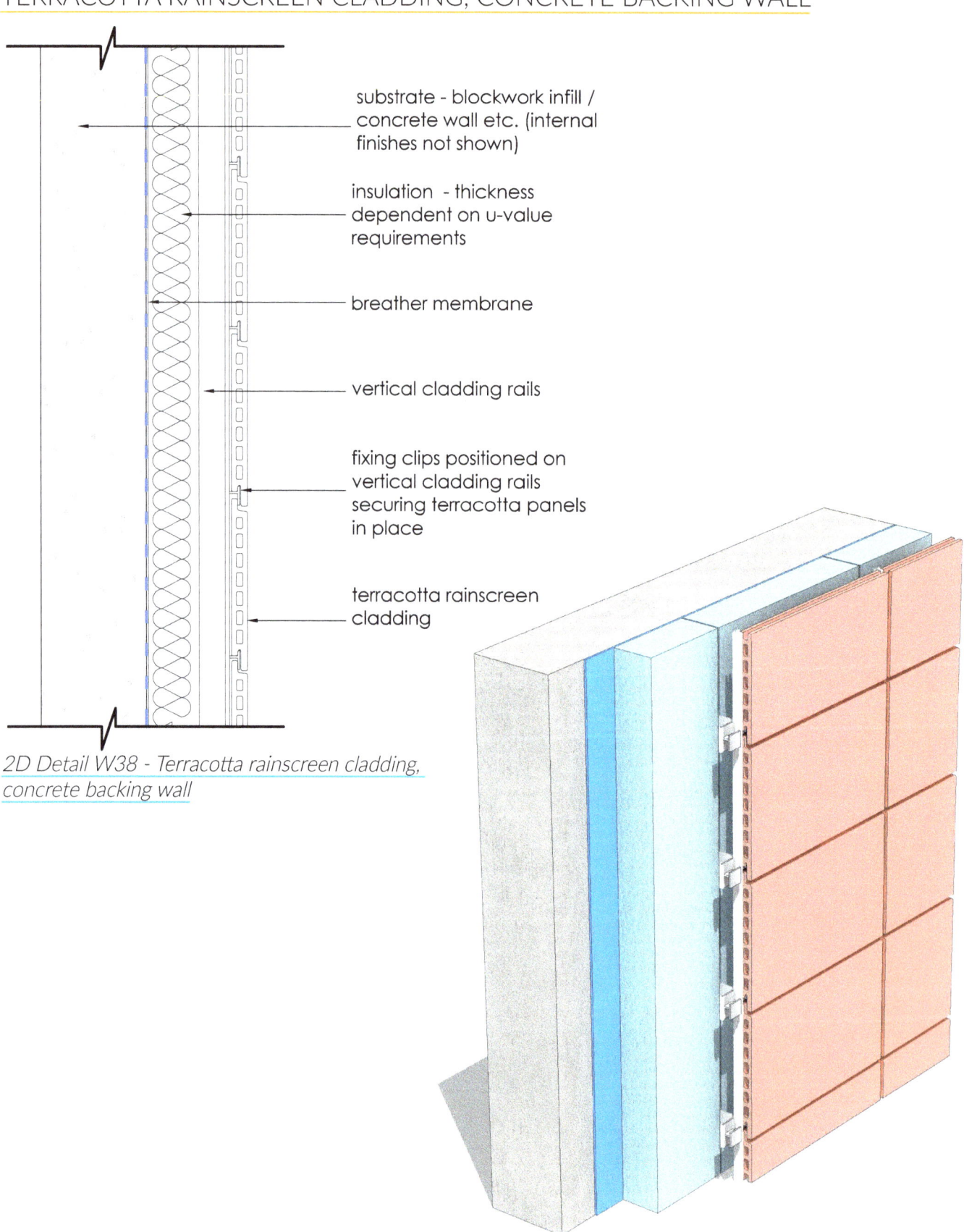

3D Detail W38 - Terracotta rainscreen cladding, concrete backing wall

SECTION 7 - WALLS

W39

TERRACOTTA RAINSCREEN CLADDING, BASE DETAIL

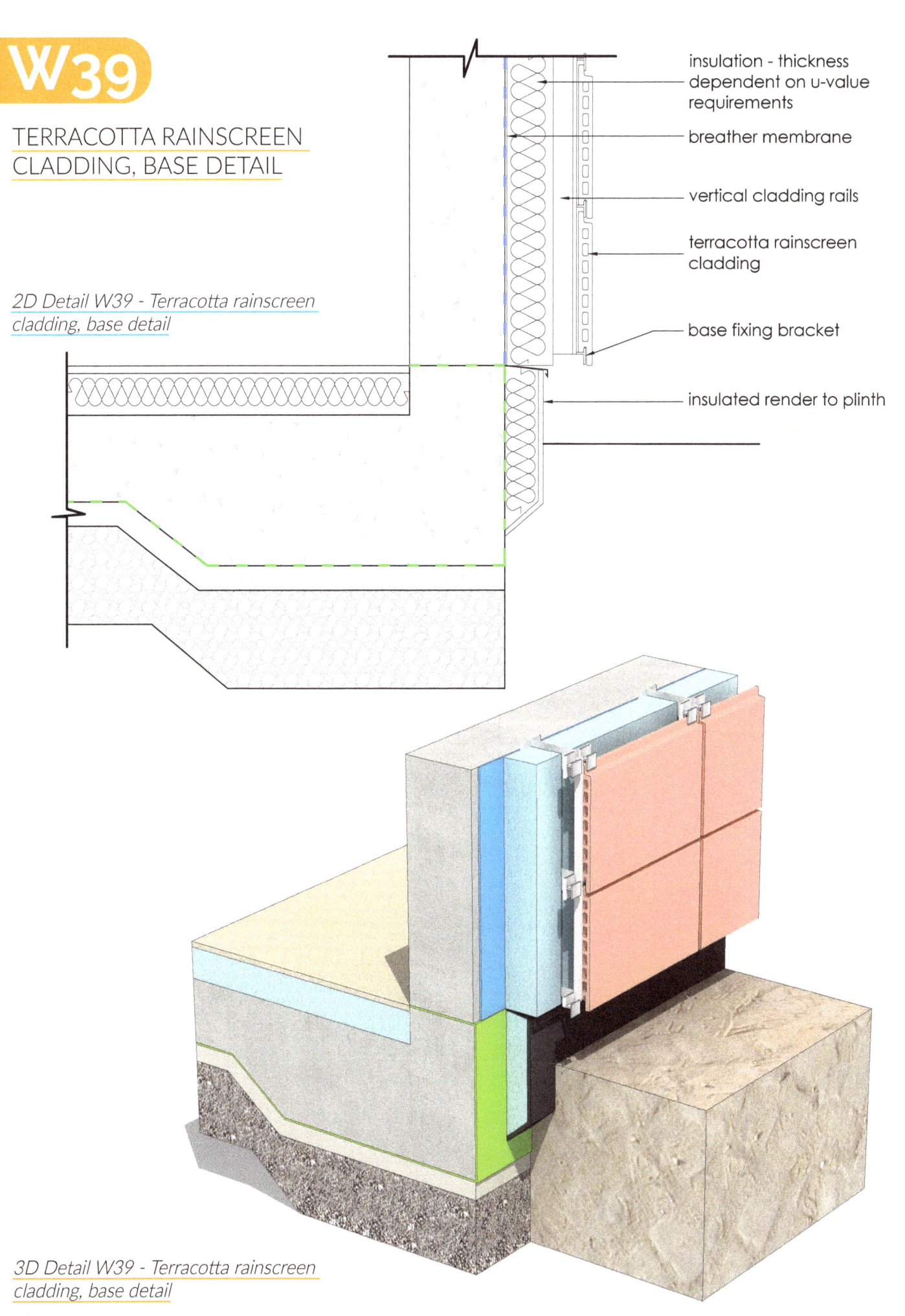

2D Detail W39 - Terracotta rainscreen cladding, base detail

- insulation - thickness dependent on u-value requirements
- breather membrane
- vertical cladding rails
- terracotta rainscreen cladding
- base fixing bracket
- insulated render to plinth

3D Detail W39 - Terracotta rainscreen cladding, base detail

W40

TERRACOTTA RAINSCREEN CLADDING, WINDOW HEAD DETAIL

- breather membrane
- fixing bracket
- vertical cladding rails
- terracotta rainscreen cladding
- fixing bracket
- insulated cavity closer
- window flashing with ventilation gaps and insect mesh

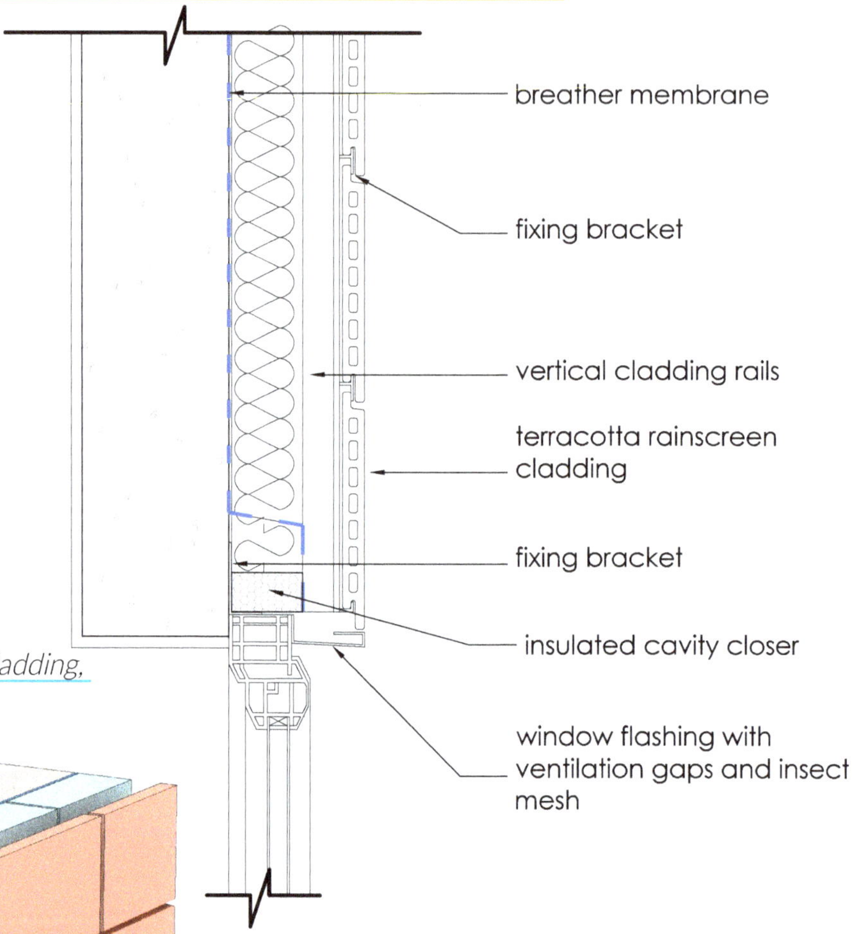

2D Detail W40 - Terracotta rainscreen cladding, window head detail

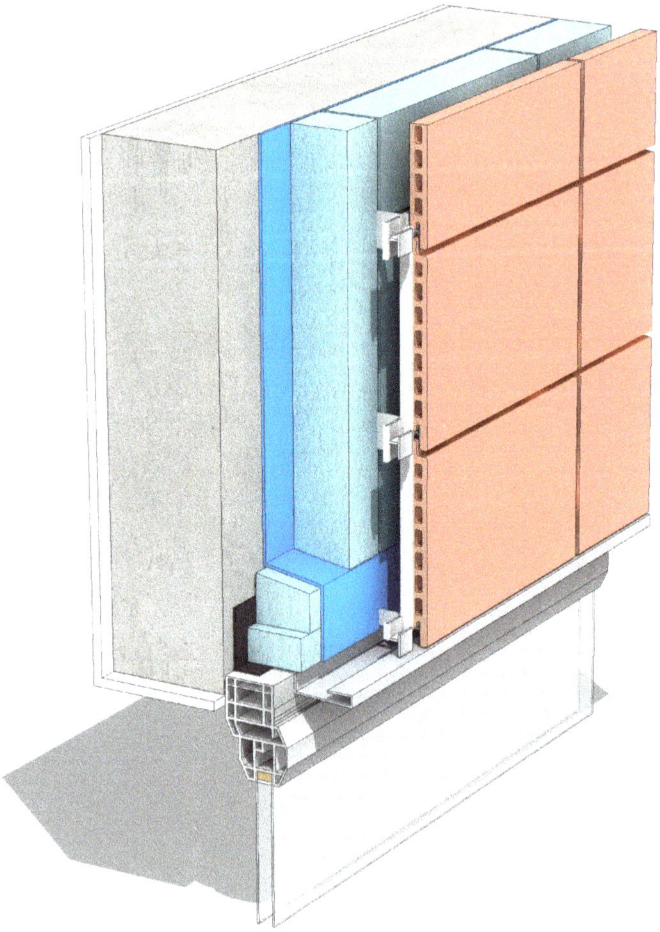

3D Detail W40 - Terracotta rainscreen cladding, window head detail

SECTION 7 - WALLS

W41

TERRACOTTA RAINSCREEN CLADDING, WINDOW SILL DETAIL

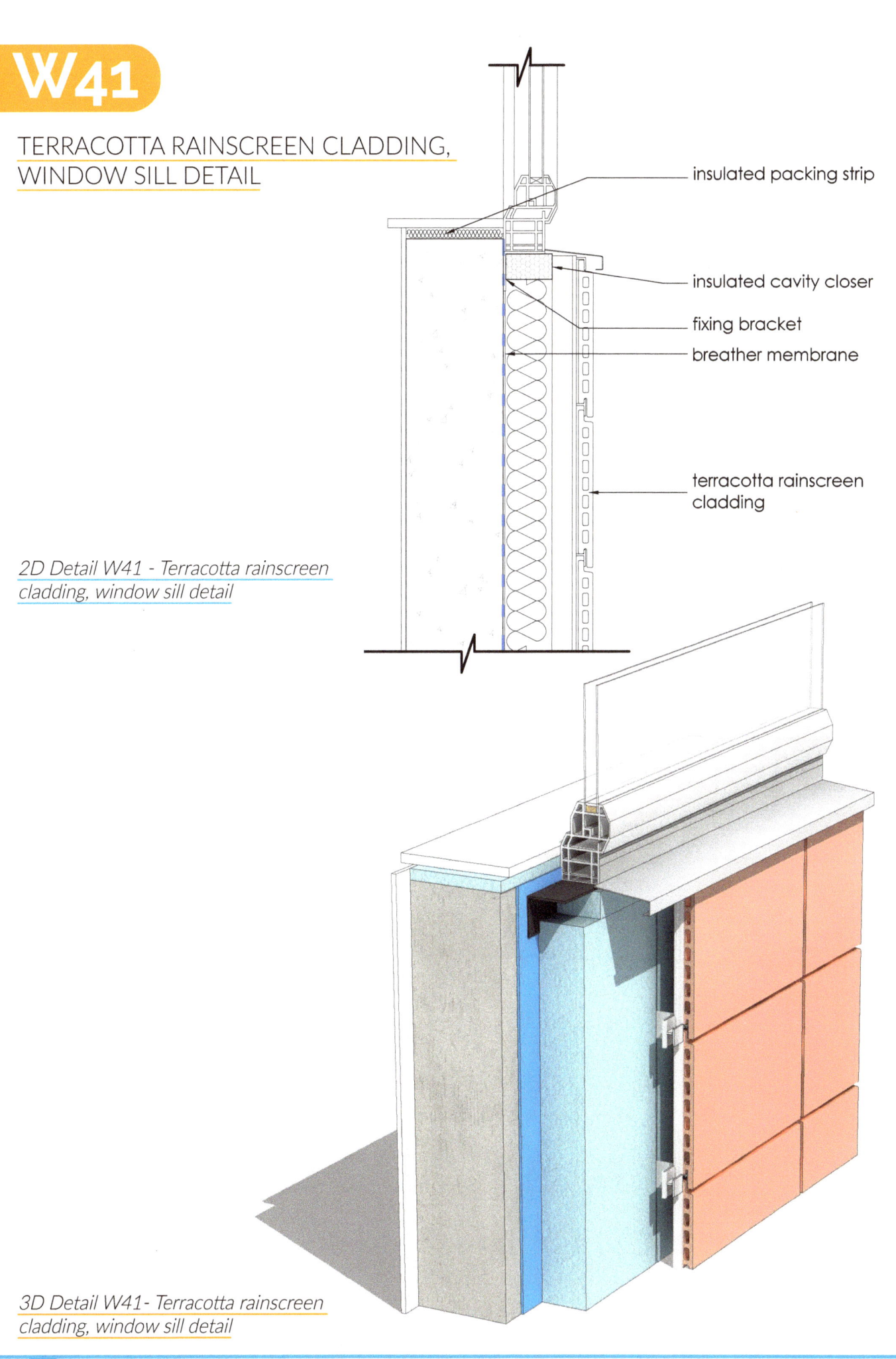

2D Detail W41 - Terracotta rainscreen cladding, window sill detail

3D Detail W41 - Terracotta rainscreen cladding, window sill detail

TERRACOTTA RAINSCREEN CLADDING, WINDOW JAMB DETAIL (PLAN)

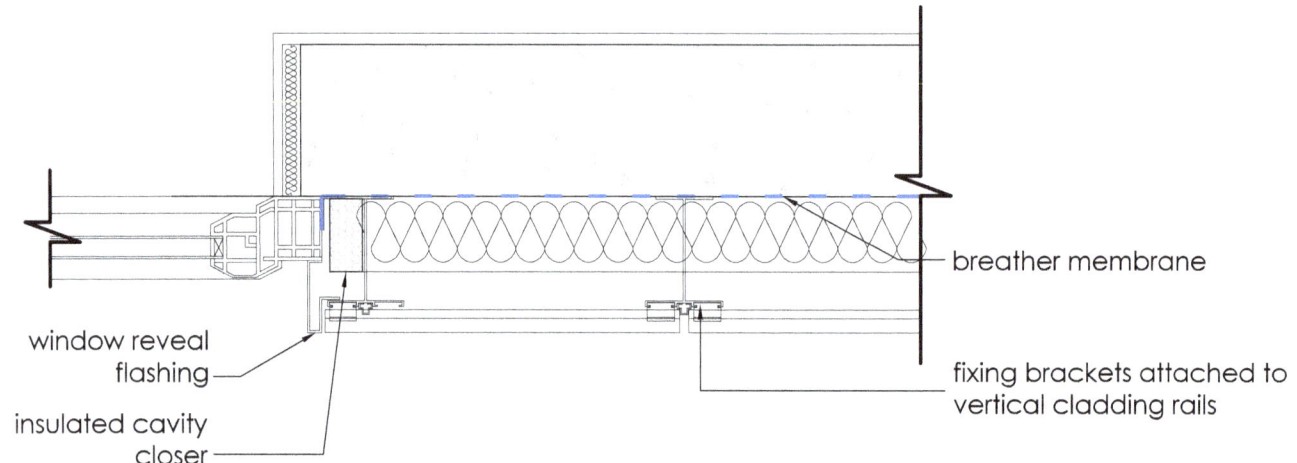

2D Detail W42 - Terracotta rainscreen cladding, window jamb detail (plan)

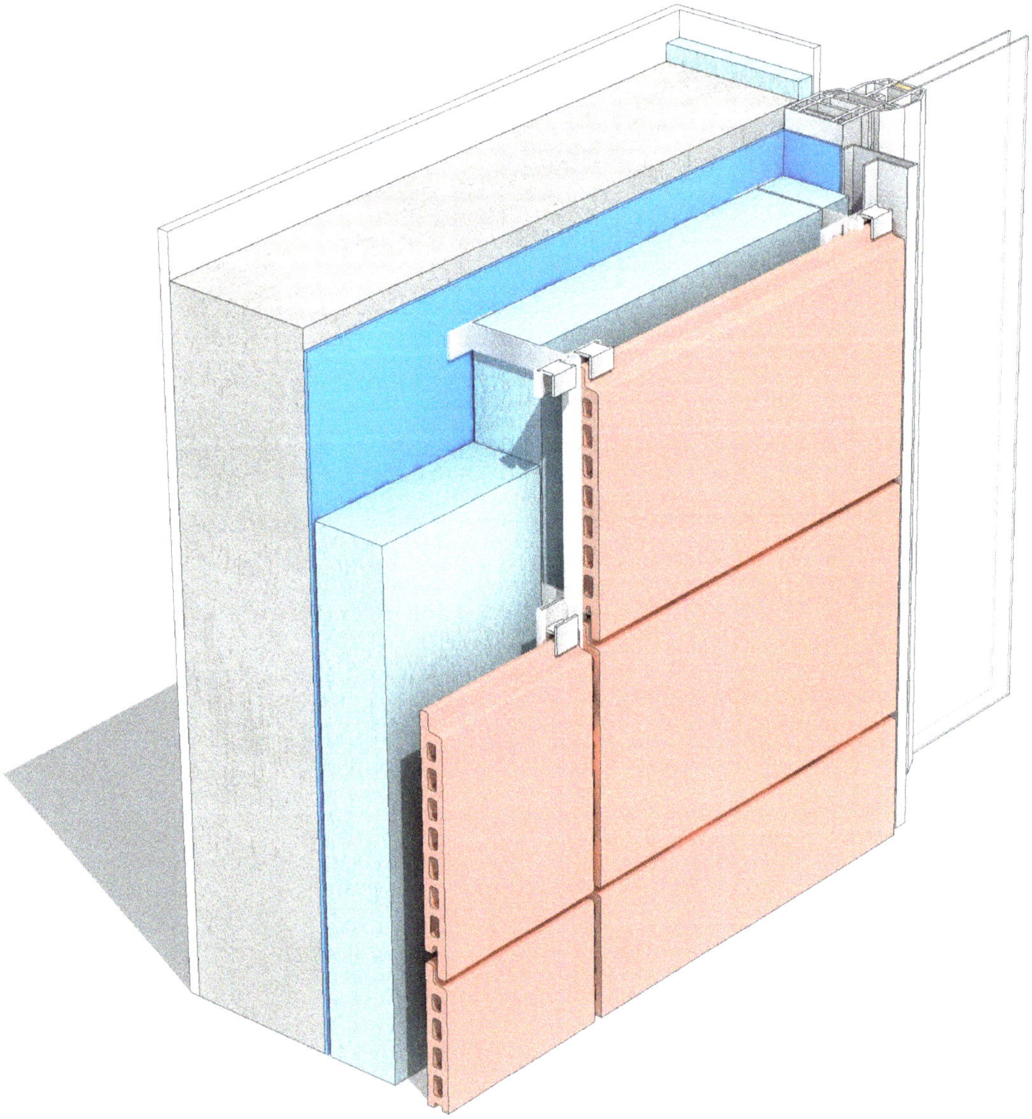

3D Detail W42 - Terracotta rainscreen cladding, window jamb detail

SECTION 7 - WALLS

W43

TERRACOTTA RAINSCREEN CLADDING, PARAPET DETAIL

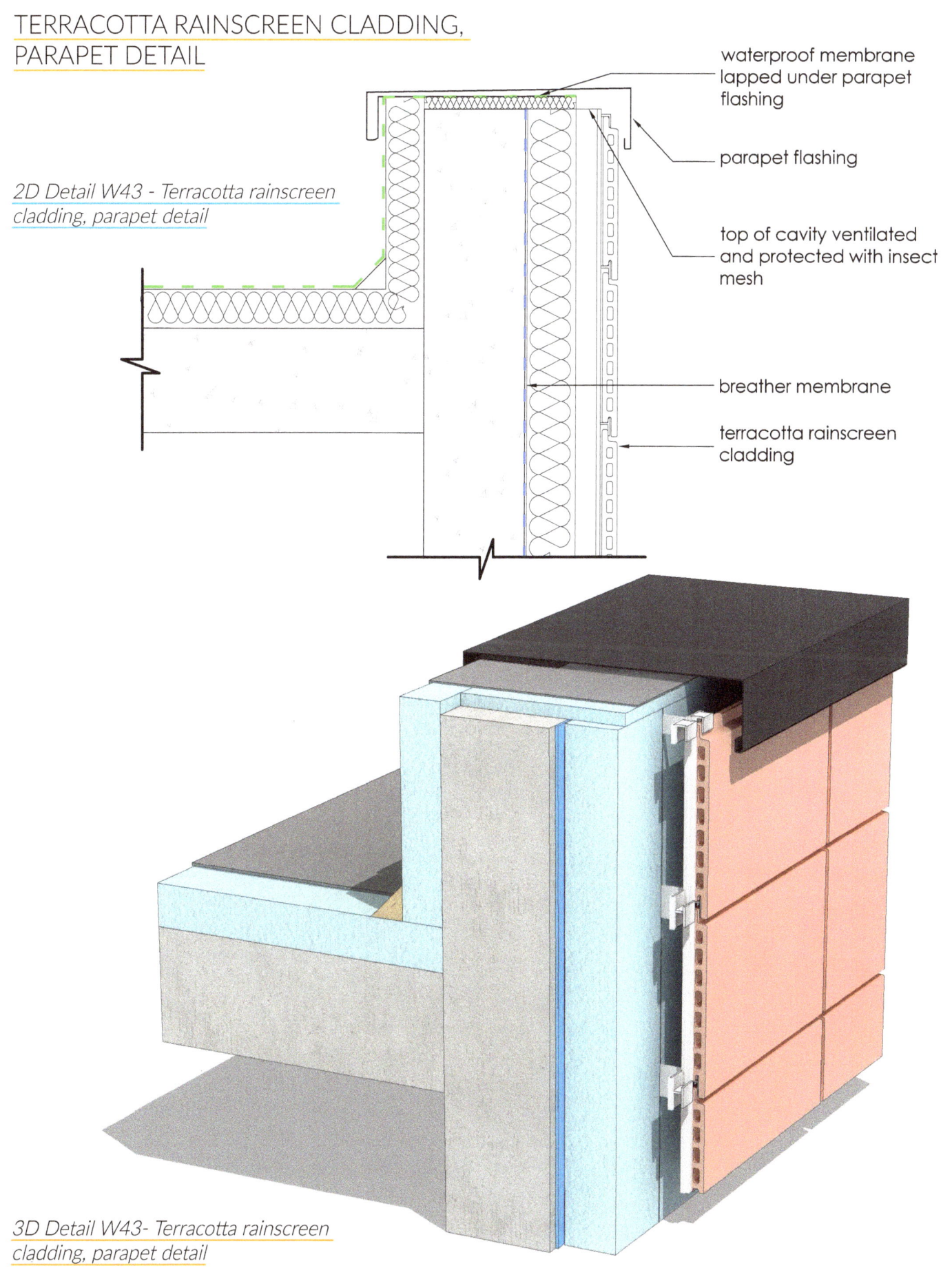

2D Detail W43 - Terracotta rainscreen cladding, parapet detail

- waterproof membrane lapped under parapet flashing
- parapet flashing
- top of cavity ventilated and protected with insect mesh
- breather membrane
- terracotta rainscreen cladding

3D Detail W43- Terracotta rainscreen cladding, parapet detail

W44

CONCRETE RAINSCREEN PANEL, LIGHT GAUGE STEEL FRAME (LGSF)

- stainless steel support bracket fixed to steel frame
- light gauge steel frame structure, with insulation between studs if required
- insulation mechanically fixed to substrate
- concrete cladding panel
- breather membrane
- vapour control layer
- joints open with cavity behind drained and ventilated

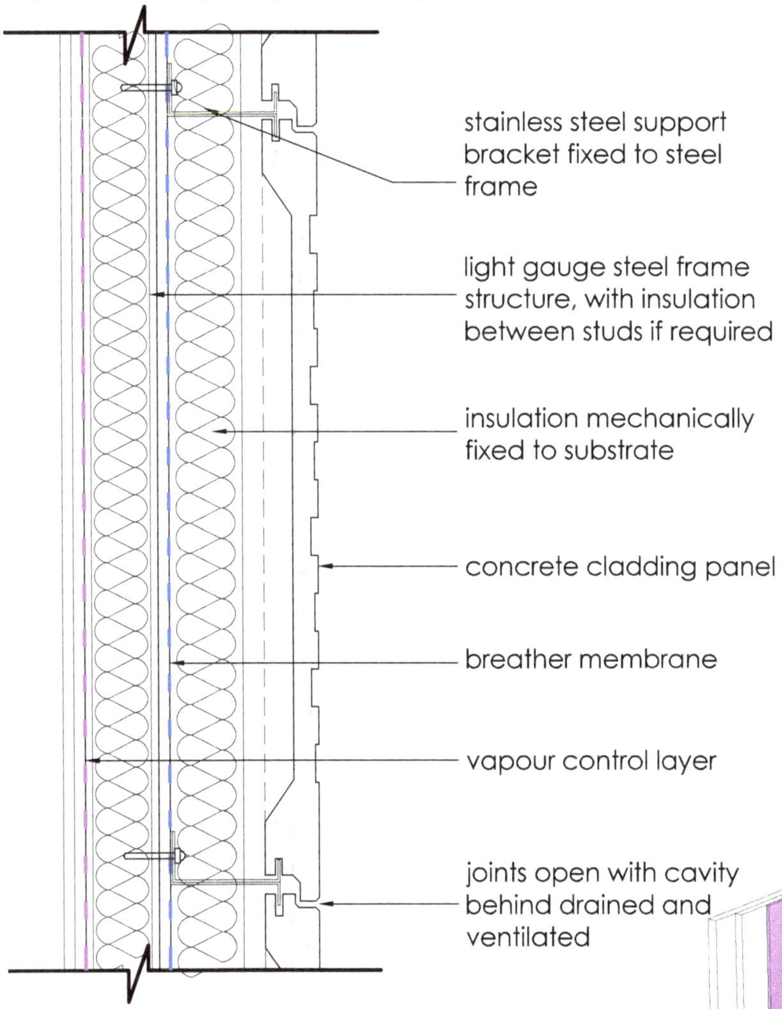

2D Detail W44 - Concrete rainscreen panel, light gauge steel frame (lgsf)

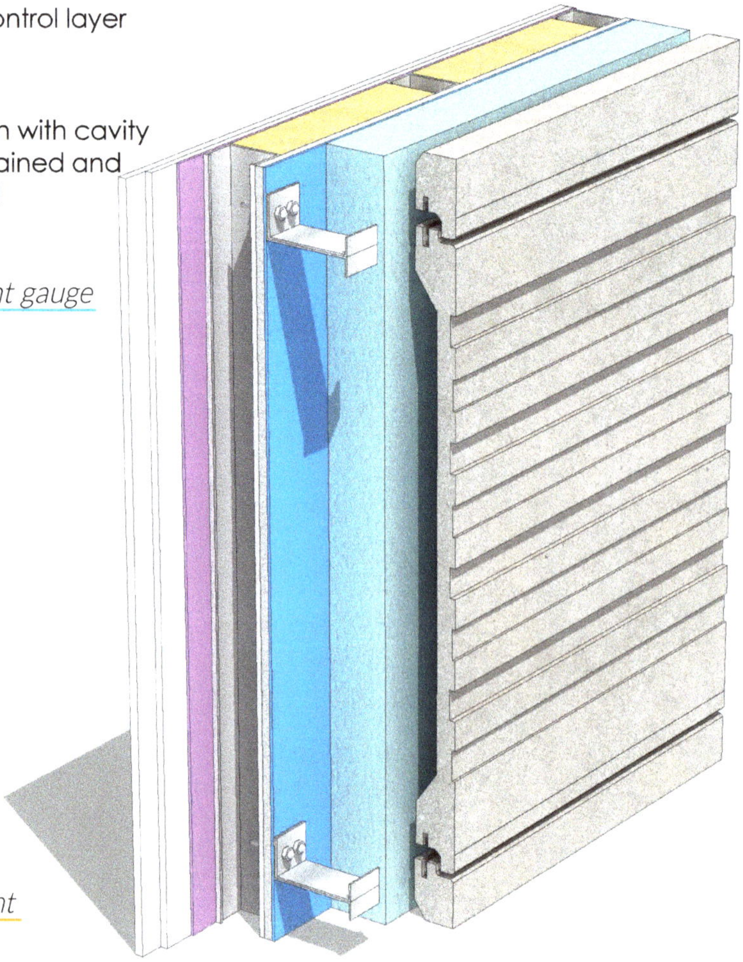

3D Detail W44 - Concrete rainscreen panel, light gauge steel frame (lgsf)

SECTION 7 - WALLS

W45

CONCRETE RAINSCREEN PANEL, LGSF, BASE DETAIL

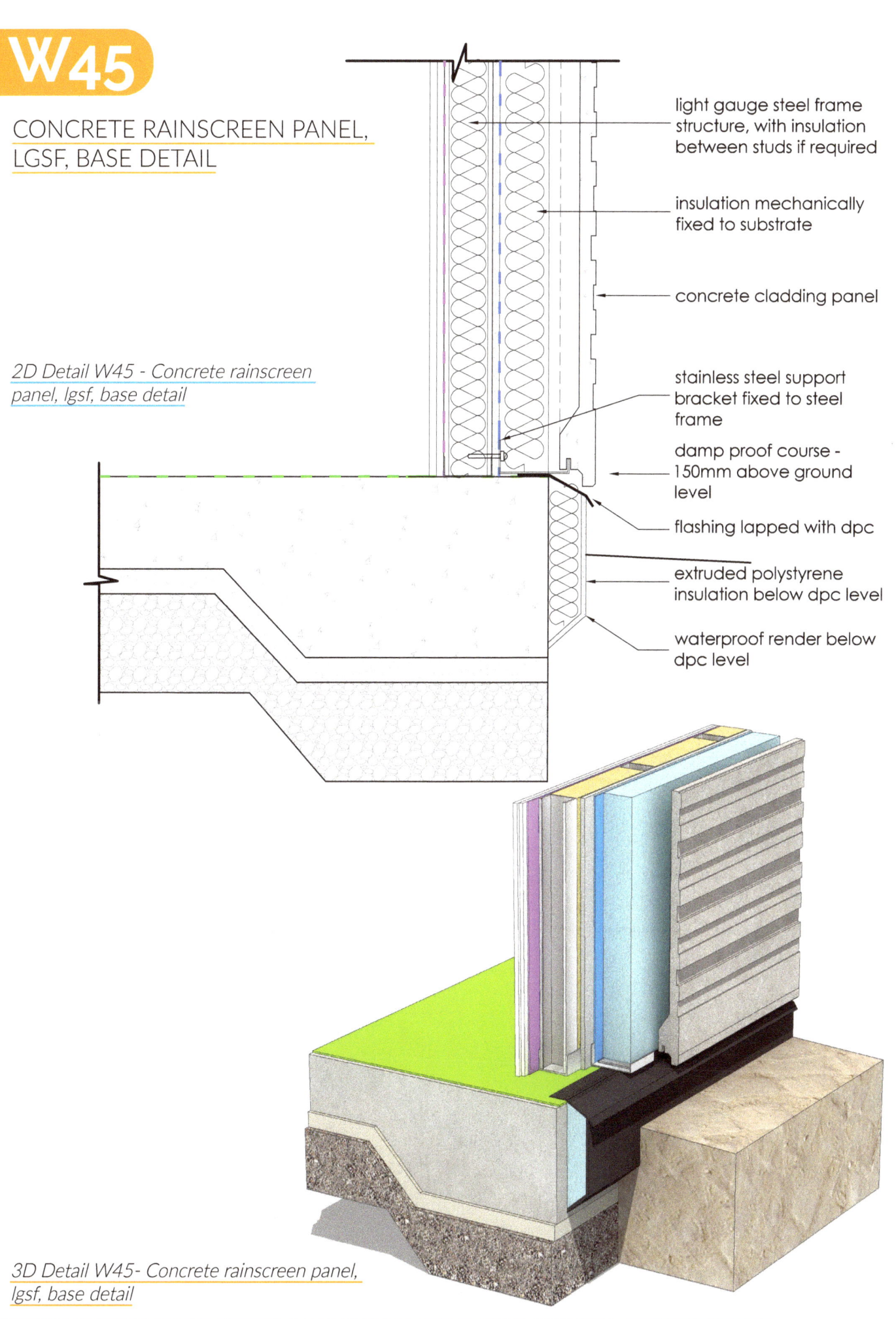

2D Detail W45 - Concrete rainscreen panel, lgsf, base detail

- light gauge steel frame structure, with insulation between studs if required
- insulation mechanically fixed to substrate
- concrete cladding panel
- stainless steel support bracket fixed to steel frame
- damp proof course - 150mm above ground level
- flashing lapped with dpc
- extruded polystyrene insulation below dpc level
- waterproof render below dpc level

3D Detail W45- Concrete rainscreen panel, lgsf, base detail

W46

CONCRETE RAINSCREEN PANEL, LGSF, WINDOW HEAD DETAIL

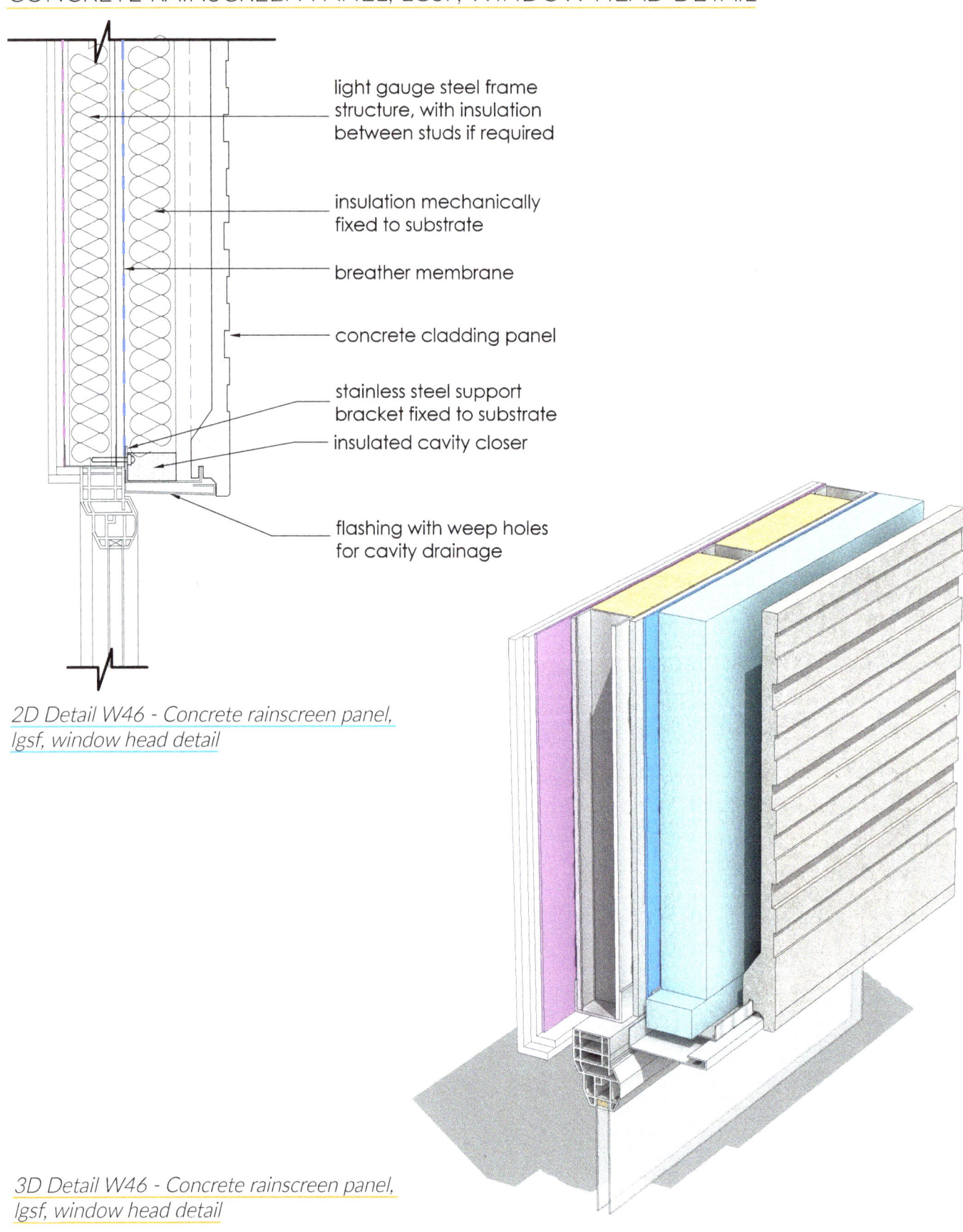

- light gauge steel frame structure, with insulation between studs if required
- insulation mechanically fixed to substrate
- breather membrane
- concrete cladding panel
- stainless steel support bracket fixed to substrate
- insulated cavity closer
- flashing with weep holes for cavity drainage

2D Detail W46 - Concrete rainscreen panel, lgsf, window head detail

3D Detail W46 - Concrete rainscreen panel, lgsf, window head detail

CONCRETE RAINSCREEN PANEL, LGSF, WINDOW SILL DETAIL

- sill overhang
- sealant strip
- insulation under sill
- insulated cavity closer
- stainless steel support bracket fixed to steel frame
- insulation mechanically fixed to steel frame
- concrete cladding panel

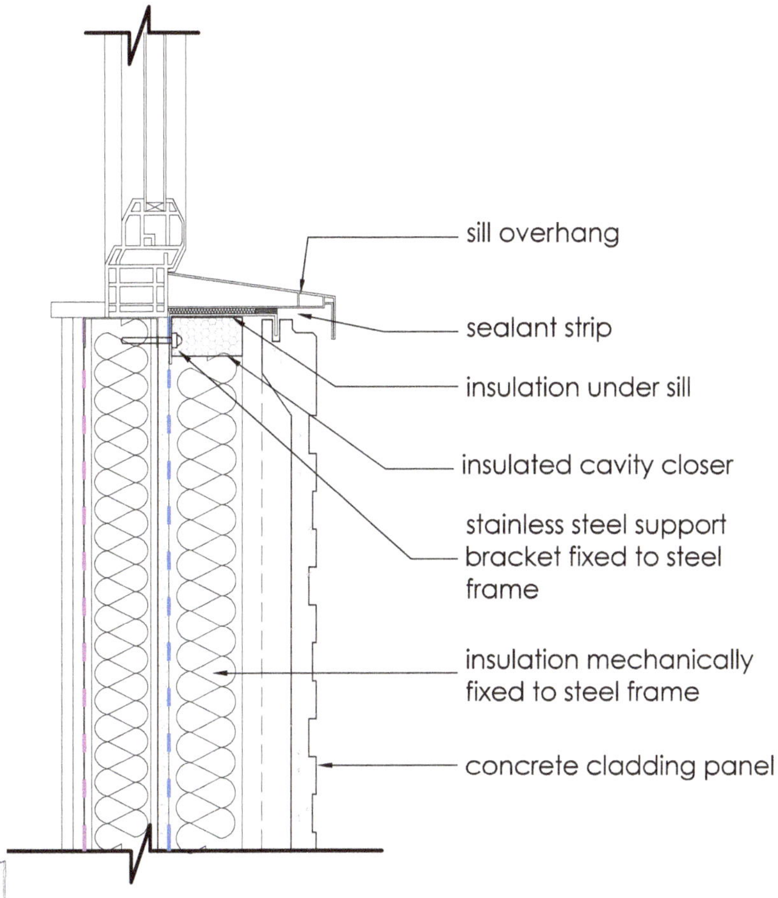

2D Detail W47 - Concrete rainscreen panel, lgsf, window sill detail

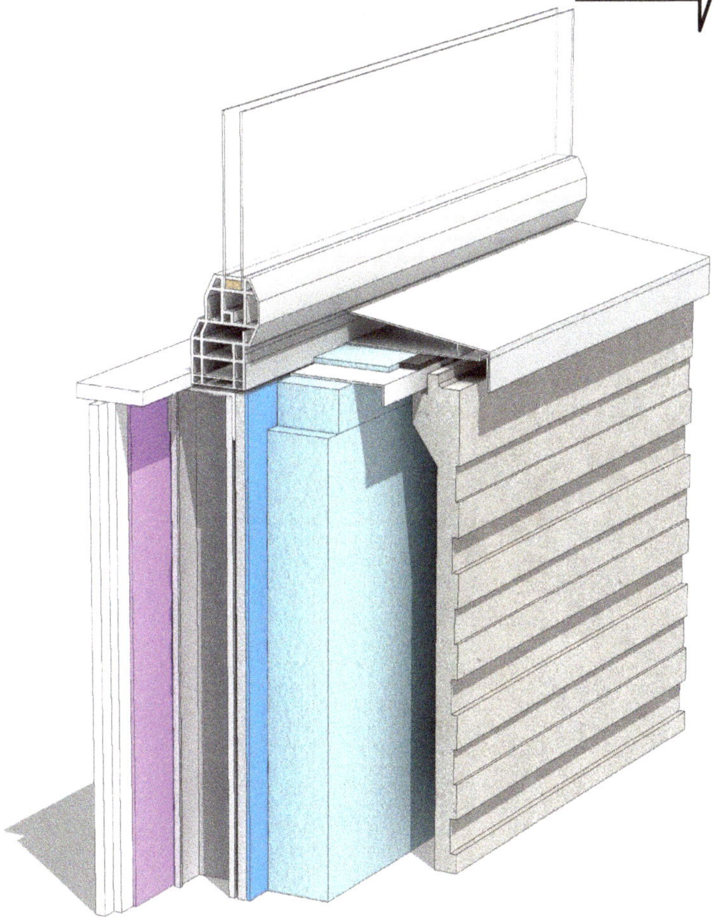

3D Detail W47- Concrete rainscreen panel, lgsf, window sill detail

272

W48

CONCRETE RAINSCREEN PANEL, LGSF, WINDOW JAMB DETAIL (PLAN)

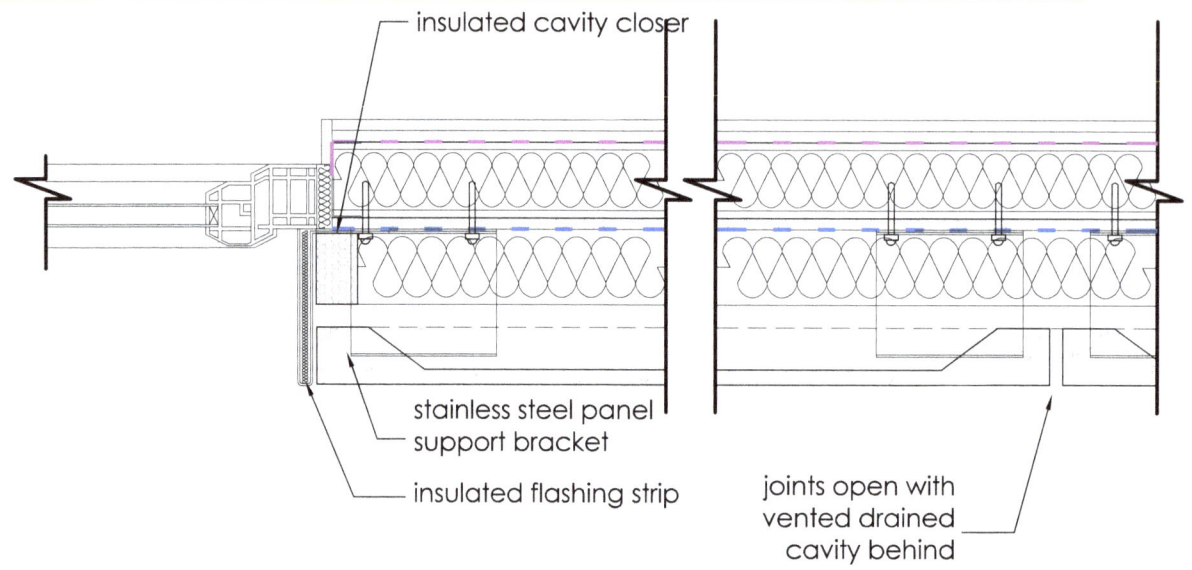

2D Detail W48 - Concrete rainscreen panel, lgsf, window jamb detail

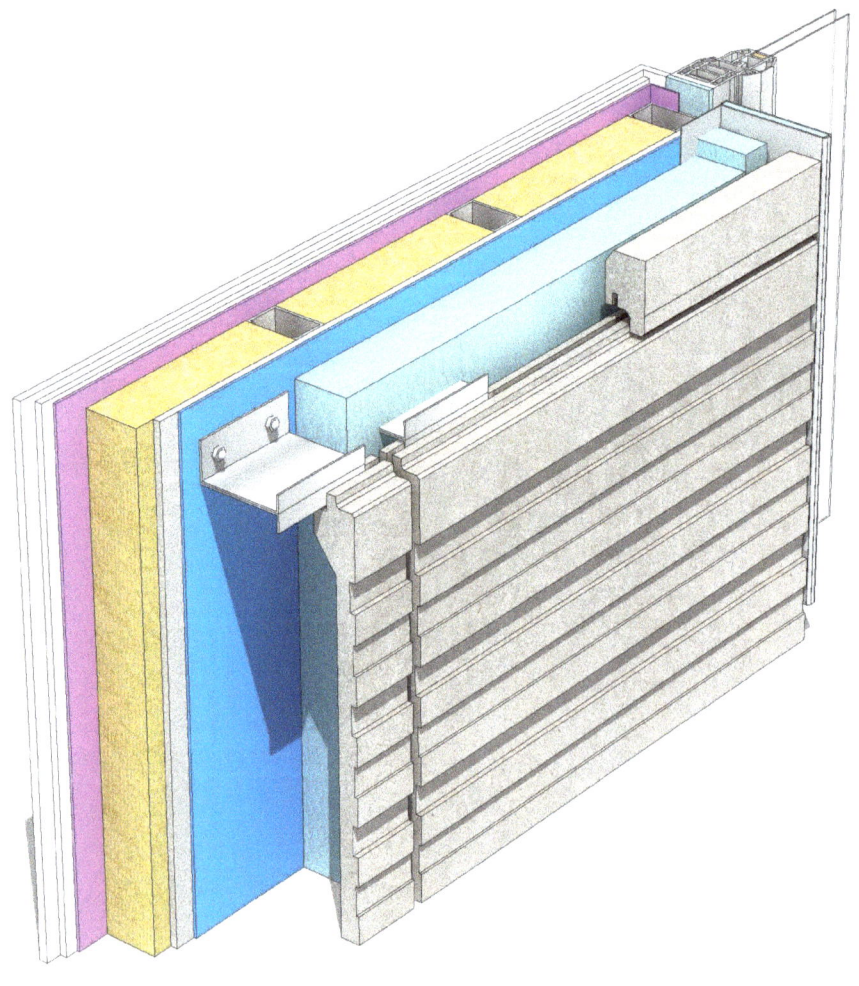

3D Detail W48 - Concrete rainscreen panel, lgsf, window jamb detail

SECTION 7 - WALLS

W49

CONCRETE RAINSCREEN PANEL, LGSF, PARAPET DETAIL

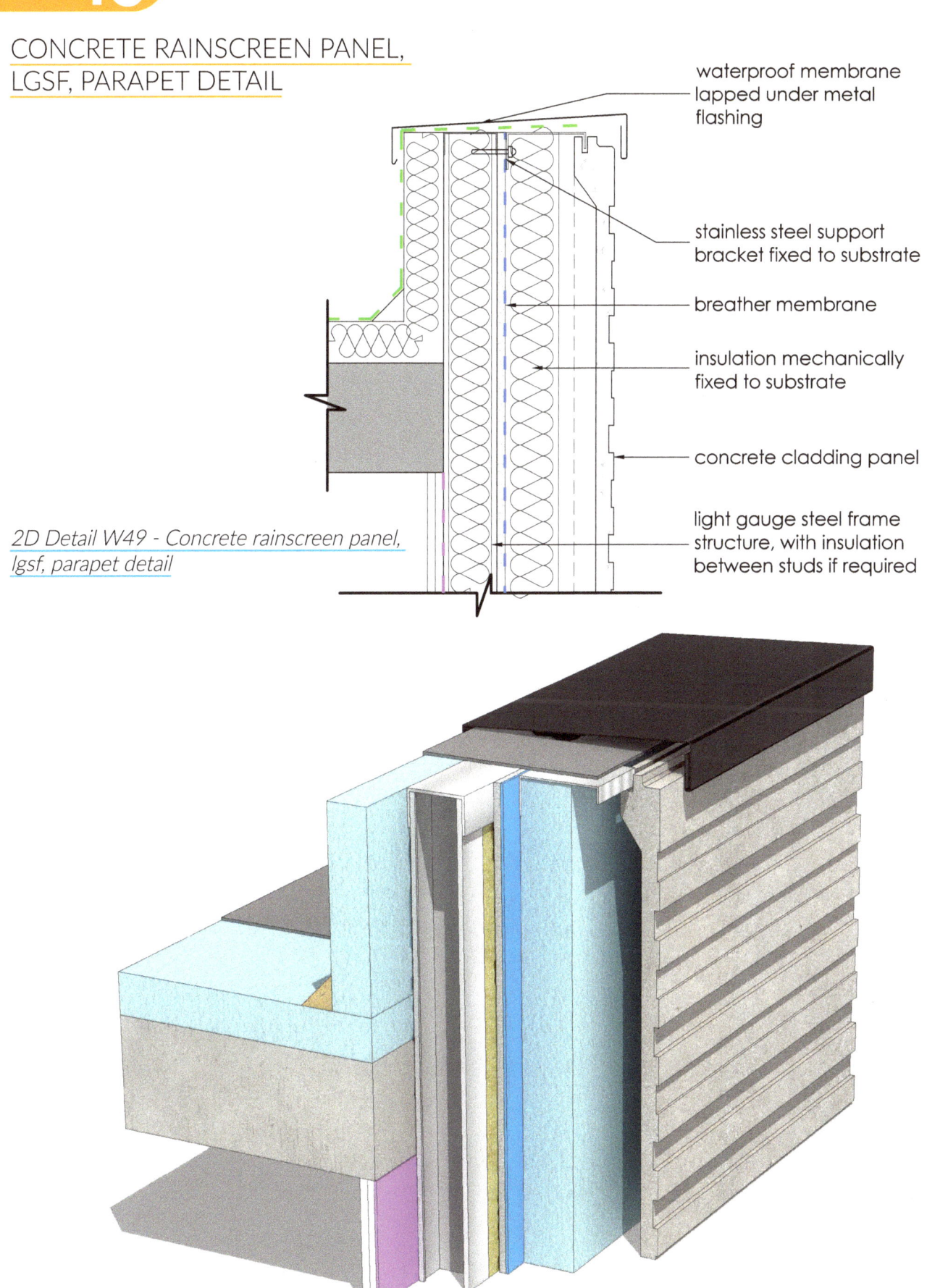

2D Detail W49 - Concrete rainscreen panel, lgsf, parapet detail

3D Detail W49- Concrete rainscreen panel, lgsf, parapet detail

METAL RAINSCREEN CLADDING, LIGHT GAUGE STEEL FRAME (LGSF)

- support bracket
- cladding rail
- rainscreen cladding panel fixed to cladding rail
- insulation to project u-value requirements
- steel frame wall
- weather resistant membrane
- vapour control layer

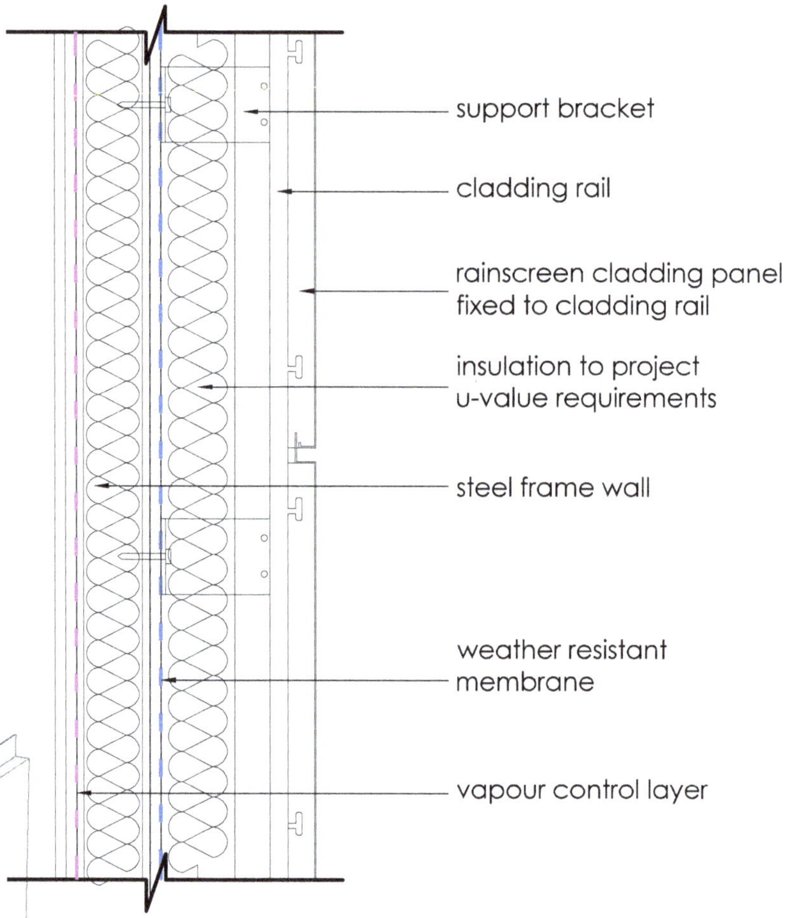

2D Detail W50 - Metal rainscreen cladding, light gauge steel frame (lgsf)

3D Detail W50 - Metal rainscreen cladding, light gauge steel frame (lgsf)

SECTION 7 - WALLS

W51

METAL RAINSCREEN CLADDING, LGSF, BASE DETAIL

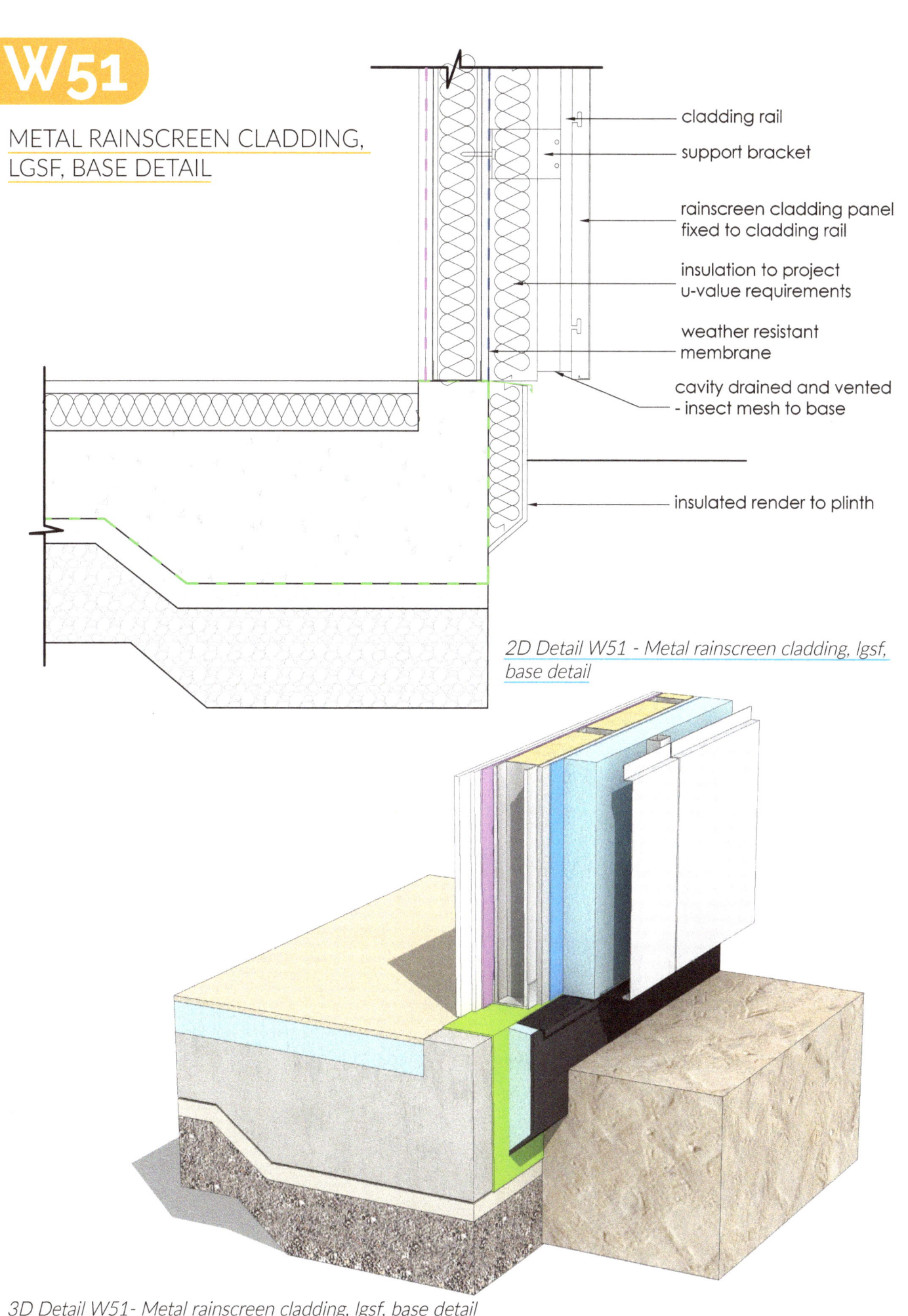

2D Detail W51 - Metal rainscreen cladding, lgsf, base detail

- cladding rail
- support bracket
- rainscreen cladding panel fixed to cladding rail
- insulation to project u-value requirements
- weather resistant membrane
- cavity drained and vented - insect mesh to base
- insulated render to plinth

3D Detail W51- Metal rainscreen cladding, lgsf, base detail

W52

METAL RAINSCREEN CLADDING, WINDOW HEAD DETAIL

- rainscreen cladding panel fixed to cladding rail
- insulation to project u-value requirements
- weather resistant membrane
- insulated cavity closer
- window flashing with ventilation gaps and insect mesh

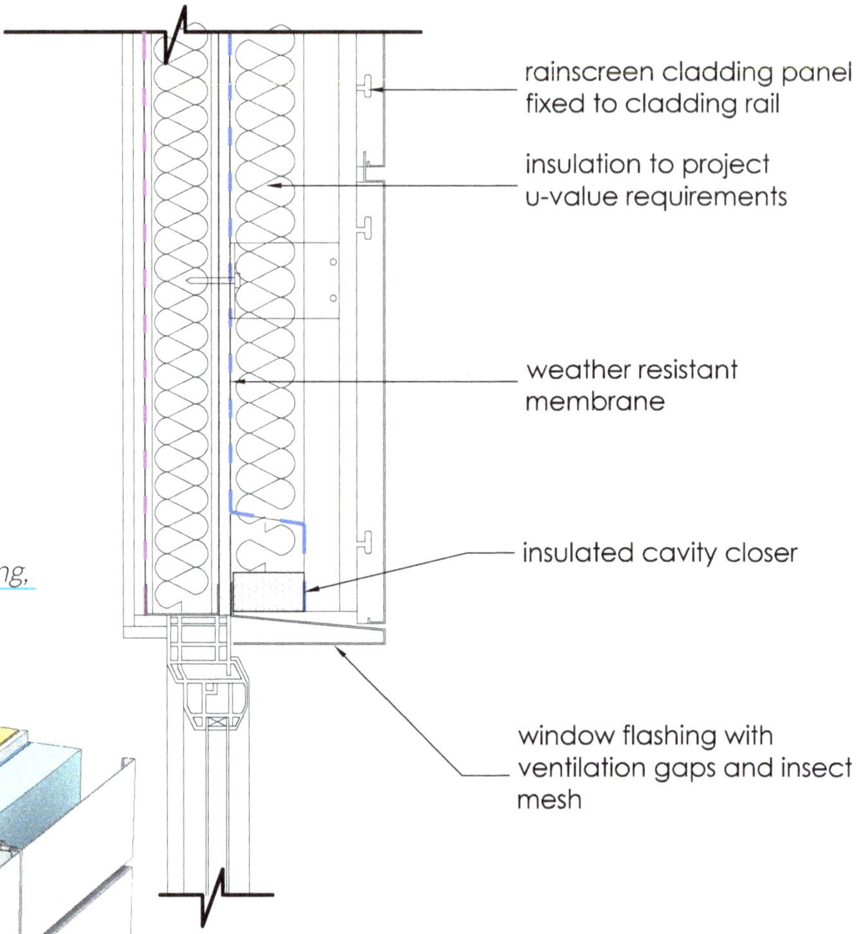

2D Detail W52 - Metal rainscreen cladding, window head detail

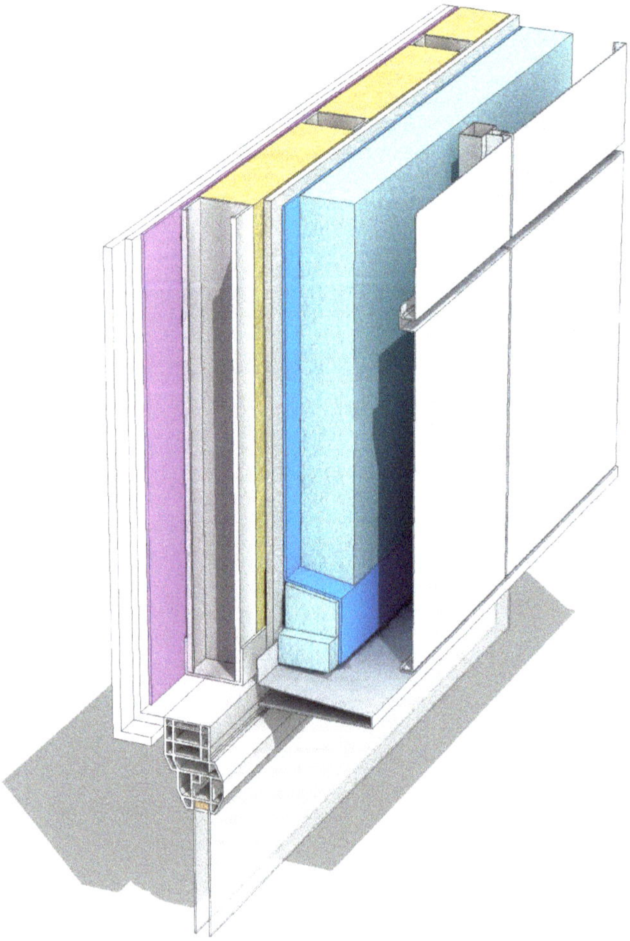

3D Detail W52 - Metal rainscreen cladding, window head detail

SECTION 7 - WALLS

W53

METAL RAINSCREEN CLADDING, LGSF, WINDOW SILL DETAIL

- insulated packing strip
- flashing lapped over cladding panel
- insulated cavity closer
- compressible insulation under sill
- weather resistant membrane
- rainscreen cladding panel fixed to cladding rail
- insulation to project u-value requirements

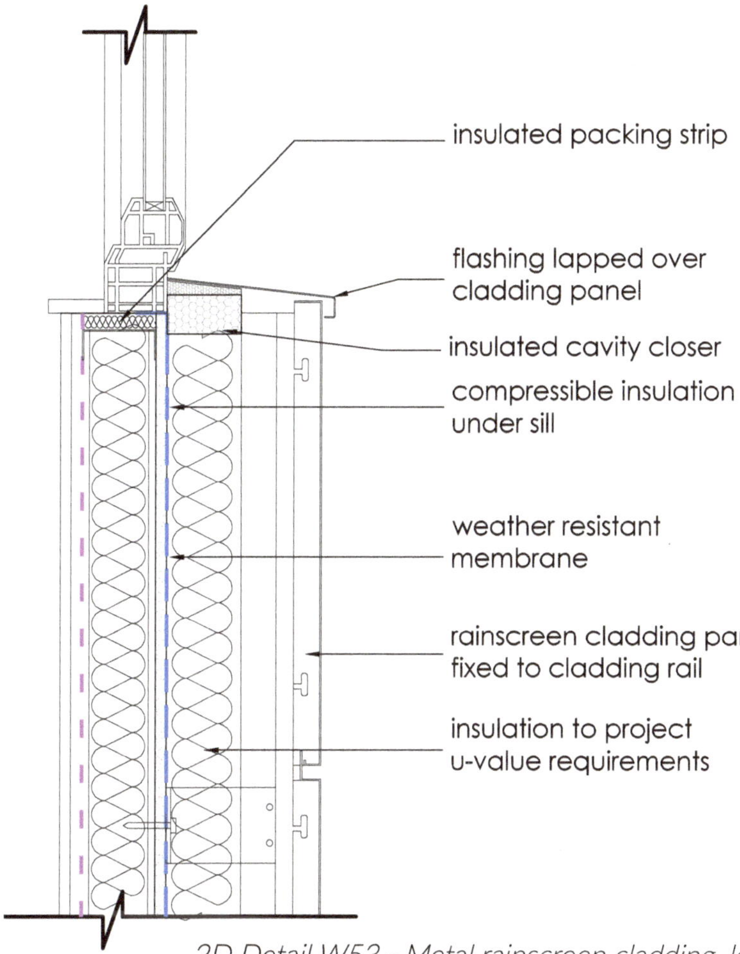

2D Detail W53 - Metal rainscreen cladding, lgsf, window sill detail

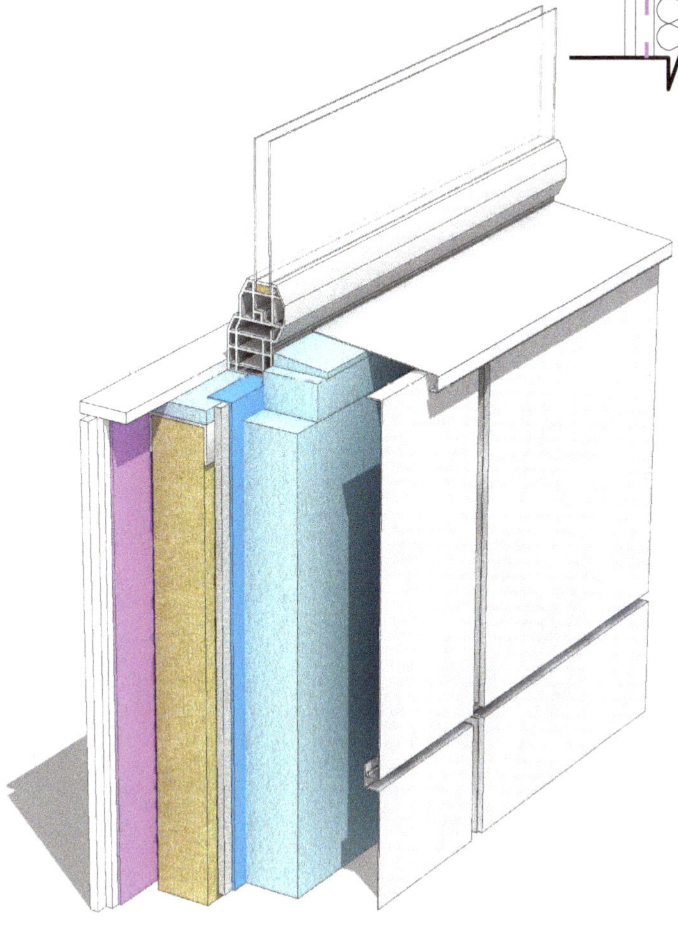

3D Detail W53- Metal rainscreen cladding, lgsf, window sill detail

278

W54

METAL RAINSCREEN CLADDING, WINDOW JAMB DETAIL (PLAN)

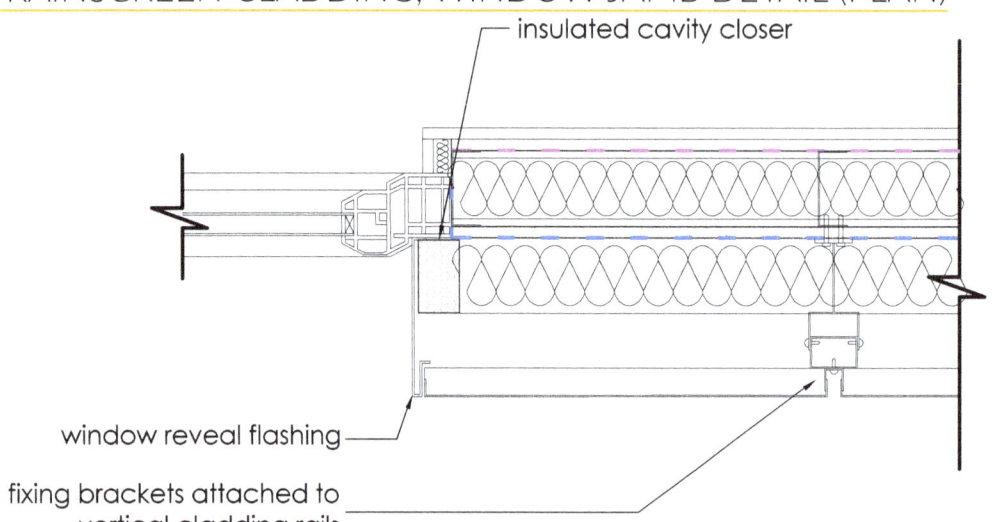

2D Detail W54 - Metal rainscreen cladding, window jamb detail (plan)

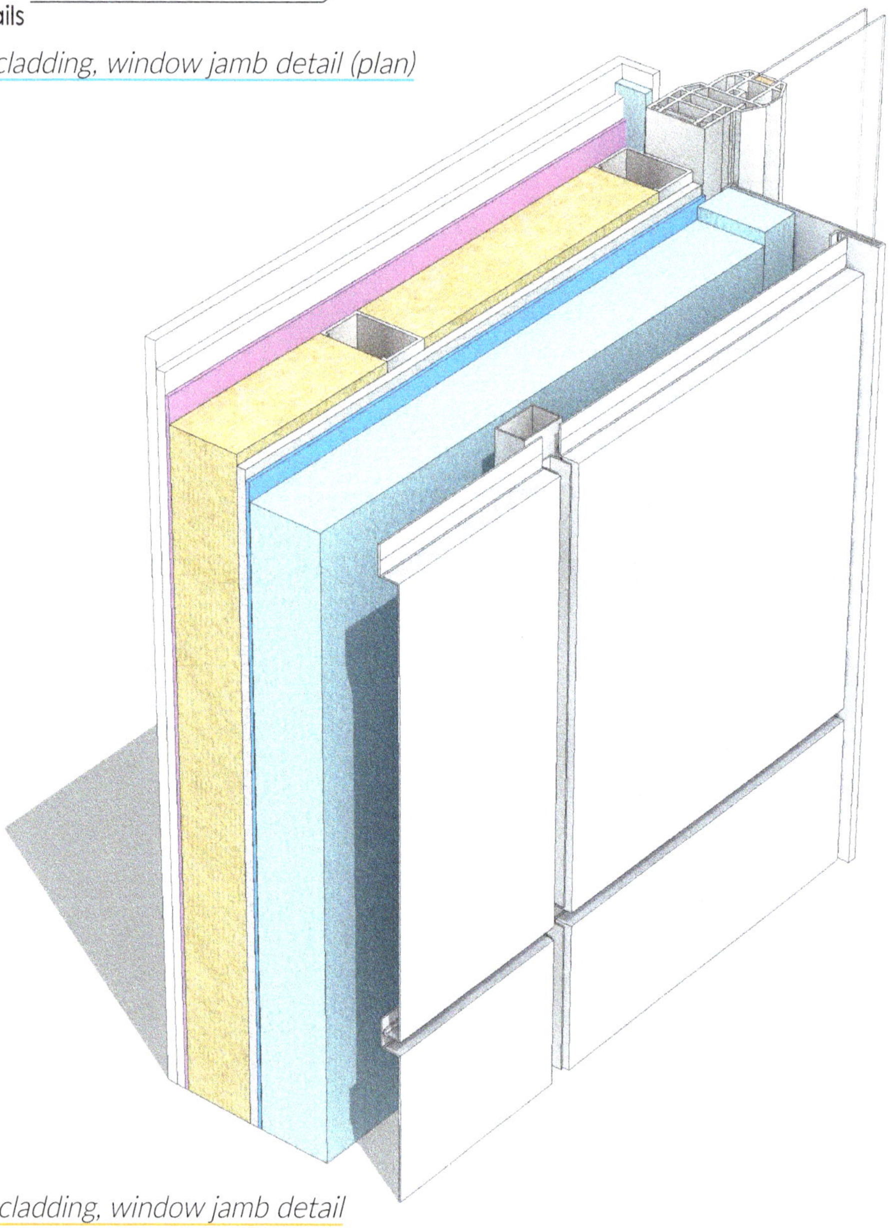

3D Detail W54 - Metal rainscreen cladding, window jamb detail

SECTION 7 - WALLS

W55

METAL RAINSCREEN CLADDING, LGSF, PARAPET DETAIL

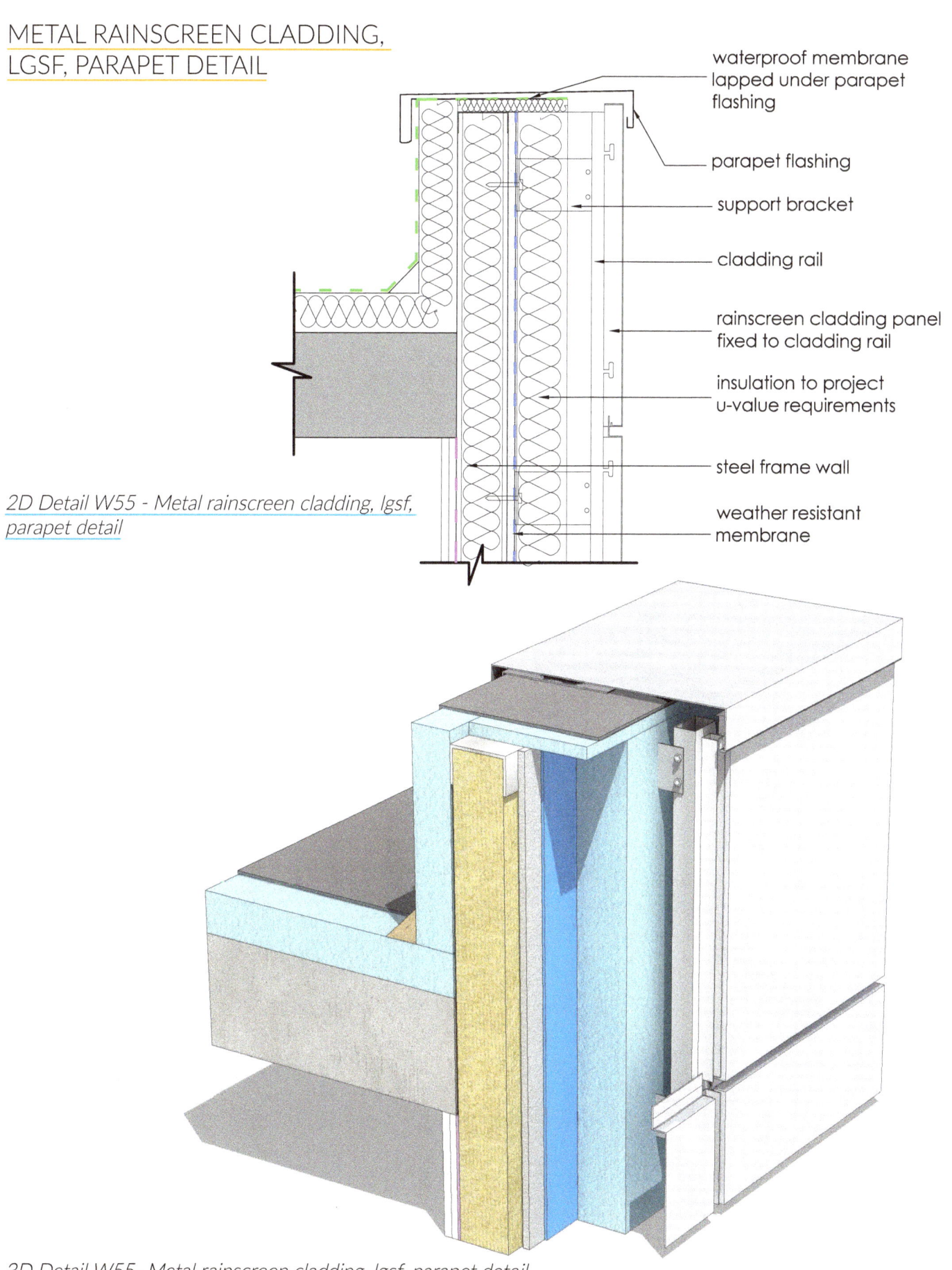

2D Detail W55 - Metal rainscreen cladding, lgsf, parapet detail

3D Detail W55 - Metal rainscreen cladding, lgsf, parapet detail

W56

TIMBER RAINSCREEN CLADDING, CONCRETE BACKING WALL

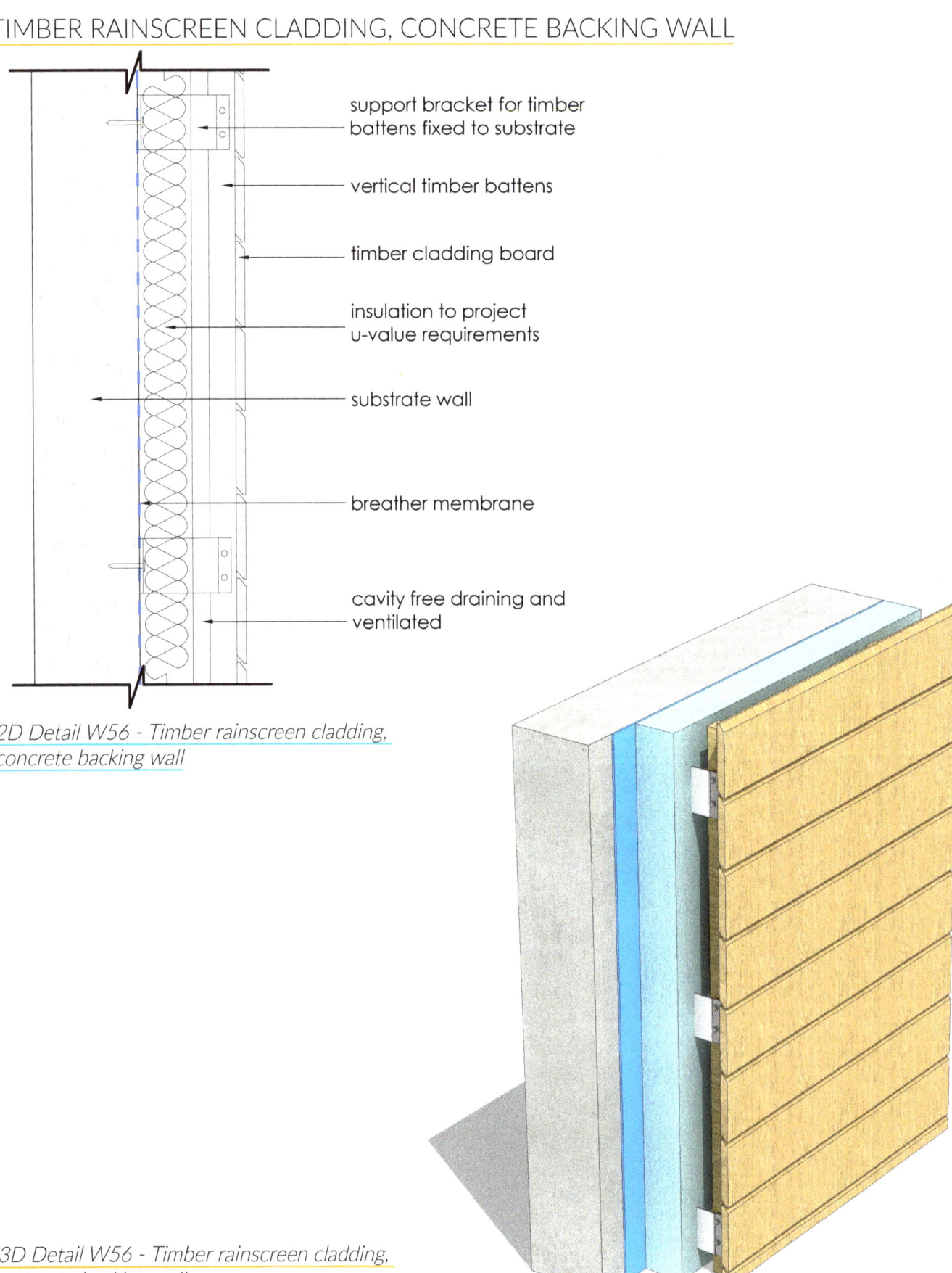

- support bracket for timber battens fixed to substrate
- vertical timber battens
- timber cladding board
- insulation to project u-value requirements
- substrate wall
- breather membrane
- cavity free draining and ventilated

2D Detail W56 - Timber rainscreen cladding, concrete backing wall

3D Detail W56 - Timber rainscreen cladding, concrete backing wall

SECTION 7 - WALLS

W57

TIMBER RAINSCREEN CLADDING BASE DETAIL

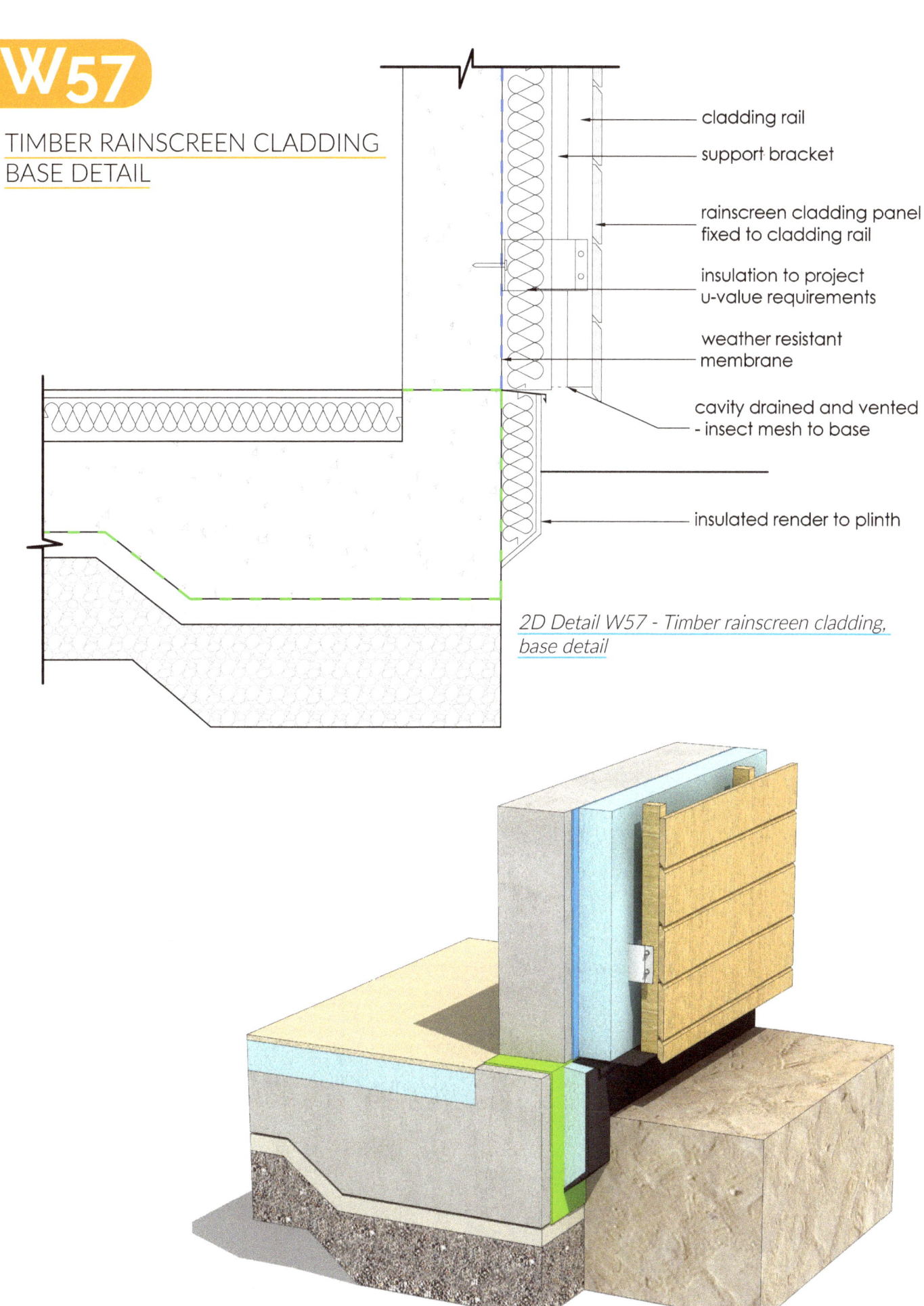

2D Detail W57 - Timber rainscreen cladding, base detail

- cladding rail
- support bracket
- rainscreen cladding panel fixed to cladding rail
- insulation to project u-value requirements
- weather resistant membrane
- cavity drained and vented - insect mesh to base
- insulated render to plinth

3D Detail W57- Timber rainscreen cladding, base detail

W58

TIMBER RAINSCREEN CLADDING, WINDOW HEAD DETAIL

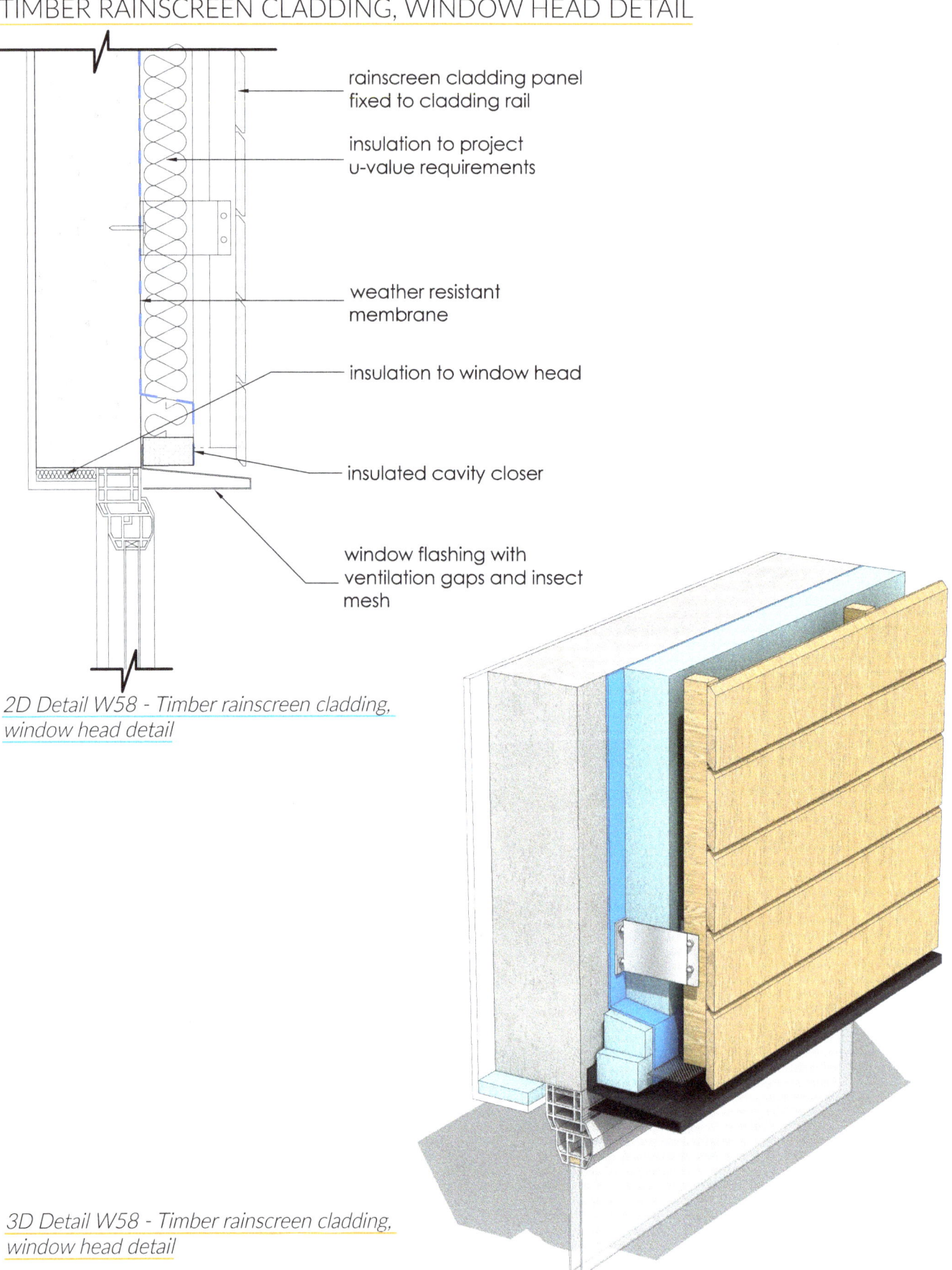

- rainscreen cladding panel fixed to cladding rail
- insulation to project u-value requirements
- weather resistant membrane
- insulation to window head
- insulated cavity closer
- window flashing with ventilation gaps and insect mesh

2D Detail W58 - Timber rainscreen cladding, window head detail

3D Detail W58 - Timber rainscreen cladding, window head detail

SECTION 7 - WALLS

W59

TIMBER RAINSCREEN CLADDING
WINDOW SILL DETAIL

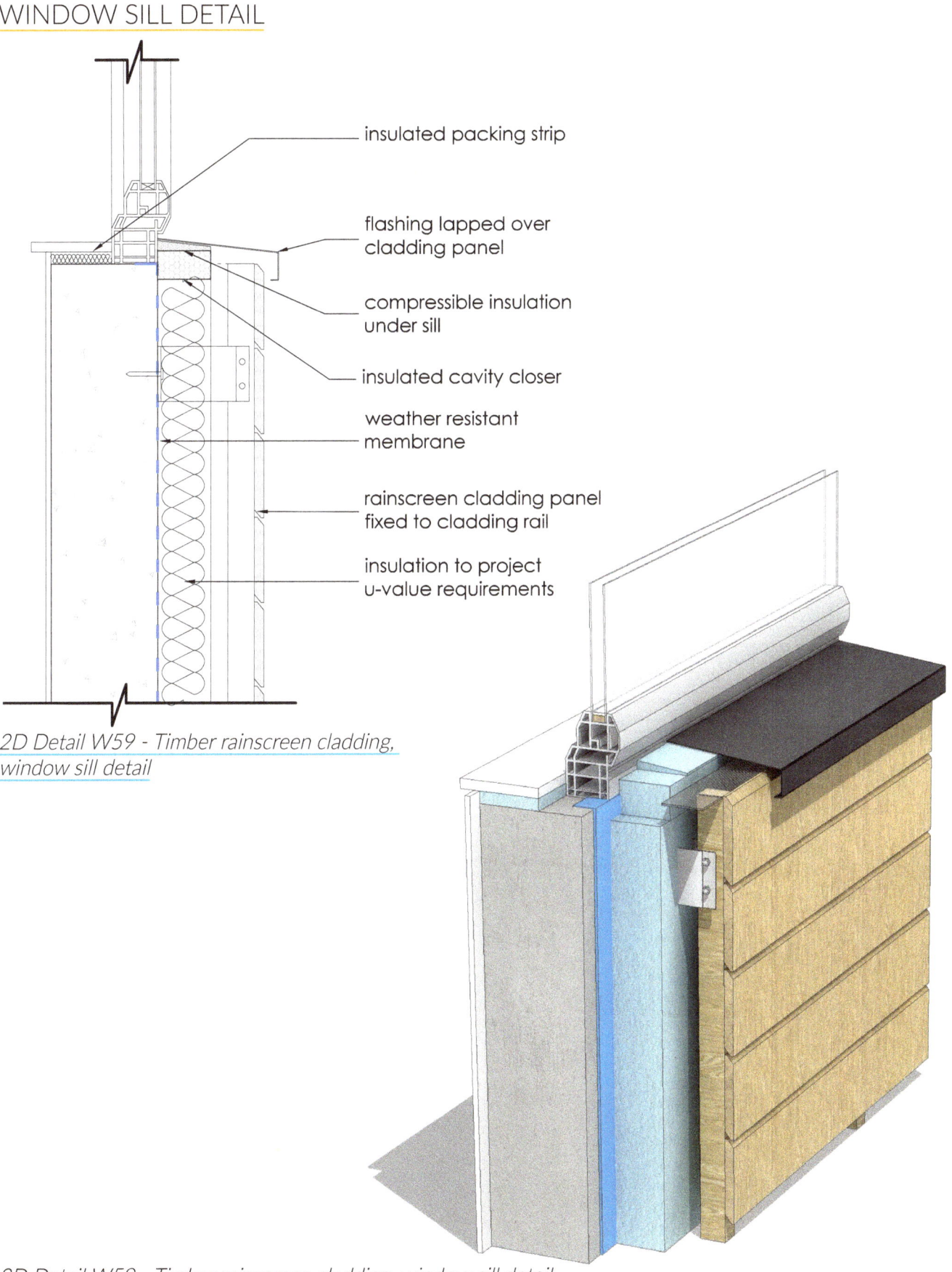

- insulated packing strip
- flashing lapped over cladding panel
- compressible insulation under sill
- insulated cavity closer
- weather resistant membrane
- rainscreen cladding panel fixed to cladding rail
- insulation to project u-value requirements

2D Detail W59 - Timber rainscreen cladding, window sill detail

3D Detail W59 - Timber rainscreen cladding, window sill detail

W60

TIMBER RAINSCREEN CLADDING, WINDOW JAMB DETAIL (PLAN)

- insulated cavity closer
- window reveal flashing
- fixing brackets attached to vertical cladding rails

2D Detail W60 - Timber rainscreen cladding, window jamb detail (plan)

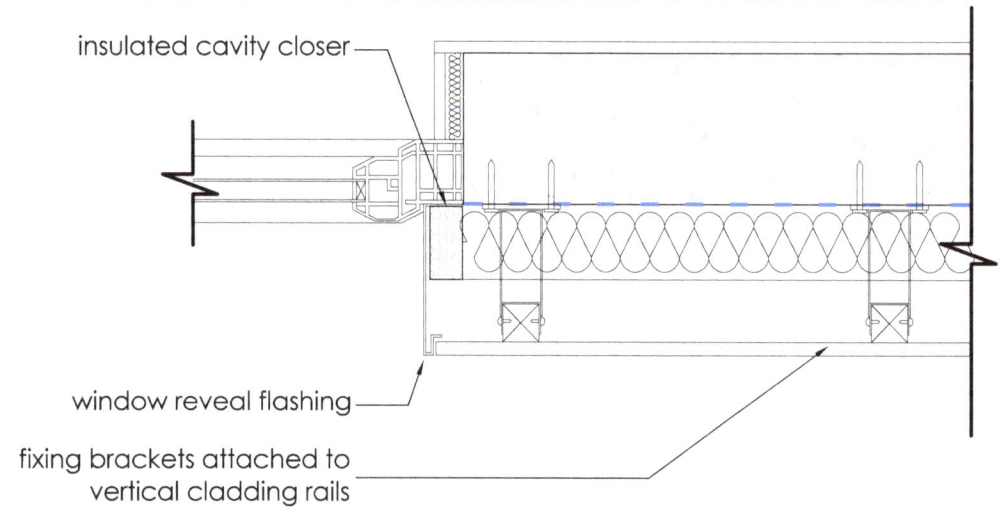

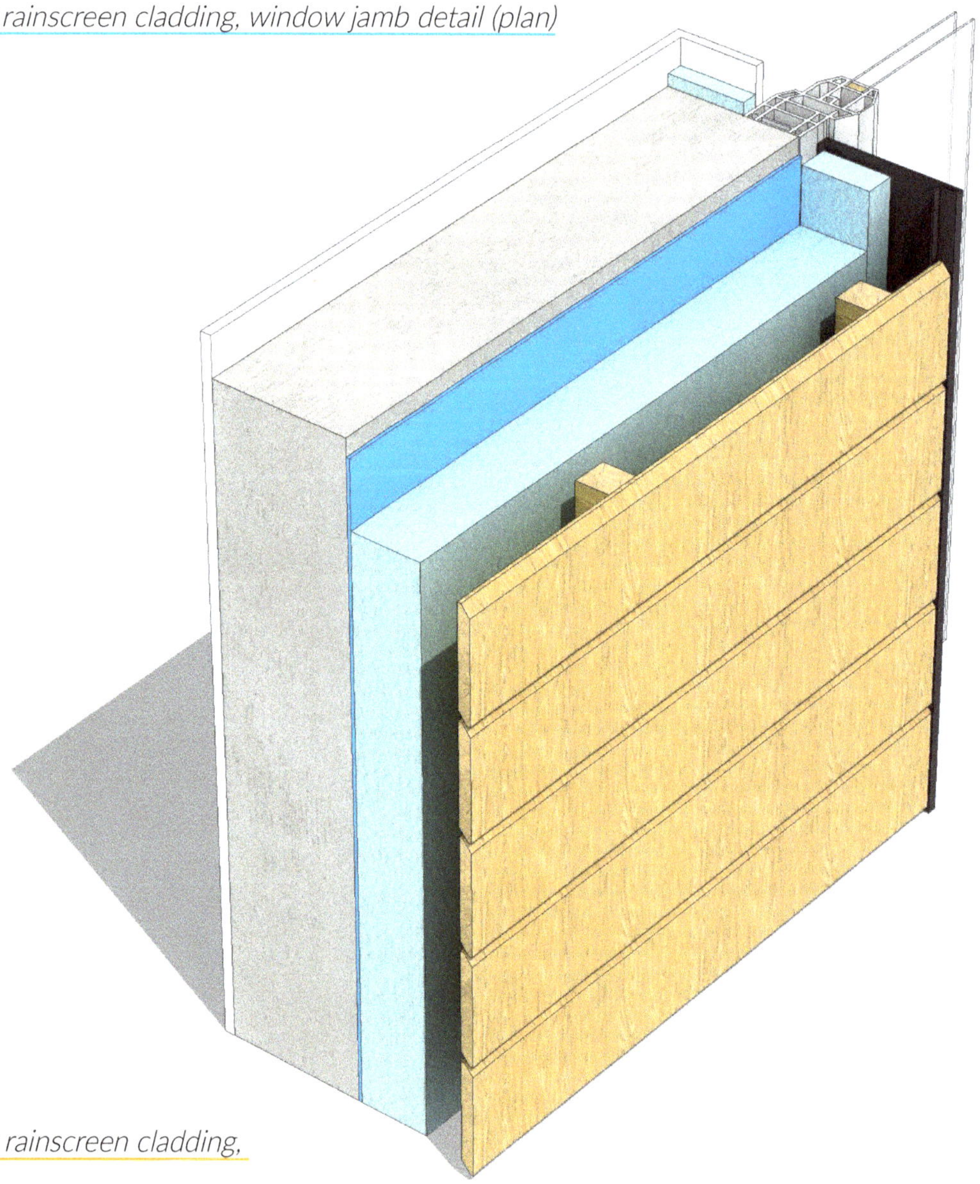

3D Detail W60 - Timber rainscreen cladding, window jamb detail

SECTION 7 - WALLS

W61

TIMBER RAINSCREEN CLADDING PARAPET DETAIL

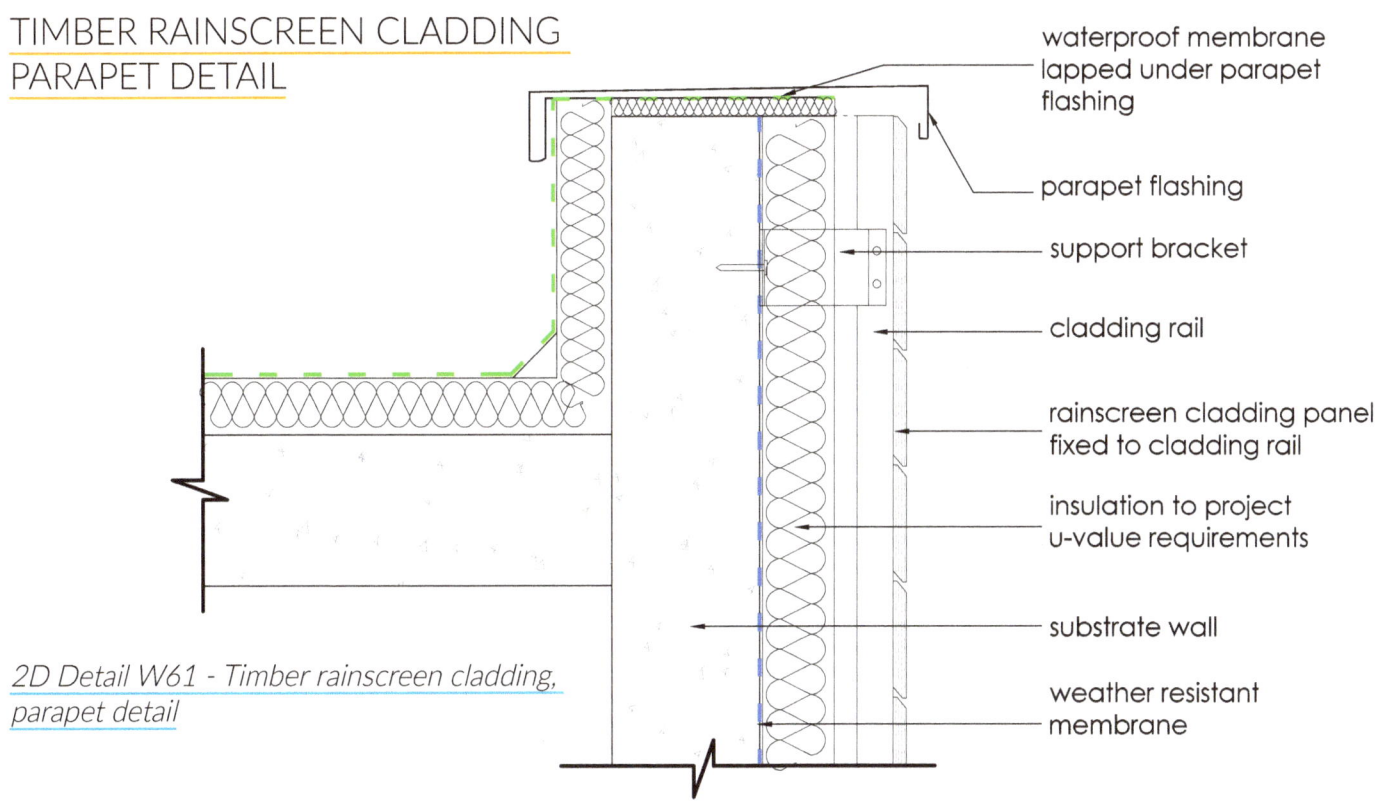

2D Detail W61 - Timber rainscreen cladding, parapet detail

- waterproof membrane lapped under parapet flashing
- parapet flashing
- support bracket
- cladding rail
- rainscreen cladding panel fixed to cladding rail
- insulation to project u-value requirements
- substrate wall
- weather resistant membrane

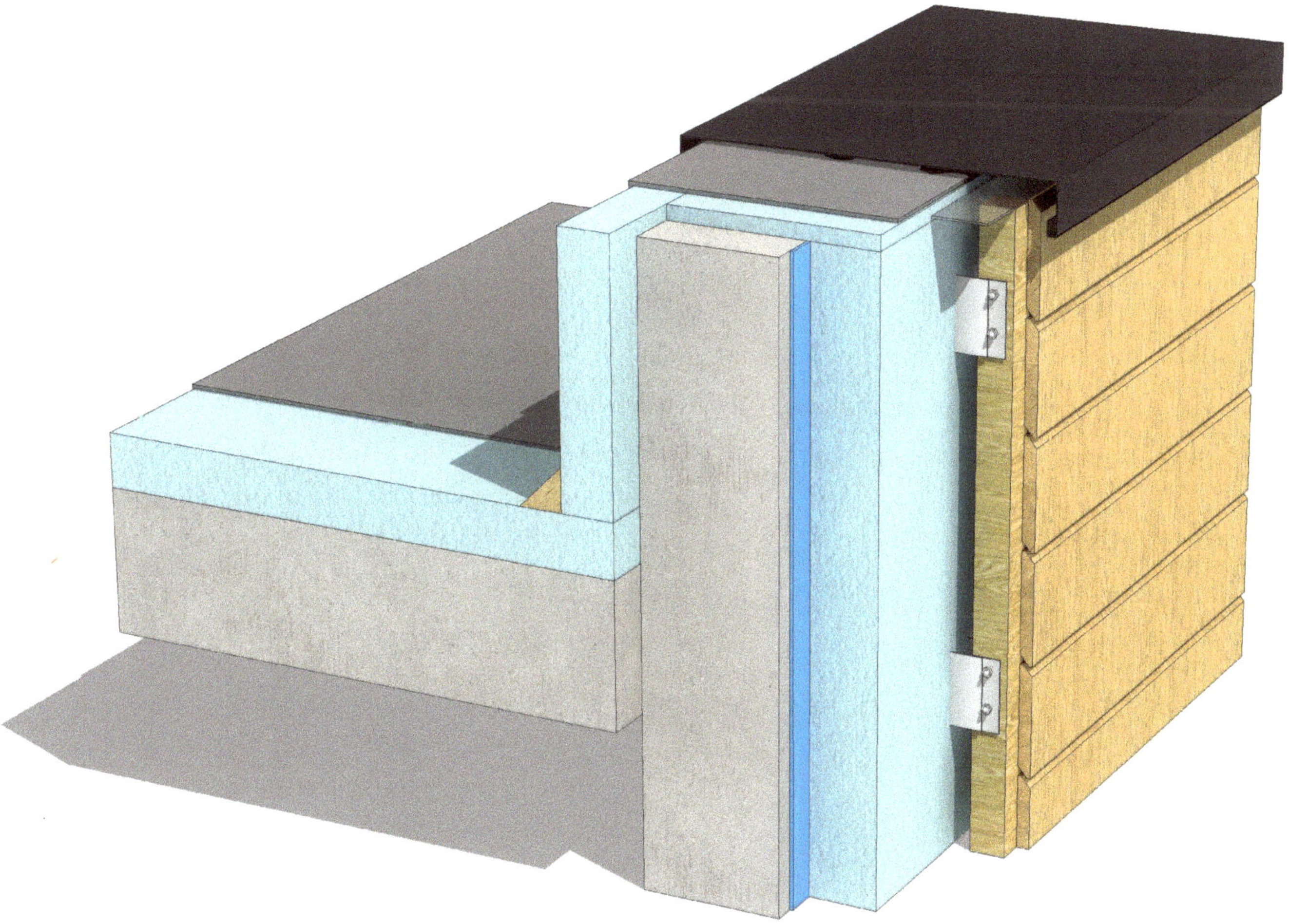

3D Detail W61 - Timber rainscreen cladding, parapet detail

W62

STONE RAINSCREEN CLADDING, CONCRETE BACKING WALL

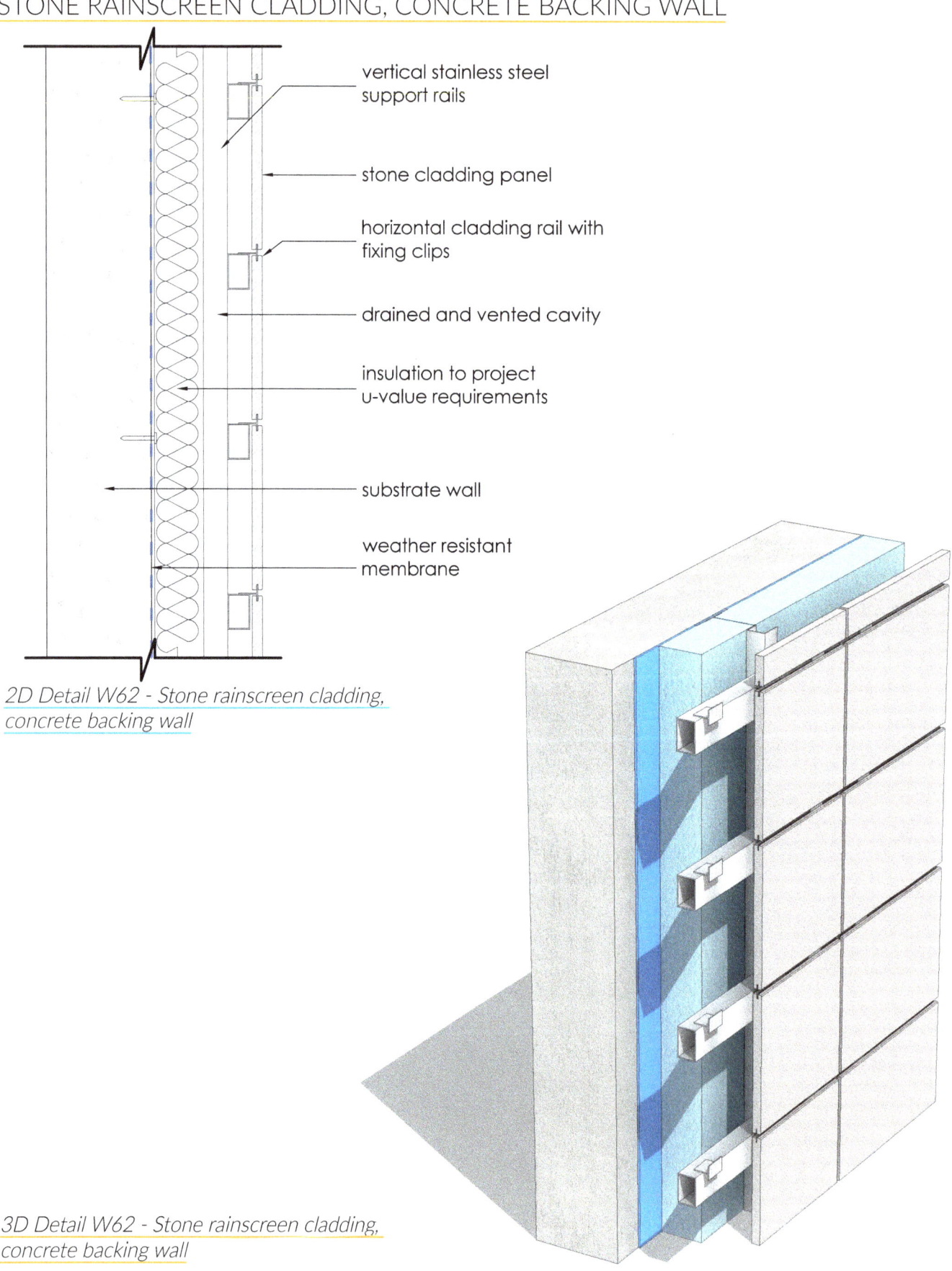

- vertical stainless steel support rails
- stone cladding panel
- horizontal cladding rail with fixing clips
- drained and vented cavity
- insulation to project u-value requirements
- substrate wall
- weather resistant membrane

2D Detail W62 - Stone rainscreen cladding, concrete backing wall

3D Detail W62 - Stone rainscreen cladding, concrete backing wall

SECTION 7 - WALLS

W63

STONE RAINSCREEN CLADDING
BASE DETAIL

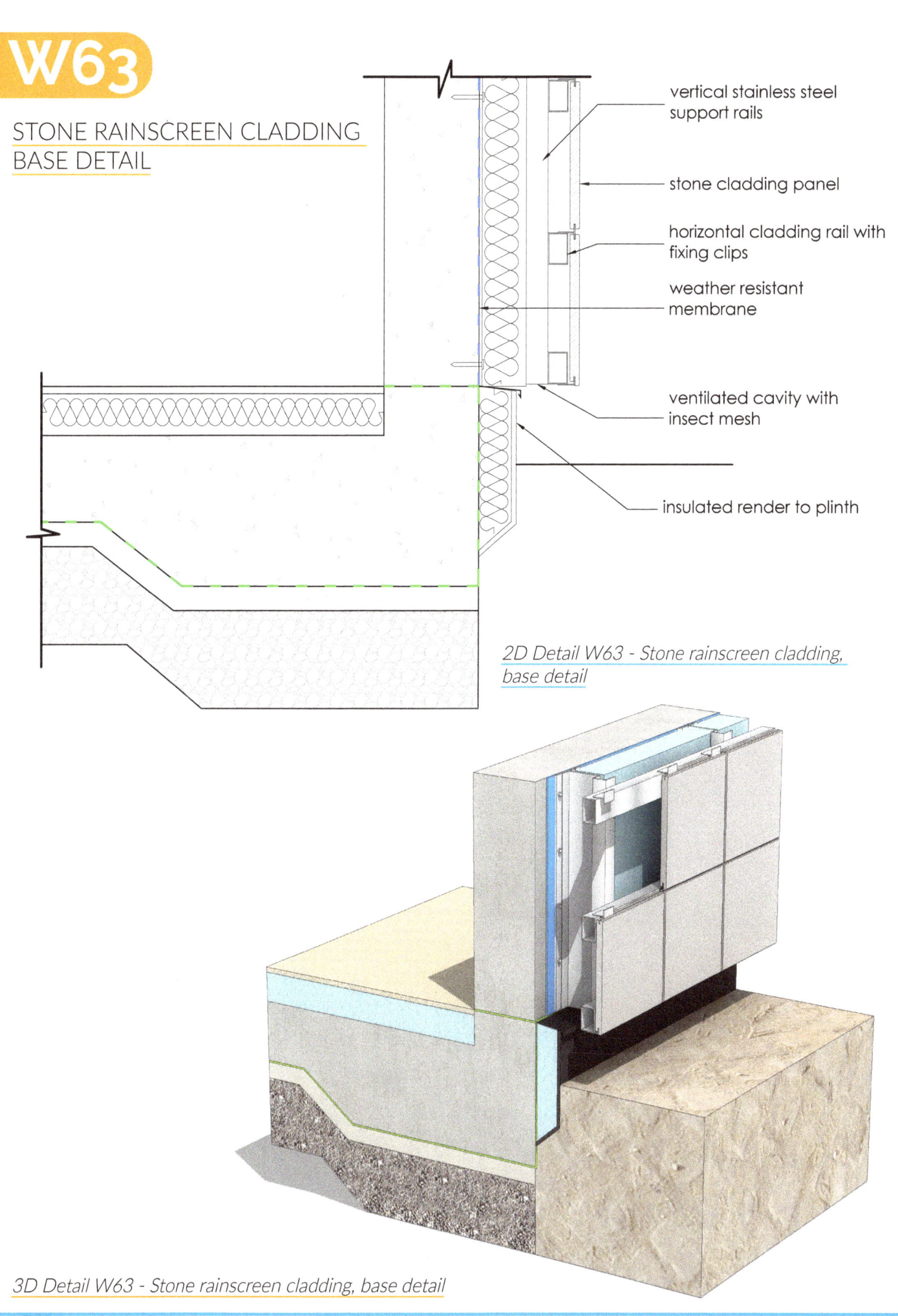

2D Detail W63 - Stone rainscreen cladding, base detail

- vertical stainless steel support rails
- stone cladding panel
- horizontal cladding rail with fixing clips
- weather resistant membrane
- ventilated cavity with insect mesh
- insulated render to plinth

3D Detail W63 - Stone rainscreen cladding, base detail

W64

STONE RAINSCREEN CLADDING, WINDOW HEAD DETAIL

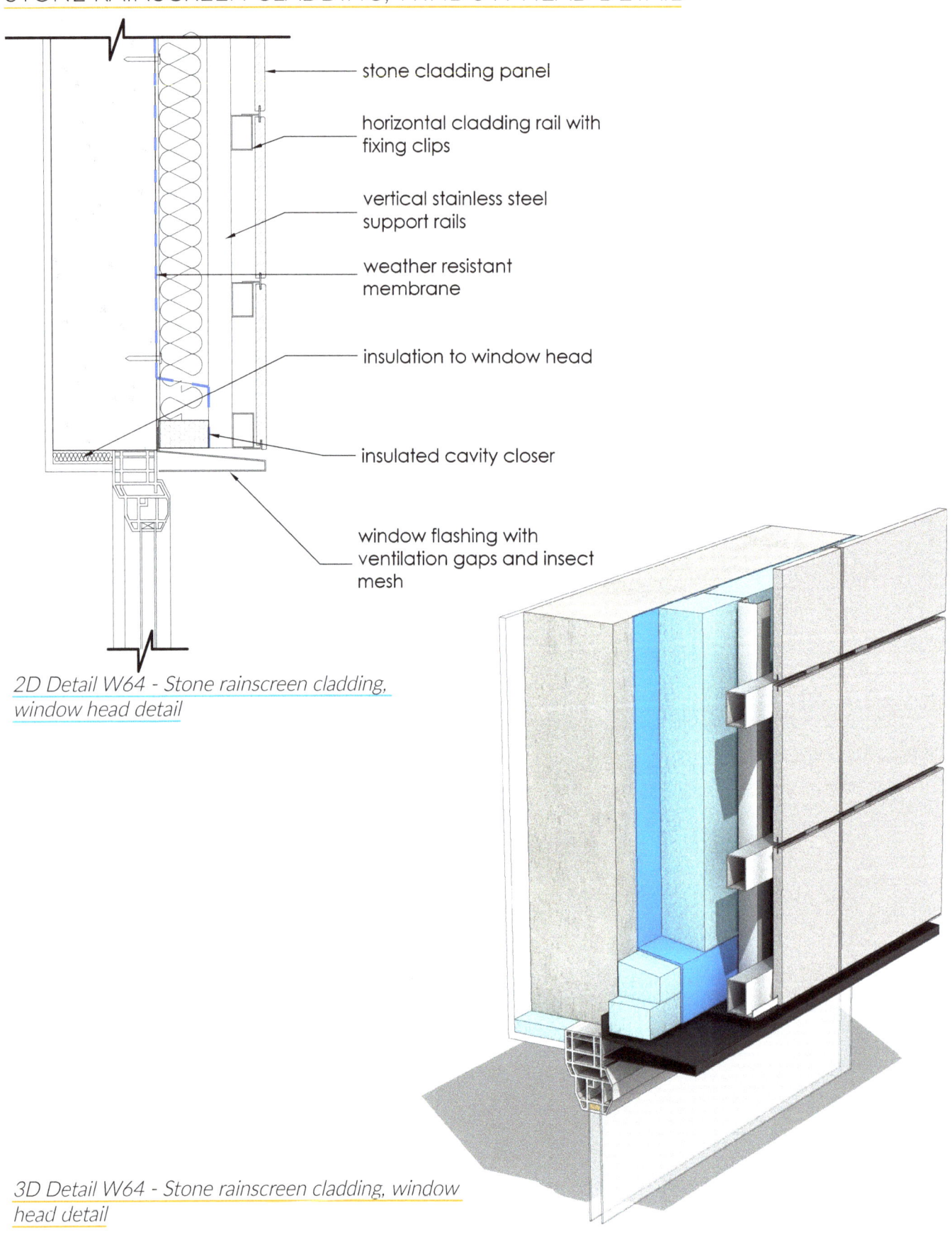

- stone cladding panel
- horizontal cladding rail with fixing clips
- vertical stainless steel support rails
- weather resistant membrane
- insulation to window head
- insulated cavity closer
- window flashing with ventilation gaps and insect mesh

2D Detail W64 - Stone rainscreen cladding, window head detail

3D Detail W64 - Stone rainscreen cladding, window head detail

SECTION 7 - WALLS

W65

STONE RAINSCREEN CLADDING
WINDOW SILL DETAIL

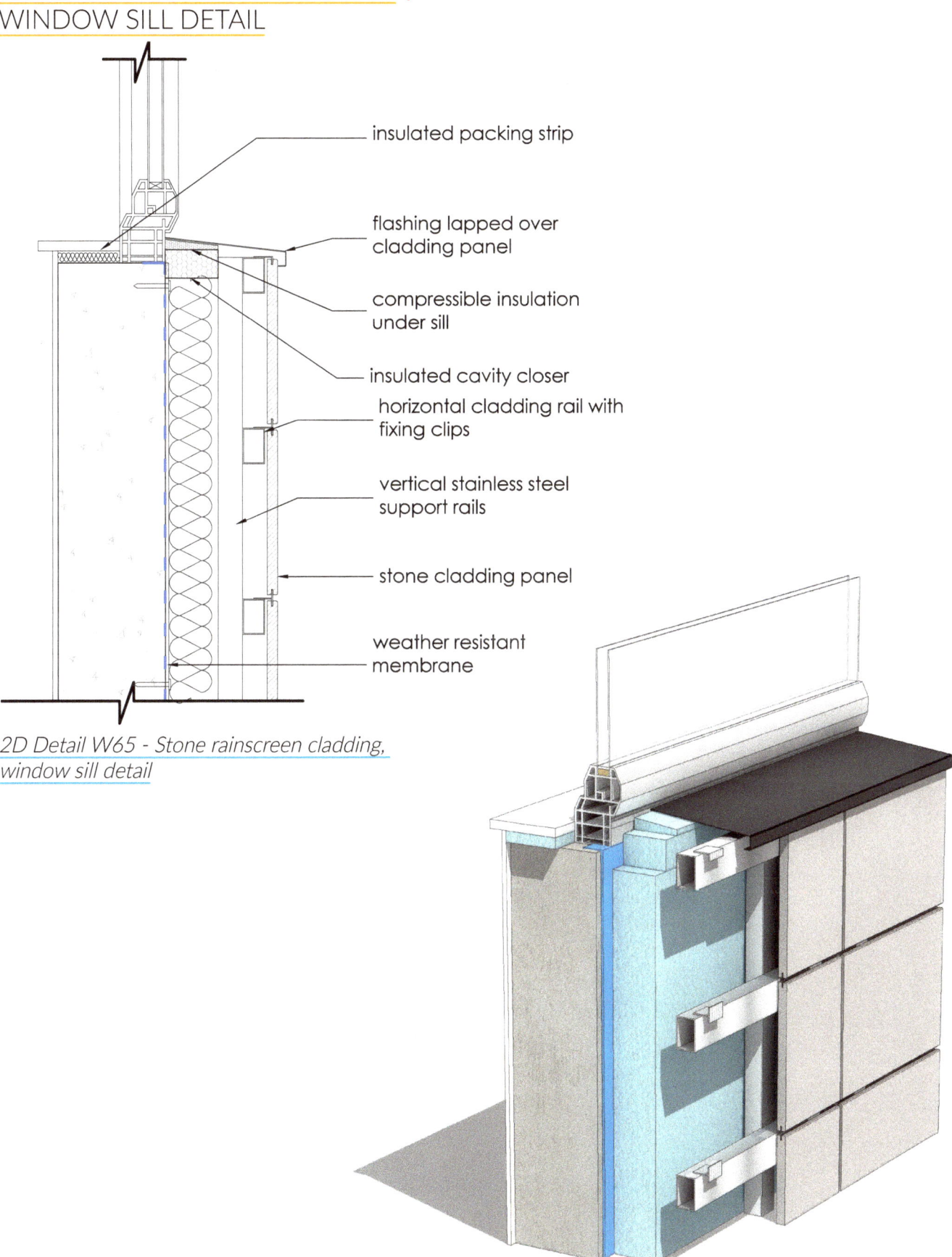

2D Detail W65 - Stone rainscreen cladding, window sill detail

Labels:
- insulated packing strip
- flashing lapped over cladding panel
- compressible insulation under sill
- insulated cavity closer
- horizontal cladding rail with fixing clips
- vertical stainless steel support rails
- stone cladding panel
- weather resistant membrane

3D Detail W65 - Stone rainscreen cladding, window sill detail

W66

STONE RAINSCREEN CLADDING, WINDOW JAMB DETAIL

2D Detail W66 - Stone rainscreen cladding, window jamb detail

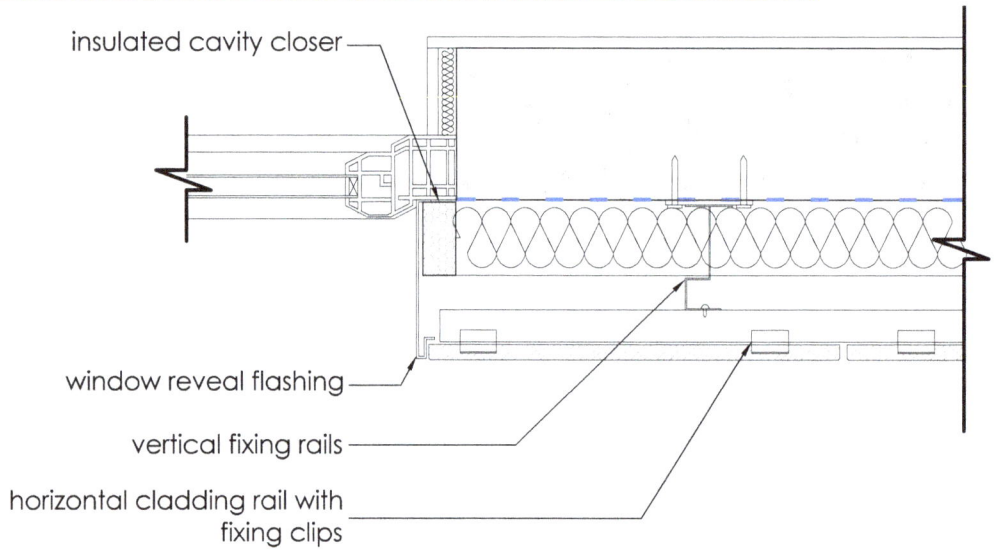

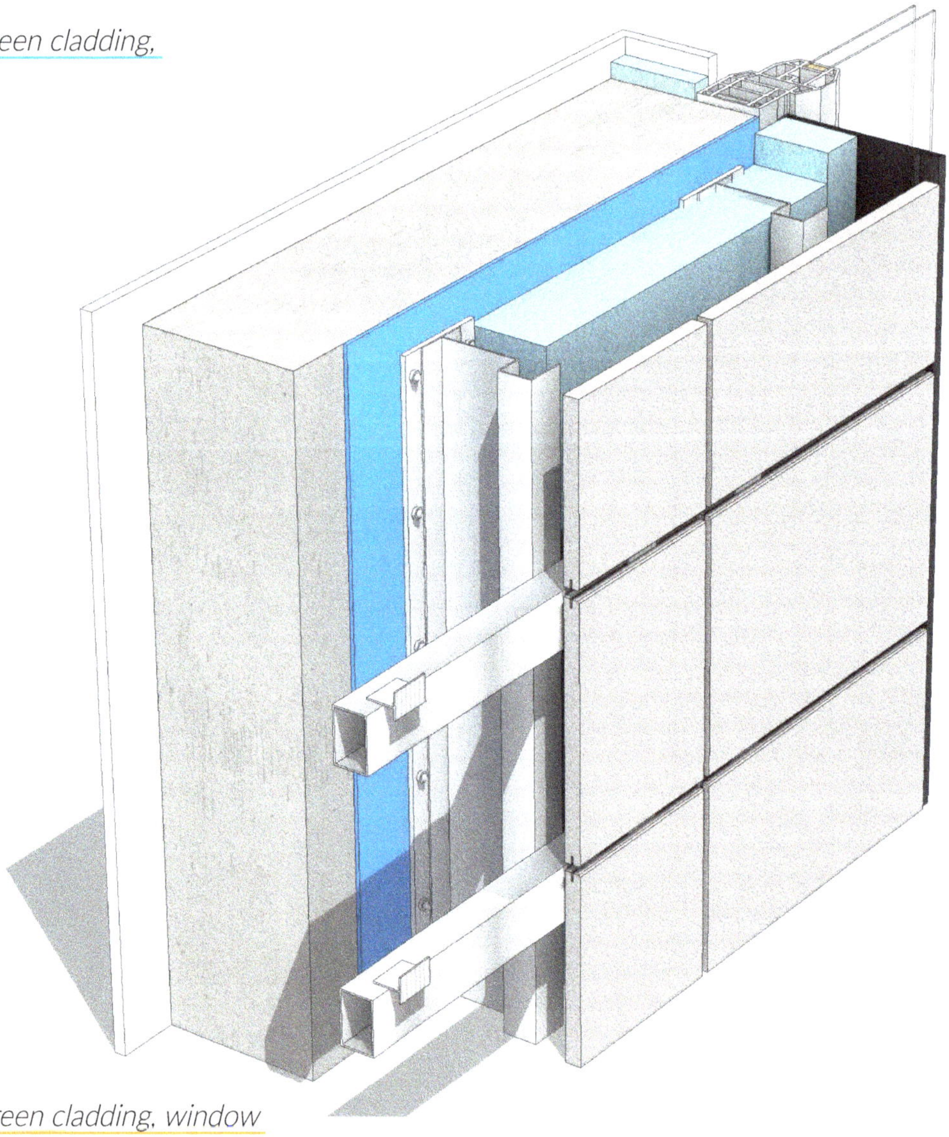

3D Detail W66 - Stone rainscreen cladding, window jamb detail

SECTION 7 - WALLS

W67

STONE RAINSCREEN CLADDING
PARAPET DETAIL

- waterproof membrane lapped under parapet flashing
- parapet flashing
- horizontal cladding rail with fixing clips
- vertical stainless steel support rails
- stone cladding panel
- substrate wall
- weather resistant membrane

2D Detail W67 - Stone rainscreen cladding, parapet detail

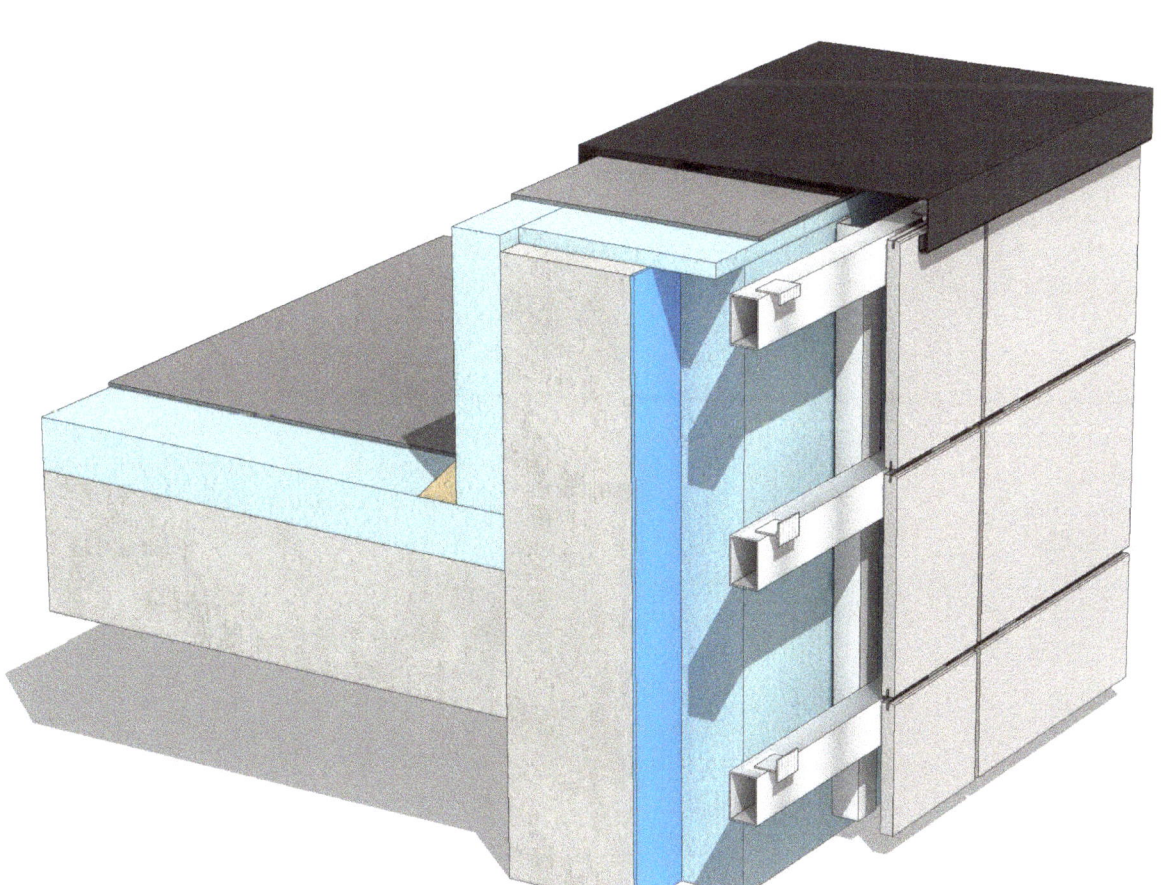

3D Detail W67 - Stone rainscreen cladding, parapet detail

W68

STONE RAINSCREEN CLADDING, LIGHT GAUGE STEEL FRAME (LGSF)

- horizontal cladding rail with fixing clips
- drained and vented cavity
- vertical stainless steel support rails
- stone cladding panel
- insulation to project u-value requirements
- steel frame wall
- breather membrane

2D Detail W68 - Stone rainscreen cladding, light gauge steel frame (lgsf)

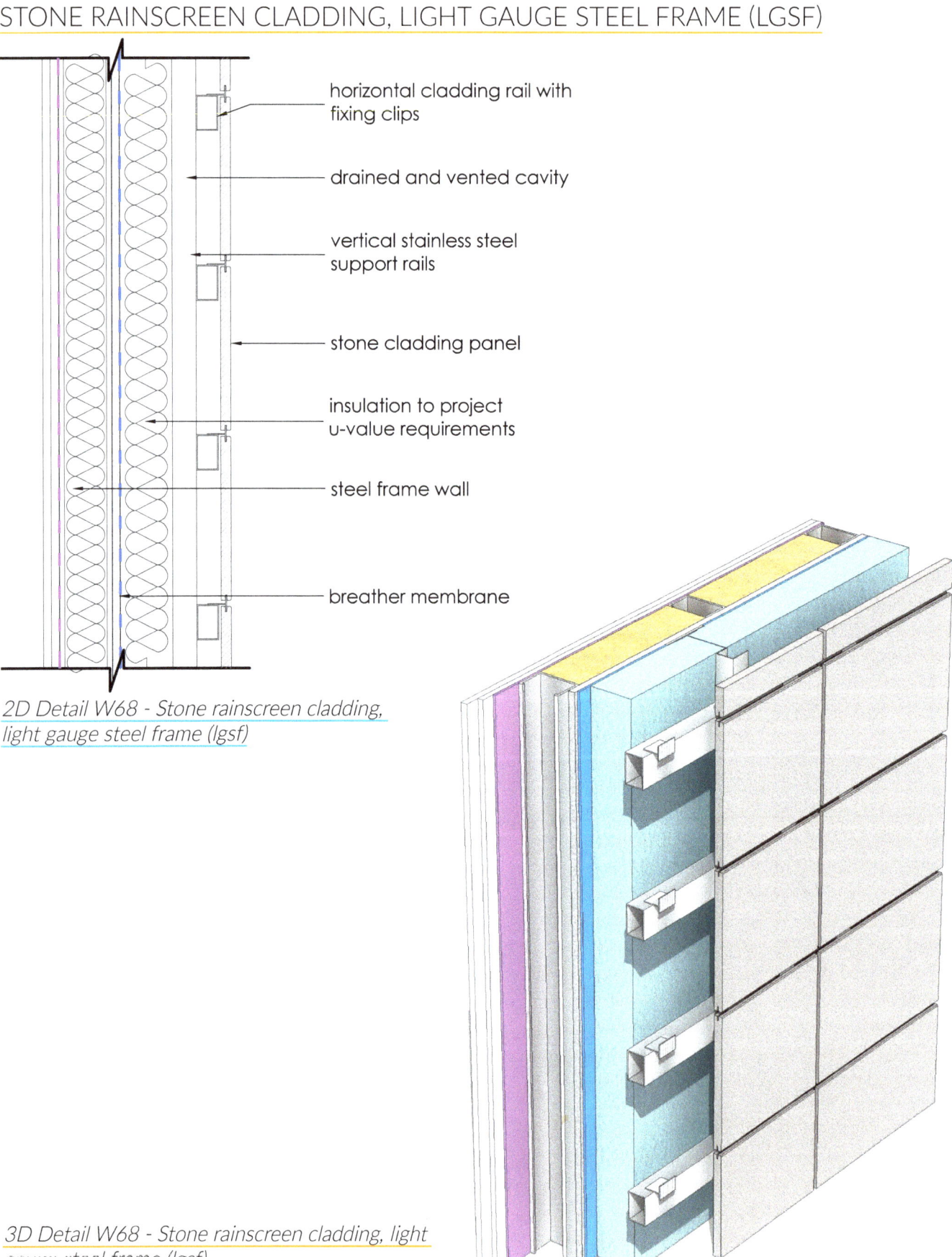

3D Detail W68 - Stone rainscreen cladding, light gauge steel frame (lgsf)

SECTION 7 - WALLS

W69

STONE RAINSCREEN CLADDING, LGSF, BASE DETAIL

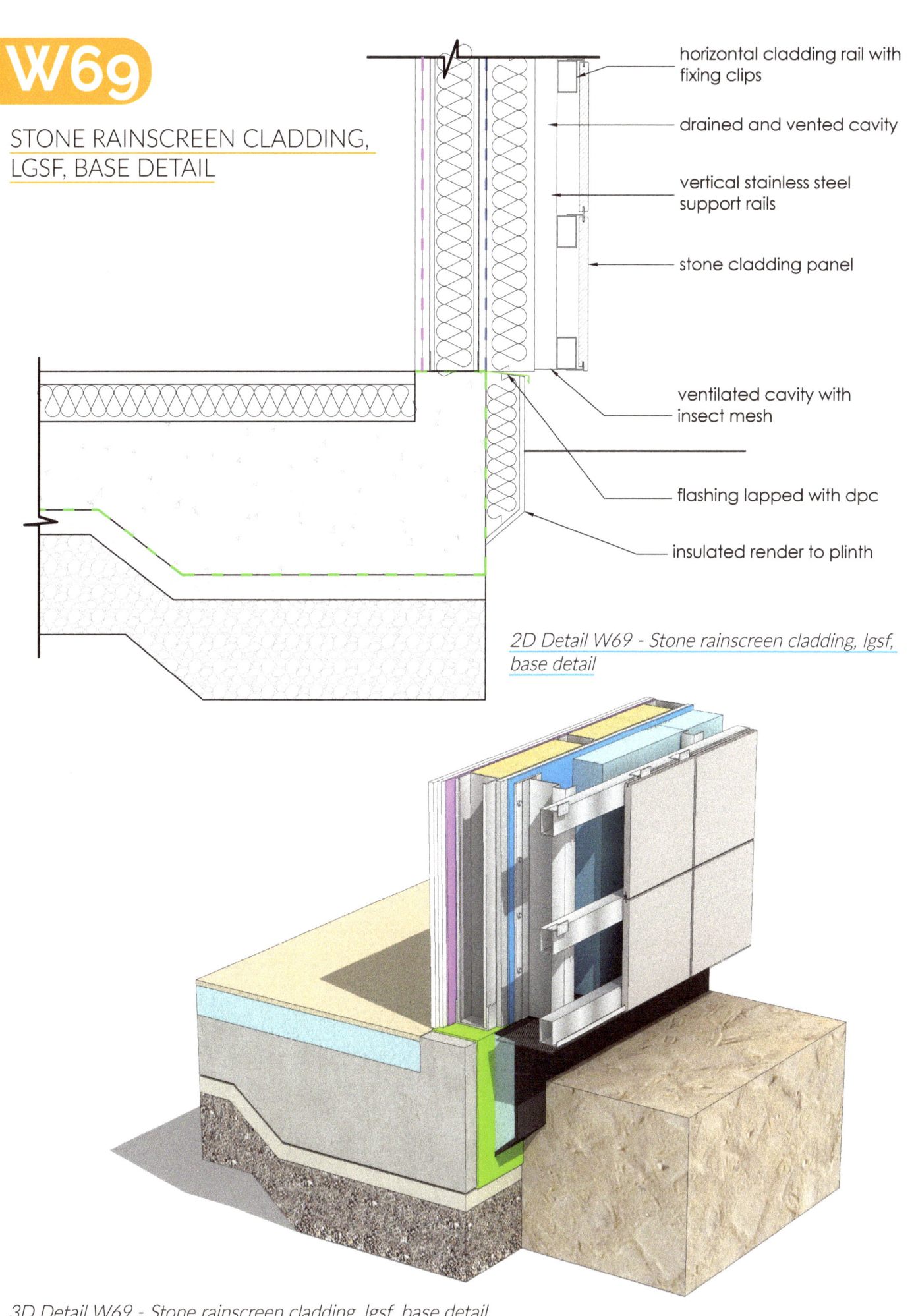

2D Detail W69 - Stone rainscreen cladding, lgsf, base detail

3D Detail W69 - Stone rainscreen cladding, lgsf, base detail

W70

STONE RAINSCREEN CLADDING, LGSF, WINDOW HEAD DETAIL

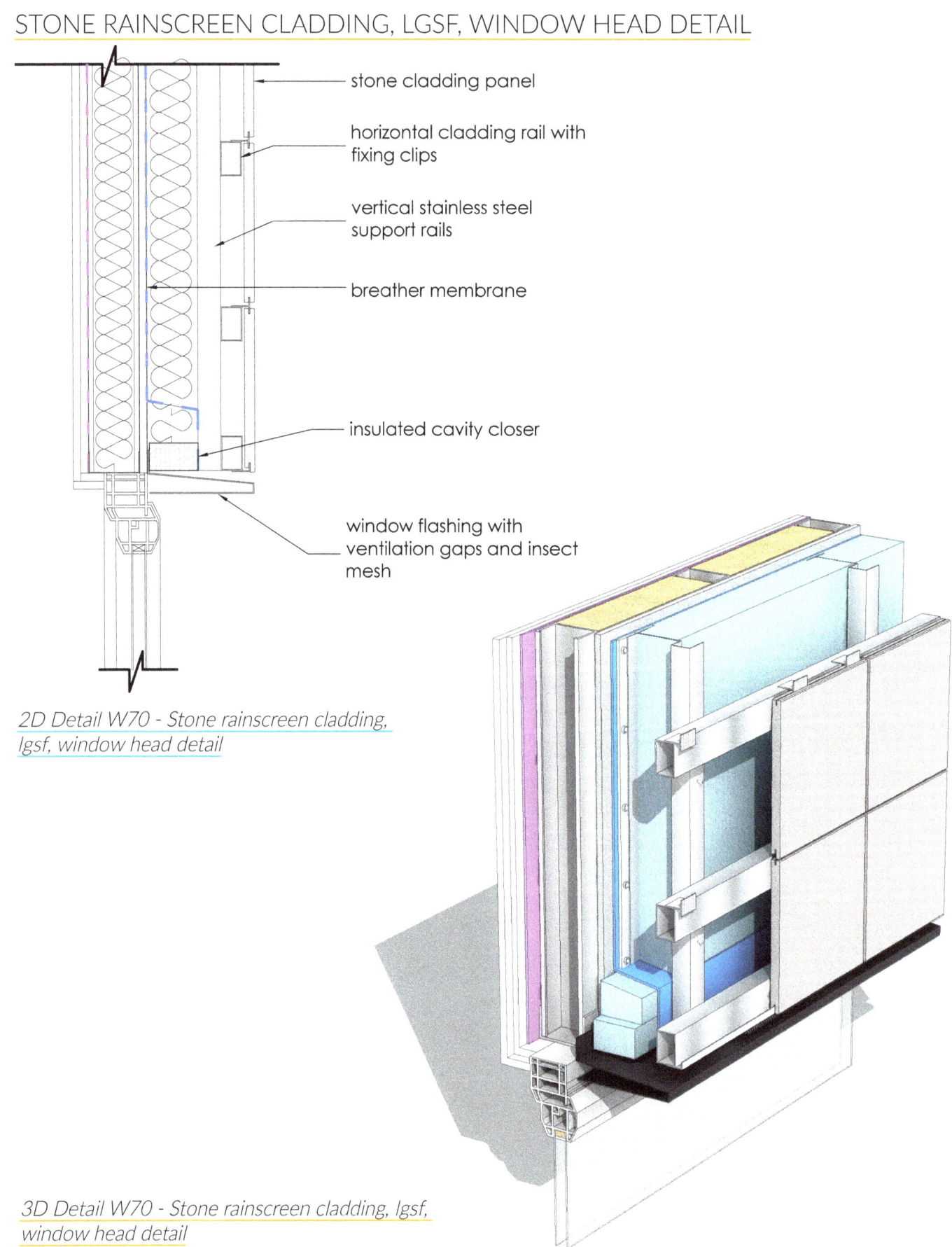

- stone cladding panel
- horizontal cladding rail with fixing clips
- vertical stainless steel support rails
- breather membrane
- insulated cavity closer
- window flashing with ventilation gaps and insect mesh

2D Detail W70 - Stone rainscreen cladding, lgsf, window head detail

3D Detail W70 - Stone rainscreen cladding, lgsf, window head detail

SECTION 7 - WALLS

STONE RAINSCREEN CLADDING, LGSF, WINDOW SILL DETAIL

- insulated packing strip
- compressible insulation under sill
- sill lapped over stone panel
- top of cavity open to allow ventilation
- insulated cavity closer
- breather membrane
- stone cladding panel

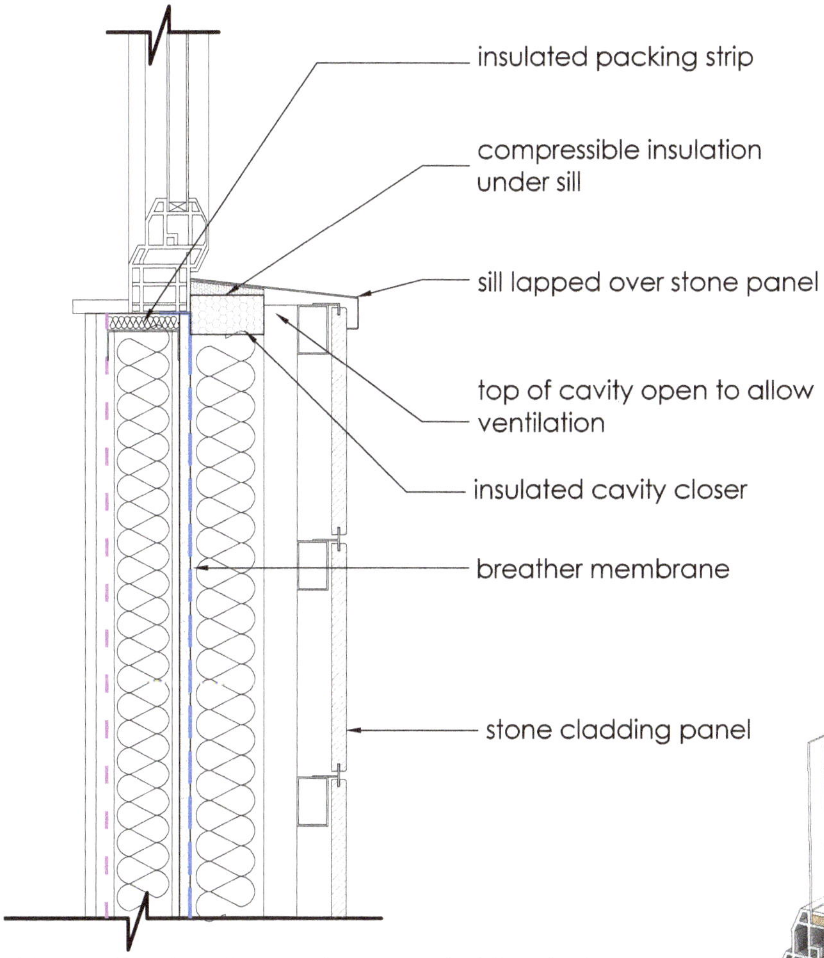

2D Detail W71 - Stone rainscreen cladding, lgsf, window sill detail

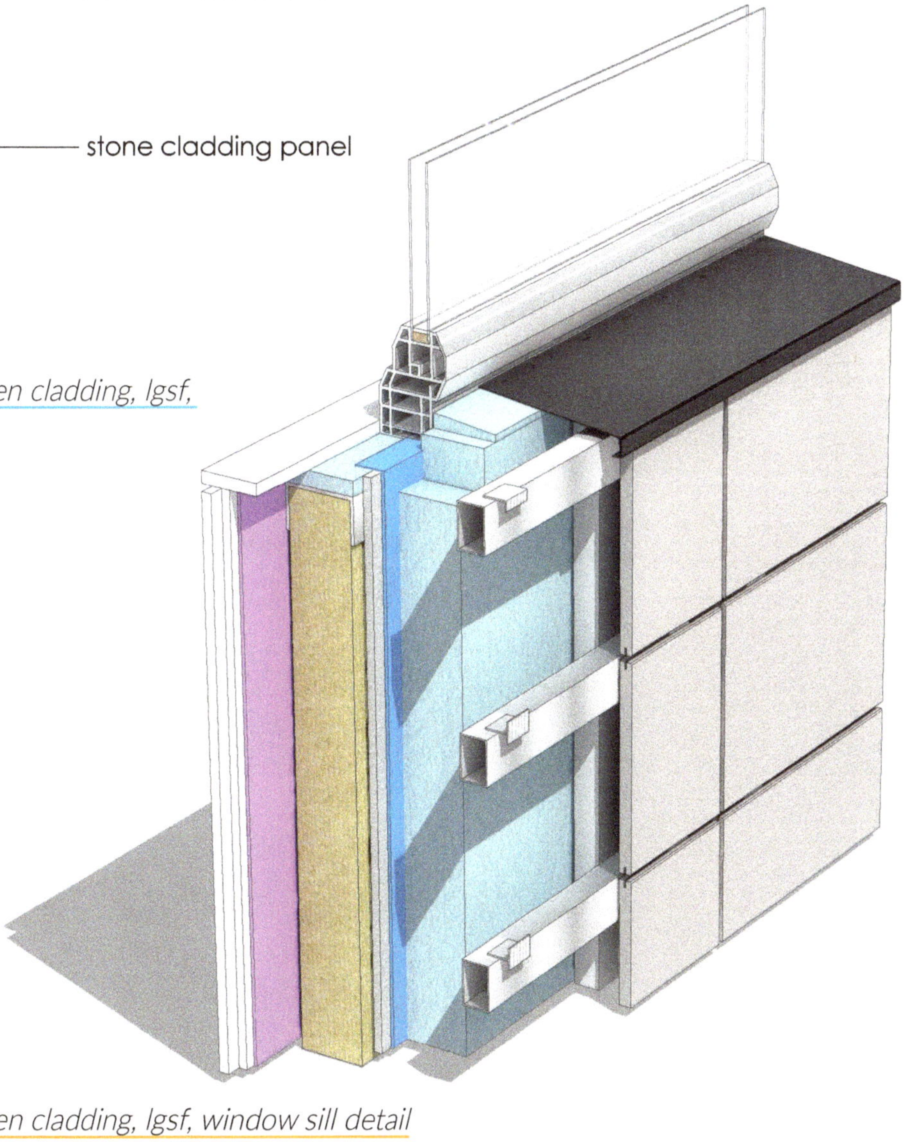

3D Detail W71 - Stone rainscreen cladding, lgsf, window sill detail

STONE RAINSCREEN CLADDING, LGSF, WINDOW JAMB DETAIL (PLAN)

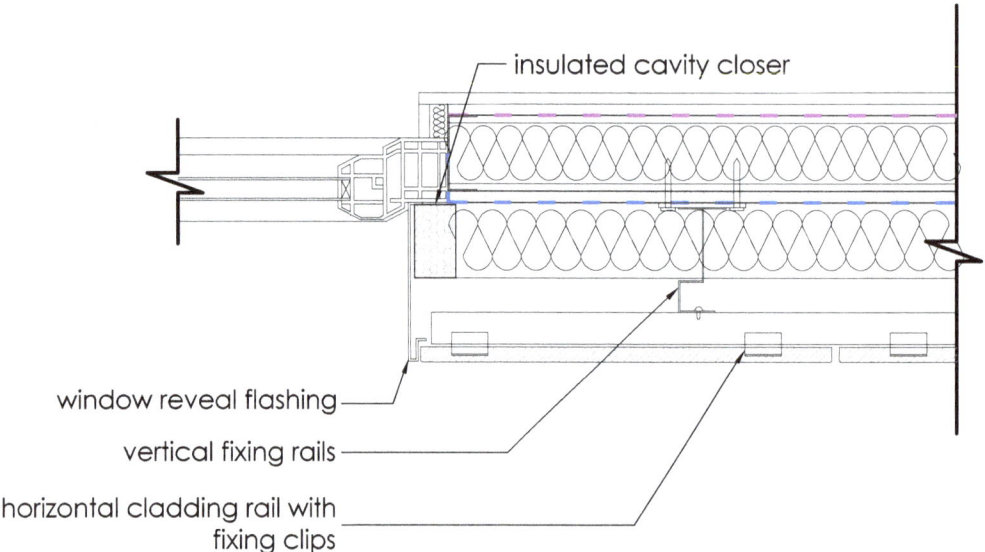

2D Detail W72 - Stone rainscreen cladding, lgsf, window jamb detail (plan)

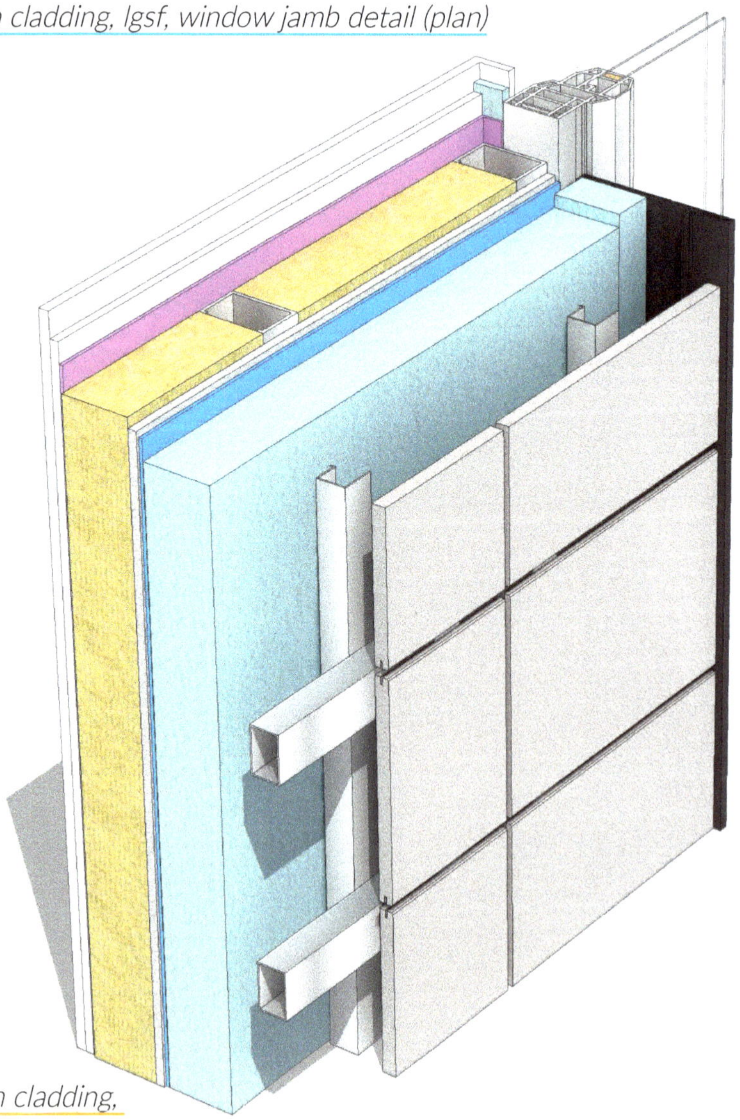

3D Detail W72 - Stone rainscreen cladding, lgsf, window jamb detail

SECTION 7 - WALLS

W73

STONE RAINSCREEN CLADDING, LGSF, PARAPET DETAIL

- waterproof membrane lapped under parapet flashing
- parapet flashing
- stone cladding panel
- horizontal cladding rail with fixing clips
- vertical stainless steel support rails
- steel frame wall
- breather membrane

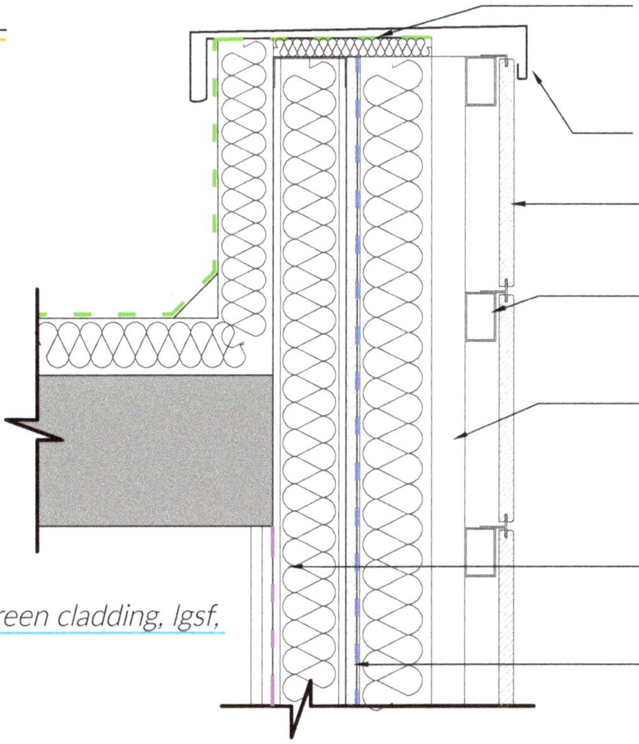

2D Detail W73 - Stone rainscreen cladding, lgsf, parapet detail

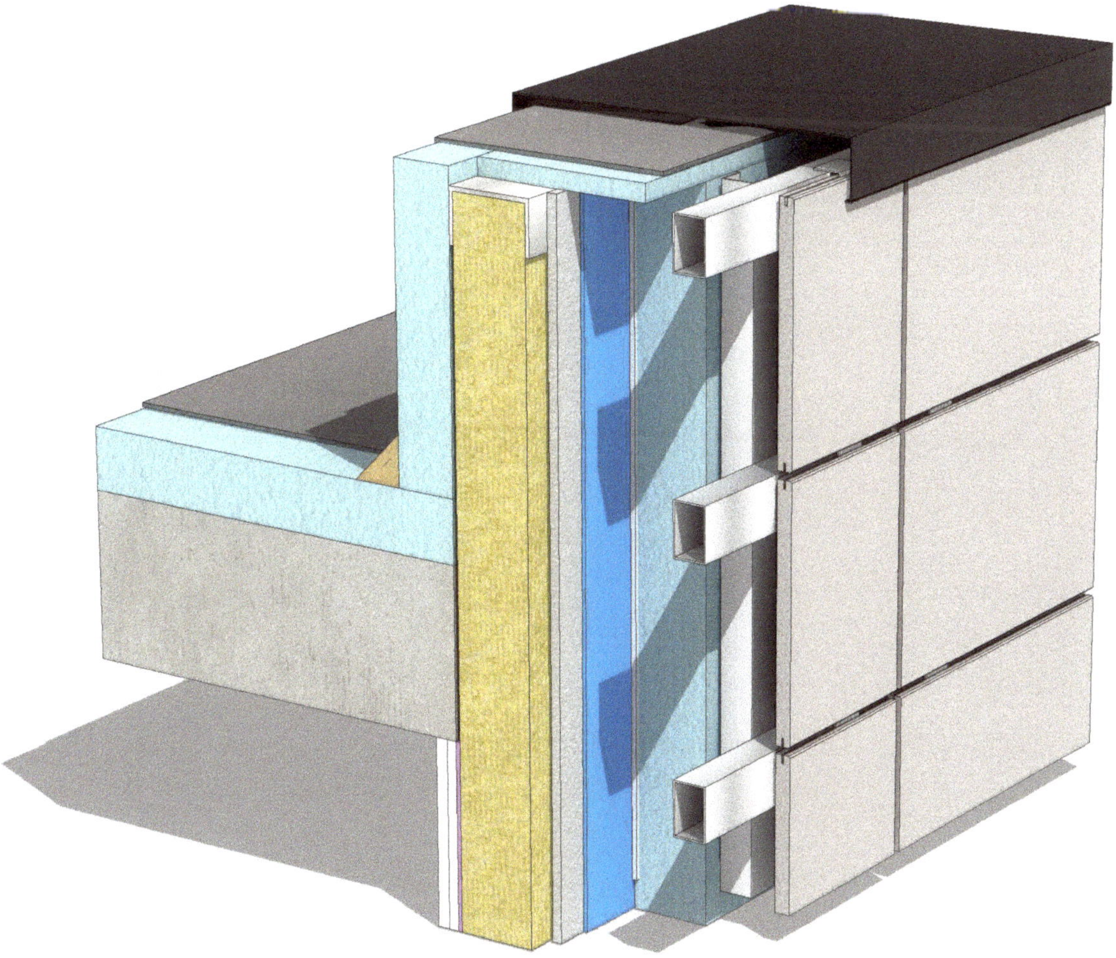

3D Detail W73 - Stone rainscreen cladding, lgsf, parapet detail

Blank Page

ROOFS

SECTION 8

INTRODUCTION TO ROOFS

FUNCTIONAL REQUIREMENTS

Although the type and style of commercial buildings can vary considerably, the functional requirements of a roof fall under the same general categories, no matter the application. Some of these functional requirements, considered alongside the site context, structural frame, and requirements of the brief, may dictate the type of roof structure specified along with the roof covering or finish.

A roof design can be studied in two parts, the structure of the roof and the covering. The functional requirements of both elements of the roof design can be described as follows:

Strength and Stability
Commercial structures are generally framed structures, made in either concrete or steel as we have explored earlier in this book. We have looked at portal frame structures and roofs in a previous chapter, so for this section we will focus on the skeleton frame roof structure. Given that the skeleton frame is usually made of steel or concrete, it is most likely that steel or concrete is used in the construction of the roof.

The structure will be required to withstand the loads generated by the roof and the external factors such as wind or snow loads. These loads all need to be transferred to the supporting structure and to the foundations below.

Weather Resistance
The main function of the roof, particularly the covering is to provide suitable resistance to the weather. A pitched roof will rely on over lapping sections that allow the water to run off the roof and away to the rainwater drainage system. A flat roof on the other hand tend to rely on a continuous impervious coating to stop water penetrating the inside of the building assembly.

Durability
The roof covering must be resistant to rain and wind, but also sun damage. It is important to ensure the roof will have the longest life possible and with minimum maintenance wherever possible. It is also worth noting that some materials will react negatively when positioned against materials that they may have a chemical reaction with or suffer differential movement in varying degrees. All of these issues must be considered in order to ensure a durable roof design.

Thermal resistance
Warm air naturally rises, and therefore the roof is of great importance when we look at heat loss in a building. The roof element must be designed to not only battle against heat loss but in some commercial buildings it is also heat gain that can be a problem. In some large commercial buildings the cost is more on cooling the building rather than heating it, as the occupants, activities, solar gain and equipment often create a naturally warm environment that requires cooling.

It is worth noting that some industrial, agricultural and warehousing buildings sometimes don't need to be heated and therefore insulation is often omitted in the roof.

Sound Resistance
The roof design must also take into account the acoustic penetration and emission from the building. The roof can help to reduce overall external sound levels to create a comfortable internal environment.

Aesthetics

Although much of the shape of the roof is determined by the layout and floor plans below along with the structure that supports it, much of the roofing finish, particularly in pitched roofs carries some aesthetic decisions. There are many roof coverings available, many of which will have a specific impact on the look, feel and context of the finished building.

STRUCTURE AND FRAMES

In residential construction the roof is often considered separately from the rest of the structure. However, with commercial buildings the roof is often considered as a complete part of the structural frame.

Due to the scale of many commercial buildings, the roof options could be considered more limiting than that of residential structures. For example, long span, low rise buildings that require large open floor spaces tend to adopt a portal frame structure with a pitched roof, whereas a complex floor plan would suggest a flat roof is more appropriate than a pitched roof. Often, a roof is used to store plant and equipment or required for maintenance access, so a suitable option in this case is a flat roof.

In more modern structures, the roof is often seen as a continuation of the wall to make a single envelope to the building. This demonstrates that roof finishes are being applied to walls, and wall finishes are being applied to roofs. We are faced with a multitude of choices for our designs, allowing us to create striking buildings by employing exciting new technologies and products.

PITCHED ROOFS

When looking at commercial and industrial structures the pitched roof is often part of the overall frame of the building, as in a portal frame, for example. However, with some high rise buildings a pitched roof can be incorporated, and this is often constructed with steel. Steel is lightweight, with a flexibility in design and assembly. Lattice frames or trusses can form the structure for a pitched roof in steelwork.

PITCHED ROOF COVERINGS

The most common pitched roof covering is the use of profiled metal sheeting, which comes in a variety of forms. These panels are able to span large areas and are considered to be an economical choice. The metal sheeting can be a single skin or double skin system - single skin being one sheet, uninsulated and most often seen in agricultural shed or unheated warehouses. The double skin system is assembled on site and allows for a layer of insulation to be fitted between the two metal sheets. The inner sheet has a lower profile and can act as the internal finish to the building.

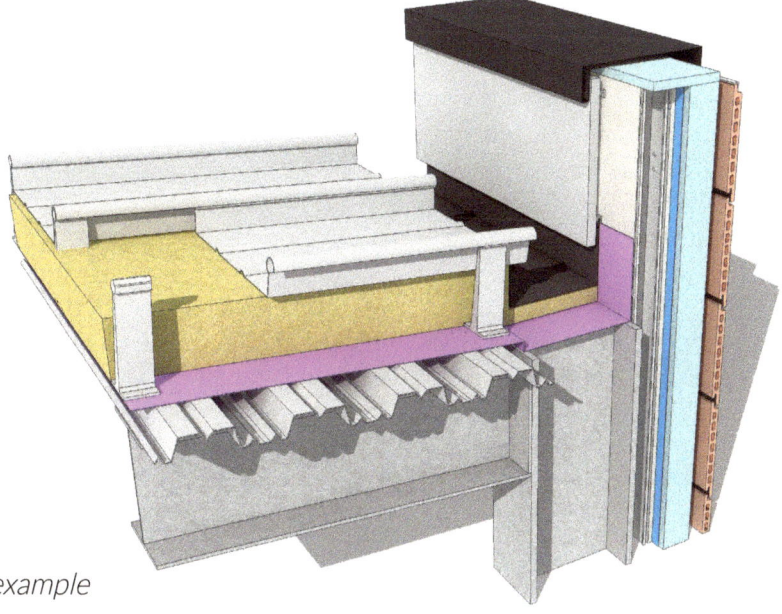

Fig 8.1 - Pitched roof example

The metal sheet systems span between metal roof purlins that are attached to the main structure. The pitch of the roof can be very low, but in most cases a pitch of 4° to 5° will be the more standard low pitch roof. These metal sheets can allow for adventurous designs where the roof becomes a continuation of the wall, and is seen as a continuous envelope.

A composite panel system is factory assembled, where the outer sheets are bonded to an insulation core. These composite panels are available in an array of profiles and finishes and are becoming increasingly popular both for wall systems and roof systems.

FLAT ROOFS

A commercial or industrial flat roof consists of three main components, the structure, the roof deck and the roof covering.

The structure of the roof transfers the loads to the main building frame and on to the foundations. The structure is often determined by the building frame.

For steel frames, the roof can also be treated in a similar manner to suspended floors. The frame will either carry precast concrete units, or a steel deck is positioned ready to receive an in situ concrete finish.

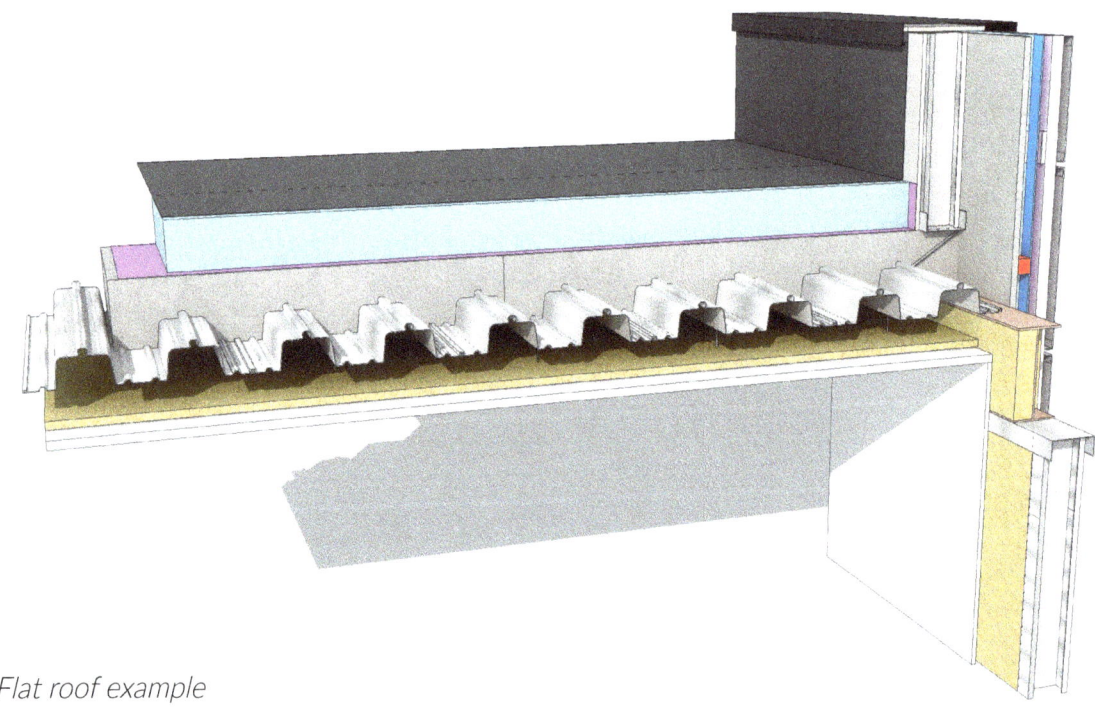

Fig 8.2 - Flat roof example

The roof deck provides a suitable surface for any insulation requirements, along with the roof covering. A flat roof will still have a slope in order to direct water away and into the drainage system and avoid standing water or pooling, this slope can be as little as 1°.

Roof Deck
A concrete flat roof will be composed of either a cast in situ or precast concrete system. The selection of this would be based largely on the structure of the rest of the building.

For example, when a frame is constructed using an in-situ concrete frame, the roof will most likely be an in situ concrete slab. This slab then makes up both the structure and the roof deck.

In other cases it would be most likely that a precast system would be adopted.

A cast in situ roof deck would be constructed using formwork and temporary support. This method has some drawbacks that include timely construction process, along with trapped moisture within the slab can expand and vaporise underneath the roof covering causing problems later on. This must be taken into account when using a cast in situ slab, and often vents are incorporated to allow for the release of any trapped moisture.

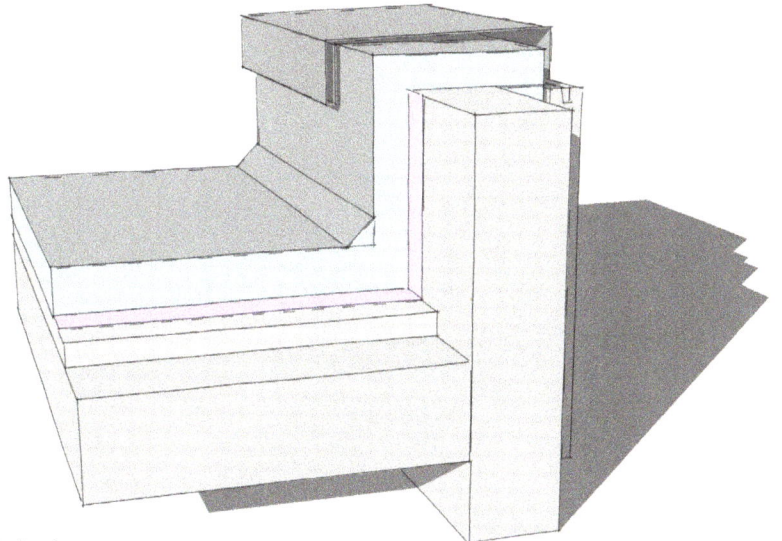

Fig 8.3 - Cast in situ roof deck

A precast concrete deck is designed in a similar way to a suspended floor. The options available include concrete plank panels, beam and block or pre stressed units.

A metal roof deck can often be described as composite deck. The reason for this is that the metal deck alone is not capable of providing a fully supporting base, and it is finished with a concrete topping to provide structural stability and strength. The steel deck is spanned between structural supports, which almost forms a permanent formwork for the concrete to be applied. After this insulation and the roof covering can be applied.

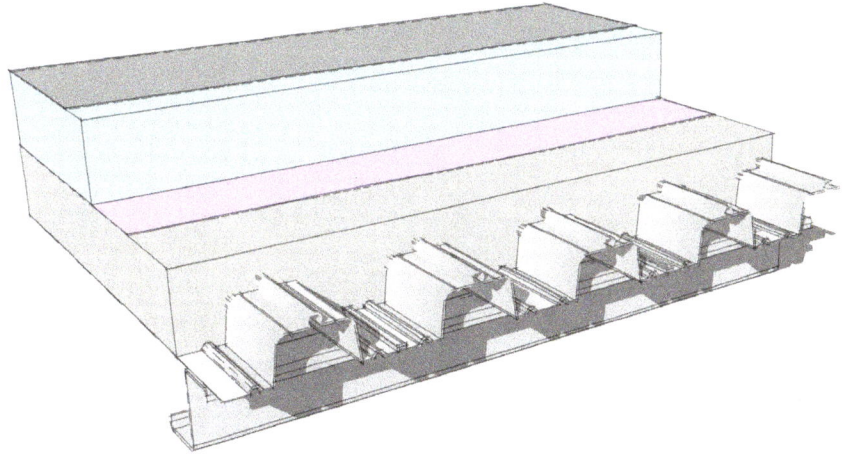

Fig 8.4 - Metal deck roof

FLAT ROOF COVERINGS

Traditionally a flat roof would be covered with a built up felt roofing or asphalt roofing, although there have been further developments in roofing technologies.

Built up roofing
Built up felt roofing uses a series of sections overlapped to form a continuous coating. The sections are partially bonded to the deck to allow for movement between the deck and the covering. The next layers will be fully bonded using bitumen to provide a two or three layer system.

Liquid systems
Asphalt or bitumen roofing is applied in liquid form to create a continuous impervious membrane to the roof. A separating layer is positioned between the roof deck and the asphalt to allow for differential movement.

The liquid system tends to soften in direct sunlight and heat, so can often be covered in stone chippings to protect it and keep the material cool. Stone chippings are not the only option, and often paving slabs can be positioned over the waterproofing layer using spacers that lift and level the slabs. This system often incorporates an insulation layer between the bitumen and the covering. These concealed membrane roofs can be termed 'inverted', where the insulation is above the waterproof covering.

Single ply
Development of rubbers and plastics has allowed materials to be produced that accommodate differential movement without disrupting the integrity of the membrane. These polymer based membranes, known as single ply membranes are durable and reliable. The membrane is applied to the deck by adhesion, mechanical fixing or loose laying.

Metal roof coverings
Traditional methods of standing seam roofing using lead, zinc and copper have seen a revival in popularity. Profiled metal roofs with standing seams have become a popular choice in roof covering for both a flat roof or pitched roof, along with wall applications.

INSULATING THE ROOF

Flat roof construction allows for three methods of insulation:
- Cold deck - the insulation material is below the roof deck
- Warm deck - the insulation is above the roof deck
- Inverted - the insulation is above the weatherproof covering

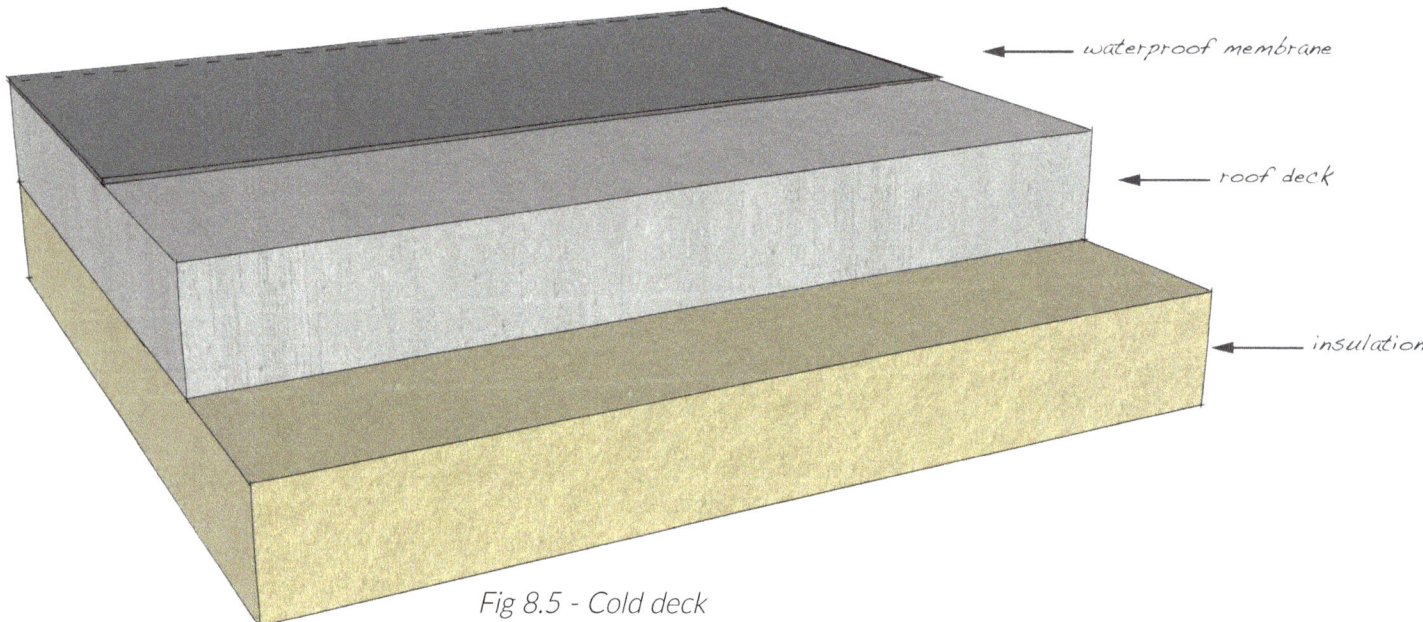

Fig 8.5 - Cold deck

Cold deck roofs are not particularly common in modern construction due to the fact that placing the insulation layer on inside of the deck, interstitial condensation may occur. To stop this, vapour control layer and ventilation must be included in the design.

A warm deck roof is perhaps the most common arrangement in a commercial setting. The insulation is placed on top of the roof deck and then protected by the weather proof membrane. A vapour barrier is usually positioned between the roof deck and the insulation. The insulation can be tapered to form the necessary falls in the roof to direct water to the outlet points. This means the structural deck doesn't have to be designed to incorporate the fall.

An inverted roof positions the insulation above the waterproof membrane. The insulation must be water resisting, and securely positioned. It is often finished with floor tiles to allow access to the roof. The membrane remains protected underneath the insulation making it a very durable option.

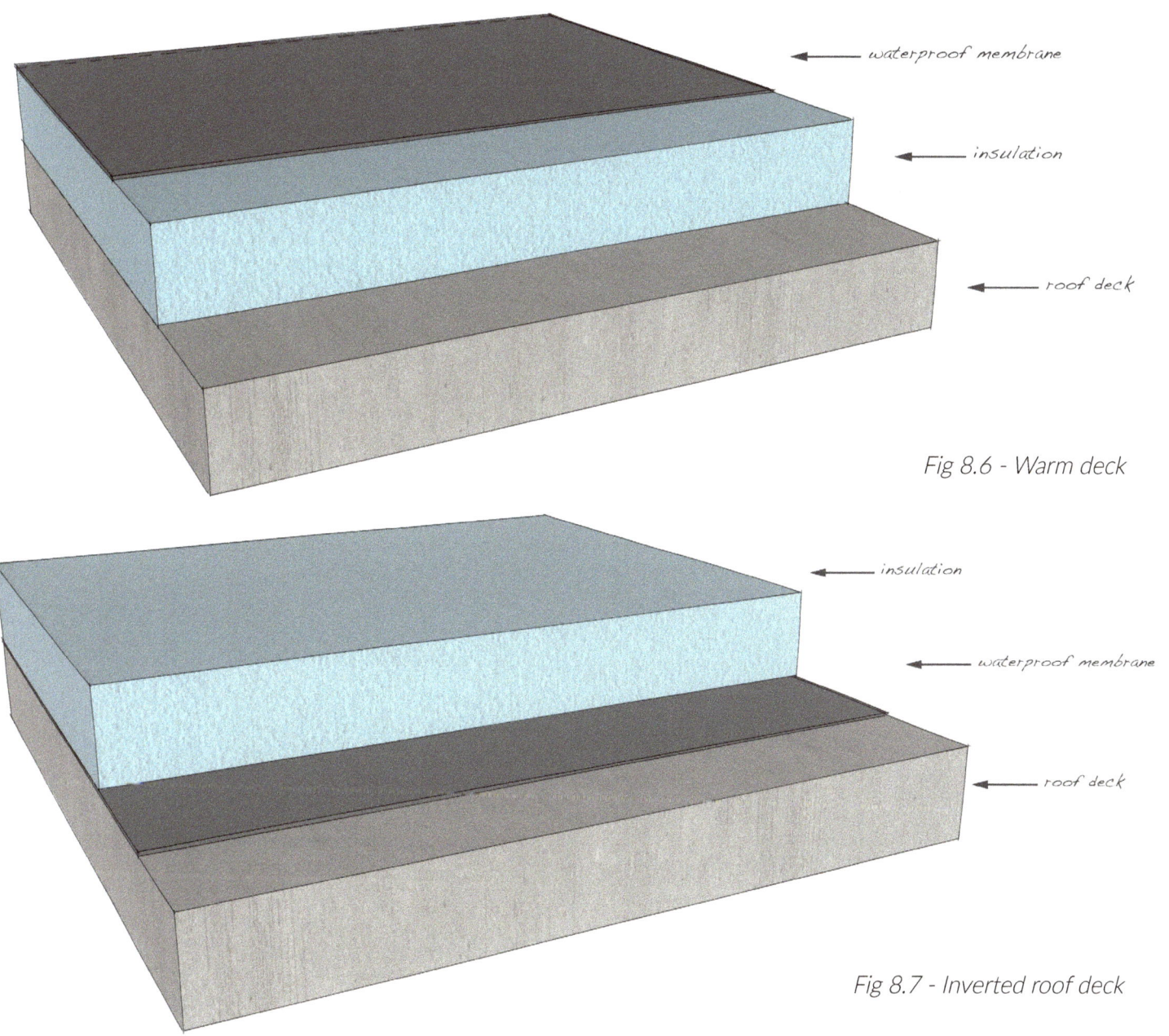

Fig 8.6 - Warm deck

Fig 8.7 - Inverted roof deck

WATER MANAGEMENT AND DRAINAGE

Commercial roofs in their nature tend to have large surface areas, and with that the rainwater run off can be substantial. Although the rainwater collection methods are similar to that of a residential design, the scale of the elements are increased and the positioning will differ. In many situations, the downpipes will be located internally.

Pitched roof drainage
A pitched roof system often consists of a gutter and downpipe arrangement. The gutter can sometimes be concealed to make for a more visually pleasing finish. In parapet arrangements the gutter can be situated behind the parapet. The downpipes in high rise buildings will be positioned inside the building, giving a number of benefits: protection from the elements, protection from vandalism, protection from freezing. The pipes are also accessible for maintenance. In long span buildings the downpipes can be positioned internally or externally depending on design requirements.

Flat roof drainage
A flat roof generally does not require gutters, and instead will have a parapet design, where the water is naturally directed to the rainwater outlets by means of falls designed into the roof structure or insulation as mentioned earlier.

Roof Type	Advantages	Disadvantages	Suitable application
Pitched Roof Structure			
Structure separate from building frame eg, lattice, truss	Flexible, lightweight, readily assembled and craned into place.	Roof span is limited, slow to construct, care required when working with connections and bracing.	Small scale roof construction for industrial buildings.
Structure as part of the building frame eg, portal	Economic option for large projects, fewer components limit possibility of quality problems, suitable for long spans	Can have long lead in times, standard frames limit shape options, transport and storage of large components	Portal frame roofs are a standard option for long span low rise buildings
Pitched Roof Covering			
Slates / tiles	Aesthetically pleasing, available in a range of sizes, easily worked on site	Expensive to large areas, slow to install, not suited to low pitch due to damage and uplift.	Generally not used in modern framed buildings but can be incorporated as a feature. Cost and time of installation is a deterrent for larger schemes.
Profiled metal sheets	A range of colours and profiles are available, good strength, few junctions due to large size of panels, economic and easy to install	Large sheets can be difficult to handle and transport, thermal movement can affect fixings.	Suited to covering large pitched roofs
Soft metal coverings	Aesthetically pleasing, durable, malleable metals make it easy to produce special shapes.	Difficult to detail, requires highly skilled installers, expensive	Used when there is aesthetic demand.
Flat Roof Structure			
Warm Deck Roof	Warm deck resists differential movement of covering, allows use of tapered insulation to create falls, can be upgraded when recovering roof.	Potential for damage to insulation when roof is under maintenance.	Most common form in commercial and industrial buildings.
Inverted Roof	Protection of membrane, insulation can be upgraded without having to replace waterproof membrane	Difficult to detect leaks, potential for damage to insulation, requires a protective surface covering and can be a costly option	A technically superior performance but best used when there is minimal risk of damage to the roof from heavy traffic.
Flat Roof Covering			
Roofing Felt	Cheap, well known technology	Older forms have a limited life span, solar degradation, problems with differential movement	Selection is usually based on familiarity of designer with the product. Losing favour to polymer based membranes
Single layer covering (polymer based)	Enhanced technology, extended life span, able to cope with differential movement	Single layer covering may suffer from localised damage	Simple to install and durable, now most popular flat roof covering option for larger buildings
Asphalt	Liquid application means asphalt is a flexible option, absence of joints, easy to detail around fixtures etc	Solar degradation, large areas can be expensive and time consuming to install	Used for areas that will receive heavy traffic or for areas that have difficult detailing.

Fig 8.8 - Factors affecting roof selection
Table adapted from Construction Technology 2: Industrial & Commercial Building - Mike Riley & Alison Cotgrave

GREEN ROOFS

Landscaping to roofs is becoming an increasingly popular option for roof coverings, and offer many benefits. The green roof is considered to offer a great sustainability rating to any development, provide much needed green space in city centre environments and increase the landscaping while maintaining the footprint of a development. The green roof can contribute to cooling in buildings, whilst also providing an outside space for occupants.

Fig 8.9 - Green roof example

Green roofs fall into two main categories: extensive and intensive.

Extensive Green Roof
Extensive roofs cover the whole roof with low level sedum type planting. These roofs are not generally accessible other than for maintenance, they require a relatively small depth of planting matter and are generally low maintenance.

Main features of an extensive roof:
- Suitable for large areas
- Lightweight
- Build up height of between 50mm-150mm
- No irrigation required
- Minimal maintenance requirements
- Simple to design
- Planting usually moss, sedum, herbs and grasses

Extensive roofs are usually used for lightweight roof decks, roofs that are inaccessible, areas where a reduced run off is required.

Intensive Green Roof

Intensive roofs, sometimes known as roof gardens provide much larger scale planting, can be landscaped with seating areas, paths and provide an amenity space for the occupants. The intensive green roof requires a larger depth of planting matter, and as such demands more from the structure in terms of loading.

Main features of an intensive green roof:
- Build up height between 150mm-1500mm
- Requires regular maintenance
- Requires regular irrigation
- Provide a mixture of soft and hard landscaping
- Planting includes lawns, shrubs, edible plants, perennials and grasses, small deciduous trees and conifers

Intensive roofs are usually used to create natural gardens that can be accessible by the building occupants, growing food, or even recreation and sporting uses.

Green Roof Construction

A typical build up for a green roof consists of:
- Roof deck - usually concrete
- Insulation
- Waterproof membrane
- Root barrier
- Filter membrane
- Water retention layer
- Planting matter
- Vegetation

The vegetation layer can be varied according to the type of roof and requirements for the particular project. The growing medium is specified according to the planting requirements.

The water retention and drainage layer will retain water on the roof and slows down the runoff. It balances the supply of water to the vegetation.

The root barrier prevents any roots damaging the waterproof membrane below and plays a vital role in the performance of the roof.

ROOF DETAILS

R01

CONCRETE CAST IN SITU, SINGLE PLY, WARM DECK

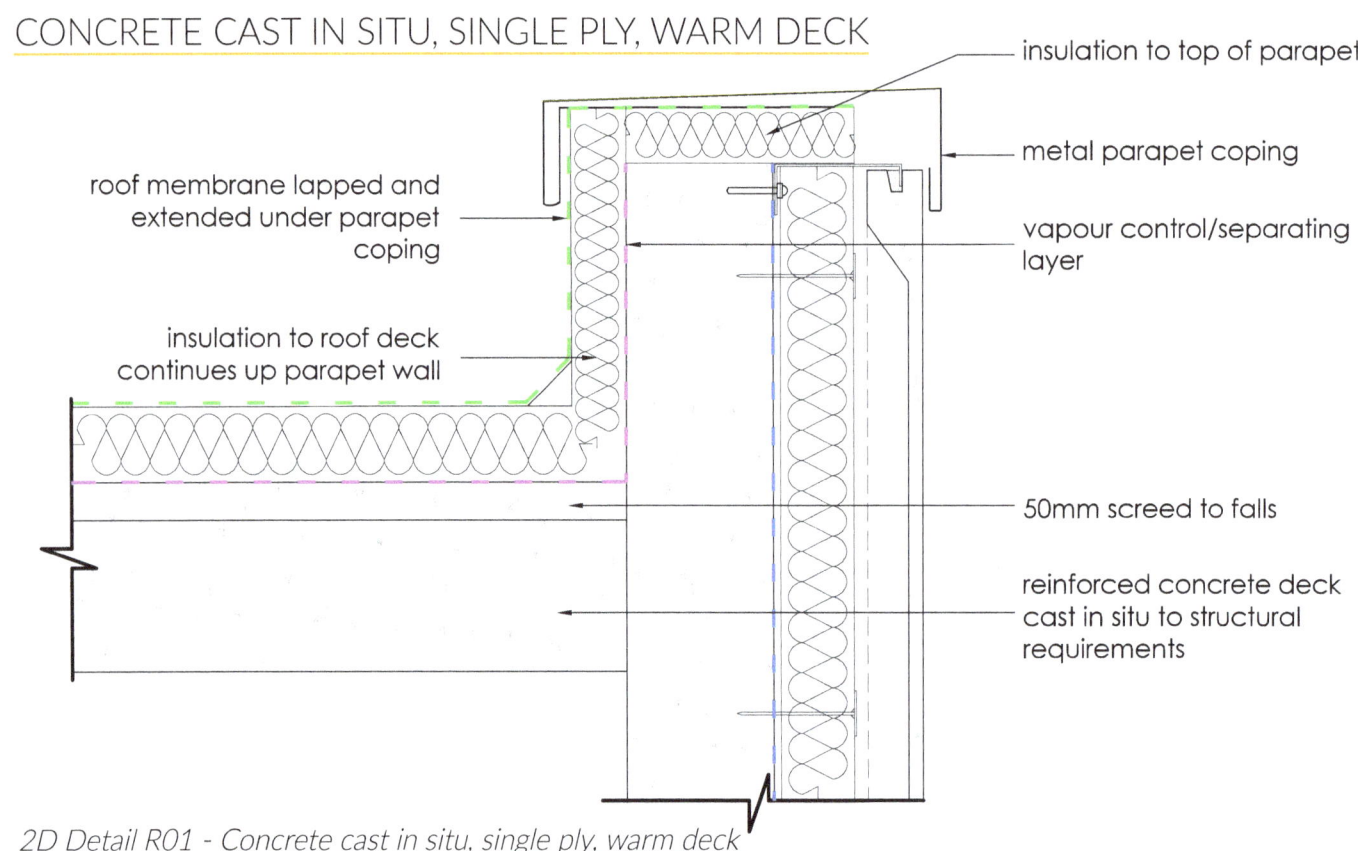

2D Detail R01 - Concrete cast in situ, single ply, warm deck

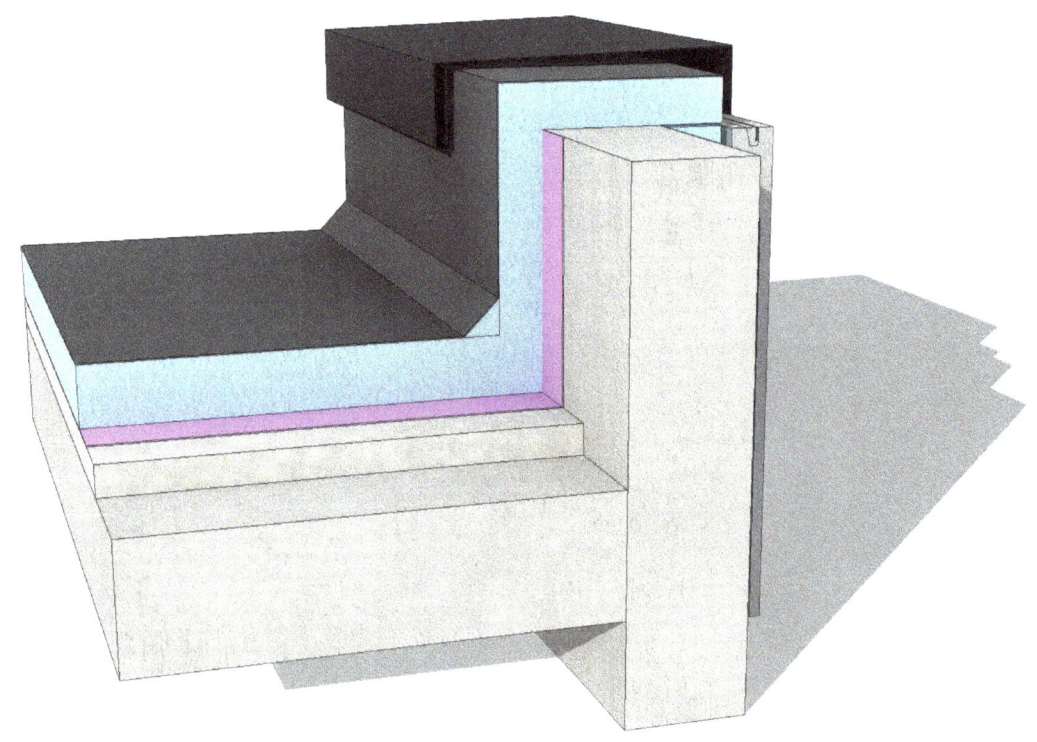

3D Detail R01 - Concrete cast in situ, single ply, warm deck

R02

CONCRETE CAST IN SITU, SINGLE PLY, RAINWATER OUTLET

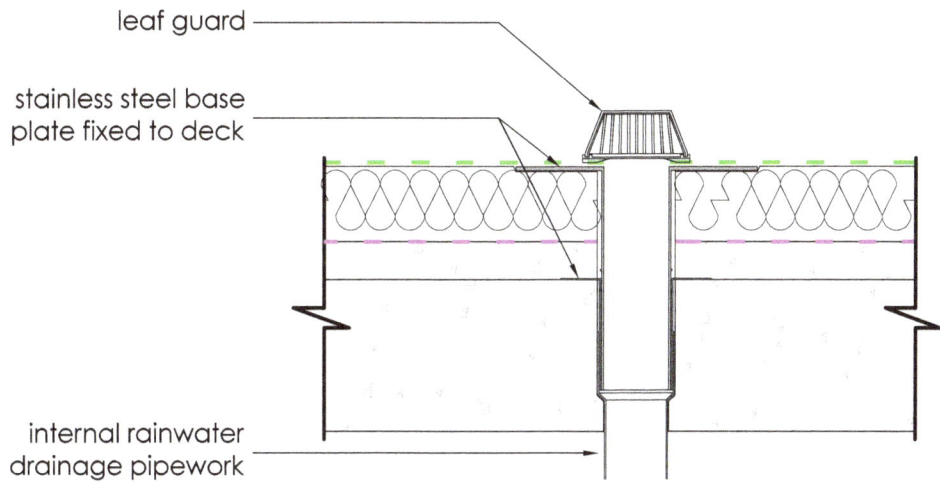

2D Detail R02 - Concrete cast in situ, single ply, rainwater outlet

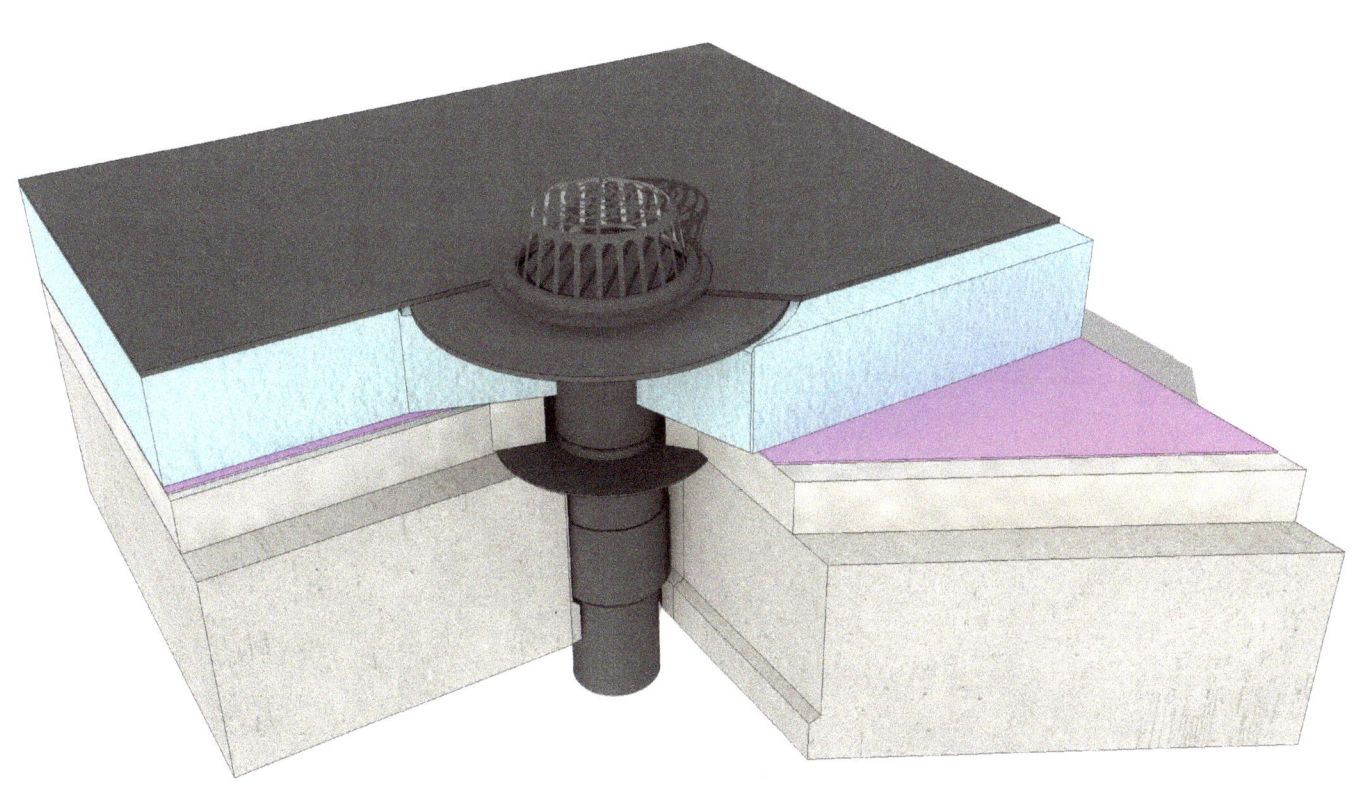

3D Detail R02 - Concrete cast in situ, single ply, rainwater outlet

R03

CONCRETE CAST IN SITU, SINGLE PLY, UPSTAND

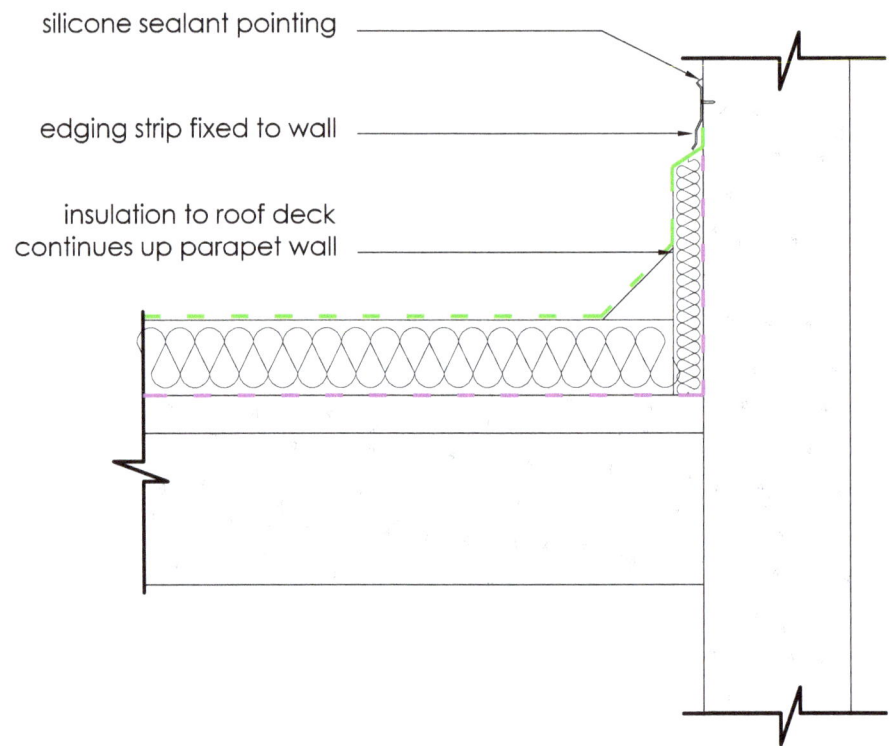

2D Detail R03 - Concrete cast in situ, single ply, upstand

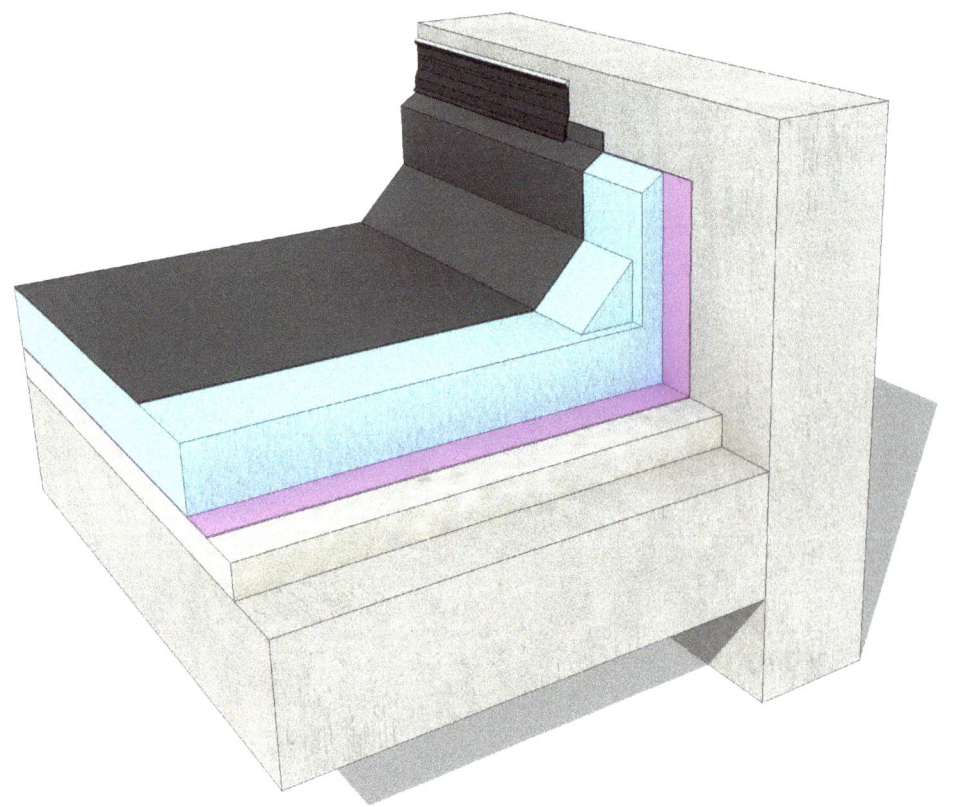

3D Detail R03 - Concrete cast in situ, single ply, upstand

R04

CONCRETE CAST IN SITU, SINGLE PLY, ROOFLIGHT

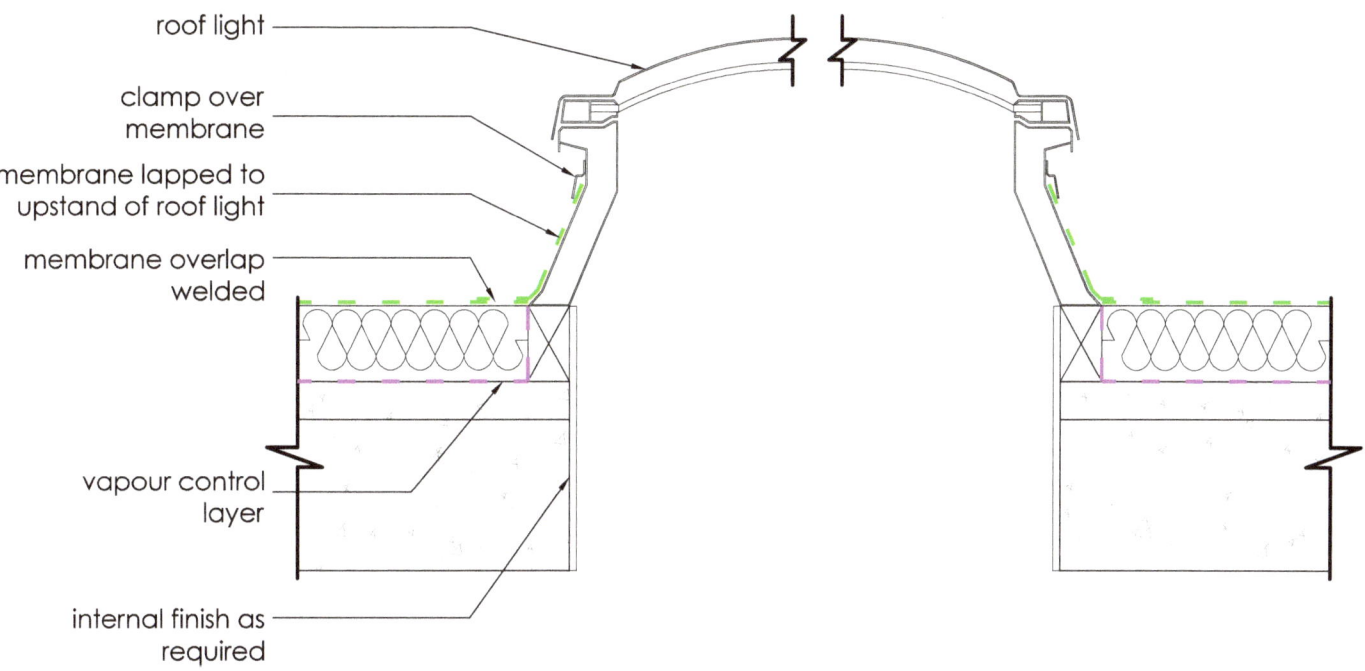

2D Detail R04 - Concrete cast in situ, single ply, rooflight

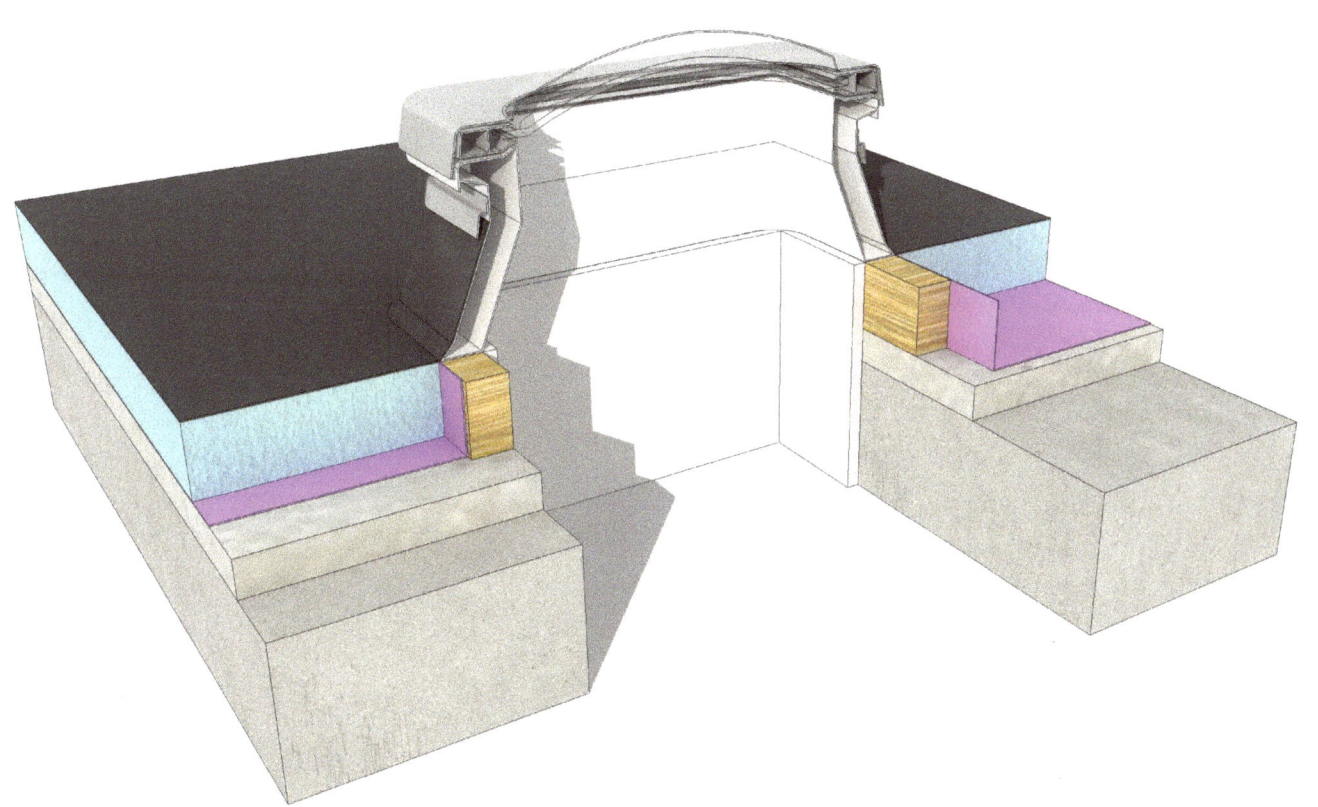

3D Detail R04 - Concrete cast in situ, single ply, rooflight

R05

CONCRETE CAST IN SITU, THRESHOLD DETAIL

waterbar

sill bedded onto sealing strip with membrane lapped under

timber decking on timber support bearers

150 min

2D Detail R05 - Concrete cast in situ, threshold detail (balcony)

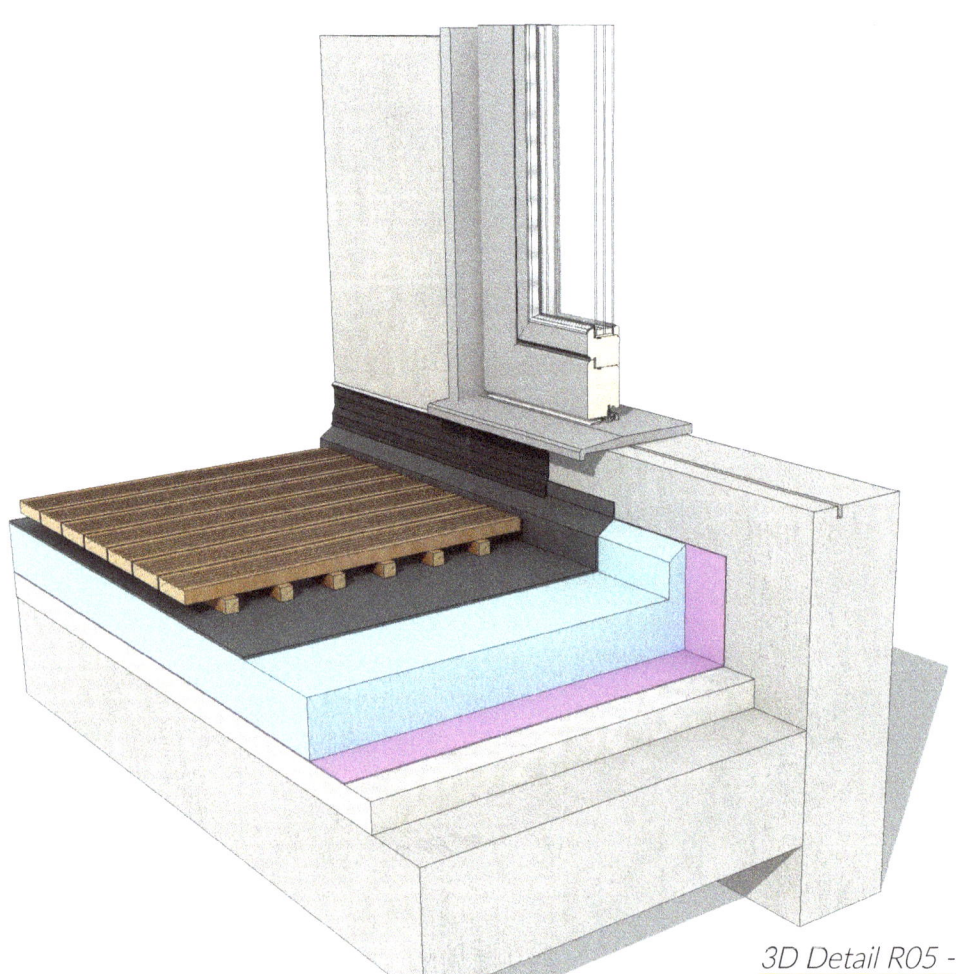

3D Detail R05 - Concrete cast in situ, (balcony)

SECTION 8 - ROOFS

R06

CONCRETE CAST IN SITU, LIQUID APPLIED, INVERTED ROOF

- bitumen applied to parapet face and under coping
- protection layer to insulation
- slabs set on spacers with pebbles to perimeter
- parapet coping
- 50mm screed to falls
- liquid applied waterproofing layer
- reinforced concrete deck cast in situ to structural requirements

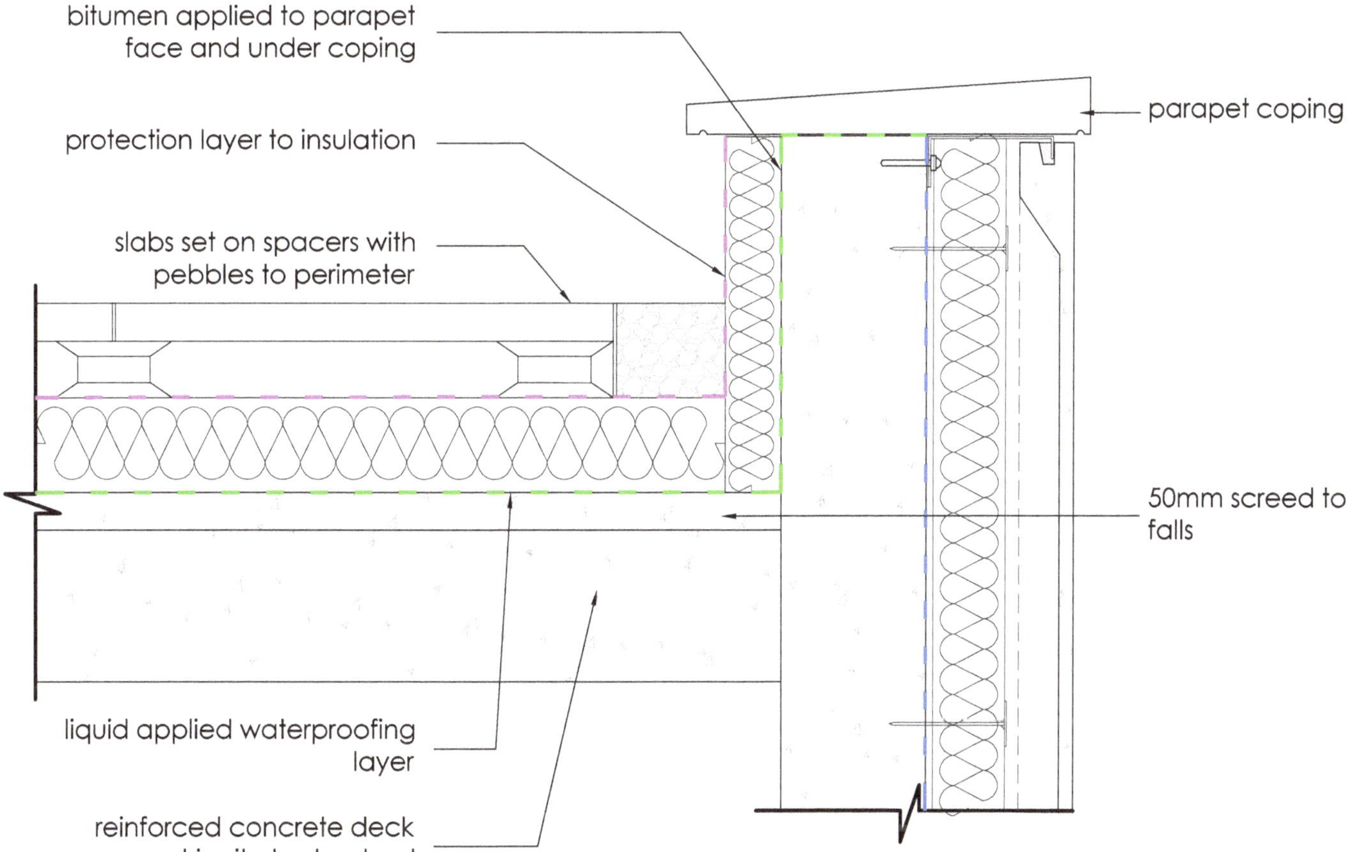

2D Detail R06 - Concrete cast in situ, liquid applied, inverted roof

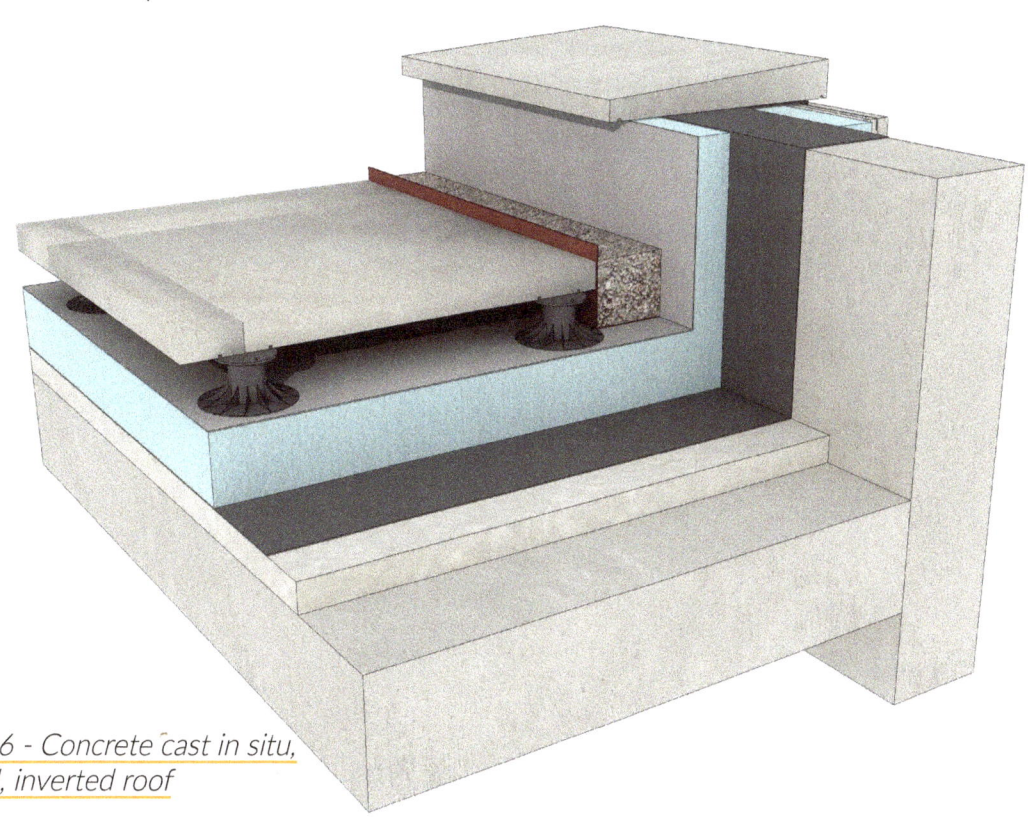

3D Detail R06 - Concrete cast in situ, liquid applied, inverted roof

R07

CONCRETE CAST IN SITU, LIQUID APPLIED, RAINWATER OUTLET

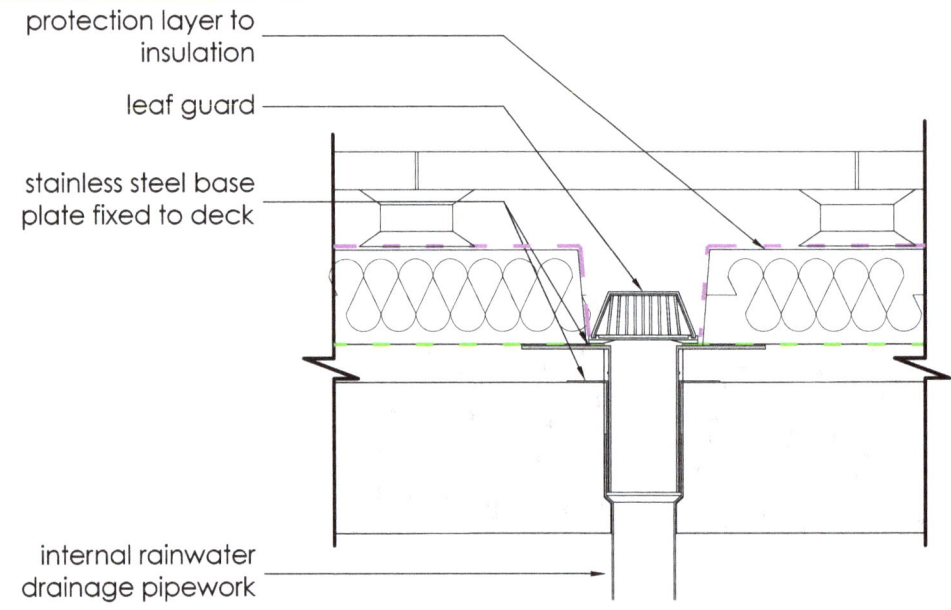

2D Detail R07 - Concrete cast in situ, liquid applied, rainwater outlet

3D Detail R07 - Concrete cast in situ, liquid applied, rainwater outlet

SECTION 8 - ROOFS

R08

CONCRETE CAST IN SITU, LIQUID APPLIED, ROOF LIGHT

- rooflight
- waterproofing layer applied to face of roof light upstand
- pebbles to perimeter
- liquid applied waterproofing layer
- internal finish as required

2D Detail R08 - Concrete cast in situ, liquid applied, roof light

3D Detail R08 - Concrete cast in situ, liquid applied, roof light

R09

CONCRETE CAST IN SITU, LIQUID APPLIED, THRESHOLD DETAIL

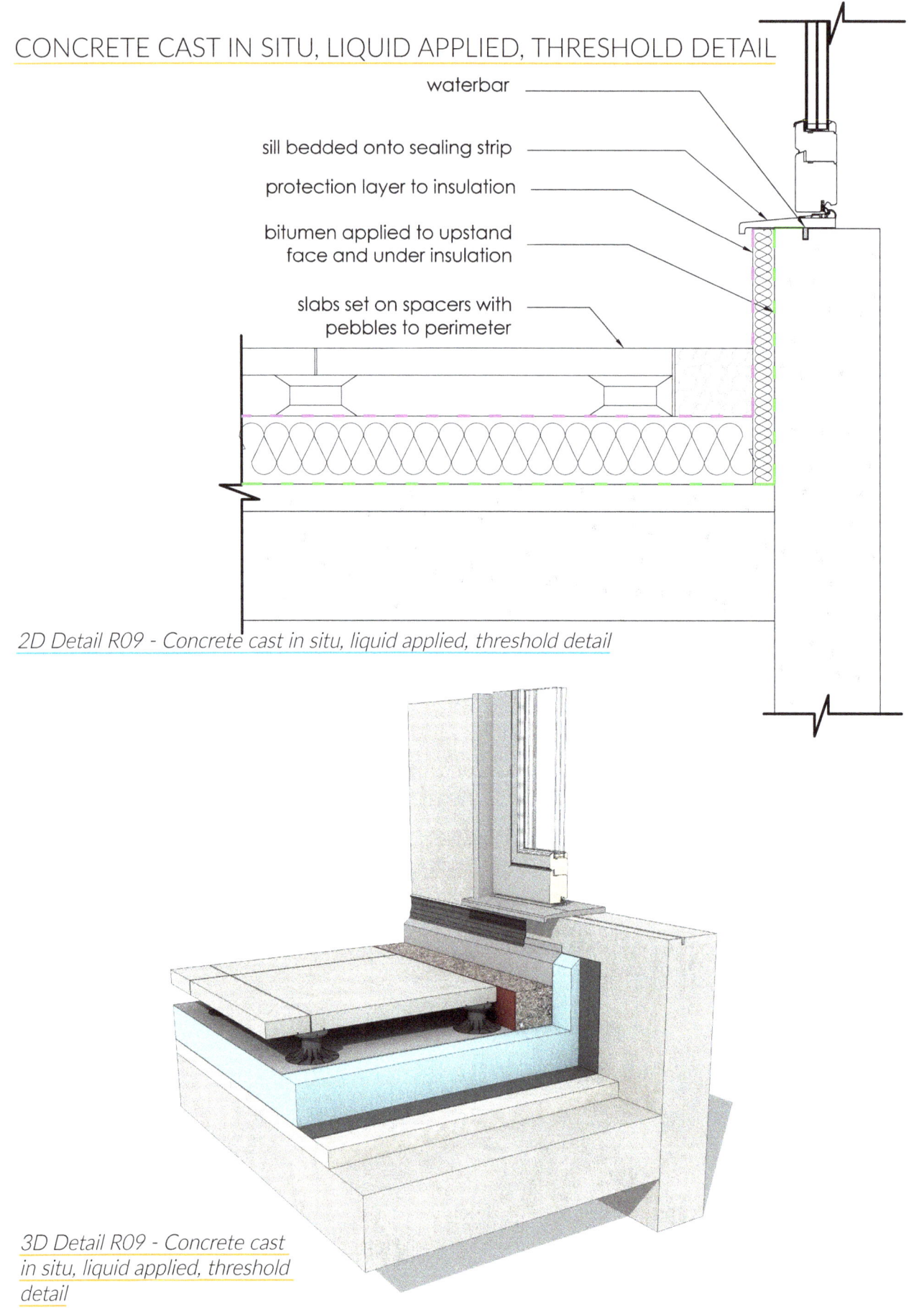

2D Detail R09 - Concrete cast in situ, liquid applied, threshold detail

3D Detail R09 - Concrete cast in situ, liquid applied, threshold detail

SECTION 8 - ROOFS

R10

CONCRETE CAST IN SITU, GREEN ROOF

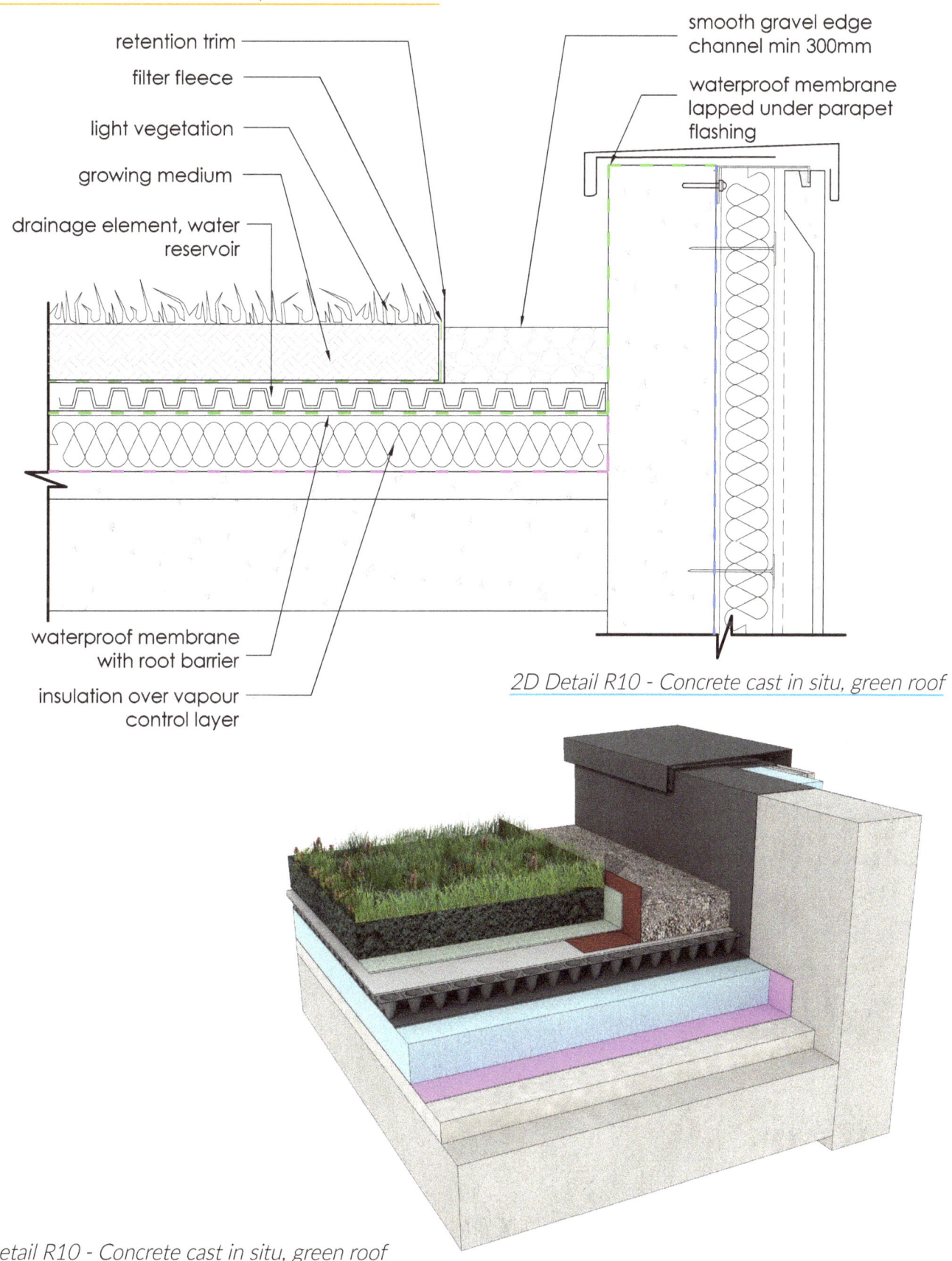

Labels (2D detail):
- retention trim
- filter fleece
- light vegetation
- growing medium
- drainage element, water reservoir
- waterproof membrane with root barrier
- insulation over vapour control layer
- smooth gravel edge channel min 300mm
- waterproof membrane lapped under parapet flashing

2D Detail R10 - Concrete cast in situ, green roof

3D Detail R10 - Concrete cast in situ, green roof

R11

CONCRETE CAST IN SITU, GREEN ROOF, DRAINAGE OUTLET

- pebbles to perimeter
- inspection chamber
- rainwater outlet
- waterproof membrane with root barrier
- insulation over vapour control layer

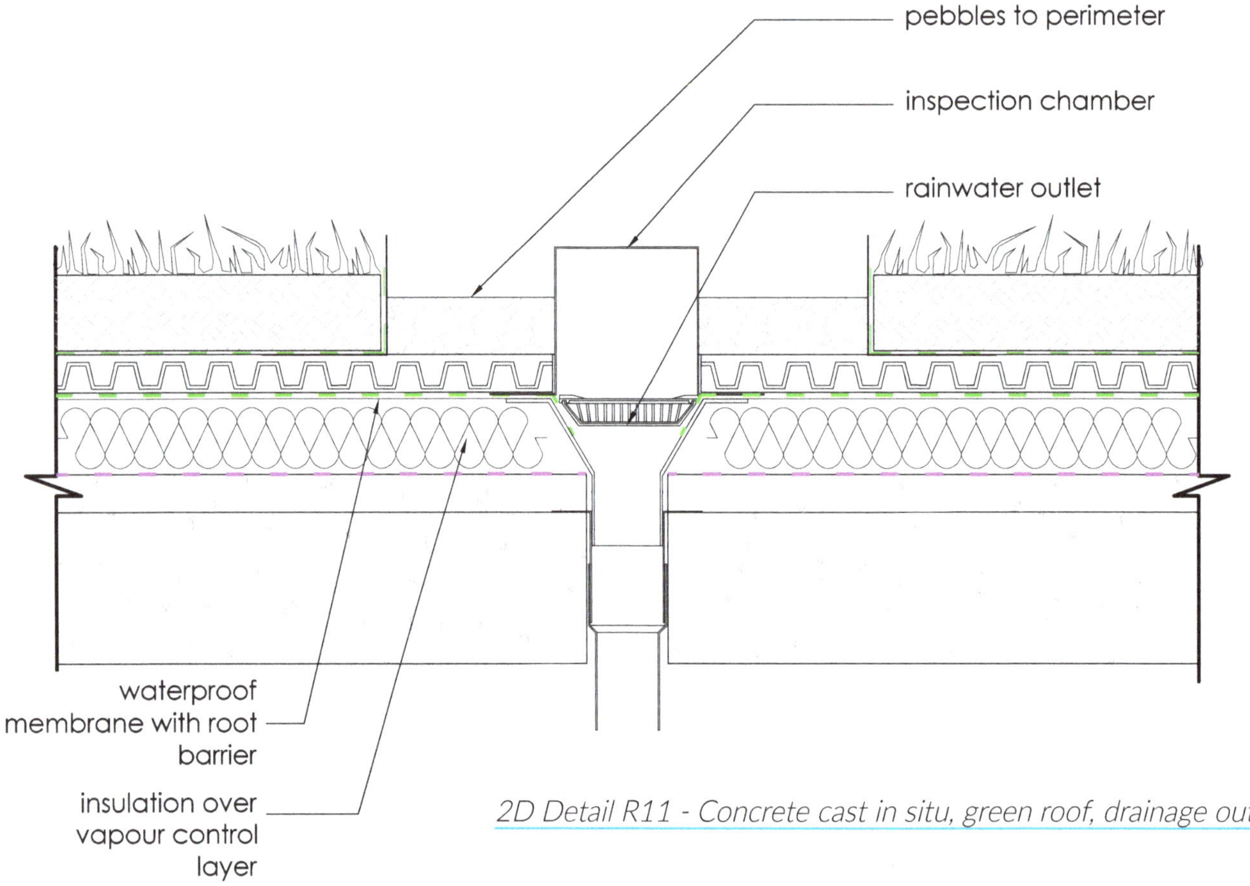

2D Detail R11 - Concrete cast in situ, green roof, drainage outlet

3D Detail R11 - Concrete cast in situ, green roof, drainage outlet

SECTION 8 - ROOFS

R12

CONCRETE CAST IN SITU, GREEN ROOF, ROOF LIGHT

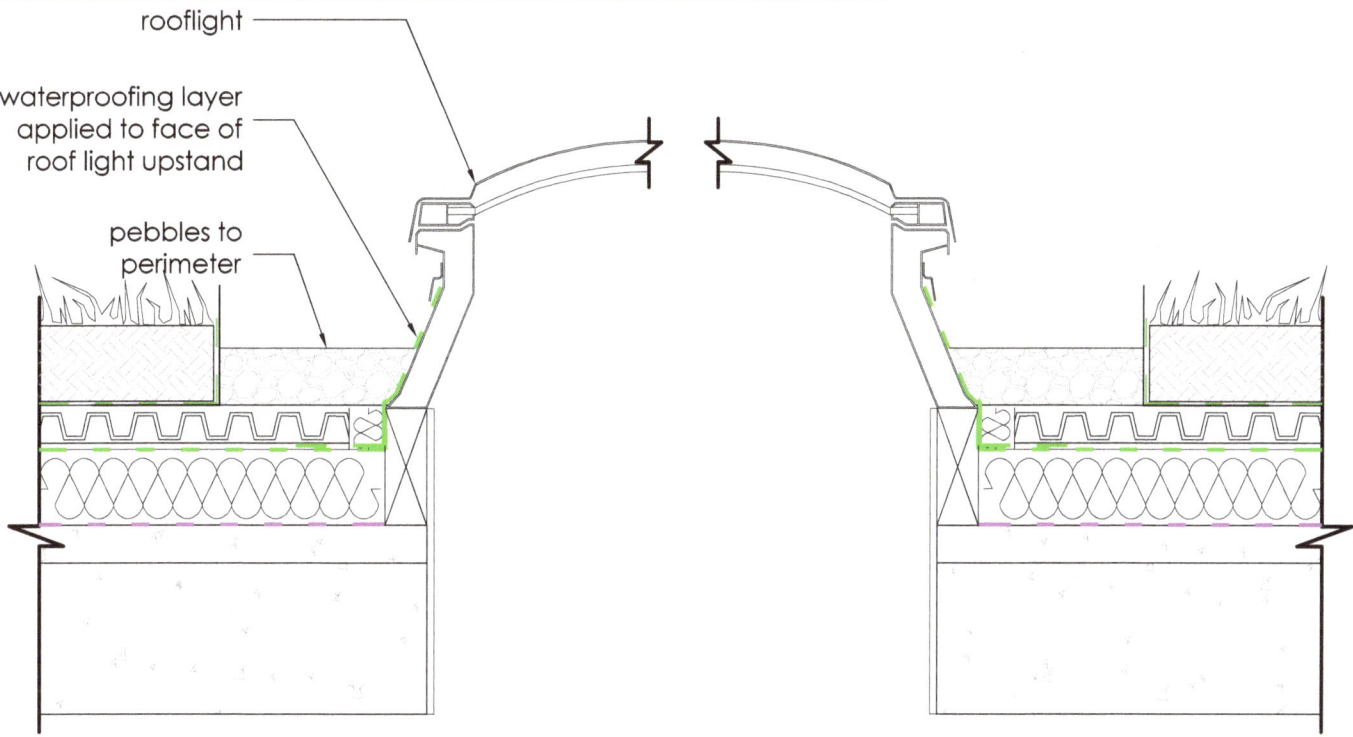

2D Detail R12 - Concrete cast in situ, green roof, roof light

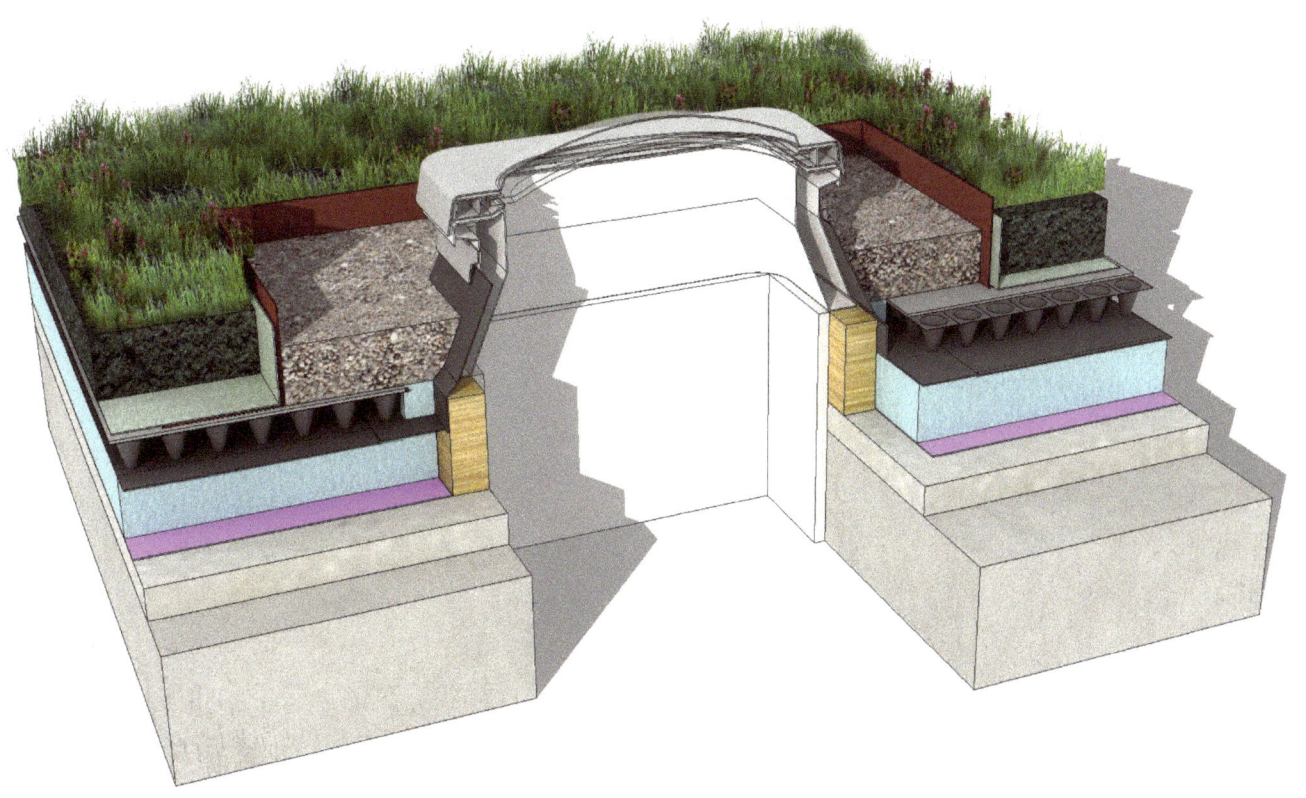

3D Detail R12 - Concrete cast in situ, green roof, roof light

R13

CONCRETE CAST IN SITU, GREEN ROOF, UPSTAND

- edging strip fixed to wall
- insulated upstand with waterproof membrane lapped over
- smooth gravel edge channel min 300mm
- retention trim
- filter fleece
- waterproof membrane with root barrier
- insulation over vapour control layer

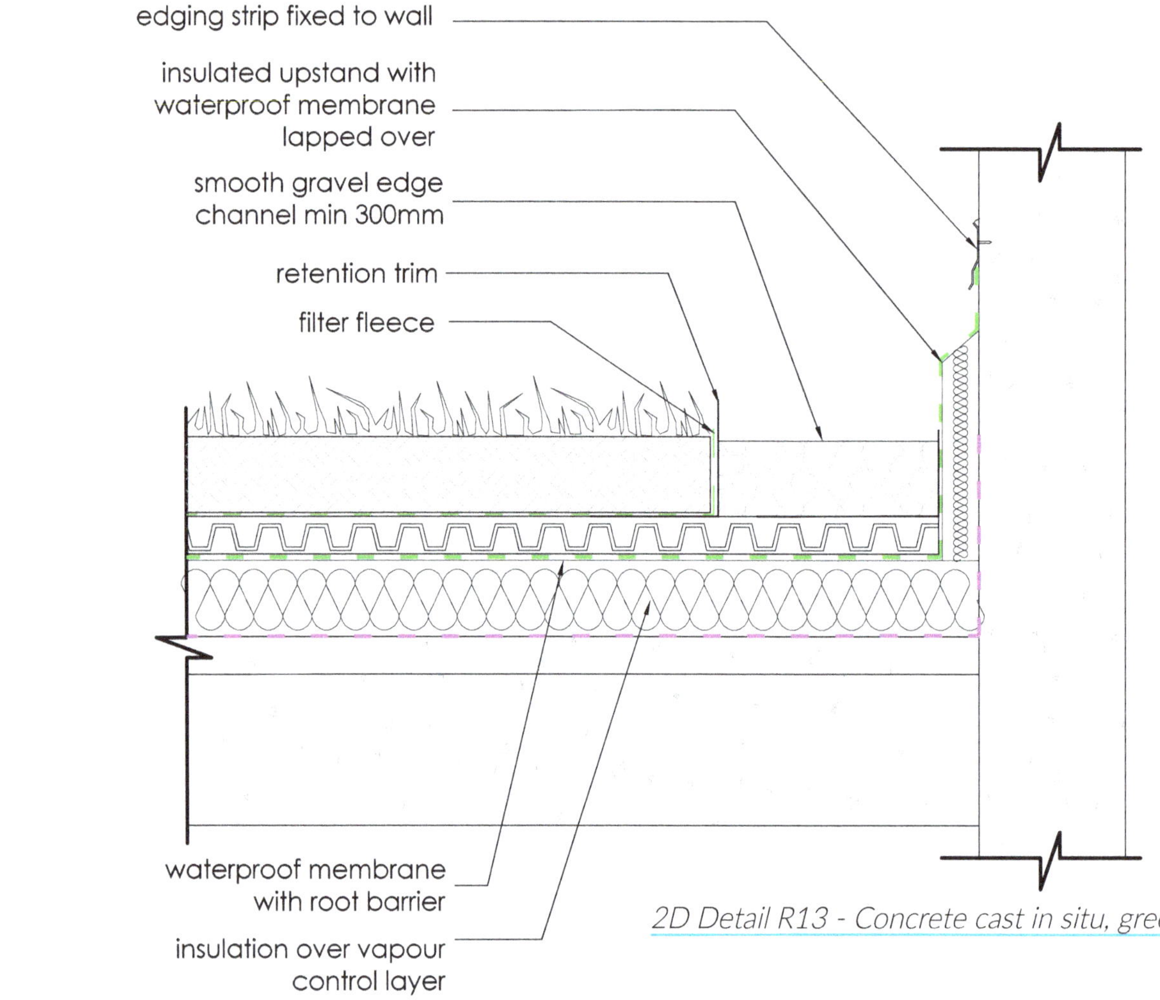

2D Detail R13 - Concrete cast in situ, green roof, upstand

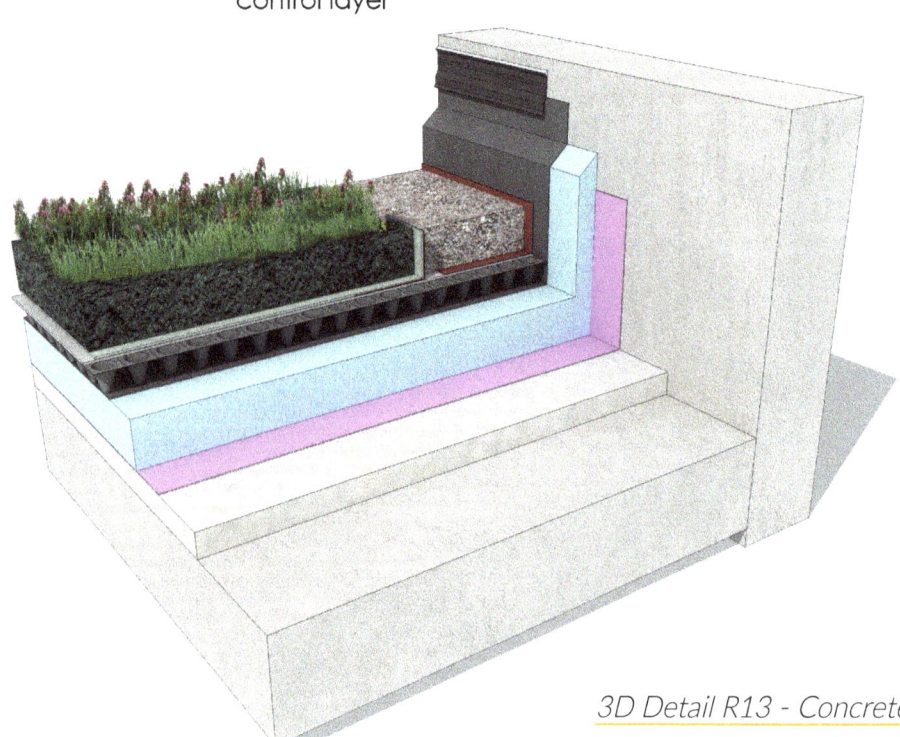

3D Detail R13 - Concrete cast in situ, green roof, upstand

SECTION 8 - ROOFS

Blank Page

R14

PITCHED ROOF, STEEL DECK, STANDING SEAM, PARAPET

- wall panel fixed to wall clips
- standing seam fixing clip secured to structural deck
- standing seam sheet
- insulation
- vapour control layer
- profiled steel roof deck
- steel roof beam
- flashing lining insulated gutter

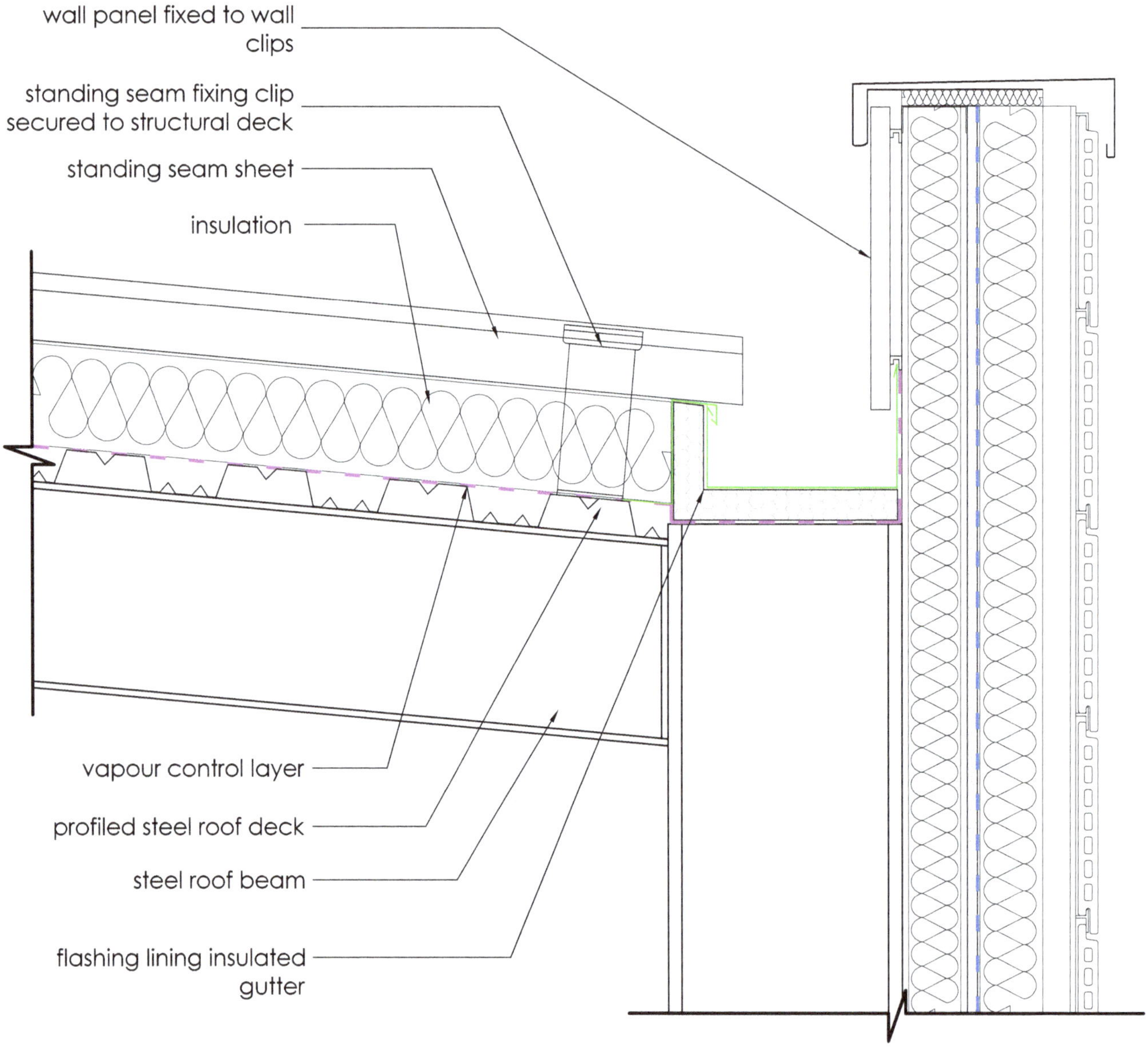

2D Detail R14 - Pitched roof, steel deck, standing seam, parapet

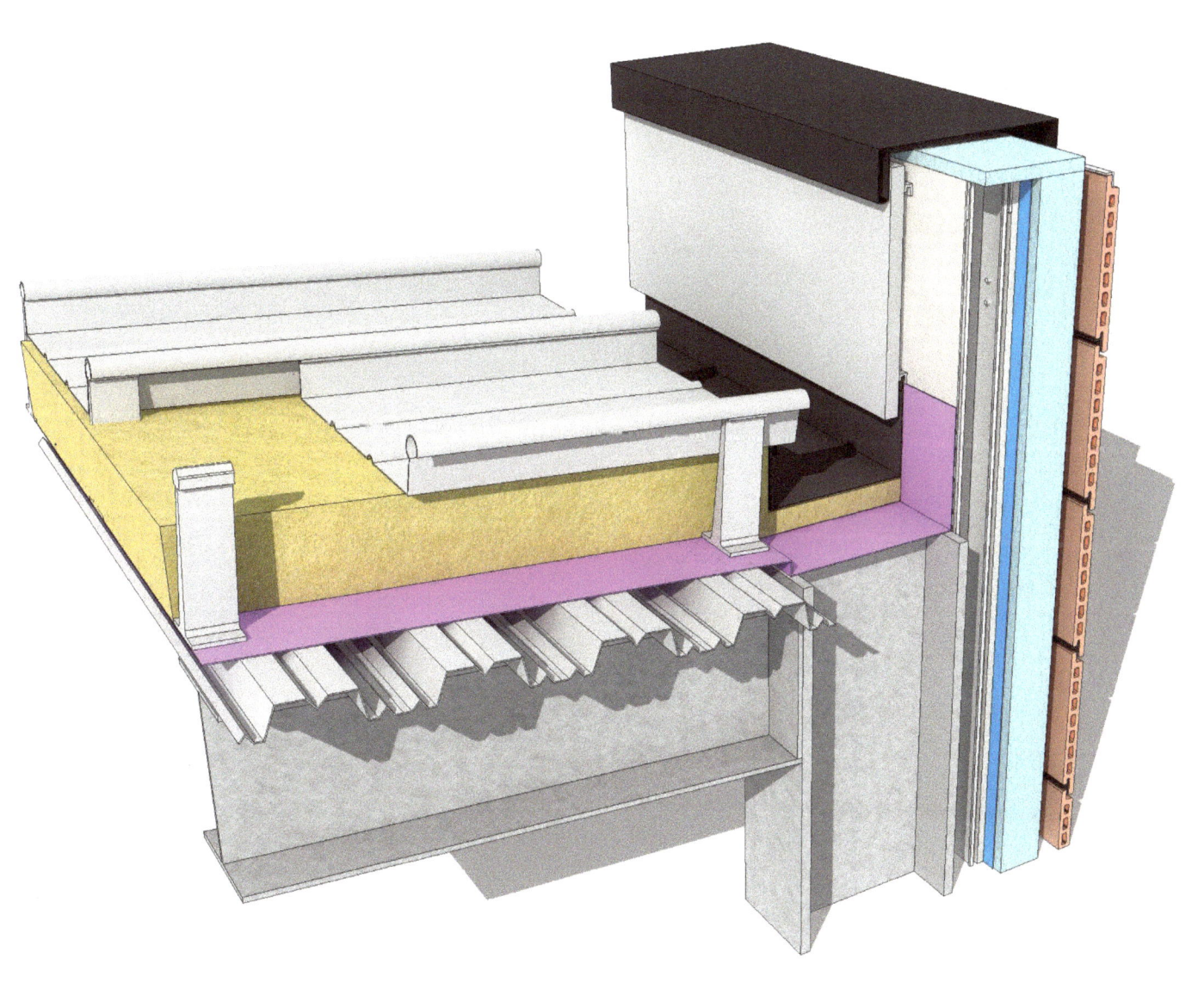

3D Detail R14 - Pitched roof, steel deck, standing seam, parapet

R15

PITCHED ROOF, STEEL DECK, STANDING SEAM, RIDGE DETAIL

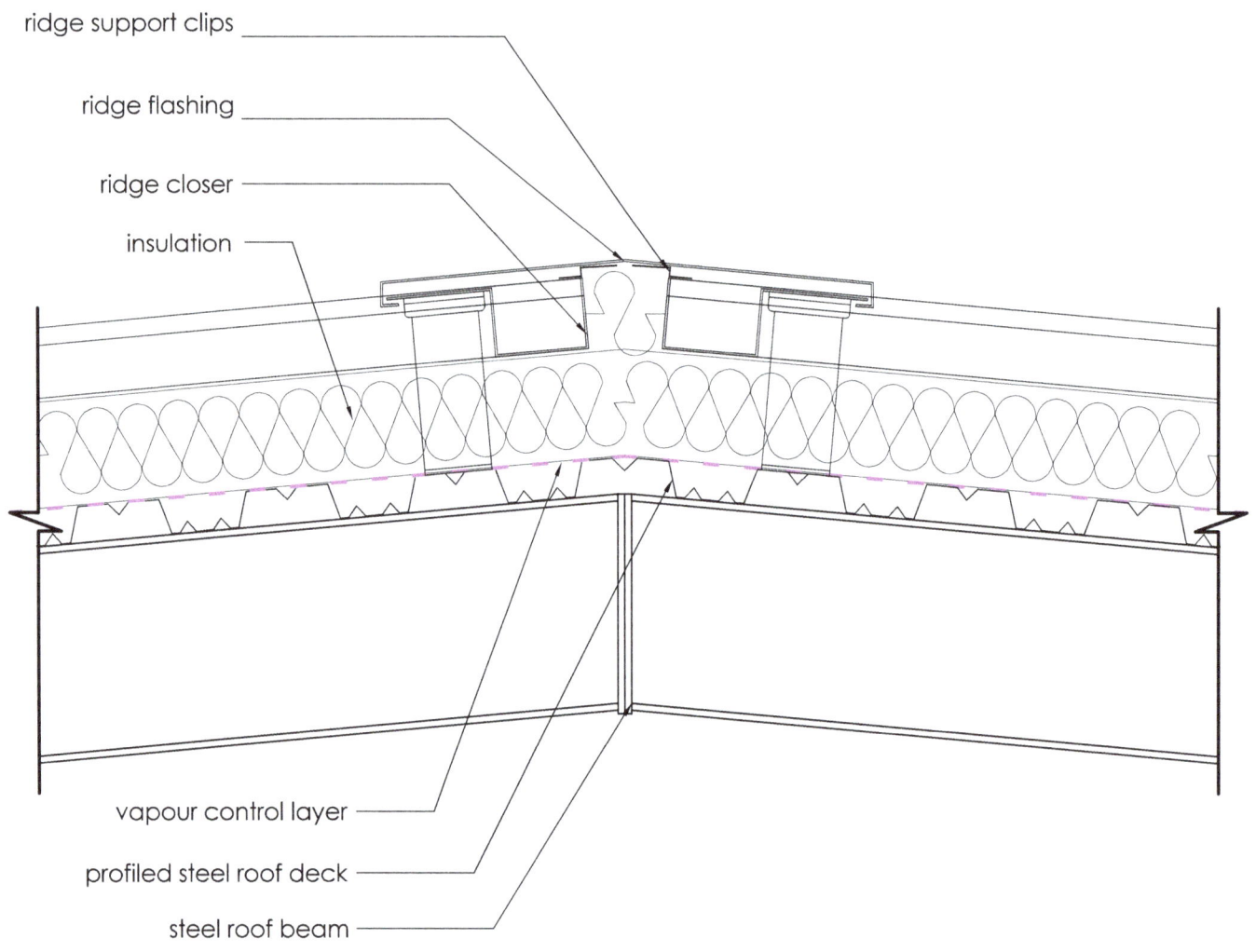

2D Detail R15 - Pitched roof, steel deck, standing seam, ridge detail

SECTION 8 - ROOFS

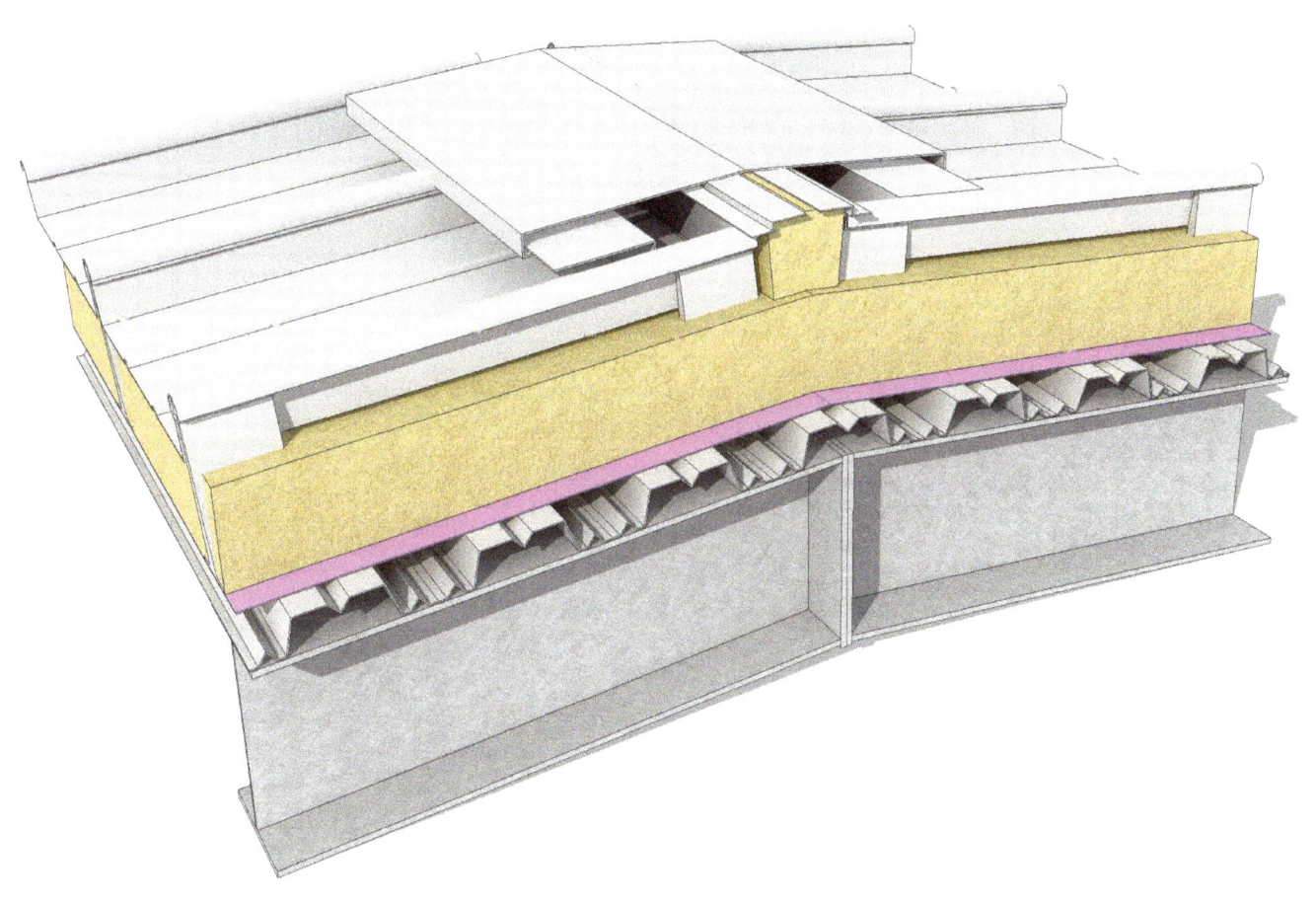

3D Detail R15 - Pitched roof, steel deck, standing seam, ridge detail

R16

PITCHED ROOF, STEEL DECK, STANDING SEAM, VERGE DETAIL

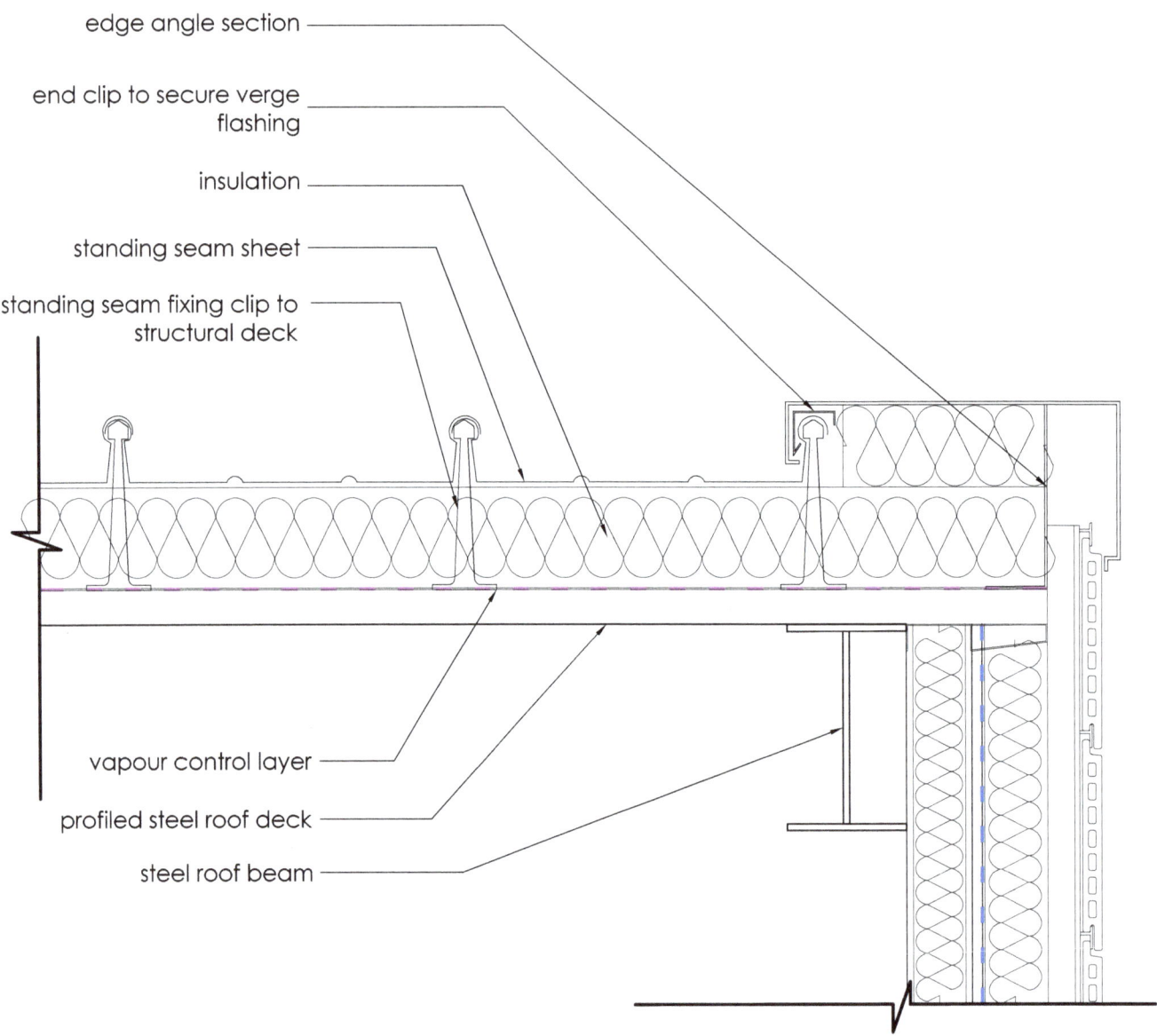

2D Detail R16 - Pitched roof, steel deck, standing seam, verge detail

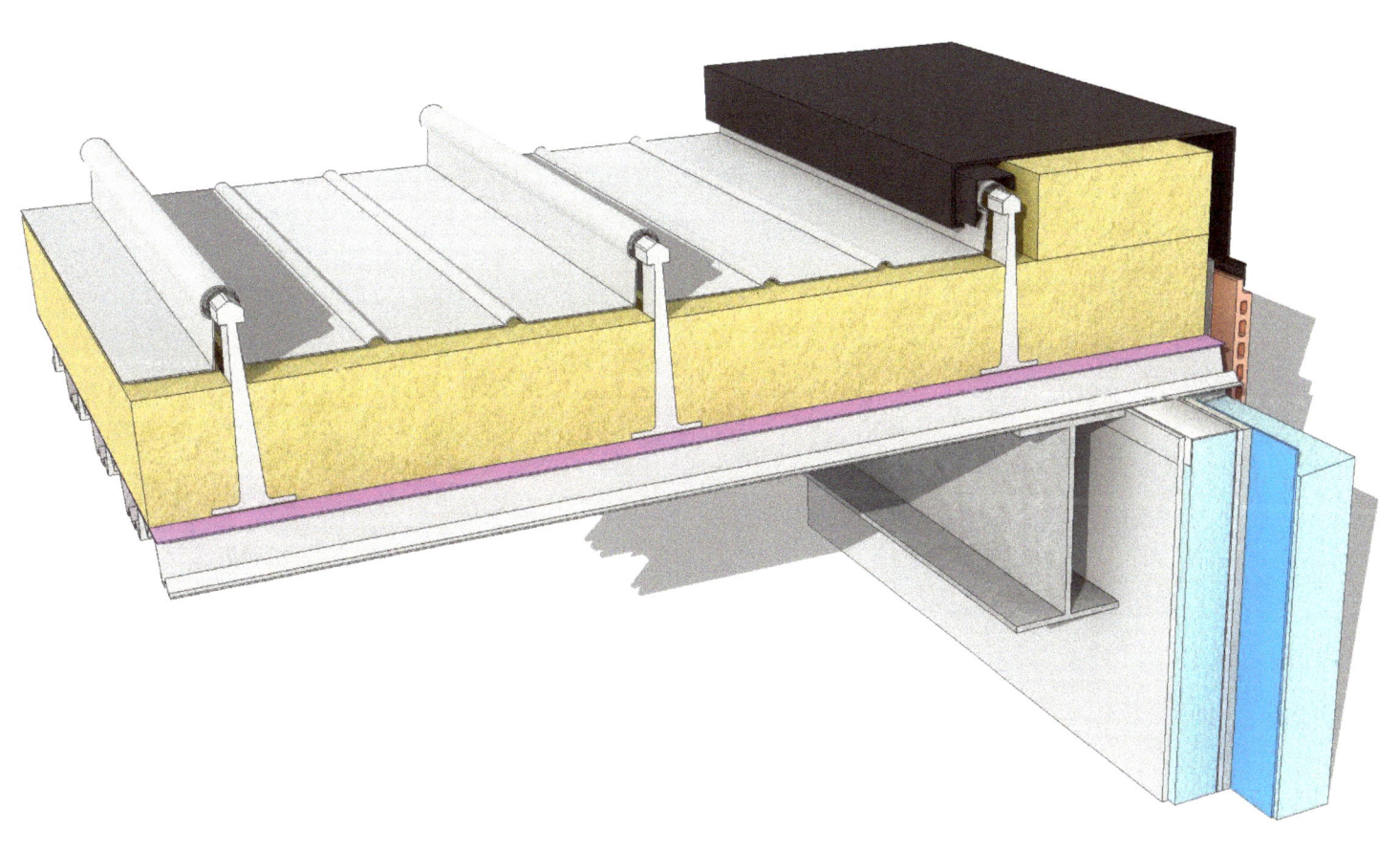

3D Detail R16 - Pitched roof, steel deck, standing seam, verge detail

FLAT ROOF, STEEL CONCRETE COMPOSITE DECK, INTENSIVE GREEN ROOF

Labels (left):
- retention trim
- vegetation
- growing medium
- drainage mat with filter fleece above
- steel deck with structural concrete finish
- vapour control/seperating layer under rigid insulation
- waterproofing layer with root barrier

Labels (right):
- smooth gravel edge channel min 300mm
- waterproof membrane lapped under parapet flashing

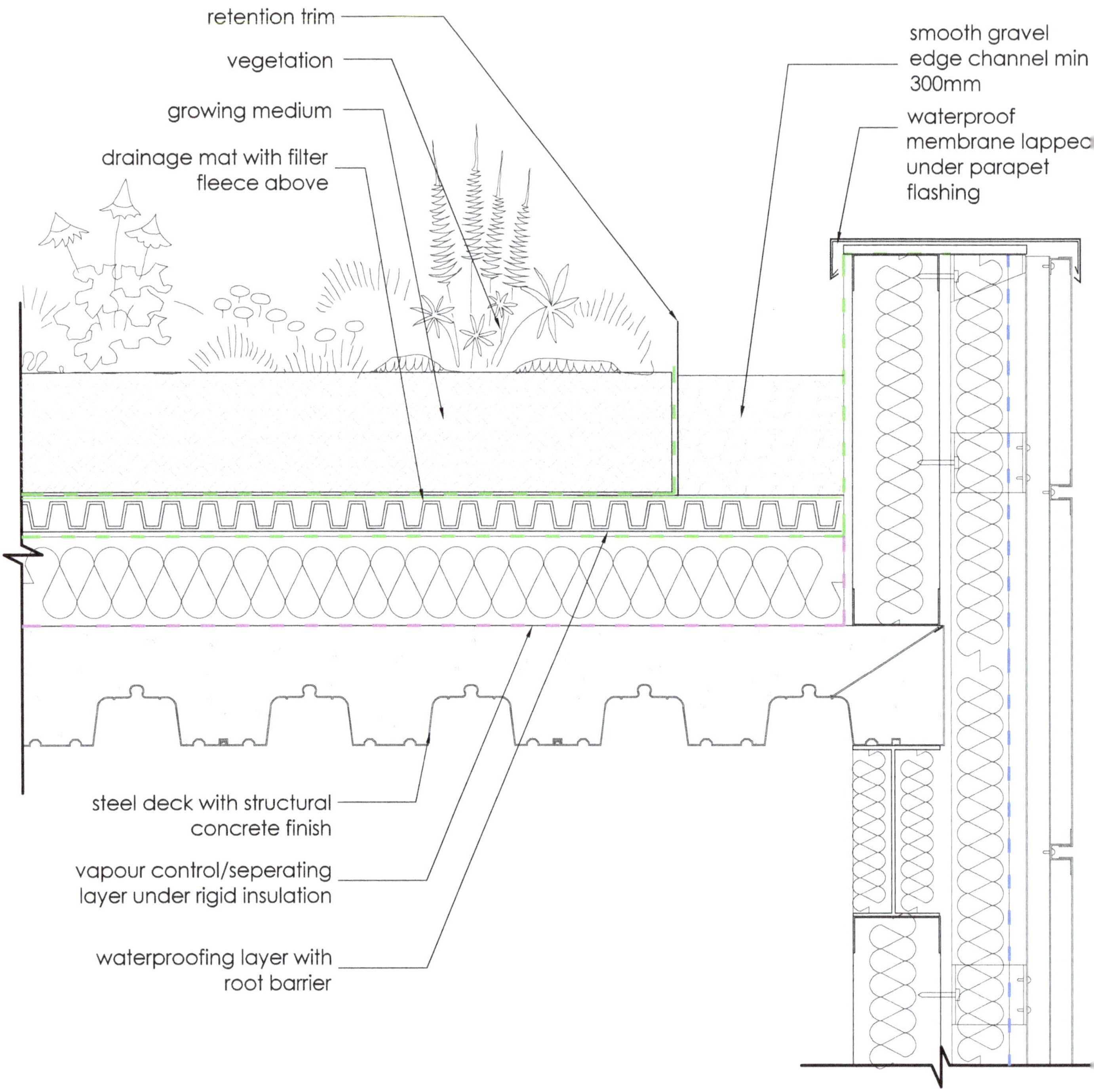

2D Detail R17 - Flat roof, steel concrete composite deck, intensive green roof, parapet

3D Detail R17 - Flat roof, steel concrete composite deck, intensive green roof, parapet

R18

STEEL CONCRETE COMPOSITE DECK, INTENSIVE GREEN ROOF, DRAINAGE OUTLET

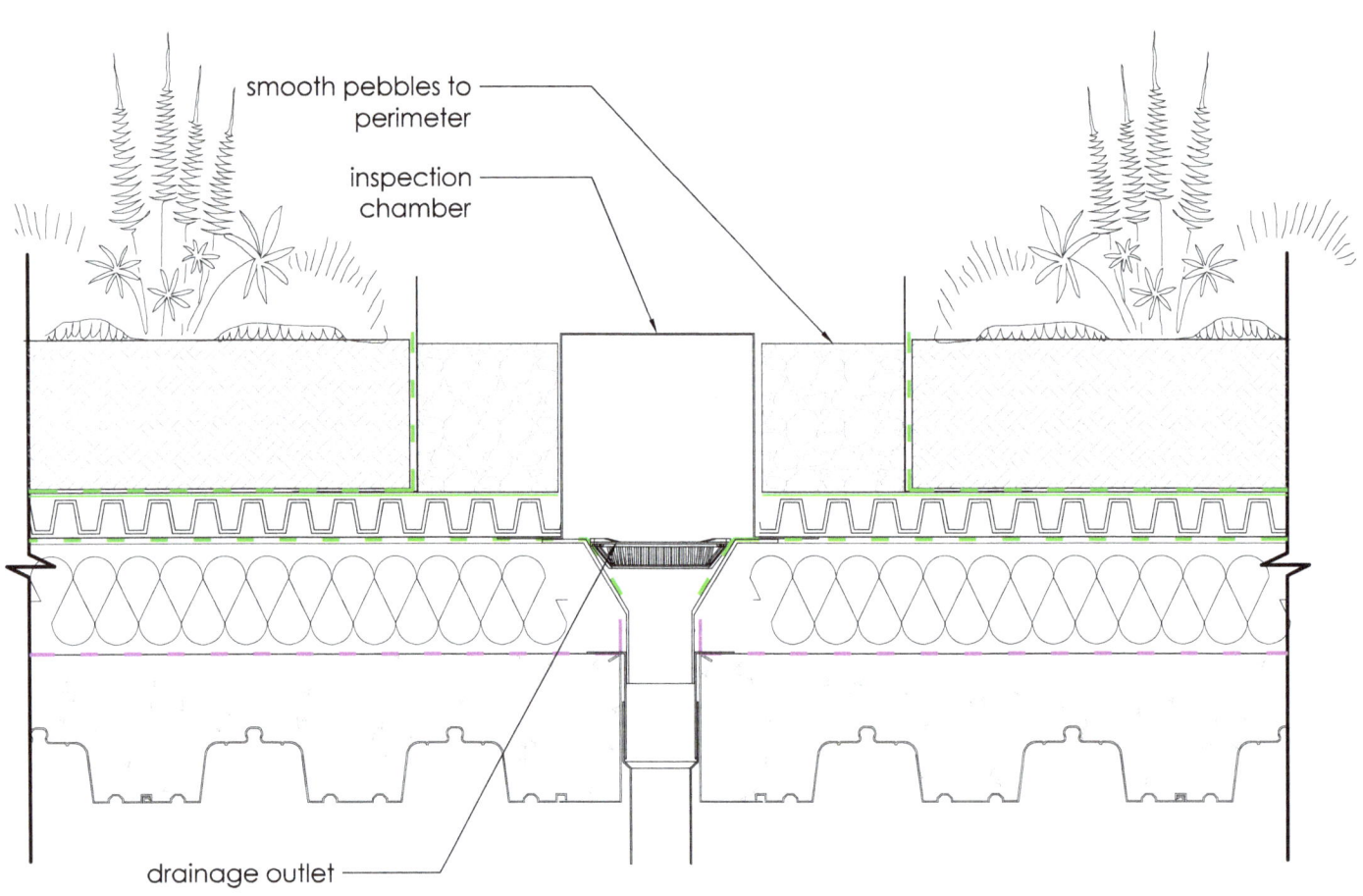

2D Detail R18 - Steel concrete composite deck, intensive green roof, drainage outlet

SECTION 8 - ROOFS

3D Detail R18 - Steel concrete composite deck, intensive green roof, drainage outlet

R19

METAL DECK, EXPOSED ROOF SYSTEM

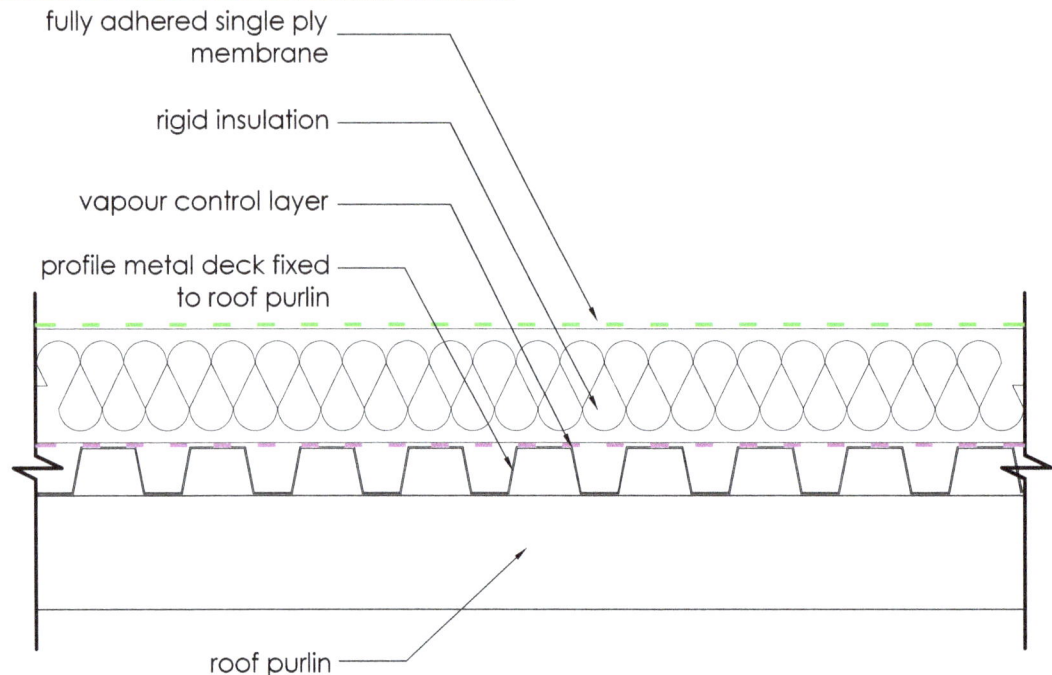

2D Detail R19 - Metal deck, exposed roof system

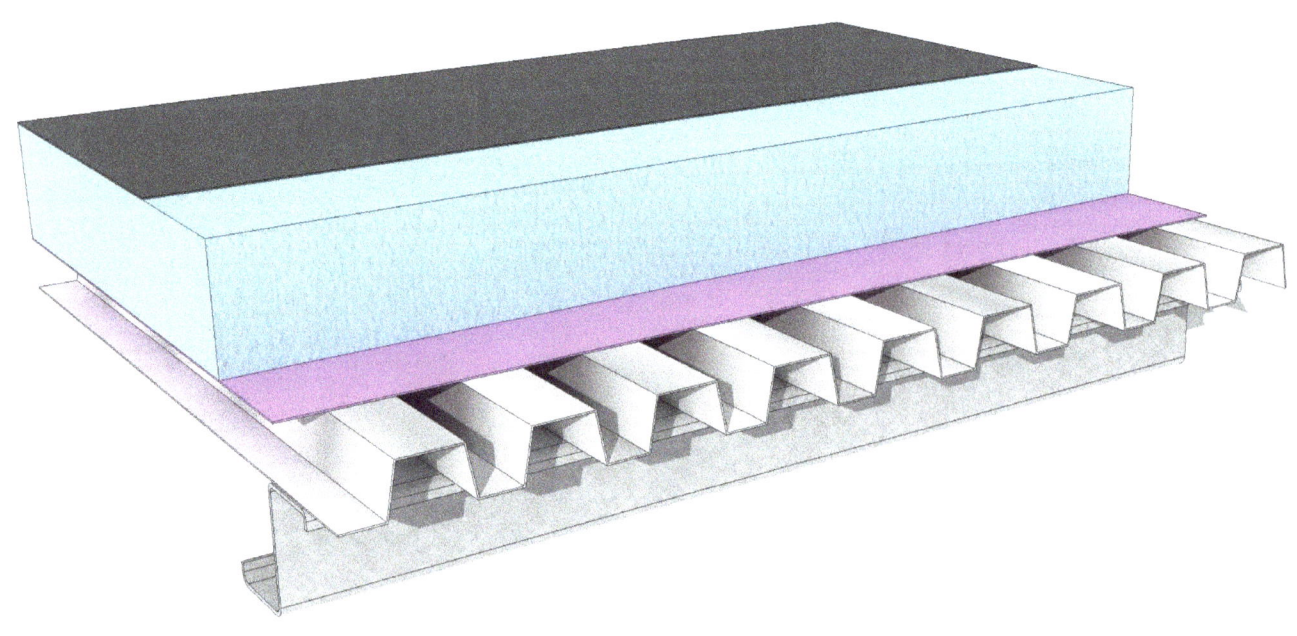

3D Detail R19 - Metal deck, exposed roof system

SECTION 8 - ROOFS

R20

COMPOSITE DECK, EXPOSED ROOF SYSTEM

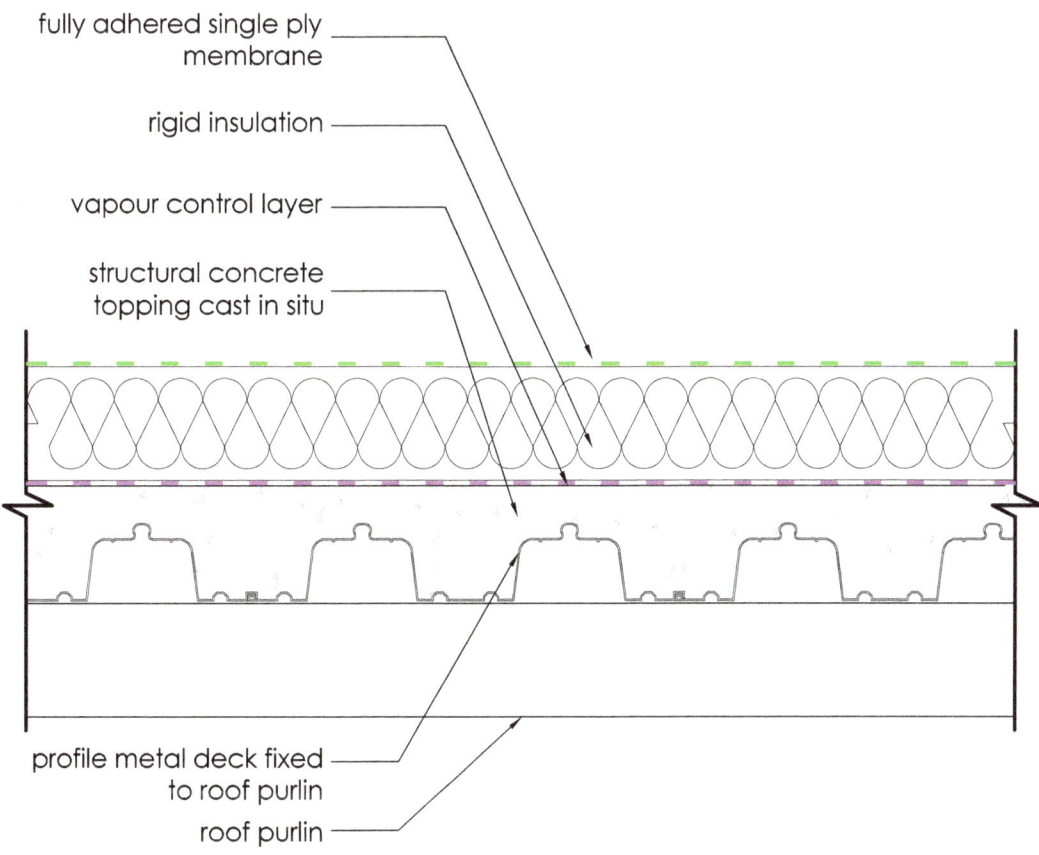

2D Detail R20 - Composite deck, exposed roof system

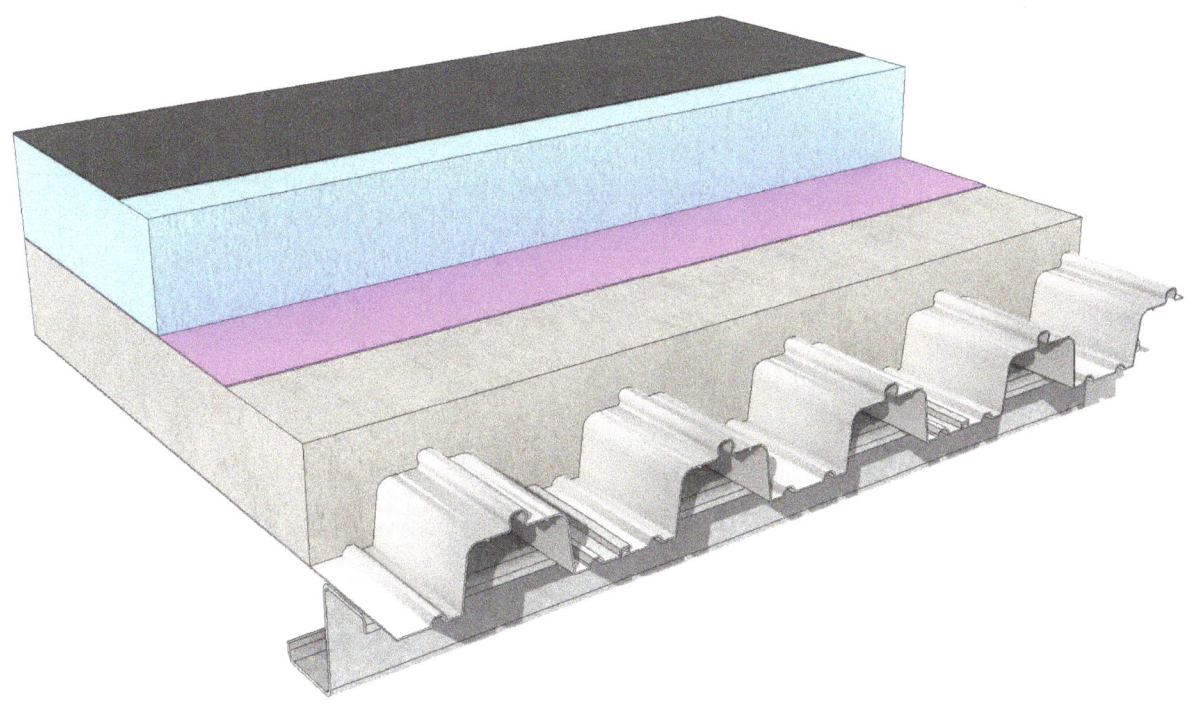

3D Detail R20 - Composite deck, exposed roof system

BIBLIOGRAPHY & FURTHER READING

BOOKS

BADEN POWELL, C., HETREED, J., ROSS, A. (2008) Architects Pocket Book. 3rd Ed. Oxford: Elsevier

CHUDLEY, R., GREENO, R., HURST, M., TOPLISS, S. (2011) Construction Technology. 5th Ed. Essex: Pearson Education Ltd.

CHUDLEY, R., GREENO, R., HURST, M., TOPLISS, S. (2012) Advanced Construction Technology. 5th Ed. Essex: Pearson Education Ltd.

EMMITT, S., GORSE C (2014) Advanced Construction of Buildings. 3rd Ed. Chichester: John Wiley & Sons Ltd.

EMMITT, S., GORSE C (2014) Introduction to Construction of Buildings. 3rd Ed. Chichester: John Wiley & Sons Ltd.

FLEMING, E (2005) Construction Technology. Oxford: Blackwell Publishing Ltd.

LYONS, A (2010) Materials for Architects and Builders. 4th Ed. Oxford: Elsevier.

MCMULLAN, R (2007) Environmental Science in Building. 6th Ed. Basingstoke: Palgrave Macmillan.

PECK, M (2014) Modern Concrete Construction Manual. Munich: Institut fur internationale Architektur-Dokumentation GmbH & Co.

RILEY, M., COTGRAVE, A. (2014) Construction Technology 2: Industrial & Commercial Building. 3rd Ed. Basingstoke: Palgrave Macmillan.

TRICKER, R., ALFORD, S, (2014) Building Regulations In Brief. 8th Ed. Abingdon: Routledge.

WATTS, A (2013) Modern Construction Handbook. 3rd Ed. Austria: Ambra |V

Also consider the wide range of well known manufacturers who have a wealth of explanatory documentation relating to their products and systems.

WEBSITES

Building Regulations Approved Documents
https://www.gov.uk/government/collections/approved-documents

British Standards Institution
https://www.bsigroup.com/en-GB/standards/british-standards-online-database/BSOL-Construction/

BRE
https://bregroup.com
https://www.brebookshop.com

Environment Agency
www.environment-agency.gov.uk

GreenSpec
http://www.greenspec.co.uk

Zinc information centre
http://www.zincinfocentre.org

TRADA (Timber Research and Development Association)
https://www.trada.co.uk

Timber Trade Federation
http://www.ttf.co.uk

Stone Federation
http://www.stonefed.org.uk

Glass and Glazing Federation
https://www.ggf.org.uk

Copper Development Association
www.cda.org.uk

Concrete Centre
https://www.concretecentre.com

FIGURE INDEX

Fig 1.1 - Factors influencing the impact of the external environment — 10
Fig 1.2 Forces leading to moisture ingress — 11
Fig 1.3 Neutralising moisture ingress — 11
Fig 1.4 - Table of U Value requirements for buildings other than dwellings — 13
Fig 1.5 - Table of thermal conductivity of common construction materials — 14
Fig 1.6 - Image showing thermal bridge at junction, and solution to improve performance — 16
Fig 1.7 - Forces driving airflow through the building enclosure — 18
Fig 1.8 - Typical leakage paths through the building envelope — 18
Fig 1.9 - Wind pressure effects — 19
Fig 1.10 - Stack effect pressures — 19
Fig 1.11 - Provisions for cavity barriers - Approved Document Part B2 — 23
Fig 1.12 - Table A1 from Approved Document Part B2 — 25
Fig 1.13 - Table A2 from Approved Document Part B2 — 27
Fig 2.1 - Forces leading to moisture ingress — 31
Fig 2.2 - Wash of a parapet flashing, and a flat roof with insulation cut to falls — 32
Fig 2.3 - Wash of a door threshold sill — 32
Fig 2.4 - Overlap of ridge flashing — 33
Fig 2.5 - Overlap flashing to roof light and tiles — 33
Fig 2.6 - Overlap flashing to edge detail — 33
Fig 2.7 - Overhang and drip of parapet coping/flashing — 34
Fig 2.8 - Overhang and drip of sill — 34
Fig 2.9 - Overhang and drip of eaves — 34
Fig 2.10 - Capillary break of window flashing — 35
Fig 2.12 - Drain and weep of rainscreen cladding — 35
Fig 2.13 - Drain and weep of cavity wall — 35
Fig 2.11 - Capillary break in vertical panel joint — 35
Fig 2.14 - Labyrinth in both vertical and horizontal joints between panels — 36
Fig 2.15 - Vapour control layer — 37
Fig 2.16 - Breather membrane — 37
Fig 2.19 - Cavity closer with PU/PIR insulation core, insulation under internal window sill — 40
Fig 2.17 - Insulated plasterboard reveal to window head with insulated lintel — 40
Fig 2.18 - Insulated plasterboard reveal and PU/PIR insulated cavity closer to window jamb — 40
Fig 2.20 - Increased insulation around parapet — 41
Fig 2.21 - Increased insulation at slab perimeter, with cavity insulation extending below floor insulation — 41
Fig 2.22 - Additional insulation on inside face of steel frame construction — 41
Fig 3.1 - Table of embodied energy of construction materials — 45
Fig 3.2 - Typical thermal conductivity of insulation materials — 59
Fig 3.3 - Laminated glass types — 60
Fig 3.4 - Table showing standard U-values for glazing systems — 61
Fig 3.5 - How low emissivity glass works — 62
Fig 3.6 - How solar control glass works — 62
Fig 4.1 - Typical subsoil bearing capacity — 66
Fig 4.2 - Types of foundation — 68
Fig 4.3 - Strip and deep strip foundation examples — 69
Fig 4.4 - Raft foundation example — 71
Fig 4.5 - Pad foundation examples — 71
Fig 4.6 - Pile foundation example — 72
Fig 4.7 - Factors affecting foundation selection — 73
Fig 4.8 - Example of ground bearing floor — 94

Fig 4.9 - Example of damp proof membrane positions	95
Fig 4.10 - Grid beam and slab floor	97
Fig 4.12 - Waffle grid slab	97
Fig 4.14 - Flat slab	97
Fig 4.11 - Ribbed slab	97
Fig 4.13 - Drop beam slab	97
Fig 4.15 - Beam and Block flooring	98
Fig 4.16 - Hollow beam floor units	99
Fig 4.17 - Rib deck concrete floor	100
Fig 4.18 - Fixing precast unit to steel beam	100
Fig 4.19 - Prestressed concrete floor units	101
Fig. 5.1 - Table of basement grades adapted from BS8102	149
Fig. 5.2 - Type A - Barrier protection	150
Fig. 5.3 - Examples of Type A tanking systems	151
Fig. 5.4 - Type B protection	152
Fig. 5.5 - Type B protection types and examples	153
Fig. 5.6 - Type C protection	153
Fig. 5.7 - Type C protection examples	154
Fig. 5.8 - PVC waterstop	155
Fig. 5.9 - Rubber waterstop	155
Fig. 6.1 - Steel frame structure with lattice beams in roof construction	178
Fig. 6.2 - Steel frame structure with lattice truss in roof construction	178
Fig. 6.3 - Portal frame structure	179
Fig. 6.4 - Skeleton frame	179
Fig. 6.5 - Flat slab construction	181
Fig. 6.6 - Ribbed slab construction	181
Fig. 6.7 - Beam and slab construction	182
Fig. 6.8 - Crosswall construction	184
Fig. 6.9 - Types of steel sections	185
Fig. 6.10 - Base connection of steel frame to concrete foundation, complete and section	186
Fig. 6.11 - Long span frame examples	187
Fig 7.1 - Solid concrete wall system	215
Fig 7.3 - Composite cladding system	217
Fig 7.4 - Concrete cladding system	218
Fig 7.5 - Brick slip cladding system	219
Fig 7.6 - Sheet metal cladding system	220
Fig 7.7 - Render cladding system	220
Fig 7.8 - Rainscreen cladding system	221
Fig 7.9 - Concrete rainscreen cladding system	222
Fig 7.10 Green wall system example	223
Fig 7.11 Green wall system example	225
Fig 7.12 Green wall system module	225
Fig 8.1 - Pitched roof example	301
Fig 8.2 - Flat roof example	302
Fig 8.3 - Cast in situ roof deck	303
Fig 8.4 - Metal deck roof	303
Fig 8.5 - Cold deck	304
Fig 8.6 - Warm deck	305
Fig 8.7 - Inverted roof deck	305
Fig 8.8 - Factors affecting roof selection	306
Fig 8.9 - Green roof example	307

2D DETAIL INDEX

2D Detail G01 - Simple strip foundation — 74
2D Detail G02 - Deep strip or mass/trench fill foundation — 76
2D Detail G03 - Simple raft foundation — 78
2D Detail G04 - Simple raft foundation with downstand beam — 79
2D Detail G05 - Simple raft foundation with downstand and toe — 80
2D Detail G06 - Simple reinforced pad foundation — 81
2D Detail G07 - Pad foundation with support piers and ground beam — 82
2D Detail G08 - Pad foundation with ground beam — 84
2D Detail G09 - Pile foundation with ground beam — 86
2D Detail G10 - Precast concrete column connection to foundation — 88
2D Detail G11 - Precast concrete column connection to foundation - alternative — 89
2D Detail G12 - Steel column connection to foundation — 90
2D Detail F01 - Ground bearing concrete floor, insulation below slab — 102
2D Detail F02 - Ground bearing concrete floor, insulation above slab — 103
2D Detail F03 - Ground bearing concrete floor, insulation above slab — 104
2D Detail F04 - Ground bearing concrete floor, strip foundation — 106
2D Detail F05 - Ground bearing concrete floor, raft foundation — 108
2D Detail F06 - Ground bearing concrete floor, raft foundation - alternative — 110
2D Detail F07 - Solid concrete ground bearing slab - timber floor on battens — 112
2D Detail F08 - Solid concrete ground bearing slab - screed finish with underfloor heating — 113
2D Detail F09 - Cast in situ reinforced concrete floor - raised access floor — 114
2D Detail F10 - Ground bearing concrete floor, typical internal load bearing wall — 116
2D Detail F11 - Ground bearing concrete floor, typical internal light load bearing wall — 118
2D Detail F12 - Ground bearing concrete floor, typical internal non load bearing wall — 119
2D Detail F13 - Suspended concrete floor, beam and block, screed finish — 120
2D Detail F14 - Suspended concrete floor, beam and block, timber floor finish — 121
2D Detail F15 - Suspended concrete floor, beam and EPS block — 122
2D Detail F16 - Suspended concrete floor, precast beam and hollow filler block — 123
2D Detail F17 - Suspended concrete floor, precast hollow floor unit — 124
2D Detail F18 - Suspended concrete floor, beam and block, ground floor — 126
2D Detail F19 - Suspended concrete floor, beam and block, beams parallel with wall, upper floor — 128
2D Detail F20 - Suspended concrete floor, precast hollow beam and block, upper floor — 130
2D Detail F21 - Suspended concrete floor, precast concrete plank system — 132
2D Detail F22 - Cast in situ reinforced concrete upper floor — 134
2D Detail F23 - Timber floor finish on battens — 136
2D Detail F24 - Insulated floating floor — 136
2D Detail F25 - Insulated floor with underfloor heating, intermittent heating applications — 136
2D Detail F26 - Suspended floor, steel deck and concrete floor composite — 138
2D Detail F27 - Suspended floor, precast hollow floor beam junction — 140
2D Detail F28 - Suspended floor, precast hollow floor beam — 142
2D Detail F29 - Suspended floor, precast beam and hollow block junction — 144
2D Detail B01 - External tanking, (with or without integral protection) — 158
2D Detail B02 - External tanking, external insulation (with or without integral protection) — 160
2D Detail B03 - Sandwich tanking, (with or without integral protection) — 162
2D Detail B04 - External tanking, insulated concrete formwork construction — 164
2D Detail B05 - External tanking, blockwork basement wall construction — 166
2D Detail B06 - Drained cavity, watertight reinforced concrete construction — 168
2D Detail B07 - Drained cavity, external tanking — 170
2D Detail B08 - Drained cavity, blockwork construction, internal insulation — 172
2D Detail B09 - Soffit detail — 174

2D Detail B10- Wall head detail	174
2D Detail P01 - Wall to floor junction with masonry wall	190
2D Detail P02 - Wall to floor junction drip detail	192
2D Detail P03 - Wall to floor junction flush drip detail	194
2D Detail P04 - Window head and sill detail	196
2D Detail P05 - Window jamb detail - plan	198
2D Detail P06- External corner detail - plan	199
2D Detail P07 - Door head detail	200
2D Detail P08- Door jamb detail - plan	201
2D Detail P09 - Ridge detail	202
2D Detail P10- Eaves detail	203
2D Detail P11 - Eaves detail with integrated gutter	204
2D Detail P12 - Parapet detail	206
2D Detail P13 - Mono-ridge detail	208
2D Detail P14 - Verge detail	210
2D Detail W01 - Concrete cladding panel, concrete backing wall	226
2D Detail W02 - Concrete cladding panel, base detail	227
2D Detail W03 - Concrete cladding panel, window head detail	228
2D Detail W04 - Concrete cladding panel, window sill detail	229
2D Detail W05 - Concrete cladding panel, window jamb detail (plan)	230
2D Detail W06 - Concrete cladding panel, parapet detail	231
2D Detail W07 - Sheet metal, standing seam	232
2D Detail W08 - Sheet metal, standing seam, base detail	233
2D Detail W09 - Sheet metal, standing seam, window head detail	234
2D Detail W10 - Sheet metal, standing seam, window sill detail	235
2D Detail W11 - Sheet metal, standing seam, window jamb detail (plan)	236
2D Detail W12 - Sheet metal, standing seam, parapet detail	237
2D Detail W13 - Sheet metal standing seam, lgsf	238
2D Detail W14 - Sheet metal standing seam, lgsf, base detail	239
2D Detail W15 - Sheet metal standing seam, lgsf, window head detail	240
2D Detail W16 - Sheet metal standing seam, lgsf, window sill detail	241
2D Detail W17 - Sheet metal standing seam, lgsf, window jamb detail (plan)	242
2D Detail W18 - Sheet metal standing seam, lgsf, parapet detail	243
2D Detail W19 - Composite cladding panel, lgsf	244
2D Detail W20 - Composite cladding panel, lgsf, base detail	245
2D Detail W21 - Composite cladding panel, lgsf, window head detail	246
2D Detail W22 - Composite cladding panel, lgsf, window sill detail	247
2D Detail W23 - Composite cladding panel, lgsf, window jamb detail (plan)	248
2D Detail W24 - Composite cladding panel, lgsf, panel joint detail	248
2D Detail W25 - Composite cladding panel, lgsf, parapet detail	249
2D Detail W26 - Insulated render, lgsf	250
2D Detail W27 - Insulated render, lgsf, base detail	251
2D Detail W28 - Insulated render, lgsf, window head detail	252
2D Detail W29 - Insulated render, lgsf, window sill detail	253
2D Detail W30 - Insulated render, lgsf, window jamb detail (plan)	254
2D Detail W31 - Insulated render, lgsf, parapet detail	255
2D Detail W32 - Brick slips, concrete backing wall	256
2D Detail W33 - Insulated brick slips, concrete backing wall, base detail	257
2D Detail W34 - Insulated brick slips, window head detail	258
2D Detail W35 - Insulated brick slips, window sill detail	259
2D Detail W36 - Insulated brick slips, window jamb detail (plan)	260
2D Detail W37 - Insulated brick slips, parapet detail	261
2D Detail W38 - Terracotta rainscreen cladding, concrete backing wall	262
2D Detail W39 - Terracotta rainscreen cladding, base detail	263
2D Detail W40 - Terracotta rainscreen cladding, window head detail	264
2D Detail W41 - Terracotta rainscreen cladding, window sill detail	265
2D Detail W42 - Terracotta rainscreen cladding, window jamb detail (plan)	266

2D Detail W43 - Terracotta rainscreen cladding, parapet detail	267
2D Detail W44 - Concrete rainscreen panel, light gauge steel frame (lgsf)	268
2D Detail W45 - Concrete rainscreen panel, lgsf, base detail	269
2D Detail W46 - Concrete rainscreen panel, lgsf, window head detail	270
2D Detail W47 - Concrete rainscreen panel, lgsf, window sill detail	271
2D Detail W48 - Concrete rainscreen panel, lgsf, window jamb detail	272
2D Detail W49 - Concrete rainscreen panel, lgsf, parapet detail	273
2D Detail W50 - Metal rainscreen cladding, light gauge steel frame (lgsf)	274
2D Detail W51 - Metal rainscreen cladding, lgsf, base detail	275
2D Detail W52 - Metal rainscreen cladding, window head detail	276
2D Detail W53 - Metal rainscreen cladding, lgsf, window sill detail	277
2D Detail W54 - Metal rainscreen cladding, window jamb detail (plan)	278
2D Detail W55 - Metal rainscreen cladding, lgsf, parapet detail	279
2D Detail W56 - Timber rainscreen cladding, concrete backing wall	280
2D Detail W57 - Timber rainscreen cladding, base detail	281
2D Detail W58 - Timber rainscreen cladding, window head detail	282
2D Detail W59 - Timber rainscreen cladding, window sill detail	283
2D Detail W60 - Timber rainscreen cladding, window jamb detail (plan)	284
2D Detail W61 - Timber rainscreen cladding, parapet detail	285
2D Detail W62 - Stone rainscreen cladding, concrete backing wall	286
2D Detail W63 - Stone rainscreen cladding, base detail	287
2D Detail W64 - Stone rainscreen cladding, window head detail	288
2D Detail W65 - Stone rainscreen cladding, window sill detail	289
2D Detail W66 - Stone rainscreen cladding, window jamb detail	290
2D Detail W67 - Stone rainscreen cladding, parapet detail	291
2D Detail W68 - Stone rainscreen cladding, light gauge steel frame (lgsf)	292
2D Detail W69 - Stone rainscreen cladding, lgsf, base detail	293
2D Detail W70 - Stone rainscreen cladding, lgsf, window head detail	294
2D Detail W71 - Stone rainscreen cladding, lgsf, window sill detail	295
2D Detail W72 - Stone rainscreen cladding, lgsf, window jamb detail (plan)	296
2D Detail W73 - Stone rainscreen cladding, lgsf, parapet detail	297
2D Detail R01 - Concrete cast in situ, single ply, warm deck	310
2D Detail R02 - Concrete cast in situ, single ply, rainwater outlet	311
2D Detail R03 - Concrete cast in situ, single ply, upstand	312
2D Detail R04 - Concrete cast in situ, single ply, rooflight	313
2D Detail R05 - Concrete cast in situ, threshold detail (balcony)	314
2D Detail R06 - Concrete cast in situ, liquid applied, inverted roof	315
2D Detail R07 - Concrete cast in situ, liquid applied, rainwater outlet	316
2D Detail R08 - Concrete cast in situ, liquid applied, roof light	317
2D Detail R09 - Concrete cast in situ, liquid applied, threshold detail	318
2D Detail R10 - Concrete cast in situ, green roof	319
2D Detail R11 - Concrete cast in situ, green roof, drainage outlet	320
2D Detail R12 - Concrete cast in situ, green roof, roof light	321
2D Detail R13 - Concrete cast in situ, green roof, upstand	322
2D Detail R14 - Pitched roof, steel deck, standing seam, parapet	324
2D Detail R15 - Pitched roof, steel deck, standing seam, ridge detail	326
2D Detail R16 - Pitched roof, steel deck, standing seam, verge detail	328
2D Detail R17 - Flat roof, steel concrete composite deck, intensive green roof, parapet	330
2D Detail R18 - Steel concrete composite deck, intensive green roof, drainage outlet	332
2D Detail R19 - Metal deck, exposed roof system	334
2D Detail R20 - Composite deck, exposed roof system	335

3D DETAIL INDEX

3D Detail G01 - Simple strip foundation	75
3D Detail G02 - Deep strip or mass/trench fill foundation	77
3D Detail G03 - Simple raft foundation	78
3D Detail G04 - Simple raft foundation with downstand beam	79
3D Detail G05 - Simple raft foundation with downstand and toe	80
3D Detail G06 - Simple reinforced pad foundation	81
3D Detail G07 - Pad foundation with support piers and ground beam	83
3D Detail G08 - Pad foundation with ground beam	85
3D Detail G09 - Pile foundation with ground beam	87
3D Detail G10 - Precast concrete column connection to foundation	88
3D Detail G11 - Precast concrete column connection to foundation - alternative	89
3D Detail G12 - Steel column connection to foundation	90
3D Detail F01- Ground bearing concrete floor, insulation below slab	102
3D Detail F02- Ground bearing concrete floor, insulation above slab	103
3D Detail F03- Ground bearing concrete floor, insulation above slab	105
3D Detail F04- Ground bearing concrete floor, strip foundation	107
3D Detail F05- Ground bearing concrete floor, raft foundation	109
3D Detail F06- Ground bearing concrete floor, raft foundation - alternative	111
3D Detail F07- Solid concrete ground bearing slab - timber floor on battens	112
3D Detail F08- Solid concrete ground bearing slab - screed finish with underfloor heating	113
3D Detail F09- Cast in situ reinforced concrete floor - raised access floor	114
3D Detail F10- Ground bearing concrete floor, typical internal load bearing wall	117
3D Detail F11- Ground bearing concrete floor, typical internal light load bearing wall	118
3D Detail F12- Ground bearing concrete floor, typical internal non load bearing wall	119
3D Detail F13- Suspended concrete floor, beam and block, screed finish	120
3D Detail F14- Suspended concrete floor, beam and block, timber floor finish	121
3D Detail F15- Suspended concrete floor, beam and EPS block	122
3D Detail F16- Suspended concrete floor, precast beam and hollow filler block	123
3D Detail F17- Suspended concrete floor, precast hollow floor unit	124
3D Detail F18- Suspended concrete floor, beam and block, ground floor	127
3D Detail F19- Suspended concrete floor, beam and block, beams parallel with wall, upper floor	129
3D Detail F20- Suspended concrete floor, precast hollow beam and block, upper floor	131
3D Detail F21- Suspended concrete floor, precast concrete plank system	133
3D Detail F22- Cast in situ reinforced concrete floor	135
3D Detail F23- Timber floor finish on battens	137
3D Detail F24- Insulated floating floor	137
3D Detail F25- Insulated floor with underfloor heating, intermittent heating applications	137
3D Detail F26- Suspended floor, steel deck and concrete floor composite	139
3D Detail F27- Suspended floor, precast hollow floor beam junction	141
3D Detail F28- Suspended floor, precast hollow floor beam	143
3D Detail F29- Suspended floor, precast beam and hollow block junction	145
3D Detail B01 - External tanking, (with or without integral protection)	159
3D Detail B02 - External tanking, external insulation (with or without integral protection)	161
3D Detail B03 - Sandwich tanking, (with or without integral protection)	163
3D Detail B04 - External tanking, insulated concrete formwork construction	165
3D Detail B05 - External tanking, blockwork basement wall construction	167
3D Detail B06 - Drained cavity, watertight reinforced concrete construction	169
3D Detail B07 - Drained cavity, external tanking	171
3D Detail B08 - Drained cavity, blockwork construction, internal insulation	173
3D Detail B09 - Soffit detail	175

3D Detail B10 - Wall head detail	175
3D Detail P01 - Wall to floor junction with masonry wall	191
3D Detail P02 - Wall to floor junction drip detail	193
3D Detail P03 - Wall to floor junction flush drip detail	195
3D Detail P04 - Window head and sill detail	197
3D Detail P05 - Window jamb detail	198
3D Detail P06 - External corner detail	199
3D Detail P07 - Door head detail	200
3D Detail P08 - Door jamb detail	201
3D Detail P09 - Ridge detail	202
3D Detail P10 - Eaves detail	203
3D Detail P11 - Eaves detail with integrated gutter	205
3D Detail P12 - Parapet detail	207
3D Detail P13 - Mono-ridge detail	209
3D Detail P14 - Verge detail	211
3D Detail W01 - Concrete cladding panel, concrete backing wall	226
3D Detail W02 - Concrete cladding panel, base detail	227
3D Detail W03 - Concrete cladding panel, window head detail	228
3D Detail W04 - Concrete cladding panel, window sill detail	229
3D Detail W05 - Concrete cladding panel, window jamb detail	230
3D Detail W06 - Concrete cladding panel, parapet detail	231
3D Detail W07 - Sheet metal, standing seam	232
3D Detail W08 - Sheet metal, standing seam, base detail	233
3D Detail W09 - Sheet metal, standing seam, window head detail	234
3D Detail W10 - Sheet metal, standing seam, window sill detail	235
3D Detail W11 - Sheet metal, standing seam, window jamb detail	236
3D Detail W12 - Sheet metal, standing seam, parapet detail	237
3D Detail W13 - Sheet metal standing seam, lgsf	238
3D Detail W14 - Sheet metal standing seam, lgsf, base detail	239
3D Detail W15 - Sheet metal standing seam, lgsf, window head detail	240
3D Detail W16 - Sheet metal standing seam, window sill detail	241
3D Detail W17 - Sheet metal standing seam, lgsf, window jamb detail	242
3D Detail W18 - Sheet metal standing seam, parapet detail	243
3D Detail W19 - Composite cladding panel, lgsf	244
3D Detail W20 - Composite cladding panel, lgsf, base detail	245
3D Detail W21 - Composite cladding panel, lgsf, window head detail	246
3D Detail W22 - Composite cladding panel, lgsf, window sill detail	247
3D Detail W23 - Composite cladding panel, lgsf, window jamb detail	248
3D Detail W25 - Composite cladding panel, lgsf, parapet detail	249
3D Detail W26 - Insulated render, lgsf	250
3D Detail W27 - Insulated render, lgsf, base detail	251
3D Detail W28 - Insulated render, lgsf, window head detail	252
3D Detail W29 - Insulated render, lgsf, window sill detail	253
3D Detail W30 - Insulated render, lgsf, window jamb detail	254
3D Detail W31 - Insulated render, lgsf, parapet detail	255
3D Detail W32 - Brick slips, concrete backing wall	256
3D Detail W33 - Insulated brick slips, concrete backing wall, base detail	257
3D Detail W34 - Insulated brick slips, window head detail	258
3D Detail W35 - Insulated brick slips, window sill detail	259
3D Detail W36 - Insulated brick slips, window jamb detail	260
3D Detail W37 - Insulated brick slips, parapet detail	261
3D Detail W38 - Terracotta rainscreen cladding, concrete backing wall	262
3D Detail W39 - Terracotta rainscreen cladding, base detail	263
3D Detail W40 - Terracotta rainscreen cladding, window head detail	264
3D Detail W41- Terracotta rainscreen cladding, window sill detail	265
3D Detail W42 - Terracotta rainscreen cladding, window jamb detail	266

3D Detail W43- Terracotta rainscreen cladding, parapet detail	267
3D Detail W44 - Concrete rainscreen panel, light gauge steel frame (lgsf)	268
3D Detail W45- Concrete rainscreen panel, lgsf, base detail	269
3D Detail W46 - Concrete rainscreen panel, lgsf, window head detail	270
3D Detail W47- Concrete rainscreen panel, lgsf, window sill detail	271
3D Detail W48 - Concrete rainscreen panel, lgsf, window jamb detail	272
3D Detail W49- Concrete rainscreen panel, lgsf, parapet detail	273
3D Detail W50 - Metal rainscreen cladding, light gauge steel frame (lgsf)	274
3D Detail W51- Metal rainscreen cladding, lgsf, base detail	275
3D Detail W52 - Metal rainscreen cladding, window head detail	276
3D Detail W53- Metal rainscreen cladding, lgsf, window sill detail	277
3D Detail W54 - Metal rainscreen cladding, window jamb detail	278
3D Detail W55- Metal rainscreen cladding, lgsf, parapet detail	279
3D Detail W56 - Timber rainscreen cladding, concrete backing wall	280
3D Detail W57- Timber rainscreen cladding, base detail	281
3D Detail W58 - Timber rainscreen cladding, window head detail	282
3D Detail W59 - Timber rainscreen cladding, window sill detail	283
3D Detail W60 - Timber rainscreen cladding, window jamb detail	284
3D Detail W61 - Timber rainscreen cladding, parapet detail	285
3D Detail W62 - Stone rainscreen cladding, concrete backing wall	286
3D Detail W63 - Stone rainscreen cladding, base detail	287
3D Detail W64 - Stone rainscreen cladding, window head detail	288
3D Detail W65 - Stone rainscreen cladding, window sill detail	289
3D Detail W66 - Stone rainscreen cladding, window jamb detail	290
3D Detail W67 - Stone rainscreen cladding, parapet detail	291
3D Detail W68 - Stone rainscreen cladding, light gauge steel frame (lgsf)	292
3D Detail W69 - Stone rainscreen cladding, lgsf, base detail	293
3D Detail W70 - Stone rainscreen cladding, lgsf, window head detail	294
3D Detail W71 - Stone rainscreen cladding, lgsf, window sill detail	295
3D Detail W72 - Stone rainscreen cladding, lgsf, window jamb detail	296
3D Detail W73 - Stone rainscreen cladding, lgsf, parapet detail	297
3D Detail R01 - Concrete cast in situ, single ply, warm deck	310
3D Detail R02 - Concrete cast in situ, single ply, rainwater outlet	311
3D Detail R03 - Concrete cast in situ, single ply, upstand	312
3D Detail R04 - Concrete cast in situ, single ply, rooflight	313
3D Detail R05 - Concrete cast in situ, (balcony)	314
3D Detail R06 - Concrete cast in situ, liquid applied, inverted roof	315
3D Detail R07 - Concrete cast in situ, liquid applied, rainwater outlet	316
3D Detail R08 - Concrete cast in situ, liquid applied, roof light	317
3D Detail R09 - Concrete cast in situ, liquid applied, threshold detail	318
3D Detail R10 - Concrete cast in situ, green roof	319
3D Detail R11 - Concrete cast in situ, green roof, drainage outlet	320
3D Detail R12 - Concrete cast in situ, green roof, roof light	321
3D Detail R13 - Concrete cast in situ, green roof, upstand	322
3D Detail R14 - Pitched roof, steel deck, standing seam, parapet	325
3D Detail R15 - Pitched roof, steel deck, standing seam, ridge detail	327
3D Detail R16 - Pitched roof, steel deck, standing seam, verge detail	329
3D Detail R17 - Flat roof, steel concrete composite deck, intensive green roof, parapet	331
3D Detail R18 - Steel concrete composite deck, intensive green roof, drainage outlet	333
3D Detail R19 - Metal deck, exposed roof system	334
3D Detail R20 - Composite deck, exposed roof system	335

End

Note all insulation thickness's should be calculated in order to achieve required u-values, according to building regulation standards.
All structural members should be calculated and assessed by a structural engineer.
These drawings MUST NOT be used as construction drawings, and are purely an educational resource.
These drawings are not finished or complete construction drawings and should not be used as such.
To read the full terms of use follow this link: http://www.firstinarchitecture.co.uk/about/terms-of-use/

All details can be purchased in dwg and skp format from
www.firstinarchitecture.co.uk
Email: emma@firstinarchitecture.co.uk

All images copyright to 'Understanding Architectural Details' & First In Architecture